DEMOCRACY AND ECONOMIC DEVELOPMENT IN ETHIOPIA

DEMOCRACY AND ECONOMIC DEVELOPMENT IN ETHIOPIA

Addis Alem Balema

THE RED SEA PRESS
TRENTON | LONDON | NEW DELHI | CAPE TOWN | NAIROBI | ADDIS ABABA | ASMARA | IBADAN

THE RED SEA PRESS
541 West Ingham Avenue | Suite B
Trenton, New Jersey 08638

First Printing 2014

Book and Cover design: Saverance Publishing Services

Library of Congress Cataloging-in-Publication Data

Balema, Addis Alem, 1957-
Democracy and economic development in Ethiopia / Addis Alem Balema.
pages cm
Based on the author's thesis (doctoral)--Erasmus Universiteit Rotterdam, 2003, issued under the title: Economic development and democracy in Ethiopia = Economische ontwikkeling en democratie in Ethiopik.
Includes bibliographical references and index.
ISBN 978-1-56902-390-7 (hard cover) -- ISBN 978-1-56902-391-4 (pbk.)
1. Democracy--Ethiopia. 2. Democracy--Economic aspects--Ethiopia. 3. Economic development--Ethiopia. 4. Ethiopia--Economic policy--1991- 5. Ethiopia--Economic conditions--1974- 6. Ethiopia--Politics and government--1991- I. Title.
JQ3760.B35 2013
963.07--dc23

2013033921

To all who sacrificed their lives for freedom and human dignity.

Contents

Preface and Acknowledgements

The interaction of democracy and economic development, and whether both endeavors have been compatible in the process of attaining structural socioeconomic transformation has been debatable among theorists. Apparently, this compatibility may differ from country to country as there are many factors, which play to a varying degree to influence the process. In addition, the compatibility side of the debate has not been consolidated beyond doubt as the astounding performers in the last three and four decades such as South Korea and Taiwan were under authoritarian regimes. That is why, the issue remains inconclusive among economic development theorists and the assertion will continue to be contestable one way or the other.

This book initially started as a manuscript for obtaining my masters degree from Amsterdam University, The Netherlands. After completing my second degree study, the director of the program, Professor Dr. Peter Malanczuk, advised me to develop it into a doctorial thesis. Under his guidance and supervision, I was able to complete my doctoral thesis and defend it in April 2003. Since then many friends and colleagues have urged me to update and broaden the thesis and publish it as a book. Understandably, it took me a couple of years to accomplish as the last few years were hectic in my work obligations.

The book extensively discusses on Ethiopia's attempt to build a democratic system concomitantly with its endeavor to eradicate poverty and achieve a respectable socioeconomic development. It analyzes the interaction between democracy and economic development in the specific situation of Ethiopia. As discussed in the various chapters of the book, Ethiopia has been faced with both challenges at the same time without any option of prioritizing them. The issue here is to analyze to what extent the interaction of democracy and economic development manifest itself in the context of the Ethiopian situations. It will also examine under what conditions are these objectives compatible and whether these conditions can be continuously and sustainable created in the country.

The history of Ethiopia has denied it the option of prioritizing the challenges of building a democratic system and attaining economic development.

Ethiopia is a country of over 80 nationalities. The recent history of Ethiopia has been shadowed with repression, war, famine and related evils that hugely challenged the unity of the country. In 1991, it was a country on the verge of disintegration. It was an open discussion that Ethiopia might follow the path taken by Liberia and Somalia at the time. Many people were fearful of chaos in Addis Ababa that was similar to what was happening in Mogadishu and Monrovia. Ethiopia has suffered more than its share both under the monarchy and the military dictatorship.

The current regime has extricated the country from disastrous decline to one of the fastest growing economy not only in Africa but also in the world. The country has been playing a pivotal role in stabilizing the Horn of Africa, and also has been contributing to the peace keeping effort in many conflict-ridden regions in the continent. It has been a leader in many international issues, from poverty eradication to the International Climate Change Conference and Summits.

The book will explore the major issues, accomplishments and challenges of the last two decades. It will start with a brief theoretical discussion on democracy, economic theories and the interaction of democracy and economic development. It will also dwell on short history of Ethiopia and the overall performances of the previous regimes, the monarchy and military dictatorship, to use it for comparison with the achievements of the current regime. The reform and democratization process is also widely addressed. In this regard, the transitional period and the major political actors, the constitution and the subsequent major political reforms, federalism and devolution of power are extensively discussed. In general, it is attempted to explain the evolving democratic process with its challenges and shortcomings.

Similarly, the economic policies and strategies adopted at the beginning of the current regime and their developments are explained. The implementation process in the last two decades and their results are also examined. The problems and challenges facing the economic development endeavor and the future prospects are also widely discussed. The major factor which has enormous influence to the effort of democratic system building and eradicating poverty has always been peace and stability in the country. The internal peace has been strengthened by the democratization process and the economic changes taking place in the country. However, the external environment, especially Horn of Africa's situation has continued to be unpredictable and volatile affecting the countries in the region. Ethiopia's relationship with Eritrea continues to be problematic causing substantial socioeconomic prices to both fraternal peoples. In this regard, the Eritrean question and the consequent conflict and the prevailing stalemate are extensively discussed. Though the border areas have been relatively quiet, the relationship between Eritrea and Ethiopia has hitherto been tense and continues to be precarious. Hence, negotiations to narrow their differences and normalize their relations are definitely advantageous to both peoples' interest.

In the end, the book attempts to compare and contrast the interaction of democracy and economic developments in the last three regimes. Above all, it analysis whether democracy and economic development can be concomitantly built at this stage. It also examines under what conditions and to what extent these endeavors can be compatible. It also attempts to draw some lessons with the intention of contributing to the discussion of whether democracy and economic development are compatible. It aims to underline that it is a worthwhile endeavor to strive for as it contributes to solving the affront challenges affecting human lives and dignity.

In the process of conducting and writing this study, many friends and colleagues contributed by providing comments and suggestions, and spending their precious time to collect documents and books pertinent to the subject matter. Without their invaluable assistance it would have been difficult to complete the study. In fact, I have received similar cooperation from those people in updating the initial study to be published as a book.

First and foremost, I continue to be deeply grateful to my doctoral studies promoter Prof. Dr. Peter Malanczuk for his encouragement and assistance from the inception of the study to its completion. His ever readiness to provide assistance, guidance and advice greatly helped me to carry out the study while doing my best to discharge my duties as a government office-holder. I will always remain indebted to his extraordinary friendship.

I remain indebted to the late Prime Minister Meles Zenawi for his useful insights that helped me to sharpen my argument and widen my view. I also want to express my gratitude to Seyoum Mesfin, Arkebe Iqubay, Addissu Legesse and Kassu Illala for their unreserved and invaluable support and encouragement that helped me to remain committed to finish the study as well as to make it useful to the current environment.

Special thanks are due to my friends and colleagues who have helped me in various ways to my effort to complete and update the thesis. I want, in particular, to thank Berhane-Tensay Wolde-Senbet, Fisseha Yimer, Graham Romanes, Yonas Zegeye, Tewolde Gebremariam, Araya Abate, Mulugeta Zewede, Getachew Iqubay, Elias Melake, Gezaee Assefa, and Melaku Petros.

My unending gratitude goes to my lifelong friends for their constant encouragement and support in every way imaginable, which enabled me to continue throughout this challenging endeavor. Specifically, I thank Abay Woldu, Tsegay Berhe, Debre- Tsion Gebre-Michael, Getachew Assefa, Tedros Hagos, Berhane Gebre-Krstos, Tekelewoini Assefa, Gobezay Wolde-Aregay, Beyene Mikru, Berhane Kidane-Mariam, Kiros Bitow, and Tewolde Gebru. I would also like to express my appreciation and gratitude to Teklebirhan Ambaye, Esayas Hadera,

Kiros Jiranie, Shewit Habte, Haile Girmay, Seifu Ambaye, Daniel Balema, Masresha Tadesse, Robel Berhane and Dawit Balema.

My heartfelt thanks also go to my dear wife, Tsehay, whose encouragement and limitless devotion were a source of immense moral support and comfort helping me to endure the formidable academic challenge. I am also thankful to my children Tedros, Senay, Wintana and Eden who have been immense sources of happiness and joy to my life. Finally, my gratitude goes to my former colleagues at the Ethiopian Embassy in Beijing and to all my current associates at the Ethiopia Commodity Exchange Authority for their exceptional support and friendship.

Chapter I
Introduction

While in the past six decades a number of developing countries have made considerable progress in terms of economic growth and human development, still nearly half of the world population has remained very poor, living off less than U.S$2 per day.[1] In particular, in Sub-Saharan Africa most people are almost as poor as they were 30 years ago. The process of economic globalization has left most of Africa marginalized. Over 300 million people in Africa continue to struggle to survive on less than U.S$ 1 a day. There is no argument about the need of significantly reducing poverty by achieving sustained and broad-based growth. This was reaffirmed in 2000 in the so-called "Millennium Declaration" which endorsed the proposal for a "United Nations Strategy for Halving Extreme Poverty".[2] The question of how best to achieve this goal, however, has remained rather controversial. This can be seen, for example, from the continuing debate on the appropriateness of the policies of the World Bank and the International Monetary Fund (IMF) relating to economic development.[3]

As suggested in the "Millennium Report" presented in 2000 to the international community by Kofi Annan, it appears that there is now widespread agreement

> That economic success depends in considerable measure on the quality of governance a country enjoys. Good governance comprises the rule of law, effective state institutions, transparency and accountability in the management of public affairs, respect for human rights and the participation of all citizens in the decisions that affect their lives. While there may be debates about the most appropriate forms they should take, there can be no disputing the importance of these principles.[4]

However, a survey of the relevant literature shows that, in particular, the relationship between democracy and economic development has remained controversial among scholars. The core issue here is whether democratization is compatible with economic development endeavours. Some scholars argue that there must be a trade-off between democracy and development. They say authoritarian governments are better suited to foster economic development.[5] On the other hand, other theorists advocate that there exists no trade-off between democracy and economic development. They argue that democratic governments perform better than authoritarian ones in promoting and achieving economic progress.[6] In other words, there is no consensus among scholars on whether authoritarian or democratic governments are better suited to advance economic development.[7]

The Problem Examined in the Present Study

The present study aims at making a contribution to the general discussion of the relationship between economic development and democracy in developing countries, particularly in Africa, by focusing upon the lessons that may be learned from the analysis of Ethiopia's experience under its last three regimes. The relevant background may be briefly summarized as follows: Ethiopia emerged as a modern state at the end of the 19th century and was able to avoid colonial subjugation through successful military and diplomatic manoeuvres. In its long history of independence, however, it achieved little in terms of socioeconomic transformation. With a population of about 84 million, Ethiopia is the second most populous country in sub-Saharan Africa. But it is also one of the poorest nations in the world. The economy is largely dominated by agriculture, which accounts for about 44 per cent of GDP, 80 per cent of export earnings and 80 per cent of total employment.[8]

After languishing for many years under an absolute monarchy, the country further suffered under military dictatorship for seventeen years. The overthrow of Emperor Haile Selassie in 1974 was followed by the flare-up of civil war and bloodshed, and adoption of irrational economic policies resembling those of the then decaying Soviet system. The restrictive economic policies and the diversion of resources to the war effort, compounded with severe fluctuations in weather conditions, brought the economy to its knees. At the end of the Derg regime, the economic situation of the country was worse than the economic hardship that led to the demise of the monarchy in the first place.

When the military government was thrown out of power in 1991, the country was on the verge of collapse and disintegration. Many people expected that another Mogadishu or Monrovia would be repeated in its worst and bloodiest form. However, such a scenario was avoided when the three major political organizations – the Ethiopian People's Revolutionary Democratic Front (EPRDF), the Eritrean People's Liberation Front (EPLF) and the Oromo Liberation Front (OLF) -agreed on an arrangement that led to the formation of a transitional government in Ethiopia.

The formation of the Transitional Government and the adoption of the National Charter, in July 1991, brought some relief to a country that had suffered enormously from protracted civil war and disastrous political upheavals. This initiative heralded the introduction of a series of political and economic reforms that led to political, institutional and economic changes in the country. In 1991, Ethiopia was faced with problems threatening the continuity of the country as a united nation. Citizens as well as the international community put the unity of Ethiopia into question. A number of liberation movements, some with a secessionist agenda, had been operating in the country and were attempting to protect their fiefdoms. On the other hand, the economic situation was extremely dismal and millions of people were once again threatened by famine that gripped most of northern and central Ethiopia. There was a sense of hopelessness in the air and people were extremely worried about the future of their country and, of course, themselves.

It was in such a grave situation that the Ethiopian government embarked on extensive political and economic reforms. In the political sphere, the National Conference convened in July 1991 and adopted the National Charter that radically changed the institutions of the country. The National Charter, in addition to adopting the Universal Declaration of Human Rights of the United Nations of 10 December 1948, recognized the right of nationalities to self-determination including the right to secede. This major political decision paved the way, not only for the formal and amicable secession of Eritrea, but also for regional administrative arrangements based on the criteria of linguistic and cultural similarities. Further attempts followed to implement the spirit of the Charter's provisions, later culminating in the adoption of a federal constitution that reinforced a series of political and institutional reforms introduced earlier.

The government also adopted major reforms to improve conditions for the heavily distressed economy. Steps were taken to transform the command economy into a market-oriented one and to create a favourable environment for better performance. The government was able to successively devise reform programs in collaboration with the International Monetary Fund (IMF). Currently, it is in the process of implementing a five-year plan, the Growth and Transformation Plan, which is ambitious in its targets. The main objective of these programs has been to encourage economic growth and reduce the widespread poverty in Ethiopia. In a country that is in international comparison at the bottom of the ladder of economic wellbeing, the process of economic development has been arduous and trying.

As indicated above, Ethiopia has embarked on two major tasks at the same time: political liberalization and economic reforms. It has been faced with the challenges of democratization and economic development simultaneously. This signifies that the country has to concomitantly advance with these two complex endeavours. Taking this into consideration, the debate of whether democracy fosters or hinders development may not be decisive in the Ethiopian political environment. However, it remains important to assess and analyse the interaction of both endeavours in the Ethiopian context. Thus, it is useful to examine whether the process of democratization is compatible with the endeavours of economic development; under what general conditions both are compatible, and whether these conditions can be created in this country. By analyzing and assessing the changes that have taken place in Ethiopia, the study contributes to the knowledge of societal transformation in important aspects. It can shed some light on whether it is worthwhile to strive for democracy while attempting to reduce, and ultimately eliminate, poverty. The study can also indicate how the objectives of democratization and economic development interact with each other, especially in a very poor country. Moreover, it should be noted that in the process of this study, many important government and other documents have been assembled that are not generally available to the public. This research may be useful as a basis for further studies of Ethiopia and for other scholars interested in studying development endeavours in similar countries.

Method of Research and Problems Encountered

Some explanation of the method of research and problems encountered is appropriate. Various methods were used to undertake the necessary research to write the study. In most of the Chapters, a theoretical framework regarding the subject matter is included. For this purpose, extensive research on secondary literature was made to understand and formulate the guiding issues on each specific subject under discussion.

The study was based on collecting and analyzing many documents dealing with relevant subject matters. Hundreds of documents regarding the Transitional Period and the years thereafter were assembled from government institutions, multilateral organizations, political parties and groups, and non-governmental organizations. Many of the documents were written in Amharic and some in Tigrigna. These documents were studied and the relevant ones identified. The researcher had no difficulty in gaining access even to the offices of the highest authorities; however, the documentation system in most of these offices and institutions has not yet developed. Such a problem makes it difficult to obtain documents easily and at short notice. Notwithstanding, the researcher believes that almost all the major documents relevant to the study were obtained and examined.

The other method employed during the research period was conducting interviews with senior government officials, parliamentarians, and the leaders of political organizations, including the opposition, the operators of non-government organizations, professionals, and other people from selected walks of life. As shown in the study, the researcher was fortunate enough to have the opportunity to interview personalities who were and have been at the helm of power, including the late Prime Minister, the Speaker of Parliament, the President of the Federal Supreme Court, Ministers, regional presidents, various party leaders and other important officials.

After analyzing the wide-range of documents, a comparison was made among the political and socioeconomic performances of the successive regimes in Ethiopia. The purpose of this comparison is to analyze the interaction of democracy and economic development under the monarchy, the military government and the current regime. In comparing the political situations, the main indicators of a democratic regime are considered. These indicators include meaningful and extensive competition among individuals and political groups; the degree of inclusiveness in electing leaders and their policies; and a certain level of civil and political freedoms exercised by the people. On the other hand, the comparison of the socioeconomic performance of each regime is discussed. The above comparison is undertaken in order to analyze the interaction of democracy and economic development in the context of the varied Ethiopian situations, and to try to answer the question under what conditions can they be compatible.

The problems encountered in the research arose mainly from weaknesses existing in the Ethiopian government institutions. As indicated above, the system of documentation is still at its infantile stage. Documents are not properly codified and are difficult to find in a single designated department. It requires extensive effort of the researcher to contact all possible departments to obtain all the necessary information. This means it demands more time, personal effort, and the cooperation of officials working in those departments. Moreover, the data produced by government institutions, banks and other organizations is far from consistent. Figures prepared by various departments on the same sector are sometimes irreconcilable. Even the same department may be publishing inconsistent figures on a specific activity within a difference of few months. Sometimes, this left the researcher to choose by himself one seemingly reliable set of data out of various alternatives, and then to ask the responsible institution to reprocess the figures anew. In solving such difficulties, the researcher has received commendable support and assistance from many government and non-government institutions throughout the country.

Structure of the Study

The structure of this book is as follows: Chapter Two addresses the theoretical framework regarding the concepts of democracy and economic development and their interaction. An important aspect of the discussion of this framework is the question to which extent these concepts can be usefully applied in view of the particular features of Ethiopian history and the nation's current structure and situation.

Chapter Three discusses the political and economic development before 1991. It summarizes the historical evolution of the modern Ethiopian state and the factors that helped the country to protect its sovereignty during the scramble for Africa. Furthermore, it reviews the political and socioeconomic situations under Emperor Haile Selassie and the causes of the demise of the Monarchy. In addition, the political nature of the military dictatorship, its disastrous economic policies and their grave consequences are reviewed. In this chapter, the role of the national as well as the Eritrean questions in shaping Ethiopian politics during the military regime is briefly discussed.

Chapter Four reviews the period of transition and the main political actors, which played major roles not only in bringing about the demise of the military government but also in shaping the political environment during the transition period. These political organizations were attempting to influence the process for the political advantage. Although the main focus is given to the most important organizations, such as the Ethiopian People's Revolutionary Democratic Front (EPRDF) and the Oromo Liberation Front (OLF), an attempt is also made to discuss the other smaller organizations that mushroomed all over the county. In this regard, the role of the nationality organizations in shaping the political and institutional make-up of the Ethiopian state is also analyzed.

Chapter Five discusses the main constitutional issues and political reforms taken place, which shaped the political and institutional framework of the nation. The electoral system and the elections held to date are discussed. The principle of the separation of powers, especially the independence of the judiciary is also reviewed. In conjunction with the above, the recognition and respect of fundamental rights and freedoms are discussed in short.

Chapter Six discusses the most important issue that changed the political and institutional architecture of the county, the introduction of the federal system. The unique nature of the Ethiopian federalism and the debate around the most controversial issues will be discussed. In addition, the devolution of power including fiscal decentralization will be extensively analyzed.

Chapter Seven will examine the thorny issue of the Eritrea question. It discusses the Ethiopian government's rationale to support and facilitate the referendum that paves the way for Eritrean secession. It analyzes the initial relationship before and after the independence of Eritrea, and the issues that started to make the close relationship sour. It explains the attempts made to ward of the winds of war and the reason they failed to result in negotiated settlement and peace. It also covers the situation during the war and its consequences in detail. The aftermath of the fratricidal war and the stalemate that ensue will be discussed. It also attempts to shade some light to the current situation and the possible resolution to the status quo, which burden high costs to both countries, most importantly to the people on both sides of the border.

Chapter Eight discusses the major economic problems and the policies devised to provide solutions. A brief review of the theory of economic development policies is presented to put the discussion into proper perspective. The 1991 economic policy is briefly reviewed to show the first steps of the Transitional Government and the general thinking of the time. The relevant policy paper was important as it served as a blueprint for the successive reform programs devised with the collaboration of the International Monetary Fund (IMF). One of the most important parts of this Chapter is the discussion of the Agricultural Development-Led Industrialization Strategy (ADLI) and the sector strategies, which have determined the path of the economic reforms. In this part, the ADLI strategy is briefly discussed and an attempt is made to review the sector strategies to show to what extent they were influenced by it and their development in the course of time, especially after the end of Ethio-Ertirean war when extensive discussions were made to clarify and enrich them. In the second part, it briefly discusses the first decade of the EPRDF's rule and the major purpose was to mitigate the deterioration of the socio-economic situation in the county and to reverse the disastrous path of the command economy. It then reviews the performance of the second decade in which rapid economic growth and tangible steps of social transformation have been registered. It reviews the achievements and attempts to analyze the shortcomings of the endeavor. It also makes an effort to draw some lessons which might be useful to expedite the process of achieving the nation's vision of joining a middle income countries' club in the near future.

Chapter Nine reviews the interaction of democracy and economic development under successive regimes in Ethiopia. By using the major political freedoms and rights, and major indicators of socioeconomic performance, it compares the situations under different regimes. It analyzes the relationship between democracy and economic development under each regime. It also attempts to draw some conclusions on whether democracy is compatible with economic development in the Ethiopian context, and how these conditions can be created and persistently strengthened.

Chapter Ten contains the conclusions of the study. It summarizes the study as a whole and attempts to draw some lessons on the interaction between the democratization process and the economic development endeavours. It briefly addresses the issue of whether these two difficult ventures are in fact progressing hand in hand to bring about better lives to the Ethiopian people who are the victims of instability and despicable poverty. It ends with some final remarks on whether it may be possible to create favourable situations that enable these noble endeavours to work together harmoniously for a better future.

Notes

1. Approximately 1.2 billion people – 500 million in South Asia and 300 million in Africa- live on less than U.S$1. Moreover, the 1 billion people living in the developed world earn 60 per cent of the world's income, while the 3.5 billion people in low-income countries earn less than 20 per cent. In this economic environment sub-Saharan Africa suffered enormously. The economic performance has failed to cope with the fast growing population. Growth in per capita income averaged 1.5 per cent in the 1960s, 0.8 per cent in the 1970s, and minus 1.2 per cent in the 1980s. (Kofi A. Annan, "We the Peoples": The Role of the United Nations in the 21st Century ("Millennium Report"), 2000, p. 19 and 30).
2. United Nations. Report of the Secretary-General on the Work of the Organization, General Assembly, Official Records, 56th Session, Supplement No. 1(A/56/1), 2001, p. 21.
3. See Stiglitz, Globalization and Its Discontents, 2001: 23-52; Lensink, Structural Adjustment in Sub-Saharan Africa, 1996: 77-108; Green, "The IMF and the World Bank in Africa: How Much Learning?", in Callaghy and Ravenhill (eds.), Hemmed In, 1993: 54-89; Loxley, John, "The IMF, the World Bank, and Sub-Saharan Africa: Policies and Politics", in Havnevik (ed.), 1987: 47-63; Bandow, Doug and Ian Vasquez, Perpetuating Poverty: The World Bank, the IMF and the Developing World, 1994; Chossudovsky, Michel, The Globalisation of Poverty: Impacts of IMF and World Bank Reforms, 1997; Hanlon, Joseph, Peace Without Profit: How the IMF Blocks Rebuilding in Mozambique, 1996: 24-37; Khan, Shahrukh Rafi, Do World Bank and IMF Policies Work?, 1999: 190-194; Caufield, Catherine, Masters of Illusion, 1996: 330-338; and Brown and Tiffen, Short Changed: Africa and World Trade, 1992.
4. Millennium Report, op. cit., p. 22.
5. See Löwenthal 1963, quoted in Sorensen, 1991:1; Rao 1984; Marsh 1979; Galenson 1959; Huntington and Dominguez, in Greenstein and Polsby (eds.), 1975; Huntington and Nelson 1976; Huntington 1993; Almond and Powell 1978; for detailed discussion, see the next section, Theoretical Framework.
6. See Dick 1974; Berg-Schlosser 1984; Diamond and Plattner 1995; Przeworski and Limongi, in Hadenius (ed.), 1997; Przeworski and Limongi, in Bagchi, 1995; Diamond 1999; Przeworski et. al., 2000; and Amartya Sen, in Diamond and Plattner (eds.) 2001; for detailed discussion, see the next section, Theoretical Framework.
7. Przeworski and Limongi, in Bagchi (ed.), 1995:11-13.
8. See MOFED, Statistical Report, 2013; World Development Report 2012, 2011: 398-400; and World Development Report 2013, 2012: 354.

Chapter 2

Theoretical Framework: Democracy and Economic Development

Democracy

Despite the continuing dispute as to its form and content, democracy can be generally described as a method of organizing government through elections and people's participation, not only in its organizational process, but also in the activities of the government. Furthermore, it is a system in which people enjoy a certain level of civil and political liberties.

Following the collapse of the Soviet Union, the global advance of free market philosophy and vast political changes in the world, democracy has attained widespread adherence in today's mode of political life and has become a criteria for determining the legitimacy of the possession of power.[1] For example, the Bucharest Declaration, adopted on 4 September 1997 by 80 states participating in the Third International Conference of the New or Restored Democracies, asserts:

> [there exists] an almost universal recognition that a democratic system of government is the best model to ensure a framework of liberties for lasting solutions to the political, economic and social problems that our societies face.[2]

The Universal Declaration on Democracy adopted by the Inter-Parliamentary Union (IPU), the world organization of more than 100 national parliaments, on 16 September 1997 even claims that democracy is a

> ...universally recognized ideal as well as a goal, which is based on common values shared by peoples throughout the world community irrespective of cultural, political, social and economic differences.[3]

Moreover, the foreign ministers and representatives from more than 100 governments who met in Warsaw from 26-27 June 2000 adopted the Warsaw Declaration, which recognizes the "universality of democratic values" and lists "core democratic principles and practices", including a number of fundamental rights of the individual.[4] Similarly, these democratic values and basic rights are reflected in the Inter-American Democratic Charter adopted in September 2001 in Lima, Peru.[5]

In view of such developments, a "democratic entitlement" school of thought has been advancing the proposition that there is even an obligation under international law for states to establish democratic systems of government. An article on "The Emerging Right to Democratic Governance" published by Thomas Franck in 1992 in the American Journal of International Law inaugurated this discussion.[6] It must be noted, however, that Franck himself does not assert that a right to democratic government exists, but that "the international system is *moving toward* a clearly designated democratic entitlement, with national governance validated by international standards and systematic monitoring of compliance" (emphasis added).[7] Moreover, as Steven Wheatley has shown in a recent analysis, particularly in view of the fact that about one-third of all states might be identified as "non-democratic", there is no evidence in state practice for an obligation of states under general international law to introduce and maintain democratic government.[8] The author shows, however, that such an obligation exists in Europe and discusses the content of this obligation, showing that

> ...democratic government involves more than free and fair elections. Democracies must be tolerant of political debate and activity, except where harmful to democracy itself. Moreover, ..., all concerned citizens must enjoy the right to participate in the decision-making processes in the state, and the state must take account of their interests.[9]

Wheatley's thorough analysis of relevant international instruments and practice leads him to conclude that "(c)onsequently, whilst it might not yet be possible to identify a general obligation on state to introduce democratic government, the evolving internal aspect of the right of a people to self-determination, the increasing numbers of states party to universal and regional human rights instruments (which all contain provisions on free and fair elections and political participation), and recognition that a democratic system of government may not legitimately be replaced by an authoritarian one, indicates a progressive and irreversible movement to a world community of democratic states."[10]

For the purposes of this present study it is more important "to recognise, in contrast to certain writings in political science, that the international legal community does not posit one paradigmatic conception of democracy".[11] In a document published in 1999 on the "Promotion of the right to democracy", the UN Commission on Human Rights has noted the "rich and diverse nature of the community of the world's democracies".[12] Furthermore, in a publication dealing with "Support by the United Nations system of the efforts of Governments to promote and consolidate new or restored democracies", the UN Secretary-General has clarified that democracy is "not a model to be copied but a goal to be attained".[13] He has also correctly observed that imposing foreign models of democracy on a society contravenes the UN Charter principle of non-intervention in the internal affairs of other states.[14] Indeed, it is noted that democracy and democratic government, can take many forms, evolving through many phases, depending on the special features and conditions of societies.[15]

Nevertheless, while accepting the need for diversity, it is necessary to identify more precisely the essential components of democracy and a democratic government for the analytical purposes of this study. In this regard, Schumpeter was one of the theorists who "criticized the classical doctrine of democracy" and embarked on defining democracy in terms of institutions and procedures.[16] Schumpeter criticized the idea of a "common good that all people could agree on or be made to agree on by the force of rational argument."[17] After rejecting this notion, he forwarded his own definition that the democratic method is an institutional arrangement for arriving at political decisions in which individuals acquire the power to decide by means of a competitive struggle for the people's vote.[18]

Schumpeter explained that the primary function of the electorates' vote in a democracy is to produce government.[19] He also dismissed the notion of "the rule by the people" as follows:

> Democracy does not mean that the people actually rule in any obvious sense of the terms "people" and "rule". Democracy means only that the people have the opportunity of accepting or refusing the men who are to rule them...Now one aspect of this may be expressed by saying that democracy is the rule of the politician.[20]

For Schumpeter, democracy was a concept that was mainly a political mechanism for choosing political leadership.

Another theorist who had a major influence in the modern formulation of the theory of democracy is Robert Dahl. Dahl emphasized that a key characteristic of a democracy is the continuing responsiveness of the government to the preferences of its citizens, considered as political equals.[21] In order to attain such responsiveness, it requires that citizens must have opportunities (1) to formulate their preferences, (2) to signify their preferences to their fellow citizens and the government by individual and collective action, and (3) to have their preferences weighted equally in the conduct of the government, that is, weighted with no discrimination because of the content or source of the preference.[22] Other theorists define democracy by giving more emphasis to accountability and the appropriateness of the mechanism of competition.[23] Some also attempt to include economic and social rights to the concept of democracy.[24]

A definition that has been recently reflected in a substantial number of studies and books is the one formulated by Diamond et al. This definition separates the notions of freedom and economic equality that it considers confused.[25] It builds on the work of Dahl and defines democracy as:

> A system of government that meets three essential conditions: meaningful and extensive competition among individuals and organized groups (especially political parties) for all effective positions of government power, at regular intervals and excluding the use of force; a highly inclusive level of political participation in the selection of leaders and policies, at least through regular and fair elections, such that no major (adult) social group is excluded; and a level of civil and political liberties: freedom of expression, freedom of the press, freedom to form and join organizations, sufficient to ensure the integrity of political competition and participation.[26]

In addition to the above definition, consociational democracy is regarded as an instrument to deliberately ease the negative effects of cultural fragmentation in building a democratic system. Lijphart defines consociational democracy as a government by elite cartel designed to turn a democracy with a fragmented political culture into a stable democracy.[27] He mentioned several requirements for the success of consociational democracy: (1) the elites should have the ability to accommodate the divergent interests and demands of the subcultures; (2) they should have the ability to transcend cleavages and to join in a common effort with the elites of rival subcultures; (3) they should be committed to the maintenance of the system and to the improvement of its cohesion and stability; (4) finally, the elites have to understand the perils of political fragmentation.[28]

Consociational democracy is defined in terms of four principles: grand coalition, mutual veto, proportionality, and segmental autonomy.[29] The primary principle of consociational democracy is grand coalition in which the political leaders of all of the segments of the plural society jointly govern the country. This principle can be applied in various forms: inclusive cabinet coalitions of ethnic, linguistic or religious parties; permanent or ad hoc grand councils, or committees with much greater influence than their formal advisory role; grand coalitions in cabinets, defined not in partisan terms but more broadly in terms of the representation of linguistic or other groups in a predetermined ratio; the allocation of top government offices, such as the presidency, prime ministership, and assembly speakership to specified ethnic or religious groups; and cabinets formed by inclusive and broadly representative parties with ministers belonging to all the main religious, linguistic, and regional groups.[30]

The second principle, segmental autonomy, entails a rule by the segment over itself in the area of its exclusive concern. The autonomy for religious and linguistic groups in power-sharing democracies has been carried out in three main forms: first, federal arrangements in which state and linguistic boundaries largely coincide; secondly, the right of religious and linguistic minorities to establish and administer their own autonomous schools, fully supported by public funds; and, third, separate personal laws, such as laws concerning marriage, divorce, custody and adoption of children, and inheritance for religious minorities.[31] As Lijphart remarked, the delegation of rule-making and rule-application powers to the segments, together with the proportional allocation of government funds to each segment, is a powerful stimulus to the various segmental organizations.[32]

The third principle, proportionality, serves as the basic standard of political representation, civil service appointments, and the allocation of public funds.[33] The principle favours the overrepresentation of small minorities and proportional representation as an electoral system. The plural electoral system and other similar methods are considered to have the tendency to over represent majorities and large parties. However, plurality does not make consociational democracy impossible to implement, its effects can be diminished in situations where there are: geographically concentrated minorities; a representative and widely inclusive party; and an electoral law that guarantees minorities a representation by providing "reserved seats" or similar treatment.[34]

Finally, the minority veto is the fourth principle that provides minorities with the right to effectively protect their autonomy by blocking any attempt to eliminate or reduce it. Usually, this principle is merely an informal understanding but in some countries in which there exists a solid majority, the minority veto is included in the constitution. The main purpose of the principle as a potential weapon for protection is to promote a feeling of security and mutual trust.[35]

The most favourable form of segmental autonomy is federalism. Since all federation systems cannot be consociational democracies, some factors are identified that would help to characterize a federation as a consociation. These are: the system should be democratic; only federations in plural societies can be consociations; all four principles of consociational democracy must be present; decentralized government; the federal system must belong to the asymmetrical category, that is, the federal and segmental boundaries should coincide as much as possible; a federation consists of relatively many and relatively small component units.[36]

Consociational democracy has presented itself as an alternative to adversary politics. Political leadership has been crucial in establishing and maintaining democracy in fragmented societies. Lijphart tries to refute the stigma attached to segmented societies as the sources of instability and fratricidal wars. He summarizes the possibility and viability of democracy in these societies as follows:

> The accommodation model provides not only an alternative model, but one for which the social prerequisites are considerably lower. Deep, mutually reinforcing social cleavages do not form an insuperable obstacle to viable democracy. The crucial factor in the establishment and preservation of democratic norms and democratic stability is the quality of leadership. The politics of accommodation opens up the possibility of viable democracy even where the social conditions appear unpromising. For those committed to the democratic creed, this is an optimistic and happy conclusion.[37]

He further emphasizes that for many of the plural societies of the non-Western World, the realistic choice is not between the British normative model of democracy and the consociational model, but between consociational democracy and no democracy at all.[38]

Applicability of the Concept of Democracy to Countries like Ethiopia

As discussed above, a precise definition of democracy is difficult to formulate since many people have different perceptions of the concept, and moreover, it is in constant change and evolution in conjunction with the overall development that takes place in the world. Although definitions differ from one another, democracy has become a cherished concept for many people in the quest for good governance and economic development.

In this regard, consociational democracy seems to have a better chance of sustaining democracy in fragmented societies of Africa. The winner-take-all model in African politics has been responsible for dislodging the opposition from the political arena and for ending the election process. Makinda rightly notes that "one of the abiding problems of political evolution in Africa...[is] the belief on the part of both the winners and the losers of elections or political competition that the winner would take everything leaving the loser with no political role, no right to question and criticize, and no security from harassment or worse".[39] However, Africans now clearly see the need for coalition building, bargaining and sharing the benefits of power. The other major issue, and a taboo in African politics, is ethnicity, which has been at the centre of conflicts since independence. The promotion of ethnic coexistence and a bargaining process for mutually accepted power and resources sharing are now issues that should be considered seriously as means of advancing democracy and stability.

The possibility of building a democratic system in sub-Saharan Africa seems to be greater in recent years. Nevertheless, there are a large number of scholars who think that it is almost impossible to have successful democracy in poor nations.[40] The scant of experience of democracy and democratic institutions presents a huge problem. This predicament may be compensated to a certain extent by a real commitment to democratic values among political leaders. However, it is obvious that the road to stable democracy is rough and full of ups and downs. In this regard, Diamond notes as follows:

> It is unrealistic to think that countries in Africa can suddenly reverse and institutionalize stable democratic government simply by changing leaders, constitutions and/or public mentalities. If progress is made toward developing democratic government, it is likely to be gradual, messy, fitful and slow, with many imperfections along the way.[41]

That is why, building democracy and ensuring good governance in Ethiopia will not be easy. It will be a process with its ups and downs. In addition, as a country with over 80 nationalities and linguistic groups, stability will continue to be paramount in building democracy in which it is basically based on the respect of vital interests of the stakeholders.

Economic Development Theories

Economic development theories originated in the 1940s and 1950s as a response to the economic predicaments of the developing countries. The attention given to these regions in the West was enhanced by the then perception of the growing threat of the expansion of Communism. On the other hand, several economists from regions like Latin America were also looking for a way out of the economic disruptions caused first by the Great Depression of the 1930s and then by the Second World War. Since then, many theoretical contributions analyzing the causes of the problem and solution recommendations have presented themselves one after the other.

Development is a very wide, dynamic and multi-dimensional concept. Many people may have different perceptions of the meaning of development. Todaro explains as follows:

> Development must therefore be conceived of as a multidimensional process involving major changes in social structures, popular attitudes, and national institutions, as well as the acceleration of economic growth, the reduction of inequality, and the eradication of poverty.[42]

Himmelstrand identifies six criteria of development as structural change: a society's capacity to feed its own people by using its resources; the ability to provide farmers with basic tools for food production; a set of shared transaction rules regulating relations of major actors; indigenous entrepreneurs and a well-organized working class; a development of reasonable trade relationships; and building democratic self-rule.[43] As defined above, development involves not only economic growth but also other concomitant changes of social and institutional processes aiming at achieving a better standard of living. Thus, the major objectives of development are to increase the availability and widen the distribution of basic life-sustaining goods, to raise the levels of living, and to expand the range of economic and social choices.[44]

Apparently, there are many theoretical approaches that deal with economic situations of developing countries and are also categorized in different ways by different theorists. The five major approaches are the modernization theory, the structuralist paradigm, the neo-Marxist paradigm, the dependency theory and the neo-classical approach. These development theories had been tried to be implemented in various countries with varying results. Nevertheless, as they were mainly ideological driven and gave inadequate attention to individual countries' differing situations and conditions they failed to bring the desired results, which have been the eradication of poverty from developing countries.

The early development strategies formulated by modernization theorists had failed to secure tangible economic progress in many developing countries.[45] These countries were faced with a deep economic crisis, and consequently, with political instability by the mid-1960s and 1970s. Other theorists whose emphasis on political stability as a determining factor in the development of developing countries was not also crowned with success.[46] Although political stability is an important factor, it is only one of the major factors that work concomitantly with the other endogenous and external ones to induce development. With the exception of a few countries' performances, authoritarian regimes were mainly engaged in suppressing their people and wasting resources in the name of economic development.[47] It then became clear that the modernization theory's prescription failed to work and many developing countries were faced with deepening economic crisis and worsening poverty.

On the other hand, the structuralists, the dependency theorists and the neo-Marxists have advocated a development strategy based on self-reliance. The structuralists' strategy of import-substitution has ended up with exacerbating the dependency, which was supposed to be reduced or eliminated.[48] The neo-Marxists' and dependency theorists' advocacy for terminating subordination to the developed world and building a new society by a socialist revolution has been unrealistic and impractical.[49] Moreover, their prescriptions for mitigating the economic debacle of the developing countries have been inadequate.[50]

The neo-classical approach had become dominant in many developing countries in the 1980s and 90s. Internal adjustments recommended by international financial institutions had had a substantial influence in the formulation of development strategies. Internal adjustments are essential but are not sufficient to ensure economic progress. Simultaneously, the external problems these countries are facing in the world market need serious attention to rectify them. A major challenge is presented in their earnings of foreign exchange, which is badly needed for imports, by restricted access to the markets of the developed world, especially in primary commodities. Moreover, the world markets of these products have continued to be depressed with their prices further declining. The debt burden is another important factor, which is compounding the development crises. Debt rescheduling has proved of little benefit to developing countries. The most realistic approach might be to encourage these countries' endeavours by cancelling the heavy debt and allowing their commodities to developed nations' market with less restriction. Moreover, the flow of foreign investment is insufficient to play a visible role. As mentioned above, serious decisions and concrete actions might be needed by the world's richest countries to complement the internal efforts of these countries to bear fruit.

Furthermore, the focus of economic development should be switched to a strategy which embraces agricultural growth as its core component. The multinational financial institutions demand for the state to withdraw and restrain itself from any economic role has been unproductive. Considering the extent of market failures in the economy and the existence of feeble private sector, the role of the state in the economy becomes indispensable.[51] The state has to invest in much selected areas that serve to bridge the gaps in the economy as well as in those sectors beyond the capability of the private sector. The multinational financial institutions' prescription of polices designed to be adopted by all developing counties irrespective of their varying conditions also failed to produce the promised results. Apparently, coherent and multi-faceted strategies and policies, which promote agriculture as the engine of growth and recognize the prudent role of the state in economic activities, and a strong determination and commitment to implement them, may produce tangible and desired results.

The Interaction of Democracy and Economic Development

The relationship between democracy and economic development has been debatable among scholars and it seems there exists substantially diverse views on the effect of the interaction.[52] On the one hand, some theorists argue that democracy and economic development are mutually reinforcing and compatible. On the other hand, others say that democracy is detrimental to development. Still, there are some who advocate that there exists no tangible relationship between democracy and economic development. In the last three decades, many researchers have attempted to seek confirmation for their respective positions, but ended up with divergent conclusions.

There has been a widespread approach, which considers democracy to be an outgrowth of socio-economic development. Lipset explains that "the more well-to-do a nation, the greater the chances that it will sustain democracy".[53] From his empirical research of various groups of countries, he concludes that economic development involving industrialization, urbanization, high educational standards, and a steady increase in the overall wealth of the society, is a basic condition sustaining democracy.[54] He argues "perhaps the most widespread generalisation linking political systems to other aspects of society has been that democracy is related to the state of economic development".[55] This approach maintains that increased national wealth creates favourable ground for the growth of the middle class, which is considered to be associated with moderation, tolerance and democracy; it reduces the conflict caused by socio-economic inequality and mitigates feelings of relative deprivation and injustice among the lower classes.[56] It also upholds that development generates the education or the communication networks required to foster democratic institutions.

Huntington explains that the correlation between wealth and democracy implies that transitions to democracy should occur primary in countries at the middle levels of economic development. He denotes that when countries attain the level of development that make them candidates for democratization, then they are most likely to transit to democracy.[57] Although these theorists agree that democracy requires as a prerequisite some level of economic development, there is no clear consensus on the level, aspect or pattern of development that would serve the purpose. Nevertheless, there is a widespread belief that poverty is a principal obstacle to economic development and democracy depends on the future of economic development.[58]

The issue of compatibility between democracy and economic development has generated an extensive debate with divergent conclusions. Some see a trade-off between democracy on the one hand and economic development on the other. These theorists see that development requires an economic surplus for investment and can be accomplished by curbing consumption, which a democratic government is unlikely to pursue. Löwenthal notes that, "every increase in freedom takes place at the cost of a slowdown of development; every acceleration of development involves less freedom."[59]

According to this viewpoint, democracy is detrimental to economic development by unleashing a wide range of pressures on the government for current consumption. Such tendencies reduce investment and thus reduce economic progress. In this regard, Galenson argues that "[t]he more democratic a government is, the easier it will be to force it to translate legislative codes into real services, and pari passu, the greater the diversion of resources from investment to consumption.[60] Similarly, Vaman Rao addresses the problems of development as follows:

> Economic development is a process for which huge investments in personnel and material is required. Such investment programs imply cuts in current consumption that would be painful at the low levels of living that exists in almost all developing societies. Governments must resort to strong measures and they must enforce them with an iron hand in order to marshal the surpluses needed for investment. If such measures were put to a popular vote, they would surely be defeated. No political party can hope to win a democratic election on a platform of current sacrifices for a "bright future".[61]

Hence, governments insulated from pressures by interest groups and democratic polities can best promote economic development. Authoritarian governments are best suited to promote policies that can squeeze maximum amount of surplus and facilitate economic growth. Marsh concludes that:

> Political competition/democracy does have a significant effect on later rates of economic development; its influence is to retard the development rate, rather than to facilitate it. In short, among the poor nations, an authoritarian political system increases the rate of economic development, while a democratic political system does appear to be a luxury which hinders development.[62]

Tavares and Wacziarg also conclude "our interpretation of the results is that democratic institutions are responsive to the demands of the poorer fractions of society by increasing access to education and lowering income inequality, but do so at expense of physical capital accumulation. When summing up the effects of democracy on growth, the negative effect through physical investment dominates. However, the higher level of human capital and a more equitable society in democracies are valued in themselves, beyond their impact on income levels. The resulting view is that democratic institutions entail a trade-off between measurable economic costs and social benefits which are harder to evaluate."[63] Similarly Barro concludes "[w]ith respect to the determination of growth, the cross-country analysis brings out favourable effects from maintenance of the rule of law, free markets, small government consumption and high human capital. Once these kinds of variables and the initial level of GDP are held constant, the overall effect of democracy is weakly negative. There is some indication of a nonlinear relation in which more democracy enhances growth at low levels of political freedom but depresses growth when a moderate level of political freedom has already been attained."[64]

Huntington and Dominguez also entertain the above assertion and explain that "[t]he preponderance of the data that exists, however, suggests that ... authoritarian and one-party systems do have an edge, although not a great one, over other types of systems in promoting economic growth in the early phases of modernization".[65] In order to allow authoritarian governments to do their job, Huntington and Nelson suggest "political participation must be held down, at least temporarily, in order to promote economic development".[66]

Some theorists not only advocate that authoritarian regimes are most likely to bring about economic development, but also the unattainableness of democracy in the Third World countries.[67] There are also those who propose for the sequencing of the two objectives: economic development first, and then democracy. This sequencing favours an authoritarian development-oriented regime followed by a democratic one as a preferable solution for the dilemma.[68] Some prominent theorists seem to favour the opinion that democracy comes second to economic reform. Huntington argues that economic liberalization, first, and then democratization, makes a great deal of sense for those who wish to achieve both goals. He further asserts that opening up the political system first is likely to complicate economic reform.[69] Similarly, Mugyenyi suggests "development leads with democracy in tow. For developing countries, the democracy in tow must be of the minimalist variety regardless of their political sloganeering and other democratic pretensions. Given the allocation of resources between development and democratic demands, development should take precedence over democratic demands".[70] Almond and Powell also denote, "state building and economy building are logically prior to political participation and material distribution, since power sharing and welfare sharing are dependent on there being power and welfare to share."[71]

On the other hand, some theorists contend that democratic government is best suited to foster sustained economic development. Furthermore, it is stated that democratic processes and the existence of political rights generate the societal conditions most conducive to economic progress. Rueschemeyer et.al. conclude "the outstanding finding is that there exists a stable positive relationship between socioeconomic development and democracy."[72] Berg-Schlosser, after examining various African countries on the basis of regime typology, also contends as follows:

> Closer analysis reveals a differentiated pattern that contradicts many commonly held assumptions concerning the developmental advantages of (civil or military) authoritarian rule in Third World countries. These polyarchic systems fare quite well both in terms of GNP growth and the improvement of the basic quality of life. They also have the best record concerning normative standards (protection of civil liberties and freedom from political repression).[73]

However, he has also indicated that authoritarian regimes are found "to have a positive effect on the overall rate of GNP growth, though their performance in terms of an improvement of the physical quality of life for a greater part of the population is fairly poor".[74]

Burkhart and Lewis-Beck, after analysing data from 131 nations argue "to the extent that this finding holds for nations currently in democratic transition, the implication is that democratic reform by itself cannot be counted on to bring about the needed economic development. However, this is no counsel to dictatorship. Just as clearly, we found that democracy, while not apparently a direct cause of economic development, certainly does it no harm. Moreover, as the lag pattern of the structural model shows, past democratic performance breeds future democratic performance. Democracy, then, can be furthered for its own sake, without sacrificing economic development."[75]

Dick has reached a conclusion that is in favour of democracy after investigating the performance of 72 countries in the period of 1959-68. He summarizes as follows:

> These results certainly do not support, and tend to refute, the view that authoritarian countries are universally capable of achieving faster economic growth in the early stages of development than countries having competitive political systems, or that underdeveloped countries face "a cruel choice between rapid (self-sustained) expansion and democratic processes".[76]

Similarly, after reviewing the performance of 115 countries over the period of 1960 - 1980, Scully contends that "political open societies, which bind themselves to the rule of law, to private property, and to the market allocation of resources grow at three times (2.7 to 0.9 per cent annually) the rate of and are two and one-half times as efficient as societies where these freedoms are circumscribed or proscribed."[77]Several theorists attempt to contest the idea that authoritarian regimes' strength makes them better candidates to promote economic development. Although they concede that economic development requires a strong state to enforce contracts, ensure law and order, and so on, they reject the idea that a strong state and an authoritarian state are synonymous. Therefore, a democratic state can also be a strong state with adequate capabilities to facilitate economic development.[78]

There have been several researches on whether democracy is compatible with economic development. The results of these researches are diverse and inconclusive. Przeworski and Limongi have examined 18 studies that generated 21 findings and noted as follows:

> Among them, eight found in favour of democracy, eight in favour of authoritarianism and five discovered no difference. What is even more puzzling is that among the eleven results published before 1988, eight found that authoritarian regimes grew faster, while none of the nine results published after 1987 supported this finding. And since this difference does not seem attributable to samples or periods, one can only wonder about the relation between statistics and ideology.[79]

On the other hand, studies show that democratic regimes, especially in developing countries, do not necessarily respond to welfare issues as the proponents of authoritarianism suspect. Williamson and Pamper, from a sample of 32 developing countries, found that the level of political democracy did not seem to facilitate social welfare programs.[80] Similarly, Sorensen presents the conclusion that democratic regimes' constraint in promoting economic development has less to do with the lack of ability to curb consumption. He deduces that the problem seems more a lack of resolve to restrict dominant elite interests that sometimes are respected at the expense of national interest.[81]

Evidently, the studies fail to provide a clear conclusion as to whether democracy fosters or hinders economic development. Some studies reveal that there has not been a one-to-one relationship between the form of regime and development, but stress more of the development capacities of regimes. As the Growth Report of the World Bank emphasizes, development requires an increasingly capable, credible, and committed government.[82] Political stability, conditions for the functioning of markets in the allocation of resources, the encouragement and mobilization of domestic savings and their effective investment, and human development aspects are generally raised as key conditions for economic progress. Sorensen observes that "democracy offers the opportunities; it does not offer guarantees of success."[83]

Przeworski et al. also observe that "political regimes have no impact on the growth of total income when countries are observed across the entire spectrum of conditions. Contrary to widespread concerns, democracies do not reduce the rate of investment even in poor countries. Indeed, it appears that when countries are poor there is little that governments can do, so that it makes little difference for economic growth whether rulers are elected or hold power by force".[84]They further declare, "we did not find a shred of evidence that democracy need be sacrificed on the altar of development".[85]

Furthermore, Amartya Sen contends "if all comparative studies are viewed together, the hypothesis that there is no clear relation between economic growth and democracy in either direction remains extremely plausible. Since democracy and political liberty have importance in themselves, the case for them therefore remains untarnished".[86] Moreover, he argues "in the terrible history of famines in the world, no substantial famine has ever occurred in any independent and democratic country with a relatively free press."[87] Shihata also explains "it is difficult ... to conclude that either process necessarily precedes the other, although recent studies suggest that economic liberalization is conducive to political liberalization and that the propensity of democracy is likely to rise with economic development".[88]

Apparently, democratization and market-oriented economic reforms seem, today, to coexist in practice in several countries. Although it has not yet been established theoretically why they are compatible, it seems clear that there is much less tangible evidence depicting democracy as an obstacle to economic progress. Diamond and Plattner observe as follows:

> Democracies can achieve lasting economic reform and sustained development, but ultimately only through the democratic process and the combined efforts of effective leaders in politics and civil society. Educating the public, persuading key constituencies, negotiating compromises, crafting political coalitions, and mobilizing new constituencies all take energy and time. But in the end, the democratic process may well produce deeper and more enduring economic reform, and certainly with fewer costs to freedom and justice.[89]

Finally, as discussed above, many theorists have diverse opinions on the interaction of democracy and economic development. The studies conducted so far are apparently inconclusive in determining whether democratic regimes have invariably performed better than the authoritarian ones. Also, the notion of the prevalence of a general trade-off between democracy and economic development does not seem to be sound. On the other hand, as Przeworski et. al. observe it seems plausible that poverty breeds poverty and dictatorship.[90] Evidently, as shown in the above discussion, it is imperative to study the interaction of these worthwhile objectives.

Conclusions

In the above sections, the study has attempted to review the main notions of democracy and economic development. The diverse conceptions of the interaction of democracy and economic development are also discussed. From the above analysis, it is not difficult to observe that these concepts create different impressions to different people. Moreover, they are dynamic and have developed in their definitions over a long span of years.

The study uses the definition of democracy provided by Diamond et al.,[91] which is quoted above in full. Thus, it adopts the main tenets of the definition: meaningful and extensive competition, a highly inclusive level of political participation and a level of civil and political liberties. Similarly, the market-oriented economic policies will be the other component in the approach used to investigate the interaction of democracy and economic development. Here, great emphasis will be given to the agricultural-development-led-industrialization strategy and subsequent sector strategies and policies.

As mentioned above, the study will mainly concentrate on the model of democracy that would possibly succeed in deeply divided societies. Ethiopia as a multi-ethnic country, and as a country that has emerged recently from three decades of civil war, needs a democratic system that includes some of the consociational principles. Therefore, the extent of the application of the principles of consociational democracy will be examined considering Ethiopia's specific conditions.

The interaction of democracy and development has been debatable for decades. The research conducted to investigate whether democracy advances or hinders development remains inconclusive.[92] Nevertheless, it is the principal purpose of this study to analyze how these concepts interact in Ethiopia, which has simultaneously embarked on the process of democratization and economic reform. It also attempts to find out under what general conditions they are compatible, and whether these conditions can gradually be created in this country.

Notes

1. See Crawford, James, Democracy and International Law, British Yearbook of International Law 1993, p. 113-133 with references to the enormous literature on these developments in note 36 at p. 122.
2. "Progress Review and Recommendations", adopted by the Third International Conference of the New or Restored Democracies on Democracy and Development held at Bucharest from 2 to 4 September 1997, UN Doc A/52/334, 11 September 1997.

3. IPU Universal Declaration on Democracy, adopted by the Inter-Parliamentary Council at its 161st Session (Cairo, 16 September 1997), at para. 1, reprinted in Netherlands Quarterly of Human Rights (2000), p. 127.
4. See the Warsaw Declaration: Towards A Community of Democracies, International Legal Materials, vol. 39, November 2000, p. 1306 – 1308.
5. Inter- American Democratic Charter, International Legal Materials, vol. 40L, November 2001, p. 1289 – 94. For example, Article 3 states as follows: Essential elements of representative democracy include, inter alia, respect for human rights and fundamental freedoms, access to and the exercise of power in accordance with the rule of law, the holding of periodic, free and fair elections based on secret balloting and universal suffrage as an expression of the sovereignty of the people, the pluralistic system of political parties and organizations, and the separation of powers and independence of the branches of government (Ibid., p. 1291).
6. Franck, Thomas, "The Emerging Right to Democratic Governance", AJIL, vol. 86 (1992), p. 46. For references to the literature see Crawford, (Democracy and International Law) op. cit., p. 122, notes 39 and 40. See also Susan Marks, The Riddle of all Constitutions: International Law, Democracy, and the Critique of Ideology, Oxford, New York: Oxford University Press, 2000; Gregory H. Fox and Brad R. Roth (eds.), Democratic Governance and International Law, Cambridge, New York: Cambridge University Press, 2000, and the review of the aforementioned two books by Richard Falk in: American Journal of International Law, vol. 96 (2002), p. 264-268, who cites additional literature.
7. Ibid., p. 91.
8. Wheatley, Steven, Democracy in International Law: A European Perspective, International and Comparative Law Quarterly (ICLQ), vol. 50, April 2002, p. 233. See also Brad R. Roth, Governmental Illegitimacy in International Law, Oxford: Clarendon Press, 1999.
9. Wheatley, p. 225.
10. Ibid., p. 234. Wheatley argues that in Europe, "this irreversible progress is complete". Reference can be made to the major regional organizations in Europe. Art. 6(1) of the 1992 Treaty of European Union states that "The Union is founded on the principles of liberty, democracy, respect for human rights and fundamental freedoms, and the rule of law, principles which are common to the Member states". New members joining the EU must show that they have a stable democracy. The European Court of Human Rights, established within the framework of the Council of Europe, has determined that "[d]emocracy....appears to be the only political model contemplated by the [European Convention on Human Rights] and, accordingly, the only one compatible with it", United Communist Party of Turkey and others v. Turkey, European Court of Human Rights Reports 1998-I, at para. 45. The member states of the Organization for Security and Co-operation in Europe (OSCE) have consented to "build, consolidate and strengthen democracy as the only system of government of our nations" and to "co-operate and support each other with the aim of making democratic gains irreversible", 1990 CSCE

Charter of Paris for a New Europe, International Legal Materials 30 (1991), p. 190.

11. Wheatley, p. 235.
12. "Promotion of the right to democracy", UN Commission on Human Rights, UN Doc. E/CN 4/RES/1999/57, 28 April 1999.
13. UN Secretary General, "Support by the United Nations system of the efforts of Governments to promote and consolidate new or restored democracies", UN Doc. A/52/513, 21 October 1997, at. para. 27.
14. UN Secretary General, Supplement to Reports on Democratization, UN Doc. A/51/761, 20 December 1996, at para. 10.
15. Ibid., at para. 4.
16. Birch, The Concepts and Theories of Modern Democracy, 1993: 51.
17. Schumpeter, Capitalism, Socialism and Democracy, 1987: 251.
18. Ibid., p. 269.
19. Ibid., p. 273.
20. Ibid., 284-85.
21. Dahl, Polyarchy, 1971: 1.
22. Since no country satisfies the above mentioned democratic ideals and countries also differ in the degree of their application, he prefers to call real world systems that are close to satisfy the requisite standard as polyarchies. Dahl applies this term to relatively democratized countries but reserves democracy for complete or almost complete responsiveness to all citizens. He further defines polyarchy as a political order distinguished by the presence of seven institutions, all of which must exist for a government to be classified as a polyarchy. These institutions are elected officials, free and fair elections, inclusive suffrage, the right to run for office, freedom of expression, alternative information and associational autonomy. The institutions constitute two dimensions of democratization: contestation and inclusiveness. Ibid., p. 4-8. See also Dahl, Democracy and Its Critics, 1989: 220-21; Dahl, Modern Political Analysis, 1991: 72-74.; Dahl, Democracy and Its Critics, 1989: 221.
23. See Bollen, Issues in the Comparative Measurement of Political Democracy." Schmitter and Karl, in Diamond and Plattner(eds.), 1996:50. (Ibid., p. 55; See also Karl, 1990:2.
24. See Ake, Democracy and Development in Africa, 1996: 132.
25. Diamond, Class, Ethnicity, and Democracy in Nigeria, 1998: 4.
26. Diamond et. al. (eds.), Democracy in Developing Countries: Africa, p. xvi. See also Diamond, 1988: 4; Diamond, 1989: 142-43; McClintock, 1989: 132-33; Sorensen, 1993: 13. Similar definitions are found in Linz, The Breakdown of Democratic Regimes, 1978: 5; and Lipset, Political Man, 1981: 27.
27. Lijphart, 1969: 216.
28. Ibid; see also Lehmbruch, 1975: 379-81.

29. Lijphart, "Consociation and Federation", 1979: 500. See also Lijphart, 1980: 25; Lijphart, 1996: 258.
30. Lijphart, 1980: 25-36. See also Lijphart, 1996: 259-60; Lijphart, 1979: 500.
31. Lijphart, 1996: 260.
32. Lijphart, 1980: 41.
33. Ibid., p. 38-41; Lijphart, 1979: 501; Lijphart, 1996: 261.
34. See Lijphart, 1996: 262.
35. Ibid., p. 261-62; see also Lijphart, 1980: 36-38; see also Dirk Berg-Schlosser, "Elements of Consociational Democracy in Kenya", European Journal of Political Research, 1985, 13, March, 95-109, where some elements of consociational democracy are discussed.
36. Lijphart, 1979: 509-12.
37. Lijphart, 1975: 195.
38. Lijphart, 1980: 238.
39. International Institute for Strategic Studies, Strategic Survey 1993-1994, 1995 quoted in Makinda, 1988: 567.
40. See Lipset, 1959; Neubauer, 1967; Lipset, 1981; Huntington, 1984 and 1991.
41. Diamond, "Beyond Authoritarianism and Totalitarianism", 1989: 24.
42. Todaro, Economic Development, 2000: 16; He further notes that the core values of development as sustenance, self-esteem, and freedom (Ibid., p.16-17).
43. Himmelstrand, in Himmelstrand, Kinyanjui and Mburugu, 1994: 18.
44. See Todaro, 2000: 18.
45. Modernization theory was the dominant school of thought on development until the early 1960s. According to this theory, economic development entails the transformation of a traditional stagnant, subsistence-oriented economy into a dynamic, capitalist economy based on wage-labour, capable of self-sustained growth and of providing, in the long term, rising real wages. Capital accumulation, availability of foreign exchange, industrialization (first of the import substitution variety and then of export oriented character), population control, human resources development, employment oriented strategies and redistribution with growth, were prescribed at various stages to facilitate the transformation. The theory emphasizes the importance of individual motivation and capital accumulation, and also encourages the flow of foreign aid, trade and investment, and technical assistance for development. Thus, the idea of building a modern society was the goal of development. See Ghai (1977), quoted in Himmelstrand et al., 1994:38; Hunt, Economic Theories of Development, 1989: 62-63; see also Tipps reprinted in Black, Comparative Modernization, 1976: 64-67. Toye explains that modern society was taken as one with typical social patterns of demography, urbanization and literacy; typical economic patterns of production and consumption, investment, trade and government finance; and typical psychological attributes of rationality, ascriptive identity and achievement motivation. (Toye, Dilemmas of Development, 1987:11).

46. Many theorists gave significant emphasis to the stability of a regime with little consideration to the government's democratic credentials. Huntington advocates that it is the degree of government and not necessarily its form that is important in determining its ability to bring about progress. However, it was not long before governments in many developing countries started to curtail civil liberties on grounds of expediting industrial development and modernization. Huntington (1965) quoted in Kamrava, Politics and Society in the Third World, 1993: 36; Donald C. O'Brien notes that the increasingly tense international situation has aroused the academic interest in political order rather than political change. (Quoted in Blomstrom and Hettne, Development Theory in Transition: The Dependency Debate and Beyond, 1984: 23).
47. Bauzon suggests some factors for the failure of the modernization theory: the mistaken belief that all societies follow a unilinear path to the same level of development; the assumption that development is primarily a function of endogenous factors; the assumption that the state is a reflection of a community-wide consensus; its teleological orientation, which ignored conflictual processes; the alienation and disaffection of a large segment of the population from the political system; and the rise of revolutionary movements in much of the Third World which reflected the above-mentioned alienation and disaffection. Bauzon, in Bauzon (ed.), Development and Democratization in the Third World, 1992: 38.
48. The structuralist approach evolved from the urge to solve the economic problems of Latin American countries due to declining primary export prices and worsening balance of payment crises. Besides, the wartime disruptions to international trade and continuing shortages of manufactured imports further worsened the economic difficulties. They rejected the theory of comparative advantage, believing that the terms of trade between the industrial and peripheral countries tend to deteriorate constantly to the advantage of the former. Several policy instruments were recommended: tariff, monetary and fiscal policy. Cutting nonessential imports; expanding primary exports, and as industrial development proceeds, manufactured goods; guiding investment to key import-substituting sectors; import control in order to counteract international trade cycles; and forming common markets in the periphery to increase the range of viable import-substituting investment, were forwarded as policy actions to be adopted to redress the difficulties caused by balance of payments. Preston, Theories of Development, 1982: 145. Hunt, 1989: 141. See also Singer and Alizadeh, reprinted in Ayres (ed.), Development Studies, 1995: 321-22; Furtudo underlines that industrial development is likely to remain blocked and economic dualism will be perpetuated unless governments come out with appropriate intervention policies. He recommends an economic strategy that places emphasis on the formation of common markets to enlarge market size and adoption of import substitution policies by the public sector in those products that show particularly high income elasticities of demand. (Furtudo, 1964).
49. The neo-Marxist theory has evolved as a subschool within Marxism with an intention to adopt classical Marxist theory in the analysisof underdevelopment in Third

World countries. Economic underdevelopment is defined as a process whose dominant feature is the persistent outflow of economic surplus generated in the periphery to the advanced capitalist economies. The underdeveloped economies are characterized by low average per capita incomes and by slow rates of accumulation. Amin explains that underdevelopment is manifested both by the outflow of surplus through trade and by a distorted and stunted process of industrial growth in the periphery. The centre exploits and blocks the development of the periphery by dominating investments in the modern sectors, controlling their composition and extracting surplus in the form of repatriated profit, and by a persistent primitive accumulation that is extraction of surplus through unequal exchange in international trade. On the other hand, Warren advocates that capitalism is serving as a bridge to socialism. He seems to believe that it is fulfilling its "historic mission" of preparing the ground for the transformation of the existing system into a socialist one. For this reason, he fails to even criticize the negative aspects of imperialism's role and places the blame on the Third World countries. Hunt, 1989: 163-64; See Amin, Accumulation on a World Scale, 1974: 86-90; Amin further explains the essence of class struggle within the centre-periphery distinction as follows: It means that, in an auto centric economy, there is an organic relation between the two terms of the social contradiction, bourgeoisie and proletariat, that they are both integrated into a single reality, the nation. In an extraverted economy, this unity of opposites is not to be grasped within the national context. This unity is broken, and can be discovered only on the world scale...unequal exchange means that the problem of the class struggle must necessarily be considered on the world scale, and that national problems cannot be seen as epiphenomena juxtaposed with the essential problem of the "pure" class struggle. (Amin, 1974: 599-600); See also Warren, 1980: 25.

50. The dependency theory emerged as a school of thought in the late 1960s. The dependency theory consists of different approaches contributed by neo-Marxists and disillusioned structuralists. Neo-Marxists' contribution evolved as a response to the criticisms that a growing number of countries in the Third World had achieved very respectable rates of capital accumulation over time, which contradicted their theory of the impossibility of local capital accumulation in the periphery. Hence, dependency is a concept which assumes that the industrial growth of some periphery countries is dependent on the world metropolitan economies for access to markets, finance and technology. On the other hand, the other version of the dependency theory emerged from the disillusionment of the import-substituting industrialization strategy, which, in the 1960s, was in disrepute. Dos Santos explains that in the post-war era, three aspects of dependence were working against the economic development of the peripheral countries. These are: (1) industrial development is dependent on an export sector for the foreign currency to buy the inputs utilized by the industrial sector; (2) industrial development is therefore strongly conditioned by fluctuations in the balance of payments; and (3) industrial development is strongly conditioned by the technological monopoly exercised by imperialist centres. Hunt, 1989: 67-68; See also Dos Santos, Theotonio, May 1970, reprinted in Seligson and Passé-Smith, 1993:

197-199. Dos Santos defines dependency as a situation in which the economy of certain countries is conditioned by the development and expansion of another economy to which the former is subjected. The relation of interdependence between two or more economies, and between these and world trade, assumes the form of dependence when some countries (the dominant ones) can expand and can be self-sustaining, while other countries (the dependent ones) can do this as a reflection of the expansion, which can have either a positive or a negative effect on their immediate development. (Ibid., p. 194).

51. The state and essential public enterprises played a pivotal role in the fast development of the East Asian countries. For some details, see Chang, Bad Samaritans, 2008:120-21; and 215-17; Lin, The Quest for Prosperity, 2012:39-42 and 97-101; see also Sainsbury, Progressive Capitalism, 2013:247-58.

52. See Lipset, 1959; Galenson, in Galenson (ed.), 1959; Lipset 1981; Dahl, 1971; Huntington and Dominguez, in Greenstein and Polsby (eds.), 1975; Huntington and Nelson 1976; Huntington, 1991; Lowenthal, 1963; Sorensen, 1991; Sorensen, 1993; Rao, 1984; Marsh, 1979; Kitching, 1983; Berg-Schlosser, 1984; Landau 1986; Dick, 1974; Scully 1988 and 1992; Przeworski and Limongi, in Bagchi (ed.), 1995; Przeworski and Limongi, in Hadenius (ed.), Democracy's Victory and Crisis, 1997; Healey and Robinson, 1992; Diamond and Plattner, 1995. Diamond, Developing Democracy Toward Consolidation, 1999; Przewoski et.al., 2000; and AmartyaSen, in Diamond and Plattner (eds.), 2001(positions of these scholars are discussed in details below). On the other hand, Warren advocates that capitalism is serving as a bridge to socialism. He seems to believe that it is fulfilling its "historic mission" of preparing the ground for the transformation of the existing system into a socialist one. For this reason, he fails to even criticize the negative aspects of imperialism's role and places the blame on the Third World countries.

53. Lipset, 1959: 75; 1981: 31; Dahl also notes that the chances for political competition depend on the socioeconomic level of the society. (Dahl, 1971: 65).

54. Lipset, 1959: 86; Lipset further explains that economic development, producing increased income, greater economic security, and widespread higher education, largely determines the form of the class struggle, by permitting those in the lower strata to develop longer time perspectives and more complex and gradualist views of politics. A belief in secular reformist gradualism can be the ideology of only a relatively well–to–do lower class. (Lipset, 1981:45).

55. Lipset, 1959: 75.

56. See Lipset, 1981: 45-53; Dahl, 1971: 81-87.

57. Huntington, The Third Wave, 1991: 60; Huntington suggests that sheer wealth may not be a crucial factor for democratization. He indicates that wealth amassed from oil sales in oil producing countries has not created the necessary broad-based economic development for transition to democracy. On the other hand, economic development involving significant industrialization may contribute to democratization.

58. Ibid., p. 311; see also Neubauer, "Some Conditions of Democracy", 1967: 1008-9.
59. Löwenthal, 1963, quoted in Sorensen, 1991: 1.
60. Galenson, Walter, in Galenson (ed.), 1959: 17.
61. Rao, Vaman, Democracy and Economic Development, 1984: 74-75; Rao further notes that curbs on democratic rights should be preceded by a national consensus on the goals and strategies of development. This consensus need not be obtained through an elaborate referendum. He argues that the process of economic development represents only a transitional stage in a nation's life and people must make extraordinary sacrifices in order to lift the economy from a lower level to a higher level. If years of exploitation and economic stagnation and decline are to be shortened, enormous sacrifices are needed. It is the only way for the Third World to "catch up". (Ibid., p. 79).
62. Marsh, "Does Democracy Hinders Economic Development in the Latecomer Developing Nations", 1979: 244; he made this conclusion after surveying 98 countries in the period 1955-70; similarly, Landau explains that "several variables were used to test for political influences on economic growth. Those that showed some significant influence were the following: the country being a democracy, the incidence of coups, and a war having been fought on the country's soil. All three were negatively correlated with the growth rate." (Landau, Daniel, "Government and Economic Growth in the Less Developed Countries: An Empirical Study for 1960-1980", Economic Development and Cultural Change, Vol. 35, No. 1, October 1986, p.70.)
63. Tavares and Wacziarg, "How Democracy Affects Growth", 2001: 1372.
64. Barro, "Democracy and Economic Growth", 1996: 23. In his another study, Barro concludes "[w]ith respect to government policies, the evidence indicates that the growth rate of real per capita GDP is enhanced by better maintenance of the rule of law, smaller government consumption, and lower inflation. Increases in political rights initially increase growth but tend to retard growth once a moderate level of democracy has been attained." (Barro, Determinants of Economic Growth: A Cross-Country Empirical Study, 1997: 119).
65. Huntington and Dominguez, "Political Development," in Greenstein and Polsby (eds.), 1975: 60.
66. Huntington and Nelson, No Easy Choice, 1976: 23.
67. For example, see Kitching, Rethinking Socialism, 1983: 48-49; Kitching further elaborates his idea as follows: In situations in which the majority of people (or even perhaps a sizeable minority) are absolutely poor, in which most people are still struggling to obtain or retain some freedom from the constraints of really basic want and deprivation, life is much more of a scrambling struggle for survival than in richer societies... people are much more prone to regard all their activities, all their investments of time and energy, from the point of view of their material 'pay off' ... The central point is simply that this kind of desperate scrambling individualism is so pronounced in poor societies, precisely because not only do winners take all, but losers lose out absolutely. The cost of failing to take advantage

of opportunities for enrichment and indeed the cost of not having access to such opportunities can be an absolute poverty: a stark, constraining and total deprivation. Thus, the stakes tend to be much higher in political conflicts: The room for manoeuvre more limited, the penalties for defeat more onerous and the rewards for victory more prized. (kitching, 1983: 58 – 59).

68. See Sorensen, Democracy, Dictatorship and Development, 1991: 13.
69. Huntington explains why economic liberalization should precede democratization as follows: China, under a communist dictatorship, and Chile, under a military dictator, introduced substantial economic reforms and have been rewarded with enviable rates of economic growth. ...if a country has an authoritarian regime, it would be lucky if its government used its coercive power to promote economic liberalization. Liberalization, first, then democratization makes a great deal of sense for those who wish to achieve both goals. Opening up the political system first, in contrast, is likely to complicate economic reform. In 1989, I was told by top advisors to Gorbachev that they had made a horrible mistake in moving ahead with glasnost and a political opening, which had unleashed all sorts of political forces, which were then making it very difficult to move toward economic reform. (Huntington, 1993: 25-26).
70. Mugyenyi, in Oyugi et al. (eds.), 1988: 182.
71. Almond and Powell, Comparative Politics, 1978: 363.
72. Rueschemeyer et. al., Capitalist Development and Democracy, 1992: 26.
73. Berg-Schlosser, "African Political Systems: Typology and Performance", 1984: 121.
74. Ibid., p. 143.
75. Burkhart and Lewis-Beck, "Comparative Democracy: The Economic Development Thesis", 1994: 907-908.
76. Dick, "Authoritarian versus Nonauthoritarian Approaches to Economic Development", 1974: 823-24.
77. See Scully, Constitutional Environments and Economic Growth, 1992: 183; see also Scully, "The Institutional Framework and Economic Development", Journal of Political Economy, Vol. 96, No. 31, 1988: 661.
78. See Sorensen, Democracy and Democratization, 1993: 66; Sirow and Inkeles, reprinted in Seligson and Passé-Smith, 1993: 391.
79. Przeworski and Limongi, in Bagchi (ed.), 1995: 11-12. Table 1.1 is a good summary of the results of the researches.
80. Williamson and Pampel, 1986, quoted in Healey and Robinson, 1992: 108.
81. Sorensen, 1991: 185; Sorensen discusses that Indian democracy has avoided policy excesses and human catastrophes such as large-scale famines. However, it has also maintained a highly unequal social structure headed by dominant elite, which resists structural change benefiting the poor. Though poverty alleviation has been the prime objective of the nation's development policy, the ruling classes are able, within the democratic structure, to resist real changes that resulted in the continuation of human suffering. (Ibid., p. 174).

82. See The World Bank, The Growth Report, the Commission on Growth and Development, 2008: 3-5 and 26-28.
83. Sorensen, 1993: 89.
84. Przeworski et. al., Democracy and Development, 2000: 270.
85. Ibid., p. 271.
86. Sen, "Democracy as a Universal Value", in Diamond and Plattner (eds.), 2001: 7; for further discussion, see also Sen, Amartya, Development as Freedom, 1999: 146-159.
87. Sen, in Diamond and Plattner (eds.), 2001: 7; The Human Development Report 2002 argues "[d]emocratic governance is valuable in its own right. But it can also advance human development, for three reasons. First, enjoying political freedom and participating in the decisions that shape one's life are fundamental human rights: they are part of human development in their own right. ... Second, democracy helps protect people from economic and political catastrophes such as famines and descents into chaos... Third, democratic governance can trigger a virtuous cycle of development- as political freedom empowers people to press for policies that expand social and economic opportunities, and as open debates help communities shape their priorities." (The Human Development Report 2002, 2002: 3).
88. Shihata, "Democracy and Development", International and Comparative Law Quarterly, vol. 46, July 1997: 637-638.
89. Diamond and Plattner, Economic Reform and Democracy, 1995: xxii; See also Diamond, Developing Democracy: Toward Consolidation, 1999: 2 - 7.
90. Przeworski et.al., "What Makes Democracies Endure?", in Diamond and Plattner (eds.), 2001: 177.
91. Diamond et. al., 1988: xvi.
92. See the above section for detailed discussion; see also Przeworski and Limongi for a short review of the studies conducted on the interaction of democracy and economic development. (Przeworski and Limongi, in Bagchi (ed.), 1995: 12).

Chapter 3

Historical Background

In order to analyse and assess the developments and changes taking place since 1991, it is essential to briefly review and summarise Ethiopia's political and socioeconomic environment of the past. Starting from the Axumite kingdom of the first century AD, which was the forerunner of the Abyssinian Kingdom, the nation passed through many ups and downs, but remained united enough to survive as independent and emerge as modern Ethiopia by becoming a participant in the 'Scramble for Africa'.[1]

The following review is divided into three main parts, which include an overview of the emergence of modern Ethiopia, of the political and economic developments under the monarchy, and of the period of the military dictatorship. Within this framework, the Eritrean and national questions are also briefly discussed because of these issues' prominence in Ethiopian politics.

Though further studies are still highly pertinent, there do exist well-researched works of Ethiopia's ancient and modern history. What is discussed in the following review is only tailored to serve the purpose of this particular research. For those interested in studying Ethiopian history further, it is advisable to look for the works of historians such as Rubenson, Pankhurst, Marcus, Erlich, Zewde, Henze and others.[2]

The Birth of Modern Ethiopia

Modern Ethiopia took its current shape at the end of the nineteenth century. The Ethiopian state that emerged as a result of the interaction of domestic and external forces was qualitatively different from its predecessor in terms of its territorial size and ethnic composition. The Abyssinian state was basically a conquest state, expanding and contracting over the ages depending on the military and political strength of the ruling elite of the time. However, geographically it did not extend to much more than those areas covering the current northern part of Ethiopia.

The Abyssinian kingdom, which traced its origin from ancient Axum, had existed for centuries before the arrival of European colonialists in the African continent. Axum was a trading state, which had contacts with various parts of the World, from Rome to the Far East.[3] The Axumite Kingdom evolved into a trading partner of other peoples towards the sixth century BC. It flourished as a trading state between the first and eighth century AD.[4] Christianity was introduced during the middle of the fourth century, which played a major role in shaping the culture of the people. In the tenth century, Axum came under pressure from the expanding Arabian forces and from those peoples under its rule in the south. That was the beginning of the eclipse of its civilisation. Marcus explains the situation as follows:

> As Muslim power and influence grew in the eighth century, Ethiopian shipping was swept from the Red Sea-Indian Ocean, changing the nature of the Axumite state. It became isolated from the eastern Mediterranean ecumene that for centuries had influenced its culture and sustained its economy... The state consequently suffered a sharp reduction in revenues and no longer could afford to maintain a large army, a complex administration, and urban amenities. The culture associated with the outside world quickly became a memory, and Ethiopia turned inward.[5]

After the collapse of Axum, the Abyssinian kingdom continued to exist confined to inland territories and at times attempted to expand towards the south whenever it felt it had the strength. There were also moments when the kingdom was threatened with extinction. It became almost non-existent in all but its name during the "Era of the Princes" between 1769 and 1855. As Keller put it, political power became decentralised as the state degenerated into feudal, regional compartments and local warlords and traditional nobility competed among them for supremacy. Consequently, Abyssinia was only nominally a state and in fact was ruled by emperors with no power whatsoever.[6]

Ethiopia experienced the re-emergence of a unified imperial rule with the usurpation of power by Emperor Tewodros in 1855. He defeated the regional rulers in various battlefields and had himself crowned as king of kings. Tewodros tried to undermine the power base of the local princes and nobility by fragmenting the traditional administrative divisions and also by attempting to create a disciplined, professional state army for the first time.[7] He also tried to establish contacts with European powers, which resulted in frustrations and bitterness.[8] As Clapham put it, Tewodros' reign is memorable more for its aspirations than for its achievements, for he lacked the resources needed to realise his plans.[9]

Yohannes IV succeeded Tewodros in 1872. Unlike Tewodros, he was willing to tolerate regional dynasties, which began to regain their strength and autonomy.[10] The opening of the Suez Canal, in 1869, started to attract foreign forces to the Red Sea and consequently, to Ethiopia's hinterlands. Soon after, the Egyptians attempted to conquer Ethiopia but were repelled in 1875 and 1876.[11] Yohannes was killed in 1889 in a battle against Sudanese Mahdists, and subsequently, Menelik was crowned as Emperor of Ethiopia.

Menelik as emperor completed the process of territorial expansion to the present boundaries of Ethiopia. In fact, while he was King of Showa, he started the expansion of territories for known economic and strategic motives. As Wubneh and Abate put it, he needed access to the rich areas of the south and the east, known for their coffee, ivory, gold, and civette gum, to finance his modernisation efforts and to buy modern European weapons.[12] Such moves enabled him to be the undisputed leader domestically, and at the same time, helped him to be in a better position to deal with European powers. Erlich describes the situation as follows:

> While rebuffing imperialism successfully in its north, Ethiopia managed to practice it to the south. During these two decades, and in fact as part of its mobilisation effort against the existential challenge presented by Europe, the kingdom itself participated in the "scramble for Africa". By conquering and annexing huge territories to the south, which were inhabited by Muslims and animists of various ethnic and linguistic origins, Ethiopia more than doubled its size. Its territorial integrity and sovereignty within these new borders were recognised and legitimised in a series of treaties signed with European powers after the Adwa victory.[13]

Menelik also pursued policies that encouraged the centralisation of authority within the empire at the expense of the regional nobility. As a result, the imperial office continued to grow. Furthermore, he imposed an imperial political economy upon his new subjects through his land distribution policies. The Emperor became the possessor of the conquered lands, from which he distributed some of the land as gult[14] or as private tenure to his local administrators, soldiers, northern aristocrats, and to some people who emigrated to the south.[15] Menelik used the land allocation to consolidate his grip on the conquered people by rewarding those who were instrumental in the realisation of the conquest. Consequently, the majority of the people were transformed into serfs with no land rights, while on the other hand, a new class of gentry and nobility, often referred to as the "balabat" and "neftegna",[16] emerged.

For those who resisted the conquest, the punishment was not only land expropriation but also physical extermination. Looting, slavery and acts of depopulation were the daily practices of the conquering army. Such actions had a serious negative impact not only on the economy but also on the social fabric of the people.[17]

Menelik made an effort to build a professional army and introduced a policy of paying its members a regular salary. He was also the first emperor who attempted to form a cabinet; however it had little meaning in practice.[18] Although extremely slow, the drive for modernisation continued to proceed.

Ethiopia's interaction with the outside world also picked up momentum during Menelik's era, but with this, complications arose. Italy's attempt to transform Ethiopia into its protectorate using the treaty of Wichale signed on May 2, 1889 was the immediate cause of the battle of Adwa.[19] The Amharic version of Article XVII of the treaty gave Ethiopia the option of using Italian good offices in the conduct of its foreign affairs, but the version of the Italian text was tantamount to making Ethiopia an Italian protectorate.[20] The disagreement led to war and Menelik was able to defeat the invading Italian army at the battlefield of Adwa in 1896.[21] Marcus describes the Italian thinking of the time as follows:

> Blinded by racism and cultural arrogance, the Italians had little respect for their enemy's modern weaponry. They also ridiculed the notion of Ethiopian nationalism, disbelieving that the Solomonic empire's masses could be united and mustered for any confrontation with European imperialism... In their immense miscalculation, they concluded that even a small force of well-trained modern and motivated soldiers would destroy Menelik's minions.[22]

At Adwa, Ethiopia's independence was saved from a dangerous onslaught from a colonial power. The victory of Adwa was a symbol of Ethiopian national political identity and integrity, which won the recognition of European powers. In the subsequent treaty of October 1896, Italy conceded the abrogation of the treaty of Wichale and recognition of Ethiopia's sovereign independence. In the same treaty, Menelik also accepted the Italian colonial possession of Eritrea and the Mareb river boundary.[23] Clapham summarises the process of the birth of the modern nation as follows:

> By 1850, the disintegrated Empire had reached its lowest ebb. Yet within fifty years, a united Ethiopia was to defeat a European invasion and more than double its territory. This was the measure of the late nineteenth century resurgence that laid the foundations of modern Ethiopia.[24]

The Monarchy and Emerging Political and Economic Forces

Political Developments

As discussed above, Ethiopia is, like other African countries, a product of the 'scramble for Africa' era. The only difference is that it was not created by European colonisers but by the conquest conducted by its last four indigenous Emperors. As Zewde put it, Adwa forms a watershed in the modern history of Ethiopia since it resolved the issue of colonial rule versus independence in favour of the latter.[25] However, the victory of Adwa did not stop the threat of colonialism altogether. In July 1906, Great Britain, France and Italy completed the Tripartite Agreement to partition Ethiopia into spheres of influence.[26] The problems associated with foreign threat and the integration of the newly conquered territories were the two most important tasks that consumed much of the energy of the Emperors of the end of the nineteenth and beginning of the twentieth century.

Emperor Menelik suffered a stroke in 1906 that left him paralysed. He died in 1913 leaving behind confusion and a discordant power struggle. It took some time and political manoeuvres for Ras Teferi, later Haile Selassie, to become first a regent and then to be crowned as Emperor. Henze explains the reason for the confusion as follows:

> Ethiopian emperors regarded themselves as representatives of a dynastic line extending back almost 3000 years, tracing their ancestry to King Solomon and the Queen of Sheba, but never assured a system of succession.[27]

After a power struggle, over a decade-long, Haile Selassie emerged as the winner and was crowned on November 2, 1930.[28] As a regent and later as Emperor, he was committed to continue the centralisation and modernisation policies started during Menelik's reign. The expansion of a modern education system especially in the capital, the construction of roads and other public works, the abolition of slavery and the initial organisation of some departments of government can be mentioned as his early achievements. His early obsession was to curb the powers of the nobility and the church, and to make himself as free as possible from them. This was formalised by provisions in the 1931 constitution.

In 1935, the Italians invaded Ethiopia from the North and South using massive air power and poison gas.[29] The League of Nations abandoned Ethiopia in order not to offend Italy and push it to side with Nazi Germany. Though the

Emperor left for Europe in 1936, the people continued to resist Italian occupation. Zewde summarizes the situation as follows:

> Almost from the arrival in Ethiopia of their first troops, the Italians were confronted with a nation-wide resistance. Their efforts to divide and rule notwithstanding, the resistance movement embraced almost all regions and ethnic groups.[30]

After Italy declared it would be an ally to Germany in 1940, the British, assisted by Ethiopian resistance forces, liberated the country in 1941 for their own reason of protecting British colonial domains from Italian expansionism. The resistance forces played a major role in preventing Italian Fascism from consolidating its hold in the country. Zewde explains the difficulty faced by the Italians:

> ... the resistance forms a glorious chapter in the history of modern Ethiopia. ... Although the patriotic bands won few major battles, the Resistance as a whole had a corrosive influence on Italian rule, both physically and psychologically. Bewildered, battered and harassed by it, Italian troops were rendered highly vulnerable when the British launched the final campaign of Liberation in January 1941.[31]

There is little doubt that the struggle waged by the patriots during five years of Italian occupation contributed to the relative ease with which the country was later liberated.

After regaining the throne, Haile Selassie attempted to modernise the country while clinging to the tenets of absolutism. He was faced with irreconcilable challenges. Modernisation without giving space to the evolving new classes sooner or later was destined to create a problem for the monarchy. The Emperor continued to curtail the power of the aristocracy by introducing some major structural reforms. He established a standing army under his complete control; a new fiscal system was introduced under the Ministry of Finance run by salaried civil servants; provincial administration was reorganised and provincial boundaries were redrawn to curtail the power of traditional governors.[32] Keller remarks:

> With the network of roads bequeathed to Ethiopia by the Italians and with the military and administrative assistance provided by the British in the immediate aftermath of the war, Haile Selassie was able systematically to begin to build an absolutist state of his own design.[33]

Haile Selassie's other preoccupation was the diplomatic front. After liberation, the British were dominant in key areas of the Ethiopian administration as judges and advisers, and in the police force and other departments. In fact, until the 1942 Anglo-Ethiopian agreement, Ethiopia was put under the control of the Occupied Enemy Territory Administration (OETA). The 1942 agreement acknowledged Ethiopia as a sovereign state; however, it contained provisions that gave the British control of some parts of the country and also limited Ethiopia's freedom of action.[34] In 1944, Ethiopia was able to negotiate a better agreement but did not acquire sovereignty over the Ogaden, which only happened partly in 1948. It had to wait until 1954 to establish its control over the whole region.[35]

The Emperor attempted to give his absolute powers a juridical framework by granting a constitution. The 1931 constitution was nothing more than a document written to provide the monarchy with a better domestic and international image.[36] It clearly confirmed that the authority of the Crown was absolute. Chapter I, Article V, states:

> By virtue of his imperial blood, as well as by the anointing which he has received, the person of the Emperor is sacred, his dignity is inviolable and his power indisputable. Consequently, he is entitled to all the honours due to him in accordance with tradition and the present Constitution. The law decrees that anyone so bold as to injure the Majesty of the Emperor will be punished.[37]

In addition, Chapter III, Article VI, states: "In the Ethiopian Empire supreme power rests in the hands of the Emperor ...He ensures the exercise thereof in conformity with the established law".[38] In terms of popular participation, Henze explains that "it [the constitution] provided for the establishment of a bicameral parliament, a senate appointed from the nobility by the emperor and a chamber of deputies to be elected indirectly on the basis of property qualifications. No law approved by the parliament could go into effect until promulgated by the Emperor. It is evident that this extremely restrictive constitution was in part intended to impress foreign countries...".[39]

With the change of situations in the fifties, and especially with the 1952 federation with Eritrea, which had a liberal constitution, a revision of the constitution was recommended to conform to internal and external expectations. The 1955 revised constitution[40] was a legal framework for the consolidation of absolutism. The difference was that the revised constitution contained provisions for human and political rights such as freedom of speech and of the press, and universal adult suffrage; however, they were grafted onto the document merely for the sake of image building. Thus, the 1955 Constitution, like the constitution of 1931, failed to impose formal restraints on the Emperor's power. Clapham explains the power configuration:

> Since the powers of the executive have been vested both in theory and in practice in the Emperor, the other major institutions of the central government have effectively been able to operate only as his delegates and advisers. The Prime Minister, who heads the government beneath the Emperor, has had wide supervisory responsibilities over the rest of the administration, but until he was enabled to select ministers in 1966, he had no substantive powers of control. For almost all of the period since the office was established in 1943, he has therefore been a chief of staff to the Emperor in administrative matters.[41]

The revised constitution of 1955 contained nothing about the formation of or the possibility of, the existence of political parties. It was only Chapter III, Article 47, which mentioned the right to form or join associations, "in accordance with the law". However, the imperial government never allowed groups to form on a social, regional or religious basis for the purposes of playing a role in politics. That is why no legal party existed in Ethiopia during the reign of the Emperor.[42]

As mentioned above, government institutions were not allowed to function autonomously. Personal connections to the palace counted more than anything else for promotion and assumption of significant office. Clapham explains the system of recruitment:

> Personal connections have still formed the chief criterion in [their] selection, and for almost every member of the post-war generation who has reached ministerial rank, a strong source of influence can be found, the most common being family connections in the government; this is true both of noblemen and of other politicians. Regional links and the patronage of existing high officials have also sometimes been important.[43]

The land tenure system and land tax have been thorny issues for the system. The land tax conflict went back to the early days of the crown's restoration after the end of the Italian occupation. After the 1942 decree, which aimed at standardising the tax structure, the people in Tigray openly challenged the imperial government. As Tareke put it, the imposition of a non-Tigrean governor and the introduction of Amharic in all state institutions, compounded with maladministration and the prevalence of banditry, were fertile grounds for resentment.[44] Above all, the infringement of Tigrean traditional autonomy was the fundamental cause of the armed insurrection, which was later quashed with the help of the British army.[45] Similarly, the government was openly challenged, as in the 1968 tax revolt in Gojam and the 1963-70 Bale insurrection over land taxation.[46] Moreover, the Eritrean resistance was gaining momentum and in the process draining the energy of the regime.

As an agrarian country, land in Ethiopia was at the centre of the sphere of power and economic activity. The land tenure system was the main cause of the perpetuation of social and economic insecurity and poverty of most farmers. In the northern part of the country, the old communal kinship system of land tenure was the major form of ownership. In the south, the main form was private tenure, which Shad several aspects. The government granted land from its large reserve to public servants and its supporters, in order to maintain and broaden their loyalty. The farmers continued to lose their holdings through purchase when they became distressed or even through forcible seizure. Landlord-tenant relationships developed as more and more peripheral land was privatised in the push to commercialise agriculture. The peasants were simple tenants and share-croppers, who tilled the land but lacked autonomy in determining how surplus production would be utilised.[47]

The issue of land reform was repeatedly hindered by Parliament, which was dominated by landowners. Any attempts to reform, even insubstantially, were utterly impossible in the face of the strong resistance of the ruling class.[48] Refort remarks as follows:

> Whether the objective was to make the rights of peasants over the land they cultivated more permanent, fixing the entitlements of landowners or penalising land left fallow, they all came up against the systemic opposition of the whole of the ruling class and the church, without the Palace ever giving the least impression that it wished to bring all its weight to bear to force these reforms through.[49]

By doing nothing, the imperial government was digging its grave through the peasant's rapid impoverishment and eviction. Though sporadic peasant rebellions were easily opposed, it was clear that the monarchy was surviving from support of the military and its security services.

On the other hand, the Emperor was very busy trying to build his image in the international arena. As mentioned previously, Ethiopia was the only black African country to join the League of Nations and subsequently became a founding member of the United Nations. He also played a major role in bringing together the Brazzaville, Casablanca, and Monrovia groups, which resulted in the formation of the Organisation of the African Unity.[50] Nevertheless, he allowed state visits to dominate his time while the nation was suffering from economic stagnation and social immobilisation.

Haile Selassie's protection of his royal absolutism did not auger well with his initiatives to modernise and develop the society. He failed to grasp the need for reforms, which go hand in hand with such societal transitions. Keller remarks as follows:

> The process of economic and political modernisation gave rise to the formation of new classes, which came into open conflict with traditional values. By the mid-1960s elements of these new classes were far more radical in their modernist orientations than the Emperor himself and eventually challenged his rule.[51]

The urban dissent came late when compared with the unrest of the peasantry in the countryside. The first open challenge from the new elites came in a coup attempt in 1960, in which the Imperial Guard was involved.[52] The coup failed due to lack of support from the other armed forces' units and from the absence of a clear direction from the coup-makers themselves. This was followed by a militant student movement, which played a major role in eroding the legitimacy of the monarchy. The student movements of 1960s and early 1970s left a distinguished legacy in the history of the people's struggle for democracy and a better life, by their unrelenting demand for democratic rights and land reform. In the early 1970s, urban dissent and rural unrest, which was compounded by the expansion and growth of the Eritrean resistance, made it obvious that the monarchy was decaying irreparably.

Economic Policy and Performance

The Ethiopian economy remained an agrarian one with feeble interaction with the global economy. There were some signs of progress at the turn of the century but these were insignificant in terms of their impact on the conditions of people's lives. Two important events were: the railway construction project granted to the French in 1897 and the establishment of the Bank of Abyssinia in 1905 under the British controlled Bank of Egypt, which later gave rise to the Commercial Bank of Ethiopia.[53]

When Haile Selassie returned to power in 1941, the fundamental nature of the economy had not changed. The Italians were able to build some important roads, establish a few small factories and introduce commercial plantation. However, Ethiopia's economy remained largely self-sufficient; trade was conducted mainly by barter; the financial economy was limited to a very small part of the population; and, of course, foreign trade was extremely insignificant.[54]

In pursuit of modernisation, the first comprehensive, integrated development plan appeared in 1957, which covered the period of 1957-1961. The main goals of the plan were to improve transportation, communication, and construction, and also to accelerate agricultural development.[55] The Second Five-year Plan (1963-1967) emphasised the development of the agricultural sector, but mostly the large-scale commercial farms and export crops, and investment in infrastructure and mining. The last imperial economic plan was the Third

Five-year Plan (1968-1973), which focused on developing the more productive sectors of the economy, namely manufacturing and agro-industry. The third plan included two objectives for the first time: the government's commitment to expanding the education sector and the emphasis given to peasant agriculture.[56]

The overall performance fell short of the targets envisaged by the plans. Moreover, their impact on the change of the economic structure and development was minimal. The first plan targeted national income growth at 3.7 per cent per year but achieved an annual rate of 3.2 per cent. The second plan's target for output growth was 4.3 per cent per annum and the result was not far off. In the third plan, an annual growth rate of 4.7 was achieved below the initial target of 6 per cent.[57]

The real gross domestic product had shown some growth between 1960 and 1974. The average annual rate of growth was estimated at 4.5 per cent between 1960 and 1968. In the early seventies, the rate of growth started to drop. As a result, the average annual growth rate between 1960 and 1974 dropped to 3.69 per cent. Since the population grew by 2.3 per cent per year in the same period, the per capita GDP rose by an annual average of 1.39 per cent. In fact, in the last years of the monarchy the average rate of annual income decreased significantly. Nevertheless, the figure was acceptable when compared to other Sub-Saharan Africa countries' performances.[58]

Agriculture contributed about 65 per cent of the gross domestic product (GDP) in 1960/61 and continued to be the largest contributor, over 50 per cent, in 1974. However, it had not received attention commensurate with its contribution to the GDP. The most neglected sector within agriculture was small-scale peasant farming. Between 1963 and 1973, only 4.2 per cent of government expenditure was allocated to agriculture, and much of this budget went to very limited large-scale agricultural development initiatives, and to the bureaucracy associated with agriculture. The government's commitment to the commercial sector and its neglect of small-scale farming can be explained by the performance of the Agricultural and Industrial Development Bank:

> By 1970, the Agricultural and Industrial Development Bank was established... and it became the governments' principal agency for mobilising and directing capital for agricultural development. In 1972, it had disbursed almost half of its original E $100 million worth of capitalisation. More than half of these funds had gone for agricultural development. Most of the loans for agriculture, however, were given to three large-scale farms and better-off individual farmers. Only 7 per cent of the loans found their way into the hands of small farmers.[59]

Furthermore, the favoured large-scale farming sector was encouraged at the expense of so many peasants. Eviction from their farming lands was the fate of thousands of poor peasants. The emphasis given to commercial farming and cash crops eventually had a negative impact on the production of food crops. Cereal production lagged behind the growth of the population. Hence, in the northern regions, lack of modern facilities and inputs, and lack of credit blocked the means for improved production. In the southern regions, the insecurity of tenure and exorbitant rents, in addition to the problems faced by their northern compatriots, hindered improved agricultural production.

The industrial sector was the other important division in imperial Ethiopia's economy. It accounted for 12 per cent of the GDP in 1960, 14 per cent in 1965, and towards the end of the reign of the monarch, it reached about 15 per cent of which manufacturing amounted to around 9.5 per cent.[60] The industrial sector, though small, benefited from the government's import-substitution industrialisation strategy with its aim of increasing domestic industrial production in order to reduce dependence on imports for basic consumer goods. These goods included processed foodstuffs, textiles, alcoholic and non-alcoholic beverages, tobacco, soap, matches, cement, metal and electrical goods, which even today dominate the manufacturing sector.

In its drive for industrialisation, the government had tried to attract foreign investment by enacting a series of legislation. The 1967 proclamation was characterised as "one of the most generous investment policies in Africa".[61] Investments for new and expanding projects exceeding Birr 200,000 were provided with five and three years' income tax exemption respectively. As well, favourable provisions were established for foreign exchange, remittance, and tariff protection.[62]

Consequently, the manufacturing sector grew at an average rate of about 10 per cent between 1967/68 and 1971/72. Nevertheless, the investment policy did not produce results as expected, and the sector's growth was generally slow. The enterprises were capital-intensive with few job opportunities and almost all necessary machinery and raw materials had to be imported. Most industries also failed to develop connections with the rest of the economy. Moreover, the industries were concentrated in only a few regions: Addis Ababa and its environs, and to a certain extent, Dire Dawa.[63] In some provinces, it was difficult to find an enterprise bigger than a flourmill.

The export of primary agricultural products and the import of finished products and cereals dominated foreign trade. Before the mid-1950s, Ethiopia had no major problems with its foreign trade, as the economy was not fully integrated into the world market. However, with its growing interaction with the rest of the world, it was not long before the country experienced an increasing trade deficit. The emergence of a new middle class with its taste for imported luxury goods and the need to import equipment and machinery for its fledgling manufacturing sector, together with the difficulties faced to diversify and expand its exports to earn the needed foreign exchange to pay for its imports, increasingly widened the shortfall. As a result, the foreign trade was consistently in deficit since 1950 except for the earliest years of 1951, 1953, 1954 and 1957, and later 1973 when the country benefited from unusual higher prices for oilseeds and pulses.[64]

Coffee has been Ethiopia's major export crop, and between 1960 and 1972, the volume of Ethiopia's coffee that entered the world market increased from around fifty thousand tons to more than eighty-two thousand tons. However, the post-1960 growth in coffee exports was offset with a steady increase in food imports. Already, Ethiopia had become a net importer of cereals in the late 1950s and remained haunted by the need to secure food supply until then. As food production continued to deteriorate, the government's imports of cereals increased steadily in order to bridge the gap. As a result, cereal imports rose sharply from fifty thousand tons in 1960 to one hundred and eighteen thousand tons in 1974.[65]

Thus, the agriculture sector suffered from misguided policy, which gave priority to the development of large-scale commercial farms and almost total neglect of small-scale peasant farming. The sector's growth was also greatly troubled by the archaic land tenure system that affected the initiatives of the peasants. Despite the great attention the industrial sector enjoyed, its growth was slow and unsatisfactory. In general, the country remained backward and waiting for a tangible economic development to begin.

The Demise of the Monarchy

Haile Selassie's drive for centralisation of the empire went too far and created dissatisfaction in the regions. The attempt to displace the language and culture of other nationalities by that of the ruling nationality, the Amhara, and the neglect of their socio-economic situations were the main causes of early revolts. The 1943 Woyane[66] rebellion, the 1963-70 unrest in Bale and the 1968 uprising in Gojam were the early symptoms of deep-rooted flaws in the system.[67] These revolts were suppressed by brute force with little consideration given to rectifying the problems.

The Eritrean resistance had been a serious challenge for the regime, which eventually drained its energy. The dubious termination of the federal arrangement established in accordance with the UN resolution of 1952 and the subsequent policies pursued by the imperial government were at the centre of the conflict. The government's resolve to quell the early peaceful resistance by force gave way to armed conflict and bloodshed with the birth of the Eritrean Liberation Front (1961) and later the Eritrean People's Liberation Front (1970).[68]

The urban opposition started with the abortive coup of 1960 led by the Commander of the Imperial Guard and his brother. This incident was followed by the student movement that emerged in 1965 with a demonstration before parliament, chanting the slogan of "land to the tiller".[69] Such demonstrations became common occurrences every year, exposing the political and socio-economic problems of the society. In fact, the opposition grew and towards the end of the 1960s it started to question the legitimacy of the monarchy as a whole.

The government was faced with many socioeconomic problems such as the archaic land tenure system, urban unemployment, and a shortage of basic commodities. However, it failed to give tangible solutions to any of the acute problems. Henze explains the situation:

> His deep-rooted habit of balancing supporters of reform and speedier progress against traditionalists persisted. Nevertheless frustrations and pressures were building up: for more educational opportunities, for more rapid development, for land reform, for wider opportunities for freedom of expression, for recognition and use of languages other than Amharic, for recognition of ethnic and religious diversity. Haile Selassie was reluctant to recognize these as serious. He adamantly opposed development of political parties. Without legitimate outlets for debate and interplay of idea, students and intellectuals resorted to leaflets, clandestine meetings and conspiracy. In this atmosphere genuinely subversive forces - indigenous and foreign - found opportunities to build tensions and clashes.[70]

The drought and subsequent famine of 1973 had a precipitating effect for expediting the downfall of the monarchy. The government knew that the main rains failed in 1972 and a massive catastrophe was looming in the northern part of the country, especially in Wollo, Tigray and Northern Showa. The Council of Ministers made a decision to do nothing instead of acting immediately to avert the danger.[71] The government not only failed to provide any relief assistance to the famine victims, but also attempted to deny its existence until the international media exposed the disaster. Such irresponsible policy greatly contributed to the delay of national and international mobilisation. Even some officials were insisting that there was nothing new about the existence of drought and famine in northern parts of the nation. One of the aristocrats is quoted explaining the situation as follows:

> First of all, death from hunger had existed in our Empire for hundreds of years, an everyday natural thing, and it never occurred to anyone to make any noise about it. Drought would come and the earth would dry up, the cattle would drop dead, the peasants would starve. Ordinary, in accordance with the laws of nature and

> the eternal order of things. Since this was eternal and normal, none of the dignitaries would dare to bother His Most Exalted Highness with the news that in such and such a province a given person had died of hunger. Of course, His Benevolent Highness visited the provinces himself, but it was not his custom to stop in poor regions where there was hunger, and anyway how much can one see during official visits? Palace people did not spend much time in the provinces either, because it was enough for a man to leave the Palace and they would gossip about him, report on him, so that when he came back he would find that his enemies had moved him closer to the street. So how were we to know that there was unusual hunger up north?[72]

The drought that was allowed to lead to famine caused the deaths of about 300,000 people. Moreover, around two million people were made destitute between 1973 and 1974.[73]

While the rural catastrophe created enormous numbers of victims, the impact in the urban areas was also profound. In the middle of such a volatile situation, the government published the Education Sector Review, which recommended the restructuring of educational priorities. It proposed the change of orientation to practical, as opposed to academic education and primary education would be the final level for most young people, which were perceived as a threat to those coming from lower classes of society. The document also made recommendations that would affect teachers, their pay and their qualifications.[74] In January 1974, teachers and students went on strike opposing the new policy, which sent another blow to an already shaken government.[75]

Staggering inflation also signalled the beginning of the final days of the monarchy. The prices of imported goods and oil rose significantly because of the Arab oil embargo. Prices overall increased by 16.5 per cent in 1973, and by 80 per cent for food in the first quarter of 1974.[76] The government announced a price increase for gasoline in response to international oil price hikes, which sent bus and taxi drivers on strike because they were prevented from increasing their fares to cover the additional costs. Although eventually the government decided to cut back gasoline prices, grant higher pay for teachers and suspend the implementation of the Education Sector Review, the crisis was worsened by the decision of the Confederation of Ethiopian Labour Unions (CELU) to hold a four-day general strike in early March by petitioning the government to ease the workers' harsh economic conditions.[77]

The death knell of the monarchy sounded loudly when the army began to show signs of unrest by joining other interest groups' opposition against the government. This became evident when a mutiny of non-commissioned officers and enlisted men occurred in a unit of the army at Neghele in Sidamo province.

The Neghele syndrome spread within a short time to other units of the army, creating a heavy pressure on the government of Prime Minster Aklilu Habte-Wolde. Thus, the public protests compounded with the military's grievances and demands forced the Prime Minister to resign. Markakis and Ayele made some observations on the Cabinet's resignation:

> The matter of the cabinet's resignation proved something of a constitutional muddle, since no one ever resigned the Emperor's service; dismissal was the only known method of release. Indeed, the word resignation did not exist in the language.[78]

Whatever changes were made, the ruling classes could not enforce law and order. The ancient monarchy was already in tatters. Knowing the weakness of the regime and the power vacuum created as a result, the military decided to fill the gap by creating a committee that became known as the Co-ordinating Committee of the Armed Forces, Police, and Territorial Army (Derg) on June 28, 1974.[79]

Not long after its formation, the Committee began to strip the Emperor of all powers and authority.[80] The Emperor was also accused of embezzlement and amassing wealth in foreign banks, while hundreds of thousands of people starved to death. On the other hand, the other interest groups such as students, labour, and teachers were not organised politically to contend for power. The military was left with no serious contender to fill the gap. Consequently, the Derg assumed power as the Provisional Military Administrative Council (PMAC) on September 12, 1974. Marcus remarks that the monarchy had created a new Ethiopia that it could not govern, and therefore, the nation required new men and new ideas.[81] As said, the people were new but there was doubt from the start concerning their 'new ideas'.

The Military Government: Dictatorship and Command Economy

The Aftermath of the Coup

The Derg issued the Provisional Military Government's Proclamation No. 1 of 12 in September 1974, which provided for the dethronement of Haile Selassie and named the Crown Prince as his successor but with no powers in the country's administrative and political affairs.[82] The monarchy was not abolished by decree until March 1975.[83] However, the Derg was very busy in trying to establish its rule.

The military government was confronted from day one with problems, which had caused the demise of the monarchy in the first place. The precipitating factors may include drought and famine, hyperinflation, military failures and other similar problems but the underlying ones include the historic inequalities and exploitation, national domination and a deplorable land tenure system. These problems are complex and difficult to solve under a military rule. Durable solutions may require citizens' open and free participation that can only happen in a democratic regime.

However, the Derg started its rule by banning peaceful opposition and demonstrations, and by sending the signal that it would not include civilian participation whatsoever. The first reaction came from the Confederation of Ethiopian Labour Unions (CELU). The CELU passed a resolution in its annual congress of 15-17 September 1974, demanding the dismantling of the Derg and the establishment of a provisional people's government, and the abrogation of the decree, which banned fundamental civil rights. The Derg ordered the trade union to withdraw its resolution, and when that was rejected, it moved to arrest the leaders.[84] The call for the hand-over of power to civilians also came from university students but received no conciliatory messages. In fact, the opposition was also shared by some military units including Army Aviation and Engineering, which demanded the reinstatement of democratic rights, the establishment of a people's government and other economic issues; however, they were suppressed by force.[85]

Not long thereafter, the Derg showed that it would not tolerate dissent even within its ranks. The first victim of such intolerance was General Aman Andom, its chairman. With Andom, over sixty detainees were summarily executed for which the Derg claimed it had made a "political decision".[86]

In terms of ideology, the Derg came to power by advocating the slogan of "Ethiopia First". Then on December 20, 1974, it announced a decree of 'Ethiopian Socialism' as the guiding ideology of revolutionary Ethiopia, which it hoped would attract the support of the intelligentsia, students and many working people. This was followed by the Proclamation of the "Zemecha"[87] on December 21. In the Zemecha, it was planned that about sixty thousand students, teachers and soldiers would participate in educating the rural dwellers on the philosophy of "Ethiopia First" and "Ethiopian Socialism". In fact, the Zemecha had dual purposes: firstly, to disseminate the philosophy of 'Ethiopia First', and secondly, to minimise the opposition as much as possible in urban centres. To this end, the Derg employed coercion, both psychological and physical, to force students to leave to their assigned districts. As Lefort put it, "...if in the broad light of the day the Derg waved the carrot, in the shadows it brandished the stick: any teacher or university or secondary school student who refused to go was threatened with being unable to continue his studies or even to work in Ethiopia".[88] However, at the end of the Zemecha the number of deserters exceeded the number of those who completed the service and the Derg was forced to withdraw its threat.

In the meantime, the Derg made continual proclamations, particularly in 1975. In April 1976, the Derg issued the Program of the National Democratic Revolution (NDRP) with the help of the All-Ethiopia Socialist Movement (its Amharic acronym is MEISON), which claimed that it was giving the Derg "critical support". The program stated "the objective of the national democratic revolution is to liberate Ethiopia from the yokes of feudalism and imperialism and to lay the foundations for the transition to socialism".[89] On March 4, 1975, the Derg declared Proclamation No. 3, which nationalised all rural land, permitting farmers to farm their share in accordance with the law and established the Peasant Associations (PA), which served as the organ of government. Proclamation No. 47 provided for the nationalisation of urban land and the confiscation of all dwellings except one. This decree also provided for the establishment of neighbourhood organisations, or kebeles, which later played a major role in destroying opposition forces as an indispensable organ of the government.

The emerging political organisations of the post-imperial regime were highly divided in their positions on the state and other timely issues. The two visible organisations of the time, the Ethiopian People's Revolutionary Party (EPRP) and MEISON, had diametrically opposite opinions on the Derg. While MEISON advocated "critical support" in the absence of an organised political leadership, the EPRP demanded the formation of a provisional people's government.[90] The polemics between the two organisations continued for some time and was then replaced by sporadic bloody encounters, assassinations, and counter-assassinations in urban areas in the autumn of 1976. Since MEISON had the support of the Derg, it was able to recruit members of the bureaucracy and kebele leaders. On the other hand, the EPRP was stronger in the student body, the working people and other city dwellers.

After Mengistu emerged as the undisputed leader of the PMAC, by killing the then Chairman of the Derg, General Teferi Benti and other power contenders on February 3, 1977, he publicly declared the start of 'Red Terror' against 'counter-revolutionaries'. Its aim was to wipe out all enemies of the Derg by any means.[91] The government empowered cadres and neighbourhood militias to expose EPRP members and sympathisers, and as a result, in the months of March and April 1977, the civilian population in Addis Ababa and other major towns was terrorised by killings, beatings, shootings and arrests. Parents were not able to mourn or bury their dead sons and daughters. For example, the army slaughtered hundreds of students and workers who attempted to stage demonstrations on May 1, 1977. The killings continued and young people were assembled and executed summarily. Lefort remarks:

> Officially there were 732 victims. In reality, a thousand, two thousand? No one can say. It was a delirious madness. The bodies of the victims were handed over only after payment for the bullets that had killed them. Addis Ababa, dazed, wore mourning for as long as it was permitted to do so.[92]

Some people blamed the EPRP's tactics for such massive killings. Although it might have had some grain of truth, it could not justify the government's madness of the 'Red Terror'. By early 1978, the EPRP was virtually wiped out from the capital city. MEISON, after playing a major role in the eradication of the EPRP, could not escape a similar fate, as the Derg started to undermine its activities in order to hinder it from becoming a dominant organisation. Soon after, the alliance came to a final point and MEISON was outlawed; many of its leaders were arrested and later executed. The other small political groupings also did not survive the intimidation and arbitrary arrests.

The victims of "Red Terror" are estimated to be as many as 32,000.[93] An entire generation of intellectuals and students was neutralised. For the time being, the Derg felt safe, especially after it was able to mobilise hundreds of thousands of militias against the Somali invasion of 1977, by exploiting the national sentiment of the people. The support from the Soviet bloc was also a boost to the regime's morale. It was in this climate that Mengistu began preparing for the formation of the sole 'legal' party in the nation.

Consolidation of Dictatorial Rule

The PMAC, after pacifying the urban centres, embarked on the effort to strengthen its legitimacy by forming a party and later on a 'republic'. The first move came in 1979 when the Derg announced the establishment of the Commission to Organise the Party of the Working People of Ethiopia (COPWE). Political groups were dissolved and membership of COPWE was possible only on an individual basis.[94] Concomitantly, the Derg created new mass organisations and attempted to consolidate the old ones such as peasant associations, urban dwellers' associations and the All-Ethiopia Trade Union. According to Proclamation No. 174 of 1979, the primary objectives of COPWE were: the dissemination of Marxist-Leninist philosophy and the formation of a political party to lead the establishment of socialism and a People's Democratic Republic of Ethiopia (PDRE).[95]

The organisational work culminated in the formation of the Worker's Party of Ethiopia (WPE), which was inaugurated in September 1984.[96] A politburo was formed consisting of 11 members; seven of who were members of the executive committee of the PMAC. The 134 member Central Committee included

29 members of the armed forces and at least another 45 ex-military officials. These military men, whether on active duty or not, comprised 55 per cent of the central committee's membership.[97] At its founding congress, the WPE adopted its own party program consisting of a draft constitution of a People's Democratic Republic, pledged to establish a socialist society, and a ten-year economic plan.[98] Although in principle it was declared the politburo would give the party guidance and government functions, the real power continued to rest in the hands of the executive members of the PMAC, especially the Chairman's. Mengistu was the Secretary General of the WPE, Chairman of the PMAC and the Council of Ministers, and Commander in Chief of the Revolutionary Armed Forces. In fact, the fate of every member of the politburo depended on the type of relation he had with the Chairman.

The WPE accepted as its primary task the conception of a new constitution inaugurating the PDRE. In June 1986 the Constitution Drafting Commission submitted the draft constitution for 'public discussion'. It was claimed that an exhaustive public debate took place and many amendments were submitted. However, it is extremely hard to accept that it was an open debate, while under the watchful eyes of cadres, who had previously terrorised the civilian population. The government declared "the amended version of the draft constitution was put to a referendum on February 1, 1987, and was approved by 81% of the voters. Of those registered to vote in the referendum...96% cast their ballots".[99] Nevertheless, the Constitution was a failure in terms of addressing the nation's acute problems. Article 1, No. 1, states "the People's Democratic Republic of Ethiopia is a state of the working people founded on the alliance of workers and peasants and the participation of the intelligentsia".[100] However, there was no sign of empowering the peasants and workers, who the Constitution described as "the major partners of power". In fact, dissent from the Derg's controlled associations was forbidden and punishable. Concerning the primary conflict in the country, the Constitution had nothing to offer. Article 2, No. 1, declares "Ethiopia is a unitary state" and Article 2, No. 2, circumscribes the Eritrean and other nationalities to "regional autonomy".[101] Chapter 11 of the Constitution also gives the President sweeping powers. Keller indicates that the Constitution resembles a hybrid of the Soviet and pre-1990 Romanian constitutions. He further remarks:

> The original draft was closely patterned on the Soviet model, but the final version departs from that model in two critical respects. First, the office of the presidency is strengthened and elevated above the authority of the Council of State. This change creates a presidency with powers similar to that of the pre-1990 Romanian chief executive. Second, the Soviet model of self-determination is consciously not endorsed.[102]

The first session of the National Assembly[103] was convened in early September 1987 and accepted the government's plan for administrative reorganisation of the regional governments. In this session, 24 administrative regions and five 'autonomous regions' were created. The 'autonomous regions' identified were Eritrea, Tigray, Assab, Dire Dawa and Ogaden.[104] "Autonomy" was granted to redress the grievances of the regions which had challenged the government with armed insurgency. Nevertheless, not only the people and the movements in the regions, but also the government, knew that 'autonomy' was nothing more than a propaganda ploy. Then, on September 10, the old government was theoretically dissolved and the "new government" of Mengistu was inaugurated, amidst the escalation of civil war in many regions of the nation.

Opposition to the regime continued to grow in spite of the extravagant celebrations in the capital city. The armed forces were amassed in Eritrea, Tigray and other Northern Ethiopian regions where they suffered continual defeat, which limited their movements to heavily barricaded towns, especially in the aforementioned regions. However, instead of negotiating a political solution, the regime continued to respond with force and bureaucratic centralism. The more force and intimidation it used to obtain compliance from the population, the faster it dug its grave. The government failed to consolidate its regime in spite of its determination to appear as though it enjoyed the support of the people. Keller remarks:

> The regime's efforts to consolidate its rule have largely failed. It lacks the legitimacy and the political and economic power to ensure citizen compliance with its policies. Consequently, it seems compelled to rely on brute force and authoritarian control to ensure its survival. In the long run, this very approach is the largest obstacle to revolutionary consolidation.[105]

As explained above, the government's heavy dependence on force to resolve differences and dissent, not only was the largest obstacle to consolidation but also one of the main factors in expediting its demise.

The National Question

Ethiopia has not been an 'ideal' nation-state resembling those to emerge in the modern history of Europe. As Ottaway put it, "the ideal type of twentieth-century state is a nation-state, with a democratic government capable of controlling the territory effectively and of satisfying at least minimally the need of its citizens".[106] Modern Ethiopia, as discussed above, was created by conquest and expansion at the end of the nineteenth century and continued to expand its territory until the 1950s and 1960s.[107] It is, as some historians call it, a "museum of peoples". Well over 75 linguistic groups with around 200 dialects are found within the territory.

Many peoples were integrated through a series of bloody and brutal conquests. Their land was taken and given to the victorious soldiers of the Emperor and his generals. The Southern peoples were reduced to almost serfdom, many were sold as slaves and their history and culture was suppressed. Markakis notes as follows:

> The state was named the Ethiopian Empire, a designation that broadened its identity without altering its essence. The essence derived undiluted from the Abyssinian core, and the process of national integration was tantamount to assimilation into the culture of the empire builders. This culture had a religious foundation, which blended together faith, state and nation...[108]

However, such fate was not limited to the southern peoples. The intensity of the oppression might have varied, but other peoples were also subjected to national oppression and discrimination. They were similarly victims of the vigorously promoted centralisation and Amharanization of Emperors Menelik and Haile Selassie. Indeed, the military government followed their lead in its intensified form.

The nationalities became victims of the successive governments' economic development policies, which prohibited them from receiving their fair share. Whatever efforts were made, they were deliberately located in Addis Ababa and its environs. Keller notes "on the eve of the revolution, 70 per cent of Ethiopia's industrial activities were clustered in Addis Ababa and Asmara. Interestingly, the concentration of industries increased after the annexation of Eritrea, as several firms operating in Eritrea either ceased to function or moved to Addis Ababa".[109] The neglect and inequalities were also reflected in the distribution of educational and health institutions. The population/doctor ratio in 1973 was about 5,800:1 in Addis Ababa, whereas it was 365,400:1 in Gemu-Gofa; 288,400:1 in Sidamo; and 739,600:1 in Bale.[110] Such imbalance was also allowed to continue during the Derg era without any tangible effort of correction. The linguistic and cultural discrimination was very intense and Markakis observes that "in imperial Ethiopia, it was easier for a non-Christian who also did not speak Amharigna to pass through the eye of a needle than to enter the charmed circle of power and privilege".[111]

The above discussed oppression and neglect made the ground fertile for fronts of different nationalities to mushroom all over the country. National fronts such as the Tigray People's Liberation Front (TPLF), the Oromo Liberation Front (OLF), The Afar Liberation Front, and later on the Oromo

People's Democratic Organisation (OPDO), and the Ethiopian People's Democratic Movement (EPDM), which was a multinational organisation but essentially formed by Amhara revolutionaries, and some other similar organisations, were instrumental in the downfall of the military regime. Some of these fronts were able to mobilise a formidable force that contributed greatly to shorten the life span of the Derg.

These fronts had varied political programs and agendas. For instance, the TPLF, the strongest nationality front, was struggling for democracy and national equality. It was founded in February 1975 and its political program stated that it was fighting for self-determination, which could result in anything from autonomy, federation, confederation, up to and including secession. The TPLF believed that "independence is taken as an alternative if and only if, all possibilities for unity based upon equality are exhausted and it becomes impossible to live together".[112]

The other major front, the OLF, was formed in 1974 with a different agenda. The OLF believed that Oromia was colonised and dedicated itself to the total liberation of the entire Oromo nation from "Ethiopian colonialism" and the establishment of an independent state called Oromia.[113] The OLF was not successful in mobilising the Oromo people to create a sound resistance to the regime. Its existence was more obvious in foreign lands than inside the country. Generally, the other political organisations also had programs that demanded democracy and equality, and the devolution of power.[114]

The other major force that shook the imperial government and then the Derg was the Eritrean resistance.[115] The Derg, as the imperial government before, concentrated on trying to suppress the resistance by force. It made successive military campaigns but failed to weaken the military capability of the EPLF. Negotiations were attempted to end the Eritrean conflict peacefully but never progressed beyond procedural talks.[116] Ultimately, the Derg was harassed by Ethiopian opposition forces and hounded in Eritrea until it collapsed; the EPLF entered Asmara on May 24, 1991.

Similarly, the Derg was determined to resolve its conflict with the nationality fronts by force. Under international pressure, there were preliminary negotiations with the TPLF but these failed to bear fruit. The Derg was not ready to give way to some transitional arrangement and then to democratic elections. It refused to accept the role of the nationality organisations in shaping the future of the Ethiopian state.

The Constitution of 1987 also failed to provide a political solution for the then intensified civil war. As mentioned above, Chapter 1, Article 2 states that Ethiopia is a unitary state and then Article 4 provides for the provision of 'regional autonomy', which was far short of the aspirations of many political organisations fighting the regime.[117] Subsequently, the government designated Eritrea, Assab, Tigray, Dire Dawa and Ogaden as autonomous regions.[118] Whatever the substance of the autonomy, there was no mention of the Oromo people who are the largest nationality in the country. Apparently, nobody took the initiative seriously, and to a large part, it remained on paper. In the meantime, the Ethiopian Peoples' Revolutionary Democratic Front was created by the joint efforts of the TPLF, EPDM, OPDO and the Ethiopian Democratic Officers Revolutionary Movement (EDORM). The EPRDF soon became a formidable force capable of ending the peoples' desolation perpetuated by the military dictatorship.

Command Economy and Its Consequences

The military government made it clear in its earliest days that it intended to establish command economy. The government declared socialism as the guiding ideology on December 20, 1974 and then attempted to elaborate its economic policies in February 1975, in which the role of the state sector, the private sector and foreign capital was delineated. The Declaration on the Economic Policy of Socialist Ethiopia stated the aims of the new course would be: to ensure that social justice and equity are promoted; to generate more resources required to accelerate economic development for improving the living standard of the people; and to expedite the construction and the management of the economy through planning and resource allocation system that would ensure a steady progress in economic and social development. In order to achieve these objectives, the Declaration emphasised the imperativeness of building a command economy as follows:

> The elimination of poverty and the prevention of exploitation of the Ethiopian people can be achieved only when the Government as the representative of the people, and in the interest of the mass of Ethiopian workers and peasants, directly owns and controls the natural resources and key industrial, commercial and financial sectors of the economy.[119]

Further the Declaration on Economic policy clearly stated the government's disapproval of private ownership by depicting it as a source of exploitation and misery to the ordinary people. The bias against the private sector was stated as follows:

> The basic cause of the economic exploitation of man by man is the private ownership of the means of production. Since such a situation leaves the masses destitute and penniless, they are forced to sell their labour for exploitation by capitalists, which cause a wide gap in the distribution of resources. Hence, the elimination of exploitation

> through public ownership and control of major means of production is one of the primary goals of Ethiopian Socialism.[120]

Consequently, nationalisation of industries, financial enterprises, rural and urban land, and other similar measures were the order of the day. These industries and institutions, as discussed in the next pages, were left to languish because of a dearth of clear objectives, capital, spare parts and professional management. Relatively, the Ethiopian economy did better before 1973 than in later years. The economy grew at an average annual rate of 2.67 per cent between 1974 and 1983, which was on equal pace with the rate of population growth. Then, by the period between 1983 and 1991/92 it had dropped to 1.52 per cent, which was well below the rate of the population growth. The rate of growth of GDP averaged 1.63 per cent per annum between 1974/75 and 1991/92, which clearly failed to match the rate of population growth believed to be over 2.91 per cent. This means that the per capita GDP declined by an annual rate of about –1.28 per cent, which created an additional burden for the average person, since the average standard of living was already one of the lowest in the world. In addition, public spending in 1974 was a relatively modest 19 per cent of the GDP when compared with the 1990's figure, which had gone up to 44 per cent. The debt had also become a hefty burden at US $ 8.6 billion in 1990. The per capita debt amounted to US $172 which was far greater than the per capita income.[121]

The government attempted to use central planning as its main instrument of economic transformation. Consequently, it published the Ten-year Perspective Plan (TYPP) as "the main instrument in the management, guidance and acceleration of the socioeconomic transformation of Ethiopia in line with the objectives of the programme of the National Democratic Revolution (NDR)".[122] However, the TYPP was not in touch with the reality of the time. The most striking side of the plan was its heavy reliance on foreign aid. First, it is difficult to imagine the government with its socialist rhetoric would be able to attract significant capital inflow. Second, if one considers foreign aid funds, they are usually tied to projects or products, or to uses according to the plans of donors. Even loans are not given without conditions. Therefore, it was hard to finance those development projects driven more by ideological wishful thinking than reality. In fact, if one attempts to consider the domestic constraints, ranging from absorption capacity to the lack of peace, the results that were achieved up to the end of regime could not be surprising.[123] Marcus says the following concerning the situation:

> The rhetoric of Mengistu's socialism scared off Western investors, and Ethiopia remained starved for capital throughout the revolutionary period. In fact, the government was so doctrinaire that it

> squandered its limited resources on propping up inefficient state farms and in sponsoring forms of collective agriculture.[124]

Thus, in the last days of the Derg the economy was close to collapse. In the next sections, the performance of the major sectors is discussed and an attempt is made to analyse the magnitude of the economic crises and the policies that caused the situation.

Agricultural Policy and Performance

Agriculture has been the mainstay of the Ethiopian people as a major source of employment, revenue and export earnings. Obviously, agriculture has to fulfil some major purposes in Ethiopia's economic development: to feed a fast growing population; to finance its own growth and structural change; to provide capital and raw materials for industrial development; and to provide cash crops for foreign exchange earnings. However, Ethiopia's agricultural sector was not even able to fulfil its main purpose, which was and still is to provide food for the fast-growing population. It had been a victim of distorted policies and climatic catastrophes during the military regime and its growth lagged behind the staggering population increase.

The first and most important policy decision was made by the decree of land reform on March 4, 1975. All rural land was nationalised without any compensation; tenancy was abolished; the hiring of wage labour on private farms was forbidden; all commercial farms were to remain under state control; and the peasants were entitled to a plot of land not exceeding 10 hectares.[125] The Proclamation provided for the formation of peasant associations, which were established on 800 hectare-areas and membership was restricted to tenants, landless labourers and small landowners with less than 10 hectares of land.[126] After the Proclamation, twenty thousand peasant associations emerged. These associations were centralised by the state-created All-Ethiopia Peasant Association, which developed into one of the primary political organs of the state. The peasants had no say in the associations' functions, and within a short time peasant leaders became agents of the state, whose daily activities were to harass the peasants and extort whatever benefits they could from the association and its membership. One Food and Agriculture Organization (FAO) study revealed "peasants complained that they felt controlled from above, and that their peasant associations had become the instruments of central control. Peasants felt harassed by leaders who had become independent of peasant support, and complained that they had lost all influence even on local decisions".[127] Lefort adds that "the institutionalisation of the peasant associations was more to serve the state, allowing it to reach into the daily life of the countryside, rather than to make it possible for the peasant communities even gradually to take over the levers of administration".[128]

The government had no clear policy of how to develop the agriculture sector beyond the abolition of the old land tenure system. Land reform alone could not produce significant additional wealth or resources for the poor peasants, although it freed them from landlords' exploitation. Dessalegn remarks that the land reform was "a redistributive and levelling reform, its strength lay not so much in having increased the resources and wealth of the rural community as in having created equal, if modest, opportunities for everyone".[129] When the issue of the agricultural development policy became pressing, the government implemented the collectivisation policy, which was declared in 1978.[130] The Proclamation required peasants to organise themselves into service co-operatives whose functions were marketing surpluses, purchase and distribute inputs, and run retail shops. By1986 some four thousand such co-operatives were formed with 4.5 million households as members.[131]

The next step, after the formation of service co-operatives, was to develop producers' co-operatives in three stages. The first stage, the Melba, was an elementary style of co-operative requiring members to pool land, oxen, and implements, while retaining up to two thousand square meters of land for private use; the second stage, the Welba, required members to transfer all their resources to the co-operative and reduce private plots to a thousand square meters; and the final stage, the Weland, established advanced co-operatives and abolished private use of land altogether.[132] Though co-operatives were receiving some privileges, including priority for credits for fertilisers, improved seed and other necessary items, their appeal to the peasants was minimal. The peasants feared confiscation of their properties and highly restricted freedom, thus, they resisted inclusion in these co-operatives. In 1987, there were only 2,821 producer co-operatives in the whole country with 215,141 households as members, which amounted to only three per cent of the total farming population.[133]

The government, busy with its ideologically driven task of establishing co-operatives and collective farms, failed to produce an appealing package of agricultural services for the peasant-farming sector. Agriculture had not performed as indicated in the development plans. Growth dropped by an annual average of -0.1 per cent between 1974 and 1978, and then revived to an average of 2.6 per cent per annum between 1979 and 1983. Then came the drastic decrease of 13.1 per cent during the great famine of 1984/85, which caused the deaths of hundreds of thousands of people. In 1986/87, growth recovered by 11.8 per cent and then dropped again to 0.1 per cent in 1988-90. As indicated above, the average annual agricultural growth rate between 1974 and 1991 was1.22 per cent, which was far below the annual rate of population growth, estimated at over 2.91 per cent. The food production per capita also decreased by an annual average rate of −1.4 per cent between 1979 and 1991.[134] As a result, cereal imports had substantially increased since the mid-1980s.[135] The available food supply per head (in grain equivalent) in 1980 was 201.4 kilograms but was reduced to about 125 kilograms in 1991. For instance, the daily calorie supply per capita in 1961 to 1963 was 1,817, but dropped to 1,634 in 1989 to 1991, far below the 2100 calories required per person per day, which was only about 78 per cent.[136]

As indicated before, between 1974/75 and 1991/92 real GDP grew by only 1.63 per cent per annum. On the other hand, the population grew at an alarming average rate of 2.91 per cent during the same period. This means that on average per capita income fell by 1.3 per cent per annum, a net welfare loss of at least 20 per cent, putting the average citizen in a worse position in 1991 than in 1974.

The most privileged but resource-wasting ventures of the government were the state farms. These farms were formed under Proclamation No. 31 of 1975, Article 7, which expropriated large-scale farms as state or co-operative farms.[137] Driven by its ideology of building state ownership in every aspect of the economy, the government allocated substantial resources and with little study or preparation, the farms were expanded from about 53,800 hectares in the first years of the land reform program to about 231,000 hectares in around 1980. In 1984, the size of state farms was reduced to 202,800 hectares, amounting to about 2.9 per cent of land used for crop production.[138]

These state farms had extensive access to bank loans to purchase their machinery, equipment, spare parts, fertilisers, pesticides and other essential materials. The principal loan provider was the Agricultural and Industrial Development Bank, which disbursed an annual average of Birr 203,618,750 to state farms out of the annual average of Birr 255,061,250 made available to the agriculture sector between 1980 and 1991. The state farms' share accounted for an average of 80 per cent of the total agricultural loans made by the Bank during this period.[139] For example, in 1980-81, state farms absorbed 80 per cent of the agricultural credit, 82 per cent of fertiliser imports, and 73 per cent of the improved seeds.[140] And yet, they were disappointing performers. For instance, the average coffee yield per hectare of land on state farms was only 65 per cent of the yield on peasant farms, and for pulses, it was only 33 per cent of the peasant farm yield.[141] Since their establishment, these enterprises were operating at a loss due to various factors. Griffin summarises some of the difficulties:

> The farms suffer from a great many difficulties, including (i) very high overhead costs, (ii) an excessive degree of mechanisation, (iii) poor capital equipment, high machine-operating costs, inadequate maintenance and consequently low capacity utilisation, (iv) short-

> ages of labour, (v) undesirable labour recruitment practices and wage payment systems, (vi) poor choice of location partly resulting from excessive rapid expansion, (vii) over-centralised management structure and (viii) an apparent disregard of financial considerations when making decisions.[142]

As a result, the annual average loss for state farms under the former Ministry of State Farms Development was about Birr 75 million.[143] Farms under the Ministry of Coffee and Tea Development incurred similar losses. Such persistent losses reached an accumulated financial deficit of Birr 777.4 million by July 7, 1991.[144] At the end of the day, they became a heavy burden on the country's economy despite their indispensable role in the ideological writings of the regime as part of the building blocks of socialism.

Low prices for agricultural products, especially food crops, and restricted market space also played a major role in the agricultural sector's weak performance. The government established the Agricultural Marketing Corporation (AMC) in 1976 aiming to stabilise producer and consumer prices; to reduce marketing margins to the producers' advantage; to ensure the timely and efficient supply of farm inputs; and to assure adequate supplies for the public distribution system. However, from its inception the AMC ensured it extracted maximum surpluses for the government. Farmers had to sell a certain quota of their grains to the AMC at a fixed price; any surplus could be sold on the free market. However, it is hard to imagine that small-holding farmers would have more grain than the required quota. Licensed private merchants were also obliged to sell 50 per cent of their grain purchases to the AMC, who was on-selling to urban dwellers' associations, state enterprises, the armed forces and other members of the society.[145]

Evidently, there was a wide gap between the AMC's farm gate price and the free market price. This shortfall was extracted from the farmers. For most of 1980/81 and 1987/88 the AMC had not altered its farm gate purchase price. Even when prices were increased in January 1988, it was only to the ridiculously small sum of 2-3 Birr per quintal for most grains.[146]

The farmers continued to protest until the government abolished its fixed price and quota system in March 1990. The AMC was transformed into a state marketing board, left to compete with private merchants on the open market. Although the government was at last forced to abandon the policy, the damage done to the farmers and consequently to their production was significant. Various taxes had also been levied on the agriculture sector: the land use fee, the tax on agricultural incomes, and taxes on exports of agricultural products, which were not easy to shoulder.[147]

The other poorly calculated policies of the government were resettlement and villagization. In November 1984, when the famine was claiming thousands of lives, the government decided to move 1.5 million people within nine months from Wollo and Tigray to South-Western Ethiopia. The program was largely driven by political motivation rather than economic necessity. According to the former head of the Relief and Rehabilitation Commission (RRC), one of the reasons for the government's resettlement program was "to depopulate rebel areas in order to deprive the guerrillas of support".[148] In fact, the government's agents made no secret of its true intentions. Many people were forced on to military vehicles when they were purchasing or selling grains and implements in market places. According to W. Giorgis, about 20,000 out of the 700,000 people moved from their villages died en route or at the new settlements because of diseases such as malaria and tsetse flies. Another 500 people were executed while trying to escape and half of the settlers were separated from members of their family.[149] However, the figures mentioned by W. Giorgis are only part of the story. The number of farmers, who died of suffocation in cargo planes and trucks, while attempting to escape en route, and in settlement sights because of various illnesses, was far higher than the published figures.[150]

Villagization was also a program that was pushed mainly because of security concerns. Between 1985 and 1986, 4.6 million people, approximately 12 per cent of the population, were forced into government designated villages. By July 1987, more than 8 million people were villagized and an attempt was made to villagize more at the end of 1987.[151] The services promised never materialised but the scheme enhanced the government's central control over the rural population, at least in the short term.

The significance of resettlement and villagization can be traced by its disruption to agricultural production and to the worsened suffering of the rural population. When the government's grip loosened, thousands of people left their resettlement sites and the newly constructed villages. Nevertheless, this outcome does not mean that these initiatives cannot be applied if they are well planned, financed, and above all, made with the free consent of the people.

The Industrial Sector

After the Derg's usurpation of power, the ownership of industry changed into the hands of the state. Proclamation No. 26/1975 provides for the nationalisation of industries in order to "give primacy to the interest of the community".[152] Article 2 detailed industrial sectors that should be owned solely by the government, which included exploration of precious metals, radioactive and nuclear minerals; large-scale mining of salt pans; basic and heavy industries such as iron and steel works, ship-building and cement production; petroleum refining and extraction of natural gas; industries such as textiles, leather and leather products, rubber and fertilisers, pharmaceutical, tobacco, glass, bottle and ceramics, printing and publishing; electric power, gas and water services; rail, air and sea transportation; radio and telecommunication services; and insurance and banking.[153] While petroleum and gas exploration, mining activities and some manufacturing sectors were available for joint ventures between the government and foreign capital,[154] smaller activities were left for the private sector.[155]

Consequently, 87 manufacturing enterprises were nationalised in 1975.[156] The government further declared Proclamation No. 76/1975 and its main purpose was to impose restrictions on the activities of the private sector. It limited the private sector's participation to small industrial activities such as grain milling, oil and seed processing, handicrafts, baking, weaving and tailoring. The capital ceiling, even in these activities, was not to exceed half a million Birr. Similarly, the capital ceiling for wholesale and retail trade was restricted to a maximum of Birr 300,000 and Birr 200,000 respectively.[157]

The average annual growth rate between 1974 and 1991 was 1.01 per cent for the industrial sector and 1.4 per cent for manufacturing. Certainly, the target of 16 per cent anticipated by the TYPP was unachievable, and in fact, from 1988 onwards growth was negative. The lack of fresh investments, raw materials and spare parts compounded with poor management and staff, and an ever-diminishing internal market, was some of the reasons for the dismal performance of the sector. Consequently, the forecasted structural change never materialised. Apparently, the share of agricultural GDP increased from 42 per cent in 1987 to 47 per cent in 1991.[158] The deceleration was indeed aggravated by the consequences of the civil war.

Trade and Service Sectors

Over 85 per cent of Ethiopia's exports have been from the agricultural sector. The stagnation of agricultural production had greatly affected the export trade. There had been a supply-side restraint, which was mainly created by drought and the marketing and other relevant policies of the government. These exports mainly produced by individual farmers were made to be collected by public enterprises, whose price offers were very low that had a negative impact on the production itself.

Exports grew rapidly in the post-monarchy period until they started declining in the 1980s. Exports grew by 21.4 per cent in 1976, but declined by 19.8% in 1985, mainly because of the 1984/85 drought. Considering the whole period between 1962 and 1990, the average annual growth rates of 5.35 per cent for exports and 8.23 per cent for imports were extremely low. Export earnings fluctuated immensely, and in fact, continued to substantially deteriorate during the Derg era. The growth rate of export earnings had steadily declined from 7.2 per cent per annum during 1962 to 1973 to 2.4 per cent during 1974 to 1990.[159] The export economy continued to be dominated by one agricultural item: coffee. The share of coffee exports had been 55.9 per cent in 1976, 84.5 per cent in 1978 and 56.8 per cent in 1988.[160] The fluctuations in the percentage of coffee's share were not results of export diversification but more of supply-side problems and world market instability. However, exports had fallen as a share of GDP from 9 per cent in the early 1980s to 7.4 per cent in the 1985/86 and 1987/88 period.[161] The external terms of trade had also been fluctuating in relation to world coffee prices, which increased in 1985 and 1986 but then collapsed damaging the country's export earnings. The terms of trade index had been below 100 (1980=100) except for the years of 1984 and 1986.[162]

The balance of payments had worsened in the 1980s because of export earnings stagnation and continued increase in imports volume as share of GDP. The problem of balance of payments had not shown any sign of abatement. In fact, it is hard to think of devising a quick solution in the near future. Ethiopia needs to import substantial quantities of industrial inputs, machinery, transport equipment and other essential items, while its exports could need a long time to become a substantial foreign exchange-earner to cover a significant part of required imports.

The overvalued exchange rate[163] had not been favourable to the export trade. The continuation of an overvalued exchange rate in the hope of developing and promoting domestic industries was counterproductive. The overvalued exchange rate reduced Ethiopia's competitiveness and discouraged official export performance. It also created an illicit market in foreign exchange where Birr was sold at a substantial discount. Since the available foreign exchange had been distributed by administrative means for the items specified by the government, other imports had to rely on the foreign exchange mainly obtained from the unofficial market. On the other hand, since the farm gate price of coffee beans was within the range of 35-45 per cent of their FOB price, the desire to evade controls in coffee marketing was very high. Consequently, large amounts of coffee beans were being smuggled to neighbouring countries, where the farmers could earn better prices for their produce. Such practices greatly hurt the nation's export trade. For example, the export quantum index (1975=100) for coffee, hides and skins, and oil seeds fell to 77.8, 63.1 and 1.7 in 1992 respectively. The general export quantum index dropped to 42.3, less than half its level in 1975.[164]

Under the military regime, public expenditure played an important role in shaping the pattern of growth. Service sectors grew more than the commodity production sectors. The size of the recurrent budget had increased from 18.6 per cent of GDP in 1980/81 to 26.1 per cent in 1987/88.[165] The greatest beneficiaries of the recurrent budget were defence and internal security, among other similar institutions. About 70 per cent of recurrent expenditures were spent on general government and social services.

The transport infrastructure has been sparse, making many parts of the country inaccessible. Until recently, Ethiopia's road network has been one of the least developed, even by Sub-Saharan African standards. The physical shortage of transport has impeded the development of an interlinked marketing system within the country. Surplus produce in one region could not be transported easily to regions where the same product was scarce. Such existing situations were aggravated by the regime's erroneous policies, which gave little space to private operators. Nevertheless, other components of the service sector had shown some progress. Apparently, the service sector was the one, which performed better than the other sectors. The services grew from 30 per cent of GDP in 1970 to 40 per cent of GDP in 1991.[166]

After suffering from economic malaise domestically and witnessing the rapid deterioration and collapse of the Soviet bloc, the Derg attempted to introduce some reforms in November 1988. These reforms were intended to make adjustments within the framework of the regime's "socialist economy". Some legislation on joint venture, small-scale industries and other issues were implemented to ease the constraints on the private sector but fell far short of creating an environment conducive to investment. When the 1988 limited steps failed to produce any tangible results, the government was again forced to adopt a reform program that was reflected in the 11th Plenum of the Central Committee of the WPE of March 1990.[167] On paper, the reform program was a departure from the command economy, and advocated the establishment of a mixed economy.[168]

Although some attempts were made to implement the reform program by passing decrees on investment and eliminate restrictions in the agriculture sector, it was hard for the private sector to have confidence. The regime's days were numbered and its capability to implement the regulations was extremely undermined by successive defeats at the hand of rebel movements. Putting aside the issue of the regime's commitment to such endeavour, its reform program came too late to be implemented in an atmosphere of uncertainty and turmoil.

In general, Ethiopia was desperately poor in the 1960s but was even poorer at the beginning of the 1990s. Its rate of development could not stay well above the rate of population growth. The country became known more for the recurrent famines and the death of millions of its people, not to mention the civil war that rocked the nation for three decades. The military government created a situation worse than when it came to power, leaving the nation with an external debt of well over four billion U.S. dollars in 1991.[169] The country was literally bankrupt with an import cover of only about a week, huge negative trade and resource balances, and a substantial budget deficit. Hence, at the end of the seventeen years of military rule, the majority of Ethiopians found their lives more miserable than they had been under the monarchy.

The End of the Military Dictatorship

The Derg, from its early days, tried to stay in power by bringing the people into submission. The summary executions, extensive detentions, and the whole senseless and wanton cruelty perpetuated by the regime were part and parcel of the conspiracy to extend its life span. Massive mobilisations and military campaigns were the order of the day to crush the resistance of liberation movements. The Derg carried out over eight massive military campaigns in Tigray and another similar number of campaigns in Eritrea including the "Red Star Campaign"[170], killing thousands of people.

The famine of 1984/85 also brought another blow to the regime. In the first place, the Derg used the cover up of the 1973/74 catastrophe by the Haile Selassie regime to usurp power. However, the same regime, which had used famine to discredit the monarchy, was caught trying to cover up the disaster in Northern Ethiopia in order not to spoil the extravagant celebration for the establishment of the Workers Party of Ethiopia (WPE). Marcus remarks "in a five and one half-hour acceptance speech, Mengistu described past achievement and future plans, never once mentioning the famine".[171] In fact, this was the time when drought-affected Ethiopians started to perish in thousands. Not only did Mengistu attempt a cover up, but he also tried his best to use food aid as a weapon against the rebel-held areas' population, intending to starve them into submission.[172] The Derg again embarked on a very controversial project of resettlement, which was intended to depopulate the already affected areas that were mainly rebel operation regions.[173]

Alienated from the people, the regime had to depend on the army and its security apparatus. The words "'negotiation" and "compromise" were not in the government's vocabulary until it witnessed the collapse of its successive military campaigns against the rebel held areas. As discussed above, in the late 1980s, negotiations started but foundered at the start of 1990, mainly because of the regime's intransigence.

In the meantime, the regime's armed forces received heavy blows from the EPLF, especially towards the end of the 1980s. In March 1988, the EPLF destroyed the army corps at Afabet, ending the regime's dream of overrunning the Sahl liberated areas.[174] Similarly, in 1989 the regime's troops sustained a humiliating defeat at the hands of the TPLF at Inda-Selassie, Western Tigray. The government panicked and withdrew its remaining army from Tigray fearing another disaster. Soon the theatre of conflict between the EPRDF[175]and the Derg's armed forces moved to the adjacent regions and then further southwards. TPLF's control of Tigray was not only a military and psychological blow to the regime but was also a loss of the only ground access to Eritrea and the signal of a near disaster for its war efforts in that region.

In 1989, frustrations within the armed forces were intensified by the successive defeats and culminated in a coup attempt when Mengistu was away on a state visit to East Germany. The coup failed due to hesitation and lack of organised moves. As a result, twelve generals and other high-ranking officers were executed without due trial. The crack within the regime started to widen, hastening its fall. Whatever Mengistu tried to preserve his position, it was too late to produce a difference. He met Siad Barre, the Somali President, who himself was under strong rebel pressure, and agreed to bridge their differences, which had affected their relations since the Somali invasion of Ethiopia in 1977. In March 1990, Mengistu declared the end of Socialism and replaced the WPE with the Ethiopian Democratic Unity Party (EDUP), but this contributed little to slow the deteriorating position of the regime.[176]

After the EPRDF's first congress of January 1991, it was decided to embark upon the last stage of the offensive against the Derg with the intention of toppling it from power. Within a short time, the "Tewodros Campaign" began which liberated Gonder, with successive victories scored in Gojam and Welaga regions. By early May, the EPRDF forces were within a 50-mile radius of the capital city, Addis Ababa. Mengistu, realising the dearth of any manoeuvring space, fled the country on May 21, 1991 to Zimbabwe. Tesfaye Gebre-Kidan replaced Mengistu but was not able to prevent the situation from deteriorating. The EPRDF forces entered Addis Ababa on May 28, 1991 ending a tyrannical rule of 17 years. Consequently, a provisional government with Meles Zenawi as president was formed on June 1, 1991. The new government promised to convene a conference within a month in which all opposition groups would participate and then form a broad-based transitional government.

Conclusions

Modern Ethiopia has emerged as a product of conquest and expansion. Although it was not a direct creation of European colonisers, its emergence had a lot in common with other 'created' nations. Ethiopian Emperors, especially Menelik and later Haile Selassie had left a strong imprint on the process of its birth. Menelik expanded the Southeast and Southern boundaries of Ethiopia to where they are today, and Haile Selassie extended them by including Eritrea under a federal arrangement and then by annexing it. None of the subjugated peoples accepted their domination by the new masters from central Ethiopia. The policies of the central government based on extraction, control, and

Amharanization were at the centre of the conflict between the Amhara rulers and other nationalities.

Despite the grievances of many nationalities, Haile Selassie continued to pursue the policy of excessive centralisation by denying regional elites the space for local administration. The imperial government imposed Amharic and the Amhara culture not only on those who were made Ethiopians at the end of the last century but also on the newly annexed Eritrea. The monarchy's lack of acceptance to reform the absolutist political system and the archaic land tenure, compounded with the civil war in Eritrea, expedited its demise.

In spite of the rhetoric, the Derg pursued the imperialist policies in Eritrea. The regime had ignored the nationalities' demands for self-determination and to the wide range of oppositions' call for the establishment of democracy. Beginning from its early days in power, the military dictatorship had responded with violence and reinforced bureaucratic centralism. Until its downfall, the Derg had never been ready for genuine political negotiation and settlement with the opposition. It had never stopped from attempting to consolidate and entrench its own rule by martial means.

The economy had performed better between 1960 and the early 1970s than under the Derg. The growth rate was at least above the annual rate of population growth. The industrial sector and commercial plantations were dominated by foreign capital. In fact, the eviction of farmers from their land together with the whole land tenure system became a breeding ground for unrest and instability. After the coup, the old land tenure was abolished but the collector of the extracted surplus changed only from a landlord to a public marketing enterprise. In both governments, small-scale farming was neglected and received little assistance from the state. Recurrent droughts were allowed to become famines, which claimed hundreds of thousands of lives. The command economy was an absolute failure, which made the people even poorer than they were in 1974. The government wasted whatever surplus accumulated in implementing its slogan of "all efforts to the War" in Northern Ethiopia and Eritrea. Military expenditure was well over 50 per cent of the annual government budget towards the end of the 1980s and continued to increase until the last days. Therefore, as a consequence of policy and the war it bred, Ethiopia had made little progress under the two successive governments.

At the end of the military rule, the country was at the verge of disintegration. The national question, which was the major cause of the demise of the regime, had to be solved in order to rectify the injustices and also accommodate the aspirations of the various armed groups. Abolishing command economy and creating an environment conducive to domestic and foreign investment had to be one of the priorities of the new government to revive the economy and create employment opportunities. Moreover, solving the Eritrean problem once and for all was one of the major challenges and then, whatever the result, Ethiopia and Eritrea needed to build a close relationship, which would ensure the free flow of goods, resources and people. Ethiopia also had to normalise its relations with its neighbouring countries that had been harmed because of the 'siege mentality' of Ethiopian leaders, and work hard to build regional economic co-operation.

Above all, the Ethiopian experience demonstrated that it is futile to attempt to achieve economic and social transformation through intimidation and brute force. Evidently, the realisation of a democratic system is a requisite for economic and social transformation in such fragmented and troubled nations. Thus, Ethiopia encountered the lone option of building a democratic system that upholds the right of nationalities to self-determination as a means of survival in the first place, and then in order to achieve genuine development, durable peace, stability and national unity.

Notes

1. See Rubenson 1964; Marcus 1994; Clapham 1970; Bulcha 1988; Erlich 1986; Henze 2000; Prouty explains "[Menelik] with full knowledge, if not the urging, of Emperor Yohannes he carried out wars of conquest between 1879 and 1882 to bring the Oromo and Guraghe peoples under his jurisdiction. Arsi, Sidamo and parts of Keffa paid tribute to Menelik, a portion of which he had to pass along to the emperor." (Prouty, Empress Taytu and Menelik II: Ethiopia 1883-1910, 1986: 23).
2. See Rubenson, Wichale XVII, 1964; Rubenson, the Survival of Ethiopian Independence, 1991; Levine, Greater Ethiopia, 1974; Pankhurst, Richard, the Ethiopians: A History, 1998; Marcus, the Life and Times of Menelik II, 1975; Marcus, Ethiopia, Great Britain, and the USA 1941-74, 1983; Marcus, A History of Ethiopia, 1994; Marcus, Haile Selassie I, 1996; Enrlich, Ethiopia and the Challenge of Independence, 1986; Prouty, Empress Taytu and Menelik, 1986; Zewde, A History of Modern Ethiopia, 1855-1974, 1991; and Henze, Layers of Time: A History of Ethiopia, 2000.
3. See Marcus, 1994: 5; Henze explains "trade was crucial for the development of Aksum. Indeed, it may have been the key factor in evolution of the city into the capital of an empire, and the empire's subsequent expansion. Red Sea trade increased steadily in the late first millennium BC and the first centuries of the Christian era. Demand grew for African goods that could only be supplied in quantity from the interior." (Henze, Layers of Time, 2000: 26).
4. See Levine, 2000: 70-71; Levine remarks that "[a] small group of Geez-speaking people established at Aksum a kingdom which flourish from the first to the sixth century A.D. and continued to play a significant role in northern Ethiopia until the tenth century. Through a series of wars the kings of Aksum extended their

boundaries in all directions. At various times they established their dominion over the Beja in the north, the Saho in the south, and the Nubians in the west. At two different periods they crossed the Red Sea to become masters of Yemen. Of more enduring importance, they consolidated a monarchical tradition and a Christian culture that would survive transplantation to the south despite the destruction of Aksum as a political centre." (Ibid., p. 70).

5. Marcus, 1994: 11; see also Henze, 2000: 44-48.
6. Keller, 1981: 526; Rubenson describes the situation as follows: From many points of view, Ethiopia of 1800 was weak state with serious internal problems and little visible cohesion. It was not, however, like many other areas of Africa, the home of a mere conglomeration of ... tribes. The many centuries of settled agricultural life in the Ethiopian highlands, the long history of the Ethiopian monarchy and the Christian Church in the area had weakened tribal structures in favour of a more regionally organized society." (Rubenson, 1976: 31-32); similarly Levine explains "[f]rom 1800 to 1850 the Solomonid monarchy was weaker than at any previous time in its history. Warfare among feudal lords raged unchecked. Islam was spreading rapidly in the south and the far north. The YejjuGalla Dynasty was undisputed master of the core provinces of Amhara and Begemdir. External Muslim threats were being revived. The Christian community was weakened by the eruption of bitter doctrinal disputes." (Levine, 2000: 90).
7. Keller, 1981: 526; Rubenson explains "Tewodros perceived as did none of his predecessors ... that the political anarchy, moral laxity, and technological backwardness of his people threatened national survival. The reforms he announced, the policies he tried to implement, the very single-mindedness and perseverance with which he tackled the problems, indicated that he aimed at nothing less than a national revival combined with the transformation of his country into a modern state." (Rubenson, 1976: 269).
8. Tewodros was extremely frustrated by the indifference of European powers and told Lejean, the French Consul, which might apply to all Europeans as follows: "I know... the tactics of the European governments when they want to seize a country in the Orient. First they send missionaries, then consuls to support the missionaries, and then battalions to sustain the consuls. I am not a Rajah from Hindustan to be made a fool of like that: I prefer to engage the battalions at once." (Lejean quoted in Rubenson, 1991: 231).
9. Clapham, 1970: 12.
10. See Haberson, 1988: 32-33; Marcus, 1994: 73.
11. Erlich, 1986: 18-25; Erlich explains the reasons for the conflict as follows: Whatever Ismail's plans concerning Ethiopia were – full destruction of its sovereignty, according to one historian, or a mere defence of his new Eritrean possessions, as concluded by another – the clash was inevitable. An Egyptian African empire including the Red Seacoast and Eritrea could not co-exist with an Ethiopia centred in Tigre. Ismail obviously sought the destruction of Yohannes. He declared that he was ready to recognise Menelik of Shoa as emperor, and indeed was probably prepared to compromise with a semi-independent, land-locked and

Egyptian-encircled Ethiopia centred on this southern province. (Erlich, 1986: 19).

12. Wubneh and Abate, 1988: 14; Menelik was building his army and expanding his territory southwards even when Yohannes was alive. Luckman and Bekele note that "... he [Menelik] was able between 1880 and 1900 to import over one million rifles, a quantity of Hotchkiss guns and artillery pieces, also making use of French and Russian military experts to train his soldiers in their use. No other precolonial African state has been able to build such an armoury." With such military strength, Menelik started his campaign of occupation of the South and Southwest of modern Ethiopia. The campaigns were brutal and bloody in which thousands of people perished who attempted to resist the new rulers. Trimingham describes that "[Menelik's] object was the permanent occupation of the conquered territories.... When they opposed him, his policy was one of ruthless extermination, as many districts which have been amongst the most fertile and flourishing in all Ethiopia bear witness. The population of Keffa, for instance, is estimated to have been reduced by two-thirds. Those who succeeded in escaping the slaughter were sold into slavery or reduced to the status of gebbar (serfs)". (Luckman, R. and D. Bekele. 'Foreign Powers and Militarism in the Horn of Africa', Review of African Economy, No. 30, 1984, p. 11; and Trimingham, J. S. Islam in Ethiopia, 1952:118).
13. Erlich, 1986: 4; see also Henze, Layers of Time, 2000: 171-76.
14. Tibebu describes Gultas tribute appropriation right granted by the Emperor to the lower echelons of the power hierarchy, such as local rulers, members of the royal family, the nobility, or priesthood as well as to religious establishments. He further explains "[i]t was the Emperor's prerogative to create and transfer gult right at will." Finally, he attempts to define gult as "the right of tribute appropriation from peasants granted by the Emperor to the various ranks of the warrior class, the Church, and others in return for military, administrative, and religious services rendered to the Emperor by the gult grantees." (Tibebu, The Making of Modern Ethiopia, 1896-1974, 1995: 78-79).
15. Haberson, 1988: 35.
16. Balabat and Neftegna are names given to a class of landowners and administrators. This class may include people ranging from petty owners to members of the feudal landed aristocracy.
17. Bulcha, 1988: 39-49.
18. Keller, 1981: 531.
19. Rubenson, 1964: 11.
20. See Rubenson, 1964 for an extensive discussion on the treaty. After extensive negotiations between Ethiopian and Italian envoys, the problem of the protectorate was impossible to solve. Finally, Menelik denounced the whole treaty of Wichale in February 1893 and informed the other European powers of this step, which led to the battlefield of Adwa. (Rubenson, 1964: 20-21). Further Rubenson notes "Salimbeni (the Italian General Resident in Addis Abeba) noted in his diary

that Menelik was alarmed, and throughout his later negotiations the Emperor maintained that it was only through these letters that he had understood that he was supposed to be under an obligation to use the Italian government as his intermediary with other powers. Menelik would accept no such obligation, and so the diplomatic struggle began. The Amharic and Italian versions of the Wichale treaty were compared, and it was soon established beyond doubt that the difference in meaning of Article XVII was considerable in the two texts." (Rubenson, 1964: 18-19).

21. Marcus explains the losses of the Italian forces as follows: The Italians paid dearly: 4,000 European men and officers and 2,000 askaris had died; 1,428 European and Eritrean soldiers were wounded. Casualties were well over 50 per cent of the force engaged. Including the 1,800 prisoners, the loss was about 70 per cent, an incredible disaster for a modern army. Ethiopian losses have been estimated at between 4,000 to 7,000 killed, and between 6,000 to 10,000 wounded. ... As the exact size of Menelik's army is unknown, it is impossible to provide a loss percentage, but after the battle his army was still in being, whereas the Italian force had been destroyed." (Marcus, The Life and Times of Menelik II, 1995: 173).
22. Marcus, 1994: 97.
23. Rubenson, 1964: 21.
24. Clapham, 1970: 12.
25. Zewde, 1991: 229; further He remarks "the results of the Battle of Adwa gave momentum to the creation of the modern Ethiopian empire-state. The era of recurrent campaigns was over. Both internally and externally, post-Adwa Ethiopia enjoyed a degree of peace that contrasted sharply with the turbulence of the nineteenth century. This situation permitted the ruling class to turn its attention to more pacific- and more profitable- pursuits." (Ibid., p. 229).
26. See Marcus, 1996: 74.
27. Henze, 1991: 37.
28. Marcus, 1994: 132; for extensive discussion, see also Marcus, Haile Selassie I, 1998: 97-123..
29. Marcus, 1994: 139-146; Alberto Sbacchi details Italian use of poison gas during its campaign of occupation as follows: On the basis of available evidence that from the conquest of Ethiopia in May 1936 to 10 June 1940, when Italy entered the Second World War, it seems that 459 poison gas bombs were used against the patriots. The estimated use of poison gas for the war of occupation by the Air Force in the Northern Front is 1,972 'C 500-T' bombs, equivalent to about 300 tons of yperite. Badoglio also fired 1,367 artillery shells loaded with arsine against the Ethiopians at AmbaAradam. On the southern front the Air Force dropped 281 yperite 'C 500-T' bombs and 325 phosgene bombs, for a total of 44 tons of poison gas. In all, between 1935 and 1936, the Italian Air Force alone dropped about 1600 'C 500-T' bombs on the Ethiopians, corresponding to 317 tons of yperite. Between 1936 and 1939 approximately 500 poison gas bombs were used against the patriots. Hence, for the duration of Italian occupation, the Ethiopians

had to suffer the bombing of 2,100 poison gas bombs, conservatively equivalent to 500 tons of poison gas. (Sbacchi, Legacy of Bitterness, 1997: 59-60).

30. Zewde, 1991: 167; he further explains "the Resistance may be divided into two phases, with the reprisals that followed the abortive endeavour to kill Graziani in February 1937 forming the dividing line. The first phase was in essence a continuation of the war. It was conventional in character, and largely led by members of the upper nobility. As a result, it was characterised by vacillation and compromise. The second phase was marked by guerrilla warfare, led in most cases by members of the lower nobility. Although, as we shall see below, it had a number of fundamental weaknesses, it was uncompromising on the issue of resistance." (Ibid.).
31. Ibid., p. 173.
32. See Keller, 1981: 532-33.
33. Keller, 1988: 69.
34. See Perham, 1969: 464-73 for the full text of the agreement; the British were able to remain in control of the Ogaden, the railway and a strip of land adjoining French Somaliland. (Ibid., p. 392).
35. See Perham, 1969: 474-78 for the full text of the agreement; see also Zewde, 1991: 180-81.
36. See Henze, Layers of Time, 2000: 207.
37. See Perham, p. 423-32 for the full text of the Constitution.
38. Ibid.
39. Henze, Layers of Time, 2000: 207.
40. Ibid., p. 435-62.
41. Clapham, 1970: 44; Henze also explains that "the constitution reaffirmed the Emperor's descent from Solomon and Sheba and confirmed his primacy in all important respects: appointment of officials, control of the armed forces and of foreign relations, and oversight of the judicial system. It went into detail on provisions for the succession and a regency in case of incapacity of the Emperor. Parliament was given the power to approve treaties, but the Emperor was empowered to dissolve Parliament." (Henze, Layers of Time, 2000: 252).
42. Lefort, 1983: 15; moreover, Henze explains that "secured in his conviction that modernization would now proceed, Haile Selassie was less concerned about the rapidity of reform than about consolidating his own power and creating a government structure amenable to control and manipulation. He was mindful to prevent any concentration of authority that could challenge his own pre-eminence. Thus he became a master at shumshir- the rotation of individuals from one position to another in both the capital and in the provinces. Loyal officials were frequently moved from one position to another" (Henze, Layers of Time, 2000: 238-39).
43. Clapham, 1970: 93-94; see also Markakis and Ayele, 1986: 35.
44. Tareke, 1991: 81-82.
45. Tareke explains the involvement of the British by quoting the British Secretary of War as follows: The War Cabinet ought to face squarely that the War Office has

a fundamental military interest in what happens in Ethiopia, owing to the key position of the country in our Middle East Strategy ... the country straddles our land communications between the Red Sea ports and the Indian Ocean. The War Office must therefore try to ensure that Ethiopia is controlled by a well desposed government which will be prepared to concede to us the rights and safeguards necessary to protect those vital military interests I have just mentioned. (Tareke, Ethiopia: Power and Protest, 1991: 105).

46. See Wubneh and Abate, 1988: 21.
47. See Keller, 1988: 61-64; see also Zewde, 1991: 191-93.
48. A relatively radical official proposal came in 1973, when the Ministry of Land Reform and Administration urged consideration of expropriation and redistribution of holdings in excess of a ceiling. However, due to parliamentary opposition and lack of political will on the part of the monarch and the executive, it remained on paper.
49. Lefort, 1983: 11.
50. Addona notes the role of Emperor Haile Selassie as follows: One of Africa's senior statesmen, Ethiopian Emperor Haile Selassie I, noted that rather than the formation of the Brazzaville, Casablanca, and Monrovia blocs, there was but one bloc for the participants- the Africa bloc. He noted further that the Ethiopian delegation at the sixteen session o the United Nations, in New York during 1961, had called for the creation of an organisation of African states. The Emperor urged the participants to agree on the structure, secretariat, and the specialised commissions inherent in the formation of such organisation. In effect, the Emperor, along with other African leaders, was reiterating the need for a body akin to the Organisation of African Unity. The Emperor was only one of many respected African leaders who urged these sentiments at the Lagos conference, but he was undoubtedly instrumental in the creation of the OAU the following year in Addis Ababa (Addona, The Organisation of African Unity, 1969: 96-97); for a brief background and aims and purposes of the OAU, and a wide-range of references on the organisation, see Bello, Emmauel G., "Organisation of African Unity", in Bernhardt, Encyclopaedia of Public International Law, vol. 3, 1997: 802-810.
51. Keller, 1990: 85.
52. Zewde, 1991: 211-15.
53. For the details of the evolution of the banking system in Ethiopia, see Teffera Deguefe, Minutes of An Ethiopian Century, 2006.
54. Wubneh and Abate, 1988: 79.
55. Keller, 1988: 99.
56. See the Third Five-year Development Plan, 1968-73, Addis Ababa, 1968: 35-41.
57. See Pickett, 1991: 104-05.
58. See World Bank: Accelerated Development in Sub-Saharan Africa, 1981, Statistical Annex, Table 2.
59. Keller, 1988: 126.

60. See World Bank, op. cit., Table 3; World Development Report, 1989, Table 3.
61. Quoted in Lefort, 1983: 24.
62. See Terfassa, in Taddesse (ed.), 1992: 143.
63. Eritrea can be mentioned here but the government had nothing to do with its industrialisation. In fact, the government was responsible for its economic decline.
64. See Report of Central Statistical Office, 1975.
65. World Development Report, 1989, Table 4.
66. Woyane was the name given to the 1943 rebellion in Tigray; for further discussion on the Woyane, see Tareke, Ethiopia: Power and Protest, 1991: 89-124.
67. See Tareke, Ethiopia: Power and Protest, Peasant Revolts in Twentieth Century, 1991; see also Henze, Layers of Time, 2000: 248-52 and 260-65.
68. For further discussions on Eritrean movements, see 3.3.3.
69. See Zewde, 1991: 222-23.
70. Henze, 2000: 259-60.
71. Keller, 1988: 166.
72. Kapuscinski, The Emperor, 1983: 111.
73. See Schwab, 1985: 15.
74. Harbeson, 1988: 86-88.
75. Clapham, Transformation and Continuity in Revolutionary Ethiopia, 1988: 38.
76. Ibid., p. 89.
77. Keller, 1988: 177-78.
78. Markakis and Ayele, 1986: 87.
79. The Committee (Derg) was created by representatives of units of the armed forces. Every unit was asked to send three representatives: a junior officer, a non-commissioned officer, and an enlisted man.
80. Clapham explains "[t]he process leading to Haile-Selassie's deposition was, it should be noted, entirely an urban one. The countryside neither came to his support, nor helped in his overthrow. The famine of Wollo was used to generate urban opposition to the regime- for example, by showing a television film which contrasted the starvation of the peasants with the luxury in which the emperor lived – rather than as a means of mobilising rural dissent, and the issue of what to do about the countryside was not confronted until after the military seizure of power. (Clapham, 1988: 40).
81. Marcus, 1994: 180.
82. See Provisional Military Government, Proclamation No. 1, Negarit Gazeta, September 15, 1974.
83. The Derg was worried about the possible reaction of the people on the abolition of the monarchy. The decree that abolished the monarchy was proclaimed six months later, after it felt secure in power.

84. See Tiruneh, 1993: 73. The government adopted proclamations on November 16, 1974 to establish special courts martial, amend the Penal Code, and public order and safety, to suppress urban dissent (Clapham, 1988: 45).
85. Tiruneh, 1993: 55-56.
86. For list of those massacred on 23rd November, 1974, see Legum, 1975: 55.
87. Zemecha literally means campaign.
88. Lefort, 1983: 99.
89. PMAC, Program of the National Democratic Revolution of Ethiopia, Addis Ababa, 1976.
90. Wubneh and Abate details the debate between the ERRP and MEISON as follows: Both the ERRP and MEISON agreed in principle that the transition from feudalism to socialism could not be accomplished by the proletariat, but by a coalition of all the progressive forces in the country. Whereas MEISON was determined that the national democratic revolution could be guided by the military as progressive members of the coalition, the EPRP refused to recognize the PMAC [Provisional Military Administrative Council] as a progressive force. ... They were diametrically opposed on the nature of the revolution: MEISON wanted a revolution guided from the top, whereas EPRP wanted a revolution guided by a coalition of grass-roots groups. The EPRP denounced the PMAC as Fascist for harassing those opposed to its leadership, for imprisoning labour leaders, and for preventing students from continuing to policize the peasantry. MEISON, in turn, labelled the EPRP as anarchist because of its demand for full and unqualified democratic rights for all citizens. The two antagonists were also divided on the question of ethnic separatist movements that were challenging the military government. ... MEISON ... held that self-determination could be exercised only within the context of a united Ethiopia in accordance with the PMAC's Programme of the National Democratic Revolution, which they (MEISON) had helped author. (Wubneh and Abate, 1988: 55).
91. Keller, 1990: 90; The "Red Terror" was a ruthless campaign waged by the government to liquidate its opponents in the urban centres throughout the country between 1976 and 1978. The campaign was not only designed to destroy the opposition but also to terrify and humiliate the people into submission. (de Waal, Evil Days: 30 Years of War and Famine in Ethiopia, 1991:101).
92. Lefort, 1983: 201.
93. Brietzke, quoted in Tiruneh, 1993: 223.
94. See Halliday and Molyneux, 1981: 142.
95. For details see Proclamation No. 174 of 1979.
96. Clapham explains "[t]he party was formed strictly along the Soviet lines, and with Soviet participation and encouragement. Even before COPWE had given way to WPE, it reached party-to-party agreements with the CPSU, rather than participating in state-to-state agreements between Ethiopia and the Soviet government–an important distinction in the Soviet system, in which party-to-party agreements are normally reserved for established Leninist parties. COPWE cadres were

trained in the Soviet Union and other socialist states. The Soviet influence was evidently exercised in the direction of haste rather than delay (Clapham, 1988: 75).

97. Harbeson, 1988: 186.
98. Ibid.
99. Ethiopia: From Feudal Autocracy to People's Democracy, Committee for the Founding of the People's Democratic Republic of Ethiopia, Addis Ababa, September 1987, p. 67.
100. Negarit Gazeta 47th year Proclamation No. 1 of 1987, Addis Ababa, September 12, 1987.
101. Ibid.
102. Keller, 1990: 92.
103. The sole right of nomination of candidates for the National Assembly rested on the WPE chapters. It was indicated that 'for each electoral district a minimum of three candidates whose competence and allegiance to the cause of the revolution as well as to the welfare of the masses had been duly confirmed, were nominated by the organs of the WPE, the mass organisations and revolutionary armed forces'. (Ethiopia: From Feudal Autocracy to People's Democracy, 1987).
104. See 'Ensuring the Rights of Nationalities', Committee for the Founding of the PDRE, Addis Ababa, September 1987.
105. Keller, 1990: 94.
106. Ottaway, in Ottaway (ed.), 1990: 4.
107. Eritrea was formally annexed in 1962.
108. Markakis, 1987: 73.
109. Keller, 1988: 138.
110. Ibid., p. 140-41.
111. Markakis, in Fukui and Markakis (ed.), 1994: 227.
112. See TPLF Program, 1979; People's Voice, April 1981: 16-17.
113. See OLF Program, 1975.
114. For detail discussions on liberation fronts, see Chapter 4.
115. For extend discussion on the Eritrean Question, see Chapter 7.
116. The early negotiations were held under the auspices of the Consolidated German Socialist Party, which were terminated in 1978 after failing to produce any tangible results. In 1985, there were several meetings between the EPLF and the government but these were no more than diplomatic games. The EPLF continued to declare its adherence to the principle of allowing the Eritrean people to choose from three alternatives: total independence, federation with Ethiopia, and regional autonomy. The government failed to prove its sincerity to solve the problem by sticking to the usual rhetoric of "autonomy", which was tantamount to asking the liberation movements for submission. In 1989, another negotiation process began with mediation from former United States President, Jimmy Carter, at the Carter

Centre of EmoryUniversity in Atlanta, Georgia, from September 7 to September 19. It was agreed that peace talks would commence without preconditions include the participation of third parties, and the talks would be publicly announced. However, the talks could not go beyond procedural issues. (See EPLF: Statement on Peaceful Solution and the Preliminary Meetings held between it and the Addis Ababa Regime, September 10, 1985;EPLF. A Memorandum on the Peace Making Process, December 30, 1988;Memorandum on the Proceedings and Assessment of the AtlantaTalks, EPLF, October 3, 1989: Final Agreement Signed by both Parties and the Mediator, September 19, 1989).

117. See the Constitution of the People's Democratic Republic of Ethiopia, Negarit Gazeta, Proclamation No. 1 of 1987, Addis Ababa, September 12, 1987.

118. See Proclamation No. 14/1987.

119. The Declaration on the Economic Policy of Socialist Ethiopia, Addis Ababa, February 7, 1975: 3 (in Amharic).

120. Ibid., p. 4.

121. Survey of Current Economic Conditions in Ethiopia, Vol. 1, No. 1, January 1993, p. 6.

122. Provisional Military Government of Socialist Ethiopia: Ten-Year Perspective Plan, 1984/85- 1993/94, Addis Ababa, September 1984: 5.

123. In this regard, Clapham remarks "[t]he National Revolutionary Development Campaigns were indeed a matter of campaigning rather than planning. Although ambitious targets were announced, there was no comprehensive ordering of available resources to achieve specific goals. ... Even before the whole process was effectively wrecked by the famine crises which struck at exactly the moment when the plan was due to come into effect, it was abundantly clear that the plan targets (which envisaged annual average growth rates of 4.3 per cent in agriculture, 10.8 per cent in industry and 6.9 per cent in services) were little more than wishful thinking, and rested on extremely optimistic assumptions about everything from the weather to the availability of foreign exchange, and on a high level of internal consistency into the bargain. ... Not only is it extraordinarily unlikely that such an increase could be obtained, but equally if it were, it would lead to a debt trap of unmanageable proportions, and even then could not be expected to generate the increases in output and employment needed to meet the plan targets." (Clapham, 1988: 116-117).

124. Marcus, 1994: 204.

125. See Proclamation No. 31 of 1975, Articles 3 and 4.

126. Article 10 provided these associations with wide-range of functions including distributing land to farmers and evicted tenants; following land-use directives to be issued by the Government; administering and conserving any public property within the area especially the soil, water and forest; establishing judicial tribunals to hear land disputes; establishing marketing and credit co-operatives and other associations; building with the co-operation of the Government schools, clinics and similar institutions; cultivating the holdings of persons who are incapable of

cultivating for themselves; undertaking villagization programmes; and excluding from distribution mining and forest lands and places of historical and antiquarian significance (see Proclamation No. 31 of 1975, Article 10).

127. See Pausewang, in Pausewang et al. (ed.), 1990: 214.
128. Lefort, 1983: 124.
129. Dessalegn, quoted in Pausewang et. al., 1990: 20.
130. See Proclamation to Provide for the Establishment of Co-operative Societies, Negarit Gazeta, March 3, 1978.
131. See IMF. Ethiopia: Recent Economic Developments, 1988: 27.
132. Wubneh, in Ottaway (ed.), 1990: 205.
133. Chole, The Ethiopian Economy: An Overview, 1988: 2.
134. See World Bank: World Tables, 1987; World Development Report, 1989; and World Development Report, 1992.
135. See1980-1989 Central Statistical Authority & FAO Crop Assessment Mission. (1990-1991 Central Statistical Authority.
136. FAO: Food Balance Sheets, Statistics Division, 1996.
137. Proclamation No. 31 of 1975. Public Ownership of Rural Lands, April 29, 1975, Article 7.
138. Ayana, Itana, 'The State and Performance of Public Enterprises in Ethiopia: The Case of State Farms', in Kello (ed.), 1994: 41.
139. Ibid., p. 53.
140. World Bank. Ethiopia: Agriculture Sector, An Interim Report, Report No. Et.3956a, January 1983: 20-21.
141. See Kebede, 1992: 19.
142. Griffin, Keith, The Economy of Ethiopia, 1992: 293.
143. Ayana, in Kello (ed.), 1994: 47.
144. Ibid., p. 64.
145. See Chole, in Pausewang et al. (ed.), 1990: 93.
146. Ibid., p. 96.
147. Ibid., p. 90-91.
148. W. Giorgis, Red Tears, 1989: 289.
149. Ibid., p. 304.
150. M. Colchester and V. Luling in their article, Ethiopia's Bitter Medicine (The Sunday Times, London, November 3, 1985) put the numbers of dead at about 50,000. (Colchester and Luling quoted in Clapham, 1988: 194); see also de Waal, 1991: 224-227; Wubneh and Abate simply noted that the victims of resettlement were in their thousands (see Wubneh and Abate, 1988: 101); see also Henze, 2000:309.
151. See Clapham, Transformation and Continuity in Revolutionary Ethiopia, 1988: 176.

152. See Proclamation No. 26 of 1975. A Proclamation to Provide for the Ownership and Control by the Government of the Means of Production, Negarit Gazeta, March 11, 1975.
153. Proclamation No. 26/1975, Article 2.
154. Ibid., Article 3; the government's share was indicated to be a minimum of 51 per cent.
155. Ibid., Article 4.
156. Terfassa, in Taddesse (ed.), 1992: 144.
157. See Article 8 of Proclamation 76/1975; at the time the official exchange rate was Birr 2.07 to US$ 1.
158. See World Development Report, 1979; World Development Report, 1986; World Bank: Sub-Saharan Africa: From Crisis to Sustainable Growth, 1989; and World Development Report, 1993.
159. Kassa, Belay, 'Instability of Ethiopia's Export Earnings: The Contribution of Major Agricultural Export Commodities', Ethiopian Journal of Agricultural Economics, Vol. 2, No. 1, January 1998: 32.
160. See Tekele, in Taddesse (ed.), 1992: 225.
161. World Bank, Ethiopia's Economy in the 1980s and Framework for Accelerated Growth, 1990: 39.
162. Ibid., p. 41.
163. The Ethiopian Birr had been linked to the U.S. dollar at a rate of Birr 2.07=1 U.S$ since 1973. The Birr was only devalued in 1992 to the rate of Birr 5 = 1 US$.
164. See National Bank of Ethiopia, Annual Report, 1992/93.
165. World Bank, op. cit., p. 35.
166. See World Development Report, 1979; World Development Report, 1986; World Bank: Sub-Saharan Africa: From Crisis to Sustainable Growth, 1989; and World Development Report, 1993.
167. Chole and Manyazewal, 'The Macroeconomic Performance of the Ethiopian Economy 1974-90', Tadesse (ed.), 1992: 36.
168. The major elements of the reform program can be summarised as follows: promotion of mixed economy; greater use of the market mechanism to guide economic decisions; active encouragement of the private sector through a series of new incentives; reorienting public sector management towards competitiveness and profitability; in the agriculture sector: abolition of Agricultural Marketing Corporation's quota levies; lifting of all inter-regional grain movement controls; allowing the private sector to operate in grain marketing; security of land tenure and investments on the land; and formation of co-operatives along strictly voluntary basis; and promotion of foreign investment. Ibid., p: 36-37; See also Ethiopia: Policy Framework Paper, 1990/91-1992/93, May 1990: 8.
169. World Bank, World Tables, 1994.
170. The Red Star Campaign was the largest campaign carried out under Mengistu's direct command in 1982. The objective was to break the backbone of the EPLF at

Nacfa and then eradicate it with successive campaigns. In defence of Nacfa, contingents of the TPLF had also participated alongside of their EPLF compatriots. From then the name Nacfa transformed into a symbol of the Eritrean resistance.

171. Marcus, 1994: 207; see also Korn, 1986: 121.
172. The government attempted to present the situation as the making of successive droughts that hit the country at the time. However, this was just part of the story, and de Waal explains that "the 1984 drought was made the culprit of a famine that had begun earlier. It proved an excellent scapegoat, as its effects were visually and statistically dramatic... The fact is, however, that a visitor can only see a single drought, and that is not enough to cause famine. Those who wish to explain the famine in meteorological terms are impelled to fall back on either convoluted arguments or blatant untruths". (de Waal, Famine Crimes, 1997: 125).
173. At the time, the TPLF was forced to evacuate over 200,000 people to the Sudan in order to save their lives.
174. After a military stalemate for several years, the EPLF destroyed the military forces stationed at the Afabet front in March 1988, and captured Afabet and the adjacent regions. Bereket remarks "the EPLF victory over Derg forces at Afabet, which has been compared to Dien Bien Phu, has altered the military balance in favour of the Eritrean struggle. It caused Mengistu, for the first time, to admit defeat and to speak reluctantly about peace, while calling for a general mobilisation". (BereketHabte Selassie, in Ottaway, 1990: 129).
175. The Ethiopian People's Revolutionary Democratic Front (EPRDF) was transformed by the TPLF and EPDM in the late 1980s and continued to expand by accepting new members like OPDO and EDORM.
176. In the late 1980s, Soviet leaders realised that Mengistu would not defeat the movements by force. The Soviets urged Mengistu to introduce economic reforms and to put an end to the civil war. Mikhail Gorbachev, while trying to show the world that he stood for glasnost and perestroika, was not permissible to tarnish his reputation by supporting a repugnant regime such as that of Mengistu's. Apparently, Gorbachev's new international image-building initiative, compounded with serious economic crises in the Soviet Union, expedited the decision to terminate assistance to several African countries, including Ethiopia. The decision came too late but played some role in hastening the demise of the regime. However, this did not mean that the Soviets had altogether stopped sending their weapons to Ethiopia, even during the Derg's last days. The effect might be found mainly in its impact on the psychological pressure it brought to the regime's faithful.

Chapter 4

The Period of Transition and the Main Political Actors

Overview of the Development

The London Peace Conference mediated by the U.S. was scheduled to start on May 27, 1991 between the military government, the Ethiopian People's Revolutionary Democratic Front (EPRDF), the Eritrean People's Liberation Front (EPLF) and the Oromo Liberation Front (OLF).[1] In the meantime, the EPRDF leadership had already decided to launch a final push in order to end the conflict on the ground before the beginning of the rainy season. The EPLF was also in final preparation to end the war in a similar way. In early May 1991, the EPLF and EPRDF leadership met in Massawa and agreed to co-ordinate their forces to shorten the life span of the regime.

On the eve of the opening of the peace talks, the conflict on the ground was almost finished. The government's delegation had very little to deliver and the talks were held among the liberation movements.[2] Averting the phenomenon of a "failed state"[3] became the imperative task of the liberation movements. On May 28, a joint statement was issued by the EPRDF, the EPLF and the OLF declaring that a conference would be held no later than July 1 to discuss the details of the transition period in general, and the formation of a broad-based provisional government in particular, with the participation of a wide range of parties and interests.[4] They also agreed that in the meantime the EPRDF would assume state responsibilities pending the formation of such a broad-based government at the proposed conference.[5] Accordingly, the EPRDF formed a provisional government after its forces entered Addis Ababa on May 28, 1991.

From the outset the provisional government was confronted with extensive difficulties and challenges. Seyoum explains that the most crucial challenge was the maintenance of peace and the establishment of the rule of law throughout the country.[6] It was at this time that one of the biggest armies in sub-Saharan Africa was scattered throughout the country with its arms. The soldiers had nothing to eat and had no shelter, and could have become a serious threat to peace and stability in their struggle for survival. The government was faced with a major difficulty in the process of the encampment of these former soldiers and in helping them to integrate back into society. Thousands of small arms also made their way into the hands of many people who could have used them for subversion. Furthermore, the collapse of government structures in almost all regions produced an administrative vacuum that could have created a breeding ground for lawlessness and public safety disruptions. In fact, it took quite some time before proper administrative structures were put in place. As Bereket noted, it was the community at large which handled its own problems in the absence of administrative organs, even in the absence of the police force. The people's desire for peace and stability was extraordinarily high[7] and in many parts of the country, peace and stability committees were elected to fill the gap. Until woreda (district) and kebele (neighbourhood or village) administrations were elected, these committees worked as administrative and policing organs, stabilizing the situation and creating a sense of security within their communities.

The other major challenge was the economic crisis left by the military government. The economy was declining rapidly and there was a serious shortage of basic commodities in the market. It was reported that the country was nearly bankrupt with an import cover of slightly over one week and a huge budget deficit. The flood of displaced people from Eritrea and other regions of the country also aggravated the situation. Many people were in transit camps with inadequate facilities. Moreover, the return of hundreds of thousands of refugees from Somalia, accelerated by the fall of the military government and the chaos in Somalia, brought another burden to the already distressed government capabilities. Besides, the need to create a breathing space for the economy was imperative. The adoption of policies that would bring relief from the command economy restraints was demanding high priority.

From the time the formation of the provisional government was declared on June 1, 1991, preparation for the national conference was in full swing. The EPRDF was busy meeting and discussing with potential participant political organisations and groupings regarding the basic agenda of the conference. These organisations and groups included liberation fronts which were more or less active in the armed struggle, groups in exile, especially those who were in Somalia, and those who attempted to organise themselves to represent an interest group or a trend in the society within that short period after the change of government. The discussions ranged from the basic issues that later made up the National Charter, to their share and scope of participation in the new arrangement. Seyoum remarks:

> One of the most accommodative and far-sighted policies of the EPRDF was that it made the participation open for those who can organise up to the conference date in order to widen the base of the transition. The thinking was as long as the EPRDF has decided for a broad based transition, and then let us make it possible for those who can regroup themselves, even within a month, be it on a national basis or on all Ethiopian political programs.[8]

Meles also explains that:

> The central point was that to have all major trends and opinions represented, and so we encouraged as many opinion makers as possible represented in the conference. The two dimensions that were important were: geographical spread and representing diverse opinions.[9]

In addition to the criteria of representing political trends and geographical spread, the criterion of commitment to peaceful competition was given strong emphasis. As a result, political organisations such as the Coalition of Ethiopian Democratic Forces (COEDF) were excluded from participation because of their unwillingness to renounce violence as a means to achieve political ends.[10]

The draft charter was discussed with political organisations and groups, and there was a genuine attempt to accommodate their opinions before the beginning of the conference. It was generally similar to the transitional program of the EPRDF in substance.[11] However, the discussions on the draft made their own contribution toward creating a working atmosphere. Leenco Lata, one of the prominent leaders of the Oromo Liberation Front (OLF) remarks:

> Until then the situation had been the traditional one in Ethiopia. The EPRDF had one political program, the EPRP had theirs, and so on. Each group proclaimed its stand and announced "all you who agree march behind me". But after the London talks the three distinct groups EPLF, TPLF, and OLF, worked very hard to put together a covenant. So coming up with this sketchy framework was a departure from the past.[12]

The National Conference was convened from 1-5 July, 1991 in Addis Ababa. Delegates from 24 national and multinational organisations, and other professional groupings were represented. It was also observed by over 20 representatives of countries, and international and regional organisations, including representatives of major religious institutions. Representatives of the EPLF also participated as observers. After intensive deliberations, the conference adopted the Transitional Charter of Ethiopia as the basic document of the transitional period.

One of the most important provisions of the Charter was Article 1, which states that "Based on the Universal Declaration of Human Rights of the United Nations adopted and proclaimed by the General Assembly by resolution 217 A (III) of 10 December 1948, individual human rights shall be respected fully, and without any limitation whatsoever...".[13] The Article was not contentious in the conference, given the nearly two decades of military dictatorship experienced by the people and their general desire to make a break with the past. The most controversial provision of the Charter was Article 2, which dealt with the right of nations, nationalities and peoples to self-determination. Although chauvinism had been defeated on the battle field by the EPRDF and other mainly nationality organisations whose major objective was to ensure the right of self-determination, it was equally important to these organisations to confirm their rights in such a conference. However, the right to self-determination was not only opposed by some multinational organisations but also by certain nationality-based political groupings. Article 2(c) was the most testing part of the Charter: it states "each nation, nationality and people... exercises its rights to self-determination of independence, when the concerned nation/nationality and people is convinced that the above rights are denied, abridged or abrogated". These organisations feared that the right to secede might jeopardise the unity of the country by encouraging some nationality-based organisations to opt for independence. However, after extensive discussions many opted for a new Ethiopia by endorsing the right to self-determination as detailed on the draft.

Based on the agreement of the London peace talks, the conference was presented with a draft paper on future Ethio-Eritrean co-operation. "The Principles of Co-operation between the Transitional Government of Ethiopia and the Provisional Government of Eritrea" contained eight points considered to be vital to the process of mutual wellbeing. Some were basic points of principle that could determine the norm of relations while others were technical issues, which could further consolidate the fundamental ones. In the discussion, those who were reluctant to fully endorse the whole principle of referendum tried to play around with the technical ones. For some organisations their earlier endorsement of the right of nations to self-determination did not deter them from expressing their reluctance to support the whole document as presented. It was clear that supporting the concept of self-determination as a theoretical principle and endorsing it as a practical means of solving the Eritrean problem were two quite different issues. The main thrust of the debate was that supporting the document was in line with the major tenets of the National Charter. However, the objective interlinkage between the right of nations to self-determination and the support for Eritrean referendum failed to produce an overwhelming support for the document as a whole from the participants. Hence, the conference agreed on the major principles which would govern the relations of the two parties, and deferred the technical ones to further sessions of the coming legislature. The amended proposal was endorsed by all, with opposition only from the representative of the university and four abstentions including the multinational organisations: Ethiopian National Democratic Organisation (ENDO) and Ethiopian Democratic Coalition (EDC). The adopted principles were as follows:

1. The Transitional Government of Ethiopia recognises the right of the Eritrean people to determine its political future by an internationally supervised referendum ... the Provisional Government of Eritrea has deferred the referendum for two years.
2. The Provisional Government of Eritrea recognises the vital importance of the port of Assab to Ethiopia's economic welfare and development, and considers it not to be a source of conflict between the peoples of Ethiopia and Eritrea. Consequently, it has deemed it necessary to make Assab a free port to Ethiopia.
3. The two sides have agreed to establish a high level Eritrean delegation in Addis Ababa to facilitate co-operation between them.[14]

Consequently, the Transitional Council of Representatives at its 10th Regular Session of August 14, 1991 further discussed the resolutions of the National Conference and decided to form a seven-member standing committee for Eritrean affairs, which included Dr. Kassu Ilala and Leenco Lata.[15] The major purposes of the committee were to formulate directives on the possible co-operation agreements between the two governments and to follow up any emerging problem in their relations.[16]

The other potentially divisive matter was the issue of land ownership. From the program of the organisations in the conference and from the debate, a resolution between those who believed in public land ownership and those who wished to treat it as a market commodity seemed unlikely. Organisations like the EPRDF were in favour of public ownership of land but with full farmers' usufructuary rights. On the other hand, groups such as ENDO, EDC, KPC and GPDO wished to reintroduce some form of private ownership of rural and urban lands. The participants agreed to defer the highly divisive issue until a time when people were able to decide how best to treat it. In the meantime, it was decided to retain the existing land ownership system.

Some important points such as the independence of the judiciary were confirmed, though the right of interpretation of the Charter was reserved to the Transitional Council of Representatives. The number of Council members was finally fixed at 87. This was the total number of seats allocated by the EPRDF to various political organisations and groups as it considered fair, according to their role in the struggle to overthrow the military government, and on the potential of their future contribution toward building a new political system. Nevertheless, in order to avoid any power accumulation by one group or nationality, it was decided that the Head of State, the Prime Minister, the Vice-Chairperson and Secretary of the Council of Representatives were to be from different nationalities.[17]

Appropriation of seats to participant political organisations and groups was another thorny issue needing extensive negotiation. Although the proposal of seat allocation came from the EPRDF, it had to be discussed with each organisation in order to ensure a successful formation of the Transitional Council. Each organisation was pressing to secure more seats than offered as it claimed to have a bigger role than the others. In particular, organisations like the OLF were difficult to convince. Seyoum remembers how the process of negotiations went as follows:

> The organisations assembled within one month of the EPRDF's rule complained they did not receive the number of seats they deserved. The OLF was also insisting on sharing seats on equal terms with the EPRDF. It was difficult to convince, particularly the OLF, and therefore we asked the EPLF to intervene and help in making its leaders understand that they were securing more seats even than that of the TPLF. The OLF was also requested to recommend personalities of their liking for cabinet and ambassadorial appointments. In general, we had difficult and time-consuming negotiations before and during the National Conference.[18]

Of the 87 seats, 32 went to the EPRDF from which the TPLF, EPDM and OPDO obtained 10 each and the Ethiopian Democratic Officers Revolutionary Movement (EDORM) two seats. The OLF also secured 12 seats and other organisations between one and three. The remaining six seats were later distributed to organisations that were not able to participate in the National Conference at the 14th Secession of the Transitional Council of Representatives on September 13, 1991.[19]

Bereket argues that the appropriation of seats was designed in such a way that one organisation might not have a dominant vote. Although the EPRDF played a leading and superior role in the armed struggle, it was allocated only 32 seats which put it in a minority position.[20] Many people might agree with such statement, but not the opposition. The Coalition of Ethiopian Democratic Forces (COEDF) declared: "the EPRDF allocated 32 of the 87 seats in the newly created assembly to itself. Additional seats were allocated to individuals and groups considered trustworthy by the EPRDF... neither COEDF nor any democratically constituted future Ethiopian government will be bound by the decisions of the Addis Ababa conference."[21] If the word "trustworthy" was meant to show similarity of political programs, it would be at least an exaggerated statement considering the different stances not only during the transition but also in the National Conference debates.

Subsequently, a 17-member Cabinet was selected by the Prime Minister and approved by the Transitional Council of Representatives. Ministers were selected in accordance with Article 9(c) of the National Charter which states that the Council of Ministers should be nominated on the consideration of ascertaining a broad national representation, technical competence and unswerving adherence to the Charter. It is clear from the list that the Ministers' ethnic composition was given greater prominence over competence and devotion to the principles of the Charter. However, the composition did not satisfy some of the member organisations. The Sidama Liberation Movement (SLM), Islamic Front for the Liberation of Oromo (IFLO) and Western Somali Liberation Front (WSLF) complained that their people were not represented in the Cabinet. Even the OLF suggested that the number of Oromos was below an appropriate representation and special consideration should be given in the appropriation of future appointments. After long discussions on the difficulties of finding the right people for the right jobs and on what should be done for the next appointments, the Council approved the nominations overwhelmingly with the exception of one abstention.[22]

The first major task of the Transitional Government was to ensure peace and stability for the implementation of its political and socio-economic programs. In order to put in place the administrative structures through elections, it was imperative to prepare the ground by minimising the possible obstacles. The Transitional Council of Representatives agreed that it would not be possible to translate the Charter fully into practice by using the previous army and security apparatus. Hence, the army of the EPRDF was accepted to serve as the state defence force for the transitional period.[23] It was also decided to encamp other organisations' armies in designated areas and provide them with some essential provisions and other assistance. However, additional personnel recruited by the armies after the fall of the military government were not recognised as members, and in fact, the organisations were supposed to disband them.[24] The criteria for the identification of organisations' armies were detailed as follows:

> Any member organisation of the Council of Representatives which declared and registered claiming to have an army shall, in addition to having participated in the Peace and Democracy Conference which adopted the Charter, prove that its alleged army:
>
> a. was established before the fall of the Derg;
>
> b. was organised and established as a regular fighter;

c. fought the Derg with full effort until the final downfall of the Derg;
d. it controlled a liberated territory administering the people therein and remained with the people in the liberated territory fighting and defen ing until the final downfall of the Derg.[25]

The Defence and Security Policy Standing Committee attempted to apply the criteria and came up with a report presented to the Council for decision. The report concluded that organisations such as the OLF, the Benishangul People's Liberation Movement (BPLM) and Gambella People's Liberation Movement (GPLM) were able to prove the existence of their armies while groups such as the Ethiopian Democratic Unity (EDU) and United Oromo People's Liberation Front (UOPLF) failed to support their claims with credible evidence. In fact, the Committee was unable to reach any conclusive decision on whether the Somali liberation movements had armed groups, or if there were, to which organisations they belonged as several of them claimed to have armed wings. The armies which clearly satisfied the criteria were recognised by the Council of Representatives and provided with camps and the necessary provisions.[26] Similarly, the directives for establishing the police force under the central and regional self-governments were detailed by Proclamation No. 9/1992. Regarding the recruitment and training of the police, Article 15 explained as follows:

1. Each region shall commence its work prior to the election period with a one-third of a police force fixed for the region by the Central Transitional Government;
2. Members of the police force shall be recruited with the participation of the people in accordance with criteria and allocation directives to be issued by the Central Transitional Government.[27]

Many people participated in meetings held to evaluate the past performance and behaviour of the members of the police force in their localities and were able to commend the better ones and reject those suspected of any involvement in corrupt practices or crimes. At the end of the exercise, many of the woredas (districts) were able to organise a police force that served as an initial component in building the institution anew.

Accomplishments of the Transitional Government should be evaluated by considering the difficulties it inherited from the previous government and the complexities of the transition itself. One of the government's major achievements was the devolution of power from the centre. The Council adopted the National/Regional Self-Governments Establishment Proclamation No. 7/1992 on November 16, 1991. According to the Proclamation, 14 regions were set up with legislative, executive and judicial powers in all aspects of government except defence, foreign affairs, economic policy, and a few other matters which were specifically reserved for the central government in the same Proclamation. Not long after, five regions decided to amalgamate and create a larger region, named Southern Ethiopian Peoples' Region, in accordance with Article 3 (26) of Proclamation No. 7/1992, January 14, 1992, which states that the self-government of adjacent nations, nationalities and peoples may, by agreement, jointly establish one larger regional self-government.

After a long delay, the first multi-party elections were held on June 21, 1992. Although the elections were the first of their type in the nation, they were marred with controversies from the outset by the boycott of the OLF, which alleged widespread intimidation. It might be hard for many people to accept the allegations of the OLF for it was itself one of the perpetrators of harassment and political killings. At the end of the elections, some irregularities were reported and in order to rectify them the Council issued the Election Review Board Establishment Proclamation No. 21/1992. Consequently, results in some districts were annulled and elections were held for the second time. It is important to note that the regional elections were the first after the downfall of the military government, and with all their shortcomings, they served quite well to establish the administrative structures that were badly needed to push through development efforts. Moreover, it was a step forward in devolving power to the grass-roots after extreme centralisation and domination of centuries old patterns of government.

The economic chaos inherited by the Transitional Government made the formulation and adoption of a new economic policy urgent. The Transitional Council adopted an economic policy in August 1991. The policy served to transform the command economy into basically a market-oriented one. The stabilisation and structural adjustment program implemented since 1992 has started to show results in rehabilitating the economy. The correction of key price distortions and the devaluation of the exchange rate from Birr2.07 to Birr5 per U.S. dollar were the centrepieces of the initial reforms. The administrative system for allocating foreign exchange was also replaced by a bi-monthly auction system in May 1993 and later by a weekly one. Furthermore, the centralised transportation system was abolished and the ceilings on transport tariffs were liberalised. Export taxes were also abolished (except for coffee) and various incentives introduced.

The government introduced several regulatory codes, including those on investment, labour, trade and others. The adoption of the Encouragement, Expansion and Co-ordination of Investment Proclamation No. 15/1992 eliminated the previous restrictive investment environment and envisaged a reduction on the bureaucratic constraint of a minimum investment. Moreover, the

Labour Proclamation No. 42/1993 entered into force on January 20, 1993 in order to provide the labour conditions for the benefit of both employees and businesses. Not only did the government attempt to abolish the restrictive atmosphere, but it also started to divest the public sector step by step. It abolished state corporations that were in control of parastatals and granted operational autonomy to enterprises under them in 1992. Since then, privatisation has been carried out under the direction of the Privatisation Agency. In general, the government guided by its development strategy, the agricultural-development-led industrialisation (ADLI)[28] has achieved tangible economic progress during the transition.

One of the major tasks of the Transitional Council of Representatives was to direct the process of constitution making and pave the way for a new national election based on the ratified constitution. Accordingly, the Constitutional Commission was formed and was entrusted with the task of drafting the constitution. After months of deliberation and collection of various interest groups' opinions, and extensive discussions in the neighbourhoods, it was able to compile a draft that was presented to the Council of Representatives for its approval as a final draft. The Council, at its 94th Session, had an extensive debate on each article. The agreed draft contained not only points of agreement, but also both majority and minority views on contentious issues, such as the right of self-determination and property rights. A Constituent Assembly was elected and after broad debate ratified the draft constitution on December 8, 1994, which came into full force and effect on August 21, 1995.[29]

On May 7, 1995 elections were held for Regional and Federal Assemblies all over the country. As before, some of the opposition parties boycotted the elections claiming that the process would not be adequately competitive. On the other hand, the government rejected the claim by declaring that the opposition stayed away for fear of a devastating defeat. According to the Electoral Commission, 19.98 million people voted out of the registered 21.3 million people, which was an overwhelming majority.[30] Based on the results of the elections, which were observed by domestic and international monitors, the Federal Democratic Republic of Ethiopia was established on August 21, 1995.[31]

The challenges of the transitional period were vastly complicated, as the institutions had to start from scratch. The collapse of the government structures and the dissolution of the army and the police force had created a vacuum. The Transitional Government was preoccupied with many problems that emerged sporadically in a climate of uncertainty and dramatic changes. The initial experiences of devolution of power have been encouraging but are far from refined, and need to be developed from the local and international experiences. Economic development has continued to be one of the most formidable challenges that preoccupied the government. Obviously, without economic improvement and tangible progress in the reduction of poverty sustaining democracy would most likely be unattainable.

The Main Political Actors and Their Policies

The Ethiopian People's Revolutionary Democratic Front (EPRDF)

The EPRDF and Its Effort to Create a United Front against the Military Regime

The EPRDF was formed by the Tigray People's Liberation Front (TPLF) and Ethiopian People's Democratic Movement (EPDM) in January 1989, following the May 1988 meeting between the leaders of the two organisations. They adopted the new Front's program and constitution, and also established a joint leadership with equal representation from both founding organisations. Such agreement brought the two organisations' close co-operation of over eight years to its highest level and further strengthened their potential to mobilise the various Ethiopian nationalities against the military government.

Convening in its first congress from 17 to 23 January, 1991 in its liberated areas, further consolidated the EPRDF. In the congress, new member organisations, the Oromo People's Democratic Organisation (OPDO) and the Ethiopian Democratic Officers Revolutionary Movement (EDORM), participated alongside the founding members. The Benishangul People's Liberation Movement (BPLM) and the Gambella People's Liberation Movement (GPLM), which were closely affiliated to the EPRDF, also participated as observers.[32] It was in this congress that the decision was made to expedite the final onslaught on the military government before the rainy season. However, the Front's desire for any possible peaceful resolution in the meantime was stressed and made open.

The united front came very late, considering its quest began much earlier in the organisations' histories. In the late 1970s the call for a united front was first made by several political organisations, although their individual concepts differed. The TPLF had attempted to form a united front with the Ethiopian People's Revolutionary Party (EPRP) starting in 1976, until their relations deteriorated irreparably in 1978. At that time, the EPRP and the TPLF had differences on the status of the national question in Ethiopian struggle. While the TPLF believed that the national question was the prime contradiction in society that could mobilise the people of Ethiopia against oppression, the EPRP maintained that it was a bourgeois concept, and a secondary one, incapable of mounting a united resistance. It asserted that class struggle should be the prior mode of opposition capable of forging joint struggle.

Consequently, the EPRP thought of itself as a vanguard of the Ethiopian People's resistance and suggested the TPLF merge with it as one mass organisation. This was perceived as tantamount to rejection by the latter. On the other hand, the TPLF insisted on the formation of a united democratic front based on a minimum political program, while each member safeguarded its organisational independence. It was impossible to bridge the differences and the chances of collaboration remained unexploited.

After keeping the initiative on the side-lines for several years, the TPLF aggressively reactivated its quest for a united front in 1984.[33] Active contacts were underway with other opposition forces. Negotiations were held with the OLF and an agreement was reached to co-operate in various fields. A TPLF contingent was sent to the OLF base area to assist in strengthening its forces and widening its base area, which was at that time limited to the borders of the Sudan in non-Oromo areas. Moreover, high-level representatives of the TPLF and All Ethiopian Socialist Movement (MEISON) met in London from 25 to 27 September, 1987. They agreed "to make a decisive contribution to the struggle of the Ethiopian people, to the unification of the fighting forces and to the creation of a democratic Ethiopia united by the free will of its peoples".[34] However, both attempts failed due to serious political differences and mutual mistrust. The TPLF was not comfortable with the OLF's collaboration with the Sudanese government against the SPLA, nor its reluctance to emerge from its border hiding place to expand its activities to the Oromo inhabited highland areas of Wellega and other adjacent regions. On other hand, the OLF was suspicious of the TPLF's stand on the Oromo issue, especially the latter's rejection of the colonial characterisation of the question by the former. These differences led the OLF to suspect the TPLF of harbouring ambition that might eventually undermine its declared course of independence.

Similarly, the leaders of MEISON failed to achieve the political comeback from their rapprochement with the TPLF after years of alienation from the Ethiopian political mainstream. The TPLF's refusal to endorse MEISON's collaboration with the Derg regime, and its pronouncement that the mistake was the result of a series of fundamental political errors made at the crucial period of the Ethiopian revolution was a major blow to the MEISON leadership. Although some communication continued between the two organisations' leadership for some time, it was clear from the start that the political gap was too wide, and their experiences were too diverse to create mutual understanding and trust.[35]

In the quest for co-ordinated struggle against the regime, the relationship between the TPLF and the EPLF had a special importance. The two organisations had passed through a difficult time in their relations between 1985 and 1988. Their differences on the right of self-determination, the Soviet Union and military strategy deteriorated and seriously damaged their relations, which had a negative impact on their struggle against the Derg. While the TPLF advocated the right of nationalities to self-determination including and up to secession as an alienable right of Ethiopian nationalities, including those in Eritrea, the EPLF argued Ethiopian nationalities have the right to self-determination but short of independence since it believed that such right would be accorded to those under colonial rule.[36] The EPLF insisted that only Eritrea had the right to independence, as its case was a colonial issue. Young rightly explains the EPLF position as follows:

> The EPLF's interpretation of national self-determination had three objectives: first, to deny Tigrayans and other Ethiopian nationalities the right to independence; secondly, to affirm the right of Eritrea as a colonial-defined territory to independence; third to deny its own nationalities the right to independence by restricting anti-colonial struggles to those of "multinational peoples" which it assumed Eritrea's to be.[37]

In addition, TPLF's open condemnation of the Soviet Union as an imperialist power was not acceptable to the EPLF, which drew some support from the Socialist block. Their difference on how best to fight the Derg's army also contributed to worsening relations. The TPLF did not appreciate the trench war, which the EPLF was conducting as it restricted the latter's capability of taking initiatives to weaken the regime. After a period of polemics, the relationship was abruptly suspended when the EPLF decided to close the cross-border route, from the Sudan to Tigray, at the height of the famine. After more than three years of lost opportunities, in 1988 the leaders of the two organisations realised the need to cooperate and coordinated their efforts. They attempted to narrow their differences and agreed to restore their relations and co-ordinate their military activities in both Ethiopia and Eritrea. The joint statement stated as follows:

> The two organisations believed that differences between them, existing as well as future, ought to be handled democratically and should not become obstacles for meaningful co-operation based on common views on basic issues. They agreed that this understanding should also serve as the basis for their future co-operation.[38]

Consequently, co-operation between the two organisations grew and made a great contribution in expediting the devastation of the government forces.

Despite the efforts of the TPLF to reach out to other groups, it achieved little success in convincing them to cooperate. Past hatred and disputes between members of various organisations hindered any real progress in reconciliation and collaboration. The TPLF's military clashes with the EPRP and the All-Ethiopia Socialist Movement's (MEISON) involvement in the "Red Terror" and the long polemics waged against each other created a big political and psychological gulf between members and sympathisers. The EPRP's characterisation of the TPLF's call for a united front was "let us co-operate now and we will destroy you later" and its intensive negative campaign strengthened the suspicions of many against the TPLF. Consequently, after delaying the launching of the united front for so long, in 1989 the TPLF was forced to start with its close ally the EPDM.

In March 1989, the Central Committee of the TPLF issued a proposal for a peaceful resolution of the conflict in Ethiopia.[39] The document proposed an immediate cease-fire on agreement of the overall peace package. It also called for the introduction of democratic rights and political freedom, the release of all political prisoners, and the formation of a provisional government comprising all political organisations leading to democratic elections and a new constitution.[40] Similarly, the Shengo[41] issued a peace proposal called a 'Six-Point New Peace Initiative'.[42] However, the Derg attempted to avoid the TPLF and only start negotiations with the EPLF.[43] After intensive campaigning by the TPLF and a change of military situations on the ground, the Derg accepted the need for negotiations. From 6 September until 2 October 1989, preliminary talks were held between the representatives of the TPLF and the Derg; they managed to agree on a time, a place and an observer.

Nevertheless, negotiations were unable to proceed beyond some procedural talks. As the peace proposal was endorsed by the EPDM and later adopted by the newly formed EPRDF, the TPLF was obliged to at least include its partner in the peace negotiations in order to achieve comprehensive peace. In fact, the TPLF was interested in inviting all warring groups to the negotiation table. However, the Derg not only refused to include the EPDM but also refused to talk with the TPLF on the agenda concerning the whole of Ethiopia. The Derg wanted to limit talks on the conflict in Tigray by claiming that nationwide issues were of no concern to the regional organisations. The central point here is that the TPLF participated in the negotiations not because it believed that peace would evolve from the talks, but rather to show the Ethiopian people and the international community that the Derg was anti-peace and the war was imposed on it by the intransigence of the regime. The Derg pushed to end the peace talks when it realised the TPLF was using the forum to pass its primary message of democratic unity of the country.

The EPRDF adopted a more detailed and developed peace proposal on March 10, 1990. The proposal for a smooth and peaceful transition was the precursor of the National Charter of the Transitional Period. The proposal called for a negotiated cease-fire and the formation of a provisional government in which all political groups, including the party in power, would participate. A referendum to resolve the Eritrean problem, writing a new constitution and conducting popular elections, which would lead to the formation of a democratic government, were some of the major points included in the proposal.[44] Based on its proposal, the EPRDF attempted to forge ties with various political groups. However, it did not succeed.. The EPRP and MEISON preferred to create their own group and present themselves as an alternative to the regime and the EPRDF. The Toronto Conference of July 1990, which brought together the EPRP, the EDU, the MEISON, the EPDA and some individuals, agreed to create a committee to prepare for the founding conference of the COEDF, which was formed on April 17, 1991. The whole exercise of the EPRP was to exclude the EPRDF, which could not compete for leadership if the latter decided to participate. In addition, the proposal was ignored by the Derg, until it was shaken by the loss of Massawa to the EPLF in February 1990 and by the capture of western Ethiopia by the EPRDF.

Consequently, the Third Emergency Session of the National Shengo of the PDRE adopted a resolution on April 22, 1991 calling for the initiation of peace talks. The Shengo's resolution states:

> The National Shengo has resolved to initiate peace talks with all opposition groups and unity forces at a joint negotiating forum with a view to reaching agreement on the establishment of lasting peace in our country, on the future political direction of the country and on the creation of a transitional arrangement that would guarantee a political solution beneficial to our people and the country as a whole.

Yet the Shengo contradicted itself by declaring "legal and organisational arrangements should be completed as soon as possible towards a nationwide mobilisation to organise, train and deploy able-bodied youth, peasants, civil servants and members of producers and service associations of 18 years of age and above and any other Ethiopian citizen".[45] The resolution called for the National Revolutionary Campaign Centre, which was established to direct and monitor the general mobilisation for the war effort, to extend its organisational structures to kebele level. It also directed the displaced party officials, government employees and members of mass organisations to receive military training and participate in liberating their regions from the rebels.[46] The regime desperately tried to avoid a humiliating defeat by pushing whatever human and material resources it could to the war front.

The resolution called for peace talks but at the same time demanded a general mobilisation, which made the peace process more complicated. Furthermore, the resolution only called for 'unity forces', which would have excluded opposition forces such as the EPLF, the TPLF and the OLF, which had been characterised by the Derg as 'anti-unity'. However, the Derg was soon forced to realize that it couldn't exclude the so called anti-unity forces from the negotiation table even if it wants to buy time for mobilization. Under the pressure of their military onslaught, it half-heartedly accepted to start negotiations with the opposition forces on the ground. That is why it reluctantly requested the United States' mediation with these 'anti-unity' forces, which eventually led to the London Conference.

The COEDF was not invited to the London Conference, in spite of its extensive campaign and lobbying the United States' administration, as it was accused of supporting the Derg's mobilisation and war decrees, and the exclusive peace call.[47] The COEDF supported the Shengo resolution and made the following statement:

> The Shengo's decision to negotiate with "all opposition sectors and forces of unity" on the peaceful resolution of the conflicts, the political future of the country...also reflects, (in conjunction with other sections of the Shengo decision), the demands of the Toronto Conference participants. As such, COEDF welcomes it.[48]

As mentioned above, the preparatory talks for the conference took too long because of too many conflicting interests. The Derg was laboriously attempting in vain to secure as much advantage as possible by raising many issues one after the other. The mediator, the United States, had its own agenda to push, especially the evacuation of the Ethiopian Jews to Israel and was playing its card to expedite the process at the expense of the regime. On the other hand, the opposition forces, the EPRDF and EPLF, were witnessing the rout of the Derg forces and were already convinced its near demise. As a result, the conference failed before it started since the regime was already on its death bed.

The EPRDF and Its Role in the Transitional Government

In accordance with the decisions of the London Conference, the EPRDF formed a provisional government after it gained control of Addis Ababa on May 28, 1991. The provisional government was confronted with the disorder left by the military government. Ensuring peace and stability was a paramount challenge, and the flow of displaced people from one region to the other, especially those coming from Eritrea, created a formidable task to the new government.

Moreover, the provision of food to drought affected regions of the country had to be intensified in order to save lives of millions of people. The overall preparation for the convening of the National Conference to form a Transitional Government had to be accomplished within the month of June.

Considering the short time-span, the achievements with all their shortcomings were considerable. Peace and stability were established in many parts of the country where most of the people live. Nevertheless, there were sizeable corners in the east, southeast and southwest of the country that remained with a power vacuum for some time, even after the formation of the Transitional Government. Feeding the thousands of displaced people in the drought-affected areas was accomplished without major disaster with the help of international donors. Bringing the dispersed members of the former armed forces to the designated camps and providing them with necessary provisions started within the first two weeks of the government.

The preparation of the National Conference that brought many of the political organisations and groups together was completed within a month. One of the most difficult tasks was to convince and bring on board the liberation fronts from southern and south-eastern Ethiopia. The Mogadishu based organisations such as the Western Somali Liberation Front (WSLF), Sidama Liberation Front (SLM) and Oromo Abbo Liberation Front (OALF) were to be convinced that the situation was different from before. It was not a change of power between two "Habeshas"[49] but a change that brought a new era of reconciliation and national equality. After they agreed to participate, they were smuggled out of Mogadishu, which was without a government at that time. The other liberation fronts, such as the Afar Liberation front (ALF), the Benishangul People's Liberation Movement (GPLM) and others, which were struggling for the recognition of the right of self-determination, had to be convinced that their interest would be best served by participating in the conference. Furthermore, the decision made by the EPRDF provisional government to encourage new political groupings to flourish made it possible for them to participate, which widened the conference base by allowing a diverse group of interests to be represented. In fact, EPRDF officials had to negotiate with each political group that wished to be represented at the conference. After extensive efforts, many political parties participated. The only visible absentee was the COEDF, which had refused to denounce violence as requested by the EPRDF.

In the Transitional Government, the EPRDF continued to be a leading player in its activities. The EPRDF led the Transitional Council of Representatives in passing proclamations and implementing them as a member of the government that transformed Ethiopia's entire political system. Devolution of power and the building of institutions were the centrepieces of the EPRDF's program and reasonable achievements have been attained on both objectives. The adoption of a constitution with a clear stand on the right of self-determination was the accomplishment of a long struggle for the EPRDF. In the meantime, its ranks were boosted by the inclusion of the Southern Ethiopia People's Democratic Front (SEPDF)[50] as a member-organisation in 1994. The EPDM transformed itself to the Amhara National Democratic Movement (ANDM) in January 1994 in order to concentrate its energy on the interests of the Amhara nationality. Many of the nationalities the EPDM attempted to mobilise established their own national organisations. According to the ANDM program, the need for a multi-national organisation has already been answered by the formation of the EPRDF. The continuation of the EPDM as a multinational organisation would be an unnecessary and overlapping endeavour. Thus the EPDM decided to become a national organisation and leave the job of co-ordination to the EPRDF.[51] The EPRDF's army also served as a national defence force for the transitional period as the Transitional Council of Representatives adopted a resolution in its 25th Session of December 2-6, 1991[52] and decreed Proclamation No. 8/ 1992 on January 16, 1992.

The EPRDF held its 2nd Congress in Awassa, the capital of the Southern Ethiopia region in January 1995. It came out with a five-year program for political and economic development.[53] The program was used as a platform for its campaign in the May 1995 elections. Since the opposition decided to boycott, the elections in many constituents were not as competitive as was desired. In fact, no force or a coalition of political groups had well organised or credible enough to challenge the EPRDF. The opposition might need to spread its reach from the cities into the countryside, where eighty-five per cent of the population live to garner enough support to win an election. The message of the time was that the opposition forces needed to coordinate and form front to challenge the EPRDF rather than bickering with each other on secondary issues.

The Oromo Liberation Front (OLF)

Background of the OLF

The OLF was formed in July 1974 a few months before the February revolution which overthrew Haile Selassie's regime. It claims to have roots to the 1960s' Matcha-Tulama self-help association of urban Oromos, which had been active in solving social problems and constructing schools, clinics and other similar service providing institutions in the Oromo areas.[54] The association was formed in 1963 and had a significant role in bringing together many Oromos from different walks of life. Bulcha explains the association:

The first Oromo organisation with roots in both urban and rural areas. Mass meetings were held in many parts of the Oromo country and taboo topics such as the exploitation of the Oromo peasantry and suppression of Oromo language and culture were raised and discussed... the continued expansion of the association worried the Ethiopian security, who had always doggedly followed its leaders to every mass meeting. 'What was especially worrisome was the fact that they (the leaders) addressed meetings in the language of the Oromo, which had been proscribed in public...'[55]

As stated, the government felt threatened by the association's activities and its ability to attract large numbers of followers. Consequently it was banned in 1967 and its leaders duly prosecuted. Although the association formally ceased to exist, its aspirations continued and the OLF was born.[56] Hassen explains the roots of the OLF and the process of its formation:

In December 1973, the leaders of the underground Macha-Tulama movement organised a secret conference in Addis Ababa itself. Among the participants, Hussein Sura (Sheik Hussein) and Elemo Qilixxu (Baker Yusuf) came from the Middle East. Several individuals from different regions of Oromia also participated in that conference, out of which the OLF was formed in January 1974. The first political program of the OLF (which was amended in 1976) was also the product of that conference. Those who formed the OLF in 1974 were card-carrying members of the Association. In short, the OLF grew out of the Macha-Tulama movement.[57]

The OLF program declared that the Oromo problem was a colonial issue and that it was struggling for the establishment of an independent republic of Oromia.[58] Later, it became one of the leading signatories of the National Charter of the transitional period by repeatedly stating its commitment to building a new Ethiopia. However, its position on various issues was always doubted because of the contradictory messages it had disseminated. The OLF declared that the main political objective was "the realisation of national self-determination for the Oromo people and their liberation from oppression and exploitation in all forms. This can only be realised through successful consummation of the new democratic revolution... and the establishment of the People's Democratic Republic of Oromia".[59] No amendment was made to the program during the transitional period and it was used by the organisation as the principal document in building its support.

There was also an attempt to convince the Ethiopian people that it was not a secessionist organisation. The OLF Central Committee statement asserts that "it is vital to emphasise at the outset that the OLF, unlike many others, has never made the promotion of the cause of secession its prime objective".[60] The struggle for the formation of an independent Oromia and the desire to build a decentralised democratic Ethiopia were not clearly delineated to the general public. Cappelli remarks: "self-determination" for the Oromo as its prime goal, the OLF's own ideology is rather nebulous. It maintains a formal secessionist stance, stating in its political program that "self-determination... can only be realised... by the establishment of the People's Democratic Republic of Oromia", but on other occasions has left open the possibility of some sort of Ethiopian political federation, a contradiction which perhaps indicates just how weak it feels its hand to be."[61] Bereket explains the mixed messages of the OLF during the Transition Period:

> Primarily, the OLF wanted to build a united Ethiopia in which its domination was well established. If such ambition was unattainable then it had a contingency plan to secede and form its own independent state. Both these objectives had been confused intentionally and unintentionally in its political manoeuvres.[62]

OLF's Relations with Other Political Organisations

The OLF started contact with both the TPLF and the EPLF when it opened an office in Khartoum in 1978.[63] This eventually grew to co-operation in various fields. In 1979, an OLF unit went to the liberated areas of the EPLF for military training. The co-operation, in fact, continued until the demise of the military government. Moreover, the OLF leadership was much more comfortable with its relations with the EPLF than with any other Ethiopian organisation. It thought the EPLF's aspirations were similar to its own, though the EPLF had never supported the characterisation of the Oromo problem as a colonial question. These sentiments are well expressed by Leenco Lata, the former deputy leader of the OLF:

> Relations between the OLF and the EPLF, on the other hand, were relatively more relaxed because of the expressed political ambition of the Eritreans; they demanded independence for Eritrea which did not appear to directly threaten the Oromos. This signalled the Eritrean leaders had no ambition to replace the Derg and rule the rest of the empire. On the other hand, their strict claim that only those nations ruled by overseas European colonizers deserve self-determination and independence did not allow them to recognize the entitlement of Oromos and others to these rights. Hence, the Eritrean leaders have always insisted that, other than Eritrea, the rest of the people should seek political settlement within the borders of the remainder of the empire... Despite the absence of reciprocity on this issue, OLF – EPLF co-operation continued to grow basically because the OLF chose to eschew the issue, insisting on a quid pro quo.[64]

Although the relations with the TPLF started in the late 1970s, they did not gain momentum until the mid-1980s. After a series of meetings in

1983, the TPLF and the OLF agreed to co-operate politically and militarily. Consequently, the TPLF sent a contingent led by one of its prominent leaders, Kinfe Gebre-Medhin, and co-operated with the OLF in waging military activities in some Oromo districts adjacent to the base area. It also helped to train members of the OLF in medical assistance, mine laying, intelligence gathering and assessment, and other fields. Kinfe was later replaced by another prominent member of the TPLF, Tadele Gebre-Selassie[65] and the contingent continued to provide further training.

In spite of co-operation in the field, attempts to bridge the political gap or at least to accommodate their differences in order to fight against the common enemy were not as successful as expected. The co-operation was terminated when the TPLF became uncomfortable with the OLF's involvement in the Sudanese civil war and their growing differences in military strategy. The OLF repeatedly clashed with the Sudan People's Liberation Front (SPLA) in the name of protecting its base areas.[66] However, the TPLF suspected the Sudanese government's involvement in the creation of a buffer zone to deter the insurgents from crossing the border into the Sudan. At the same time to serve its own interest, the TPLF pushed the OLF into leaving the lowlands of the border areas and expanding its operations in the highlands of the Oromo region. Such operations would undoubtedly weaken the government, while at the same time strengthening the OLF by widening its mass support. Nevertheless, the TPLF failed to convince the OLF leadership and subsequently decided to withdraw its forces. The TPLF cited the cause of failure as the OLF's reluctance to involve itself in the turbulent process of struggle. Unlike the leaders of the EPLF and the TPLF, most of the OLF's leaders were living abroad, which made striving for liberation difficult.[67]

Leenco Lata argued that relations were already damaged "when the TPLF drew up its own agenda for the whole of the empire and decided to project itself as the sole champion of the Oromo cause, relations started to sour".[68] Moreover, he stated they further deteriorated when in the late 1980s "the TPLF formed its Oromo wing, drawing members from prisoners of war of the TPLF and the EPLF".[69] Suspicion and mistrust played a major role in the deterioration of their cooperation; however, the major factor was the OLF's reluctance to shoulder the heavy burden of an armed struggle and regarded the TPLF's insistence as distasteful interference in its organisational as well as Oromo matters.

In 1986, the TPLF published its stand on the Oromo question and its recommendations of how to mobilise and organise the Oromo people against the military dictatorship. It also exposed the weakness of the OLF, especially its failure to properly lead the Oromo struggle and to command it in the future.[70] The OLF accused the TPLF of arrogance and conspiring to destroy the "vanguard" of the Oromo people and their aspiration for freedom. Leenco Lata interpreted the presentation of the TPLF as follows: "the Oromo nation is by nature incapable of producing an effective leadership".[71] Such interpretation was not in any way related to the statement but made out of context to arouse Oromo nationalism against the TPLF. Some people, including members of the OLF, claimed that the main reason for the failure to mobilise the Oromo people, as accomplished in Tigray and Eritrea, was the geographical vastness and inaccessibility of the Oromo region. However, critics doubted the wisdom of such a claim as a major obstacle. Accepting its negative role, they argued that had there been a clear strategy and an action-oriented leadership, it would have been possible to build a formidable army and a strong base area in some parts of the region, especially in those with less access problems. Alex de Waal explains the failure of the OLF to mobilise the large Oromo population:

> The OLF was unable to build a strong united leadership, and was unable to move beyond shallow nationalist politics towards a deeper articulation of the needs of the Oromo peasantry ...the organisation was unable to build upon the concrete experiences of Oromo peasants to build a political programme. The OLF programme still consists largely of platitudes about democracy and human rights and a general commitment to self-determination for the Oromo people.[72]

The weakness of the leadership handicapped the OLF from exploiting the potential of the Oromo people in its fight against the military government. The discrepancies between what the OLF leadership propagates and the actual strength of the organisation have been quite extensive. Cappelli remarks:

> The OLF was unable to commence substantive military activities until the early 1980s when it began operating out of bases in the Sudan, and its mediocre performance in the field from then until Mengistu's fall makes its claim of having mobilised "millions of peasant masses" a hollow one. Long confined to two cul-de-sacs in the extreme west (Wollega) and east (Hararghe) of the country, it never posed a serious threat to the military regime...[73]

In the meantime, the TPLF was involved in assisting some Oromos in organising themselves, which culminated in the formation of the Oromo People's Democratic Organisation (OPDO) in 1989. As a result, relations between the TPLF and the OLF further deteriorated and stayed low until the last days of the Derg.

The debate on the characterisation of the Oromo problem ("colonial versus national question") has been a dividing source of recriminations within the Oromo intellectuals and members of various organisations. Those who have defined the Oromo question as a national one run the risk of being called a "Gobena"[74] by the one side, and those who have characterised it as a colonial question are "narrow nationalists" to the opposite side. The agreement on the right of the Oromo people to self-determination up to and including secession was not enough to bring them together and create a united front or co-operation. According to the OPDO, the OLF has never been ready to work with other Oromo organisations on an equal basis. When the OPDO forwarded the idea of a united front, it claimed that the OLF demanded its abolition and its members join it as individuals.[75] The absence of consensus on the question has been visible in Oromos living abroad and continues to divide agreement even on a minimum common stand. Baxter notes the different views:

> Most Oromos in exile have been concerned, with varying degrees of passion and commitments, to establish Oromo autonomy. They have not all, of course, agreed about its extent and its form but all, at the least, have wanted to see the Oromo language and Oromo customs given equal status with those of the north... Others argue that cultural autonomy is not possible without political autonomy, that is, the creation of an independent state of Oromia, which has been the declared goal of the Oromo Liberation Front.[76]

The OLF and the Transitional Government

Although the OLF failed to emerge as one of the decisive forces in fighting the military government, it was made to participate in the London Conference mainly for the recognition of the Oromo people's role in establishing a new Ethiopia. In fact, the OLF participated through the initiation and persistent request of the EPRDF to United States government representatives. The OLF was not included in the proposal of the U.S. representatives for they did not consider it as one of the warring factions, which could have a role in a conference for peace. The conference with the military government did not take place, but the liberation movements, the EPRDF, EPLF and OLF, came out with an agreement for the future process.[77] Despite the OLF's participation and agreement on the formation of a one-month EPRDF's provisional government and the convening of a national conference for a formation of a Transitional Government, it came out with a statement that repudiated the same agreement. The statement indicated the OLF's opposition to the U.S. invitation of one of the contending parties, the EPRDF to assume state responsibility and confirmed that it would not compromise on the Oromia's independence.[78] At the time, the statement upset the other parties of the agreement. Later, negotiations resumed on how to organise the national conference and other pertinent issues.

Leenco Lata stated, "assurance by the U.S. Government played a critical role... in persuading the OLF to consider becoming a party to the program of peacefully reforming the empire, despite the history of numerous age-old bitter Oromo experiences with Abyssinian treachery".[79] In addition, he detailed some factors that compelled the OLF to participate in the Transitional Government. These were: the collapse of the Somali state, which he characterized as a traditional ally of the Oromo people; the pressure from the Sudanese government, which made it known that it would not support any force against the new government; the Western powers' (especially the U.S. government's) insistence on the participation of the OLF to reform the state; and the EPLF's assurance to the OLF that they would not allow any domination to emerge in Ethiopia.[80] Of course, these factors might have been helpful in convincing the OLF that the era of achieving one's political objective through arms was almost over. The OLF was also confident that the new platform would provide it with the opportunity to be in touch with millions of Oromos, which was unthinkable a few months before. The opportunity to transform itself into a strong organisation and formidable power was present and the OLF decided to take it. Hence, it was the new conducive environment in the Ethiopian political climate that attracted the OLF to join the Transitional Government.

Within the weeks before the conference, the OLF was able to discuss every issue of the draft charter, including the distribution of seats between the intending participant organisations. The EPRDF proposed to take 32 seats for its four-member organisations and 12 for the OLF. However, the OLF refused to accept this distribution since it demanded similar numbers of seats as the EPRDF. The EPRDF believed that the OLF was garnering seats more than it deserved. The point was that it was getting more seats than the TPLF, which played a significant role by far. In the end, the discord was resolved with the intervention of the EPLF, and the OLF accepted the allocated seats. Furthermore, they were able to present their list of ministerial and ambassadorial posts, which they intended to occupy and, in fact, they were considered seriously in the selection of high office-holders of the Transitional Government.[81]

After the formation of the Transitional Government, the relationship between the EPRDF and the OLF was not easy. The OLF was accused of recruiting ex-soldiers of the Derg into its own ranks and disrupting peace and stability. Its army grew from a few thousand into tens of thousands in a matter of a year. Keller notes the sudden growth of the OLF as follows:

> The OLF had expanded the ranks of its military wing two-to three-fold from its maximum strength of about eight thousand in 1991. This expansion was made possible in part by the attraction of new recruits in areas heavily populated by the Oromo, and also in part

> by the incorporation of Oromos who had formerly been soldiers in Mengistu's army.[82]

The Council of Representatives passed Proclamation No. 8/1992, which provided for the need to reach agreement on the size of the army each organisation should maintain, based on the size of the army each had on the eve of the final downfall of the military government.[83] Negotiation with the OLF was arduous and ended with the involvement of the EPLF as a mediator. Though the EPRDF believed that the OLF's army was not more than seven thousand, it agreed to accept the number as twenty-four thousand.[84] In fact the agreed number was a compromise as the OLF claimed to have more than thirty-seven thousand soldiers.[85]

Recriminations between the EPRDF and the OLF, the Benishangul People's Liberation Movement (BPLM) and the OLF started immediately after the formation of the Transitional Government. The EPRDF accused the OLF of violating the Council of Representatives' resolutions by mobilising ex-soldiers and members of the Workers Party of Ethiopia (WPE), destroying bridges, mining roads, conducting hit and run operations, destroying government property and by its involvement in black market activities.[86] Similarly, the BPLM repeatedly requested the Council of Representatives to take action against the OLF for allegedly burning Benishangul villages, wanton killings, and looting public property. The Council condemned the conflict at its 32nd Session on January 22, 1992.[87] In response, the OLF accused the EPRDF of closing its offices, killing its members, cadres, sympathisers and supporters, and of imprisoning and killing of civilians.[88] It was common knowledge that OLF members were involved in subversive activities and the EPRDF army was after those units for the purpose of maintaining peace and stability as a defence force. Usually, in the middle of such conflicts the civilian population was the victim. Alex de Waal attempts to explain the situation:

> The OLF recruited more troops to its army, repeatedly attacked EPRDF military positions and destroyed more bridges in the year after the fall of Mengistu than in the 17 years of his rule. This, in turn, has given ample excuses for the EPRDF forces to refuse to encamp, and to engage in military actions against the OLF.[89]

The worst political blow came when the OLF was accused of massacring over 150 people at Bedeno County in Hararghe administrative region between March 14 and April 10, 1992, when the area was under its control. The OLF admitted to this charge, but its leadership denied responsibility, claiming it had already taken necessary measures against the perpetrators; however, it failed to provide evidence to support the statement.[90] After a long debate, the Council held the OLF responsible and condemned its failure to bring the perpetrators to justice. It also demanded that the OLF immediately hand over the alleged criminals to the authorities.[91] Such widely reported incidents tarnished its image, not only in the non-Oromo population but also in the Oromo nationality, which it expected to amass its support from.

Rapid deterioration of relations between the OLF and the Transitional Government (the EPRDF) was creating uncertainty in the country. Negotiations were continuing and an agreement was made between the two organisations on April 15, 1992. The agreement mediated by the U.S. Government and the Provisional Government of Eritrea demanded the EPRDF and the OLF encamp their armies within a week for the safe conduct of regional elections.[92] Soon the OLF was accused of failing to garrison some units of its army, which were alleged to be involved in disrupting peace and stability in the Southern regions.[93] On the eve of the polling day on June 20, 1992, the OLF decided to boycott elections. It alleged the violation of electoral procedures and accused the EPRDF of controlling the powers.[94] It also announced its withdrawal from the Transitional Government and its army left its camps, which brought the country into the brink of a civil war. However, the armed conflict was over within weeks and as a result the OLF lost most of its army.

The OLF Secretary General, Gelassa Dilbo, pointed out three "fundamental errors" as causes of the problems encountered:

> First, the TPLF formed a provisional administration alone after the London conference of May 28, 1991...The TPLF's assumption of having a prerogative on who to include and who to exclude coupled with a seats allocation that tilted in its favour paved the way for the formation of a legislature, the Council of Representatives, under its sway. The second most important error emanated from a recognition given to the TPLF militia as the defence force of the country for the transition period... Third, while still doubting the TPLF leadership's commitment to uphold laws and agreements, we decided to take the risk of encamping our troops as the ultimate proof of our commitment to bring about a peaceful democratisation of the country.[95]

On the other hand, the EPRDF leaders claimed that the OLF problem emanated from its confused political stand and illusions of power. They stated the OLF had thought of all Oromos as its supporters and that divergent attitude was not tolerated. They also pointed out that the OLF misperceived its military capabilities and its belief that by withdrawing, the government would collapse, bringing about a reign of confusion, which would enable the OLF to realise its dream of controlling an independent Oromia. Moreover, it took the support of the international community for granted. Indications from some quarters suggested a desire for the OLF to emerge as a strong challenging force to the EPRDF. The OLF could create a deterrent effect upon a "one party domination" of the EPRDF as a formidable opposition force.[96]

Beyond the recriminations, it is important to mention that the OLF would have benefited from its commitment to the system. It could have used the parliamentary platform and found other ways to promote its political positions. With all its shortcomings, the democratic process would have provided it with better opportunity to garner support and eventually implement its program. The resolves to violence have put the OLF's sincerity and commitment to the democratic process in question.

Nationality Organisations

As stated above, debate on the nature of the principal contradiction in the country and how it ought to be tackled was at the centre of Ethiopian politics in the 1970s and early 1980s. Nationality-based organisations believed that society's prime contradiction was the national question, which should be resolved by Ethiopian revolutionaries before attempting a unified struggle on class platforms. Conversely, multinational organisations argued that the national question was a derivative of class oppression and could be eliminated when the class contradiction was resolved. Hence, all nationalities had to unite in a class struggle, which could also satisfy their rights of self-determination.[97] The debate continued to divide opposition forces and even later became the source of armed conflicts among the organisations. In the process, while the nationalist organisations continued to grow, the multinationals advocating the primacy of class struggle failed to create a reasonable force and a reliable political base. Analysing the situation and reaching the right conclusion was not enough to lead to a successful opposition. Formulating strategies, progressing with changes in the political environment, and the emergence of a strong political leadership are some of the highly important points necessary to build a reasonable mass base. This suggests why, within organisations of similar political objectives, a range of diversity in their degree of achievements is evident.

The Role of Other Nationality-based Groups in the Armed Struggle

There were nationalist organisations that were engaged in the armed struggle against the military government other than the nationalist fronts within the EPRDF and also the OLF. Armed movements such as the Western Somali Liberation Front (WSLF), the Sidama Liberation Movement (SLM), the Somali Abbo Liberation Front (SALF), and the United Oromo People's Liberation Front (UOPLF) had some activities in the Southern and South-Eastern part of the country, especially before the Somali invasion was beaten back in early 1978. Since then their existence was mainly a political one, which was largely limited to maintaining offices in Mogadishu, Somalia. The Islamic Front for the Liberation of Oromo (IFLO) has existed as an armed movement after their split from the OLF in 1978. It also had limited activities in the eastern and south-eastern regions.

In the western and south-western parts of the country, the Benishangul Peoples' Liberation Movement (BPLM) and the Gambella People's Liberation Movement (GPLM) had armies, mainly stationed near the border of the Sudan. These organisations had a close relationship with the EPRDF and participated in its first congress as observers. Though their military role in the downfall of the regime was insignificant, it had a visible contribution in demonstrating that the resistance was not confined to limited regions. The Afar Liberation Front (ALF) had also some armed activities in the eastern part of Ethiopia. There was some co-operation between the ALF and TPLF in the latter's military operations in the Assab-Dese road, which was the major route connecting the country to its outlet to the sea. However, it remained a small organisation drawing its support from a few clans in the Afar nationality.

After the demise of the military government, the EPRDF had to convince these armed groups to participate in the National Conference. It needed to assure these organisations that the situation was different, and that the motive was basically to discuss a future contract of the peoples of Ethiopia that would enable them to live together in harmony. After a general understanding was reached, representatives of the Somalia-based organisations were evacuated from Mogadishu, which had already been in chaos after the downfall of Siad Barre's regime. The IFLO also agreed to participate in the conference with the help of the Sudanese government. The other armed groups, which had a pre-existing relationship with the EPRDF were not difficult to convince. They were aware that by participating in the Conference their objectives could be fulfilled as the right of self-determination would be high on the agenda. Consequently, all these groups did participate in the National Conference and later in the Transitional Government.

Nationality-based Organisations and Their Role in the Transitional Government

Other than the aforementioned organisations, other nationalist groups were able to participate in the process. These organisations were more or less formed within the one-month period of the EPRDF's provisional government or at least began to be constituted. Although some of them claimed they had an earlier history of covert resistance, it is difficult to verify this claim from other sources and one prefers to ignore it since the grip of the former regime in the capital was very strong. Whatever the background of the organisations, the Harrari, Gurage, Hadiya, Omotic, Issa and Gedebursi, Kembata and the Wollaita groups' representatives participated in the process which brought the Transitional Government into existence. Later on, the Transitional Council of Representatives accepted the application of some organisations from unrepresented nationalities at its 14th Session of September 13, 1991.[98] Accordingly, the Agew People's Democratic Movement (APDM), the Burji People's Democratic Organisation (BPDO), the Gedeo People's Democratic Front (GPDO), the Kaffa People's Democratic Union (KPDU) and the Yem People's Movement (YPM) were able to fill the seats that were reserved for unrepresented peoples. While KPDU received two seats out of the six, the other organisation got one each.[99]

The mushrooming of nationality organisations continued in almost all nationalities, except in Tigray and to a certain extent in the Amhara Region.[100] The All-Amhara People's Organisation (AAPO) was formed in February 1992 with the objective of protecting the right of the Amharas in the various regions of the country. According to its program, one of the main objectives is to resolve the religious and tribal conflicts that were sparked during the transitional period.[101] The organisation has been working as one of the vocal opposition groups in the country. It was accused of involvement in illegal activities such as being an accomplice in some armed subversive actions. One of its leaders was convicted of such involvement and had served lengthy prison sentence. Its support is mainly based on the Amhara elite, especially those whose interests are affected by the transitional process.

The formation of political groups had become widespread in the Southern People's region and other minority areas. The Election Commission's list of political parties and organizations showed the extent of the proliferation of diverse political groupings. The Commission registered over 80 political parties and organizations as of August 2002. In fact, the list shows groups that were formally registered with the Election Commission; however, their actual number was far more than those registered.

There was a striking difference between the nationality organisations, which participated in the National Conference, and those that were locally organised and presented themselves at the regional elections of 1992. The former were mainly constructed of urban-based intellectuals with little political base in the rural constituencies. In contrast, the post national conference-formed organisations, especially in the Southern Peoples' Region, were affiliated to the EPRDF and mainly targeted the rural and small town populations as their mass base.

As witnessed in the regional elections of 1992, the newly formed organisations swept the votes in the whole Southern Peoples' Region. Moreover, the diversity of political positions was the most important aspect of the competition. The political differences of the Southern Ethiopia Peoples' Democratic Coalition (SEPDC)[102] and the Southern Ethiopia Peoples' Democratic Front (SEPDF)[103] focus on issues like the right of self-determination and property rights. The SEPDC advocated the rights of nationalities to self-rule short of secession[104] while the SEPDF as a member of the EPRDF endorses the right of self-determination up to and including secession.[105] Furthermore, while the SEPDC stood for the private ownership of urban and rural lands, the SEPDF favours public ownership of land, which includes the right of free use of land in accordance with the law. Other political and economic policy differences are also exhibited in their political programs.

Other Southern peoples' organisations such as the Gurage People's Democratic Front (GPDF), Kembata People's Congress (KPC) and Wolayta People's Democratic Front (WPDF) formed the Ethiopian National Democratic Party (ENDP) together with the Ethiopian National Democratic Organisation (ENDO) and Ethiopian Democratic Coalition (EDC) in April 1994 and fielded joint candidates for the 1995 elections. These nationality organisations advocated similar political stances as the SEPDC except for some tactical issues and minor political differences. These organisations played a major role in the drafting process of the constitution and the implementation of other tasks of the Transitional Council of Representatives.

The member organisations of the SEPDC, particularly the Sidama Liberation Movement (SLM), the Omotic Peoples' Democratic Front (OPDF), the Hadya National Democratic Organisation (HNDO), the Gedeo People's Democratic Front (GDPF) and the Yem People's Movement (YPM) came into conflict with the Transitional Council of Representatives when they participated in the "Paris Conference of Peace and Reconciliation",[106] and supported its call for the replacement of the Council by a new one. At its 65th Session the Council made it clear that organisations which are members of the SEPDC, and at the same time, members of the Transitional Council which endorsed the Paris decision, had to choose between continuing as members or withdrawing from the government Some organisations such as the KPC, the BPDO, the GPDF, the WPDF and the KPDU, which were also members of the SEPDC dissociated themselves from the decision of the Coalition. On the other hand, the SNM, the OPDF, the HNDO, the GDPO and the YPM confirmed their support. After long discussions, the Transitional Council of Representatives decided on April 1, 1993 to expel the organisations but indicated the possibility of presenting an 'appeal' or opposition to the decision taken within seven days.[107] The resolution was passed by 37 in support, 9 opposed and 2 abstentions. In accordance with the resolution only the Yem People's Movement (YPM) presented an opposition to its expulsion and then declared its rejection of the Paris Conference resolution, which paved the way for its reinstatement to the Council.[108]

The SEPDC with its remaining member organisations and other opposition groups organised the National Conference for Peace and Reconciliation in Ethiopia in December 1993. The Conference declared that "the democratisation process was aborted by the ruling party to consolidate its power to the detriment of the fundamental rights and interests of the people". It also rejected the Transitional Government's efforts to draft a new constitution for not including "independent political organisations and prominent personalities". Hence, it decided to establish a "Council of Alternative Forces of Peace and Democracy in Ethiopia" (CAFPDE)[109] and this was formed in March 1994. The Council had been considered by some people as a political group able to challenge the EPRDF. During the transitional period, its call for the formation of an alternative transitional government made little sense for many since its mandate would have been a repetition of the existing government's. Besides, the main drive for another transitional government seemed to be no more than an ambition for power. As a coalition, its support within the population was never seriously tested because of its repeated tactics to boycott elections. It was only in 2005 some of its members participated for federal and regional parliament seats in the name of United Ethiopian Democratic Forces when it won 52 seats, and in 2010 in a broad coalition named the Ethiopian Federal Democratic Unity Forum (FORUM) in which it won only a seat from the 547 seats of the House of People's Representatives which were open for contention.

Other than the OLF and OPDO, several Oromo organisations had participated in the Transitional Government. One of these organisations, the Islamic Front for the Liberation of Oromo (IFLO) had been active in the eastern part of the Oromo region. The IFLO had a mixture of religious and political objectives. It had a tendency to take Islam as the Oromos' sole religion and to a certain degree it wished to convert others.[110] It was also advocating the right of self-determination of the Oromo people since it emerged as a splinter group from the OLF in 1978. After staying as a member of the Transitional Government, it decided to withdraw from it by accusing the EPRDF of failing to honour the provisions of the National Charter.[111] Consequently, it reverted to armed activities, which it was unable to sustain because of the swift action by the government forces. Remnants of the OLF have been supported and trained by the Eritrean government as an instrument of its proxy war with the Ethiopian government. Despite a number of attempts to cross the border from Kenya and other neighbouring countries to carry out their mission, they have failed to have any impact on the political environment of the country. Other organisations such as the Oromo Abbo Liberation front (OALF) and United Oromo People's Liberation Front (UOPLF) were too small to have a significant political impact, and remained small to have any visible role. Moreover, the proliferation of organisations like the Oromo Liberation National Party, Oromo Federalist Democratic Movement, Oromo Liberation Party, Oromo People's Congress, All Oromo People Democratic Party and Geda System Advancement Party still continues.[112] As mentioned before, OPDO is member of the EPRDF, and Oromo People Congress and Oromo Federalist Democratic Movement are members of the main opposition political grouping, the Ethiopia Federal Democratic Unity Forum (FORUM). Nevertheless, they have to strive in order to survive and sustain their activities before making any impact on Ethiopian politics, and particularly in the Oromo affairs.

The proliferation of parties in the minority nationalities and relatively backward regions raises the issue of whether their development is facilitated or delayed by spreading the already minuscule skilled manpower. In the Afar region, there were four organisations working within the framework of the National Charter and the new constitution. The Afar Liberation Front Party (ALFP) was the former ALF which was dominated by the family of Sultan Ali Mirah and a few elites of the nationality. It had dominated the legislative and executive organs of the regional government up to the end of the Transitional Period. Consequently, the leadership of the party, particularly the family members of the Sultan, were accused of corruption, nepotism, and inefficiency in running the regional administration. After the elections of 1995, the ALFP lost most of its seats to rival parties.

The Afar People's Democratic Organisation (APDO) was formed before the downfall of the Derg in the northern part of the Afar region. It was not a member of the Transitional Council of Representatives and was not successful in the 1992 elections; however, it was able to become the largest organisation in the regional council after the 1995 elections. This political group claimed to have the support of the lower strata of the Afar population. In its administration, some reports indicated that there are some improvements in the allocation of funds, implementation of programs and the overall control. However, the shortcomings have still been visible, and they have attracted the attention of the Federal Government.[113] Furthermore, the Afar National Liberation Front (ANLF) had a significant number of seats in the regional council. The Afar National Democratic Movement (ANDM) had also a few seats.

The other development in the Afar region was the decision made by the Afar Revolutionary Democratic United Front (ARDUF) to join the peace process. In its 4th congress at Assayta, it abandoned armed struggle as a means of achieving its political goals and also amended its political program, which was designed to create a greater Afar region including the Afars in Eritrea.[114]

It declared its willingness to join hands with other Afar political groups to enhance development. The most important point here is that the four organisations claimed they represented the needy and the disadvantaged part of the population, however, it was not easy for them to come together, and at least, attempt to cover part of the dearth of skilled manpower. Evidently, tribal and clan disputes played a negative role in forging joint effort. After two years of arduous negotiations, the above-mentioned organisations, the AFLP, the APDO, the ANLF, the ANDM, and the ARDUF agreed to merge and form a united organisation. The founding conference took place between November 1-3, 1999 and a new organisation called the Afar National Democratic Party (ANDP) was formed.[115] The formation of this organisation has made a considerable contribution to the development of the region by bringing together the scarce human resources.

Nevertheless, there are still smaller political parties in Afar that are not part of ANDP. The Afar Revolutionary Democratic Unity Front (ARDUF), the Afar Liberation Front Party (ALFP) and the Afar National Revolutionary Democratic Front (ANRDF) have some activities but not enough to win them regional or federal parliament seats. They usually complain about narrowing political space in Afar region. Apparently, there might be some violations perpetuated by members of the ruling party, but the organizations rather seem too weak to spread their influence to the population in the first place.

In other regions, as in the Benishangul Gumuz region, various organisations agreed to form a joint front and work together to compensate the disadvantageous position of their region. The four political groups agreed to form a joint front named the Benishangul Gumuz People's Democratic United Front. However, such unity was not able to break the barriers of the member organizations to bring them into unity of purpose. Narrow tribal and regional affiliations compounded by corruption continued to persist throwing the front into crises. The crises led to a rectification process at the end of which a united organization, the Benishangul Gumuz People's Unity Democratic Party (BGPDP) was formed in October 2010. It is expected that the united party would reduce the tribal and regional frictions and bring together the scarce trained people together to change their region. In the Gambella region, the two parties with seats in the Regional Assembly were the Gambella People's Liberation Party (GPLP) and the Gambella People's Democratic Unity Party (GPDUP). The GPLP which has dominated the regional administration however failed to maintain a regional government with a reasonable efficiency and credibility. As in the other peripheral regions, the scarcity of trained manpower had played a major role in slowing down development efforts.[116] In 1998 the GPLP and GPDUP merged to form the Gambella People's Democratic Front (GPDF). However, the created front was not able to reduce the corruption, tribalism and regionalism that had been rampant in the region. Such adverse situation led to a crisis in which the front was dissolved in a meeting held in November 2007 but end up with the creation of three nationality organizations. The formation of the three organizations representing the Mezzenger, Agnwak and Nuer nationalities were part of the problem from the start. Recognizing the gravity of the predicament, the rank and file of the organizations and the people at large pushed for a unified organization. As a result the current ruling organization, the Gambella People's Unity Democratic Movement was formed in November 2008. The unity of the organisations would play a positive role in improving the state government's performance for it would benefit from the emerging unity of purpose within the existing meagre supply of skilled manpower.

Similarly, there have been several political groups in the Somalia region. The WSLF has transformed itself into the Western Somalia Democratic Party (WSDP). It was formed by people mainly from the Ogaden tribe though it also included some members from other clans. Most members were disillusioned after the fall of the Ziad Barre government. Currently it has little following, and only won none of the seats in the regional parliament. The only issue in its political program that differs it from others is that it advocates the private ownership of land.[117] However, it was not clarified how private ownership of land could be practised in a region where the majority of the people are nomads, and tribal and clannish relations are still strong.

The Ogaden National Liberation Front (ONLF) was formed by members mainly from the Ogaden tribe. It won the majority of seats in the regional council in the 1992 elections. Its administration was repeatedly shaken by corruption and ineptitude in the implementation of development projects. Subsequently, the ONLF was split into two groups; those who wanted to function peacefully within the framework of the Constitution and those who advocated armed struggle in order to "liberate" the Somali region. In the 1995 regional elections, it lost its majority control of the regional council to the Ethiopia Somali Democratic League (ESDL). The ESDL was consisted of 11 clan-based organisations. The regional government led by the ESDL has registered better achievements in development activities[118] than its predecessor but it failed to escape the usual allegations of corruption and wastefulness. Instability of administrations has become endemic to the region. Furthermore, the Ogaden tribe members who are the largest group in the region were complaining that they were not well represented in the ESDL administration.[119] Negotiations between the ESDL and ONLF to form a common front and eventually a united organisation resulted in the two organisations deciding to merge and form the Somali People Democratic Party (SPDP).[120] The merger has provided the region with a unified leadership and relatively benefited from the joint effort of its limited skilled manpower in running the badly managed development ventures. The organisation faces a formidable challenge of building itself into a real unified party. Any sign of proliferation of clan-based factions would spell disaster to the party, and evidently, would be a setback to the betterment of the Somali state. The merger is a good achievement; however, the remaining task will not be easy and needs a great deal of patience and skill.

The ruling party, the SPDP, keen to differentiate itself from other Somali organizations in Ethiopia and neighbouring countries, has changed its name into Ethiopian Somali People Democratic Party (ESPDP) in July 2009. The party claims that it will contribute to developing belongingness and commitment to the betterment of Somali region and Ethiopia at large. Its effect is going to be seen in the future. Other smaller groupings like the Somali Democratic Alliance Forces still exist. However, their political influence in the region is extremely limited.

Multinational Organisations

The Role of Veteran Multinational Political Groups

Several multinational organisations have a relatively long history in Ethiopia's political environment. The Ethiopian People's Revolutionary Party (EPRP) and the All-Ethiopian Socialist Movement, better known by its Amharic acronym, MEISON, were quite visible in the mid-1970s. The EPRP claimed to have started in 1972 but the party program was not released until August 1975. In September 1976, the Derg in collaboration with MEISON started killing and incarcerating EPRP and other opposition members under the "Red Terror" campaign. By 1977, the EPRP's urban party organisation was almost crippled and those who remained from the assault fled to the rural areas of northern Ethiopia. The EPRP's military wing, the Ethiopian People's Revolutionary Army (EPRA), had some activities in the Tigray and Gondar regions and was able to increase its numbers by the influx of "Red Terror" escapees from the cities. Its presence in Tigray was terminated when it came into conflict with the TPLF in 1978. By the end of 1978 and early 1979, the EPRP lost most of its rank and file members, who crossed the border to the Sudan or who surrendered to the government. By the early 1980s, it was again expelled from its base areas in Wolkait and Tsegede of the Gondar region. Since then its existence is reflected better on paper than on the ground.

After MEISON helped the Derg to destroy the EPRP and weaken other opposition forces, it became the next victim of the government's crackdown. MEISON had a similar background to that of the EPRP's, arising from the Ethiopian student movement. When the military government came to power, MEISON decided to give "critical support" to the new regime, which it thought to be an easy road to usurp power. This position came into conflict with the EPRP's call for the immediate formation of a "provisional people's government". The polemics between them became bitter and deteriorated into shootings and killings. As stated previously, MEISON collaborated with the Derg in its efforts to destroy the EPRP, and of course, it succeeded. Soon after, the Derg became uncomfortable with MEISON and started to restrict its activities by creating confrontation. The collaboration reached its final phase and the leadership of MEISON fled. Many of them were captured and mercilessly killed. By early 1979, MEISON was destroyed and except for those who had managed to escape abroad, there were a few who changed their allegiance to the powerful Derg.

Putting aside their feud and differences, remnants of the EPRP and MEISON agreed to co-operate and form a joint coalition with the participation of other small groups and individuals in order to challenge the perceived threat from the EPRDF's success. The EPRP and MEISON, including other exiled political groups, formed the Coalition of Ethiopia Democratic Forces (COEDF) and released their program on April 17, 1991. The formation of the COEDF was the result of the Toronto Conference of the previous year. The major force in the Coalition was the EPRP, which was determined to avoid negotiating with the EPRDF. The EPRP knew that it could not have a leading role in a coalition in which the EPRDF was a party. The avoidance of rapprochement was not new since it was the extension of past conflicts.

Despite the on-going polemics, physical confrontation did not occur until the EPRDF started moving to western Ethiopia as part of its strategy to finalise the armed conflict in the country. The EPRP took the move as a conspiracy to eradicate it as a political movement. It declared that "the TPLF war against the EPRP, which is being backed directly or otherwise by other forces, is in actual fact an attempt to strike at the democratic forces and the alternative they present for Ethiopia".[121] On the other hand, the EPRDF accused the EPRP of helping the military government by attacking its forces, ambushing its convoys and mining the roads to create problems with the delivery of its logistics.[122] The recriminations continued when the COEDF declared that it supported the Derg's parliament resolution for negotiating with opposition "unity forces", and at the same time, calling for general mobilisation to crush the armed opposition groups.[123] The EPRDF accused COEDF of supporting the Derg's war decrees.[124] The COEDF condemned the outcome of the London talks, which it could not attend. Nevertheless, the COEDF declared its intention to participate in the planned conference.[125] The EPRDF demanded that the COEDF should renounce violence and publicly commit itself to peaceful political struggle. The demand was not accepted by the Coalition, and it was barred from participating in the National Conference. Though some negotiations were taking place between the COEDF and the EPRDF with the mediation of the U.S. government, they did not produce any tangible results. The COEDF remained an exiled organisation with little influence in the dynamics of Ethiopian politics.

The Ethiopian Democratic Unity (EDU) was a member of the COEDF until the last days of the Derg but it decided to participate in the National Conference by opposing the Coalition's position. The Chairman of the EDU, Mengesha Seyoum, publicly accused the COEDF of retreating from the peaceful process and advocating to continue the armed struggle against the newly formed provisional government.[126] The EDU was formed in the mid-1970s, mainly by high officials of the Haile Selassie regime. In the early years, the organisation's main slogan was against "land to the tiller", which was meant to protect the interests of the traditional landowners. Its advocacy to preserve the old system brought it into conflict with the TPLF and they fought bloody battles between 1977 and 1978. As a result, EDU's army was defeated and driven not only from Tigray region, but also ceased to exist as a relevant armed group in Ethiopia. As mentioned above, the exiled leadership decided to participate in the National Conference and obtained one seat on the Transitional Council of Representatives. It remained on the Council until it participated in "the National Council for Peace and Reconciliation in Ethiopia", which called for the dissolution of the Transitional Government. The conference resolution states that "the two and a half years set by the supreme law of the transition period expires in January 1994 and there is no legal provision in the Charter for extending the term of office". Consequently, the Transitional Council of Representatives at its 85th Regular Session debated the position of the EDU and decided to take it as the organisation's decision to terminate its membership in the government.[127] Since then the EDU has a mediocre existence with little influence in the political spectrum.

Newly Formed Multinational Political Groups and the Transitional Period

The other multinational organisations with a visible contribution in the transitional period were the Ethiopian National Democratic Organisation (ENDO) and the Ethiopian Democratic Coalition (EDC). These organisations mainly played the role of advocacy for diverse political stances from that of the EPRDF in the legislative body. From their political programs, it would not be difficult to deduce that they represented a certain sector of society, which believes in the benefit of the State's complete withdrawal from economic activities. They supported the right of nationalities to self-rule but stop short of the right to secede. In addition, they supported the right to own both urban and rural land, which included the right to acquire, use, mortgage, sell, and transfer by succession or other means. These were the organisations whose opinions were presented as an alternative minority position to the Constituent Assembly.[128] Joined by the GPDF, the KPC and the WPDF, they formed the Ethiopian National Democratic Party (ENDP) to field candidates for the 1995 elections but were unsuccessful in winning seats. They were not able to build their constituency outside a few urban centres. In fact, in an agrarian country like Ethiopia, the rural support is essential in winning elections. Hence, it needs a lot of effort to build the party machinery and gradually establish a political constituency. Part-time politics do not suffice as a credible party for government. Nevertheless, their contribution in the attempt to build a political culture of democratic competition had been worth mentioning.

The Council of Alternative Forces for Peace and Democracy in Ethiopia had been working as an opposition force outside the parliamentary process. The main force in the Council is the Southern Ethiopia People's Democratic Coalition (SEPDC), which as discussed above, was expelled from the Transitional Government for calling for the dissolution of the transitional arrangement. It was conducting public meetings and demonstrations against government policies and actions, particularly in the capital city of Addis Ababa. It accused the EPRDF of aborting the democratisation process to consolidate its power and imposing its party program on the Ethiopian people as a constitution.[129] Though endorsing the right of nationalities for self-rule, it opposed the existing method of demarcation of regional states as a ploy that serves to aggravate nationality antagonisms and negatively affects their unity. On the economic field, it advocated the right to private land ownership, including the right to sell, mortgage and transfer by succession or inheritance.[130] It boycotted the 1995 elections alleging the existence of unfair practices and despite its claims to have wide ranging support, it had difficulty to substantiate. The Council then ceased to exist and many of the member organizations participated in the 2005 elections by forging new alliances and some on their own.

The Moa Anbessa organisation was also worth mentioning in order to address the political current entertained by the aspirants of the return of the monarchy. The organisation advocated for the establishment of a constitutional monarchy. The program known as "The Conquering Lion: Ethiopians for Constitutional Monarchy" declares that the monarchy is essential to safeguard the country's unity. However, Ethiopians generally seem to have little predilection for the reinstitution of a monarchy, which was partly to be blamed for the country's backwardness and extensive suffering. It was clear from the start that the organization would not last long considering the rarity of support for the defunct Monarchy.

The countrywide organisations with substantial support are mainly coalitions or united fronts of various nationality-based political groups. The multinational organisations with countrywide programs have not been able to build a broad mass base. In fact, many of them have little influence beyond the capital city. These types of organisations have a long way to go before securing credible support. Current political trends in the country favour those who are attempting to build constituencies based on nationalities. However, this does not mean there is no place for the evolvement of a multi-national organisation with respectable credibility and a reasonably large constituency.

Relationship of Actors

The relationship of political groups has not been smooth since student movement took a prominent place in Ethiopian politics. Almost all left-wing movements originated from the student movement of the 1960s and 1970s. Although these organisations advocate for change and the betterment of the people, they failed to co-ordinate their forces against the common enemy. In fact, the failure of these forces to form a united front had contributed to prolonging the life span of the military government and as a consequence the sufferings and agony of the Ethiopian people.

The recriminations and political violence was first aggravated by the deterioration of relations between the EPRP and MEISON. As discussed above, MEISON collaborated with the Derg in the name of a "critical support" to root out its competitor and prime antagonist. The EPRP attempted to usurp power through urban insurrection, which it thought of as the shortest path to destroy an opponent and gain ascendancy. The conflict caused the extermination of thousands of young people accused of sympathising with both organisations. Such a disastrous fight was again followed by the dispute between the EPRP and the TPLF, which ended the role of the former as an important player in the country's politics. These conflicts could have been avoided, had there been a reasonably developed culture of tolerance and management of differences. In the midst of squabbling and feuding, the common enemy was free to attack the opposition forces one by one.

Hostile Relations between the EPRDF and the COEDF

The political conflict between the EPRDF and the COEDF has a lot to do with their past relations. Their failure to come to terms with the existing capabilities and conditions has been affecting the COEDF in its dealings with the EPRDF. The polemics between the organisations had been there in the 1980s, but they had not been in physical contact for years, until early 1991. When the EPRDF swept through the northern regions and began to attack government positions in central and western regions of the country, the EPRP claimed that the offensive was targeted at its army, which had an insignificant presence in the border areas.[131] Consequently, the EPRP was involved in some armed activities against the EPRDF, which pushed the latter to clean its rear before proceeding to further engagements with government forces. Then the support of the COEDF to the Derg's parliament resolution was interpreted by the EPRDF as an endorsement of the government army mobilisation efforts. The circumstances were followed by the COEDF's condemnation of the London Conference. Then the EPRDF sent its representatives to Washington, D.C. and asked the COEDF to join in the peaceful competition, which the latter refused. It even vowed to continue its struggle to quash the "EPRDF and American conspiracy".[132] When the COEDF announced it had had a change of heart and decided to join national conference, the EPRDF demanded a public repudiation of violence, which did not happen. In the meantime, the EDU left the Coalition and decided to participate in the conference by denouncing the insincerity of the Coalition's claim of standing for peaceful competition. Consequently, it became the only noticeable organisation to remain out of the national conference.

There have been several attempts to mediate between these organisations by foreign parties, especially the U.S. While the EPRDF insisted on the COEDF's renunciation of violence and participation in the Ethiopian political platform as any organisation, the COEDF demanded revision of the Constitution to which it was not a party. It also called for the formation of a new transitional government to facilitate drafting a new constitution and conducting fresh elections. The EPRDF was not ready to discard whatever it has endeavoured since 1991 in order to attract an organisation which it believes has little influence in Ethiopian politics except for its external profile. Furthermore, it was not prepared to guarantee some of the COEDF leaders, especially MEISON cadres, immunity from prosecution for their role in the infamous "Red Terror".[133] As the negotiation proved fruitless, the gulf between them further widened and the efforts vanished from the mediators' agendas of the last few years. The COEDF seems to remain an exiled group, able to make opposition statements but too weak to make a political difference in the country.

The EPRDF and the OLF: An Attempt of Co-operation under Mutual Mistrust

The two parties which could be considered as the major actors of the Transitional Government until June 1992 were the EPRDF and OLF. The OLF participated in the process starting as a junior partner in the London Conference. As discussed above, the past relations between the two organisations had never been smooth. Although there has been some co-operation since

1983, it was difficult to develop it to a satisfactory level for both organisations. Furthermore, suspicions and mistrust shadowed timely co-operation, particularly after the OPDO was formed in 1990. Nevertheless, the EPRDF insisted on the participation of the OLF in the London talks, and with the EPLF, the three organisations were able to agree on the future process. In spite of the joint statement, the OLF issued its own statement that could have jeopardised the collective agreement. The EPRDF was uncomfortable with the repeatedly changing stances of the OLF. Within a few weeks negotiations began between the two organisations but it was difficult to reach agreement until the EPLF was asked to mediate. Issues ranging from the content of the Charter to the allocation of seats in the Transitional Council of Representatives, and cabinet and ambassadorial positions had to be settled by arduous negotiations.

After the formation of the Transitional Government, the EPRDF and OLF negotiated and agreed on how to administer the South-East regions. The OLF argued that its forces liberated the areas, but the EPRDF refused to accept this, claiming these areas were under the military government and the OLF had only entered its forces after the regime's downfall. Subsequently, the OLF withdrew its forces from the main towns, major roads and economic installations to rural areas in accordance with the agreement of August 1991. In the 25th Regular Session of Transitional Council of Representatives, the member organisations, including the OLF, voted in support of Proclamation No. 8/1991. This stated that the EPRDF army was entrusted to serve as the nation's defence force and required other organisations to encamp their armies in designated camps.[134] However, armed clashes between the two forces were frequent, causing security and economic concerns. In February 1992, in accordance with the decision of the Council, the two organisations, mediated by the EPLF, agreed on the encampment of their forces and on a dispute-resolving mechanism, which included the formation of committees comprising members from the EPRDF, the OLF and the EPLF. Nevertheless, the armed clashes and mutual recriminations resumed, culminating in the OLF's boycott of the June 1992 regional elections. It also withdrew from the government and its forces left their camps, which brought them into full armed conflict with the EPRDF forces. After several weeks of armed clashes, most of the OLF armed units were taken prisoner and were encamped for months at a centre called the Hurso Rehabilitation Camp. After finishing the courses,[135] most of them were released to return to their normal lives. In just a short period, the OLF was reduced to a number of small units wandering in some remote areas of southern Ethiopia. The leadership that was in the capital city during the crises was not the target of the government actions against the OLF. Seyoum explains the situation:

> Even during the crises and when fighting was continuing with the OLF army, negotiations were proceeding with the mediation of the EPLF until the OLF leadership walked out. Yet, we helped them to leave the country without any problem by providing them passports. Most important of all, the dream that the government would collapse in the wake of their withdrawal did not happen.[136]

Attempts at improving the disrupted relations continued until the end of 1997. Informal meetings had taken place between the EPRDF and the OLF representatives in the presence of the former German Ambassador to Ethiopia, Mr. Horst Winkelmann. Both organisations presented their conditions for a possible reconciliation. The EPRDF asked that the OLF recognise the Constitution; openly renounce violence; revise its 1976 program that envisaged the establishment of an independent Oromo state; and retract its pronouncements of the existence of political prisoners under government custody as the EPRDF considered them to be criminals who should face trial. On the other hand, the OLF demanded the release of all OLF prisoners; the reinstatement of partnership in government; immunity from any prosecution; the reorganisation of state institutions as it believed that they were dominated by the EPRDF; and the further devolution of power, since it regarded the present decentralisation as an exercise inadequate for a real and substantial autonomy.[137] It also raised the issue of its army's existence and the ways in which it could be accommodated, together with other economic issues surrounding privatisation and the activities of trading companies, which were in some way related to the ruling party. The EPRDF rejected the notion of the existence of the OLF army, and explained the legal circumstances and proper activities of the Privatisation Agency and the mentioned trading companies.[138] After three rounds of meetings and long debates, the two sides failed to narrow their differences. The OLF side wanted to secure some face-saving concessions from the government, which the latter regarded as unacceptable considering the OLF's past activities and unclear future role in Ethiopian politics. The last meeting was held on October 6, 1997, and there had been additional factors, such as the change of leadership within the OLF[139] and the conflict between Ethiopia and Eritrea, which made the possibility of reconciliation even more remote.

Although the government kept the negotiations secret, the OLF expressed its frustration on the results of the meetings through a formal statement. The OLF statement explains the situation as follows:

> ... beginning from February 1997, held three rounds of preliminary talks with representatives of the regime in the presence of an intermediary in Germany. The third round was held early this month. Unfortunately, once again the talks reached a deadlock despite our

> efforts and those of the intermediary. The regime failed to respect understanding already reached during the previous two rounds of talks. They reneged on agreement to negotiate all contested issues without any preconditions as well as the confidentiality of the talks.[140]

The heaviest blow to the reconciliation attempt came when the OLF made a statement aimed at siding with Eritrea in the conflict with Ethiopia. The OLF statement called "the Oromo and other peoples in the Empire of State of Ethiopia to alienate themselves from this conflict which does not bring any positive economic or political change to their way of living".[141] Soon Eritrea started to train OLF insurgents and attempted to infiltrate them through Somalia to southern Ethiopia. The attempt was not successful as many of them fell to the ambushes of government forces. The military operations were not only disastrous but also caused irreparable damage to further rapprochement between the EPRDF and the OLF.

These days, the OLF's chances of survival as a political force are limited. Its interests would be best served if it could negotiate with the government to go back into a peaceful political environment and competition. The idea of waging an armed struggle to achieve political objectives seems unattainable in today's Ethiopia. Hence, grasping the chance of negotiation, which could bring it back to peaceful competition, seems the only viable option remaining for the OLF. The government has repeatedly indicated that everybody is welcome to peacefully compete, including those who rejected the process in the past.[142] Of course, its flirtation with the Eritrean government has made the chance of reconciliation extremely remote. Such situation has been further exacerbated by the House of Representatives' designation of OLF as a terrorist organization in 2009.[143] Nevertheless, when the dust settles the opportunity of peacefully resolving the conflict might rekindle.

The EPRDF and the Southern Ethiopia Organisations

The relations between the EPRDF and Southern nationalities' organisations began after the former took power defeating the military government. Some organisations created within the short provisional government's stay in power negotiated with the EPRDF and agreed on the draft charter, which enabled them to participate in the National Conference. Even from the start there were visible political differences, which in fact crystallised in the process of the transitional period. Differences on the issues of self-determination, economic policies and property rights, especially on land ownership were some of the issues that widened the gulf between them. In the meantime, the EPRDF was busy helping other organisations from the same nationalities that might have similar political programs. The Southern nationalities, which were members of the SEPDU and the Transitional Government, felt abandoned by the EPRDF in favour of the newly formed groups. Tesfaye Habisso, former Secretary of the Transitional Council of Representatives explains their feelings:

> The Southern nationalities' organisations in the Transitional Council of Representatives were expecting that the EPRDF would help them to strengthen themselves. However, the EPRDF side-lined these organisations and was busy organising its own creations by bringing together former prisoners of war and other uninformed people.[144]

Bereket Simon, member of the Executive Committee of the EPRDF, denies any wrong doing in the actions taken by the EPRDF. He explains the process:

> An organisation is formed by certain people who have similar political stances, and similarly, a common umbrella organisation is created by organisations that have similar objectives. With members of the SEPDU, we have had differences in our political stances and we made it clear to them from the start that we could not ally with them in a common organisational framework. Moreover, it is natural for the EPRDF to seek alliance with those who have similar political viewpoints. Hence, we have to compete for the population's support and they have to accept it as one face of democracy.[145]

The SEPDU, after leaving the Transitional Government, with the exception of those members who dissociated themselves from the Paris declaration, did not participated in the subsequent elections. The negotiations conducted to encourage the opposition did not bear fruit. Consequently, the SEPDU alleged that the electoral process was not open and democratic enough to be worth participating and boycotted the 1995 elections. Since then, there have been no serious negotiations that take place between the party in government and the SEPDU, especially with those who later formed the United Ethiopian Democratic Forces until the eve of the 2005 elections.

OLF's Relations with Oromo and Other Political Groups

It is also important to discuss the relations between the OLF and organisations other than the EPRDF. The OLF and the Southern and South-Western nationality organisations were not able to build a working relationship based on mutual trust. These nationality organisations were not comfortable with the OLF's designation of the whole of Southern Ethiopia as Oromia. The "threat" of the OLF was exacerbated by its frequent statements of describing the Southern nationalities as "pockets of other people within Oromia".[146] There were many skirmishes between peoples incited by the OLF that caused the deaths of many and thousands were displaced in the region.

The Transitional Council of Representatives' attention was also attracted by the numerous clashes between the OLF and the Benishangul People's Liberation Movement (BPLM). As a result, many people died and property was destroyed, especially at Assosa, in the Benishangul-Gumuz region. The BPLM and the OLF clashed over the control of the town, and the existence of an OLF army in the region was taken by the former as a threat. The BPLM continued to accuse the OLF of destroying infrastructure, including schools, health centres and buildings, and of kidnapping young people from Benishangul for conscription and killings.[147] In November 1991, the situation was aggravated and armed clashes were frequent. In the incident of December 3, 1991, the OLF was accused of burning more than 200 civilians' houses and looting and burning over 30 shops. In Kushmengel, a village outside Assosa, over 40 houses were burnt and six people were killed.[148] The Council at its 32nd Regular Session approved the recommendations of the Defence and Security Committee which stated that the fundamental solution was the quick implementation of the encampment of the armed groups, meaning the Assosa-based armies would be placed in designated camps. Moreover, it asked the organisations to bring to justice those who were involved in killings and destruction and looting of property.[149] Nevertheless, the relationship between these organisations had been destructive until the encampment of the armed groups and later the disappearance of groups' armies by various means.[150]

The OLF was also criticised by other Oromo organisations for its "arrogance" and "domineering" attitude. When the OPDO issued a 'Proposal for Creating Unity among Oromo Organisations'[151] in early 1991, it was expecting some sort of reaction from the OLF. However, the OLF demanded the dissolution of the OPDO as an organisation and asked members of the latter to join its ranks as individuals.[152] The talks on a united front could not proceed because of the OLF's rejection of the existence of another organisation in Oromia other than itself. Similarly, the IFLO had been complaining about the OLF's "misconception" of it and "domineering attitude". Moreover, the statement indicated that their differences had become more serious and became the cause of some instances of armed clashes.[153] It is not difficult to understand that the OLF's relations with the far smaller organisations such as the OALF and UOPLF were not smooth. The OLF's attitude seemed to be that it was the only organisation which could represent the "real" aspirations and interests of the Oromo people.

Concluding Remarks

By early 1991, there were clear signs of the Derg government's collapse and a serious danger was looming, threatening the country's unity and existence. Various liberation movements were gaining ground and the government's forces were limited to a number of urban areas. Consequently, the economy was in deep crisis and worsening rapidly with the political uncertainty that gripped the nation. The question that occupied most of the people was the survival of the country and whether the scenarios of Liberia and Somalia would be repeated in Ethiopia. Fortunately, the situation began to improve with the establishment of EPRDF's Provisional Government and its successful efforts to enforce law and order throughout the country.

The EPRDF handled the situation with a firm conviction to fundamentally restructure the state and its institutions. It believed that the "old" thinking of building the Ethiopian nation by assimilating the tens of nationalities into the Amhara culture had failed to deliver the intended results. In fact, it became the main cause of the mushrooming of nationality-based liberation movements. With this in mind, it organized the National Conference of July 1-5, 1991, which adopted not only the right of nationalities to self-rule but also the exercise of their rights to self-determination, including secession.

As discussed above, the implementation of the transitional program was not easy, as it was a new venture where there had been little experience in such affairs of great magnitude. In addition, many political organisations and groups with diverse political and economic programs constituted the Transitional Government. The Transitional Government encountered one of its most difficult challenges when the OLF decided to withdraw from the government and ordered its armed units to leave their camps. Although the OLF was one of the signatories of the London agreement, it was consumed by a dilemma that arose from its program, which advocated for the establishment of an independent Oromia state. Throughout its stay in the Transitional Government, its main occupation was strengthening itself militarily and politically with the ultimate objective of achieving an independent state. Such tendencies were also compounded with the practice of employing force to achieve political goals and silence opponents. Of course, this does not mean the EPRDF and other members of the Transitional Government were free of any blame. However, the difference is that they may have made mistakes within the implementation process of the Charter while the OLF was accused of working against the agreed program.

The relationship between the internal actors was not straightforward, and there were instances when many people were concerned with the continuity of peace and stability in the country. The most serious challenge came from the OLF but it was resolved in a relatively shorter period than many expected. The other problem that needed addressing was the boycott of elections by opposition forces such as the SEPDU, AAPO, and other small organisations. These organisations accused the government of foul play, an accusation rejected by the government. On the other hand, the EPRDF argued that these organisations had little support and were afraid of facing the electorate, and prefer to hide themselves behind such fabricated pretexts. As discussed, the opposition organizations have started participating in elections since 2000 and began take their seats in the House of Peoples' Representatives except CUD's boycott in 2005. CUD's boycott was detrimental to its reputation as well as organizational standing. Moreover, it played a negative role to the development of multi-party system in Ethiopia. With the reputation of the opposition in tatters and EPRDF's remarkable success in economic growth performance and some improvements in governance, the electorate vote in 2010 deny the opposition parliamentary seats except one.

The past two decades' lessons from the political process should contribute to Ethiopia's economic growth, and development of the democratic process and good governance. They are beneficial not only to the ruling party to remain in power but also to the opposition to challenge the status quo. They also provide the people with better options to choose from and the capacity of choosing what is favourable for their livelihood. This requires political leaders and activities to think and work for the long term interest of the country rather than squabbling for short term sectarian advantages.

Notes

1. The U.S. moved to arrange the London Conference. Cohen explains that "government officials urged the U.S. to help facilitate a peaceful transition. They affirmed a keen desire to include rebel groups and others in a restructured regime". It was the U.S. administration's goal to arrange a peaceful transition in Ethiopia. On the other hand, the U.S used the Derg's weakness and desperate situation to pressure it to agree to the exodus of Ethiopian Jews to Israel. In fact, the administration was indicating unless the evacuation of the Jews was expedited, the U.S. could withdraw from the proposal of the May 20 meeting. As a result, about 15,000 Ethiopian Jews were evacuated by a huge airlift launched by Israel (Cohen, Statement, June 18, 1991; see minutes on the meetings of Ethiopian government officials and U.S. diplomats on the preparation for the London Conference of May 20, 1991, Ministry of Foreign Affairs of Ethiopia; and see Newsweek, June 3, 1991: 27). On the other hand, the initial U.S. proposal of participants to the conference included the major warring groups, namely the government, the EPRDF and the EPLF. The Oromo Liberation Front (OLF) was included, due to the insistence of the EPRDF. In fact, initially the U.S. representatives were not comfortable with the inclusion of the OLF for they thought in order to organ-

ise a conference for peace, only the principal warring factions were needed and other groups could be included at later stage (Meles, former Prime Minister and Seyoum, former Foreign Minister, interview).

2. Herman Cohen reported to the Sub-Committee on Africa of the Committee on Foreign Affairs, House of Representatives, on the peace talks and how they ended as follows: On the 27th, acting President Tesfaye Gebre-Kidan told us the Ethiopian Army had virtually disintegrated, and that he and senior government officials were concerned about their ability to provide for law and order. The acting President said that the government intended to broadcast a call for a unilateral cease-fire and an appeal to the citizens of Addis to accept the EPRDF when they entered the capital. The EPRDF decided to move into the city that night. The United States strongly agreed with that decision, because the EPRDF was now left as the only disciplined force capable of keeping order in the capital. At that point the Addis regime effectively ceased to exist and their delegation in London dropped out of the talks. The final part of the London meeting began with the United States no longer in a mediation role between the government and the insurgents, but in a de facto advisory role for the three opposition groups about to inherit all military and political power. Our London meeting thus ended without the appointment of a Transitional Government as we had envisaged. But it ended with something perhaps even better. The insurgent groups themselves argued that a Transitional Government was not possible until more political factions were present and participating. In a joint statement, they themselves called for a meeting of a wider range of political parties and interests to establish a broadly based Transitional Government. (Cohen, Statement on June 18, 1991).

3. The phenomenon of a failed state or state collapse is explained by Zartman as "a situation where the structure, authority (legitimate power), law, and political order have fallen apart and must be reconstituted in some form, old or new". (Zartman, in Zartman (ed.), 1995:1). He further elaborates that "collapse" means that the basic functions of the state are no longer performed. He focuses on three functions: "the state as the sovereign authority- the accepted source of identity and the arena of politics; the state as an institution- and therefore a tangible organisation of decision-making and an intangible organisation of decision-making and an intangible symbol of identity; and the state as the security guarantor for a populated territory". (Zartman, in Zartman (ed.), 1995:5).

4. Seyoum remembers the negotiation on the transitional arrangement as follows: The Americans initially proposed that it would be advisable for the EPRDF to establish the Transitional Government for four or five years in order to control the volatile situation in the country. The EPRDF did not accept because it had its own program of transition that envisaged the participation of all political groups. We told them that we would establish a broad-based government after a one-month provisional government of the EPRDF. We believed, within one month, we could organise a national peace conference to decide on the transitional arrangement. The proposal was agreed between the EPLF, the OLF and ourselves, and was declared by Herman Cohen (Seyoum, interview).

5. Joint Statement by EPRDF, EPLF and OLF, London, May 28, 1991; concerning the major results of the conference, Meles remarks as follows: The Americans made a basic shift of policy on the Eritrean question, which had been in place for decades. The EPLF's decision to organise an orderly referendum and to accept the choice of the Eritrean people was a logical and acceptable political formula for them. On our side, we got the American and other Western powers' conditional support depending on our commitment to a democratic transition (Meles, interview); On the other hand, Herman Cohen also explains the major accomplishments of the London meeting as follows: First, the Mengistu regime, dead by its own misguided policies, is gone but without the pitched battle for Addis that some had feared. Second, there is an interim administration in place that is temporary and solicitous of wider membership and political participation. It seeks Western help in forming a true Transitional Government. Third, and most important, in this fragile transitional stage in Ethiopia, the juridical issue of Eritrea's future did not really arise among the parties in London...But there is general, if tacit, agreement that the long-sought referendum and the final determination of Eritrea's status can await a more stable situation emerging in Addis (Cohen, Statement on June 18, 1991).
6. Seyoum Mesfin, former Minister of Foreign Affairs, interview August 16, 1997; many soldiers were roaming in towns and even some selling their weapons for small amounts of money. Apparently, they could have been involved in looting and other criminal activities.
7. Bereket Simon, Member of the Executive Committee of the EPRDF, interviews August 17, 1997.
8. Seyoum Mesfin, interview
9. Meles Zenawi, interview.
10. The COEDF had been insisting on holding the conference outside Ethiopia and being mediated by a team of mediators, which was apparently unacceptable to the Provisional Government. When COEDF announced its decision to participate at the eve of the conference, it failed to address the concern of the EPRDF that was its public rejection of violence as a form of political struggle.
11. See EPRDF's Proposal for a Smooth and Peaceful Transition in Ethiopia, March 10, 1990.
12. Leenco Lata, quoted in Sarah Vaughan, 1994, p. 35.
13. The Transitional Charter is attached as an appendix.
14. For details see the draft proposal on 'the Principles of Co-operation between the Transitional Government of Ethiopia and the Provisional Government of Eritrea', July 1991; In order to see the details of the proceedings, it is advisable to see the video tapes of the Conference, but the summary of the decisions of the Conference can be found in the Minutes of the 10th Regular Session of the Transitional Council of Representatives (TCR), August 14, 1991.
15. Kassu Ilala is a former Minister and now Ambassador to EU, and LeencoLata was the Deputy Secretary-General of the OLF.

16. See Minutes of the 10th Regular Session of the TCR, August 14, 1991.
17. See Article 9 of the Transitional Period Charter of Ethiopia, July 22, 1991.
18. Seyoum, interview.
19. For further information, see Minutes of the 14th Regular Session of the TCR, September 13, 1991.
20. Bereket Simon, interview.
21. COEDF. Statement on the Addis Ababa Conference of July 1-5, 1991, July 6, 1991.
22. See Minutes of the 8th Regular Session of the TCR, August 10, 1991.
23. Proclamation No.8/ 1992. A Proclamation to Provide for the Deployment of the State Defence Army of the Central Transitional Government and the Establishment of Police Force, January 16, 1992, Article 3 (1).
24. Ibid., Article 10.
25. Proclamation No. 9/ 1992. A Proclamation to Provide for the Creation of Expeditious Conditions for the Election on National/ Regional Self-Governments, January 18, 1992, Article 20 (2).
26. For further details of the debate, see Minutes of the 39th Regular Session of the TCR, April 14 and 16, 1992.
27. Proclamation No. 9/1992, Article 15.
28. ADLI promotes the productivity increase of small holder agriculture and industrialisation bases on utilisation of domestic raw materials with labour intensive technology; encourages exports of agricultural and mineral commodities in order to expedite an interdependent agricultural and industrial development (see Chapter IV, the ADLI).
29. See Proclamation No. 1/ 1995. Proclamation of the Constitution of the Federal Democratic Republic of Ethiopia, August 21, 1995.
30. Report of the Election Commission, September 1996, pp. 207.
31. See Proclamation No. 2/ 1995. Declaration of the Establishment of the Federal Democratic Republic of Ethiopia Proclamation, August 22, 1995.
32. EPRDF. Resolutions and Political Stand of the First Congress, February 1991.
33. Proposal for the Formation of a United Resistance Force presented by the TPLF, May 8, 1984.
34. MEISON and TPLF. Joint Declaration, September 1987.
35. The two organisations agreed to wage a common struggle against the Derg but failed to forge a similar position on the unfortunate collaboration of the MEISON with the Derg in causing immense sufferings to the Ethiopian youth. The MEISON's hard-sought desire to leave behind its past 'crimes' did not materialise as a result of its rapprochement with the TPLF. The Joint Statement, in fact, brought forward the harboured feelings as follows: 'TPLF still argues that the policy of alliance with the Derg was the result of a series of fundamental mistakes in the political line advocated by the MEISON. The errors led the organisation to

join the counter-revolutionary camp, thus causing serious harm to the Ethiopian revolution' (See Joint Statement, September 1989). The MEISON rejected the position of the TPLF and insisted that it did not commit any fundamental political errors. The difference of positions on this issue gave the signal that the TPLF would not support any drive to exonerate the suspects of the 'Red Terror' campaign after a change of government. In addition, the primacy of the oppressed nationalities' struggle for self-determination in the Ethiopian revolution was also a point of disagreement. The MEISON did not 'consider [the national question] to be the main aspect of the class struggle in Ethiopia' (ibid.). The disagreement did not help to change the reputation of the MEISON as a 'chauvinist' organisation in the TPLF circles. Hence, the Joint Statement failed to serve as a ground to build confidence and initiate co-operation between them.

36. Adulis, May 1985.
37. Young, Peasant Revolution in Ethiopia, 1997:153.
38. EPLF and TPLF. Joint Statement, April 24, 1988.
39. Proposal of the Tigray People's Liberation Front for a Peaceful Solution to the Situation in Ethiopia, March 1989.
40. Ibid.
41. Shengo is an Amharic word for Assembly.
42. For details, see Resolution of the Shengo: 'Six-Point New Peace Initiative', 1989.
43. BehanBayed, the Dreg's Foreign Minister, claimed that the peace call was for the Eritrean insurgents and refused to recognise the urgency of starting negotiations with the TPLF and other Ethiopian organisations in his press statement of early 1989. It was only on August 18, 1989 the same Foreign Minister publicly accepted the necessity of beginning negotiations with the TPLF.
44. EPRDF's Proposal for a Smooth and Peaceful Transition in Ethiopia, March 10, 1990.
45. Resolution of the Third Emergency Session of the National Sheng of the People's Democratic Republic of Ethiopia, A (1), April 22, 1991, Addis Ababa.
46. Ibid.
47. The COEDF campaigned very hard to be included in the London talks. For example, MershaYosef, the Chairman of the Executive Committee of COEDF wrote to Herman Cohen as follows: "The peace efforts begun by the USA following the Ethiopian Shengo resolution have justifiably aroused COEDF's interest too. We have learnt from the media and other sources that the U.S government has invited certain Ethiopian opposition forces to peace talks to be held under U.S. auspices and tentatively planned for May 20, 1991 in London. A similar invitation to attend the planned London talks has not been extended to COEDF to date. COEDF hopes the U.S. will encourage the participation in the peace forum of as many Ethiopian opposition forces as are willing. Such a move would help to avoid future entanglements" (Letter to Heman Cohen, May 13, 1991).
48. COEDF. Statement on the Decision of the Third Emergency Session of the National Shengo of Ethiopia, April 24, 1991.

49. Habesha is a name given to the peoples of Northern Ethiopia, especially to the Amharas and Tigrians and other related nationalities.
50. SEPDF is an umbrella organisation for over 23 nationality-based political groups.
51. The Political Program of ANDM, January 1994: 10-11.
52. The Proclamation was approved by all members of the Council except for one abstention that was a representative of the Sidama Liberation Movement (SLM), who claimed the decree did not provide enough powers for the regional administrations. (See Minutes of the Regular Session of the TCR, December 2-6, 1991).
53. The main points of the five year program are to give priority to rural development, encourage private investment in the economic sector, emphasis on the development of infrastructure, education and preventive health care, primarily support to the most underdeveloped areas of Ethiopia and devolve power from the regional to the local level, meaning towards the grass roots.
54. Jalata, 1993: 154-55.
55. Bulcha quoted in Jalata, 'The Emergence of Oromo Nationalism and Ethiopian Reaction', in Jalata (ed.), 1998: 6.
56. The enormous exploitation by the landlords had become unbearable to ordinary and poor peasants. Scattered and spontaneous resistance was erupting here and there and was suppressed by the government without ever trying to review the situation and introducing any tangible solution to the plight of the peasants. The Bale peasant resistance that took place between 1963 and 1970 was significant in not only presenting an enormous challenge to the government but also brought the extent of oppression and misery of the peasants and nomads in the region to the forefront. It took the government over six years to squash the rebellion and as usual the measures employed were harsh and brutal. Evidently, the other face of its response to such rebellion and dissension had been to increase central control and to reduce local autonomy. (For extensive discussions on the Bale revolt, see Tareke, 1991: 125-59; see also Baxter, in Fukui and Markakis (eds.), 1994: 170).
57. Hassen, Mohammed.' The Macha-Tulma Association 1963-1967 and the Development of Oromo Nationalism', in Jalata (ed.), 1998: 213-14.
58. See the OLF Program, 1976.
59. Ibid.
60. Oromo Liberation Front, Central Committee: Statement on the Current Situation in Ethiopia, February 1992.
61. Cappelli, Vanni. 'The Oromo of Ethiopia- Africa's Nation Manqué'. Horn of Africa, Vol. XV, Numbers 1, 2, 3, 4, December 1997, p. 87.
62. Bereket, interview.
63. Markakis, 1987: 263.
64. Leenco Lata, 'The Making and Unmaking of Ethiopia's Transitional Charter', in Jalata (ed.), 1998: 52-53; however, the same author expressed a different opinion on the EPLF's role in the mediation talks between the OLF and EPRDF. He stated his disappointment as follows: There is no question that the EPLF leaders

were completely aware of TPLF/EPRDF violations of the bilateral agreements and did not pull their weight to deliver the promises they made to entice the OLF to join and invest in the transitional arrangement... when the agreement collapsed, the EPLF tried to shift the blame to the OLF for the failure of the co-operation that it reluctantly entered into mainly as a result of EPLF assurances and encouragements. Oromo political opinion that asserts that the EPLF partnership is restricted to their Tigrayan cousins is vindicated (Ibid., p. 67).

65. Tadele was later the leader of the Ethiopian army contingent to the Rwandan peace keeping mission of the United Nations in 1994-95.
66. Interviews with Seyoum, Berket, and Kinfe (Former Security Chief).
67. Ibid.
68. Leenco Lata, in Jalata (ed.), 1988: 53.
69. Ibid.
70. TPLF. The Oromo Question, 1986.
71. Leenco Lata, "Peculiar Challenges to Oromo Nationalism", in Jalata (ed.), 1998: 147.
72. Alex de Waal, in Gurdon (ed.), 1994: 33.
73. Cappelli, December 1997: 85.
74. Ras Gobena was Emperor Menelik's general of Oromo origin that played a major role in the conquest of the Oromo lands and other Southern regions.
75. OPDO.Results of the OPDO's initiative for the formation of a united front, 1992.
76. Baxter, in Fukui and Markakis (eds.), 1994, pp. 170-71.
77. See Joint Statement by the EPRDF, EPLF and OLF, London, May 28, 1991.
78. OLF. Statement at the conclusion of the London talks, May 29, 1991.
79. Leenco Lata, in Jalata (ed.), 1998: 60.
80. Ibid., p. 54 - 56.
81. Seyoum, interview.
82. Keller, in Zartman (ed.), 1995: 135.
83. See Proclamation No. 8/ 1992.
84. Bereket, interview.
85. Ibid.
86. Statement of the Executive Committee of the EPRDF, March 29, 1992.
87. See Minutes of the 32nd Regular Session of the TCR, January 22, 1992; and also the Report of the Defence and Security Standing Committee of the Council, January 1992.
88. OLF Central Committee. Statement on the current situation in Ethiopia, February 1992.
89. Alex De Waal, in Charles Gurdon ed., 1994, pp. 34.
90. See Minutes of the 44th Regular Session of the TCR, May 26, 1992.

91. Ibid.
92. See Minutes of the 40th Regular Session of the TCR, April 21, 1992.
93. Statement of the Southern Command of the Defence Forces, May 8, 1992.
94. Statement given by Leenco Lata, Deputy Secretary-General of the OLF, June 17, 1992.
95. OLF Central Committee. Statement of the Secretary General on the State of the Oromo People's Struggle, March 1, 1993.
96. Interviews with most of the EPRDF leaders indicate that the OLF failed to grasp the essence of the dynamics of the Ethiopian political environment; Tesfaye Habisso the leader of the Kembata People's Congress and former Secretary of the TCR also indicated similar reasons for the OLF's actions (interview, August 12, 1997).
97. See the Ethiopian People's Revolutionary Party Program, August 1975; All Ethiopia Socialist Movement (MEISON) and TPLF, Joint Statement, September 1987; Araia, Ethiopia: The Political Economy of Transition, 1995: 127; See also Markakis, National and Class Conflict in the Horn of Africa, 1987: 254-55.
98. See Minutes of the 14th Regular Session of the TCR, September 10 and 13, 1991.
99. Ibid.
100. Most of the political groups formed mainly by Amharas adopted the name Ethiopia and claim that they are multinational organisations. Even the All Amhara People's Organisation (AAPO) is registered as a countrywide organisation with the Election Commission.
101. See the Political Program of the AAPO, April 22, 1994.
102. SEPDC was formed by sixteen nationality-based groups of the Southern Region in March 1992. About ten organisations of the Coalition were members of the Council of Representatives until 1993. Some organisations that chose to remain as members of the government left the Coalition.
103. SEPDF was organised by more than twenty-three nationality-based groups and became member of the EPRDF in 1994. It has won the majority seats of the regional parliament and has been able to form the regional government.
104. See the Political Program of the SEPDC, April 2, 1994.
105. SEPDF Political Program, 1994.
106. The 'Paris Conference on Peace and Reconciliation' constituted by groups such as COEDF, OLF and other foreign-based organisations. Among the organisations that were members of the Transitional Government only SEPDC leadership participated. In the Conference resolutions such as the need to organise another broad-based transitional government was adopted and also blamed the EPRDF for irresponsibly disbanding the former armed forces.
107. For details of the debate and the full text of the resolution, see the Minutes of the 65th Regular Session of the TCR, March 18, 25, and April 1, 1993.
108. For details see Minutes of the 66th Regular Session of the TCR, April 8, 1993 and the Minutes of the 68th Regular Session of the TCR, April 27, 1993. The

most important point here is that the four organisations argued that they support the National Charter and they did not support the dissolution of the Transitional Government, but at the same time, they declared that they support the general message of the conference and the need to organise a peace and reconciliation conference in Ethiopia, which would allow the inclusion of the opposition groups in order to ensure peace and stability in the country. Nevertheless, in essence the statement called for the dissolution of the existing Transitional Government and for a change with a new one.

109. Resolutions of the National Conference for Peace and Reconciliation in Ethiopia, December 22, 1993.
110. IFLO was accused of masterminding the massacre of several people from the Yem nationality in the name of 'Jihad' in the Illubabor region. For details see the Minutes of the 46th Regular Session of the TCR, June 16-20, 1992 and the Report of the ad hoc committee sent to investigate the incident, May 20, 1992.
111. See letter written to the President of the Transitional Government by Abdulkarim Ibrahim, Chairman of the IFLO, August 13, 1993.
112. See Election Board, Political Parties that are Actively Participating in the Upcoming Elections, 2012.
113. The Federal Government has decided to form the Project Contract Administration Office within the fiscal year of 1997/98 in order to help the regional administrations of Afar, Somali, Benishangul-Gumuz and Gambella. The capacity building projects have also been continuing to address the serious shortages of manpower in these four regions.
114. Resolutions of the 4th Congress of ARDUF, October 3-4, 1997, Assayta, Afar region.
115. See Resolutions of the Founding Conference of the ANDP, November 3, 1999.
116. The Ethiopian Herald, Vol. LIV, No. 300, September 5, 1998.
117. The Western Somali Democratic Party, 1995.
118. Abdel Mejid Hussein, former Minister, interview, August 21, 1997.
119. Peter Gebriel, former Ambassador to EU, interview, October 2, 1997.
120. See the Ethiopian News Agency (ENA), June 27, 1998.
121. EPRP. Communiqué, May 10, 1991.
122. See EPRDF News Bulletin, December 5, 1991.
123. Resolution of the Third Emergency Session of the National Shengo of the People's Democratic Republic of Ethiopia, April 22, 1991; and see the Statement of the Executive Committee of the COEDF, April 24, 1991.
124. COEDF's statements were sending the wrong signal to other opposition groups, especially to those engaged in armed struggle. It was taken that COEDF was attempting to align itself with the Derg using whatever excuses surfaced in the rapidly changing circumstances. Its statement of May 21, 1991 that states "Mengistu was the main obstacle to the peaceful resolution of the conflicts in Ethiopia and the eventual transition of the country to a democratic state.

Therefore, COEDF views Mengistu's removal from power as an important positive step that could enhance the effort to bring about peace in Ethiopia" was perceived as a desperate declaration in search of rapprochement with the successors of Mengistu who were of similar credentials.

125. COEDF statement on the July 1, 1991 Conference in Addis Ababa, July 6, 1991.
126. The COEDF denied the allegations in its statement of June 22, 1991.
127. See Minutes of the 85th Regular Session of the TCR, January 3, 1994.
128. See the draft constitution of Ethiopia approved by the Council of Representatives, May 1994; for the details of the debate in the Council, see the Minutes of the 94th Regular Session, April 12-May 3, 1994.
129. See the Political Program Amendment of the Council of Alternative Forces for Peace and Democracy in Ethiopia, March 3, 1996.
130. Ibid.
131. See EPRP Communiqué, May 10, 1991.
132. At that time Dawit Yohannes (former Speaker of the Federal Parliament) and Berhane Gebre Christos (former Ambassador to the U.S) were sent to encourage various organisations and groups to join the new platform. They also met COEDF representatives but were told its resolve to continue its struggle in all means. (Seyoum, interview, August 16, 1997); See Alex de Waal, in Gurdon (ed.), 1994: 25; Henze, in Gurdon (ed.), 1994: 24; and see also the various statements made and press releases distributed by the opposition groups in Europe and North America. Alex de Waal argues that "this is of course an absurdity: if anything, the diplomatic intervention of the State Department under Ambassador Herman Cohen served to slow down rather than hasten the advance of the EPRDF. The EPRDF and EPLF had won the war in February and March following an extraordinary violent and protracted struggle over the previous decades and it only remained for the former government of President Mengistu Haile Mariam to acknowledge the fact". (Ibid.).
133. Dawit Yohannes, interview.
134. For details of the debate, see the Minutes of the 25th Regular Session of the TCR, December 2, 4 and 6, 1991.
135. The courses provided at the Hurso Rehabilitation Camp covered the government's policy of self-determination, how the Oromo cause should be addressed, issues of conflict between the government and the OLF, the benefits of peace and stability, the economic program of the government, the issue of integration into the society and other relevant issues. (See Ethiopian Herald, Vol. XLIX, No. 88, December 25, 1992).
136. Seyoum Mesfin, interview.
137. Negasso Gidada, former President and now opposition leader and Kuma Demeksa, Mayor of Addis Ababa, interview.
138. Ibid.

139. The OLF at its congress held in Mogadishu between May 12 and 18, 1998 made a radical change on the composition of its leadership. Prominent leaders such as Leenco Lata, the former deputy leader, Taha Abdi, Zegeye Asfaw, Tadesse Eba, Abiyu Geleta, Ibsa Gutema, Dima Nogo, Fekadu Wakjira, and Kuleni Gudina were dropped from the new elected national council. The above mentioned people were familiar to Ethiopian politicians, which had made it easier to communicate. On the other hand, the absence of personal acquaintance may present additional difficulties in the organisations' future attempt for reconciliation. (See The Indian Ocean Newsletter, July 18, 1998).
140. OLF, Central Committee. Statement on the Talks with the Regime in Ethiopia, October 13, 1997.
141. The OLF National Council. OLF Statement on the Current Ethio-Eritrean Conflict, May 21, 1998.
142. Meles, interview, September 2, 1997.
143. See House of Peoples' Representatives, Resolution No. 13/2011, June 14, 2011.
144. Tesfaye Habisso, interview.
145. Bereket, interview.
146. Tesfaye Habisso, interview.
147. BPLM. Letter to the TCR, October 16, 1991.
148. See Report of the Ad hoc Committee sent by the TCR, December 1991.
149. Minutes of the Regular Session of the TCR, January 22, 1992.
150. The BPLM army was later integrated to the national defence force at the end of the transitional period and the OLF army basically disappeared after its armed clashes with the EPRDF army, the national defence force for the transitional period.
151. For details of the Proposal, see EPRDF News Bulletin, 1 (2), March 5, 1991.
152. See Results of the Proposal for Creating Unity among Oromo Organisations, OPDO, 1991.
153. The statement of IFLO on its relations with the OLF, April 16, 1992.

Chapter 5

Main Constitutional Issues and Political Reforms

Political and constitutional reforms have started taking place since the convention of the June 1991 Conference on Peace and Democracy. As mentioned above, the Conference adopted the Transitional Period Charter, which became the first guiding document in initiating and implementing political reforms in the country. The political reforms carried out during the transitional period brought radical change to the structure of the government and its institutions precipitating a break with the past.

The reforms enacted and implemented during the four-year transition were reinforced by the adoption of a new constitution in 1994, paving the way for nation-wide elections and the establishment of an elected government. The Constitution confirms and enriches the restructuring of the Ethiopian State on the basis of a federal arrangement based on linguistic and cultural diversity of the people. It recognises the existence of diverse identities and uses them as the foundation of the new contract. It also contains vital provisions that establish numerous institutions safeguarding human and democratic rights, and promoting the rule of the law, and the evolvement of democratic governance.

The constitution serves as a tool to initiate institutional changes and innovation. The demanding challenge is to translate the written provisions into practice and consolidate and institutionalise the new achievements. A constitution will be declared successful when its provisions are well institutionalised and serve as a guide to the nation's political life. Nevertheless, it is evident that a successful adoption of constitutional reforms by itself is a step forward in the arduous task of realising a clear break with the past and institutionalising the new. In addition, the implementation activities have been progressing and new institutions have already taken their place although the institutionalisation process is at an early stage.

This part of the study discusses the major political and constitutional reforms that have mainly taken place after the Transitional Period. The constitutional drafting and ratifying process and the some of the contentious issues are addressed briefly. It also attempts to review the major political reforms and their implications, and their future prospects.

Ethiopia's Constitutional Experience

Constitutions are defined as "codes of norms, which aspire to regulate the allocation of power, functions and duties among the various agencies and officers of government, and to define the relationships between these and the public".[1] Wheare also defines a constitution as "the rules which establish and regulate or govern the government".[2] Hence, a constitution is a framework from which other items of law flow and from where they drive their validity. Moreover, it portrays how a state is constituted and operates.

Most states, with the exception of few such as the United Kingdom, have a written constitution and derive their laws and rules, at least theoretically, from the same document. Even in the United Kingdom, in spite of the lack of a single formally enacted constitutional document, there exists a wide-range of documents, which regulate the behaviour of the government. The Magna Carta of 1215, the Habeas Corpus Act of 1679, the Bill of Rights of 1689, the 1832 reform of the House of Commons and the 1911 reform of the House of Lords and the recent European Union laws are some of the constitutional documents that determine the activities of the government and the rights of citizens.[3] The various conventions and set of customs, in practice, play the role of a formally enacted constitutional document.

A written constitution is expected to contain rules that regulate the powers of the state in relation to society and at the same time allocate these powers to the major political actors. It mainly consists of rules that address four objects: (a) the nature of the state; (b) the rights of individuals; (c) the powers of the state; and (d) the process of changing the constitution.[4] However, the substance of constitutions and the various institutions that emerge as a result differ from country to country. As Lane indicated, the two crucial problems in writing constitutions are: the delineation of the overall powers of the state in relation to the individual, and the allocation of state powers between the major players, namely the legislative, executive and judicial branches.[5] Such delineation and allocation of powers are mostly affected by the relationship of various actors in the society, the nation's historical experience, and the external influence on the same society.[6]

The other important point is that a constitution has to be accepted by the people since a government draws its power and legitimacy to govern from the constitution. A constitution is in essence a contract between the government and the people. Hence, it must be comprehended and approved as fair, responsive and democratic. Calvert remarks:

> In the ultimate analysis, the constitution consists of those rules according to which effective government enjoys at least the minimum acquiescence of the vast mass subjects.[7]

As in the rest of Africa[8], Ethiopia's constitutional development has been disappointing and the one ratified in 1994, which came into full force in August 1995, has a long way to go before proving itself as an effective constitution, contributing fully to the political development of the nation.

The Ethiopian Constitution under the Imperial Regime

Ethiopia's experience with making formal written constitutions started in 1931[9] when Emperor Haile Selassie "granted" a constitution to the Ethiopian people.[10] The Constitution was enacted as a result of Ethiopia's interaction with the rest of the world and was driven by the desire of becoming a modern state and accepted as a "civilised" independent nation by the international community. Only a few years before that it became a member of the League of Nations, over some nations' objections that it was not " civilised enough" to join the club of the civilised nations.[11] However, the Constitution was designed to curb the power play of the nobility and the church and secure their formal subordination. The Constitution unequivocally declared that the sole basis of legitimate authority was the Emperor, and that all titles and appointments descended from him. Article 6 declares as follows:

> In the Ethiopian Empire supreme power rests in the hands of the Emperor. He ensures the exercise thereof in conformity with the established law.[12]

One of the significant innovations of the Constitution was the creation of the deliberative Chamber of the Empire: Chamber of the Senate and Chamber of the Deputies.[13] The role of the Chambers was limited to an advisory one and they were prohibited from initiating new laws or questioning the existing ones. Members from the nobility appointed by the Emperor constituted the Chamber of the Senate.[14] The selection for the Chamber of Deputies was not essentially different. Article 32 states as follows:

> Temporarily, and until the people are in a position to elect them themselves, the members of the Chamber of Deputies shall be chosen by the Nobility and the local Chiefs.[15]

The 1931 Constitution served more for the Emperor to polish his image internationally and weaken the other power players, the nobility and the church, than ensuring the rights of the people. In reality, it had little influence on the functions of the government and the way politics had been conducted in the Empire even after the Imperial restoration in 1941.[16]

In December 1950, the United Nations General Assembly approved the Federal Act that later federated Eritrea with Ethiopia. The Ethiopian Government along with the British and later the elected Eritrean Assembly approved the Eritrean Constitution drafted by the UN Commissioner for Eritrea in 1952. The Eritrean Constitution contained democratic principles and rights, which the 1931 Ethiopian Constitution was lacking.[17] In fact, it was one of the factors that forced the Emperor to revise the Constitution in 1955. Clapham indicates some of the factors, which made the constitutional revision essential:

> Firstly, the applicability of the 1931 Constitution to Eritrea was questionable, given that Eritrea had not been part of Ethiopia when it was introduced, and no explicit action had been taken to extend it to Eritrea. Secondly, the democratic principles of the Eritrean Constitution clashed embarrassingly with the absence even an elected legislative in the rest of Ethiopia. Thirdly, a new constitution could covertly be used to undermine the powers of the Eritrean government. Furthermore... the Ethiopian Empire was by the mid-1950s looking dangerously anachronistic in the light of the demands for self-determination then sweeping the rest of Africa.[18]

The Revised Constitution of 1955 was again another gift of the Emperor to his subjects on the twenty-fifth anniversary of his coronation.[19] The Constitution contained many of the political freedoms and rights of the Federal Act. However, it failed to mention the existence of a federal arrangement with Eritrea.[20]

Chapter 2 of the Constitution detailed powers and prerogatives of the Emperor, which indicated absolute power was vested in him. The Constitution incorporated provisions allowing the election of members of the Chamber of Deputies by universal adult franchise for a four-year term. On the other hand, the Senate remained the prerogative of the Emperor to fill it with his appointees.[21] The Parliament had mostly acted as a rubber stamp for imperial decrees and proclamations until nearer the demise of the monarchy, when some dissent voices were heard as a result of popular discontent and pressures. In addition, it was only in 1966 that the Emperor allowed the Prime Minister to nominate ministerial candidates for his approval.

In the early 1970s, public unrest and discontent continued to rise in many parts of the country. Student demonstrations mainly under the slogan of 'land to the tiller' and the growing sympathy of the rest of the population for their cause compounded with the worsening of the rebellion in Eritrea, shook the monarchy to its foundation and brought forward the question of its relevance to the Ethiopian people. The Emperor, threatened by the tide of change, offered to revise the constitution and appointed a Constitutional Commission in 1973. The draft constitution, which proposed the establishment of a constitutional monarchy, was finalised but it was too late to stop the brewing revolution. By the time the draft was published it was already obsolete. Popular demand had already been transformed to calls for a radical change and the total demise of the feudal regime.

The Military Government and Its Savour to Rule by Decree

In 1974, the Emperor was overthrown and the military junta suspended the Constitution. The Provisional Military Government issued Proclamation No. 1/1974 on September 12, 1974, which declared the overthrow of Emperor Haile Selassie and his replacement by the Crown Prince. Article 5 declared the suspension of the 1955 Constitution and promised to expedite the drafting process of a new constitution, which would be "suitable for the political, economic and social conditions of modern Ethiopia and appropriate to the respect and protection of human rights". On the other hand, Article 8 of the Proclamation banned any opposition against the military government's directives, labour strike, peaceful public demonstrations, and any "illegal" activities. Except for Article 8, all remained on paper and when the long awaited constitution came out in 1987, it was a replica of the other former Soviet bloc countries' constitutions.[21]

The military government declared that its guiding ideology was socialism as early as December 1974 and issued the Program of the National Democratic Revolution in April 1976. The Derg attempted to apply the Soviet model system in all sectors of social and economic activities. The 1987 Constitution was only an attempt by the government to gain legitimacy to what it was trying to implement for over a decade. A constitutional commission was formed to prepare the draft and discussions in neighbourhood associations were held under the supervision of the regime's notorious cadres. Finally, it was declared that the overwhelming majority of the people endorsed the Constitution in the referendum of February 1, 1987.[22]

The Constitution inaugurated the establishment of the People's Democratic Republic of Ethiopia as a state of the working people, designed to accomplish the National Democratic Revolution and lay the foundation for the construction of Socialism.[23] The Constitution also declared the Workers' Party of Ethiopia guided by Marxism-Leninism was the vanguard party dedicated to serve the working people and protect their interests.[24] As expected, Article 3 explained that the state would control key production, distribution and service enterprises, which legalised the massive nationalisation of private businesses after the government came to power in 1974. Commenting on the principal cause of the civil war, the Constitution recognised the existence of nationalities but reaffirmed that Ethiopia would remain a unitary state.[25] In the same Article the formation of regional autonomy was indicated, and subsequently, five 'autonomous' regions were mentioned, however, the Amharas, the Oromos and other nationalities were not on the list. It failed to be consistent with the recognition of the existence of various nationalities, and even for the mentioned candidates the intention remained on paper.[26]

Although the Constitution placed some division of power as a structure, the reality was that all powers converged into the hands of a single person. The Secretary General of the Worker's Party was also Chairman of the National Shengo (the parliament), the Executive President of the Republic and the Commander-in-chief of the armed forces. The President practically accumulated as much power as the Emperor except for the alterations of names and the rhetoric embodied in the Constitution. Failing to address the grievance of various nationalities, the civil war escalated and as a result the government collapsed in May 1991 with the entry of the Ethiopian Peoples' Revolutionary Democratic Front (EPRDF) to Addis Ababa.

Constitutional Experience after 1991

After a one-month rule of the Provisional Government of the EPRDF, a national conference was convened from July 1-5, 1991, in which various political organisations and groupings came together to discuss on the future of the country. The Conference adopted a Transitional National Charter, which laid out the rules governing the Transitional Government and detailed the principles for the Transitional Period. The Transitional Charter contained a number of principles, which signified a total break with the past. Some of the principles were quite controversial and became contentious issues when the Federal Constitution was drafted.[27]

One of the major commitments for change was manifested in Part Four of the Charter. The Council of Representatives, created in accordance with the spirit of the Charter, was entrusted with the formation of a Constitution

Commission to draft a new constitution. The Commission was expected to submit a draft to the Council of Representatives, which would present it to the people for discussion. After the draft constitution was finalised, the Charter required the election of a Constituent Assembly to ratify it.[28] The Council of Representatives debated the draft presented by the Commission from April 12 to May 10, 1994. As discussed above, the most contentious issues were the ones that divided the Commission in its drafting endeavour.[29] In both cases, Articles on self-determination, including secession and the right to property, the Council showed its preference by majority votes but decided to include both majority and minority positions in the draft constitution. The Council's intention was to present the Constituent Assembly with major trends on the above contentious issues not only in the Council itself but also in the society as a whole for its deliberations. Such decisions were made to expand the debate towards the majority position, which in fact later on allowed for more extensive debate from all directions of the political spectrum.[30]

Accordingly, the new Constitution was ratified by the Constituent Assembly on December 8, 1994, paving the way for national elections and the formation of the federal and regional state governments.[31] In fact, the Transitional Period did not come to an end as envisaged in the Charter, within the two-year period (or the two-and-a-half years if the need for an extension arose). It took almost four years for a national election to be held due to several factors that were difficult to predict during the convention of the National Conference. Difficulties related to security, devolution of power, the drafting process of the constitution and the preparation for national elections, were some of the challenges which contributed to the extension of the Transitional Period.

National elections were held on May 7, 1995 for regional and federal parliaments. The new parliament was convened and the Federal Democratic Republic of Ethiopia was inaugurated on August 21, 1995 bringing the Transitional Period to conclusion. As discussed above, the Transitional Period Charter of Ethiopia had served, for over four years, as the constitution of the country and became the basis for the new federal constitution and structure which is now in place.

Electoral System and Elections

Elections and electoral systems are two of the most important facets of democratic systems. Without both, it would be difficult to imagine the existence of a democratic system. Holding elections and adopting electoral laws alone are not sufficient to build democracy. Among other factors, elections should be competitive enough to at least solicit the respect of the contenders, the voters, as well as the observers.

Ozbudun details three conditions required to define competitive elections: "universal adult suffrage; fairness of voting as guaranteed by such procedures as secret ballot and open counting, as well as by the absence of a significant degree of electoral fraud, violence, or intimidation; and the right to organise as political parties and to put up candidates, which gives voters a choice among different groups of contenders, if not necessarily among different public-policy programs".[32] He further adds two factors required to identify the competitive elections held in democratic political systems as the periodicity and inclusiveness of the elections.[33] The electoral process needs to be institutionalised and it takes time to become well established. A level of acceptable competitiveness might not be attainable in a short span of time. It would be gradual, as the level of institutionalisation would be to a certain level determined by the outcome of the experiences acquired by the polity and the people as a whole.

Electoral systems are defined as the practical instruments through which notions such as consent and representation are translated into reality.[34] They determine how votes are translated into seats and they affect the behaviour of the voter. There are various types of electoral systems. They differ one from the other in the method by which they allocate seats. Accordingly, there are plurality, majority and proportional systems. Countries adopt one or a combination of two electoral systems depending on their internal conditions and on their perception that one or the other suits their country's situation.

The so-called plurality systems or first-past-the-post systems are linked to territorial representation and are aimed at producing a government. They are systems in which a candidate is awarded with a seat for winning the largest number of votes. Its main purpose is to manufacture a parliamentary majority based on the choice of government.[35] Similarly, majority systems are related to plurality systems but are aimed at avoiding the notion of a winning candidate with the largest minority vote. In order to produce a majority winner, there are two types of electoral systems: the alternative vote used, for example, in Australia and the second ballot, for example, used in elections for the French National Assembly.[36]

Proportional systems attempt to translate votes into seats proportionally. The two most widely used methods of proportional systems are the single transferable vote and the allocation of seats based on party lists. In the list system, the parties nominate lists of candidates in multimember districts. Voters are required to cast their ballots for one or the other party list and the seats are allocated to the party list in the proportion of the votes they have won. There are various ways of allocating votes practised in different countries, however, the general system is relatively constant world-wide.[37] The other system, the simple transferable vote, requires voters to cast their ballots to individual candidates. The voters are required to number the candidates in the order of preference.

The surplus votes to the quota collected by a candidate are allocated according to second preferences, and in the process, the candidates with the smallest numbers of votes are successively eliminated and the voters' preferences are redistributed until all seats are filled.[38]

The debate on choosing one or the other electoral system revolves on the number of parties it produces and its effect on the political stability of a country. Supporters of the plurality system evidence their choice on four factors: first, it helps elect a governing majority, and as a result a government; second, it reduces party fragmentation; third, it creates a more direct relationship between voters and their representatives; fourth, it improves the quality of the elected office holders.[39] On the other hand, it is criticised for being unrepresentative. The system seeks to produce effective government by manufacturing governing majorities. Critics indicate that the representative distortion possibly goes as far as allowing a party to win the absolute majority of seats without winning the largest number of popular votes.[40]

The proportional representation systems are upheld for several reasons: first, they are credited for reducing polarisation; second, they foster national alliances; third, they create a political climate in which it is easier to make and sustain fair claims; fourth, they encourage issue-based politics and make it possible for the parties to bargain over issues that cut across plural boundaries; and fifth, they promote coalition behaviours in spite of a tendency to generate multiple political parties.[41] On the other hand, proportional representation methods are criticised for producing weak governments; generating too many political parties; and complicating the calculation of election results.[42]

There are some who call for the adoption of the combination of both in order to benefit from the positive sides of these electoral systems. In fact, in some countries, both plurality and proportional methods are employed in combination. For example, in Germany the list proportional representation system is used for those who obtain at least 5 per cent of the popular vote to share the seats according to the votes they managed to collect. On the other hand, plurality elections are held for half of the seats, but the seats won are subtracted from the total number to which the party is entitled according to proportional representation. After these single-member district seats have been subtracted, the remaining seats earned by the parties are filled from party lists.[43] Similarly, Italy adopted a mix of 75 per cent plurality and 25 per cent proportional representation recently. As Sartori remarked, its plurality part has not produced any cohesive bipolar realignment, while its proportional part would maintain party fragmentation at damaging levels.[44] The left-wing coalition government, which came to power in the 1996 elections, had to depend on the good will votes of the Re-founded Communist Party to stay at the helm. Even in 2011 the government of Silvio Berlusconi fall down in the wake of debt crisis and sex scandals.

His party was dependent on the support of the Lega Nord and the right wing National Alliance. The defection of deputies to the opposition hastened his resignation. Apparently, the predicament of fragmentation and proliferation of parties seems to increase with little sign of abating.

As discussed above, there is no perfect formula for designing electoral systems. Each country designs what suits its conditions. It is also true that reforms of electoral systems are not easy since not all political parties will benefit equally from changes. Every party would strive to protect its advantages and it would not adopt a new one that costs it some seats. Nevertheless, it would be advisable for those who embark on a new beginning to be more flexible in adopting electoral rules that would produce stability as well as a reasonable level of representativeness, and gradually improve them based upon experience.

Electoral systems are highly connected with party politics. The existence and survival of parties depends on the electoral rules practised in the country. As discussed above, electoral laws play a significant role in the proliferation or regrouping of political parties and groups. On the other hand, they to a certain extent determine the "rules of the game" for elections. McDonald and Ruhl remark that "there is no such thing as a 'neutral' electoral system; whatever decisions are made will encourage some groups and restrain others".[45] Hence, they have to receive as much support as possible in the whole political spectrum, whatever changes are intended to be introduced.

The other salient feature of democratic systems is the accountability of the government once put in power by competitive elections. As Finer remarked, the primary meaning of democracy is the existence of a government, which is derived from public opinion and is accountable to it.[46] Hence, it would not be sufficient to win by competitive elections. The government's accountability should be checked through freedoms of speech, press, assembly and association as well as the right of the people to be informed. Besides, the checks and balances of various state organs, at a national or sub-national level, would contribute to this effect.

Ethiopia's Electoral System

The Ethiopian electoral system has been elaborated by several Proclamations since the establishment of the Transitional Government. First, Proclamation No. 64/1993 declares that any election should be based on free, direct and equal popular suffrage.[47] Furthermore, it embraces the plurality system by stating that "a candidate with more votes received than that by other competitors within the constituency shall be declared the winner".[48] The electoral law indicates that the constituencies should be based on the territory of the country taking districts (woredas) as a basis without affecting regional boundaries.[49] It also specifies that each constituency should be made up of one hundred thousand inhabitants.[50] However, it stipulates that minority nationalities which are believed, by the Council of Representatives or its successor, to require separate representation shall be made to elect and send their respective representatives.[51]

Proclamation No. 111/1995 confirms the plurality electoral system and other provisions mentioned in Proclamation No. 64/1993.[52] The electoral system has been reconfirmed by subsequent proclamations. The latest proclamation, Proclamation No. 532/2007 declares that "(a) candidate who received more votes than other candidates within a constituency shall be declared the winner."[53] As mentioned above, despite the Proclamations' insistence that the plurality system is the preferred method in elections, they also provide for the special representation of minority nationalities, which could not have the required number, one hundred thousand people, to elect a representative. Hence, the electoral law is not purely a pluralist system.

The electoral law was first enacted by the Council of Representatives, which was formed by organisations with variant political persuasions and programs. Both Proclamations were issued by the same transitional legislature. During the drafting and the ratification process of the Constitution, the electoral system was not considered a contentious issue. However, this does not mean that there exists a consensus about the system. There have been some complaints from certain opposition groups concerning the choice of the electoral system. They argue that the plurality system favours the largest party, the EPRDF, to win in most of the constituents. The smaller parties, which can garner some votes here and there, but unable to win a constituency are disadvantaged by the existing rules. Apparently, the proportional representation may enable them to win certain seats in parliament. Hence, they insist on changing the electoral system from the plurality one to a proportional representation method.[54] However, it is unlikely that the issue will soon come to the forefront of the political debate and change in favour of the opposition groups' argument and proposal.

Electoral Laws and Their Implementation

The elections for the establishment of the national/regional and woreda (district) councils were conducted in accordance with Proclamation No.7/1992, which established fourteen national/regional self-governments.[55] The regions were created by taking the borders of the woredas that existed prior to 1974 as the basis for delimitation. Similarly, the woreda constituencies were created on similar basis of the woredas that existed prior to 1974.

Building a conducive environment for elections required designation of the army that could serve as a national defence force, the encampment of other armies of liberation movements, and the establishment of the police force, Proclamation No. 8/1992 provided for the army of the EPRDF to serve as defence force for the Transitional Period. It also provided for the encampment of the armies of other liberation movements.[56] The Proclamation enabled national/regions self-governments to form their police forces to preserve peace and security in their respective regions. In addition to the above, Proclamation No. 9/1992 was issued to create the necessary conditions for the elections of national/regional administrations. It provided for the disarmament of former government and party officials but exempted those armed at their own expenses and who were able to produce proper evidence and license.[57] Furthermore, it detailed the criteria to be fulfilled by those organisations that claimed to have armies of their own.[58]

The Electoral Law in its full form was enacted by Proclamation No. 64/1993 after the first elections were held to establish regional and lower levels of administrations. The National Electoral Board, accountable to the Council of Representatives of the Transitional Government, was formed not only to conduct elections but also to have a judicial role concerning election complaints.[59] The Board was given far-reaching powers, including the power to interrupt the electoral process or nullify the electoral result and to order re-elections, as well as to rectify electoral irregularities and rule on complaints.[60] The Electoral Law upheld the woreda constituencies without affecting the regional boundaries and the one hundred thousand inhabitants' figure for each constituency. Furthermore, the special representation for minorities was reaffirmed.[61] Accordingly, 525 regular constituencies for the House of Peoples' Representatives and 22 minority nationalities' constituencies were created to bring the total figure to 547. The Transitional Council decided on which minority nationalities should be accorded the special representation at its 89[62] Regular Session. Minority nationalities with over ten thousand inhabitants were entitled to a special representation.[63] In the same Proclamation, it was stipulated that the members of the Constituent Assembly would be elected in accordance with the provisions in the Law, and the powers and duties of the Assembly were detailed.[64]

Subsequently, Proclamation No. 111/1995 was enacted to make the Electoral Law conform to the Constitution of the Federal Government. In addition to the textual changes and clarifications in certain cases, it adds some provisions to enrich the Law and omits others which have become obsolete. In Proclamation No. 64/1993, Article 46 provided for a government employee registered as a candidate with the right to be released from duty during the course of the election and with all employment benefits intact.[65] This provision was amended in the Proclamation No. 111/1995, which states "any government employee serving in any state administration, and any judge, public prosecutor, soldier or policeman shall, unless he is a political appointee, resign from his post if he runs for election as a private candidate or as a candidate of a political organisation".[66] The provision was enacted in order to protect the civil service from political intrusion. However, the Law does not forbid them from being members of political parties, short of assuming leadership roles or being visible activists.[67] Furthermore, Proclamation No. 120/1995 was issued to limit the ceilings on election expenses by a candidate; to clarify government assistance which may be provided to candidates; and also to establish an Election Assistance Fund that is to be administered by a board and finance the activities of candidates in accordance with the rules set by the same Proclamation.[68]

Proclamation No. 187/1999 and Proclamation No. 438/2005 were issued to amend the Electoral law.[69] The main objectives of the amendments were to make the law conform to the Constitution and also include some of the best practices of the past elections. Latest amendment was done by Proclamation No. 532/2007 to consolidate and clarify some of the provisions of the electoral law.[70] It further consolidates the rights of nations and nationalities to exercise their rights through their elected representatives. It also made inclusion and amendments of some provisions to bring them up to international standards and put in place instruments that enable political parties and individual candidates to play constructive role in dispute mitigation and resolving election result disagreements.

After thorough discussions and reached agreements, Proclamation No 662/2009 was adopted to bolster peaceful political struggle and civilized competitions. It contains code of conduct for political parties and their candidates; establishes joint council of the contending parties to promote dialogue, consultation and resolution of disputes on the process as well as results of the elections; enacts procedures of dispute resolution mechanism; and also explains the details of electoral violations and their means and processes of handling, and legal resolutions and measures.[71]

The Constitution confirms the establishment of a National Election Board, which is independent of any influence, and capable of conducting free and fair elections in federal and state constituencies in an impartial manner. Article 102 stipulates that the members of the Board should be appointed by the House of Peoples' Representatives upon recommendation of the Prime Minister.[72] In fact, the Constitution has only adopted what was practised during the Transitional Period. The Board has consistently insisted that it has accomplished its tasks impartially and prudently. However, every political group does not necessarily agree with the reports and claims of the Board. Some opposition groups have accused the Board of partiality and non-accommodative attitudes.[73]

The other issue worth mentioning is the party law and its implementation. In accordance with the Transitional Period Charter, Article 1(a),[74] Proclamation No. 46/1993 was enacted to implement the provision the right to association.[75] The Proclamation defines a political party as "a social group formed in accordance with this Proclamation by specified persons within the society having a program of its own reflecting its political belief and objective, and which participates in country-wide or regional political activities for the purpose of achieving political power through the democratic process".[76] It also details the criteria for the recognition of parties on a countrywide basis or on a regional one.[77] On the other hand, it bans groups that preach hatred and animosity among nationalities from organising themselves as parties, and armed groups and organisations inclined to achieve their goals using subversive means.[78]

The other requirement for a party to commence its activities is to register with the Office of Registration and receive a certificate of legal personality.[79] Sources of finance for political parties are detailed as membership dues collected from members; subsidy and grants from government; and donations from others.[80] Donations from foreign nationals, foreign government or foreign political parties, welfare and religious organisations, and prisoners of law are forbidden.[81]

Proclamation No. 82/1994 was issued to make some amendments to Proclamation No. 46/1993. Mostly, the amendment was introduced to bring the party law into conformity with the enactment of the Electoral Law. Part 6 of the previous Proclamation that provided for the objective and functions of the Registration Commission was replaced by a provision, which requires political parties to register with the National Electoral Board.[82]

The latest party registration law was enacted by Proclamation 573/2008. Articles 32-35 dwell on the union of parties, formation of front and the establishment of coalition of political parties. It explains that a front is an organization formed by two or more parties, without prejudicing each constituent party's individual legal existence, which decided to have a common name, political program and by-laws. The coalition is also defined as a temporary collaboration for defined an objective.[83] Furthermore, the Proclamation details the principles, objectives, and requirements for providing government financial grants and support to enable political parties to effectively participate in elections as well as run their day to day activities. It also enacts the accountability of parties and measures to be taken in time of non-compliance with the regulations and default of their obligation regarding the financial grant. [84]

In accordance with the Proclamations, 57 regional and 7 nation-wide political organisations were registered as of August 1997.[85] The numbers vary from time to time because of newly formed parties, the disappearance of some parties and the mergers among parties that have taken place due to similarities in political viewpoints and even as a survival strategy. As a result, there were 73 regional and 8 nation-wide organisations as of August 2002,[86] and similarly the number of national and regional political parties that were registered with the Electoral Board was 79 as of December 2012.[87]

Several elections have been conducted since the establishment of the Transitional Government. The first election was held on June 21, 1992 to establish regional and district (woreda) councils. It was the first multi-party election held in the country. The elected councils were to assume the duties and powers provided by the initial federal structure promulgated by Proclamation No. 7/1992. This was reinforced by Proclamation No. 41/1993, which defined the powers and duties of the central and regional governments, and by Proclamation No. 33/1993 which determined the sharing of revenue between them.[88]

The 1992 elections, although they introduced the era of the formation of government through democratic competition for the first time, were not free from controversy. The Oromo Liberation Front (OLF), one of the major actors in the Transitional Government, boycotted the elections alleging widespread intimidation.[89] Moreover, some irregularities were reported and the Transitional Council of Representatives formed an Election Review Board by Proclamation No. 21/1992.[90] The Review Board submitted its hearings and decisions on complaints filed by some political organisations and individual candidates, which were decided upon in the 55th Regular Session of the Transitional Council of Representatives.[91] As a result, some election results were annulled and re-elections were conducted to the satisfaction of the contenders. Nevertheless, the significance of the 1992 elections was that it was the first of its kind and it provided vital experiences to the Electoral Board, the political parties, and, above all, to the electorate.

The other major elections were conducted on July 5, 1994 for the convention of the Constituent Assembly to ratify the Constitution. The overall preparation and logistical distribution was better than the previous elections.[92] The debate on constitutional issues enabled many voters to distinguish various party positions from one another. The efforts made by the National Electoral Board to provide candidates with the opportunity to introduce themselves and their programs, through the media, to the electorate was better than before. Some opposition groups like the CAFPD chose to boycott the elections. They opposed the way and the manner the Constitution was being drafted and ratified. They accused the EPRDF of controlling all the countryside through the regional district administrations as a result of the June 1992 elections, which they considered fraudulent.[93] Accordingly, they thought the playground was in favour of the EPRDF.

The elections for the members of the Constituent Assembly were conducted as planned and there were a few complaints of irregularities submitted to the Board. These complaints included some illegal activities to deliberately restrict the forums by which a competitor could meet the electorate; doubt about the accuracy of the counting of ballots; violation of the secrecy of the voting process; instances of harassment of candidates.[94] These were addressed in accordance with the facts obtained during the investigations.[95] Elections were delayed for several weeks in the Somali region due to logistical problems. Finally, 547 representatives, including 22 representatives of minority nationalities comprised the Constituent Assembly that ratified the Constitution in December 1994.

Based on the new Constitution, the 1995 elections were conducted to end the Transitional Period and replace it with an elected government. The preparations seemed better than the previous elections. The platforms defining the positions of the various parties were discussed starting from the drafting process of the Constitution to the eve of the elections. Donor countries, especially the United States and the European Union member nations, worked hard to convince the opposition parties, which boycotted the elections for the Constituent Assembly, to participate in the important election that would determine the path of the country for at least five years. They encouraged the government to help the opposition groups open regional offices and work without political intimidation. On the other hand, the donor countries clearly indicated to some of the opposition forces such as COEDF, OLF, AAPO and SEPDU that non-participation would play an insignificant role in illegitimating the government in power. It was impossible to deny legitimacy of the elections by avoiding them.[96] However, the above-mentioned groups again decided to boycott the elections based on similar pretext.

Nevertheless, the elections were conducted as planned with the participation of several observer groups. The boycott of certain groups had an effect on the evaluation results of some of the observer groups. The absence of some strong contenders in many constituencies cast a shadow over the inclusiveness and competitiveness of the elections. The donor countries evaluated the elections as "technically right".[97] In their report, they declared that "elections however, are about choice. For the reasons stated in this report, the ability of the Ethiopian people to use the ballot effectively to choose their leaders is still limited. Until alternative political organisations participate, however, such choices will remain restricted".[98]

However, they recognised the efforts of the government to accommodate the opposition forces in order to encourage broader participation.[99] They were dissatisfied by some of the opposition groups, especially the SEPDU's decision to boycott the elections. The European Union also declared that "its desire to see Ethiopia fully and definitively embarked on the democratic path".[100] Apparently, the statement indicates that though the process is on the move, more has to be done in order to make the path irreversible.

On the other hand, the Organisation of African Unity (OAU) pronounced the elections as free and fair.[101] Of course, some irregularities were reported in some districts; however, the boycott issue seemed to influence the donors in passing their judgement. Many people seem to agree in calling it the first democratic election, but there was also agreement that there was room for further improvement in the future elections.[102]

The elections for the House of Representatives and Regional State Councils were conducted simultaneously. There were 547 constituencies, including 22 minority nationalities for the House of Representatives and 569[103] constituencies for the Regional Councils, which presented a strong challenge not only to the supply of election logistics but also to monitoring the elections and rectifying any deviation from the rules and regulations set by the Proclamations and the National Electoral Board. It was a difficult venture for a country with little exposure to competitive elections and inexperienced institutions to administer and run them properly. Considering the situation, it would have been strange not to have observed some shortcomings in the preparation as well as in the conduct of the elections. With all its weaknesses, it would be proper to call them the first democratic elections, but needing further improvement both in the application of the rules and regulations of conducting elections, and in the inclusiveness of various alternatives. The task will need the co-operation of both the government and the opposition parties, including those which boycotted the elections.[104] The opposition will be required to have a strategy to win seats in the parliament and regional councils and to commit their long-term contribution towards strengthening democracy, and developing a culture accommodating diversity.

In the second national election of May 14, 2000, the main opposition parties participated, which meant more realistic competition. Although the country was at war with Eritrea, it was decided to hold elections according to the established schedule. Opposition parties came up with better organisational and campaign strategies. They rigorously challenged the ruling party in substantial numbers of constituencies, especially in Addis Ababa and the Southern Ethiopian Peoples' Regional State. There were reports of intimidation and harassment prior to the election date in some constituencies, especially in Southern Ethiopia's Hadya, Sidama and North Omo zones. Although the election went relatively well in most of the constituencies, similar problems persisted in the above-mentioned zones, and as a result, the Election Board was forced to stop the voting process or annul the outcome in some areas.[105]

Consequently, re-elections were held in 16 constituencies of the Southern Ethiopia Regional State on June 25, 2000, in which the opposition won most of the seats. Similarly, re-elections were held in one constituency in the Harari regional state on July 23, 2000.[106] Although rectified, the attempt made to rig the elections in these constituencies showed that there were still major deficiencies in the democratisation process, which required more attention. The problems might arise from lack of democratic culture and commitment to the democratic process, but they were also a product of the limited economic space in the country, in which elected officials were tempted to cling to power using any means available. Some local officials might feel that they had little opportunity of employment if they lost their offices.

One important point was, although the lower house was still dominated by the ruling party, the opposition, independents and non-EPRDF parties had a total of 68 members out of 547. The opposition had been able to use the parliament forum to oppose government policies and practices. The problem that continued to persist was the opposition's lack of an alternative coherent strategy and program of action.

The 2005 election were conducted in a different environment from the past elections. Both the ruling party and the opposition took the elections seriously and had early preparations. The EPRDF taking lessons from the past elections decided to make the 2005 elections as much as possible free and fair. It unilaterally issued code of conduct regarding campaigning and relations with the opposition to provide no excuse for sceptics. Moreover, the EPRDF decided to use the election process in addition to promoting the democratic process for image building. It was hopeful to show the world that the democratic process was gaining momentum. In order to create conducive atmosphere for a free and fair competition, the EPRDF pushed for negotiations to improve the electoral law as well as to formulate agreed code of conduct for all contenders.

The United Ethiopian Democratic Forces (UEDF) negotiated and signed an agreement on the amendment to the electoral law except on the one issue of electoral system. The UEDF prefers the proportional representation while the EPRDF has been in favour of the first-past-the-post system. The negotiations were held after over a decade of distance, hence, it was taken by many as a good sign of civility. On the other hand, the other major opposition group, the Coalition for Unity and Democracy, was not willing to negotiate with the EPRDF by indicating it wanted to talk with the government. The Coalition did not want to commit itself to agreed code of conduct, as it was harbouring the option of waging a "colour revolution". From the start, there were signs of defying the law to achieve their objectives, which was not only usurping power but also throwing out the constitution.[107]

The debates between the parties were held for almost nine months and covered all relevant issues. It was a good opportunity for the Ethiopian people to know the diverse stances of the political parties. However, the opposition was mainly keen in exploiting and aggravating the grievances of the people, especially the youth against the ruling party. The youth was not able to see the light at the end of the tunnel as the economic benefits and creation of jobs were at their initial stage. With election day approaching, the situation between the ruling party and the opposition became tense and there were already agitations of civil disobedience indicating signs of rejecting whatever the outcome of the election would be.

The elections were not smooth as they were held under high tension and suspicion. The opposition almost won Addis Ababa except for one seat in the city administration council. It was able to win significant number of seats all over the country, especially in major cities and towns. The Coalition for Unity and Democracy (CUD) won 109 seats while the United Ethiopian Democratic Forces won 52. However, the EPRDF retain its majority by winning 327 seats, which was 59.8 per cent.[108]

Both the ruling party and the opposition complained that there were election rigging, harassment and misconduct. The opposition claimed there were election fraud in 299 constituents, meaning in all they were defeated. On the other hand, the ruling party complaint was on 22 constituents. Notwithstanding, the opposition were only able to support their claims with evidence on 144 constituents while the ruling party presented on 19. The surprising assertion was the opposition claimed that they won in 127 polling stations in which they never participated in the first place. In the end, the Election Board decided re-election in 31 constituents.

On August 21, 2005, the re-run elections in 31 constituencies, and elections for the House of Representatives and the State Council of the Somali State were held. In the re-run elections, the EPRDF won in all 31 constituencies and able to get additional 24 seats in the House of Peoples' Representatives. In addition, the EPRDF allied Somali People's Democratic Party (SPDP) won all 23 seats to the House of Peoples' Representatives and 161 out of 182 seats in the regional council.[109]

All observers agreed the pre-election and the Election Day process were without any major shortcomings. The problem started during the tabulation period and declaration of results. The EU Election Observation Mission (EU EOM) declared that voting on 15 May was conducted in a peaceful and largely orderly manner, the counting and aggregation processes were marred by irregular practices, confusion and a lack of transparency.[110] On the other hand, the Carter Centre Observation Team explains that "the majority of the constituency results based on the May 15 polling and tabulation are credible and reflect competitive conditions. However, a considerable number of the constituency results based on the problematic CRB[111] and CIP[112] processes lack credibility."[113] As can be deducted from the two statements, the EU Election Observation Mission's message was totally negative while the Carter Centre's assessment was more or less balanced.

The ruling party vehemently rejected the total admonition of the EU EOM. The EPRDF explains that the report didn't reflect the situation on the ground but it was an instrument for other hidden objective. It was reported the

EU EOM leader was pushing for the establishment of a "unity government" that would allow the opposition groups to have a role in the new government.[114] Such overture of the mission was unacceptable to the ruling party. The ruling party accepted that there were some problems here and there but were not significant enough to annul the outcome of the elections.

Apparently, the opposition's wining of 174 seats was not the result of the electorate support for their policies and programs. It was a protest vote against the EPRDF rule.[115] However, they were not content with their gains and increases from 12 seats in the past parliament to 174 seats, which was 32 per cent of the total seats. In addition, they were able to absolutely dominate the capital city administration. Instead of using their windfall as leverage for future victory, they decided to agitate the people, especially the youth that they were robbed their victory by the ruling party. Such fermentation of unrest and disinformation led to violent street protests, which resulted in bloodshed and destruction of property. The House of Peoples' Representatives established investigation commission reported that six policemen and 193 civilians were killed, and 71 policemen and 763 civilians sustained light and heavy wounds in the riots between June and mid-November 2005 in Addis Ababa and several towns. Millions worth of property was destroyed.[116]

As a result, the government decided to incarcerate the leaders of the riot and 35 leaders of the opposition were persecuted and sentenced for life and others to serve terms by the high court on July 16, 2007. They were later pardoned after they plead guilty and asked for clemency. [117] The main purpose of the pardon was taken as an important step to leave behind the chaos and recrimination of the past and looked forward towards the future.

As discussed above, the 2005 elections were marred with controversies and violence. The ruling party's desire of moving forward with democratic process and building the image of the country was faced with setback. The opposition was preoccupied with its plan of usurping power either by ballot or street protest. The opposition lacked the vision of using its gains to further expand its influence on the population and start preparing to win the next elections. The hidden ambition of waging "colour revolution"[118] blinded them to properly assess the situation, and decide on the right path that would strengthen their position. In the end, the CUD leadership decided to boycott parliament and reject the offer of taking over the Addis Ababa administration. It was a fateful decision that shadowed on the emergence of a credible loyal opposition.

On the other hand, the UEDF, the Oromo Federalist Democratic Movement and one of the CUD member organizations, the United Ethiopian Democratic Party-Medhin Party and some individuals from the other CUD member organizations decided to take their seats in the House of Peoples' Representatives. Notwithstanding, the chance of having a formidable opposition group in parliament was lost. The EPRDF prepared a draft, based on international experience, to make parliamentary discussions, debates and procedures more democratic and participatory. The draft was then discussed with parliamentary opposition groups. After long negotiations, the House of Peoples' Representatives adopted the agreed draft rules to conduct its day to day business.[119] In addition, Addis Ababa was left for a care-taker administration until it was replaced by an elected one after two years.

The election results gave proper lessons to the ruling party. The overall message was unless it hastens the progress of the economic growth and ensures the benefit of the population from the economic development, the peace and stability of the country would be at risk. Secondly, the results also reminded it that it should better communicate with the population, and listen and improve problems of governance in its ranks, especially in the lower levels of government.

The 2010 elections were held in a very different environment from that of the 2005 elections. The EPRDF after the 2005 elections held neighbourhood, town and village meetings and discussed on the grievances of the people. Learning from the opinions of the participants, it improved its policies, rectified errors of governance and also promised to deliver better results in its socio-economic endeavours. It has also worked on the youth and women by trying to address their role in the development of their country.

As a result, popular participation in the business of their communities improved; the economy continues to grow registering its seven year of double digit growth; jobs creation especially organizing and supporting macro and small business gained momentum; efforts made to solve housing problem started showing results as condominiums have been made available to urban residents; and massive infrastructural projects were constructed and some were also under construction improving provided services. All in all, people started to witness significant improvement and were already longing for better and larger achievements.

On the other hand, the opposition after squandering its election results in 2005 were almost in disarray. They were not still organized enough to present alternative policies and development directions to the electorate. Secondly, they had little at hand to mobilize protest votes as the socio-economic change started, to a certain extent, benefit the people as well as the promise of growth and poverty eradication has begun to sound lauder.

The 2010 elections provided the EPRDF and its allies with almost total victory. Only one independent, one opposition, and one from a very small organization named the Argoba People's Democratic Organization (APDO) candidates won seats in the House of Peoples' Representatives. The EPRDF and its allies won 544 of the 547 seats in the House.[120] The EU EOM as usual alleged that "the electoral process fell short of international commitments for elections...".[121] On the other hand, the African Union Observer Mission declared "the Ethiopian Legislative Elections were organized and conducted in accordance with the constitutional and legal provisions and the rules and regulations governing the conduct of election in the country and were largely consistent with AU guidelines and standards for the conduct of democratic elections."[122] Notwithstanding, all agreed that the elections were peaceful and better organized than before.

The overwhelming victory of the EPRDF indicates that the people wanted to see faster economic growth, poverty reduction, good governance and accelerated social transformation. It was an acknowledgement for the results so far achieved but it was, at the same time, an obvious demand for better performance in all fields in the next five years. Apparently, the people's patience for low performance and bad governance seems extremely low. Hence, the EPRDF is expected to deliver its promises of economic growth, poverty reduction, democratic system and good governance, and social transformation. That is the Ethiopia which graduated from the least developed country's classification.

Separation of Powers and the Independence of the Judiciary in Ethiopia

The Concept of Separation of Powers and Independence of the Judiciary

The emergence of the concept of separation of powers goes back to the 17th and 18th centuries. The two leading political theorists of the time, Locke and Montesquieu, discussed the concept of divided powers in the hands of separate state organs. Although they had different approaches, they agreed on the necessity of a separation of powers in the modern state based upon the rule of law.[123] Montesquieu explained why he favours a constitution embodied with the separation of powers:

> All would be lost if the same man or the same body of principal men, either of nobles, or of the people, exercised these three powers: that of making the laws, that of executing public resolutions, and that of judging the crimes or disputes of individuals.[124]

Modern democratic constitutions, in one way or the other, adopted the concept of the separation of powers in their task of combating tyranny, and strengthening democracy and the rule of law. The theory of separation of powers suggests the means by which state power is constrained by allocating specific competence to the main organs of the state: the legislature, the executive and the judiciary.[125] The separation of powers is one of the methods of political checks and balances, which are important to promote individual and group fundamental rights and freedoms. Other methods are the creation of two Houses of Parliament and the devolution of powers. Finer explains that "the essential point of all of these devices - the separation of powers, the creation of Upper and Lower Houses, territorial division or devolution of powers - is to bring friction, delay and the necessity for consultation and compromise into the operation of government".[126]

In the concept of the separation of powers, the independence of the judiciary has received close attention recently. The Basic Principles on the Independence of the Judiciary endorsed by the General Assembly of the U.N. in 1985 is one of the conventions on the issue of human rights in the administration of justice.[127] Judicial independence signifies that the judiciary has to be shielded from any executive pressures and legislature interference. The concept also comprises the notion of internal independence within the judiciary itself, meaning the independence of the judge from his judicial colleagues or superiors.[128]

Several scholars attempt to define the concept of judicial independence in terms of impartiality of the judiciary and its insularity from any political interference. Rosenn defines judicial independence as "the degree to which judges actually decide cases in accordance with their own determinations of the evidence, the law and justice, free from the coercion, blandishments, interference, or threats from governmental authorities or private citizens".[129] Similarly, Taipale defines judicial independence as a concept in which "the organs administering justice can only be subordinate to the law, and that only the law can influence the contents of the decisions made by these organs. No other state authority, not even the highest, is allowed to influence the decisions made by the judicial organs".[130] After reviewing other definitions Larkins attempts to define it as follows:

> Judicial independence refers to the existence of judges who are not manipulated for political gain, who are impartial toward the parties of a dispute, and who form a judicial branch which has the power as an institution to regulate the legality of government behaviour, enact "neutral" justice, and determine significant constitutional and legal values.[131]

Separation of Powers in Ethiopia

In Ethiopia, the Constitution does not provide for the full separation of powers. It is stipulated that the form of government of the Federal Democratic Republic of Ethiopia is a parliamentary one.[132] The House of Peoples' Representatives is the highest authority of the Federal government, and its powers are limited to the functions of the centre determined by Article 51 of the Constitution.[133] Although the Constitution provides for the three branches of government, the executive is established by a party or a coalition of political parties that has the greatest number of the seats in the House of Peoples' Representatives.[134] The fusion of the legislature and the executive, which exists in many parliamentarian democracies, is also reflected in the Constitution.[135] Members of the executive can also be members of parliament, which is in contrast to the United States' rule of separation of personnel between the three branches of government.[136]

The President is the head of the state but has little executive powers.[137] He is nominated by the House of Peoples' Representatives and is elected by a two-thirds majority vote of the joint session of the House of Peoples' Representatives and the House of the Federation.[138] If the elected President is a member of either House, he is required to vacate his seat.[139] The highest executive officer of the government is the Prime Minister.[140] Article 72 (2) states that "the Prime Minister and the Council of Ministers are responsible to the House of Representatives".[141] This Article clearly indicates that the parliament is supreme and the executive has to rely on its support to stay in power. Moreover, Article 73 (1) affirms that the Prime Minister should be elected from among members of the House of Peoples' Representatives, and in contrast to the President, continues to keep his seat in the House.[142]

As in some parliamentary democracies, the Prime Minister's dependence on the vote of confidence of the legislature is not counter-balanced by an outright power of dissolution of parliament by the Prime Minister. Article 60 (1) states that "with the consent of the House, the Prime Minister may cause the dissolution of the House before the expiry of its term in order to hold new elections".[143] As indicated, the Prime Minister needs the agreement of Parliament for its dissolution, and it can reject the call and form a new government to replace the outgoing one. Accordingly, Article 60 (2) confirms that the President may invite political parties to form a coalition government within one week. It is only if the legislature fails to agree to the continuation of the previous coalition or to form a new majority coalition, that it would be forced to dissolve.[144] Such provisions are, to a certain extent, similar to the German Constitution, Article 68 (1), where the Bundestag can reject the dissolution by electing a new Chancellor to replace the outgoing one within twenty-one days.[145]

The Independence of the Judiciary in Ethiopia

The Ethiopian Constitution declares that an independent judiciary is established and judicial powers both at federal and state levels, are vested in courts.[146] It is also indicated that supreme federal judicial authority is vested in the Federal Supreme Court and that the House of Peoples' Representatives may, by two-thirds majority vote, establish the Federal High Court and First-Instance Courts where they are needed.[147] Similarly, the states are also required to establish State Supreme, High and First-Instance Courts.[148] However, it is forbidden by the Constitution to set up special or ad hoc courts, which take judicial powers away from the regular courts.[149] The only exceptions are religious and customary courts that had state recognition and functioned prior to the adoption of the Constitution, and the federal and state legislatures may also recognise or establish such courts in the future.[150] The overall direction is a new trend in the Ethiopian justice system. There has never been a situation where the independence of the judiciary was respected. Practically, the judiciary was being administered as a department under the Ministry of Justice until recently.[151]

The Constitution provides for the insularity of the courts from any interference or influence of other government bodies.[152] Judges are supposed to perform their powers and functions in full independence and should be directed solely by law.[153] The other provision considered enhancing to their security of tenure states that judges should not be removed from duties before reaching the retirement age determined by law.

Judges can be removed not simply by the decisions of the Judicial Administration Council but such decisions must be endorsed by the legislature.[154] The provision provides for a stringent process in order to strengthen their sense of security and gives "the judiciary a very important and independent chance to develop the legal system".[155]

As in many constitutional democracies, the judges are nominated by the executive to be appointed by the legislature.[156] Article 81(1) states that the President and Vice-President of the Federal Supreme Court are appointed by the House of the Peoples' Representatives upon recommendation by the Prime Minister.[157] The other federal judges are selected by the Federal Judicial Administration Council and submitted by the Prime Minister to be appointed by the House.[158] Similarly, the State Councils upon the recommendation by the chief executives of the states appoint the Presidents and Vice-Presidents of the State Supreme Courts.[159] State Supreme and High Court judges are also selected by the State Judicial Administration and appointed by the State Council. In these selections, the views of the Federal Judicial Administration Council are required unless it failed to provide such views within three months.[160]

Furthermore, the Constitution attempts to make the courts financially independent of the executive. The Federal Supreme Court should draw and submit the budget for the Federal Courts to the House of Peoples' Representatives for approval and is responsible for administering it.[161] The State Supreme Courts should also follow the same procedures.[162] The House of Peoples' Representatives is also required to compensate for the expenses state courts incur in adjudicating disputes on federal matters.[163]

Proclamation No. 24/1996 established the Federal Judicial Administration Commission to implement the constitutionally guaranteed independence of the Judiciary.[164] The establishment of such an institution, which is envisaged to be free from the influence of other organs of government, is the first of its kind in the country. In the past, there had been a judicial commission that was led by the Ministry of Justice, which made it an appendage of the executive.[165]

Proclamation No. 24/1996 was amended by Proclamation 684/2010 to further insure the independence of the judiciary, widen the council's composition by including members from civil society, and better institutionalize it by providing the necessary structures.[166] In addition to the President of the Federal Supreme Court, the Vice President of the Federal Supreme Court, three members of the House of Peoples' Representatives, the Minister of Justice, the President of the Federal High Court, the President of the Federal First Instance Court, and a judge selected by all the federal judges, it also includes a lawyer, a law academic and a distinguished citizen appointed by the Council to its ranks.[167] It is also indicated the representation of women should be ensured.[168] Apart from selecting nominees to the federal courts and forwarding opinions on regional court nominees, the Council has the power to issue Disciplinary and Code of Conduct Rules for federal judges, and to decide on the transfer, salary, allowance, promotion, medical benefits and placement of federal judges.[169] The Proclamation also institutionalizes the function of the Council by providing for the establishment of a secretariat. The secretariat receives complaints and petitions and disseminates decisions render on them to the concerned persons and organs. It, in general, follows up the day to day functions of the Council.[170]

In the Constitution, it is stipulated that the Federal Supreme Court should have the highest and final judicial power over federal matters while the State Supreme Courts have similar powers over state matters.[171] The Federal Supreme Court has the constitutional authority, in cassation, to review and correct any final decisions of a "basic error of law".[172] This was further elaborated by the amendment to Proclamation No. 25/1996. Proclamation No. 454/2005, Article 4 denotes that "interpretation of a law by the Federal Supreme Court rendered by the cassation division with not less than five judges shall be binding on federal as well as regional courts at all levels."[173] It also obliges the Federal Supreme Court to publish and distribute decisions of the cassation division that contain binding interpretation of laws to all levels of courts and other relevant bodies.[174] The State Supreme Courts are also delegated to hear cases that fall under the jurisdiction of the Federal High Court, matters within the prerogatives of the Federal Government but arising in the states. This provision helps to expedite court decisions and minimise difficulties arising from travelling long distances as courts within the states handle the cases. Later on considering the constraints in available capacity, the House of Peoples' Representatives in accordance with Article 78(2) of the FDRE Constitution decided to establish federal high courts in the relatively less developed regions.[175] Proclamation No. 322/2003 provides for the establishment of Federal High Courts in Afar, Benishangul, Gambella, Somali and Southern Nations, Nationalities and Peoples.[176]

Proclamation No. 25/1996 specifies the jurisdiction of the federal courts.[177] Article 3 of the Proclamation states that the federal courts should have jurisdiction over: cases arising under the Constitution, federal laws and international treaties; parties specified in federal laws; and places specified in the Constitution or in federal laws.[178] Furthermore, the criminal and civil jurisdiction of the federal courts is detailed in order to delineate their functions from that of the state courts.[179] The other point worth mentioning is the Federal Supreme Court Plenum, which comprises the President, the Vice-President and judges of the Supreme Court, the Presidents of the Federal High Court and the Federal First Instance Court, and the Presidents of Regional State Supreme Courts.[180] In this Plenum the Minister of Justice and other representatives of appropriate institutions can participate without the right to vote.[181] The Plenum can deliberate on the difficulties encountered by the judiciary and work out remedies. It can also examine and approve directives, regulations and decisions that help to improve judicial practices, and also submit proposals to the legislature for the enactment of new laws or an amendment to the existing laws.[182] This Plenum exchanges experiences and opinions, and works towards making the judiciary strong as well as efficient.

In the States, the judicial branch is comprised of the state supreme court, zonal high courts and woreda (district) courts. As mentioned above, the state supreme courts have the highest and final jurisdiction over state matters.[183] The state constitutions also provide for the establishment of kebele (neighbourhood) social courts. The judges of these social courts are elected by the kebele shengo (council) and their term of office is similar to the term of the council of the kebele, which in most of the states is five years.[184] These courts are essential to solve many but small and time-consuming cases, which arise from day to day interactions among people who reside in relatively small surroundings.

According to the Constitution, the courts are required to submit cases that need constitutional review to the Council of Constitutional Inquiry, which in turn has to present its recommendations to the House of the Federation for final decisions.[185] It is argued that as the Constitution is a contract between various nations and nationalities in Ethiopia, it would be safe to treat constitutional disputes politically since legal deliberations can possibly create a deadlock on the peaceful resolution of conflicts.[186] The state constitutions also provide for similar mechanisms for the purpose of the interpretation of their respective constitutions. The ultimate interpreters of state constitutions are the State Councils, which are the legislatures of the Regional States.[187]

As discussed above, the Constitution and the relevant Proclamations provide essential provisions for the emergence and development of an independent judiciary. However, much remains to be done not only by the judiciary but also by the legislature and the executive to promote the quality and the integrity of the country's judges. The challenges facing the judiciary are mainly constraints of human and material resources. Although the judiciary has to prepare its budget, the legislature has to approve it in relation to the needs of the other organs of the state and the availability of resources. It is difficult to expect that an adequate budget could be allocated to the judiciary in cash-starved countries like Ethiopia. The resources are always inadequate in spite of the significant increases made in the past few years. As for building human resources capacity, the government has established training centres for judges, prosecutors, and other professionals of the justice system which have been active in the last few years.[188] The graduates from these centres have been filling the gap created by shortage of trained people. It is reported that signs of improvement are gradually materialising and the prospect for the consolidation of the judiciary in the coming years appears brighter.

Fundamental Rights and Freedoms

The concept of human rights has started to occupy an important place in the international arena after the Second World War. The horrendous crimes carried out during the war have brought the issue of protecting individuals from their states and other abusers to the forefront.[189] The signing of the United Nations Charter in 1945 can be considered a benchmark of initiatives to protect the rights of the individual. The adoptions of a number of international treaties and conventions, which have become instrumental in the promotion and protection of human rights and human dignity, have followed the Charter.

The notion and scope of human rights have been changing and expanding with the ever-changing and developing situations on our planet.[190] Certainly, the advocacy for human rights has benefited from the end of the Cold War. The campaign for promoting and protecting human rights has gained momentum and drawn the attention of governmental and non-governmental actors. However, there are still persistent problems in finding a full global consensus on the meaning and substance of human rights because of the cultural, economic and political diversity within the international community.[191] The main purpose of the various Conventions and Declarations of the United Nations[192] is the protection of the individual's rights from abuse, in particular by state institutions. Accordingly, every person has certain rights that are inherent and should be enforceable in courts of law. Malanczuk notes that "every individual has certain inalienable and legally enforceable rights protecting him or her against state interference and the abuse of power by governments".[193]

In Ethiopia, after the demise of the military government, the Transitional Charter as a "mini-constitution" for the Transitional Period, it contained the main political, economic and social policies of the government. The Charter adopted the Universal Declaration of Human Rights and attempted to use it to restore peace and dismantle the institutions of dictatorship. Article One of the Charter declares as follows:

> Based on the Declaration of Human Rights of the United Nations, adopted and proclaimed by the General Assembly by resolution 217 A (III) of 10 December 1948, individual human rights shall be respected fully, and without any limitation whatsoever. Particularly every individual shall have:
> a) The freedom of conscience, expression, association and peaceable assembly;
> b) The right to engage in unrestricted political activity and to organise political parties, provided the exercise of such right does not infringe upon the rights of others.[194]

During the Transitional Period, the Council of Representatives ratified the International Covenant on Civil and Political Rights, the International Covenant on Economic, Social and Cultural Rights, and the Convention Against Torture and Other Cruel, Inhuman or Degrading Treatment or Punishment.[195] Although the Transitional Government was occupied with the most important tasks of restoration of peace, stability and the rule of law, it made substantial strides in opening the system and encouraging the participation of the people in the political process.

As the transition was difficult and complex, there were reports of human rights abuses, (although most of them were not verified). In the aftermath of the change of government, it was not easy to put in place administrative structures that had collapsed during the war. The organisation of the police force and other law and order institutions took time. In the meantime, the task of policing fell on the shoulders of the EPRDF army. Although known for their discipline and good manners, the fighters were not trained for police duties.

The situation was also aggravated by some political organisations that were members of the Transitional Government but were acting in opposition. One of these organisations was the Oromo Liberation Front, which was responsible for many atrocities in the Oromia region.[196] Consequently the government had the task of controlling not only its own structures but also the activities of other fronts, which, especially in the early days, were acting as the ultimate power in their "liberated areas".

As mentioned above, there were visible developments in encouraging political participation of the people and respect for human rights. However, it would be naive to assume that there would not be any human rights violations in a country where there has not been any tradition of democracy, and which was traumatised by civil war and horrifying experience under a cruel military dictatorship. As the U.S. Department of State reported in 1995; "the Government continued its stated commitment to human rights but serious problems remain. There were credible reports that members of the security forces physically abused some criminal suspects and detainees, although these practices do not appear widespread".[197]

Although Sorenson's details of human rights abuses were taken from opposition reports and appear to be exaggerated, the conclusion he draws illuminates the situation further:

> Clearly, the transition to democracy was not a smooth one. However, it would be remarkable if no such violations occurred in the aftermath of Mengistu's rule, given Ethiopia's poverty, recent history of violence, intensification of ethnic hostilities over the last decade, militarization of the region and competition for power. Abuses must not be overlooked but should be seen in the context of an overall improvement in human rights within an atmosphere of insecurity and tension; the early 1990s were a period of social upheaval resulting from the change from a centralised state-dominated economy to a more market-oriented system.[198]

The present Constitution was ratified in December 1994 and entered into force on August 21, 1995. The Constitution has incorporated many provisions of the international human rights covenants. As mentioned above, Article 3(2) states that "the fundamental rights and freedoms specified in this Chapter shall be interpreted in a manner conforming to the principles of the Universal Declaration of Human Rights, International Covenants on Human Rights and international instruments adopted by Ethiopia".[199] Thirty-two of the Constitution's 106 Articles contain detailed human rights provisions and 16 of them are classified under that heading.[200]

The Constitution also provides for the establishment of an independent judiciary and Article 79 confers all judicial powers, both at federal and state levels, to the courts.[201] Additionally, the House of Peoples Representatives is empowered to establish institutions that would encourage the promotion and respect for human rights. Article 55(14) states that the House of Representatives "shall establish a Human Rights Commission and determine by law its powers and functions".[202] Similarly, Article 55(15) provides for the House to "establish the institution of the Ombudsman, and select and appoint its members. It shall determine by law the powers and functions of the institution".[203] The above mentioned human rights provisions are also reflected in the constitutions of the regional states.[204]

The Transitional Government and later the Federal Government were confronted with the issue of human rights abuses of the military government and perpetrators of horrific crimes. Human rights treaties explicitly or implicitly require states to prosecute violations of rights contained in those international instruments. In addition, Ethiopian law has long recognised a duty to prosecute crimes against humanity in its Penal Code of 1957.[205] The Transitional Government, as discussed before, committed itself not only to the respect of human rights in the future, but also to draw appropriate lessons from the past.

From the experiences of many countries there have been several options of handling past atrocities, ranging from massive criminal prosecution of former officials to unconditional pardon. The granting of absolute amnesty as practised in some Latin American countries under a strong pressure from the military could have been an option.[206] The other choice was the formation of a truth commission as in South Africa with the aim of forgiving, but not forgetting the past.[207] However, Ethiopia chose to bring all offenders, including high officials and field commanders, to trial. From the start, it was clear that the task was enormous and international financial and technical assistance was sought.

The Special Public Prosecutor's Office was created in accordance with Proclamation No. 22/1992.[208] The Proclamation states that "the office shall, in accordance with the law, have the power to conduct investigation and institute proceedings in respect of any person having committed or responsible for the commission of an offence by abusing his position in the party, the government or mass organisation under the Derg-WPE regime".[209] Accordingly, a Special Prosecutor was appointed in September 1992 and the Office began its functions subsequently. The Office was able to organise lawyers, investigators and support staff, and set about learning from the experience of foreign consultants.

Most of the suspects were under custody before the creation of the Office. This was due to the change of the government, since at the time, the former officials were detained to prevent them from fleeing, and in many cases to protect them from retributive violence. It took some time to charge them, for obvious reasons, as the Office must collect evidence of crimes perpetrated over a period of almost two decades, by thousands of suspects. Some human rights organisations, such as Amnesty International had complained about the delay, but criticisms failed to consider the size of the task and the available manpower, and did not appreciate the complexity of the endeavour.[210]

On October 25, 1994, charges against 73 high level officials, including policy and decision-makers, senior government officials and military commanders, were filed. Only 46 were in the country and the rest, including former President Mengistu, were tried in absentia. On February 13, 1997, the Special Prosecutor announced that a total of 5,198 people were charged. Only 2,246 were charged in detention, while the rest, 2952 people, were charged in absentia.[211] Most of the defendants were charged with committing genocide and war crimes, and alternatively faced charges of committing aggravated homicide and wilful injury.[212] According to the Special Prosecutor's Office (SPO), the defendants were classified into three major categories: first, the policy makers who were responsible for the formulation of "the plan of genocide in their effort to eliminate their political opponents" and organizing the necessary institutions for its implementation; second, the "field commanders" who were responsible for "transmitting orders from the policy makers to the material offenders and by issuing fresh orders of their own"; and third, those who were involved in the actual implementation of the plan.[213]

After lengthy process, in December 2006, 73 top officials of the Derg were found guilty of crime against humanity and genocide. Many of them were sentenced to death on May 26, 2008. According to the Special Prosecutor's Office report, as of May 2008, 3583 suspects out of which 1308 in abstentia were found guilty. In the whole process, 51 suspects were found guilty of genocide and were sentenced to death, 182 suspects to life imprisonment, 921 were sentenced between 15 to 25 years imprisonment and 1539 suspects were set free. [214]

In June 1, 2011, the President pardoned the 23 Derg top officials and commuted their sentence of death penalty to life imprisonment.[215] The President stated in a statement the pardon was necessary to close the horrible historical chapter and encourage unified sprit of the nation to speed up economic development, democracy and good governance. Obviously, it was a difficult decision for the government and was much more hard for the tens of thousands victims and their families to accept, although many would not want to live in the past. Nevertheless, it has to be seriously taken as a lesson to future generations. Everyone should be accountable to one's own action.

Some of the top Derg Officials were eligible to be set free on parole after serving 20 years in prison. As a result, 16 of them were freed on October 4, 2011. As discussed above, though it took long time, the main idea of being held accountable for their actions would contribute to the development of democracy and good governance in the country.

The Ethiopian government has been criticised by a number of international human rights groups. Amnesty International has accused the government over the delay in the trial of former officials, some human rights violations, not responding for its call to abolish the death penalty and other misdeeds.[216]

Similarly, Human Rights Watch claimed that the slow pace of the trials of the former government officials would violate Article 9(3) of the International Covenant on Civil and Political Rights.[217] It also reports a number of cases of human rights violations.[218]

The government has attempted to rectify violations by concentrating its efforts on strengthening the institutions and training its officers. Several courses and seminars have been provided to members of the judiciary, the police force, prison officials and also local administrators and functionaries. However the government resents the reports made by human rights groups on unverified and unsubstantiated incidents and then on the failure to retract them when the reports are proven false. The former Prime Minister remarked that "these human rights organisations work by receiving allegations they have not got the institutional capacity to check. Once published, these allegations become treated as fact. But if there are violations, they can never be systematic and we will do all we can to improve the situation".[219] The government repeatedly admits that there are some human right shortcomings but without building the institutions of the police and the judiciary, it would be hard to achieve an improved result. That is why it is endeavouring to strengthen these and other related institutions and if any country or organisation is interested in the improvement of human rights in the country then it should participate in moving such efforts forward.

The Human Rights Commission and the Ombudsman has been active since their establishment in 2000.[220] They have been given wide-range responsibilities and powers to help safeguard and promote the rights of the people. Apparently, these institutions should be further strengthened and discharge their responsibilities to contribute better to enhance the democratic process and promote good governance.

Similarly, efforts have been made to promote the democratic rights of the people. The Transitional Charter embraces, in its Article one, the freedom of conscience, expression, association and peaceful assembly. It also stipulated "the right to engage in unrestricted political activity and to organise political parties, provided the exercise of such right does not infringe upon the rights of others".[221] Article Two stated "the right of nations, nationalities and peoples to self-determination is affirmed".[222]

The Constitution further details those rights and added other rights that were not mentioned in the Charter. Article 29 lays down the rights of thought, opinion and expression as follows:

1. Everyone has the right to hold opinions without interference.
2. Everyone has the right to freedom of expression without any interference...

> 3. Freedom of artistic creativity is guaranteed. Freedom of the press shall Specifically include the following elements: a) Prohibition of any form of Censorship; b) Access to information of public interest...[223]

The right of assembly, demonstration and petition is recognised in the Ethiopian Constitution as long as such a right is exercised peacefully and without arms. The Constitution also states that "this right does not exempt from liability under laws enacted to protect the well-being of the youth or the honour and reputation of individuals, and laws prohibiting any propaganda for war and any public expression of opinions intended to injure human dignity".[224] Every individual has also the freedom to form or join an association except those organised in violation of appropriate laws or to illegally subvert the constitutional order.[225]

The rights of nationality; marital, personal and family rights; the rights of women; the rights of children are provided for. The right of access to justice; the right to vote and to be elected; the rights of nations, nationalities, and peoples; and the right to property are detailed. Other socio-economic rights, such as economic, social and cultural rights; the rights of labour; the right to development; and environmental rights are also included under democratic rights.[226] These rights are also enshrined by the regional state constitutions.[227]

Several proclamations have been promulgated to implement the democratic rights provided by the Transitional Charter and subsequently by the Constitution. The first of these instruments is Proclamation No. 3/1991, which details the procedures for peaceful demonstrations and public political meetings.[228] The Proclamation reaffirms that any individual has the right to organise and participate in peaceful demonstrations and public political meetings.[229] The obligation attached to it is that the organisers have to give written notice 48 hours before the intended event.[230] However, it prohibits some events that are characterised as non-peaceful and against the well-being of the people such as discrimination on race, colour, religion, sex or similar offences.

Proclamation No.34/1992 was promulgated to implement the freedom of expression provided by the Constitution.[231] Article 3 of the Proclamation declares that "freedom of the press is recognized and respected" and "censorship of the press and any restriction of a similar nature are hereby prohibited."[232]

The right of the press to seek, obtain and report any information from government agencies is recognised. The press and its agents are encouraged to disseminate any information in their possession.[233] However, the press is reminded that its press products have to be free from:

a) any criminal offence against the safety of the State or of the administration established in accordance with the Charter of the national defense force;
b) any defamation or false accusation against any individual, action/nationality, people or organization;
c) any criminal instigation of one nationality against another or incitement of conflict between peoples; and
d) any agitation of war.[234]

Although the Press Law was enacted during the Transitional Period, it continued to apply after the Constitution entered into force. The criminal and civil liability part of the Law continues to be controversial as some opponents present the Article as a tool for harassing the press.[235] On other hand, the use of the state owned mass media was another concern of the advocates of fair play. Accordingly, a number of proclamations were enacted which provide for the media agencies their organisational and operational autonomy from the government.[236] Such a move would not by itself ensure the agencies' autonomy and independence, but it can be taken as a step in the right direction as the media has traditionally been the mouthpiece of the government of the day.

In addition, Proclamation No. 178/1999 was promulgated to establish the Ethiopian Broadcasting Agency and to mainly define the rights and obligation of the stakeholders in the broadcasting service.[237] The Proclamation further elaborated and amended by proclamation No. 533/2007. The powers and duties of the regulatory body were further detailed and it was changed into an Authority. It also further defines the rights and obligations of persons undertaking broadcasting service.[238]

Moreover, Proclamation No. 590/2008 reaffirms that "freedom of the mass media is constitutionally guaranteed. Censorship in any form is prohibited."[239] It indicates that restriction should only be by laws issued based on the Constitution.[240] Restriction on obtaining information are to issues related to privacy, information related to third party, commercial information of the third party, law enforcement proceedings and legal investigation, and national security.[241]

Proclamation No. 46/1993 was enacted to implement the right to participate in any political activity and to organize political parties.[242] The Proclamation was revised and amended by Proclamation No. 573/2008.[243] Article 4(2) declares that any Ethiopian aged 18 and above has the right to party membership.[244] It also indicates that a political party can register as country wide organization if it has at least 1,500 found members; at least 40 per cent of its founding members are residents of the same regional state; and the remaining founding members reside in at least four regional states.[245] On the other hand, regional parties required at least 750 founding members and more than 60 per cent of the founding members are residents of the same region.[246]

Furthermore, it asserts that parties that ferment conflict and war by preaching hatred and enmity among the people; organized to achieve their political objectives by force of arms and also aim to overthrow the government through violence; have foreign nationals in their ranks; involved in unlawful activities and organized to illegally violate the constitutional order are barred from registration.[247] It also declares that, apart from fraudulent practices and non-compliance of detailed regulations, if a party fails to participate two successive general or local elections, it would be cancelled from registration.[248] The other important point is that the Proclamation details the conditions by which political parties form union, front and coalition.[249]

In accordance with the freedom of the press recognised in the Transitional Charter and Proclamation No. 34/1992, independent media started to thrive even before the licensing and judicial frameworks were put in place. Tens of private papers and party journals started to circulate within a short period. The freedom of expression and of the mass media was further bolstered by the issuance of Proclamation No. 533/2007 and Proclamation No. 590/2008. Currently, apart from government television and radio services, five commercial radio broadcasters and eight community radios are actively working. In addition, 33 periodicals and 19 magazines are circulating in the country.[250] Evidently, the radio is the most far-reaching medium in the country. Hence, the participation of the private sector in radio broadcasting, with their limitation of reach, will have a commendable impact on information dissemination. As for the quality of the content of the information spread by journalists, a lot is to be desired and issues of capacity building and promoting professional integrity should be highly pursued to better serve the people.

The private press' access to government officials has been very limited. Many officials have been avoiding the private press since they believe their interviews and opinions are not properly reflected. However, the reluctance of officials to provide information is not limited to the private press. They are not even forthcoming to the government media. Proclamation No. 590/2008 has made it abundantly clear that access to information should be respected.[251] It declares that "all persons have the right to seek, obtain and communicate any information held by public bodies, except as expressly provided for by this Proclamation."[252] The restrictions are detailed from Articles 15 to 29.[253] It also provides an appeal process by which the head of the public institution is obliged to provide an explanation. It further indicates a person not satisfied by the explanation of the institution can appeal to the Ombudsman.[254] The aggrieved person, if disagrees with the decision of the Ombudsman, can appeal to the court.[255] On the other hand, the government has established Communication Affairs Office not only to properly communicate to the public but also promote and develop media that is commensurate with the current technological age.[256]

As discussed, the Constitution provides for the freedom of association, the right of peaceful assembly and the right to engage in unrestricted peaceful political activity. Political pluralism is considered to be a major ingredient in the consolidation of a democratic system. Democratic constitutions accord a special role to political parties organised by individual citizens in order to run or oppose the government.[257] The creation of an environment in which opposition groups function properly and contribute to the enhancement of a democratic system has been one of the challenges facing countries in transition. On one hand, governments need to dismantle obstacles that impede the activities of opposition groups, and on the other hand, the latter have to use lawful means in promoting themselves. In this regard, Tomuschat remarks that "lawfulness of political opposition is a distinctive criterion of every truly democratic society, one which permits competition between all of its societal groups and refrains to the greatest extent possible from imposing on its members values and principles that may not be challenged and are surrounded by a protective wall of sanctity".[258] Hence, open competition under consensually accepted rules of the game will help democracy to take roots. From such an atmosphere both the government and the opposition would benefit and consolidate their support, and above all the system would be strengthened. Tomuschat further puts it as follows:

> The right to political opposition is a necessary ingredient of a democratic system. On the other hand, it should not be ignored that every country is at the same time in need of law and order. Government must be able to discharge their functions in an effective manner. Advocates of dictatorial or authoritarian rule often fail to understand that a government that accepts public criticism of its actions is not weakened, but strengthened by such openness.[259]

As of December 2012, 79 political parties and organisations have been registered with the National Electoral Board.[260] Moreover, there are 2813 non-governmental organizations (NGOs) registered with the Charities and Societies Agency as of December 2012. 397 of them are foreign NGOs working in different fields. The government promulgated Proclamation No. 621/2009 with the aim of enabling charities and societies to work legally, and in a transparent and accountable way to achieve their stated objectives. Article 88(1) instructs charities and societies to allocate only 30 per cent of their budget to administrative activities. Many charities and societies claim that such regulation restricts their activities and want some of their activities and purchases such as consultancy fee, remuneration of project managers, purchase of vehicles and other similar expenses not to be included in administrative expenses. On the other hand, the government intends to minimize unnecessary wastages and abuses, and enlarge the portion of the budget to be as much as possible spent on the intended objectives.

Similarly, Article 2(2) forbade Ethiopian charities to receive donations from foreign sources exceeding 10 per cent of their budget. Many of them present it as an instrument to narrow the political space in the country while the government insists that political activities are solely citizens' business and should be funded by citizens only. Provided reputation of many NGOs for wastage and abuse, many people desire that the money should spent on the declared objectives rather than fattening the pockets of individuals. Similarly, it will be sustainable and beneficial when political activities are funded and performed by citizens. It will protect the country from any unwarranted foreign influences and intervention.

As the Constitution provides for the right to peaceful assembly and demonstrations, the government generally allows political and other interest groups to assemble and demonstrate against any government policy or action. The only major obligation is Article 4 of Proclamation No. 3/1991 which requires the organizers to notify the relevant government institution in advance.[261] It is evident that the police do stop demonstrations such as opposition parties' rallies held without permits and made in defiance of the Proclamation. Such police measures might not be considered as a breach of the groups' right unless the permits are deliberately delayed by the administration to frustrate the requested activities. However, the police have to be trained and equipped to contain violent protests and unauthorised demonstrations. Lack of professionalism in such events may cause unnecessary consequences that might hurt the democratic process as a whole.

Concluding Remarks

As discussed above, reforms began with the adoption of the Transitional Charter and have been deepened and strengthened by the ratification of the Constitution and the practices made to interpret it. Ethiopia has passed through a number of constitutions, none of which had much impact on the lives of the broad masses of the people and the political atmosphere in the country. The 1931 and the 1955 constitutions mostly remained on paper, and if they had any effect, it was no more than giving a cosmetic face lift to the autocratic monarchical regime in the eyes of its foreign allies. Similarly, the military government's 1987 constitution did not have any influence in changing the behaviour of the regime in its relations with the people. The government attempted to accord legitimacy to the chaotic and disruptive administration of over a decade, but with little success.

The Federal Constitution further deepened the reforms initiated by the Charter by detailing and enriching the direction already set. It also brought forward the nationality issue, addressed in the Charter by clarifying the scope of the right and the method of its interpretation. It details the principles on which the federal arrangement is built and delineates the division of power between the federal and state governments. The other significant point in the Constitution is the issue of land ownership, which has remained unchanged under the state's prerogative. Although the above issues remain controversial among the political elite, the majority of the people basically support them, and with time and more experience, they are undoubtedly taking root. The Constitution also provides for a wide range of human and democratic rights that reflect the contents and language of international human rights instruments.

Elections have been conducted in order to enable the people to voice their choices. The 1992 elections were held to create the structures of government in the regions and districts and the 1994 elections were held for the purpose of convening the Constituent Assembly to ratify the Constitution. The 1995 elections were held under the new Constitution to form the federal and state governments. The elections were not free from allegations of mal-practice but in large they were instrumental in establishing a reasonably effective government. The boycott by certain opposition groups narrowed the choice of the people and had a negative impact on the democratisation process. The obstacles faced by the opposition did not amount to a deterrent from participating, as there was no systematic violation of the electoral law.

The decision of a number of opposition groups to participate in the 2000 elections was a positive step to Ethiopia's democratization process. Although the elections generally went well, they also showed serious weaknesses, especially in some zones of the Southern Ethiopia Peoples' Regional State. Lessons were drawn from such experience and were used to improve the electoral law and the electoral process. The 2000 elections were of benefit to the opposition groups in gaining them seats and giving them a voice in parliament. As detailed above, the 2005 elections saw a very competitive atmosphere and the process was very educating to the people. However, the subsequent violence and the refusal of the main opposition group, the CUD, to take up its spoils in parliament were a set back to the democratization process. The CUD failed to capitalize its gains of "protest vote" to further its political objectives. The EPRDF learning from the 2005 elections attempted to show the people that there is light at the end of the tunnel. Successive impressive double digit percentage of economic growth, commendable job creation effort, improvement in governance issues, better communication with urban dwellers especially the youth and women and other activities made the EPRDF better prepared and organized for the 2010 elections. The 2010 elections provide the EPRDF with overwhelming mandate to rule for the next five years. It presented the opposition with a valuable lesson if they commit themselves to learn and rectify their past blander. However, the opposition still lacks a coherent strategy and program of action that can be presented to the people as an alternative. It is clear that just opposing whatever the ruling party presents will not widen the opposition's constituency and their credibility in the eyes of the electorate.

Human and democratic rights are widely provided for in the Constitution, further reinforcing the provisions which were initiated by the Transitional Charter. As discussed above, the Ethiopian people are enjoying these rights in spite of cases of violations reported by some human rights groups and the opposition. Such shortcomings might not be surprising considering Ethiopia's economic situation and its lack of experience of democracy. The prevalent abject poverty and the centuries-old rule of absolute monarchy and the recent dictatorship have left the people without experience of any form of democracy. Thus, in the absence of favourable socio-economic conditions and supporting institutions, Ethiopia's record of recent years can be taken as a positive step in the right direction. This does not mean that Ethiopia should not be criticised for violations of human and democratic rights, but it should be evaluated by putting the whole context into perspective.

In general, Ethiopia has managed to register substantial results in its key political reforms. By dismantling the hundreds of years of centralisation and national oppression, it not only devolved power from the centre to the nationalities but also brought peace and stability by endeavouring to close the chapter of its troubled past. Of course, the success of the process needs the concerted effort of the Ethiopian people, especially the political elite. Enormous efforts are needed to change the behaviour of political groups which has been negatively witnessed in recent years. An atmosphere of moderation, accommodation and compromise should reign among the political groups to enable them play a constructive role in strengthening the democratisation process. Besides, state institutions and political organisations have to discharge their responsibilities in educating the people to exercise their rights and safeguard their achievements. Diamond explains this important task as follows:

> People must come to learn not only the value of democracy but the ways of democracy: the importance of voting and being informed; the need to temper partisanship with respect for opposing parties and viewpoints; the means through which grievances and needs can be brought before elected officials, both directly and through the mass media; the techniques by which communities can organise themselves to achieve common ends; and the details of how their own electoral system, legislature, bureaucracy, local government and legal system work.[262]

The people should not be left to be spectators if the democratisation process is going to succeed. As Linz stated "ultimately, the success of a society is not the result of activities of the state or even the best possible government, but of the efforts of the whole society".[263] The Ethiopian political elite needs not only to create an atmosphere of co-operation and tolerance among itself but also to involve the millions of people in the political process in order to succeed in the endeavour of building a democratic system. Moreover, Ethiopia requires a stable external environment to enable it to concentrate on its political and economic development.

Notes

1. See S. E. Finer et al., 1995: 1; S. E. Finer, 1979: 15; Bogdanor (ed.), 1988.
2. Wheare, 1966: 1.
3. Lane, 1996: 6. Bagdanor explains why Britain lacks an enacted constitution as follows: "Constitutions are generally drawn up to symbolise the birth of a nation, a new beginning in the aftermath of war or revolution. A constitution marks the start of a new political order, a new epoch in a nation's development. A document, so it is generally held, is an essential pre-requisite to the legitimisation of a new regime... A constitution, therefore, marks a sharp discontinuity in the history of a state, a radical break with previous practice. England, however, has been spared such discontinuities since the seventeenth century. Its progress has been evolutionary, unpunctuated by revolutionary upheaval or foreign occupation". (Bagdanor, in Bogdanor (ed.), 1988: 53-54).
4. Lane, 1996: 110; Magdwick and Woodhouse, 1995: 5.
5. Lane, 1996: 111.
6. The American Constitution indicates that the founders were determined to limit government and design three branches of power with a strong system of checks and balances devised to ensure that neither legislature nor executive acquires an upper hand. The German Constitution contains provisions that reflect the rejection of the abuses of the past and the federal system was to a certain extent imposed by the occupiers though it was also favoured by some of the Christian Democrats. The parliamentary sovereignty in the British system also evolved from the struggle to curb the powers of the king. (See Finer, et al., 1995; Magdwick and Woodhouse, 1995; Bogdanor, ed., 1988).
7. Calvert, 1985: 35.
8. African countries have not been deficient in making constitutions but almost all failed to last long. Many countries were quick to suspend or change their constitutions, which were in fact inherited from their former colonial masters. By the early 1970s, military or one party rule was the dominant form of government in Africa. The Independence Day constitutions literally failed to thwart authoritarianism. (See Diamond et al., 1988; Lane 1996).
9. Constitutionally significant documents had existed for centuries in Ethiopia. They contained rules such as the succession to the throne through the Solomonic dynasty, the relationship between the Emperor and the regional princes, the role of the Ethiopian Orthodox Church and the Emperor's absolute fidelity to the Church, and an imperial court system.

10. Emperor Haile Selassie in his speech of July 16, 1931 mentioned the evolution of the constitution as follows: "The idea which has dominated us, bearing in mind the interests of Ethiopia and of Our beloved people, and which has been the object of Our ceaseless endeavours, is as follows: 1) To grant a constitution to the whole of the Ethiopian people. 2) To secure that it be observed and maintained". (Perham, 1969: 424).
11. For details, see League of Nations, Official Journal, Special supplement, No. 19, 1923.
12. Perham, 1969: 427.
13. Ibid., Article 30, p. 429.
14. Ibid., Article 31.
15. Ibid.
16. The Constitution was abolished by the Italian invaders in 1935 but was again restored in 1941.
17. For full text of the Eritrean Constitution, see Final Report of the United Nations Commissioner in Eritrea, United Nations General Assembly, Official Records: Seventh Session, Supplement No. 15, New York, 1952.
18. Clapham, C. "Constitutions and Governance in Ethiopian Political History", in Constitutionalism: Reflections and Recommendations, May 1993.
19. See Revised Constitution of Ethiopia, Negarit Gazeta, 15th Year, No. 2, Addis Ababa, November 4, 1955.
20. Ibid; Article 1.
21. Ibid., Articles 101-07.
22. Proclamation No. 1/1974: Proclamation of the Establishment of the Provisional Military Government, September 12, 1974.
23. See Preamble of the 1987 Constitution, Negarit Gazeta, 47th Year No. 1, Proclamation No. 1 of 1987, Addis Ababa, September 12, 1987.
24. Ibid., Article 1.
25. Ibid., Article 6.
26. Ibid., Article 2.
27. The administrative structures were announced in September 1987 and five autonomous regions, namely Eritrea, Tigray, Assab, Dire Dawa and Ogaden were mentioned. On the other hand, the Oromo, the Amhara and other nationalities were divided among a number of regions. (See 'Ensuring the Rights of Nationalities', Committee for the Founding of the PDRE, Addis Ababa, September 1987).
28. Within the Constitution Commission and in the public discussions, the most controversial issues were the rights of nations and nationalities to secede, and land ownership.
29. Ibid., Part Four, Article 10-11.
30. For details of the debate on the right of nations and nationalities, see the Minutes of the 94th Regular Session of the Council, p. 108-125. In the Council, 33

members voted for the inclusion of the right of nations and nationalities to secede while 9 voted against, and there were also 3 abstentions. Though the preference of the Council was clear, it decided overwhelmingly to include both recommendations in the draft for consideration by the Constituent Assembly. Only two members opposed the decision. (Ibid., p. 125). Similarly, the land ownership issue was voted in the Council. 34 voted in support of the public ownership and 7 voted for the other recommendation with two abstentions. Both recommendations were also forwarded to the Constituent Assembly. (Ibid., p. 138) In fact, the debate on the land ownership can bc found in the same document, see p. 126-138.

31. For contrast, part of Article 39 of the draft constitution was formulated as follows: 1. Every nation, nationality or people in Ethiopia shall have the unrestricted right to self-determination up to secession; 2. Every nation, nationality and people shall have the right to speak, write and develop its language and to promote its culture, help it grow and flourish, and preserve its historical heritage; 3. Every nation, nationality or people in Ethiopia shall have the un-restricted right to administer itself; and this shall include the right to establish government institutions within the territory it inhabits and the right to fair representation in the federal and state governments... On the other hand, the alternative supported by the minority of the Council was stated as follows: Every nationality in Ethiopia shall have the right to speak and write in its own language, and express, promote and develop it. Every nationality in Ethiopia shall have the full right to administer itself. This right shall include the right to establish government institutions within the territory it inhabits and the right to fair representation in the federal and state government. As indicated above, though the two recommendations agreed on the right of nations to self-rule, the alternative draft clearly avoided the right to secede as a cardinal principle of the Constitution. It indicated, in the rest part of the Article, how it would be handled when and if the demand for secession arises. Similarly, in the other contentious issue, the ownership of land, there existed a striking contrast between the two viewpoints. The majority-supported draft of Article 40, the right to property, was stated as follows. 1. The right of every citizen to own property is guaranteed. Unless the law provides otherwise in the public interest, this right shall include the right to use and enjoy property, and, in so far as it does not violate the rights of others, to sell, transfer by succession or by any other means.... 2. The right to own rural and urban lands as well as natural resources belongs only to the state and the people. Land is an inalienable common property of the nations, nationalities and peoples of Ethiopia. 3. The right of Ethiopian peasants to free allotment of land and not to be evicted therefrom is guaranteed... On the other hand, the alternative supported by the minority was as follows: Every Ethiopian citizen of either sex shall have the right to own property, including the ownership of both urban and rural land. This right includes the right to acquire, use, mortgage, sell, transfer by succession or by other means...The State may, in public interest and in particular, to ensure that Ethiopian citizens shall have an equal opportunity to gain a living and an equal access to housing, determine the size of ownership of both rural and urban land (The Draft Constitution of Ethiopia. A Draft Approved by the Council of Representatives, May 1994, p. 17-21).

32. The Constitution is included in the Appendix part; In addition, the donor countries' envoys had followed the deliberations of the Constituent Assembly and at its conclusion issued a statement to encourage not only the constitution making but also the aftermath process as follows: This is an important milestone on the path towards the establishment of democracy in Ethiopia and during the assembly's deliberations we were especially impressed with the open debates on serious issues with minority views receiving a full hearing. Free, unhindered expression of dissenting views is the essence of a healthy constitutional democracy (A Group of 18 Embassies, Press Release on the Constitution and Forthcoming Elections, December 14, 1994, Addis Ababa).
33. See Ozbudun, in Weiner and Ozbudun (ed.), 1987: 393.
34. Ibid. The periodicity of elections is that they should be held regularly at legally prescribed intervals and inclusiveness means that the principal public-policy makers in a political system should be chose by competitive elections.
35. Bogdanor, in Bogdanor and Butler (ed.), 1983: 1.
36. Sartori, 1997: 3.
37. The alternative vote is intended to produce a winner with an absolute majority, at least more than 50 % of the total. The voters are asked to indicate their first preference, the second one and others. If the winner candidate fails to obtain 50 % then the last candidate is dropped to distribute the votes to the remaining. The process continues until a majority winner appears. The French system calls for two-ballot process. The highest two vote earners would contest for the second time to produce a clear majority winner. (Rose, in Bogdanor and Butler (ed.), 1983; Sartori 1997; and Lijphart 1984).
38. Ibid. There are several methods of practising list proportional systems in translating the votes into seats. The d'Hondt or 'highest average' method; the Sante-Lague formula; and the method of 'largest remainder'. The d'Hondt method favours larger parties, the largest remainder system is said to favour the smaller parties and the Sainte-Lague system is less proportional than the largest remainder system but more proportional than the d'Hondt system. (Sartori, 1997: 8).
39. Rose, in Bogdanor and Butler (ed.), 1983: 34-40.
40. Sartori, 1997: 55.
41. Sartori 1997: 53-61; Lijphart 1984: 150-68; and Bogdanor and Butler (ed.), 1983. 30-43.
42. Ibid.
43. Ibid.
44. Lijphart, 1984: 432; and Sartori, 1997: 73-74.
45. Sartori, 1997: 74.
46. McDonald and Ruhl, 1989: 346.
47. Finer, 1978: 63.
48. Proclamation No. 64/1993. Electoral Law of Ethiopia, Negarit Gazeta, August 23, 1993, Article 13 (1).

49. Ibid., Article 13 (2).
50. Ibid., Article 15 (1).
51. Ibid., Article 15 (2).
52. Ibid., Article 15 (3).
53. See Proclamation No. 111/1995. Proclamation to make the Electoral Law of Ethiopia Conform with the Constitution of the Federal Democratic Republic of Ethiopia, NegaritGazeta, February 23, 1995, Articles 13 & 15.
54. Proclamation No. 532/2007, June 25, 2007, Article 25.
55. Dawit Yohannes, a former Speaker of the House of Peoples' Representatives, interview, December 19, 1997.
56. Proclamation No. 7/1992.A Proclamation to Provide for the Establishment of National/Regional Self-Governments, Negarit Gazeta, January 14, 1992, Article 3 (1).
57. The Provisional Government of the EPRDF formed the Commission for the Rehabilitation of Former Members of the Army and Disabled War Veterans on June 14, 1991 even before the establishment of the Transitional Government. In the first demobilisation and reintegration program 455,000 former soldiers and 21,200 OLF combatants were targeted. The total costs of the Ethiopian demobilisation and reintegration programs between mid-1991 and early 1995 are estimated at Birr 518 million (approximately US$195 million), of which Birr 474 million (91.5 per cent) was for program interventions. The expenditure for the programs was much less when compared with similar programs conducted in Namibia and Uganda. Ethiopia spent approximately US$195 million for almost half-million soldiers, while Namibia spent approximately US$41.3 million and Uganda about US$43.2 million for 49,500 and 36,358 soldiers respectively (World Bank. Case Studies in War-to-Peace Transition, 1996: 2 and 19-20). The other face of the above process was the demobilisation of the EPRDF fighters that was carried out before some years. The objective of the program was to create proportional representation of the various nationalities in the army and also to transform the force into a regular army with the required physical fitness. A total of 24,593 fighters were demobilised and the nationality composition of them was worked out in order to address the existing imbalance within the national defence force. Out of the mentioned total figure, 21,026 of them were from Tigray, 2806 from Amara, 735 Oromos and 26 from Southern Nationalities (Report on the Demobilisation of Members of the Ethiopian National Defence Force, Ministry of National Defence, 1998).
58. Ibid., Articles 10, 11, and 12.
59. Ibid; Article 20; the alleged army should fulfil the following conditions: it was established before the fall of the Derg; it was organised and established as a regular fighter; fought the Derg with full effort until the final down fall of the Derg; and in its struggle against the Derg it controlled a liberated territory administering the people therein; and remained with the people in the liberated territory fighting and defending until the final down fall of the Derg (Article 20 (2)). Moreover,

the size of the alleged armies was determined based on the following criteria: the size and organisational set up of the army should be close to the fighting strength it revealed when fighting against the Derg; the size and organisational set up of the army should be close to the size of manpower required to liberate and defend the area it liberated; and the size of the army should be close to the size of the force known to the forces of other organisations which came to their knowledge as a result of co-operating and operating together in the armed struggle. (Article 21 (3)); for further details and debates on the subject, see minutes of the 30th Regular Session of the Transitional Council of Representatives, January 1,1992.

60. See Proclamation No. 64/1993. Electoral Law of Ethiopia, Negarit Gazeta, August 23, 1993, Article 3.
61. Ibid., Article 5.
62. Ibid., Article 15.
63. For more details and the debate on the issue, see the Minutes of the 89th Regular Session of the Transitional Council of Representatives, January 27, 1994; and also the Report of the Election Board to the House of Peoples' Representatives, September 1996, p. 40 (both in Amharic). See also the Minutes of the House of Federation, August 21-23, 1995.
64. Ibid., Article 74; and Article 75 details the powers and duties of the Assembly as follows: It should 1) elect its officials; 2) draw up its own rules of procedure; 3) form such committees as may be necessary for the performance of its functions; 4) determine the procedure for submission of a draft constitution for its consideration; 5) deliberate upon the contents of the draft constitution submitted to it and alter, modify, or adopt same, as the case may be; 6) officially declare the constitution it finally adopted in whole; and 7) fix the time-table for elections to a National Assembly to be held pursuant to Article 12 of the Transitional Period Charter.
65. See Proclamation 64/1993, Article 46.
66. Proclamation No. 111/1995, Article 46 (1).
67. Ibid., Article 46 (2).
68. See Proclamation No. 120/ 1995. Financing and Administration of the Election Assistance Fund, NegaritGazeta, April 8, 1995; Article 4 (1) states 'no candidate can spend for his or her election campaign in cash or in material or a combination of the two valued in excess of Birr twenty thousand (Birr 20, 000)'. That means the ceiling was put at the time at four thousand U. S. dollars (Birr 5 was approximately equal to U. S. $ 1).
69. See Proclamation No.187/1999, Proclamation to Make the Electoral Law of Ethiopia Confirm with the Constitution of FDRE (Amendment), December 2, 1999; and Proclamation No. 438/2005, January 18, 2005.
70. Proclamation No. 532/2007, A Proclamation to Amend the Electoral Law of Ethiopia, June 25, 2007.
71. Proclamation No. 662/2009, A Proclamation to Provide for the Electoral Code of Conduct for Political Parties, August 28, 2009.

72. See Proclamation No. 1/1995, Article 102.
73. Tesfaye Habisso, Leader of the Kenbata National Congress, interview, August 12, 1997; Statements made by the Council of Alternatives Forces for Peace and Democracy in Ethiopia (CAFPD) allege similar conduct; and also statements made by the opposition in 3rd and 4th national elections.
74. See the Transitional Period Charter of Ethiopia, July 22, 1991, Article 1 (a).
75. Proclamation No. 46/1993. Political Parties Registration Proclamation, Negarit Gazeta, April 15, 1993.
76. Ibid., Article 3.
77. Article 4(2) details the criteria to be fulfilled by a party to attain country-wide personality as follows: a) it has at least 1,500 founding members; b) the number of founding members who are residents of one region does not exceed forty per cent (40%); c) the rest of the founding members are residents of at least four regions within Ethiopia; d) the number of members registered as founders in each region as laid down in sub-article 2 (c) of this Article constitutes at least fifteen per cent of the total founding members. On the other hand, regional personality can be obtained where the party has at least 750 founding members and more than forty per cent of the founding members are residents of one region. (Article 4 (3).
78. Ibid., Article 5.
79. Ibid., Article 22; the Office of Registration was later abandoned and the task was given to the National Electoral Board.
80. Ibid., Article 28.
81. Ibid., Article 29.
82. See Proclamation No. 82/1994. Political Parties Registration Amendment,, January 28, 1994, Article 4.
83. See Proclamation No. 573/2008., A Revised Political Parties Registration Proclamation, September 24, 2008, Articles 32-35.
84. Ibid., Articles 42-50.
85. List provided by the office of the National Electoral Board, August 1997.
86. See Annex for the list of nation-wide and regional parties, and for mergers of organisations as of August 2002.
87. See the website of National Electoral Board of Ethiopia, www.electionethiopia.org.
88. See Proclamation No. 41/1993. A Proclamation to Define the Powers and Duties of the Central and Regional Executive Organs of the Transitional Government of Ethiopia,, January 20, 1993; and Proclamation No. 33/1992.A Proclamation to Define the Sharing of Revenue between the Central Government and the National/Regional Self-Government,, October 20, 1992.
89. See the statement given by LeencoLata, Deputy Secretary-General of the OLF, June 17, 1992.
90. Proclamation No. 21/1992. Election Review Board establishment,, July 30,1992; Article 9 indicated that the Board should have twenty-one members who

represented the judges of the Supreme Court; the Ministry of Justice; the Bar Association; the Faculty of Law of Addis Ababa University; the Labour Unions, the Ethiopian Chamber of Commerce; the Ethiopian Teachers Association; the four Ethiopian religious organisations; the Ethiopian Medical Association; the National Observers Group; and the Joint International Observers Group (as non-voting member). Each organisation was asked to present a list of three candidates from which the Council of Representatives chose 21 voting members.

91. For more details on the Report of the Election Review Board and the debate on the decisions, see Minutes of the 55th Regular Session of the Council of Representatives, October 13, 1992 (in Amharic).
92. See Report of the Ethiopian Independent Election Observers Association on the Elections for the Constituent Assembly, June 1994 (in Amharic).
93. An interview with BeyenePetros, opposition leader, the Courier, No. 145, May-June 1994.
94. See Report of the National Electoral Board, September 1996:7-27.
95. Ibid.
96. See Minutes of the Meeting between the Foreign Minister and Ambassadors (mainly the United States and the E. U. member countries' Ambassadors) on the Issues of Elections, on October 21, 1994 and February 2, 1995.
97. Hiruy Amanuel, former Director General of the American and European Affairs, Foreign Ministry of Ethiopia, interview, August 15, 1997. The evaluation is based on his discussion with the U.S and E.U. member countries' Ambassadors. They had little complaint on the technical conduct of the elections. Their reservation referred to the narrow choices the people were offered because of the boycott by some of the opposition forces, especially the Southern Ethiopia Peoples' Democratic Unity. Nevertheless, there was a consensus in calling the election as 'the first democratic election' held in the country.
98. See the Donor Election Unit's Final Analytical Summary of Donor Election Reports on the May 7, 1995 Ethiopian Elections, May 30, 1995, p. 15.
99. See the covering letter addressed to the Ethiopian Foreign Minister signed jointly by the Ambassadors of Britain, the U. S., the Netherlands, Sweden, Canada, Italy, and Germany, May 31, 1995.
100. Statement of the European Union on the Elections, October 2, 1995.
101. Statement by the OAU Observer Group on Elections of May 7, 1995.
102. Ibid.; Legum, Colin. Third World Reports, May 24, 1995; and various local observer groups' statements indicated that the elections were a step in the right direction.
103. Additional nine minority nationalities got a special representation to the Southern Nations, Nationalities and Peoples' Regional Council.
104. Supporters of the EPRDF and other political organisations reject the claim by the boycotting organisations that they do not want to participate in order to deny legitimacy to the EPRDF's rule. They claim that these organisations do not have

mass support and prefer to shy away from elections in order not to expose their little following. Whatever the case, these organisations have to decide on participating in the elections, not only to test their mass support but also to contribute to the democratic process.

105. See Report of Ato Kemal Bedri, October 2000.
106. See Report of Ato Kemal Bedri, Chairman of the Electoral Board to the House of Representatives, October, 2000; See also Tronovoll, Voting, Violence and Violations: Peasant Voices on the Flawed Elections in Hadiya, Southern Ethiopia, Journal of Modern African Studies, Vol. 39, No. 4, 2001: 667-716.
107. For detail discussion of the pre and post 2005 elections, see Bereket Simon, The Tale of Two Elections, 2011 (in Amharic).
108. See Electoral Board, Report on Election Results, September 2005.
109. See Electoral Board Report of the Re-run Elections and the Somali Region, 2005.
110. Ethiopia: Legislative Elections 2005, European Union Election Observation Mission Final Report, 2005.
111. The Complaints Review Body
112. Complains Investigation Panels.
113. Final Statement of the Carter Centre Observation of the Ethiopia 2005 National Elections, September 2005.
114. See Letter by Prime Minister Meles Zenawi to the Editor of the Ethiopian Herald, August 31, 2005.
115. Election Board, Report of Final Results, September 5, 2005.
116. See Report of the Independent Investigation Commission Submitted to the House of Peoples' Representatives, September 2006.
117. The Ethiopian government announced that it pardoned 38 opposition leaders on July 20, 2007.
118. A Colour revolution is a term used by the media and concerned change leaders to describe the movements that were happening in the former Soviet Union counties during the early 2000 to change governments through street violence and demonstrations. (Like the 2003 Rose Revolution of Georgia and the 2004 Orange Revolution of Ukraine).
119. See House of Representatives, Regulations for the 3th Working Season, 2005.
120. See the National Electoral Board of Ethiopia, Official Results of the 23rd May 2010 General Election, June 21, 2010.
121. See Ethiopia: Final Report, House of People's Representatives and State Council Elections May 2010, European Union Election Observation Mission, 2010.
122. See the African Union Observer Mission Report, May 26, 2010.
123. Lane, 1996: 37.
124. Montesquieu, 1989: 157. He based his argument in his assessment that 'in each state there are three sorts of powers: legislative power, executive power over things

depending on the right of nations, and executive power over the things depending on civil right. (Ibid., p. 156).

125. Finer, 1978: 71.

126. Ibid., p. 73.

127. See Basic Principles on the Independence of the Judiciary, Adopted by the Seventh United Nations Congress on the Prevention of Crime and the Treatment of Offenders held at Milan from 26 August to 6 September 1985 and endorsed by General Assembly Resolutions 40/32 of 29 November 1985 and 40/146 of 13 December 1985.

128. Shetreet, in Shetreet and Deschenes (ed.), 1985: 590.

129. Rosenn, quoted in Larkins, 1996: 610.

130. Taipale, quoted in Shetreet, 1985: 594-95.

131. Larkins, "Judicial Independence and democratisation", 1996: 611.

132. See Proclamation No. 1/1995, Article 45; Lane details a number of institutions that govern the relationship between the people in the executive and legislative branches in a parliamentary system. Some of the significant ones are: the vote of no-confidence on the part of parliament towards the cabinet; the right to dissolve parliament on the part of the premier; the right to call a vote of loyalty towards the cabinet on the part of the premier; and the right of the premier to appoint ministers in the cabinet. Since different countries exercise parliamentarism in a way that suits their situations, there is hardly a uniformity of institutions being involved. Hence, the British parliamentary democracy may satisfy the mentioned criteria but other countries practise it differently and with less emphasis. For example, Article 67 (1) of the German Constitution provides for the possibility of a no confidence vote by the Bundestag against the Chancellor but at the same time protects him by stipulating that the majority of the members must agree on an alternative Chancellor before outvoting him. Article 68 (1) also stipulates that the Federal President may dissolve the Bundestag upon the proposal of the Federal Chancellor (See Finer et al., 1995: 156). Similarly, the Italian Head of State has the power to dissolve parliament after a government's collapse and when the formation of a new one becomes impossible. On the other hand, the Prime Minister may at any time dissolve parliament in Canada, Denmark, Ireland, Spain and Sweden. However, in Norway parliament cannot be dissolved, and in Belgium and the Netherlands parliament can only be dissolved in situations when there is a constitutional revision. (Lane, 1996: 133-34).

133. Ibid., Article 50 (3) and Article 51. The parliamentarism employed in the Ethiopian Constitution has its own characteristics for it is practised in a federal system. Parliament may pass laws that concern the powers given to the federal government under the Constitution. The amendment of the Constitution has also to pass through stringent approvals of not only the House of the Federation, which is the representative of the member states, but also garner the endorsement of the member states. Hence, it would not be difficult to see that the powers of the parliament are limited. On the other hand, one can see how powerful the

British parliament is. Dicey explains the British parliament sovereignty as follows: "The principle of parliamentary sovereignty means neither more nor less than this, namely, that parliament thus defined has, under the English constitution, the right to make or unmake any law whatever; and, further, that no person or body is recognised by the law of England as having a right to override or set aside the legislation of parliament". (Dicey, 1959: 39).

134. Ibid., Article 56; The Constitution provides for a two "Federal Houses: the House of Peoples' Representatives and the House of the Federation". It is stipulated that members of the House of Representatives, on the basis of population and a special representation for minority nationalities, would not exceed more than 550. Currently, the House is consisting of 546 members directly elected by constituencies of 100,000 inhabitants and representatives of 22 minority nationalities for five-year term (Proclamation No. 1/1995, Article 53-54).

135. Ibid., Article 73 and 74; as in many parliamentary democracies, there is no strict separation of personnel between the legislative and executive branches and many of the members of the cabinet could be members of the legislative branch. The executive is formed by a political party or a coalition of political parties that have the greatest number of seats in the House of Peoples' Representatives' as well as 'lead it'. However, the cabinet is not required strictly to be composed of members of the two Houses. Non-House members with required qualifications could join the cabinet as long as they got the approval of the House of the Peoples' Representatives (Ibid., Articles 56 and 74).

136. See Finer, 1978: 71.

137. Proclamation No. 1/1995, Article 69 and 71. The powers and functions of the President are mainly proclaiming the laws and international agreements passed by the House; appointing ambassadors and other envoys upon recommendation by the Prime Minister; receiving credentials of foreign ambassadors and foreign envoys; granting high military titles upon recommendation of the Prime Minister; awarding prizes; and granting pardon in accordance with the procedures of the law. In addition, he opens the joint session of both Houses at the beginning of their annual sessions. (Article 71).

138. Ibid. Article 70 (1 & 2).

139. Ibid., Article 70 (3).

140. Ibid., Article 72 (1); Article 74 (1) states that the Prime Minister is the Chief Executive, the Chairman of the Council of Ministers, and the Commander-in-Chief of the national armed forces.

141. Ibid., Article 72 (2).

142. Ibid., Article 73 (1).

143. Ibid., Article 60 (1); in some parliamentary democracies such as Canada, Denmark and Sweden, the Prime Minister has the power to dissolve parliament at any time. Countries such as France and Germany have constitutions, which provide for the Prime Minister or the Chancellor respectively to require the President to dissolve the legislature and call new elections. In Britain, the Prime Minister has the right

to require the Queen to dissolve parliament and issue the writs for new general elections. (Finer et al., 1995; Lane 1996).

144. Ibid., Article 60 (2).
145. Finer et al., 1995: 156.
146. Proclamation No. 1/1995, Articles 78 (1) and 79 (1).
147. Ibid., Article 78 (2).
148. Ibid., Article 78 (3).
149. Ibid., Article 78 (4).
150. Ibid., Article 78 (5). This sub-Article is stipulated in relation to Article 34 (5) of the Constitution, which states the adjudication of disputes relating to personal and family laws can be handled in accordance with religious or customary laws, with the consent of the parties to the dispute.
151. Kemal Bedri, President of the Federal Supreme Court, interview, December 23, 1997. The Constitution of the People's Democratic Republic of Ethiopia (the constitution under the military government) declares that judicial powers are vested only in the courts, but failed to stress that they are independent from both the legislature and the executives (Article 100). Article 101 indicates that judges of the Supreme Court should be elected by the legislature, and at the same time, the legislature has the right to recall the judges it elected. Moreover, the judicial administration formed was led by the Minister of Justice and only two judges were members. (See the Constitution of PRDE, 1987).
152. Ibid., Article 79 (2).
153. Ibid., Article 79 (3).
154. Ibid., Article 79 (4). The grounds for the termination of the tenure of any federal judge is detailed by Proclamation No.24/1996, Article 9 as follows: 1) upon resignation, subject to a two-month prior notice; 2) where he has attained the age of 60; 3) where it is decided that he is incapable of properly discharging his duties due to illness; 4) where he has committed a breach of discipline; 5) where it is decided that he is of manifest incompetence and inefficiency; 6) where he has transgressed the Disciplinary and Code of Conduct Rules for judges.(Proclamation No. 24/1996. Federal Judicial Administration Commission Establishment Proclamation, Federal, February 15,1996); and for further details of the debate, see Minutes of the 23rd Regular Session of the House of Peoples' Representatives, February 14, 1996 (in Amharic).
155. Scholler, "Strengthening and Capacity building of the Regional Judiciary in Ethiopia", Recht in Africa, 1999: 61; Shetreet explains that the independence of the judiciary is comprised of two aspects, which are the independence of the individual judges and the collective independence of the judiciary as a body. The individual judge should enjoy substantive independence, which means that in the making of judicial decisions and exercising other official duties, he is subject to no other authority but the law. Besides, his personal security should be assured by judicial appointment during good behaviour terminated at retirement age, and by protecting judicial remuneration from encroachment (Shetreet, in Shetreet and

Dachenes, 1985: 598). This is in fact reaffirmed by the international instrument on the Basic Principles on the Independence of the Judiciary, Article 11 that states "the term of office of judges, their independence, security, adequate remuneration, condition of service, pensions and the age of retirement shall be adequately secured by law" (Basic Principles on the Independence of the Judiciary, 1985, Article 11). Furthermore, Article 7 states that "it is the duty of each Member State to provide adequate resources to enable the judiciary to properly perform its functions" (Ibid., Article 7). This is to ease the pressure that can be created through material constraints. Governments are supposed to provide the judiciary with resources that may enable it to function properly within the countries' capabilities.

156. See Finer et al., 1995: 88-89.
157. Proclamation No. 1/1995, Article 81 (1).
158. Ibid., Article 81 (2).
159. Ibid., Article 81 (3).
160. Ibid., Article 81 (4).
161. Ibid., Article 79 (6).
162. Ibid., Article 79 (7).
163. Ibid.
164. The Constitution provides for the formation of a council but the Proclamation calls it a commission. It is the same institution in spite of the variation in name.
165. Fasil Nahum, Legal Advisor to the Prime Minister, interview, August 12, 1997.
166. Proclamation No. 684/2010, Amended Federal Judicial Administration Council Establishment Proclamation, July, 24, 2010.
167. Ibid., Article 5.1.
168. Ibid., Article 5.2.
169. Ibid., Article 6.
170. Ibid., Article 9 and 10.
171. Proclamation No. 1/1995, Article 80 (1 & 2).
172. Ibid., Article 80 (3) (a).
173. Proclamation No. 454/2005. A Proclamation to Re- amend the Federal Courts Proclamation, June 14, 2005, Article 4.
174. Ibid., Article 5.
175. Article 78(2) states "supreme federal judicial authority is vested in the Federal Supreme Court. The House of Peoples' Representatives, may, by two-thirds majority vote, establish nationwide or in some parts of the country only, the Federal High Court and First Instance Court it deems necessary. Unless decided in this manner, the jurisdictions of the Federal High Court and of the First-Instance Courts are hereby delegated to the state courts." See proclamation No. 1/1995. Proclamation of the Constitution of the Federal Democratic Republic of Ethiopia, August 21, 1995.

176. Proclamation No. 322/2003. A Proclamation to provide for the Establishment of Federal High Court in some Regions, April 8, 2003; Article 2.
177. Proclamation No. 25/1996. Federal Courts Proclamation, Federal, February 15, 1996.
178. Ibid., Article 3.
179. Ibid., Article 4 and 5. Some of the Sub-Articles in Article 4 are amended by Proclamation 321/2003. See Proclamation No. 321/2003. A Proclamation to Provide for the Amendments of the Federal Courts Proclamation, April 8, 2003.
180. Ibid., Article 32 (1).
181. Ibid., Article 32 (2 & 3). The institutions may include government offices, associations, organisations, law faculties, and scientific institutions, and even individuals who can contribute to the purpose of the Plenum.
182. Ibid., Article 33.
183. See the Constitution of the Amhara National Region, Article 63. In case of the Southern Regional State, the Constitution in addition provides for the establishment of Special Woreda High Court, where a relatively small nationality enjoys its woreda self-administration. (See the Constitution of the Southern Nations, Nationalities, and Peoples, Article 62 (1).
184. For example, see the Constitution of the Southern Regional State, Article 94. Similar provisions are provided by all state constitutions.
185. Proclamation No. 1/1995, Article 83; in times of disagreement, various countries employ diverse methods of constitutional review to determine whether the issue at hand is constitutional or not. In countries like the United States, the Federal Supreme Court has the ultimate power of judicial review of the constitution. As a result, not only the Supreme Court but also lower federal courts have the power to declare congressional or presidential acts unconstitutional. On the other hand, in some countries such as the United Kingdom and New Zealand, the parliament is the ultimate interpreter of the Constitution. Others have created constitutional courts or councils to review issues arising from the Constitution. Regular courts do not have the power to decide on constitutional issues other than submit them to the constitutional courts or councils (see Finer et al., 1995: 28-29; Lijphart, 1984: 191-93; Woll, 1986: 7; and Murphy, in Greenberg et al. (ed), 1993: 15). Articles 134-137 of the Italian Constitution establish a constitutional court, which is composed of jurists who serve for twelve years and are nominated by the President, the Parliament and the judiciary one-third each. (Friedrich, in Zurcher (ed.), 1976: 21); similarly, the German Basic Law establishes judicial review and vests it in the constitutional court (Articles 92 & 93). Article 94 (1) states that 'the Federal Constitutional Court shall consist of federal judges and other members. Half of the members of Federal Constitutional Court shall be elected by the Bundestag and half by the Bundestrat' (see Finer et al., 1995: 174-75). Furthermore, the Parliament enacted the Federal Constitutional Court Act of 1951 that states 'the decisions of the Federal Constitutional Court shall be binding upon the constitutional bodies of the Federation and of the Lander

as well as upon all law courts and public authorities'. (quoted in Murphy, in Greenberg et al. (ed.), 1993: 15). In France, Article 56 of the Constitution of the Fifth French Republic of 4 October 1958 provides for the establishment of the Constitutional Council. It states that 'the Constitutional Council shall consist of nine members, whose term of office shall last nine years and shall be renewable... Three of its members shall be appointed by the President of the Republic, three by the President of the National Assembly, and three by the President of the Senate'. Prior to the 1974 amendment, those who can submit questions of constitutionality to the Council were only the President, the Prime Minister and the Presidents of the two chambers. The amendment added to the list a group of sixty deputies or sixty senators, however, it seems the channels for submitting constitutional questions are limited (see Finer et. al., 1995: 230-31; and Lijphart, 1984: 194). The above examples are mentioned here in order to show that there is no uniformity of institutions entrusted with the interpretation of constitutions. The institutions are devised in a way each country thinks suitable to serve the purpose.

186. Dawit Yohannes, Former Speaker of the House of Peoples' Representatives, interview, December 19, 1997 (He was Secretary of the Constitution Commission, which drafted the Constitution).

187. For example, see the Constitution of the TigrayNationalState, June 19, 1995, Article 66; and the Constitution of the Afar National State, June 1995, Article 68.

188. For further reading of the objectives of the training and its function, see Proclamation No. 364/2003, A Proclamation to Provide for the Establishment of Justice Organs Professionals Training Centre, September 9, 2003.

189. See Malanczuk, Akehurst's Modern Introduction to International Law, 1997: 209; Birch, The Concepts and Theories of Modern Democracy, 1993: 120-121; Hannum (ed.), Guide to International Human Rights Practice, 1992: 4-6; the rights that are heralded by the international conventions are, to a large extent, rights against the state. In this respect, the state is ought to respect and fulfil its human right obligations. Eide remarks "the role of the states is...a dual one. The state must respect human rights limitations and constraints on its scope of action, but it is also obliged to be active in its role as protector and provider". Therefore, the state is expected not only to refrain from any violations, but also to promote and protect the rights of the individual as provided by international conventions and national constitutions (see Eide, in Eide and Hagtvet (ed.), Human Rights in Perspective: A Global Assessment, 1992: 5).

190. Malanczuk, The Universality of Human Rights and Differences in Asian and European Values from the Perspective of International Law, Paper for the Informal ASEM Human Rights Seminar, Beijing, 28-29 June, 1999: 5.

191. Ibid., p. 36. The debate on the primacy of one category over the other has also been part of the polemics between the West and the rest of the world on human rights. Evidently, the West regards civil and political rights as central to human dignity while others accord primacy to economic and social rights (Ghai, "Human Rights and Governance: The Asia Debate", Australian Yearbook of International Law, 15, 1994: 24; Monshipouri, 1995: 17). In addition, cultural, economic and political

diversities present a strong challenge to the notion of the universality of human rights. Such factors are put forward against any scrutiny on human rights practices in many countries. In this respect, Mahbubani's remark is representative of the Asian elite's viewpoint: "There is only one force that has the power to 'liberate' the Third World. Economic development is probably the most subversive force created in history. It shakes up old social arrangements and paves the way for the participation of a greater percentage of society in social and political decisions. The Chinese Communist Party can no longer regain the tight totalitarian control it enjoyed in Mao Zedong's time. Deng Xiaoping's reforms have killed that possibility. Hence, if the West wants to bury forever Mao's totalitarian arrangements, it should support Deng's reforms to the hilt, even if he has to occasionally crack down to retain political control" (Mahbubani, Can Asians Think?, 1998: 76).

192. These rights are reflected in international instruments such as the Universal Declaration of Human Rights, 1948; the International Covenant on Economic, Social and Cultural Rights, 1966; the International Covenant on Civil and Political Rights, 1966; and other relevant conventions. For details, see The United Nations, Human Rights: A Compilation of International Instruments, Vol. 1, 1994; see also the African Charter of Human Rights and Peoples' Rights adopted at the 18th Summit of the Heads of State and Government of the OAU in June 1981(for the full text of the Charter, see Ambrose, Democratization and the Protection of Human Rights in Africa, 1995: 181-93).
193. Malanczuk, 1997: 209.
194. The Transitional Period Charter of Ethiopia, July 22, 1991, Article One.
195. The International Covenant on Civil and Political Rights and the International Covenant on Economic, Social and Cultural Rights were ratified on June 11, 1993. The Convention against Torture and Other Cruel, Inhuman or Degrading Treatment or Punishment was also ratified on March 14, 1994. (See Ministry of Foreign Affairs, List of International Human Rights Instruments Ratified by Ethiopia, August 2002). See also letters signed by the President of the Transitional Government on May 26, 1993 to accede to the mentioned covenants (Letters provided by the Ministry of Foreign Affairs, August 2002).
196. For further information, see 4.12.2.
197. U.S. Department of State.Ethiopia Human Rights Practices, 1995, March 1996: 3.
198. Sorenson, in Sorenson (ed.), Disaster and Development in the Horn of Africa, 1995: 8.
199. Proclamation of the Constitution of the Federal Democratic Republic of Ethiopia, August 21, 1995, Article 13 (2).
200. See Ibid., Articles 13-44.
201. Ibid., Articles 78-79; See also Proclamation No. 24/1996. A Proclamation to Provide for the Establishment of the Federal Judicial Administration Commission, which has the purpose of protecting the judiciary from the encroachment of its powers by the other branches of government.

202. Ibid., Article 55 (14).
203. Ibid., Article 55 (15).
204. For example, see Proclamation No. 1/1995. Constitution of Southern Nations, Nationalities, and Peoples' Regional State Proclamation, Debub Negarit Gazeta, June 22, 1995; and Proclamation No. 2/1995. A Proclamation to Provide for the Establishment of the Constitution of the Amhara National Region, Zikre Hig, June 22, 1995.
205. See Human Rights Watch, Ethiopia Reckoning under the Law, Vol. 6, No. 11, December 1994: 18-25.
206. See Dritz, N. J. (ed.), Transitional Justice. How Emerging Democracies Reckon with Former Regimes, Vol. I, II, and III, Washington D. C: United Institute of Peace, 1995.
207. For detail information on the South African Truth and Reconciliation Commission (TRC), visit the TRC's home page at http://www.doj.gov.za/trc/index.html; see also Nattrass, Nicoli, "The Truth and Reconciliation Commission on Business and Apartheid: A Critical Evaluation", African Affairs, vol. 98, no. 392, July 1999: 373-391.
208. Proclamation No. 22/1992.A Proclamation to Provide for the Establishment of the Special Public Prosecutor's Office,, August 8, 1992.
209. Ibid., Article 6.
210. See Amnesty International Reports, 1992-97; for example, see Amnesty International Report, 1995: 128-31; Amensty International Report, 1996: 148-51 and Amnesty International Report, 1997: 149-52.
211. Announcement by Girma Wakjira, Special Prosecutor, on February 13, 1997 to diplomats and the press.
212. Ibid.
213. Trial Dateline, Consolidated Summary of Red Terror Trials, Trial Observation and Information Project, No. 1, Addis Ababa, March 1999: 2.
214. SPO Blood-Soaked Files, list of convicted Derg Officials, January 2009 (in Amharic). The book explains in details horrific crimes perpetuated by the Derg officials during their stay in power, especially during the shameful "Red Terror" Period between 1977 and 1978.
215. For the basis and procedure of the pardon process, see Proclamation No. 395/2004. A Proclamation to provide for the Procedure of Granting Pardon, April 17, 2004.
216. See Amnesty International Report, 1997: 149-52.
217. Human Rights Watch. Ethiopia: The Curtailment of Rights, December 1997.
218. Ibid.
219. Interview, Financial Times, March 2, 1998.
220. See Proclamation No. 210/2000, A Proclamation to Provide for the Establishment of the Human Rights Commission, July 4, 2000 and Proclamation No. 211/2000,

A Proclamation to Provide for the Establishment of the Institution of the Ombudsman, July 4, 2000.

221. See The Transitional Period Charter of Ethiopia, July 22, 1991.
222. Ibid.
223. Proclamation No. 1/1995, August 21, 1995, Article 29.
224. Ibid., Article 30.
225. Ibid., Article 32.
226. Ibid., Articles 33-44; the right to development and environmental rights are included in the Constitution as mere declaration, which can be reflected in development programs of the country. There exists a controversy in their status as the third generation of human rights between developing and Western countries. (For further discussion, see Malanczuk, The Universality of Human Rights and Differences in Asian and European Values, 1999: 18-23).
227. See the constitutions of the nine regional-states. There is no any variation even in the wording of the mentioned articles.
228. Proclamation No. 3/1991.Proclamation to Establish the Procedure for Peaceful Demonstration and Public Political Meeting,, August 12, 1991.
229. Ibid., Article 3.
230. Ibid., Article 4.
231. Proclamation No. 34/1992. A Proclamation to Provide for the Freedom of the Press,, October 21, 1992.
232. Ibid., Article 3.
233. Ibid., Article 8.
234. Ibid., Article 10 (2).
235. The arguments of the supporters and opponents of the Article are discussed below.
236. See Proclamation No. 113/1995. Ethiopian Press Agency Proclamation, March 1, 1995; Proclamation No. 114/1995.Ethiopian Radio and Television Agency Proclamation, March 1, 1995; and Proclamation No. 115/1995. Ethiopian News Agency Proclamation, March 1, 1995.
237. See Proclamation No. 178/1999. A Proclamation to Provide for the Systematic Management of the Broadcasting Service, June 29, 1999.
238. See Proclamation No. 533/2007. A Proclamation on Broadcasting Service, July 23, 2007.
239. Proclamation No. 590/2008. Freedom of the Mass Media and Access to Information Proclamation, December 4, 2008, Article 4(1)
240. Ibid., Article 4(2).
241. Ibid., Articles 11-31.
242. Proclamation No. 46/1993 Political Parties Registration Proclamation, April 15, 1993, Article 4.
243. Proclamation No. 573/2008. The Revised Political Parties Registration Proclamation, September 24, 2008.

244. Ibid., Article 4(2).
245. Ibid., Article 5.
246. Ibid., Article 6(1).
247. Ibid., Article 11.
248. Ibid., Article 40.
249. For details, see Articles 32-36.
250. Broadcasting Authority, List of Broadcasters, Periodicals and Magazines, December 2012.
251. Proclamation No. 590/2008. Freedom of the Mass Media and Access to Information Proclamation, December 4, 2008.
252. Ibid., Article 12.
253. See ibid.
254. See ibid, Articles 31-33.
255. Ibid., Article 34. See also Proclamation No. 211/2000. A Proclamation to Provide for the Establishment of the Institution of the Ombudsman, July, 4, 2000.
256. Council of Ministers Regulation No. 158/2008. Government Communication Affairs Office Establishment Council of Ministers Regulation, January 1, 2009.
257. Finer et al., 1995: 39.
258. Tomschat, in Rosas and Helgesen (eds.), 1992: 27.
259. Ibid., p. 46.
260. See NEB, List of Political Parties and Organization, December 2012.
261. See Proclamation No. 3/1991. Proclamation to Establish the Procedure for Peaceful Demonstration and Public Political Meeting,, August 12, 1991.
262. Diamond, in Diamond (ed.), 1992: 17.
263. Linz, 'Transitions to Democracy', 1990: 161.

Chapter 6
Devolution of Power

Federalism and Federal Systems

The devolution of power in Ethiopia was carried out by adopting a federal system. Assessment of the extent of the devolution of power can be made by looking at the federal system provided by the Transitional Period Charter and then reinforced by the Constitution of 1994. The federal arrangement and its implementation need also to be analysed in relation to federal systems existing in other countries. Federal systems in different countries have their own history of evolution. Some federations such as the United States, Switzerland and Australia were created by aggregation of previously established political units while others have been created by devolution of a unitary state as it was in Germany. The Ethiopian experience resembles the latter one.

As federalism is practised in many countries, it would certainly have certain variations of content from one country to the other. However, it may be possible to define it in its most common features. Wheare defines a federal system as "an association of states, which has been formed for certain common purposes but in which the member states retain a large measure of their original independence".[1] A broader view is provided by Elazar that defines federalism as "the mode of political organisation which units separate politics within an overarching political system so as to allow each to maintain its fundamental political integrity".[2] Similarly, Riker explains federalism as "a political organisation in which the activities of government are divided between regional governments and a central government in such a way that each kind of government has some activities on which it makes final decisions".[3]

These definitions indicate the existence of the division of powers between the central and regional governments, in which the latter are territorially defined, and the arrangement is fundamentally unchangeable as long as the system continues to be a federal one.[4] In addition to this primary federal principle, Lijphart identifies other five secondary characteristics: a written constitution; bicameralism; the right of the component units to be involved in the process of amending the federal constitution but to change their own constitutions unilaterally; equal or disproportionally strong representation of the smaller component units in the federal chamber; and decentralised government.[5]

Usually, a federal system is adopted in countries where a unitary system is incapable of satisfying the aspirations and needs of the people. These aspirations might evolve from cultural, political or social cleavages that cannot be accommodated in unitary structures. The United States, for example, chose a federal arrangement to satisfy the diverse interests of the previously existing independent entities. On the other hand, Canada had not only to accommodate several independent entities but also the cultural and linguistic diversity of Quebec, which is largely a French-speaking territory.[6] Nevertheless, there is a wide-range of variations in the application of the federal system depending on the diverse situations of each and every nation. Accordingly, there are federations composed of territorial units with "cultural patterns, social groupings and political institutions" that are similar in each of the units and in the federation as a whole, which Tarlton named symmetrical federations.[7] In this category, one may include relatively symmetrical federations such as Australia, Austria and Germany. On the other hand, asymmetrical federations are "composed of political units corresponding to differences of interest, character, and make up that exist within the whole society".[8] The latter category is relatively complex and prone to instability for it involves religious, ethnic and cultural cleavages, which require a high degree of systemic accommodation. Countries with segmented societies based on ethnic or strong religious divisions are included in this category and the arrangement is required to protect their distinct features within the federation.

Federalism emerges out of necessity, crisis-situation, or compulsion. It evolves from concrete and tangible needs or pressures.[9] Some factors such as similarity of feelings, mutual economic needs, defence and security concerns, cultural similarities, historical background and mutual heritage can serve to create the foundation for a federal arrangement.[10] All factors have not received equal weight in causing the institution of federal arrangements. Riker emphasises that the vulnerability of the individual member state makes the necessity of a collective defence policy a prime motive for any movement towards a federal structure.[11] As Riker pointed out, it was a driving factor in the formation of the Canadian Confederation, but it might not be a dominant factor in the formation of federations in other countries. In some countries, economic needs or the preservation of diversity within unity was the driving factor. One factor alone cannot produce the intended results and has to be enforced by other concerns.

Cooding explains that the Swiss Constitution framers were faced with the task of creating "a system of government that would provide security against external enemies and internal conflicts and furnish the conditions necessary for the attainment of a good life for a maximum number of individuals".[12] He further explains that the emphasis on federalism was considered not only to create unity but also to recognise the historical importance of the cantonal units and the cultural differences that existed among them.[13] The above mentioned factors cannot by themselves be the right foundation for the creation of federations. They need to be politically articulated and used as a basis for political bargaining and accommodation.

The institution of federal structure provides several advantages to the population who opted to adopt the arrangement based on the above-discussed necessities. Some of the advantages are detailed as follows: enhancing citizen participation, building sub-national "laboratories of democracy"; making government relevant to localised needs; placing greater restraints on the central government; providing greater avenues for protection of minority identity, rights and interests; promoting diversity and experimentation; and enhancing efficiency and performance by bringing government closer to the population.[14] Similarly, proponents of federalism argue that a federal arrangement is a form of empowerment, by which the voices of regional actors are heard and addressed prudently. Moreover, federalism has to provide for substantial devolution of power to the grassroots in which they would be encouraged to handle their local affairs by themselves. In this regard, Elazar explains that "the federalist revolution has been directed toward serving the cause of equality by creating better instrumentalities for citizen involvement in public affairs through the development of governmental arenas of differing size and scope, ranging from the immediately local to the most general".[15]

As mentioned above, by constraining the powers of the centre and diffusing the powers to the constituent units, federalism helps to mitigate conflicts and promotes accommodation. Specifically, it provides the mechanism to protect the rights and freedoms of multi-ethnic societies, especially minorities. Accordingly, "as an ideology, federalism assumes that the retention of some degree of group liberty is a democratic requisite in territorially-fragmented societies and that compound politics are better safeguards against the abuse of political power in general".[16] Furthermore, the federal structure facilitates the development of various institutions that would help the people to exercise their self-rule and also promote their language and culture. Based on the experiences of many federal countries, Elazar remarks that "federal ideas have made possible the development of new forms of community with new instruments for local self-government by making it possible to build new societies through contractual relationships rather than relying on kinship or other traditional ties".[17]

One other point worth mentioning concerns the fiscal relationships between the federal and regional governments. Federal constitutions are usually designed to reflect the allocation of autonomous revenue resources to both levels of government to cover their expenditures and the mechanism of transferring resources between them to correct imbalance.[18] Such relationships include the need to correct horizontal imbalances relating to disparities in the revenue capacity of different member units by means of general equalisation transfers and grants to support certain development programs. Watts states that "most federations have established federal governments with sufficient authority to play a substantial redistribution role through broad equalisation schemes and weighted specific grants intended to assist the less wealthy constituent units".[19] The effective division of revenue complimented by substantial transfers and grants might enable regional governments to function in accordance with powers accorded to them by the constitution. Without adequate resources, the constituent units would have difficulty to protect and defend their powers and rights enshrined in the constitution.

Federal systems do not follow similar patterns in dividing state powers between the centre and the constituent units. In countries such as the United States, Switzerland and Germany the residual legislative powers have been left with the constituent units. Article 3 of the Swiss constitution reads: "the cantons are sovereign so far as their sovereignty is not limited by the federal constitution, and, as such, they exercise all the rights which are not delegated to the federal power".[20] Similarly, Article 30 of the German Constitution declares "except as otherwise provided or permitted by this Basic Law, the exercise of government powers and the discharges of governmental functions shall be incumbent on the Länder".[21] In fact, the provision is further made clear by Article 79 (1) that states "the Länder shall have the right to legislate in so far as this Basic Law does not confer legislative power on the Federation".[22] On the other hand, the Canadian Constitution has left the residual legislative powers with the federal government rather than the states.[23] Similarly, the Indian Constitution, after detailing the Union List, the State List and the Concurrent List, the residuary powers are vested in the centre.[24]

Federalism has been applied in conjunction with consociational arrangements[25] in some countries. Of course, consociational arrangements do not exist in all federalist countries. For instance, there is no sign of such arrangement in countries like Germany while substantial elements of consociational democracy have been reflected in India and other multi-ethnic societies.[26] Provided the segments of the multi-ethnic societies are geographically concentrated and the boundaries of the component units follow the segmental borders, a federation with its principles applied can also be a consociation.[27] The two crucial principles of federalism are also consociational elements: the component units enjoy a high degree of secure autonomy in organising their internal affairs; and they all participate in decision-making at the central level of government. However, every consociation is not a federation, and at the same time, a federation is not necessarily a consociation. Hence, a federation can be a consociation if it is a democratic system, which exists in pluralist societies. Furthermore, all four principles of consociational democracy should be applied: a substantial segmental autonomy; a formal or informal grand coalition of government at the centre; a formal or informal veto power for the minority segments; and proportional representation or overrepresentation of the minority in all affairs.[28]

The federal solution has had its own ups and downs in this century. After the Second World War, it was applied in many newly independent countries, in South and South-East Asia and Africa. By 1960s, many of the federal experiments faced difficulties and as a result some of them were dissolved or suspended. Some of the federal systems were able to reconcile "the desire, on the one hand, for larger political units required to build an efficient and dynamic modern state, and the search, on the other, for identity through smaller self-governing political units more responsive to the individual citizen and the desire to give expression to primary group attachments, distinctive religious, linguistic, cultural, social and historical traditions".[29] Hence, there have been successful federations, which have proved to be innovative enough in tackling the difficulties encountered and in strengthening their systems to face further challenges. Watts summarises the lessons obtained from the experiences of the post Second World War federal systems as follows:

> First, federal political systems do provide a practical way of combining, through representative institutions, the benefits of unity and diversity, but there are no panaceas for humanity's political ills. Secondly, the degree to which a federal political system can be effective will depend upon the degree to which there is acceptance of the need to respect constitutional norms and structures and an emphasis upon the spirit of compromise and tolerance. Thirdly, the extent to which a federal system can accommodate political realities is likely to depend not just on the adoption of federal arrangement but upon whether the particular form or variant of federal system that is adopted or evolved gives adequate expression to the demands and requirements of the particular society in question.[30]

The success of some countries in maintaining their federal systems has been mainly dependent on their ability to manage conflicts. The existence of different identities and interests has made it evident that conflicts are inherent components of federal systems. The main factor that helped the successful ones is not "they have eliminated conflict but because they have managed it".[31] In this case, the ability to develop self-restraint and accommodative political culture plays a significant role in managing conflicts that may surface with time and socio-economic changes. Elazar remarks that "federalism can exist where there is considerable tolerance of diversity and willingness to take political action through conciliation even when the power to act unilaterally is available".[32] Thus, the federal institutions need to be flexible enough to adapt to changing situations, which are usually applied in incremental adjustments over a long span of time. With all its shortcomings, federation has presented itself as one of the alternatives of government and especially as the best alternative form of government for countries with strongly fragmented communities, which have the desire to protect their identity and interests while recognising the benefits of forming and preserving a larger unit. Elazar remarks the relevance and contribution of federalism as follows:

> Federalism has had a tendency to attract adherents who are searching for panaceas. As in every other human situation there are no panaceas. But federal principles, arrangements and practices, like those of democracy itself, applied however imperfectly, often have strengthened the forces of peace and democracy in the world.[33]

The Evolution of Federal System in Ethiopia

Ethiopia's experience with devolution of power and federalism began in 1991 after the military government was overthrown and a Transitional Government was installed. The decision made at the National Conference, which formed the Transitional Government, was designed to reverse the process of excessive centralisation perpetuated for the last hundred years. Many nationalities raised arms against the central government to secure their autonomy and self-rule. The main force that challenged the central government and caused its demise came from those organisations that fought for self-determination. It was critical for the new administration to address the issue of devolution of power from the start.

The National Conference of July 1-5, 1991 adopted Article Two, which declared that the right of nations, nationalities and peoples to self-determination was affirmed. The nationalities right to preserve their identity, to promote their respective cultures and history, and use and develop their languages was recognised. Moreover, the Charter upheld the right to self-rule, and fair and proper representation of the nationalities in the central government.[34] Based on the principles of the National Charter, Proclamation No. 7/1992 was enacted to institute the devolution of power from the centre and to create the regional self-administrations.[35] The Proclamation represented an important departure from the strong tendency of centralising government under previous regimes and a decisive step towards the establishment of a federal state.

Article 3 (1) provided for the establishment of fourteen national/regional self-governments. It enumerated 63 nationalities, which were incorporated in the fourteen regional administrations.[36] Furthermore, it provided for 48 of the identified nations, nationalities and peoples the right to establish a form of self-government at woreda (district) level or above.[37] It also left open the opportunity for adjacent self-governments to jointly establish a larger self-government within any of the fourteen administrations mentioned above.[38] The regional self-governments were vested with legislative, executive and judicial powers but they were "in every respect, entities subordinate to the Central Transitional Government".[39] From this sub-Article, it was clear that the self-governments would enjoy extensive powers but the ultimate power remained in the hands of the central government.[40]

One of the contentious provisions was Article 4, which provides for the delimitation of the borders of the national self-governments. The provision was in line with Article 3 of the National Charter, which states "there shall be a law establishing local and regional councils for local administrative purposes defined on the basis of nationality".[41] For clarity purposes, Proclamation No. 7/1992 defined nation or nationality as "a people living in the same geographical area and having a common language and a common psychological makeup of identity".[42] Hence, Article 4 (1) of the same Proclamation stated, "the adjacent of territory settled by a nation, nationality and people shall be the basis for the delimitation of the borders of a National Self-Government".[43] The borders of the woredas that existed prior to 1974 were taken as a basis for the delimitation and woredas with more than one nationality were incorporated to the adjacent self-government of the nation, nationality or people of which more than fifty per cent of the woreda is composed. In spite of the provisional status of such arrangements of delimitation,[44] the problem arose in woredas where none of the nationalities in the respective woreda was more than fifty per cent. It was stated that the problem should be solved by agreement between the two adjacent self-governments. For instance, the Bege Special Woreda case was one example where the two adjacent self-governments, the Oromia and Benshangul-Gumuz states, could not agree on its status. Finally, the problem was solved through a referendum of the woreda people, in which they voted overwhelmingly to be incorporated into the Oromia State.[45]

The Proclamation also specified the powers of the self-governments by stating that "the National/Regional Transitional Self-governments shall have legislative, executive and judicial powers in respect to all matters within their geographical areas except such matters as defence, foreign affairs, economic policy, conferring of citizenship, declaration of a state of emergency, deployment of army where situations beyond the capacity of National/Regional Transitional Self-government arise, printing of currency, establishing and administering major development establishments, building and administering major communications networks and the like, which are specifically reserved for the Central Transitional Government because of their nature".[46] The Article at first glance seemed to provide that the residual powers rest with the self-governments, however, the broad concepts such as economic policy, establishing and administrating major development establishments, including the words "such matter as" and "the like" signify that the list was not exhaustive.[47] Thus, the provision did not provide a strict delineation of powers in unequivocal terms. Such a perception might be reinforced by assessing sub-Article 9 (2) which indicated that the powers and responsibilities of the central organs would be proposed by the Council of Ministers and decided upon by the Council of Representatives of the Central Transitional Government, which vested the final say in the hands of the central legislature.[48]

The special powers of the national/regional self-governments are listed in Article 10 of the Proclamation. The powers vested in the self-governments need to be implemented in line with the general policies and regulations of the central government. The power and duties of the self-governments are: to borrow from domestic lending sources and levy taxes; to issue and implement laws and rules relating to public services; to plan, to direct, and supervise social and economic development programs; to establish, direct and supervise social and economic enterprises; to prepare, approve and implement their own budgets; to administer, develop and protect natural resources; to employ and administer the personnel of their own self-governments; to establish and direct the security and police force ; and to establish a judicial organ with regional jurisdiction. In addition, they are entitled to own property and have the right to transfer ownership when the need arises.[49]

The Proclamation declared that judicial power in any region should be exclusively vested in courts and confirmed the independence of the judiciary.[50] Apart from the Regional Council, the other structure provided by the Proclamation was the woreda administration.[51] In fact, it was up to the Regional Council to organise and decide upon the structure of administration in between the two levels wherever needed. In practice, zonal administrations were established without elected councils and legislative powers except in nationality based zones.

Proclamation No. 7/1992 is the first attempt to devolve power from the centre to the regions since the emergence of modern Ethiopia. It is evident that the implementation process was difficult and it required strong commitment and patience. The devolution process had a number of critics. There were political groups like the All Amhara People's Organisation (AAPO) and the royalist

Moa Anbessa Organisation, who regarded the devolution of power as a ploy to disintegrate the unity of the country, and also, as a tactic employed by "the Tigrians to divide the nation and sustain their rule".[52] Others such as the Council of Alternative Forces for Peace and Democracy in Ethiopia (CAFPDE) while supporting the devolution of power objected to the delimitation of borders along ethnic lines claiming it would harm the unity of the country.[53] On the other hand, the Oromo Liberation Front, though its representatives were active in the drafting and approving the Proclamation, was not enthusiastic for its implementation. Many suspect that the OLF was not satisfied because it did not go far enough to weaken the powers of the centre.[54]

As discussed above, elections were held in June 1992 to implement the devolution of power provided by Proclamation No. 7/1992. The major contribution of the 1992 elections was that it enabled the regions to establish their own governments, and also provided the opportunity to create government structures down to the level of kebeles. Despite the boycott of some organisations and some reports of election irregularities, it created the minimum condition for carrying out administrative and economic development activities. Proclamation No. 41/1993 was enacted to define the powers and duties of the central and regional executive organs.[55] It envisaged the creation of 20 bureaux, which corresponds with the number of ministries at the centre.[56] The bureaux had the power to execute their respective functions within the region and were required to submit periodic activity reports to the regional executive organ as well as to the concerned central executive authority.[57]

Similar to the democratic transition, the devolution of power has also been a new venture to Ethiopia. In the last hundred years, modern Ethiopia was ruled by an absolute monarchy, which consolidated its power at the expense of the regional polities who had traditionally enjoyed a wide-range of autonomy and little interference in their domains by the centre. The same line was followed by the pro-Soviet military dictatorship in the midst of the emergence and consolidation of regional resistance against centralisation. Consequently, the excessive centralisation and the repression perpetuated to remain in power brought the country to the verge of disintegration in 1991. The only option for democratic transition and peaceful reconciliation was the adoption of the right to self-rule. Of course, no one could fully predict the implications of the concept applied in the process. Nevertheless, in the short term it brought peace to the troubled country, and the experience obtained in the implementation of the Proclamation and other related instruments contributed to the drafting process of the Constitution and to the refinement of the functions of the federal system.

The Constitution articulates a more advanced federal framework, compared with the earlier Proclamations. Accordingly, the relationship between the states and the federal government is substantially different from that between the pervious self-governments and the central government. The first Article of the Constitution declares that a federal and democratic state structure is established.[58] The Federal Democratic Republic is comprised of states, which are "delimited on the basis of the settlement patterns, language, identity and consent of the people concerned".[59] Subsequently, Article 47 states that the federation is comprised of nine member states: the State of Tigray; Afar; Amhara; Oromia; Somalia; Benshangul-Gumz; the Southern Nations, Nationalities and Peoples; the Gambella Peoples; and Harari.[60] The Constitution declares that the nations, nationalities and peoples within the enumerated states have the right to establish their own states if the need arises.[61] The procedures for acquiring the statehood status are detailed in the same Article.[62] The capital city, Addis Ababa, has an extensive self-government, but short of attaining statehood and the administration is responsible to the federal government.[63]

The federal government and the states have legislative, executive and judicial powers.[64] The State Council is the highest organ of the state authority and is responsible to the People of the state.[65] The State Council is sovereign in matters that rest within the jurisdiction of the state powers, and above all, has the exclusive power to draft, adopt and amend the state constitution.[66] Further, the notion is confirmed by Article 50 (8) that states "Federal and State powers are defined by this Constitution. The States shall respect the powers of the Federal Government. The Federal Government shall likewise respect the powers of the States".[67] Thus, the devolution of power is no mere decentralisation; it is devolution of rights to the states, which are protected by the Constitution from encroachment by the central government.

The Constitution delineates the powers and functions of the federal and state governments. As discussed, the governing principle of the division of power is that the states are sovereign in matters that fall within their jurisdiction while the federal government is mandated with full responsibility for common matters as well as for matters affecting more than one state.[68]

The radical departure from the previous arrangement that was provided by Proclamation No. 7/1992 is Article 52 (1) that states "all powers not given expressly to the Federal Government alone, or concurrently to the Federal Government and the States are reserved to the States".[69] This is, in fact, similar to Article 70(1) of the German Basic Law which states "the Länder shall have the right to legislate in so far as this Basic Law does not confer legislative power on the Federation".[70] Having secured the residual powers at the hands of the states, the Constitution articulates some of the powers and functions of the states in Article 52 (2).[71]

The Constitution does not provide any structure for the devolution of power within the states. The task of establishing other levels of administration is left to the states. However, Article 50 (4) states "adequate power shall be granted to the lowest units of government to enable the people to participate directly in the administration of such units".[72] However, the states took relatively longer time to devolve power to the lower levels of administration. It was only in the second-half of 2001 that the constitutions of the major regional states were amended to devolve more powers to woreda (district) councils.[73]Similarly, the constitutions of the regional states were slow to clearly separate legislative and executive branches of government. For some years, the president of the state was also the chairman of the regional council, which compromised the independence of the legislature to oversee the activities of the executive branch.

Nationalities within the states are entitled to have their own zonal or special woreda councils with a substantial autonomy.[74] Except for those zones constituted by distinct nationalities, zonal administrations do not have councils and plenums of their own. The zonal administration members are appointed by the president of the region except for the Chief administrators who are required to be confirmed by the regional councils.[75] On the other hand, the nationality zones councils are comprised of representatives elected by the people and those elected by the zone for the state council.[76] Unlike the other zonal administrations, the nationality zonal councils have legislative, executive and judicial powers. They determine their working language, levy and collect duties from specified activities by the state constitution, and organise executive and judicial organs within the zone. Special woredas, which are also constituted by minority nationalities, are entitled to similar rights and powers.[77]

The other administrative level with elected council is the woreda administration. The woreda council is elected by the people from among kebele (neighbourhood) residents within the locality of the woreda.[78] The woreda councils are important low-level administrative organs with elected members and officials, where major governmental activities are led and performed.[79] The lowest and basic administrative organs are the kebele councils, which are elected by the people of the neighbourhood and perform government affairs at grassroots level.[80] They play a significant role in mobilising and organising the people to participate in developmental and other local activities. The regional state constitutions were later amended to facilitate the smooth functioning of the various levels of government. For instance the Tigray regional state was amended in March 2005 and April 2005.[81]Some of the amendment deals with clarifying woreda councils' powers and their relations to the regional council. Article 73(3) states that woreda council is accountable to the regional council as well as to the woreda people.[82] In addition, Article 52(3) and 77(3) were amended to bring about solutions to council sessions' quorum difficulties. It lowers the required quorum from two-third members to 50 per cent plus one and it allows the possibility of passing decisions by majority vote of those in attendance.[83] It also included some articles that allow the regional council to appoint interim administrations in times of failure of the elected administration to properly function in adverse situations. It further details the powers and functions of the interim administrations. Moreover, some articles were amended that were found to be impediments to providing responsive and effective governance.[84]

Undoubtedly, there is a growing drive to devolve more power downward to bring the affairs of government "nearer to the people". The design has been to create the conditions for the most local decisions to be handled at grassroots level with direct participation of the concerned people. Gradually, the people are more participating in their local affairs in a meaningful way. The recent drive to enhance production and productivity are led with full participation of the rural population. The soil and water conservation initiatives performed with full participation of the local people have produced commendable results in many regions. The notion of acting together based on these decisions is a good sign of popular participation in their own governance. In fact, such experience should be made to encompass other daily livelihood of the people.

Fiscal Decentralisation and Its Development

The Concept of Fiscal Decentralisation and Experiences of Federal Countries

Fiscal decentralisation is one of the most important aspects of federalism to be examined in order to determine whether there is real devolution of power to regional governments. The trend of devolution of the powers of spending and raising revenues to lower levels of government has increased in recent years in many countries. While there may be many reasons for this in differing countries, a key factor is the recent drive towards more democratic and open government. Ter-Minassian explains that "this trend is partly a reflection of the political evolution toward more democratic and participatory forms of government, seeking to improve the responsiveness and accountability of political leaders to their electorate, and to ensure a close correspondence of the quantity, quality, and composition of publicly provided goods and services to the preferences of their beneficiaries".[85]

In fiscal decentralisation the main issue is the division of responsibilities among the various levels of government concerning taxation, expenditure and regulatory powers. Such assignment of functions is usually linked with a structure or a mechanism of resource transfers between those level of government.[86]

Expenditure assignments are mostly related to the responsibilities of each and every level of the government and are defined by the constitution or relevant law of the country. Oates promotes "the decentralisation theorem" to be applied in the attempt to divide expenditure assignments between various levels of government. It is stated that " for a public good- the consumption of which is defined over geographical subsets of the total population, and for which the costs of providing each level of output of the good in each jurisdiction are the same for the central or the respective local government- it will always be more efficient (or at least as efficient) for local governments to provide the Pareto-efficient levels of output for their respective jurisdictions than for the central government to provide any specified and uniform level of output across all jurisdictions."[87] From the above argument, the states should be responsible for the provision of public goods that can be provided efficiently and effectively at their level. Accordingly, the states would be responsible for providing local services including health care, education, welfare services, state transportation and communication, family and child support services, natural resources management, and other local utilities.[88]

On the other hand, Oates argues that "the central government should assume primary responsibility for resolving the stabilisation and distribution problems and for providing efficient outputs of those public goods that significantly affects the welfare of individuals in all jurisdictions".[89] Hence, the responsibilities of the federal government are mostly set in relation to the tasks of the provision of national public goods and services, the maintenance of the efficiency of the internal market and the objective of achieving redistributive equity in the country as a whole. Accordingly, the federal government would be responsible for sectors such as defence, foreign affairs, international trade, macroeconomic stability, and other services that transcend state borders.[90]

Division of expenditure assignments between the central and sub-national governments varies in its extent from one country to the other depending on historical, political and cultural circumstances. Ahmed *et al* note that "among the six industrial federations (Australia, Austria, Canada, Germany, Switzerland, and the United States), the share of local (municipal) expenditures in total government expenditures varies from 7 per cent in Australia to 24 per cent in Switzerland; the state or provincial share of total expenditures varies from 14 per cent in Austria to 43 per cent in Australia".[91] As indicated, the share of federal expenditures is a significant part of the total expenditures in all the mentioned countries because of the high costs of the assignments such as defence bestowed on the central governments.[92]

The issue of financing the expenditure tasks assigned to all levels of government is another important aspect of decentralisation addressed by constitutions in many federal countries.[93] The financing sources are mainly tax assignment and the arrangements of transfers of resources from one level to the other level of government. Boadway et. al. note that "the nature of the decentralisation of revenue raising responsibilities will depend upon the role of the federal government in addressing the problem of redistributive equity".[94] On the other hand, the decentralisation process has to take into account that the state governments need to finance some of their expenditures with their own resources. Hence, four general principles are consider in allocation of taxing powers, which are economic efficiency, national equity considerations, administrative feasibility and fiscal need or revenue adequacy. In this regard, Musgrave suggests the following principles, which are basically based on equity and efficiency criteria as follows:

1. Middle and especially lower level jurisdictions should tax those bases which have low inter-jurisdictional mobility;
2. personal taxes with progressive rates should be used by those jurisdictions within which a global base can be implemented most efficiently;
3. progressive taxation, designed to secure re-distributional objectives, should be primarily central;
4. taxes suitable for purpose of stabilisation policy should be central, while lower-level taxes should be cyclically stable;
5. tax bases, which are distributed highly unequally among sub-jurisdictions, should be used centrally; and
6. benefit taxes and user charges are appropriate at all levels.[95]

These principles are useful to the discussion of allocation of revenue sources to each and every level of government. Direct taxes such as corporate taxes, capital taxes, personal income taxes, taxes on wealth and wealth transfers, and trade taxes are good candidates for the central government and indirect taxes such as excises and general sales, and property taxes and users' taxes are suitable for state and other lower levels of government.[96] Based on the above principles, Musgrave and Musgrave summarise the approximate tax assignments by level of government as follows:

Central level	Middle Level	Local Level
1. Progressive income tax	1. Income tax on residents	1. Real property tax
2. Death Duties	2. Income tax on income due to factors owned by residents and on income accruing to non-residents but originating within the jurisdiction	2. Payroll tax
3. Natural resources taxes	3. Retail sales tax	3. Benefit charges
	4. Origin-type product tax as benefit charge	

Source: Musgrave and Musgrave, 1989: 470.

Although the general trend is as discussed above, experiences differ from one country to the other depending on historical, geographical, ethnic, and constitutional particularities of a specific country. Australia has a two-tiered highly centralised system. The commonwealth government administers and collects about 80 per cent of the taxes. Its dominance is created because of its control of the major sources of tax revenue such as the personal income tax, customs and excise, company income tax, and sales tax.[97] On the other hand, Canada has a two-tiered highly decentralised system where the provinces have substantial revenue collection powers. Taxes such as the personal income tax, the corporate income tax, the goods and services tax are at the hands of the federal government while the personal income tax and the corporate income tax (collected by the federal government but remitted in part to provinces), the retail sales tax, and resource taxes are the prerogatives of the provinces. The property tax is left to lower local administrations.[98]

Germany has a three-tiered tax assignment system where tax legislation is fully centralised. The federal government is in control of taxes such as surcharge on income and corporation tax, road transport tax, customs tax, excises on mineral oil, tobacco, and alcohol (except beer), capital transactions tax and insurance tax. The Länder collect revenue from net wealth tax, motor vehicle tax, beer tax, real property transfer tax, and betting and lottery tax while municipalities administer business profits tax, property taxes and communal levies on public services (utilities).[99] In addition, taxes such as wage tax, assessed income tax, non-assessed taxes on earnings, corporation tax, turnover tax (VAT), and import turnover tax are common taxes or shared taxes between the federal and Länder governments.[100]

The above-discussed expenditure and tax assignments to various levels of government usually create vertical and horizontal imbalances in their fiscal capabilities. Vertical imbalances emerge when the revenues and expenditures at particular levels of government within a federation are unequal. On the other hand, horizontal imbalances evolve when the own fiscal capabilities of various subnational governments of the same level show disparity.[101] Federal countries normally attempt to address the imbalances by adopting a variety of resource transfer and borrowing mechanisms in order to bridge the gap between expenditure responsibilities and resource capabilities of subnational governments.

Bahl and Linn explain that intergovernmental grants are "a compromise solution in the debate over the division of revenue-raising authority and expenditure responsibility. They permit national governments to retain the authority to tax productive resource bases, but guarantee state and local governments a flow of revenues".[102] These intergovernmental resource transfer mechanisms are supposed to be designed to advance equity and, at the same time, efficiency of the economy. These grants are needed to address inter-jurisdictional spill overs;[103] bridge the fiscal gap between revenue means and expenditure needs, attain minimum standards of services all over the country; narrow differential net fiscal benefits across subnational territories;[104] and to achieve economic stabilisation objectives.[105] These transfer mechanisms can be grouped in to two categories: conditional transfers (or specific purpose payments) and unconditional transfers. Conditional transfers include various types of grants such as matching grants, non-matching grants for specific purposes, and block grants. In these types of grants, the grantor defines, to a certain extent, their specific purposes. On the other hand, unconditional transfers include revenue-sharing mechanisms, with or without distributional criteria, and general-purpose grants. These grants are usually provided to the recipients to use them according to their own priorities.[106]

Federal countries employ different resource transfer mechanisms depending on their internal situations and their respective policies. As discussed above, Australia's vertical imbalance is wider than many federal countries and resource transfers from the Commonwealth government play a larger role in enabling the subnational governments to cover their expenditures. Resource transfers are handled by a permanent institution, the Commonwealth Grants Commission (CGC), which assesses the claims forwarded by the states. The CGC functions in accordance with the terms of reference provided by the commonwealth after consultation with states and territories.[107] The CGC determines the needs according to the principle "that each State should be given the capacity to provide the same standard of state-type services as the other states, if it makes the same effort to raise revenues from its own sources and conducts its affairs with the same operational level of efficiency".[108] The assessment includes both revenue-raising capacities and expenditure needs. The CGC produces recommendations and usually, but not automatically, accepted by the Commonwealth and state governments.[109]

In Switzerland, the need for revenue transfers to the disadvantaged cantons is reflected in the Constitution. Article 135 of the Constitution notes that "the Confederation shall issue regulations on the equitable equalization of financial resources and burdens between the Confederation and the Cantons as well as among the Cantons."[110] Article 135(3) further indicates that "the funds for the equalization of financial resources shall be provided by those Cantons with a higher level of resources shall amount to a minimum of two thirds and a maximum of 80 per cent of the payments made by the confederation."[111] Revenue transfers are made with the objective of enabling the cantons to provide similar levels of services without forcing them to levy taxes that are heavier than the other better-endowed cantons. Such redistributive objectives are implemented through three types of vertical financial adjustments: federal tax reimbursements, tax sharing, and specific purpose grants.[112] These redistributive grants are partly based on a cantonal fiscal capacity measure, which is determined by a formula. The formula contains four ingredients: the cantons fiscal revenue per capita, the canton's GDP per capita, regional (cantonal and local) tax effort, and the canton's specific expenditure requirements.[113]

Similarly, the German Constitution contains provisions that provide for equalisation considerations among the Länders. Article 107(2) of the Basic Law states that "Such statute [federal statute with the consent of the Bundesrat] shall ensure a reasonable equalisation between financially strong and financially weak Länder, due account being taken of the financial capacity and financial requirements of communes or association of communes... Such statute may also provide for grants to be made by the Federation from federal funds to financially weak Länder in order to complement the coverage of their general financial requirements (supplementary grants)".[114] The Federal Government provides grants that are conditional and intended to co-finance specific state projects. These conditional grants are mainly provided for education, health, welfare, and infrastructure. It also provides unconditional grants to support the poorer states of the federation. Both these grants have distributional objectives on the provision of public services.[115]

In addition, horizontal grants and equalisation schemes are applied to enhance the distributional mechanism. First, the Länder share of the turnover tax (VAT) which is about 45 per cent of the total is shared among the Länders using an equalising method. About one quarter of the Länder VAT share is distributed to support the financially weaker ones and the rest is distributed according to the population of the Länders. Secondly, a horizontal scheme of interstate equalisation without federal government interference provides another source of revenue for the relatively poorer Länders. Revenue transfers are made from the richer to the poorer in order to bring the fiscal capacity of the latter to an acceptable standard.[116]

In India, as discussed above, the revenue sharing scheme created vertical imbalances that have to be narrowed through grants by the central government. These are several groups of grants provided to the state governments. The grants-in-aid account for about 7 per cent of the transfers, which are recommended by financial commissions in order to address the residual deficits of non-plan revenue accounts of state governments.[117] There are also grants decided by the Planning Commission on the condition that it approves the state development programs. These grants are provided in accordance with a formula that comprises weights of 60 per cent for population, 25 per cent for per capita income, 7.5 per cent for a combined index of tax effort, literacy, and completion of foreign aid projects, and 7.5 per cent for special problems.[118] In addition, transfers are made for specific purpose programs such as assistance for hill area development, matching grants for foreign aid projects, emergencies and to improve specific services. Although these transfers are made by taking into consideration the need to favour relatively poorer states, there exist substantial horizontal imbalances among them.[119]

The other means of closing the gap between expenditures and revenue resources available to subnational governments is borrowing either in the open market or from central government funds if these are available. In most cases, borrowing is not left to subnational governments to decide. The approaches used by various countries in respect of control of subnational borrowing can be grouped into four broad categories. Of course, countries are not confined to using one or the other but to a mix of them. These categories are: 1) sole or primary reliance on market discipline; 2) co-operation by different levels of government in the design and implementation of debt controls; 3) rules-based control; and 4) administrative controls.[120] Although the first approach has been used in countries like Canada and Brazil until recently, most countries exercise some level of controls to avoid unnecessary subnational indebtedness.[121] These controls of borrowing take various forms such as setting of annual limits on the overall debt of each subnational government; reviewing and authorisation of individual borrowing undertakings; and/or centralising all government borrowings with the objects of lending subnational government for approved investment projects.[122]

Fiscal co-ordination among central and subnational governments is important to ensure fiscal discipline and stability. In Switzerland, fiscal co-ordination is advanced through some budget directives: a) the growth rates of public expenditures should not exceed the expected growth of nominal GNP; b) the budget deficit should not be higher than that of the previous year; c) The number of civil servants should stay the same or increase only very slightly; d) the volume of public sector building should remain constant and an inflation indexation clause should be avoided.[123] In Germany, the Constitution stresses that "the Federation and the Länder shall have due regard in their budget management to the requirements of overall economic equilibrium".[124] It further indicates that "through federal legislation requiring the consent of the Bundesrat, principles applicable to both the Federation and the Länder may be established governing budgetary law, responsiveness of budget management to economic trends, and financial planning to cover several years ahead".[125] As mentioned, an effective federal-länder co-ordination is ultimately ensured through the Bundesrat where the Länders send their representatives.

As discussed above, fiscal decentralisation is a complex and difficult undertaking but imperative for building a federal system. Experiences indicate that achieving a satisfactory and smooth working mechanism needs time and learning on the job. In addition, it requires hard work and consensus building not only on revenue sharing and resource transfers but also in achieving a reasonable fiscal harmonisation and discipline at all levels of government. On the other hand, lack of local administrative experience, institutions, and competence should not be used as an excuse for not decentralising responsibilities to subnational governments.

The Development of Ethiopia's Fiscal Decentralisation

In Ethiopia, fiscal decentralisation began during the transitional period and continued in its stronger form after the establishment of the federal government. The process of fiscal devolution began in 1992 after the promulgation of Proclamation No. 33/1992, which defined the sharing of revenue between the central government and the national/regional self-governments.[126] The revenue instruments were categorised as central, regional and joint, and the objectives of the revenue sharing were to: enable the central and the national/regional governments to efficiently carry out their respective duties and responsibilities; assist national/regional governments develop their regions on their own initiatives; narrow the existing gap in development and economic growth between regions; and encourage activities that have common interest to regions.[127] The central government was charged with the powers to determine the policies applied not only to its own but also to the joint ones. Besides, it was also charged with ensuring the measures enacted by the regions and the central government were consistent with a unified tax policy base.[128] In fact, the powers of the regions to pursue independent revenue policies are practically limited as the economic base still remains relatively small.

As discussed above, the Constitution provides the states with extensive expenditure powers. It also specifies that "the Federal Government and the States shall respectively bear all financial expenditures necessary to carry out all responsibilities and functions assigned to them by law".[129] Accordingly, the states enjoy reasonable powers in determining revenue policies and collecting taxes. Article 95 of the Constitution states that the sharing of revenue has to take the federal arrangement into account.[130] Accordingly, the federal government collects revenue from levies on imports and exports; personal income tax on employees of the federal government and international organisations; income, profit, sale and excise taxes on enterprises owned by the federal government; taxes on national lotteries; taxes on the income of air, rail and sea transport services; the rental income taxes for houses and properties owned by the federal government; fees and service charges on services provided by the federal government; taxes on monopolies; and federal stamp duties.[131]

On the other hand, the state revenue instruments include: income taxes on employees of the state and of private enterprises; fees for land usufructuary rights; the agricultural income taxes; the profit and sales taxes on individual traders; taxes on income from transport services rendered on waters within their territory; the rental income tax from private houses and other properties, and also collect rent on houses and other properties they own; the profit, sales, excise and personal income taxes from enterprises owned by the states; taxes on income, royalties and land rentals of mining operations, which are applicable in conjunction with Article 98 (3); charges and fees for licenses and services rendered by state organs; and royalty for use of forest resources.[132]

The joint taxation powers apply to the profit, sales, excise and personal income taxes from jointly established enterprises, the taxes on the profits of companies and on dividends due to shareholders, and on incomes derived from large-scale mining and all petroleum and gas operations, and royalties on such operations.[133] Later, Article 98 was amended because of the difficulty it caused in implementation. According to the Constitution, the House of Peoples' Representatives and the State Councils are the only authorities with the powers of levying taxes in their respective domains. Hence, levying jointly means that the two levels of legislatures have to meet to decide on such matters, which is difficult to implement. In order to avoid such complications, it was decided that the federal government would levy and collect the taxes and royalties and the sharing of the revenue between the federal and state governments would be decided by the House of the Federation in accordance with Article 62 (7) of the Constitution.[134] The joint session of the House of the Federation and the House of Peoples' Representatives decides on the ownership of unallocated taxes by a two-thirds majority.[135]

Apparently, the states' exclusive domain of tax bases is currently small. The federal government, in 2010/11, collected 83 per cent of the aggregate tax revenue and 75 per cent of the aggregate non-tax revenue. For example, the federal government collected the export and import taxes, which accounted about 40 per cent of the country's aggregate tax revenue in the same year. It also collected over 80 per cent of the indirect domestic taxes, which are 27 per cent of the total tax revenues.[136] The future expansion of the economic base and the gradual improvement of the regional tax administrations would narrow the wide disparity. However, such developments are likely to take place gradually and might not radically change the overall standing of both levels of government in terms of their resource capabilities in the near future. The states will continue to be mainly dependent on the resource transfers from the centre.

Harmonised and standardised tax bases are envisaged at the federal and regional levels.[137] The Council of Ministers Regulations No. 17/1997 indicates that consultations between federal and state governments should take place on all new or changed taxes at both levels of government to ensure that the tax bases are harmonised and standardised. Hence, the Ministry of Finance is expected to provide the required research and administrative support to that effect.[138] Such tax harmonization process was reaffirmed by Council of Ministers Regulation No. 190/2010.[139]

The revenues collected by states only cover a small part of their expenditures. On the other hand, the block subsidy to regions annually increased on average of 28.9 per cent between 2006/07 and 2010/11. Similarly, the average annual subsidy for regions was 31.4 per cent of the total federal expenditure within the same period.[140] In 2011/12, subsidy to regions that includes block subsidy and special subsidy to support millennium goals initiatives reached 39.4 per cent of the total expenditures. In 2012/13, it was increased to 41 per cent.[141] As indicated, the share of the federal government is still greater because of its undertakings of major capital and infrastructural projects. However, the expenditure responsibility assigned to the regional governments is considered to be "close to what is found in a highly decentralised system".[142] Moreover, the areas devolved by the federal government are regarded to be extensive in relation to other developing countries and any further devolvement has to be done gradually, while giving more attention to enhance efficiency in the already devolved areas.[143]

In accordance with Proclamation No. 41/1993, regions started preparing their budgets, for the first time, for the 1993/94 budget-year.[144] Each region had to prepare and implement its own capital and current budget proposals and was included in the overall consolidated budget of the central government. Since the Constitution entered into force in 1995, the states have to prepare and implement their own budgets[145]and the federal government's powers are limited to the preparation and implementation of its own budget.[146] Neverthcless, the federal government is expected to advise the state governments of their budget subsidy ceilings in time for them to prepare their regional budgets, based on their subsidy share and the availability of the resources. [147] Some of the regions have had some difficulties in preparing their budgets and had to be assisted by the centre. Substantial improvements have been achieved since the early years. However, the minority states still face enormous difficulties because of the shortage of skilled manpower.[148]

As mentioned above, these regions have had to rely on central government's transfers including foreign assistance. The resource transfers of the states are determined, first, by estimating the total resources available, which include domestic revenues, counterpart funds, loans and assistance. Then the federal government requirements, both recurrent and capital budget, are deducted to give the total remaining resource available for state transfers. These transfers have been made using a formula that has been changing in the past years in order to find one that can satisfy the various participants.

The grant system has been in place since 1993/94 and the formula to determine the share of the regions has been developing with time.[149] The 1993/94 subsidy gave priority to projects in agriculture, education, public health and rural roads and was distributed on the basis of first, the on-going projects transferred from the central government to the regional governments and second, an assessment of the regions' capacities to implement projects.[150] In the 1995/96 budget-year, three variables were used for the determination of the amounts of allocations for each region: population, the regional revenue budget in 1994/95, and the I-distance indicator.[151] These three variables were given an equal weight of 33.3 per cent each.[152] Of course, there were some shortcomings in the formula, which needed to be addressed. For the 1995/96 allocations outdated population data was used, data which was also used for the 1992 elections. The I-distance indicator used very heterogeneous variables, which had some deficiencies in assessing the actual situations in the regions. For example, road density in sparsely populated desert areas and highly populated highland and urban areas cannot have the same meaning. In 1996/97 the same formula and weightings were used, although the I-distance indicator was simplified by using only five variables instead of the eight. The indicator was changed with a new name, the development index. The variables used were number of health clinics, number of primary schools, number of telephone lines, electricity consumption and road density. Except for using a reduced number of factors, the formula was more or less the same in its content with the previous one. The reasons mentioned for using the same criteria of the previous year were inadequate information on the variables that constitute the I-distance indicator, constraint of time and the delay of the population census that was underway at the time.[153] After a long debate on the issue it was approved unanimously by the House of the Federation with the exception of one abstention.[154]

An attempt to improve the grant system was again made in the 1997/1998 budget-year. Similar variables were employed but with different weightings. Accordingly, 60 per cent was given to population number, 25 per cent to development index and 15 per cent to the amounts of revenues contributed by each region.[155] There was a slight change made to the development index by using six factors. These variables were education level, health sectors indicator, road density, electricity consumption, water supply and telephone coverage. Representatives of minority regions were uncomfortable with the overwhelming weight given to the population size and argued that the criteria showed double counting as the populous regions are the relatively developed ones in the country.[156] Many representatives were not satisfied with the criteria and the weight accorded to them; however they chose to endorse the proposal because of the absence of other alternatives and the limited service of the proposal for only the 1997/1998 budget-year. The proposal was approved by 73 in favour, 1 against and 5 abstentions.[157] The same formula was used for the 1998/99 and 1999/2000 resource transfers to the regional states.

Certainly, the formula suffered from a number of shortcomings. One was that the formula lacked adequate provision for measuring revenue-raising capacity of the regional states as well as rewarding better performing state governments. Second, the formula failed to include other major indicators of expenditure needs, such as the size of the people under poverty line, vulnerability to drought, variations in unit costs of construction, distance as a measure of additional cost, or variation in recurrent cost need and indicators of project and program implementation. Third, the development level index included variables such as electricity consumption, telephone lines, and asphalt roads, which are under central government jurisdiction and do not have any impact on the expenditure responsibilities of state governments.[158] These and other deficiencies such as the level of transparency of the formula and its application were raised and the House of Federation had instructed the Ministry of Economic Development and Cooperation to review the formula and come up with proposals to improve it at its Third-year Second Regular Session between April 9-10, 1998.[159]

As mentioned above, a formula was designed for the years between 2000/2001-2002/2003 was presented to the House of the Federation and was approved after extensive deliberations.[160] The new formula was intended to address the above-discussed shortcomings and also attempted to incorporate some experiences from other countries such as India, Australia, Germany and Switzerland. In this formula, poverty level was included in addition to the previous three indicators: population, level of development, and revenue-raising effort. In addition, the development index consisted of five variables including education, health, rural road, water and recurrent or administrative cost indicators. These variables were made to address the expenditure pressures of regional governments by adding unit cost of construction for education, health and rural road sectors as it varied from region to region. The population indicator was also based on the projection for 2001/2002 rather than taking the 1994 census and attempts were made to update the overall data concerning the other variables.[161] The weights assigned to indicators were 55 per cent to population, 10 per cent to the level of poverty, 20 per cent to the level of development (expenditure needs) and 15 per cent to revenue raising effort and sectoral output performance indicator. Out of the 15 per cent, 11 per cent was assigned to revenue-raising effort and the remaining 4 per cent to sectorial output performance indicator.[162]

Similar attempt was also made in 2003/04 budget year. The difference was that the poverty-level indicator was dropped. The three previous indicators, population, expenditure needs, and revenue raising effort and sectorial output performance with 65 per cent, 25 per cent and 10 per cent respective weights were used. [163] The next one was the 2006/07 formula which was prepared for the first time by the House of Federation with the support of the Ministry of Finance and Economic Development. The formula was based on the regions gap of fiscal capability to finance their expenditures. This means it based itself on the gap created between the regions' expenditure needs and their revenue raising potential. In addition, it reserved 1 per cent of the total subsidy resource to exclusively support the relatively less developed four regions: Somalia, Afar, Benshangul Gumuz, and Gambella regions.[164] The revenue collection effort and the performance level indicators were dropped. Although it solved some regions' objections on the previous one, the formula still didn't satisfy to those who better use their capital expenditures and attempted to relatively narrow their gap in capital needs by involving various initiatives with the participation of the people. The formula seemed to benefit those who showed wider capital needs gap as it took country-wide standard as a measurement. Moreover, there was no adequate mechanism to regulate the 1 per cent additional subsidy provided to the four regions whether it was used for its intended aims.

The House of Federation recently approved a grant allocation formula that would be used for budget years between 2012/13 and 2016/17. The House of Federation in collaboration with relevant institutions made an extensive study to identify and explain the bases of the formula. The revenue potential and expenditure needs of the regions were taken as the two factors to design the formula. The revenue potential of each region was determined by considering the major revenue sources of the region and application of appropriate tax rates. It took a revenue source with most lucrative potential that accounts for highly substantial percentage of the total revenue collected by the regions as a "representative" one. The approach called the Representative Tax System (RTS) uses a designated potential tax base with the application of appropriate tax rate to attain the revenue potential. Accordingly, pay-roll tax, agriculture income tax, land use fee, livestock tax, profit tax, turnover tax and value added tax (VAT) were used to arrive at the revenue potential of a region. [165]

On the other hand, the expenditure needs of the regions were assessed using the sectors that usually take on the average of over 90 per cent of the regions' expenditure resources. The sectors designated to indicate the expenditure needs were general administration including state institutions, justice, security and general service; primary and secondary education, including TVET; public health; agriculture and rural development; environmental protection, drinking water development; rural road construction and maintenance; urban development; and development of micro and small-scale enterprises. [166] Apparently, the fiscal gap was calculated by deducting revenue raising potential of the regions from their total expenditure need. The final subsidy percentage of the region was reached by applying adjusted relative spatial relative price index[167] to the 50 per cent of the estimated expenditure need.

As shown in Table 6.2, the House of Federation considering the above factors and applying some adjustments, the shares of the regions were computed. It was decided that the formula and the percentage of the shares from the total resource would be applied for the next five years.

Table 6.2. Percentage share of each region from the overall resource pool

Regions	Percentage of shares
Tigray	7.18
Afar	3.15
Amhara	23.17
Oromia	32.50
Somalia	8.14
BenshangulGumuz	2.10
SNNP	20.10
Gambela	1.50
Harari	1.00
Dire Dawa	1.16
Total	100.00

Source: The Federal Budget Grant Distribution Formula, 2012/13 – 2016-17, January 2012.

Evidently, the current formula is situated to better address the needs of the regions. It has been the product of enormous effort and extensive studies. However, it is still handicapped by the weakness of capacity to compile adequate and reliable data in the country. This weakness is not only manifested in the regions but also in the federal institutions which are supposed to compile adequate data for usage of pertinent institutions. Without minimizing such detrimental deficiencies, it will be farfetched to present such formula as one reflecting the actual situations. Notwithstanding, it can be considered as one that can be considered nearer to reflect the reality based on the existing environment.Undoubtedly, the formula needs further refinement by undertaking additional studies in light of future experience. In the future, other forms of grants, such as specific purpose transfers, need to be considered to address some of the uneven and disparate developments in economic betterment or provision of services. On the other hand, institutionalisation of the scheme is very important, which also requires the establishment of an independent grant commission or committee. The commission or committee would be in a position to make the necessary studies for improvement and also prepare the proposal for the yearly transfers made to the regions rather than having these tasks done by an ad-hoc one. The proposal, of course, has to be approved by the House of Federation in accordance with Article 62(7) of the Constitution.[168]

Subnational borrowing is provided for in the Constitution, but limited to domestic sources. Article 51 of the Constitution states that "it [the Federal Government] shall determine by law the conditions and terms under which States can borrow money from internal sources".[169] This provision is further explained by Proclamation No. 57/1996 that states "the Regional Governments shall provide the Ministry [Federal Ministry of Finance] with all information required to allow it to determine the amounts to be borrowed by individual Regions, taking into account national fiscal policy and borrowing limitations imposed by law or agreements".[170] The Council of Ministers Regulation No. 190/2010 states that "where state governments experience budget shortfall in any fiscal year, the government may give them loan in the form of advance to be charged to their budgetary subsidy of the following year."[171] Clearly, the federal government has some control on the ability of regional governments to borrow from internal resources. However, regional governments have not used their right to borrow to finance their projects or to fill gaps in their budgets except for some regional governments which provided credit, with the concurrence of the Federal Ministry of Finance and Economic Development, to farmers in the form of loan guarantees to commercial banks. At this stage, the federal government's control on the borrowing capabilities of the regional government is important for maintaining fiscal discipline and stability. Notwithstanding, the federal government might eventually need to put in place further detailed rules and regulations in which the regions' need of borrowing can be addressed by taking their capabilities into consideration.

Devolution of Power: Challenges and Prospects

Initially, the performance of the regional governments was not satisfactory because of skilled manpower shortages, scarcityof essential materials for project work, lack of experience in the newly elected leadership, compounded problems accumulated during the previous regime and other related difficulties.[172] However, these difficulties are being overcome and the performance of the regions, especially the bigger ones, has significantly improved. Their ability to collect revenue has also increased. Initially the States had the incentive of using revenues collected beyond the quotas for their own programs without affecting their share of subsidy from the federal government. This has been currently replaced by revenue raising potential which indicates that the benefit will be more if they exert maximum effort in raising taxes. Notwithstanding, they have not yet exhausted their revenue collecting potential and of course, will considerably expand with the fast and sustainable growth of the economy. Additionally, the tax bases left for the regions are yet to develop with the economic growth and the reduction of Ethiopia's level of dependence on trade taxes. Until then, they will remain highly dependent on the transfers made from the centre.

As mentioned, budget administration and implementation has reached satisfactory levels in some of the regions, particularly the Amhara, Tigray, Oromia and the Southern Nations, Nationalities and Peoples' States.[173] Visible progress has been made in providing social services and building infrastructure. The drive to improve food production has received the highest attention of the states' organs. Thousands of farmers have been provided with fertilisers, selected seeds and agricultural experts' advice and substantial increases of food production have been reported.[174] Extensive activities in water and soil conservation and building of small dams have been carried out. There have been substantial moves in capacity building activities such as training technicians of various levels, health professionals, agricultural experts, and lower and medium level managers. Nevertheless, the problem of capacity in running overall state affairs will continue to remain a major challenge in all states and human resources development will be at the top of the agenda for long time to come.

Apart from the capacity problem, there is a wide range of problems facing regional governments. Corruption and mal-practices are not yet in the past. Accountability among elected officials and civil servants has yet to develop. In addition to the usual checks and balances, the government has formed an independent corruption fighting institution. The institution has been working in educating civil servants and the people for some time now. It has also investigated and persecuted officials on corruption and bad governance practices. However, it requires enhancing its activities and making an impact on the improvement of transparency and accountability in the delivery of government services.

Initially, the bureaucracy inherited from the previous government was not ready to embrace the devolution of power and civil servants were reluctant to be transferred to regional or state organisations. The notion that states are peripheral and impose hardships remained in their minds and some were also politically opposed to the new system. In many cases, inexperienced graduates had to fill sensitive vacancies in the regional states. Gradually, the situation has been significantly changed. Regional governments have achieved visible progress in capacity building of their institutions and civil servants which resulted in the betterment of the delivery of services. Apparently, there have been signs of bad governance, and of course, the pace of improvement differs from region to region. Currently, the drive to introduce and build change, and organizing and facilitating the participation of major stakeholders around not only elevating the state of government services delivery but also to the standard that deserves the complements of the beneficiaries is underway. This initiative brings together the efforts of the ruling party, government institutions and the people to achieve good governance and socioeconomic transformation. The initiative might be in its early stage but its development and expansion seems inevitable since it continues to be at the top of the government's priority list.

The problems faced by the larger states have sometimes been exacerbated in the smaller states, which were previously known as the "peripheries". The basic difficulty in these regions, (namely Somali, Afar, Benshangul-Gumuz and Gambela) is the low level of capacity induced because of neglect and deprivation during the previous regimes. The difficulty has been compounded by the desire of the local elite to capture the state and use its resources for personal benefit.[175]Consequently, the federal government have been helping these regions by providing expertise in plan and project preparations as well as their implementation. Later, it has institutionalized the support by enacting the Council of Ministers Regulation No. 103/2004, which was later replaced by Regulation No. 242/2011.[176] Based on these regulations, a high level board has been established to follow and coordinate the support provided to these regions. Although a long way before reaching up to expectations, the support has been instrumental in the improvement of governance as well as the implementation of socio-economic programs and projects. Nevertheless, much is required to bring about tangible and qualitative change in the affairs of these regions.

Overall, much has been achieved in the improvement of self-government in all regions. Significant improvements have been witnessed in their human and material resources capacity in recent years. Apparently, the performance differs from region to region; however, it would be safe to indicate that the regional states are brining tangible socio-economic progress to their respective states. Evidently, Ethiopia's recent economic growth comes from the improved performance of the regions, especially in agriculture, micro and small enterprises, health and education, and other relevant sectors. While the so far achievements are commendable, there is still plenty of room for improvement.

The devolution of power, and in general, the federal system is taking root and has irreversibly changed the Ethiopian system of government. The federal system, as discussed, contains substantial elements of consociational democracy. As expected, it will play a significant role in managing conflicts that are inherent in segmented societies like Ethiopia. The composition of the Cabinet and other high official appointments reflect, apart from the necessary qualifications and personal merits, the nationalities' representation. In addition, the special representation of minority nationalities in the House of Peoples' Representatives and their overrepresentation in the House of the Federation confirms that the elements are seriously applied. Evidently, such practices have a long way to go to be irreversibly consolidated and become the ingrained feature of the country's political system.

As democracy and federalism are relatively new to Ethiopia, it is an uneven learning process. Devolution of power is not only a choice but also the only solution to bring a break with the past as the result of the disastrous evils of the former systems. Of course, it has never been nor will it be a panacea for all the country's ills. However, it has undoubtedly brought a relatively high degree of internal stability and peace to the country. In addition, if successful, it can provide a useful practical experience to many African countries, which have been troubled by ethnic tensions, but have not yet been bold enough to address them.

Notes

1. Wheare, 1963: 1.
2. Elazar, 1972: 65.
3. Riker, 1975: 101. King also defines federation using a different approach, but with more or less similar content as follows: "Federation is to be regarded primarily as an institutional arrangement...distinct national and regional units of government are assigned somewhat distinct powers within a perhaps new sovereign whole. At least some of the powers of the regions are entrenched, not by virtue of rendering the regions sovereign, but by constitutionally incorporating them into the decision-making procedure of the federal centre". (King, 1982: 89).
4. There have been some theorists who advocate what they call "corporate" federalism, which suggests the possibility of providing autonomy to geographically interspersed groups. However, the existence of such theory is unlikely to affect the general theory that a federal system is made up of territorially defined entities. (see Lijphart, 1984: 183-85).
5. Similar characteristics are also detailed by Watts as follows: 1) two orders of government each acting directly on their citizens, a formal distribution of legislative and executive authority and allocation of revenue resources between the two orders of government, including some areas of autonomy for each other; 2) Provision for the representation of regional views within the federal policy-making institutions; 3) a written supreme constitution not unilaterally amendable and requiring the consent of all or a majority of the constituent units; 4) an umpire (courts or referendums) to rule on disputes between governments; 5) process to facilitate intergovernmental relations for those areas where responsibilities are shared or overlap. (Watts, in Bertus De Villiers (ed.), 1994: 8-9).
6. See Boase, in Bertus De Villiers (ed.), 1994: 91.
7. Tarlton, Charles D. 'Symmetry and Asymmetry as Elements of Federalism', 1965: 868.
8. Ibid.
9. Simpson argues "devolution through the vertical distribution of government may be a way of pre-empting precipitous resort to violence in situations where there are a number of national entities coexisting precariously within one state. Devolution is the dispersal of power to non-state groupings whether on the basis of regionalism, federalism, or subsidiarity. As such, it may prevent a more catastrophic fracturing of government through revolution, secessionist interethnic conflict or political disintegration." (Simpson, "The Diffusion of Sovereignty: Self-Determination in the Post-Colonial Age", in Sellers (ed.), 1996: 53).

10. Wheare details some factors that led for the formation of a federal arrangement as follows: A sense of military insecurity and of the consequent need for common defence; a desire to be independent of foreign powers, and a realisation that only through union could be independence be secured; a hope of economic advantage from union; some political association of the communities concerned prior to their federal union... geographical neighbourhood; and similarity of political institutions- these half-dozen factors all operated in the United States, Switzerland, Canada and Australia, to produce a desire for union among the communities concerned. (Wheare, 1963: 37.)
11. Riker, 1964: 11-12.
12. Codding, Jr., 1961: 35.
13. Ibid.
14. See Agranoff, in Bertus De Villiers (ed.), 1994: 80.
15. Elazar, 1987: 262-63.
16. Hueglin, T. 'Legitimacy, Democracy and Federalism', 1987: 35.
17. Elazar, 1987: 262.
18. Tripathy, 1982: 31.
19. Watts, in De Villiers, 1994: 19.
20. The Federal Constitution of Switzerland, quoted in Codding, Jr., 1961: 43.
21. Finer et al., 1995: 143.
22. Ibid., p. 153; in the United States, the Constitution reserves residual powers to the states. The Xth Amendment states 'the powers not delegated to the United States by the Constitution, nor prohibited by it to the States, are reserved to the States respectively, or to the people'. (Ibid., p. 118).
23. See Bertus De Villiers (ed.), 1994.
24. Sarkar, 1991: 36-38.
25. For detailed discussions on consociational democracy, see Chapter One.
26. See Lijphart 1996.
27. Lijphart, 1979: 505.
28. Ibid., p. 509-10.
29. Watts, in Bertus De Villiers, 1994: 3.
30. Ibid., p. 6.
31. Ibid., p. 15.
32. Elazar, 1972: 360.
33. Elazar, 1993: 190-95.
34. The Transitional Period Charter of Ethiopia, July 22, 1991, Article 2.
35. Proclamation No. 7/1992, January 14, 1992.
36. Ibid., Article 3 (1).
37. The remaining 17 nationalities and peoples having a small-size of population, which are less than fifty per cent of the population of self-government woredas

were incorporated into the bigger woredas. For these minority nationalities sub-Article 5 (3) provided them with the right to be represented properly. It stated that 'minority nationalities within the Woreda shall, irrespective of the small size of their population; have appropriate representation in the Woreda Council for the purpose of achieving national composition thereof'. (Ibid., Article 5 (3).

38. Ibid; Article 2(b). Not long five National/Regional Self-Governments (Region Seven, Region Eight, Region Nine, Region Ten and Region Eleven) came together to form a larger self-government named the Southern Ethiopia Nations, Nationalities, and Peoples' Self-Government, which is comprised of over 45 nationalities.

39. Ibid., Article 3.

40. In this respect, sub-Article 9 (3) made it clear by stating that 'a National/ Regional Transitional Self-Government shall be accountable to the Council of Representatives of the Central Transitional Government and to the people of the region and the nation that elected it'. (Ibid., Article 9 (3).

41. The Transitional Period Charter of Ethiopia, July 22, 1991, Article 13.

42. Proclamation No. 7/1992, Article 2 (7).

43. Ibid., Article 14 (1).

44. The woreda as a basis for delimitation was taken as a temporary solution until the study was finished which later enabled to lay down the specific geographical borders of each nation, nationality and people. (Ibid., Article 2 (a).

45. The district was the Bege Special Woreda and the Oromia and Benshagul-Gumuz states were in disagreement and could not solve it bilaterally. Hence, the Transitional Government's Prime Minister's Office decided a referendum to be held and until then a neutral body administered the district. The referendum was held on July 2, 1995 and the majority of the people voted to be included to the OromiaState. 90% of the people were registered to vote, and 81% of them voted on their future status. Accordingly, an overwhelming majority of 67% voted for Oromia and the results were accepted by both states.

46. Proclamation No. 7/1992, Article 9 (1).

47. The Article was too ambiguous to clearly delineate the powers between the two levels of government. Besides, the Proclamation did not clearly protect the National/Regional Self-Governments from any encroachment from the centre.

48. Ibid., Article 9 (2).

49. Ibid., Article 10.

50. Ibid., Article 23 and 26.

51. Ibid., Article 38.

52. Various statements made since the adoption of the Transitional Period Charter have entertained the viewpoints. (See the statements of the All Amhara People's Organisation and the Moa Anbessa Organisation).

53. See the Political Program of the Council of Alternative Forces for Peace and Democracy in Ethiopia, March 3, 1996 (in Amharic).

54. The OLF boycotted the election designed to implement the Proclamation No. 7/1992 alleging a widespread intimidation and violation of electoral laws by the EPRDF. However, the OLF has never changed the prime objective of its political program, which has been to establish an independent Oromia and it would not been surprising if it thought that the Proclamation fell short of its desires. (See the Political Program of the OLF, 1975).
55. Proclamation No. 41/1993. A Proclamation to Define the Powers and Duties of the Central and Regional Executive Organs of the Transitional Government of Ethiopia,, January 20, 1993.
56. Ibid., Article 33.
57. Ibid., Article 34 (3); however, Article 55 stated that each bureau head should be accountable to the Executive Committee of the region. There was no mention of the concerned ministry's control other than receiving periodic activity reports.
58. Proclamation No. 1/1995, Article 1.
59. Ibid., Article 46.
60. Ibid., Article 47 (1).
61. Ibid., Article 47 (2).
62. Article 47 (3) details the procedures to be adhered as follows: "a) when the demand for statehood has been approved by a two-thirds majority of the members of the Council of the Nation, Nationality or People concerned, and the demand is presented in writing to the State Council; b) when the Council that received the demand has organised a referendum within one year to be held in the Nation, Nationality or People that made the demand; c) when the demand for statehood is supported by a majority vote in the referendum; d) when the State Council will have transferred its powers to the Nation, Nationality or People that made the demand; and e) when the new State created by the referendum without any need for application, directly becomes a member of the Federal Democratic Republic of Ethiopia".
63. Ibid., Article 49; Proclamation No. 87/1997 states that the Addis Ababa city government has executive powers on all matters other than those falling under the jurisdiction of the federal executive organs. (See Proclamation No. 87/1997. A Proclamation to Provide for the Charter of the Addis Ababa City Government, Federal, July 7, 1997, Article 3 (1).
64. Proclamation No. 1/1995, Article 50 (2).
65. Ibid., Article 50 (3).
66. Ibid., Article 50 (5).
67. Ibid., Article 50 (8).
68. Ibid., Article 51.
69. Ibid., Article 52 (1).
70. Finer et. al., 1995: 157.
71. Ibid., Article 52 (2). Kifle Wodajo, President of the Constitution Commission explained why it was needed to enumerate some powers of the States after stating that the residual powers rest within the jurisdiction of the states in its pedagogical role.

He said that the enumeration was not exhaustive but as the Constitution would play an educating role in societies like ours, an attempt was made to mention the major powers and functions of the States. (Kifle Wodajo, interview, August 15, 1997).

72. Ibid., Article 50 (4).
73. See the Amended Constitution of the Tigray National Regional State, Proclamation 45/2001, November 15, 2001; The Amended Constitution of the Amhara National Regional State, Proclamation 59/2000, November 5, 2001; and The Amended Constitution of the Oromia National Regional State, Proclamation 49/2001, October 27, 2001.
74. See Proclamation No.2/1995. A Proclamation of the Constitution of the Amhara National Region, Zikre Hig, Bahir Dar, June 22, 1995, Article 45 (1) and Article 45 (2) states that the Himra, Awi, and Oromo peoples within the region have their own zonal councils. Similarly, in the Southern Nations, Nationalities and Peoples' state, the many nationalities within the state have their own zonal or special wereda councils, (See Proclamation No. 1/1995. Constitution of Southern Nations, Nationalities, and Peoples' Regional State Proclamation, Debub Negarit Gazeta, Awassa, June 22, 1995, Article 45.)
75. See the constitution of Tigray Regional State, 2002 Articles 58(4) and 58(6)
76. The Constitution of the Southern Nations, Nationalities and Peoples', Article 68 (5); the Southern State has nine zones, which are constituted by distinct nationalities. As the state is comprised of over 45 nationalities, others also have their own special woredas that enjoy similar privileges. Such features make it different from other states.
77. Ibid., Article 69.
78. Ibid., Article 78.
79. Ibid., Article 80 and 81.
80. Ibid., Article 88 and 89.
81. See Proclamation No. 98/2005, Amendment to the Constitution of Tigray National Regional State, Tigray Negarit Gazeta, March 15, 2005 and Proclamation No. 105/2005, Amendment to the Constitution of Tigray National Regional State, April 08, 2005.
82. Proclamation No. 98/2005, Article 73.
83. Ibid, Articles 52(3) and 77(3).
84. See Proclamation No. 98/2005 and No. 105/2005.
85. Ter-Minassian, "Intergovernmental Fiscal Relations in a Macroeconomic Respective: An Overview ", in Ter-Minassian (ed.), Fiscal Federalism in Theory and Practice, 1997:3.
86. See Boadway, et. al., The Reform of Fiscal Systems in Developing and Emerging Market Economies, February 1994:3.
87. Oates, Fiscal Federalism, 1993: 35.
88. See Boadway, et. al., the Reform of Fiscal Systems in Developing and Emerging Market Economies, February 1994: 30.

89. Oates, Fiscal Federalism, 1993: 31-32.
90. See Boadway et. al., 1994:30; see also Ahmad et. al., "Assigning Expenditure Responsibilities", in Ter-Minassian (ed.), 1997: 25-30.
91. Ahmed et al., in Ter-Minassian (ed.), 1997:28.
92. See Musgrave and Musgrave, Public Finance in Theory and Practice, 5th edition, 1989:475.
93. See the Basic Law for the Federal Republic of Germany of 23 May 1949 (Finer et. al., 1995); The Australian Constitution (Sawer, 1995); The Nigerian Constitution, 1989; for the Swiss Constitution, see Cooding, Jr., 1961; and The Constitution of India (Sarkar, 1991).
94. Boadway et. al., 1994: 23.
95. Musgrave, Richard A. "Who Should Tax, Where, and What?", in Oates (ed.), 1998: 72. For similar discussions, see Norregaard, "Tax Assignment" in Ter-Minassian (ed.), 1997: 54; Oates, "Federalism and Government Finance", in Oates (ed.), 1998: 15; and Shah, the New Fiscal Federalism in Brazil, 1990: 9.
96. Boadway et. al., 1994: 62-64; see also Musgrave, in Oates (ed.), 1998: 72 –75.
97. See Craig, "Australia", in Ter-Minassian (ed.), 1997: 177.
98. See Krelove et. al., "Canada", in Ter-Minassian (ed.), 1997: 205.
99. Spahn and Föttinger, "Germany", in Ter-Minessian (ed.), 1997: 228-230.
100. Ibid.
101. See Ahmed and Craig, "Intergovernmental Transfers", in Ter-Minassian (ed.), 1997:73.
102. Bahl and Linn, "Fiscal Decentralisation and Intergovernmental Transfers in Less Developed Countries", in Oates (ed.), 1998:632.
103. Inter-jurisdictional spill overs occur in situations when the benefits of a locally provided good or service spill over beyond the local jurisdiction to benefit those not contributing to the costs (e.g. benefits from control of air and water pollution, and locally educated students who relocate) and because non-residents come to the locality and enjoy the public services provided (Shah, 1990:58).
104. Differential net fiscal benefits across states arise because of various reasons:
    a) Some states are better endowed in natural resources which provide them with a better revenue base;
    b) Some states have relatively higher income which are normally a source of higher revenues;
    c) Some states have higher cost of disability factors such as lacking the minimum threshold for scale economies or difficult terrain factors or other costly disadvantages. (Ibid., p. 63).
105. For detailed discussions, see Shah, 1990:58-64; and Boadway et. al., 1994:37-40.
106. See Ahmad and Craig, "Intergovernmental Transfers", in Ter-Minassian (ed.), 1997:86-87; and Oates, Fiscal Federalism, 1993: 65.
107. Craig, "Australia", in Ter-Minassian (ed.), 1997: 184.

108. Quoted in Ibid.
109. Ibid., p.185.
110. Federal Constitution of the Swiss Confederation, April 18, 1999, Article 135(1).
111. Ibid., Article 135(3).
112. Spahn, "Switzerland", in Ter-Minassian (ed.), 1997: 331.
113. Ibid., p. 333.
114. Finer et. al., Comparing Constitutions, 1995: 184.
115. For details, see Spahn and Föttinger, "Germany", in Ter-Minassian, 1997: 532.
116. Ibid.
117. Hemming, Mates, and Potter, "India", in Ter-Minassian, 1997: 532.
118. Ibid., p. 532-533.
119. Ibid., p. 533.
120. Ter-Minassian, "Intergovernmental Fiscal Relations", in Ter-Minassian (ed.), 1997:18.
121. In Canada, each province has the right to borrow overseas or domestically without limit; in Australia a co-operative approach is followed in which the annual debt ceilings are set with state governments helped by a National Loan Council established to co-ordinate and control such undertakings; and in India only the central government can borrow overseas. (See Ter-Minassian and Craig, "Control of Subnational Government borrowing", in Ter-Minassian (ed.), 1997:159-161). Swiss practices also indicate that borrowing by cantons and communes is restricted to capital projects, which should be financed on a pay-as-you-go basis and requires popular referenda for approval (Shah, 1998: 13-14).
122. Ter-Minassian, "Intergovernmental Fiscal Relations", in Ter-Minassian (ed.), 1997; 19.
123. Shah, Fiscal Federalism and Macroeconomic Governance, 1998: 14.
124. Basic Law for the FederalRepublic of Germany, Article 109(2), Finer et. al., 1995: 185.
125. Ibid., Article 109(3).
126. Proclamation No. 33/1992. A Proclamation to Define the Sharing of Revenue between the Central Government and the National/Regional Self-Governments,, October 20, 1992.
127. Ibid., Article 3.
128. Ibid., Article 8.
129. Proclamation 1/1995, Article 94(1).
130. Ibid., Article 95.
131. Ibid., Article 96.
132. Ibid., Article 97.
133. Ibid., Article 98.

134. See Minutes of the Second Joint Session of the House of Peoples' Representatives and the House of the Federation, 2nd Year, April 10, 1997.
135. Proclamation 1/1995, Article 99.
136. The World Bank, Ethiopia: Regionalization Study, June 15, 2000: 17.
137. Proclamation No. 57/1996. Federal Government of Ethiopia Financial Administration Proclamation, Federal, December 19, 1996, Article 58.
138. Council of Ministers Regulations No. 17/1997. Council of Ministers Financial Regulations, Federal, July 1, 1997, Article 76.
139. See Council of Ministers Regulation No. 190/2010 Council of Ministers Regulation to Provide for the Financial Administration of the Federal Government, October 4, 2010, Article 53.
140. See FDRE 2012/13 Budget Summary, June 2012.
141. See Proclamation No. 719/2011, 2011/12 Fiscal Year Federal Government Budget Proclamation, July 26, 2011, Article 2.
142. Gupta, Sanjeev et. al. Ethiopia: Issues in Intergovernmental Fiscal Relations, International Monetary Fund, January 1996, p. 11.
143. Ibid., p. 19.
144. Proclamation No. 41/1993. A Proclamation to Define the Powers and Duties of the Central and Regional Executive Organs of the Transitional Government of Ethiopia, January 20, 1993, Articles 20 and 52.
145. See Proclamation 1/1995, Article 52 (1) (e).
146. Ibid., Article 51 (10).
147. Council of Ministers Regulations No. 17/1997, Article 77 and see also Council of Ministers Regulation No. 190/2010, Article 54.
148. Ismael Ali Sero, President of the AfarState, interview, December 16, 1997.
149. Proclamation No. 7/1992, Article 36 stated that "the central government had to allocate grants to the National/Regional Governments that cannot undertake by themselves basic social services and economic development programs". Subsequently, Proclamation No. 33/1992 indicated that the National/Regional Governments should receive subsidies from the central government where deemed appropriate. (Article 7 (1).
150. See Gupta et al., 1996: 21.
151. See the Minutes of the 2nd Regular Session of the House of the Federation, April 1 and 2, 1996, p.103 (in Amharic). The I-distance indicator is a synthetic variable that seeks to capture the regional differences in the levels of social and economic development among the states. It is based on eight distinct, quite heterogeneous variables: length of rural roads, share of rural population in total population, per capita industrial production, per capita crop food production, density of telephone lines, number of post offices, hospital beds in relation to total population, and pupils in elementary schools in relation to total population.
152. Ibid., P. 101.

153. Ibid., p. 106.
154. Ibid., p. 111.
155. See Minutes of the 2nd Regular Session of the House of the Federation, 2nd Year, April 8-10, 1997, p. 54 (in Amharic).
156. Ibid., p. 52-74.
157. Ibid., p. 74.
158. The Federal Budget Grant Formula in Ethiopia, Ministry of Economic Development and Co-operation, 2000: 5; see also Crosio and Gupta, "Ethiopia", in Ter-Minassian (ed.), 1997: 515-519.
159. See minutes of the House of Federation, 3rd year, Second Regular Session, April 9-10, 1998.
160. See Minutes of the House of Federation, Fifth year, Second Regular Session, April 12-13, 2000.
161. See the Federal Budget Grant Formula, 2000: 17-20.
162. Ibid., p. 22.
163. House of Federation, Intergovernmental Fiscal Transfer System, May 2003
164. Ibid.
165. For details, see the House of Federation, the Federal Budget Grant Distribution Formula, 2012/13 -2016/17, January 2012.
166. Ibid
167. Spatial price index is computed by taking the national general average price level as 100 per cent. If then calculates each region's price index by considering the price differences in the regions and also the distance and remoteness of the regions. It shows by how much a given region's price differs from the national average price which is taken as 100 per cent
168. See Proclamation 1/1995, Article 62(7).
169. Proclamation No. 1/1995, Article 51(7).
170. Proclamation No.57/1996, Article 59 (1)
171. Council of Ministers Regulation No. 190/2010, October 4, 2010, Article 52(2).
172. See the Minutes of the Joint Meeting of Senior Officials of the Central and Regional Administrations, DebreZeit, February 1993.
173. See Reports of Economic Sector's Performance, 2012.
174. Ibid.
175. Bereket, interview.
176. See Council of Ministers Regulation No. 103/2004; No. 128/2004 and the recent one, Regulation No. 242/2011

Chapter 7

The Eritrean Question and the Aftermath of its Independence

The Concept of Self-Determination

The concept of self-determination has evolved through time and has become a fundamental principle of international law.[1] Nevertheless, the concept has continued to elude specific definition and explanation as it remains ambiguous. Self- determination was employed in some treaties before 1945 such as the Treaty of Versailles[2] and also as a fundamental principle in the Atlantic Charter, which advocated the return of the rights of choosing and establishing self-governments for those peoples who were under alien domination.[3]

The United Nations Charter indicates that peaceful and friendly relations among nations are "based on respect for the principle of equal rights and self-determination of peoples".[4] The same principle is also implicitly reflected in Articles 73 and 76 (b), which deal with colonies and other dependent territories.[5] Although mentioned in several documents before, the right to self-determination become an international legal instrument after the UN General Assembly adopted Resolution 1514 (XV) in 1960, which acknowledged the right of peoples under colonial administrations to independence. Resolution 1514 (XV) declares that "[a]ll peoples have the right to self-determination; by virtue of that right they freely determine their political status and freely pursue their economic, social and cultural development".[6]

As self-determination has evolved from a political principle into a legal right, various scholars, depending on their field of study, look at it differently. Scholars have defined the concept of self-determination with varying content and scope. Johnson defines self-determination as "the process by which people determine their own sovereign status".[7] This definition is not only too general, but also equates self-determination solely with independence. Similarly, Walker defines the right to self-determination as "[t]he claim of a group of people having some degree of national consciousness, to form their own state and govern themselves".[8] Although the definition implies that people are entitled to attain independence and also participate in their own government, it is somewhat unclear when it attributes the right to "a group of people having some degree of national consciousness". The meaning of "some degree of national consciousness" is imprecise in this context.

Krys, on the other hand, attempts to give a wider definition by stating that "the right of peoples to self-determination as the right of a group of people having a degree of national consciousness based on, among others characteristics, common language, political heritage, customs and religion, to pursue their political, cultural and economic wishes without interference or coercion by outside States, and the right of all segments of the population to influence the constitutional and political structure of the system under which they live".[9] The definition is able to fill the gap left by Walker by explaining what "national consciousness" does mean. Moreover, it stresses that self-determination is not only a right to determine a people's political process in relation to any foreign influence but also the rights of participation in the internal administration of the entity.[10] The two aspects are identified as external and internal self-determination. Similarly, Przetacznik defines the concept with the same content but in a more concise way as follows:

> The right to self-determination may be defined as the right of people or a nation to determine freely by themselves without any outside pressure their political and legal status as a separate entity, preferably in the form of an independent State, the form of government of their choice, and the form of their economic, social and cultural system.[11]

From this definition one may deduce that the choices include not only independence but also any form of autonomy such as federation, confederation or any lesser form of local autonomy.[12] The people[13] have the right to form their government without any pressure from outside, including the use of their resources. The details may be determined in their constitution or legal instrument they would freely adopt to govern their sovereign state or some form of entity within a larger state.[14]

Eritrea before 1991

Eritrea was a product of the Italian colonial ambition in African that started in the 1880s. After occupying the territory, the king of Italy issued a decree creating the colony of Eritrea on the 1st of January 1890. Although, the Italian expansion was thwarted by the defeat at the battle of Adwa in 1896, Eritrea remained under Italian colonial administration. Menelik signed the Treaty of Peace of Addis Ababa on the 26 October 1896 in which Italy recognized Ethiopia's sovereign independence. The peace treaty also "accepted Eritrea's Mareb frontiers."[15] Subsequently, a treaty was signed between Ethiopia and Italy to delimit the border between Eritrea and Ethiopia in 1900.[16]

The Italians occupied Eritrea until they were defeated by the Allied Forces in the Second World War. The British then established the Occupied Enemy Territory Administration (OETA) and continued their presence in Eritrea. In 1947 with the signing of the Treaty of Peace with Italy, the Italian government renounced all the rights and title to the Italian territorial possessions in Africa.[17] Since the four powers were unable to reach agreement on the disposition of Eritrea, the matter was referred to the General Assembly and by Resolution 289A (IV), Section C, of 21 November 1949, the United Nations Commission for Eritrea was created to resolve the final status of the colony.[18]

After consultation with the population and also considering the Ethiopian claims, Resolution 390 A (V) was adopted by the General Assembly on December 2, 1950 which recommended the establishment of a federal arrangement between Ethiopia and Eritrea.[19] In this regard, the Resolution reads that "Eritrea shall constitute an autonomous unit federated with Ethiopia under the sovereignty of the Ethiopian crown". Accordingly, it notes that the Eritrea government would possess legislative, executive and judicial powers in the field of domestic affairs.[20] These provisions were reflected in the Eritrean Constitution, which was adopted by the Eritrean Constituent Assembly on July 15, 1952.[21] Article 8 declared that Paragraphs 1 to 7 of the resolution constitute the Federal Act which should be submitted to the Emperor for ratification. Accordingly, the Federal Act was formally ratified by Emperor Haile Selassie on 11 September 1952. Similarly, the Eritrean constitution was approved by the Emperor which heralded its entry into effect. However, the Revised 1955 Constitution of Ethiopia failed to mention the federal arrangement with Eritrea. Article 1 declared that "the Empire of Ethiopia comprises all the territories, including the islands and territorial waters, under the sovereignty of the Ethiopian crown. Its sovereignty and territory are indivisible. Its territories and the sovereign rights therein are inalienable".[22]

However, the Eritrea government from the start was riddled with ethnic, religion and regional cleavages, which negatively affected its performance. As the Imperial government was unhappy with the arrangement, the representatives of the Emperor exploited the divisions and feuds within the Eritrean groups. When confronted with interference in the domestic affairs of Eritrea, the Emperor's representative was quoted stating as follows:

> Neither I nor my assistants would understand, nor did anyone explain to us the meaning of the allegation that the Office of H.I.M.'s Representative has intervened in the internal affairs of Eritrea and has attempted to corrupt the faith of the Members of the Assembly. In any case there is no internal or external affairs as far as the Office of H.I.M.'s Representative is concerned and there will be none in the future. The affair of Eritrea concerns Ethiopia as a whole and the Emperor.[23]

Tekeste Negash contends that the relationship between Ethiopia and Eritrea could not be included in the family of "federations". He notes that "even according to the intentions of the UN, Eritrea was not granted a federal status but only a status of autonomy. Yet the UN and its advisors, including the Commissioner for Eritrea, Anze Matienzo, insisted on using the term "federation" without having to bother about laying down the appropriate infrastructure for its proper functioning".[24] As mentioned above, the Imperial government was helped by local bickering in its effort to dismantle the federation. As a result, the federal arrangement was formally dissolved on November 14, 1962 and Eritrea became one of the provinces of Ethiopia.

Apparently, the decision to dissolve the federation was done without proper popular consultations. The so-called decision of the Eritrean parliament was not "consultation" with the people. The dissolution of the arrangement constituted a unilateral abrogation of the Federal Act, which was an international instrument, by Ethiopia.

Soon the Eritrean opposition to the imperial domination turned into armed resistance by the formation of the Eritrean Liberation Front (ELF) in 1961. On the other hand, the merger of splinter groups from the ELF formed Eritrean People's Liberation Front (EPLF). The early 1970s were marked by the fratricidal fighting between the two organizations.[25] Eventually, the ELF was weakened mainly by its internal problems and disintegrated in its conflict with both EPLF and TPLF in 1981. The EPLF was able to forge a close co-operation with the EPRDF in the late 1980s, which expedited the demise of the military government.[26] On the 24th May 1991, the EPLF entered Asmara and formed a provisional government.

Independent Eritrea

The need to conduct a referendum in Eritrea[27] was agreed among the EPRDF, OLF and EPLF at the London Conference.[28] Subsequently, the agreement was reflected in the Principles of Co-operation between the Transitional Government of Ethiopia and the Provisional Government of Eritrea, which was adopted by the National Conference convened from the 1st to the 5th of July 1991.[29] The Agreement states that "the Transitional Government of Ethiopia recognizes the right of the Eritrean people to determine its political future by an internationally supervised referendum... the Provisional Government of Eritrea has deferred the referendum for two years".[30] Accordingly, the President of the Transitional Government of Ethiopia wrote a letter to the Secretary General of the United Nations on December 13, 1991 recognizing the right of the Eritrean people to a referendum by stating that 'the people of Eritrea have the right to determine their own future by themselves and accepted that the future status of Eritrea should be decided by the Eritrean people in a referendum to be conducted in the presence of international observers'.[31] Subsequently, the PGE established the Referendum Commission of Eritrea on April 7, 1992. Proclamation No. 22/1992, which established the Commission, details its functions as follows:

a) guaranteeing a referendum that is free and fair;
b) identification and regulation of eligible voters;
c) creation of the mechanism of the referendum;
d) publicizing the referendum and informing the voters.[32]

The choice presented to the people was limited to one by the Proclamation. Article 3 indicated the single question to the voter as "[d]o you approve Eritrea to become an independent sovereign state?" and the voter had to place a mark in either yes or no box, and any other alternative to appear on the ballot was prohibited.[33] Proclamation No. 21 attempted to answer the question of who is an Eritrean with a right to vote in the referendum. The Eritrean Nationality was accorded to those who resided in Eritrea before 1933 or if he or she were the offspring of such a person; had exercise his or her right to become a citizen by collective naturalization; and exercised his or her right to become a citizen by naturalization.[34] However, it was difficult to identify Eritreans, especially living in Ethiopia because of the cross-migration and most of all the close relationship between the two peoples.

The referendum was conducted between April 23 and 25, 1993. Various international groups, including the United Nations and the Organization of African Unity, and the delegation of the Ethiopian government observed it. At the end of the referendum, it was declared as free and fair, though some criticized it for its narrow choices and strong bias towards independence. The Commission announced the results and it was declared that 99.805 per cent had voted "yes" and 0.165 per cent voted "no".[35]

The Transitional Council of Representatives discussed the referendum results and the position on the referendum outcome on April 29, 1993. The Council approved the process and the result of the referendum unanimously except for two abstentions.[36] Subsequently, the Ministry of Foreign Affairs of Ethiopia issued a statement recognizing the sovereignty and independence of Eritrea.[37] The Statement indicates the desire of the Ethiopian government to strengthen the relations between the two peoples as follows:

> The past two years of peace and co-operation between the Transitional Government of Ethiopia and the Provisional Government of Eritrea have made it abundantly clear [that] the opportunities for expanding the areas of co-operation between Ethiopia and Eritrea in all fields are limitless and that the prospects for further enhancing ties between the two are bright.[38]

Eritrea officially became independent immediately after the results of the referendum were declared. The EPLF convened its third congress to adopt a national charter to formulate the structure of the government and its policies. The EPLF transformed itself into "a broad-based movement" and the Charter explains that "given the Front's extensive objectives and the structure of our society, given the absence of any positive experience of a multi-party system in the country, the Front... should as much as possible be broad-based, embracing all patriotic Eritreans who have at heart the welfare of Eritrea and its people".[39] The Charter further indicated that "the front must be the center of political gravity in Eritrea guaranteeing peace and stability, promoting and strengthening nation-building, healthy democracy and political progress".[40] The name of the Front was changed to People's Front for Democracy and Justice[41] and the Congress decided to establish a national assembly whose composition was stated as follows:

> 1. Affirms that the decisions of the seventh meeting of the Central Committee regarding the Proclamation on the Government of Eritrea and the establishment of the National Assembly were appropriate and timely;
> 2. Resolves that the National Assembly be constituted 75 representatives of the People' Front for Democracy and Justice (PFDJ), and an equal number of representatives elected by the population;
> 3. Resolves that the 75 representatives of the PFDJ shall be the Members of the Central Council elected by the Congress.[42]

While attempting to build some structures of government, the PFDJ has not left any room for other political organizations to function in independent Eritrea. Eritrean groups such as the ELF Central Command, the ELF-United Organization, the ELF-Revolutionary Council and the Eritrean

Democratic Liberation Movement have been barred from participating in the political process. As a result, political violence has persisted in some parts of the country.[43] The government has attempted to address ethnic divisions by prohibiting the formation of political groups based on ethnicity and redrawing provincial lines by mixing various ethnic groups into a district.[44] The regime claimed that rearranging provincial entities was carried out as a mechanism to reduce ethnic segregationist tendencies and promote all-inclusive national construction. However, it is clearly a far-fetched and wishful policy considering the level of ethnic divisions and tensions among the Eritrean society today.

In April 1994, the Eritrean government proclaimed the establishment of a Constitutional Commission to prepare a draft for the approval of the National Assembly.[45] Subsequently, the Constitution was ratified on May 23, 1997 after three years of drafting process. As discussed above, the desire to narrow the diversity of ethnic groups in Eritrea is reflected in Article 1(5) of the Constitution. It states that "the state of Eritrea shall have a unitary government divided into units of local government. The powers and duties of these units shall be determined by law".[46] Article 19 provides for the freedom of conscience, religion, expression of opinion, movement, assembly and organization. Specifically, Article 19(6) provides for the right of association, which is explained as the right to form organizations for political, social, economic and cultural ends.[47] The official interpretation of the above mentioned Article can be deduced from the following speech made by the President during the sixth anniversary celebrations of Eritrea's liberation:

> Our constitution allows for multi-partyism. These parties must be real and grow out of Eritrean realities for we would not like to establish cosmetic parties. We will not permit the existence of parties driven by external forces and which serve as a political camouflage for others... In my opinion, our constitution will provide a conducive atmosphere for the emergence of political parties... Once again, I would like to reiterate that we do not want to establish political parties in order to please external powers. Let me say with all certainty that political parties will emerge in Eritrea...as a natural outcome of the engagement of our society.[48]

In line with the speech, none of the opposition Eritrean organizations has been allowed to freely function and the PFDJ remains the sole legal political organization in the country.[49] Usually, citizens are expected to conform to the pronouncements and preferences of the government in the name of national unity and solidarity. In general, the Constitution has not been put in practice and the envisaged institutions have never come into existence.

Ethio-Eritrean Cooperation and Its Difficulties

As mentioned above, the co-operation between the Ethiopia and Eritrea was not limited to the implementation of the referendum. The two governments agreed to work together in almost all spheres for mutual benefit. There were several agreements signed by the two governments to concretize the reigning spirit of co-operation reigning since the joint struggle to defeat the military dictatorship. Both governments believed that the economic co-operation between Eritrea and Ethiopia has been a necessity for a number of reasons: the long common borders of the two countries; the historical and cultural ties between their peoples; the existence of transport and communication links facilitating the movement of persons and the exchange of goods between them; and the shared awareness on the part of the governments of both countries of the advantages to be gained from gradual economic integration.[50]

One of the most important agreements between the two countries was the Trade Agreement signed on September 27, 1993. The crucial provision in the Agreement was Article 2(1) that states "there shall be free movement of goods and services for local consumption in the respective countries of the contracting parties, except for the goods in short supply whose movement shall be determined by the competent authorities of the respective countries".[51] Furthermore, Article 2(3) indicated that "there shall be no re-exportation of goods and services originating from Contracting Parties countries to [a] third country".[52] The Memorandum of Understanding signed on October 7, 1994 has a provision that read "both parties agree [that] free movement of goods and services should not be distracted by "short supply".[53] With the intention of deepening the economic integration between the two countries, an agreement to form a Free Trade Area (FTA) was signed on April 3, 1995. The main provisions of the agreement are summarized as follows:

a) Removal of tariff and non-tariff barriers on all goods and services produced and exchanged by the two countries;
b) Periodic review to include new products and services produced and exchanged between the two countries;
c) Harmonization and simplification of customs documents and procedures, introduction of common classification of goods, common instruments for data collection and a system of exchange of trade data;
d) Appropriate payment system of the flow of trade in goods and services.
e) Establishment of a FTA Secretariat.[54]

In order to facilitate the proper flow of goods and services, customs agreements were signed between the two governments on January 20, 1993 and November 11, 1993 respectively.[55]

In accordance with the above agreements, there had been progress towards removing tariff barriers, but not as far as it was reflected on the Agreements. A provision that provides for the prohibition of additional intermediate and local payment from being imposed on goods and services traded between the two countries has not been fully implemented.[56] Above all, there seemed to exist a difference on the interpretation of the above quoted Article 2 of the Trade Agreement of September 27, 1993. Eritrea complained that it was facing restrictions and outright prohibitions on its imports of Ethiopia's exportable products throughout the implementation period.[57] The Eritrean side also opposed the Ethiopian decision to prohibit franco-valuta imports as a measure which would hinder re-export trade and would be a cause for the widening of illegal trade along the borders of the two countries. On the other hand, Ethiopia insisted that the restriction of exportable goods was in line with the above mentioned agreements. It also indicated that the prohibition of franco-valuta did not violate the agreements, and in fact was consistent with Article 2 (2) of the 1993 Agreement.[58] Moreover, Ethiopia complained about the absence of co-operation in combating illegal trade, especially in smuggling its exportable products.[59]

After the high level meeting, from August 15 to 16, 1996, it was decided to form a joint review committee to identify the problems encountered in the implementation of the agreements and to come up with solutions. The Joint Review Committee identified some constraints in the implementation process:

a) divergence in the economic policies of the two countries;
b) difference in their trade regulatory systems;
c) difference in the interpretation of various articles of the agreement;
d) gaps in the agreements which provide loopholes for maintaining or introducing tariff and non-tariff barriers; and
e) failure to establish in time the institutional mechanism for following up the implementation of the agreements.[60]

Due to the differences in policies and also in interpretation of the agreements, the Free Trade Area Agreement mainly remained on paper. The Agreement seemed to be far-fetched, as the initial agreements were not properly implemented. However, it did at least signify the political will to strengthen and broaden the co-operation between the two countries.

One of the agreements that remained mainly on paper was the Protocol Agreement on Harmonization of Economic Policies signed on September 27,

1993. The harmonization provisions include exchange rate policies and interest rate structures, tariffs and taxes, and also investment policies.[61] Article 4 of the Agreement indicated that "the contracting parties agree to harmonize their investment policies, basic regulatory framework.... Further, the parties in principle agree that national investors of both countries should have the same and equal treatment in each other's territories".[62] The Eritrean side was pushing for the adoption of a policy that would open investment opportunities to resident nationals in both countries without restrictions made on foreigners. Nevertheless, the Ethiopian side indicated that it would make certain restrictions particularly in banking and insurance sectors.[63] The Ethiopian investment code reserves some areas for Ethiopian nationals only; however, it did not affect many people of Eritrean origin as their choice of citizenship had not been determined until the conflict.[64] Therefore, the Eritrean government was not worried about Eritreans residing in Ethiopia, as they were practically enjoying the same rights as Ethiopians. It was only trying to acquire similar privileges for non-resident Eritrean nationals and also the right to invest in banking and insurance sectors. The Eritrean government was proposing to sign a comprehensive bilateral investment promotion and protection agreement with the intent of including the above-mentioned sectors, which the Ethiopian side was not ready to yield. On the other hand, the Eritrean government from the outset restricted the involvement of Ethiopians residing in Eritrea in any relevant economic activity.

Similarly, there were difficulties in the implementation of other agreements.[65] As discussed, the divergent interpretation of some of the provisions, the failure to update the agreements with the adoption of new economic policies and reforms by both countries, and lack of a strict implementation process were among other factors that hampered the full implementation, or affected the results of the agreements. The Joint Review Committee evaluated the implementation of the agreements as ranging "from poor in the area of harmonization of macro-economic policies to fairly good in the area of road transport, and port and transit services".[66] Apparently, the initial strong desire to co-operate for mutual benefit and the actual implementation process did not go hand in hand and eventually become a source of mistrust and conflict.

The other contentious issue was related to the issuance of a new currency, the Nakfa, by Eritrea and the debate surrounding the system of exchange between the currencies of the two countries. The Ethiopian government insisted on making the necessary preparation before the new currency was introduced as the two countries were using the Ethiopian Birr. The Eritrean government was not enthusiastic in devising precautionary measures at the time of currency conversion. On the other hand, when the issue of trade in the new situation of having two currencies arose, the position of the two governments failed to reconcile in successive meetings. The previous agreements were made in an environment of a common currency arrangement, which stipulated the regime of free movement of goods and services, and trade and service transaction between the two countries should be made in Birr.[67] When Eritrea issued its currency in November 1997, the Ethiopian government decided that all transactions should be in hard currency through letter of credit.[68] The Eritrean government opposed the use of hard currency and instead proposed for the direct exchange and free circulation of the two currencies in both countries. The Ethiopian government persisted with its position but allowed for small border trade using local currencies. According to the directive of the Ethiopian Ministry of Trade and Industry, the border trade would be allowed as long as the amount of transaction was up to two thousand Birr.[69] Prime Minister Meles argued that the border trade transaction was considered because of the special relationship between the two peoples and such measure was in addition to the exemption of customs duty on exports between the two countries.[70]

However, the Eritrean authorities did not appreciate the Ethiopian position. In fact, it was taken as a protectionist policy and deliberately applied to hurt the Eritrean economy. In an interview with Aser magazine President Isaias Afwerki argued that "the basis of the policy is to limit Eritrean competitiveness in Ethiopia... The policy is fundamentally protectionism.... The volume of business between the two countries is so small that there is no trade transaction that would require L.C. (letter of credit). If we are going to introduce L.C., it will have to be explored 3 to 4 years from now.... The Ethiopian government can make restriction on the trade of goods that harm the Ethiopian economy, why make restriction on the rest. There is no need to make a two thousand Birr limit. There is no need for L.C".[71] The Eritrean government was not ready to allow trade transactions through letter of credit and the border trade directive remained mainly on paper. As a result of the disagreements, trade between the two countries came into standstill and relations between the two governments started to deteriorate. It seems that Eritrea expected that Ethiopia would allow the free circulation of Nakfa and may be at a fixed exchange rate, and most probably at a one-to-one basis. That is why Eritrean leaders were accusing Ethiopia of creating a stumbling block to the expansion and increase of trade and services traffic between the two countries.

Evidently, the abrupt termination of trade exchanges has caused more difficulties for Eritrea. Eritrea used to earn up to 50 per cent of its foreign trade revenue from export sales to Ethiopia, but for Ethiopia it was only 10 to 15 per cent of its foreign trade revenue from the sale of agricultural products to Eritrea.[72] Moreover, Ethiopia's boycott of the Eritrean ports has dried up about one billion Birr in revenue for the Eritrean government.[73] Of course, this does not mean it would not affect Ethiopia's trade for all its foreign trade has to pass through the Djibouti Port. It only means that the situation had limited effect on the economy. Eritrea has been basically dependent on remittances from its nationals residing abroad.[74]

The Conflict and Its Consequences

With relations souring due to trade disagreements, border problems started to gain prominence. Although there exist a number of maps and agreements between Ethiopia and Italy, the borders have never been demarcated. The first agreement was signed on the 10th of July 1900 between Emperor Menelik and Italy, which attempted to delineate the boundary.[75] The boundary was modified by the Treaty of 15th May 1902 between Italy, Great Britain and Ethiopia.[76] As mentioned, the boundary was defined in the agreements but Italy didn't want to be contained in Eritrea. Hence they were not interested to demarcate their colony's frontiers with Ethiopia. Further territorial encroachments can be easily seen from the Italian maps of Eritrea in the 1930s. In fact, after the Italian occupation of Ethiopia, the whole region was included in one map that depicted Colonia Italia Africa Orientale.[77] Whatever the case, border disputes should not be a source of armed conflict as there are various mechanisms of resolving them peacefully.

Blunders against its neighbors have put Eritrea's reputation as a peaceful and co-operative neighbor into question. In December 1994 diplomatic relations with the Sudan were severed after Eritrea accused Sudan of training and supporting rebels and the Sudanese Embassy premise in Asmara was given to the opposition alliance. In 1995 the Eritrean government started to attack Islamic groups in border areas of the Sudan. Subsequently, the Eritrean government not only declared its dislike of the Khartoum regime but also openly vowed to dismantle it from power. The Eritrean President was quoted by the Economist magazine stating his design for the Sudanese government. He declared that "we are out to see that this government [the Sudanese government] is not there anymore. We are not trying to pressurize them to talk to us, or behave in a more constructive way. We will give weapons to any one committed to overthrowing them".[78] The open declaration to dislodge a foreign government from power was a breach of international law, and it was not well received by other neighbors as well as the international community.

The other neighbor that became a victim of Eritrea's belligerent policy was Yemen. In December 1995 Eritrea invaded and occupied the Hanish islands. The looming war between the two countries was averted due to mediation efforts of countries like France and Ethiopia. As a result, the two countries agreed to resolve the conflict through arbitration. The International Tribunal meeting in London on October 9, 1998 awarded Yemen the sovereignty over the Hanish islands.[79] As agreed, Eritrea accepted the verdict of the International Tribunal. However, the issue raised by many people is whether it was necessary to invade the islands and cause the death of tens of soldiers in the first place. It should have been solved through peaceful means without creating the cloud of war in the region.

In April 1996, Djibouti complained about Eritrea's aggression on its territory. It was reported that the late President Gouled Aptidon rejected a map, produced by Italy in 1935, submitted by the Eritrean Foreign Minister. The Djibouti authorities claimed that the Eritrean map included almost 500 square kilometers of their territory. The Djibouti Foreign Minister remarked that "Djibouti does not want to get involved in a dispute on the borderline... but asks before any discussion for the withdrawal of the new Eritrean map".[80] Ethiopia played a major role in diffusing the tension and Eritrean troops were withdrawn from the disputed border area.[81] Nevertheless, two years later Eritrea accused Djibouti of siding with and helping Ethiopia's war effort against it, and relations have been severed since November 18, 1998.[82]

As mentioned above, the relationship between Ethiopia and Eritrea started to encounter problems with the increase of trade and other economic related disagreements. Such disagreements brought the border issue to the forefront and tensions began to rise around the disputing areas.[83] Consequently, the two governments agreed to form a joint commission to seek a lasting solution. The Commission held its first meeting on November 14, 1997 in Asmara and devised its program of action, and also agreed that both sides had to respect the status quo and took measures to alleviate any dispute until a lasting solution was attained.[84]

The Commission was to hold its second meeting on May 8, 1998 when border skirmishes started on May 6, 1998. The May 8 meeting was held as scheduled and it was agreed to meet after two months, and that the Eritrean forces, which entered the Ethiopian territory were to pull back to their positions in Eritrea.[85] However, the agreement was not implemented and in fact a larger force occupied the disputed territories of Badme and its environs. The unexpected show of force triggered a strong reaction from the Ethiopian Council of Ministers and the Parliament on May 13, 1998. Although the commitment for peaceful solution of the conflict was reflected, the resolutions passed called for the immediate and unconditional withdrawal of the Eritrean forces.[86] When Prime Minister Meles was asked why it happened, his remark was "I don't have any concrete answers as to how it reached such a scale with Eritrea. It can be suggested that it might have been influenced by the feelings created as a result of the currency change. It may also be influenced by different problems that arose in the area.... There is no sufficient reason to cause the occurrence of such an incident. Whatever the reason behind may be, a grave historical blunder is committed".[87]

On the other hand, the Eritrean government denied occupying Ethiopian territory. President Isaias said that according to the maps Badme was inside Eritrea and Eritrean forces did not cross the border.[88] The Cabinet of Ministers of Eritrea reacted to the accusations of Ethiopia by stating that "there have been, and continue to exist, border disputes in certain localities along the common borders between Eritrea and Ethiopia. These problems have been instigated by the unlawful practices of the Ethiopian army, which occasionally made incursions into these Eritrean territories...".[89] Furthermore, it proposed to proceed to peacefully resolve the border issue ignoring the call for the return of the status quo ante.[90] In fact, the Eritrean government issued a statement denying its occupation of Ethiopian territory, which said "the Government of Eritrea categorically asserts that it has not made any incursion into Ethiopian territory and reaffirms its readiness to facilitate inspection by any third party to verify the facts on the ground".[91]

After the crisis unfolded, the governments of Rwanda and the United States attempted to facilitate the peaceful resolution of the conflict. At the end of their facilitation process, they came up with recommendations presented to the parties for their consideration. The main sticking part read as follows:

> ... that within 24 hours of the arrival of the Observer Team, Eritrean forces begin to redeploy to positions held before May 6, 1998, and that immediately following, the civilian administration in place before May 6, 1998, return, and that there should be an investigation into the events of May 6, 1998.[92]

The facilitation process continued until May 29, 1998, in which Ethiopia accepted the recommendations and Eritrea rejected them. In his interview with the BBC, President Isaias declared that "to withdraw from Badme is morally unthinkable and physically impossible".[93] The rejection of the recommendations was followed by armed clashes from May 31- June 6, 1998 between the two countries. Ethiopia accused Eritrea of invading Ethiopian territory in order to create new facts on the ground. Consequently, the 68th Ordinary Session of OAU Council of Ministers meeting in Ouagadougou, Burkina Faso appealed to the two parties "to put an end, concurrently and simultaneously, to all hostilities, accept and implement the recommendations of the [US and Rwanda Governments] facilitators".[94] The crisis was further seized by the Summit of the Heads of the State and Government who expressed deep concern over the escalation of the conflict. They also endorsed the resolution of the 68th Ordinary Session of the Council of Ministers and appealed to the two parties to put an end to all hostilities and implement the recommendations of the Facilitators (the United States and Rwanda). Moreover, they decided to send an OAU missions of Heads of State led by the Chairman to both countries.[95]

Subsequently, during a meeting of the Central Organ of the OAU Mechanism for Conflict Prevention, Management and Resolution held at summit level, it was decided that an OAU High Level Delegation would be led by the Chairman, President Blaise Compaore of Burkina Faso, and comprise the Heads of State of Djibouti, Zimbabwe and Rwanda, as well as the Secretary General of the OAU.[96] The High Level Delegation visited Ethiopia and Eritrea on 18 and 19 June 1998 and its mission failed to end the deadlock. The statement of the High Level Delegation declared that "the Ethiopian side reiterated its acceptance of the proposals of the Facilitators. The Eritrean side stated clearly that the Facilitation was over. From this point of view, therefore, the Delegation was not able, at this junction, to make headway with respect to the Facilitators recommendations".[97] However, it decided to establish a Committee of Ambassadors to collect information relevant to the ways and means of solving the conflict, and also to determine the authority, which was administering Badme before 12 May 1998.[98]

The resolution made by the Summit of Heads of State and Government and the efforts of the High-Level Delegation was also complemented by the Resolution of the Security Council of June 26, 1998. The Resolution stated that the Security Council "expresses its strong support for the decision of the Assembly of the Heads of State and Government of the OAU on 10 June 1998 (S/1998/494) as well as for the mission and efforts of the Heads of State of the OAU and urges the OAU to follow up as quickly as possible".[99] However, Eritrea was not ready to accept the facilitators' recommendations and in fact, President Isaias Afwerki was quoted by the Reuters News Agency as saying "... the problem with the peace process is the hasty way it was managed by the Americans...they believe in quick fixes and bulldozing and that does not work. It is not our culture".[100]

Subsequently, the Committee of Ambassadors presented its report to the Ministers of Foreign Affairs of Burkina Faso, Djibouti and Zimbabwe as well as the OAU Secretary General at their meeting in Ouagadougou from 1st to 2nd August 1998. The Ministers endorsed the report, and enriched and approved the recommendation presented by the Committee of the Ambassadors.[101] One of the findings of the Committee of Ambassadors was concerning the status of Badme before the conflict and stated that "on the basis of the information at our disposal, we have reached the conclusion that Badme town and its environs were administered by the Ethiopian authorities before 12 May, 1998.... It is ... of the view that what happened in Badme between 6 and 12 May constitutes a fundamental element of the crises".[102] The findings were rejected by the Eritrean Minister but were well received by the Ethiopian Minister.[103] At the end of the meeting, the Ministerial Committee concluded that there was no visible change on the positions of the disputing parties.

The OAU High-Level Delegation met in Ouagadougou on 7 and 8 November 1998 to once again try to broker peace between the parties. After consulting with the disputing parties and considering the recommendation of the Ministerial Committee, the Delegation approved a set of proposals for a framework agreement and presented it to the parties for their consideration. The proposal for the Framework Agreement asked Eritrea to withdraw its troops from Badme town and its environs and redeploy them to positions they held before 6 May 1998.[104] The Ethiopian government accepted the proposals by calling them consistent with the previous OAU resolution. The statement stated that "considering the proposal and the satisfactory clarification of these points, Ethiopia fully accepted the proposed OAU plan".[105] The Eritrean government, on the other hand, proposed other points to be included in order to "provide a sound basis for a lasting peaceful solution to the border conflict".[106] In other words, the Eritrean government was not ready to accept the proposal as presented by the High-Level Delegation.

The other important occasion in which the OAU attempted to bring peace to the region was the 4th Ordinary Session of the Central Organ of the OAU Mechanism for Conflict Prevention, Management and Resolution held from 17 to 18 December 1998 in Ouagadougou, Burkina Faso. On 12 December 1998 the Eritrean government handed over a document that detailed questions asked for clarification from the High-Level Delegation.[107] The document showed Eritrea's implicit rejection of the proposal by stating that "... the OAU Summit in Ouagadougou adopted a resolution on the basis of the misguided approach and report of the Facilitators' Team. This has posed and remains a major handicap to the OAU initiative, severely limiting a fresh and independent approach. Indeed, while Eritrea had made it clear that the facilitation process was over and it regarded the OAU initiative as a new one, the recommendations by the Committee of Ambassadors revolved around the same parameters that had led to the failure of the facilitation process".[108]

In the Summit the two parties continued to advocate their already held positions. The Eritrean President, ignoring the call for the withdrawal of his troops, simply repeated his earlier position as follows:

> In regard to redeployment, Eritrea holds that, with a cease-fire in place and military observers on the ground, demarcation can be done expeditiously without the complicated and time consuming disengagement of hundreds of thousands of troops. Eritrea, however, has no objection in principle to redeployment in the framework of demilitarization... it cannot countenance alien administration on its own territory and over its own population.[109]

The Ethiopian Prime Minister, on the other hand, explained Ethiopia's position regarding the border dispute as follows:

> Having a border dispute is something that we unfortunately have to live with all over the continent and try to resolve it peacefully. Invading your neighbor because of such dispute is an altogether different thing so we asked the Eritrean government to withdraw from the territory that it has occupied by force and agree to resolve the problem peacefully including through international mediation, to delimit and demarcate our boundaries.[110]

He pleaded with the members of the Central Organ to stick to the proposals made by the High-Level Delegation by remarking that "four of Eritrea's five neighbors have been assaulted. Three of the five members of the delegation that you appointed to help us have been assaulted. This is a pattern of behavior. This is an unacceptable pattern of behavior. This is a source of continued instability in the region".[111] At the end of the Summit, the Central Organ endorsed the proposal submitted by the OAU High-Level Delegation to the parties and urged them to commit themselves to the peace process.[112]

The Resolution of the Central Organ was backed by the UN Security Council Resolution, which called the Framework Agreement "the best hope for peace between the two parties".[113] It also welcomed Ethiopia's acceptance and urged Eritrea to accept as soon as possible.[114] In fact, the European Union in its statement of 15 January 1999 also shared the spirit of support for the Framework Agreement.[115] Moreover, the Governments of Italy, Netherlands, the United Kingdom and other friendly countries openly asked Eritrea to accept the OAU Framework Agreement.[116]

Despite the international community's support for the Framework Agreement, the two parties remained apart in their attitude towards the peace process. Prime Minister Meles at his briefing to the African diplomatic community, described the Framework Agreement as follows:

> Like all compromise proposals, it was much less than perfect, from our point of view. Nevertheless, we felt obliged to accept this proposal, not only out of respect for those who devoted their time and effort to help us resolve this problem but also, and perhaps more importantly, because we felt that the proposal, whatever its shortcomings, was firm on the principles that mattered most to us and, I believe, to Africa. This is that border disputes cannot and must not, be resolved by force.[117]

President Isaias, on the other hand, had a different view on the Framework Agreement and continued to have until the February armed clash broke out. In an interview with the national TV (ERI-TV) on January 31, 1999, he argued as follows:

> The OAU Framework Agreement is not a take it or leave it package but an open-ended peace proposal subject to discussion and clarification.[118]

After playing with words and facts, war once again erupted on February 6, 1999. Both parties accused each other of first launching the offensive.[119] As late as February 8, 1999, the Secretary General of OAU urged Eritrea to accept the Framework Agreement to avoid the unfolding war. He stated that "the OAU High-Level Delegation awaits the response which the Eritrean side undertook to communicate to it after receiving the clarifications sought on the elements of the Framework Agreement".[120]

Undoubtedly, the war was bloody which cost the lives of thousands of combatants. After weeks of battle, Ethiopian forces were able to break the strong trenches of the Eritrean army, which resulted in the expulsion of the latter from the disputed territory of Badme and its environs. As a result, President Isaias wrote a letter to the UN Secretary General and the OAU President his acceptance of the Framework Agreement reversing his long perceived rejection. In his letter to the Secretary General, he declared that "the Government of Eritrea strongly rejects the attempts by Ethiopia, before and now, to impose a solution through the use of force. Nonetheless, the Government of Eritrea accepts the OAU framework agreement to pave the way for an expedited demarcation".[121]

Although the international community applauded the sudden Eritrean acceptance of the Framework Agreement, the Ethiopian authorities did not take the new Eritrean move as sincere. In his letter to the President of the Security Council, Prime Minister Meles noted that "a Framework agreement which only six days previously the Eritrea President had told an EU Troika was unsatisfactory became by some miracle acceptable to Eritrea. Its author, the OAU, which the Eritrean President told the Troika was a fickle organization suddenly, became credible in the eyes of the Eritrean authorities".[122] He stressed that "no wisdom is required... for realizing that the Eritrean acceptance of the Framework Agreement is a tactical ploy they decided to resort to after they saw what was coming and a tactical move for buying time".[123] He further requested the Security Council to call on Eritrea "to withdraw its forces from all remaining occupied Ethiopian territories and to uphold that Eritrea bears responsibility for the loss of human lives, the humanitarian crisis and for the destruction of property caused by its aggression".[124]

However, the Ethiopian conditions were not acceptable to Eritrea. The Eritrean Foreign Ministry repeatedly stated that "Eritrea is ready to implement redeployment in all contested areas along the common border within the framework of demilitarization of the entire common border".[125] In another interview with the National Television, President Isaias Afwerki rejected the withdrawal of Eritrean forces from occupied Ethiopian territories, the restoration of Ethiopian civilian administration and the acceptance of responsibility for the damages inflicted because of the border dispute.[126] He simply remarked that "the answer is simple. If Eritrea says that it accepts the OAU Framework Agreement, the next step is finding ways and means to implement it".[127] The Ethiopian side, on the other hand, argued that the unconditional withdrawal of Eritrean forces had been part of the OAU Framework Agreement, which for the Prime Minister asked for clarification before his acceptance.[128] If not, Ethiopia reiterated that it has the right to self - defense in accordance with the UN Charter.

Ethiopia claimed it had the right to self-defense under Article 51 of the UN Charter that states "nothing in the present Charter shall impair the inherent right of individual or collective self-defense if an armed attack occurs against a Member of the United Nations, until the Security Council has taken measures necessary to maintain international peace and security." Although the drive had been to resolve the dispute peacefully, it repeatedly warned the players such as the U.S and the European Union that the use of force could not be discounted.[129]

Differences of interpretation of the provisions of the Framework Agreement started to surface when the High Level Delegation attempted to move the peace process forward. Ethiopia continued to insist that Eritrean forces had to withdraw not only from the Badme area but also from the other areas occupied after May 6, 1998. On the other hand, Eritrea as mentioned above, persisted arguing that it had already fulfilled as required by the Framework Agreement, the withdrawal of Eritrea forces from the Badme area. Concerned by the confusion created by different interpretations, President Blaise Compaore, the then Chairman of the OAU, wrote a letter to President Isaias Afwerki that stated "I submit to you a solemn appeal, in the name of the OAU and its High-Level Delegation, that you accept our proposal that the Eritrean government agree to redeploy its troops out of Ethiopian territories occupied after May 6, 1998".[130] Once again, President Compaore wrote a letter that underlined "in the interim, the concern which preoccupies the High Level Delegation is that of creating necessary and favorable conditions for that implementation, notably a return to the status quo prior to May 6, 1998".[131] However, such pleadings played little to change the stance of the Eritrean government.

Amid such differences and diplomatic maneuver, the Eritrean government resorted to a military solution intended to retake the Badme area from the Ethiopian army in mid-June 1999. After intense fighting, the Eritrean army not only failed to achieve its objective but was also forced to retreat from a number of strategic positions within Eritrea.

As the military option failed to produce the upper hand on the ground, the diplomatic option started to get some momentum. As a result, the 35th Assembly of Heads of State and Government of the OAU convened in Algiers from 12 to 14 July, 1999 endorsed the Modalities for the Implementation of the OAU Framework Agreement on the Settlement of the Dispute between Ethiopia and Eritrea.[132] The Modalities for the Implementation of the OAU Framework Agreement confirmed the imperative of the two parties returning to positions held prior to 6 May 1998. In this regard the first two provisions read as follows:

1. The Eritrean Government commits itself to redeploy its forces outside the territories they occupied after 6 May 1998.
2. The Ethiopian Government commits itself to redeploy, thereafter, its forces from positions taken after 6 February 1999 and which were not under Ethiopian administration before 6 May 1998.[133]

The terms "occupied" and "positions taken" were not simply a choice of words. They were put deliberately to indicate that there was an invasion carried out by Eritrea, and the advances of the Ethiopian forces in Western Eritrea was a matter of military expediency. On the other hand, the document postponed the details of the modalities for the re-establishment of the civilian administration and population in the concerned territories to be worked out at a later date. Of course, the re-establishment of the civilian administration was to be preceded by cessation of hostilities.[134]

According to the Transcript of the Proceedings, the Eritrean President attempted to amend the Modalities while declaring that he accepted them. He insisted that the principle of "non-acquisition of territory by force" should also apply to "those areas which changed hands between July 1997 and May 1998".[135] Furthermore, he stated, among others, the principle of non-acquisition of territories by force applies equally to both sides and to all territories seized since 1997. Such statement was opposed by the Ethiopian Prime Minister who declared that the Eritrean government was attempting to put new substance to the document, and if they accepted the Modalities, it should be with "no ifs and buts".[136] Then, the President of Eritrea withdrew his amendments by calling them "side issues" and declared that he wanted to see the implementation of the Framework Agreement.[137] Ethiopia also wrote a letter to the President of Algeria confirming its acceptance of the Modalities for the Implementation of the OAU Framework Agreement. In the letter, Prime Minister Meles Zenawi expressed his concern by stating "the Eritrean Government is "interpreting" the "Modalities" in a manner that is completely contrary to the letter and spirit of the "Modalities". It has endeavored to change the cut off dates in the "Modalities", changing the carefully crafted wording to obliterate the difference between invasion and legitimate defense, and has introduced a completely new issue of compensation".[138] He pleaded that such conduct should not be allowed to continue in order to protect the integrity of the peace process.[139] Evidently, from the above statements and counter-statements, it is not difficult to notice the precarious position of the mediators in this highly sensitive dispute.

Subsequently, the special envoy of the Algerian President visited the two capitals, Addis Ababa and Asmara, to discuss the formulation of the implementation plan. He invited both leaderships to submit their inputs to help the OAU in its Endeavour to prepare the implementation document. Before long, the Prime Minister of Ethiopia sent a letter to indicate some of Ethiopia's concerns that it wanted to be reflected in the implementation document. He underlined that "it is my conviction that no movement forward will be possible, without first verifying the areas from where re-deployment will be undertaken".[140] He further suggested that "the OAU establish a team of verifiers through consultation with the parties. The team would then collect evidence from both parties and undertake consultations with them in order to arrive at an agreed list of the areas from which re-deployment is to take place on the basis of Paragraphs 1 and 2 of the "Modalities".[141] The expectation of the Ethiopian side was that the mediators would, at least, formulate some of the most sensitive issues through shuttle diplomacy and consultations. On the contrary, the implementation plan, the Technical Arrangements for the Implementation of the OAU Framework Agreement and its Modalities, was formulated as a "collective work of the OAU, the United Nations, the United States and other interested partners",[142] and presented to the parties as binding and unamendable document.

Convinced that its concerns were unheeded and the document contained provisions that depart from the Framework Agreement and Modalities, the Ethiopian side asked for clarifications, which were in essence requests for amendment. The Ethiopian side opposed the prior signing of cessation of hostilities and waiting another 50 days for the redeployment to start, and of course, without knowing the areas from where the Eritrean forces would be redeployed.[143] It also questioned the need for the establishment of a peacekeeping force[144] since the Ethiopia side believed as the primary purpose of such a body was to assist in the verification of the implementation of the Framework Agreement and the Modalities, and as there was no need to keep the peace between the two parties, it was unnecessary and a departure from the abovementioned basic documents. The idea was that an observer mission was proper for the task. The other points raised were concerning the restoration of the status quo ante where the Ethiopian side felt some of the provisions infringed its sovereignty. One of these provisions is Article 9 (a) (2.1) that provided for "prohibitions on displacement and deportation of civilian populations".[145] Article 9 (a) (2.3) that stated "prohibition of display of weapons by militia in populated areas where civilian administration is restored" and Article 9 (b.2) that provided for "the grievance resolution mechanisms" were considered to be in contravention with the principle of fully restoring the Ethiopian sovereignty.[146] There were also additional issues from demilitarization of the border areas to humanitarian concerns raised for clarification.

On the restoration of the status quo ante, the Ethiopian side complained that article 9 (a) (2.1) denied the right of Ethiopia as a sovereign country to deport undesirable aliens and persons posing a security threat to the nation. It also rejected Article 9 (a) (2.3) as an infringement to the restoration of the civilian administration with its law enforcement institutions functioning in accordance with the laws and regulations as in the rest of the country. Similarly, the establishment of the grievance resolution mechanism that replaced the proposal of the deployment of a team of human rights monitors as provided by article 8 (c) of the OAU Framework Agreement[147] was considered by the Ethiopian side as a parallel structure to the local administration with a potential of encroaching the latter's sovereignty.[148]

On the other hand, the Eritrean government promptly declared that it accepted the Technical Arrangements as they were presented. On Eritrea's acceptance, Eritrea's President remarked that "the first minutes I was handed over the document, it took me about 10 minutes to read the document. And I said, "well, this is almost a perfect document, and there is no room for maneuvering, asking questions or demanding clarifications on any issue put in that document". I refrained from saying, "I accept the document", because politically or as a matter of courtesy, I have to say, "I will study the document with my experts and come back to you with an answer." I have to take time and go sleep for about two hours and come back again to tell the delegation that we officially have accepted the document. There was no reason to delay".[149]

Before long, the OAU provided Ethiopia with the clarifications regarding the questions presented by the Prime Minister's letter of August 13, 1999. Although the document attempted to address the concerns of Ethiopia, it failed to satisfy the leadership, especially on the most sensitive questions such as the verification of the areas from where Eritrean forces would be redeployed prior to signing of cessation of hostilities. The document continued to uphold the signing of the cessation of hostilities as requisite for the commencement of the implementation process.[150] When it became clear that Ethiopia would not accept the Technical Arrangements as they were clarified by the OAU, negotiations started to accommodate the concerns of Ethiopia, which produced a document called the "Consolidated Technical Arrangement" after almost eight months.[151] This document was a proposal, which had to be presented to Eritrea for its consideration and reaction.

After another round of shuttle diplomacy from February 23 to March 5, 2000 by the representative of the Algerian President, it was reported substantial progress was made towards narrowing the differences. The OAU issued a press release appreciating the progress as follows:

> 1. both parties reaffirmed their acceptance of the Framework Agreement and the Modalities for its implementation;
> 2. with regard to the Technical Arrangements submitted by the OAU and accepted by Eritrea, a consensus was reached on some of their provisions while others require additional efforts in order to secure the common acceptance of the full document by both parties;
> 3. the two parties reaffirmed their will to see that Technical Arrangements are consistent with the letter and spirit of the Framework Agreement and the Modalities.[152]

Based on the above consensus, the then chairman of the OAU invited the two sides for proximity talks that would have been held on March 25, 2000. In the meantime, the Eritrean Cabinet of Ministers declared that "the OAU should officially announce that the Technical Arrangements, which had been submitted as non-amendable, are now open for discussion by both sides since the TPLF has rejected the original document".[153] This was, of course, a setback for the OAU, which a few weeks earlier announced that there was an agreement on negotiating to make the Technical Arrangements consistent with the already agreed two documents. Consequently, the Eritrean side failed to confirm its participation in the March 25, 2000 talks and it was postponed.

After the failure of the first attempt, once again diplomatic activities continued to bring the parties to proximity talks and it was agreed to hold on April 29, 2000. Although the two delegations stayed in Algiers from April 29 to May 5, 2000, no substantial talks were held. At the end of the exercise, the OAU current Chairman issued a communiqué that started as follows:

> [T]he proximity Talks held in Algiers were intended to assist the two parties to arrive at Consolidated Technical Arrangements on the basis of positions acceptable to each of them... Unfortunately, those substantive discussions could not be started because Eritrea requested, as a pre-condition, the signing of the Framework Agreement, the Modalities and the cease-fire while Ethiopia maintained its position of July 1999 namely, that the said signing should take place only after the finalization of the Technical Arrangements.[154]

The unexpected Eritrean pre-condition seemed to catch the mediators and the U.S by surprise, and the negotiations were postponed to unspecified date.[155] As usual, both countries accused each other for the failure of the proximity talks.[156] At the time a delegation of the Security Council that was in a mission to Central Africa came to the Horn of Africa after the Algiers proximity talks failed. The delegation attempted to bridge the differences but the positions remained unchanged. As its mission failed to bear fruits, it only resorted to issuing warnings of sanctions in case one of the parties turned to military solution.[157]

The Ethiopian Prime Minister remarked on the action of Eritrea as based "in their analysis of the Ethiopian situation, the leaders in Asmara expect the international community to prevail upon Ethiopia to unconditionally "close the military option". They have taken their cue from the statements of governments, media coverage of the situation of Ethiopia, and from views expressed in the UN Security Council... if the military option is ruled out the occupier could take his time till a "friendly" peace plan makes an appearance".[158] He further argued "what we cannot afford is the prolongation of the status quo... This country cannot continue to divert its meager resources for defense purposes at the same time as has been denied international development assistance. At the very least we need to use our all resources where they make the most differences. And that is in food security... Those who are suggesting that a peaceful option is the only option will have to show us how they are going to do it quickly. How they are going to reverse the aggression peacefully and quickly".[159] Apparently, Eritrea did not expect Ethiopia would resort to a military option at a time when it has been severely affected by drought and was also under heavy international pressure. However, it proved to be a grave miscalculation and once again war broke out between them on May 12, 2000.

This round of fighting was triggered by Ethiopia's frustration with the stalled peace talks and the inaction of the Security Council on the matter. It can easily be observed from his letter to the President of the Security Council when the Ethiopian Foreign Minister stated "Can Ethiopia, even at this stage, expect justice from the Security Council? Does the violation of international law in Africa matter to the Security Council? Can we believe that the Security Council abhors aggression wherever it is committed?"[160] The Security Council passed Resolution 1297 (2000) condemning the renewed fighting and called for the resumption of talks without precondition.[161] This was also followed by the Communiqué of the OAU Mechanism for Conflict Prevention, Management and Resolution that called for the halt of hostilities and the resumption of the peace talks.[162] However, the Ethiopian government was convinced that it would not make any headway in the talks, intensified its offensive and declared that it broke the Eritrean defensive lines on the Western front, Badme-Mereb front, on the 13th of May 2000,[163] and was followed by the fall of the town of Barentu, a strategic regional center in Western Eritrea.

As Resolution 1297 (2000) remained unheeded, the Security Council began deliberations on a U.S proposed draft resolution mainly intended to punish Ethiopia, which in legitimate exercise of its right of self-defense started the recent offensive. The draft resolution not only demanded for arms embargo ostensibly on both sides putting aggressor and victim on equal footing but was also intended to deny Ethiopian officials from travelling to other countries.[164] On the other hand, the Russians tabled another draft that called for the resumption of the peace talks and the dispatch of envoys of the current Chairman of the OAU and the U.N Secretary General.[165] After intense negotiations and diplomatic manoeuvres among the members of the Security Council, it was only agreed that the resolution would contain an arms embargo provision for a limited period.[166]

Furthermore, the Security Council adopted a time limit of 12 months and at the end of the period would decide on whether to terminate the sanctions or to extend them depending on both governments' compliance of peaceful resolution of their dispute.[167] In addition, it declared that the embargo would be immediately terminated if the Secretary General reports that a peaceful definitive settlement of the conflict has been concluded.[168]

Both parties angrily protested on the handling of the conflict by the UN Security Council. Each side claimed that it has been the victim of the other side's aggression and the measures should target the culprit. President Isaias Afwerki wrote to the UN Secretary General explaining that "[t]he United Nations is now at a critical juncture of its history. It is clear that any failure by the United Nations to apply the principles of collective security and to reverse Ethiopia's aggression today will result in the forfeiture of its moral and legal authority to maintain and ensure intentional peace and security".[169] Ethiopia's Foreign Ministry also rejected the Resolution by declaring that "as a matter of principle the people of Ethiopia condemn, with all their strength, this unjust and unfair resolution adopted by the Security Council".[170] The Statement further accused the U.S and the U.K for attempting to deliberately hurt Ethiopia by stating "[t]he United States and the U.K who had wanted even a far harsher punishment to be meted out on Ethiopia did not succeed. As such, Security Council Resolution 1298 is a defeat for the United States and the U.K, and a victory for those on the Security Council who were determined to protect the credibility of the United Nations".[171] Apparently, those countries praised by the statement were Russia, China, France and some members of the Security Council from developing countries.

Resolution 1298 (2000) had little effect on the war. Ethiopia openly declared it would continue fighting until it regained its occupied territories. The

Ethiopian Prime Minister declared that "we will negotiate, negotiate in good faith. But we will not cease-fire until one thing happened. The jack boots of the invader are removed from our territory".[172] Accordingly, the offensive on the second front, the Aiga-Mereb defense lines, began on May 23, 2000, in which the Ethiopian Prime Minister declared that "the next hours, at most, over the next twenty-four hours, that defense line will also totally crumble".[173] With the resumption of fighting in this major front, it was clear that the intensity of the war dramatically increased, and of course, its current and potential consequences.

In the meantime, the envoy of the Chairman of the OAU, Mr. Ahmed Ouyahia, was shuttling between Asmara and Addis Ababa from May 21-24, 2000 seeking an agreement for cease-fire and the resumption of the proximity talks. As a result, the OAU issued a communiqué that stated Eritrea's willingness to cease-fire and resumption of proximity talks but Ethiopia, while agreeing to participate in the proximity talks refused to cease-fire till the restoration of its territorial status quo prevailing at 6 May 1998.[174] The mission of Mr. Ouyahia was, in fact, followed by the visit of President Abdelaziz Bouteflika to give more backing to the peace process on May 24, 2000.[175]

As Ethiopia was declaring the Eritrean defense lines were crumbling, Eritrea issued a statement indicating that "for the sake of peace, ... in accordance with the second requirement of the OAU Communiqué that it has decided to re-deploy its forces to positions held before 6 May 1998. Eritrea will begin this redeployment at midnight 25th May on the Zalanbessa area".[176] This, in fact, was scorned by Ethiopia which said the Eritrean forces were routed.[177] The next day, the Eritrean President informed the current Chairman of the OAU that "Eritrea commits itself to re-deploy its troops from Bada and Burrie in order to deny Ethiopia any pretext",[178] areas which Ethiopia indicated earlier that they were still under Eritrean occupation. Ethiopia did not take the Eritrean statements as dependable. A statement by the Foreign Ministry of Ethiopia indicated that "Eritrea is engaged in a play to buy time in order to save its battered army so that it would continue with its aggressive behavior".[179] It further declared that "Ethiopia wishes to make it clear that even now large chunks of territory in the eastern and north-eastern part of Ethiopia, in the Afar Regional State, are still occupied by Eritrea. The war can only come to an end when Ethiopia has verified that Eritrea has removed its forces of occupation from all the remaining Ethiopian territory under their control".[180] Notwithstanding, it repeatedly indicated that Ethiopia has never had any desire to remain in Eritrean territory and it would withdraw when its military objectives are fulfilled.[181] Accordingly, on May 30, 2000, Ethiopia declared that its forces had withdrawn from Western Eritrea after fulfilling their mission.[182] The announcement was confirmed by the statement of the Ethiopian Foreign Ministry of May 30, 2000. It stated that "the mission had two objectives: 1) To destroy enemy forces that were in retreat in the area; 2) To facilitate the realization of the return of Ethiopian territories along the border...".[183] Fulfilling its mission, it was time to, at least, withdraw from Western Eritrea.

On May 31, 2000, the Council of Ministers of Ethiopia indicated that the forces in the Northern front were instructed to stand down and the forces in the Eastern front were ordered to verify whether the areas were evacuated by Eritrean forces. It further declared that "as the crisis presently moving from the military to the diplomatic arena, Ethiopia is attending the Algiers talks with an approach that would enable her to safeguard her legitimate rights and interests."[184] Later, the Prime Minister confirmed that he verified all Ethiopian territories were cleared from the Eritrean forces and the attention would be focused on the diplomatic negotiations to find a definitive settlement of the conflict. However, he reiterated that Ethiopian forces would stay in the Zalanbessa-Senafe area until an agreement was reached.[185]

After the OAU delegation's shuttle diplomacy, as discussed above, both parties agreed to resume their proximity talks in Algiers on May 29, 2000. The talks were held from 29 May to 10 June 2000, and as a result, the OAU was able to prepare a proposal for the signature of the parties. The Proposal reaffirmed the parties' acceptance of the previous main documents, the OAU Framework Agreement and the Modalities for its Implementation.[186] It underlined for immediate cessation of hostilities starting from the signature of the document, which was the main purpose of the negotiations. According to the Proposal, a Peacekeeping Mission would be deployed by "the United Nations under the auspices of the OAU", and would be in place until the delimitation and demarcation of the border is completed.[187] Paragraph 9 of the Proposal provided for the redeployment of Ethiopian forces to positions of Ethiopian administration before May 6, 1998.[188] On the other hand, in order to satisfy Ethiopia's demand for "security guarantees" as a condition for withdrawal from Eritrean territories, Paragraph 12 provided for the creation of a "buffer zone" inside Eritrea. Paragraph 12 read as follows:

> In order to contribute to the reduction of tension and to the establishment of a climate of calm and confidence, as well as to create conditions conducive to a comprehensive and lasting settlement of the conflict through the delimitation and demarcation of the border, the Eritrean forces shall remain at a distance of 25 km (artillery range) from positions to which Ethiopian forces shall redeploy in accordance with paragraph 9 of this document. This zone of separation shall be referred to in this document as the "temporary security zone.[189]

This was an enormous setback for Eritrea as it was even resisting discussing on the substance of the "Consolidated Technical Arrangements" unless Ethiopia signed a cease-fire and the previous documents as a precondition at the failed proximity talks from April 29 to May 5, 2000. Such unexpected acceptance of a "buffer zone" in its territory came as a result of the facts on the ground. Eritrea paid a huge price from the re-ignited fighting that started on May 12, 2000, and was desperate to stop the war from causing further havoc in the country. In his letter of acceptance of the Proposal, Eritrean Foreign Minister decried that Ethiopia's "precondition for withdrawing from Eritrean territory, namely the provision by the international community of "security guaranties" is preposterous and totally unjustified. It was also a ploy to torpedo the Algiers proximity talks".[190] On the other hand, Ethiopian authorities rejected the accusation and attempted to justify the necessity of "security guarantees" since they could not trust the Eritrean regime. The Proposal was only designed to stop the war and make some ground works for the final resolution of the conflict. The details of the settlement of the conflict had to be negotiated and both parties had to reach a comprehensive agreement to find a lasting solution to the problems.

Such fierce conflict and the irreconcilable and strongly held positions of the parties had caused the war to rage for over two years, which resulted in the death of thousands of people, hundreds of thousands displaced and millions of dollars worth of property destroyed. According to the Ethiopian Office of the Government Spokesperson, as of 7 March 1999, around 381,677 people were displaced of which 343,156 were internally displaced and the remaining 38,021 were expelled from Eritrea.[191] The Eritrean government, on the other hand, indicated that over 50,000 people of Eritrean origin were expelled from Ethiopia.[192] Although the numbers might be inflated for propaganda purposes, the numbers of people affected were evidently high. The Ethiopian government justified its expulsion for security reasons as the Eritrean government had a wide spread political network inside Ethiopia.[193] Apparently, political organizations in the region have had a long tradition of attempting to attain political objectives by using clandestine networks. Nevertheless, it would not be hard to observe that many innocent people were caught in the middle of such complicated crises. On the Eritrean side, the Ethiopians residing in Eritrea were harassed and persecuted in order to make them leave. In fact, for Ethiopians residing in Eritrea, this was the second exodus as thousands of them were expelled in 1991 by the EPLF after it entered Asmara.

The eruption of the conflict on May 12, 2000 further created a major displacement for an estimated of 750,000 Eritreans, mainly from the Gash Barka region of Western Eritrea, which became a huge humanitarian crisis. In addition, over seventy-three thousand people were reported to flee to the Sudan.[194] On the other hand, Ethiopia complained that the Eritrean government and its supporters terrorized and killed Ethiopian citizens residing in Eritrea. According to an Ethiopian report, after May 12, 2000, seventy-nine Ethiopians were killed and more than seven thousand out of the estimated eighty thousand Ethiopians living in Eritrea were rounded up and confined to camps.[195] The Eritrean government did not deny the detention of Ethiopians in camps but argued that they were detained for their own safety as their lives were in danger of reprisals from Eritrean citizens angered by the Ethiopian military offensive.[196] Whatever governments' statements advocated, it was clear that the civilian population have paid a heavy price from the conflict that should not happen in the first place.

Furthermore, it is obvious the economy of the two countries was a victim of this horrible war as the parties spent a lot of wealth on armaments and maintaining huge armies. Above all, the war and its consequences would leave an enormous scar on the relations of the two peoples that would take a long time to redress.

The Stalemate

No war No peace

As discussed above, Ethiopia's last push came on the 12th of May 2000, which not only breached the strongly defended trenches but also chased the Eritrean army from all fronts and occupied large parts of Eritrea. After the creation of new reality on the ground, Eritrea dropped its preconditions and pressed to sign the proposal. On 18 June 2000, both countries signed the cessation of hostilities in Algiers that ended the war. This was followed by the Agreement of 12 December 2000 that was intended to bring peace between the warring parties. Article 3 of the agreement provided for an investigation to be carried out on the incidents of 6 May 1998 and on any other incidents prior to the mentioned date that might contribute to evolvement of the crises.[197]

Moreover, the most important article, Article 4, provided for the establishment of a neutral Boundary Commission with a mandate to delimit and demarcate the border in accordance with pertinent colonial treaties and applicable international law.[198]

The Commission started its work after completing its constitution on 20 February 2001 in The Hague, The Netherlands. The parties presented their written pleadings and supporting documents to the Commission. The Commission also heard oral argument of the parties in its various sessions. On the 13th of April 2002, the Commission deliberated its delimitation decision. After studying the ruling, Ethiopia's misgivings were clear when it presented its request for "interpretation, correction and consultation "on May 13, 2002.

The request included clarification of issues of the ruling in relation to the ground and the rectification of the error made on the geographic position of Fort Cardorna. It also included that the need to undertake careful fieldwork and the necessity of consulting the parties during the demarcation process.[199] However, the Commission rejected Ethiopia's plea by stating that "the concept of interpretation does not open up the possibility of appeal against a decision or the reopening of matters clearly settled by a decision... the Ethiopian request is inadmissible and no further action will be taken upon it."[200] On the other hand, it admitted the error it made on the geographic position of Fort Cardorna but downplayed the flaw by stating it had no effect in changing its prior decision.

Subsequently, the Commission proceeded with its preparation to demarcate the boundary in the absence of clear agreement from the parties.[201] Ethiopia, once again, declared the necessity of considering the human and physical geography through the study of facts on the ground during the demarcation process.[202] It further appealed that adjustments should be made to basically avoid unnecessary situations such as dividing villages, homestead or roads by the boundary.[203] However, the Commission refused to entertain such requests unless authorized by both parties.[204] On the other hand, Eritrea advocated that the delimitation decision should be implemented without any alterations.

The accusations between the parties as well as the Commission continued unabated, which further complicated the situation. Ethiopian Prime Minister in his letter to the Secretary General of the UN stated that the key to the crisis of the work of the Commission was the totally illegal, unjust and irresponsible decisions on Badme and parts of the Central sector. He further admonished the Commission's decision for ending up splitting a single village and even a single homestead between the two countries. Consequently, it would be anathema to the achievement of durable peace and stability in the region. Such letter was followed by another letter from the Minister of the Foreign Affairs, which attempted to refute the decision of the Commission in details.[205] However, the Commission was busy defending its decision,[206] and similarly, Eritrea was not interested to provide any room for any considerations.

In the meantime, the Commission started its preparation for demarcation in the Eastern Sector, however, Eritrea informed the Commission that it objected the work if it didn't cover the entire boundary in October 2003. When the situation falls in stalemate, the Ethiopian government attempted to break the deadlock by proposing a peace plan intended to resolve the differences between the two countries. The Prime Minister of Ethiopia in his speech to the House of People's Representatives proposed a five point peace initiative, which included to resolve the dispute between Ethiopia and Eritrea only and only through peaceful means; to resolve the root causes of the conflict through dialogue with the view to normalizing relations between the two countries;

Ethiopia's acceptance, in principle, the Eritrea-Ethiopia Boundary Commission decision; its agreement to pay its dues to the Commission and appoint field liaison officers; and to start dialogue immediately with the view to implementing the Commission's decision in a manner consistent with the promotion of sustainable peace and brotherly ties between the two peoples.[207]

Later, the Ethiopian position was changed from accepting the decision in principle to accepting it without precondition[208] in order to pave the way for dialogue and then enable the demarcation process to proceed based on the reality on the ground. However, Eritrea was not interested to involve itself in a dialogue and rejected any initative other than the Commission's platform. It also rejected the United Nations Secretary General Special Envoy's attempt to bring together the two parties. The call of the Security Council for Eritrea to enter into dialogue and cooperation with the Special Envoy produced nothing in terms of changing Eritrea's stance.

The situation started to get worse when Eritrea started to put restrictions in the activities of the United Nations Mission in Ethiopia and Eritrea (UNMEE) since early 2004. On 5 October 2005, Eritrea banned all UNMEE helicopter flights within Eritrean airspace as well as those coming to Eritrea. Subsequently, on 6 December 2005, Eritrea order members of UNMEE who were nationals of the United States of America, Canada, Europe, and the Russian Federation to leave the country within ten days. After evident non-cooperation of the Eritrean government, the Security Council was force to relocate the staff of UNMEE from Eritrea to Ethiopia.[209] The future and role of UNMEE had been extensively discussed between the parties and the United Nations to enable it to discharge its responsibilities. The Secretary General stated that "the Military occupation of Eritrea of the TSZ and the restrictions it has imposed on UNMEE are a violation of the Agreement on Cessation of Hostilities and have undermined the very basis of the Mission's mandate". [210] When Eritrea was asked to reconsider its position and lift the restrictions, and rectify the violations of the Agreement on Cessation of Hostilities, the President of Eritrea contended that the presence of UNMEE was prolonging the occupation by Ethiopia of territory awarded to Eritrea. On the other hand, Ethiopia did not want to accept the long-term deployment of UNMEE on the Ethiopian side only. It argued that "such a deployment would effectively create a new security zone on Ethiopian territory, with serious legal implications for the status of the Agreement on Cessation of Hostilities and the Temporary Security Zone."[211] When all the options failed to materialized, the United Nations had no alternative but to terminate the Mission. Accordingly, the Security Council passed Resolution 1827(2008) to terminate UNMEE's mandate effective on 31 July 2008.[212]

Such provocative posturing was earlier accompanied by the violation of the Temporary Security Zone (TSZ) by Eritrean forces in October 2006.

Initially the Eritrean government sent armed personnel in the name of militia using the pretext of farming activities.[213] On 16 October 2006, the Eritrean defense forces openly violated the TSZ by moving in hundreds of well-armed soldiers. Consequently, the Ethiopian government condemned the incursion and reminded the international community that it was a violation of the Algiers Agreement. It also sent a notification to the Eritrean government which stated that it decided to notify the State of Eritrea of its material breaches of the Algiers Agreements and of Ethiopia's entitlement to invoke the breaches as grounds for considering its legal and peaceful options, including terminating the Agreements or suspending their operation in whole or in part.[214] On the other hand, Eritrea responded that as soon as all of the arrangements for demarcation were in place, it would remove its forces from the TSZ as long as it affected the operations of the Commission. Apparently, the actions that transpired around the TSZ contributed to the aggravated tensions between the two counties, notwithstanding, the two countries didn't allow the situation to further deteriorate and cause another round of bloodshed.

In the meantime, the Eritrea-Ethiopia Claims Commission which was established in 2001 in accordance with the Algiers Agreements of December 12, 2000 decided to partially award Ethiopia on its claim that Eritrea was liable for loss, damage and injury it and its nationals suffered by Eritrean aggression. On December 19, 2005, the Commission decided that Eritrea "violated Article 2, paragraph 4, of the Charter of the United Nations by resorting to armed force on May 12, 1998 and the immediately following day to attack and occupy the town of Badme, then under peaceful administration by the claimant, as well as other territory in the Claimant's Tahtay Adiabo and Laelay Adiabo Woredas."[215] Evidently, the Claims Commission's decision of finding Eritrea as the aggressor had no effect on the Eritrea-Ethiopia Boundary Commission's decision. However, it would help to rest Eritrea's persistent prevarication of the start of the war and who started it. Notwithstanding, the verdict did not deter Eritrea from its actions that incapacitated UNMEE and invading the TSZ, which grossly violated the Algiers Agreements.

The Eritrea and Ethiopia Boundary Commission claiming it received no cooperation from the parties to demarcate the physical border, decided to resort to "virtual demarcation". In its 30 November 2006 Press Release, it declared that "it would instead use modern techniques of image processing and terrain modeling, combined with high resolution aerial photography, as well as knowledge acquired on the ground by the Commission field staff, to identify the locations where the line of the boundary changes direction, and where boundary pillars would otherwise be located."[216] It proceeded with virtually "demarcating" the border citing the demarcation of the Iraq-Kuwait border in 1993 as precedence. It is clear that the action of the Commission didn't contribute to peacefully resolving the dispute.

The differences of stances concerning the "demarcation" of the Commission continued. The Eritrean President declared that "I choose simply to affirm, at this stage, Eritrea's acceptance of this procedure as an important step forward towards the demarcation on the ground. But since virtual demarcation does not represent completion of the process, I urge the Commission to persist until erection of pillars to bring the process to its natural conclusion."[217] On the other hand, Ethiopia argued that "these demarcation coordinates are invalid because they are not the product of a demarcation process recognized by international law." [218] As shown above, the Commission continued to be part of the problem and contributed little to the peaceful resolution of the conflict.

The Eritrean President started accusing Ethiopia that its "refusal to vacate Eritrean territory constitutes a gross violation of the Charter of the United Nations."[219] On the other hand, Ethiopia contended that the demarcation process remained impossible unless and until Eritrea fully accepted its fundamental obligations and restored the full integrity of the Algiers Agreements.[220] When the Commission decided to terminate its existence and business on 30 November 2007, it seems that it was not missed by many stakeholders. The issue of dialogue among the parties has been advocated not only by Ethiopia but also by the Algiers Agreements guarantors, facilitators and witnesses. The Security Council pleaded with both countries to start dialogue by repeatedly passing resolutions.[221] On 29 January 2004, the United Nations Secretary General appointed Lloyd Axworthy as his Special Envoy to assist both parties in implementing the peace agreements. Ethiopia welcomed the initiative but Eritrea refused to cooperate with the Special Envoy. The Security Council expressed its support for the Special Envoy and disappointment on Eritrea's refusal to engage with the Envoy by Resolution 1531(2004).[222] Despite Security Council's repeated resolutions urging it to engage with the Envoy, Eritrea showed no interest in getting involved in a dialogue with Ethiopia.[223] As mentioned above, the stalemate and the exacerbation of the tension with the violation of TSZ continued.

When the process of solving the conflict through the Commission came to an end in 2007, the Secretary General of the United Nations once again offered to send his representative to talk to the parties. Ethiopia accepted the proposal but it was rejected by Eritrea which stated that it would not accept alternative mechanisms to the Commission.[224] In fact, Eritrea's position was earlier explained by the President in his letter to the President of the Eritrea-Ethiopia Boundary Commission. The letter stated that "Eritrea is prepared to consider normalizing its relations with Ethiopia and engage in any necessary discussions pertaining to normalization as soon as the demarcation of the boundary is completed and when a conducive environment for normalization is established. It must indeed be clear that dialogue on normalization would not be acceptable as a precondition for demarcation."[225] The Eritrean President's statement is evidently in stark contrast to Ethiopia's position that the demarcation should be carried out after discussions in order to avoid any problems that may cause potential conflicts on the ground. In addition, Ethiopia does not see demarcation as separate issue from normalization of relations.

By rejecting dialogue, Eritrea is in effect insisting on a "virtual demarcation" of the boundary. Regrettably the Boundary Commission seemed to adopt the same approach to defend its flawed decision. There is no such practice in boundary demarcation under international law as a "virtual demarcation". Despite its flaws which the Ethiopian government pointed out in detail in its memorandum of May 2003 to the Commission, it accepted the decision on delimitation but called for dialogue on its implementation. It may be worth recalling that Nigeria and Cameroon settled their boundary dispute amicably by engaging in dialogue on the implementation of the International Court of Justice decision which favored Cameroon.[226] In contrast there have been cases where, unlike Ethiopia, one of the parties rejected in toto, giving their detailed reasons, the unfavorable decision and called for a fresh arbitration to settle the issue. This was the boundary case decision of the Court of Arbitration on the conflict between Argentina and Chile on the Beagle Channel rendered on 2 May 1977. It was totally rejected by Argentina in January 1978. Although Chile insisted on the implementation of the arbitration decision, it agreed to a fresh arbitration by the Pope which settled the matter to the satisfaction of both parties by signing a Peace and Friendship Treaty on 29 November 1984. The Beagle Conflict resolution process started in the court but ended by negotiated settlement. Although the defective decision by the Eritrea-Ethiopia Boundary Commission justified such course of action by Ethiopia, the Ethiopian government did not reject the decision but merely called for dialogue on demarcation. As discussed above, border demarcation leads to sustainable peace when the conflict is amicably put to rest. Therefore, it is prudent to give dialogue a chance to solve such fratricidal conflict which should not happen in the first place. Notwithstanding, considering the immense mistrust between the parties, the end of the impasse does not seem at the moment in sight.

The Proxy War

It has been a tradition among the region's countries to harbor and support the enemies of one's perceived or actual enemy for political purposes. When the relationship between Ethiopia and Eritrea started to decline, Eritrea started to gather opposition groups for a mission intended to weaken the Ethiopian government. It harbors, trains and provides military and financial support to groups such as the Ogaden National Liberation Front (ONLF), Oromo

Liberation Front (OLF), Tigrayan People's Democratic Movement (Demhit), Ginbot Sebat (G7) and Afar Revolutionary Democratic Unity Front(ARDUF). Moreover, it supports almost non-existent groups such as Arbegnoch (Ethiopian Patriots), Debub-Hizboch and Benishangul rebels. It repeatedly tried to deploy especially ONLF and OLF forces through Somalia to Ethiopia. Some of the armed men caught by the Ethiopian army confirmed that they were trained and given support by the Eritrean army.

Eritrea trained those groups not only to wage guerilla warfare but also for terrorist activities. They were provided with bombs and other explosive materials to cause massive mayhem on the Ethiopian people and destroy economic and communication installations. One unbelievable and atrocious attempt made by Eritrean intelligence officials was intended to disrupt the January 2011 African Union summit in Addis Ababa with a bombing and killing campaign in the city. It indicated how desperate the Eritrea government has become because of its alienation and excommunication from the world community of states caused by its irresponsible and rogue policies and practices. Such behavior and actions have not helped Eritrea to sell its perceived grievances to the community of nations and remained a pariah state with little support.

The other front where Eritrea has been waging a proxy war against Ethiopia was in Somalia and through Somalia. Initially, it armed and financed the United Islamic Courts (UIC) with the intention of opening a front against Ethiopia through Somalia. The UIC was able to defeat the various war lords in Southern Somalia including Mogadishu and consolidated its grip on most of the Somali population. The UIC then started moving north and fighting was raging against the Somali Transitional Government forces, which has had the support of the African Union and the international community. As expected, the UIC forces not only threatened to cross the Ethiopian border and create instability in the border areas but also declared and made calls for Jihad against Ethiopia.

Faced with a major disaster in its doorstep and its unimaginable consequences, Ethiopia was forced to send its troops to fight on the side of the Transitional Government in 2006. The UIC forces were defeated and driven from the major cities and regions of Somalia. Consequently, the UIC was split and the moderate faction negotiated with the Transitional Government and joined to establish a new government, the Transitional Federal Government, in which one of the former UIC leaders, Sharif Sheik Ahmed, was elected president in February 2009.

Eritrea still continued to support off shoot of remnants of the UIC, which evolved into Al-Shabaab, which imposed a strict Sharia law in areas it controlled and openly declared its allegiance to Al-Qaeda. It declared Jihad against the TFG and the African Union Mission for Somalia (AMISOM) which was deployed to contribute to peace and stability in Somalia. Eritrea, despite receiving strong condemnation for its support to those extremist terrorists from the international community, it has continued to support them with armaments and other essentials. They fought against the TFG and African contingent and widen their control of many parts of Somalia, including part of Mogadishu. They terrorized the people under their control and forced them to adhere to their extremist interpretation of Islam. Such atrocities continued until the TFG and the African Union contingents forced Al-Shabaab to retreat and lose most of its territorial control. The advance of the government side was helped by the decision of the African Union leaders to expand AMISOM's mandate from a peacekeeping one to a peace enforcement focus. In spite of the African Union's resolve to defeat Al-Shababa and strengthen peace and stability in Somalia, Eritrea has continued to play the spoiler role by shipping arms and supplies to the terrorist group.

Alarmed by the irresponsible and outrageous actions of Eritrea, the international Community started to seriously scrutinize its involvement and the consequent complications. The situation was further exacerbated by Eritrea's clash with Djibouti at Ras Doumeria border region causing loss of lives. The military clashes were waged between June 10 and 13, 2008. Earlier when the situation was growing tense, Ethiopia was seriously concerned and its Prime Minister called the situation a threat to peace and security of the whole Horn of Africa, and warned Ethiopia would secure its trade corridor in the event of war. As usual, Eritrea denied sending troops to the area. The Africa Union Peace and Security Council seized the matter and announced that it "strongly condemn Eritrea's military action against Djibouti in Ras Doumaira and Doumeria Island and demand Eritrea withdraw immediately and unconditionally from the Djiboutian territories it occupies.[227] The Communiqué supported the efforts of AU Chairperson but Eritrea refused to receive the mission of the Commission. Similarly, the statements of the Security Council President also fell on deaf ears. While Djibouti withdrew its forces to the status quo ante and cooperated with fact-finding mission, Eritrea refused to take any action to diffuse the situation. Consequently, the Security Council adopted Resolution 1862(2009), which demanded Eritrea to withdraw its forces and also engage in dialogue to defuse the tension, and also find a means to determine the border in a mutually acceptable settlement.[228]

Eritrea has also been repeatedly urged to desist from supporting and training opposition forces with the intention of destabilizing the region. The African Union, IGAD, the Security Council and the Secretary General of the United Nations again and again asked Eritrea to stop its arms delivery and support to the extremist forces in Somalia. They also encouraged it to make peace with Djibouti by amicably settling the border conflict. However, Eritrea refused to cooperate with all the institutions responsible for regional and international peace and stability.

Eritrea's intransigent position and its disrespect and non-compliance to decisions of the African Union and its other institutions pushed the 13th African Union Summit to call on the Security Council to impose sanctions on Eritrea for its support to armed groups destabilizing Somalia and undermining the regional peace and stability efforts.[229] Accordingly, the Security Council passed Resolution 1907(2009), which imposed arms embargo and travel restrictions and a freeze on assets of Eritrean political and military leaders as designated by the Sanctions Implementing Committee.[230] In the absence of any tangible movement to compliance and change of behavior, the Security Council passed Resolution 2023(2011) to strengthen and expand the sanctions imposed by Resolution 1907 (2009).[231] The Security Council based its decision on the report of the Somalia/Eritrea Monitoring Group that confirmed the continuation of the Eritrean political, financial, training and logistical support to armed opposition groups, including Al-Shabaab, which are engaged in undermining peace, security and stability in Somalia and the region.[232] It also noted the decision of the 18th Extraordinary Session of the Assembly of the Heads of State and Government of the Intergovernmental Authority on Development (IGAD), which called on the Security Council to take measures to ensure Eritrea stop from destabilizing the Horn of Africa.[233] Resolution 2023(2011) also condemned the planned terrorist attack of January 2011 to disrupt the African Union Summit in Addis Ababa. It also condemned the imposition of the "Diaspora tax" on Eritrean diaspora and decided that Eritrea should cease collecting those funds by use of extortion, threats of violence, fraud and other illicit means. The Resolution also expressed the Council's concern on the potential use of the Eritrean mining sector as a financial resource to destabilize the Horn of Africa, and called on Eritrea to show transparency in its public finances. Moreover, it expressed its intention to apply targeted sanctions against individuals and entities if they met the criteria detailed in Resolution 1907(2009).[234]

Evidently, the Resolution indicates there will follow serious consequences if Eritrea fails to comply. It was welcomed by the 20th Extraordinary Session of the IGAD Assembly of Heads of State and Government.[235] However, after all those diplomatic and political pressures, Eritrea has continued to pursue its destructive and disruptive activities in the Horn of Africa. Eritrea has failed to desist from its support of armed groups including extremists and terrorists with the intention of destabilizing the region. According to the Monitoring Group report, an Eritrean General and his collaborators continue to be engaged in arms and people trafficking to the Sudan.[236] Although the Monitoring Group indicated that arms shipment to Somalia declined, it did not show that it has completely stopped and also is far from exhibiting change of policy and practice of the Eritrean government. The decline of shipments seems to have been caused by coordinated and intensified international scrutiny of its actions. On the other hand, the Monitoring Group noted that the Eritrean government violated the Resolution by providing support to armed groups with intention of destabilizing Ethiopia.[237] Moreover, an Eritrean supported, trained, armed and financed armed group, the Afar Revolutionary Democratic Unity Front (ARDUF) raided a tourist camp during the night of 17 January 2012 and killed five Europeans and wounded others. Ethiopia held Eritrea responsible[238] and Ethiopian troops raided three Eritrean military bases in retaliation with limited objectives on 16 March 2012.

As mentioned above, Eritrean government failed to comply with the resolutions of the Security Council. It has continued to play a destabilizing role in the region by hosting armed groups. It has also become a major actor in the arms and ammunition trafficking and sale through the Sudan. The Monitoring Group confirmed that Eritrea has been collecting "Diaspora taxes" by involving threats, harassment and intimidation. Since such practices are under scrutiny and some countries like Germany and Britain forbade the Eritrean officials from collecting the "taxes", the Eritrean government agents will undoubtedly devise a system that is clandestine to collect the money. Evidently, these "taxes" and contributions constitute a major part of the government's budget, and thus, the Eritrean authorities will not easily give in.

Some people consider Eritrea's reopening of its mission to Africa Union and some statements indicating its desire to rejoin the IGAD as positive steps towards ending its rogue behavior. However, many veteran observers of Horn of Africa's politics and political actors do not buy such optimistic view. The Eritrean government looks flexible in tight situations and in the absence of other alternatives. Otherwise, rather than addressing its internal problems and the country's thirst for development and change, it looks determine to prolong its stay in power by now and then creating external crisis and fabricating enemies.

Conclusion and the way forward

As discussed above, the beginning of the transitional period was crafted in agreement with EPLF as it accepted the process of referendum to settle the issue of Eritrean question once for all.

Many people in both countries had high hopes that relations between Ethiopia and Eritrea would be based on a new foundation of brotherhood and friendship. The initial signs of the cooperation and the signing of many agreements and protocols in all sectors showed the heralding of a new relationship based on mutual cooperation and for mutual benefit. Apparently, the relationship started to show some rifts as the mutual confidence on each other and the perceived as well as the actual economic and trade relationship started to exhibit some divergence.

Evidently, the differences on economic policies and lack of commitment on mutual benefit and sincere cooperation were the decisive factors that brought up the conflict. Although there have been border issues and disagreements since the 1970s, it would be a mistake to treat them as the casus belli of the conflict. Border issues got prominence after attempts to bridge the differences in economic issues became unattainable.

It is difficult to know why the Eritrean government decided to solve it differences by using brute force. In this age, it is difficult to imagine border problems can be solved through force. If the intention was to get permanent settlement and stability, the only option that exists is dialogue and the will to meet your antagonist half way. Many observers of the region suspect that Eritrea crossed the border to pressurize the Ethiopian government to cave in to some of its positions. Others believe that Eritrea thought the Ethiopian government was fragile and would not risk putting up major resistance and would sit to negotiate based on its terms a more likely miscalculation. Apparently, there could be many factors that swayed the Eritrean leadership to follow the road it took. However, it is incomprehensible why it took that unfortunate path knowing the EPRDF leadership would not give in to blackmailing and coercion.

As indicated above, the fratricidal war caused the death of tens of thousands people, the displacement of hundreds of thousands citizens of both countries, hundreds of millions worth of property, and above all, it left a repulsive scar on the brotherly relationship of the two people. To make matters worse, such situation was aggravated by the fateful and flawed decision of the Eritrea-Ethiopia Boundary Commission, which is devoid of becoming a basis for lasting settlement and peaceful co-existence. Such irresponsible and amateurish decision brought the situation to standstill.

The price of the stalemate is growing day by day hurting the opportunities of the two peoples to eradicate poverty and prosper together on the basis of extensive cooperation based on mutual interest. The Horn of Africa is continuing to be unstable; both countries are forced to maintain big armies which are not helpful to the economy; the economies of both countries has been devoid of the contribution of the one economy to the other; and relatives on both sides have been separated from one another with dire consequences to the historical and cultural relationship. In addition, as discussed above, the proxy war will not produce any advantage to either side in a substantial way. In this case, Eritrea's harboring and supporting any fringe group opposing the Ethiopian government haven't helped its cause. In fact, it has been alienated from the international community and has been exposed to international sanctions. It is in Eritrea's interest to stop destabilizing the region and start to be a responsible member of the regional as well as the international organizations. After all, it hasn't been more than an irritation to the Ethiopian government.

In addition to desisting from attempts to destabilize neighboring countries, the other major element to making peace between the countries is trust and confidence on one another. Mistrust and suspicion of one another's motive has pushed both countries to harbor antagonistic disposition which most of the time end up in disastrous results. Hence, the first step should be to enhance trust and confidence between the parties. Such move should include desisting from attempting to hurt the interests of the other side that ranges from stopping unfavorable propaganda to ending providing support to anti-peace groups and elements.[239]

As the border issue was a byproduct of differences in economic and trade policies, the demarcation process should be closely linked with decisions and appropriate actions to normalize the relationship. The Eritrean President's argument that Eritrea will "engage in any necessary discussions pertaining to normalization as soon as the demarcation of the boundary is completed and when a conducive environment for normalization is established,"[240] seems a non-starter to the Ethiopian side. Truly, all sides know that there needs to be a dialogue before demarcating the border to avoid any potential source of conflict and make it a permanent settlement. Therefore, leaders of both sides should rise above animosity and squabbling and decide on building the common destiny of both peoples. The destiny of both sides is to live in harmony, eradicate poverty and build a very strong economic cooperation that leads to common prosperity.

Notes

1. See Malanczuk, Akekhurst's Modern Introduction to International Law, 1997: 326-27; Tomuschat (ed.), Modern Law of Self-Determination, 1993: 1-2; Cassese, Self-determination of Peoples, 1995: 11-33; Hannum, Autonomy, Sovereignty, and Self-Determination, 1996: 27-49; Krys, "The Right of Peoples to Self-Determination", 1985: 289; Menon, "The Right to Self-Determination", 1975: 183; and Przetacznik, "The Basic Collective Human Rights to Self-Determination of Peoples and Nations as a Prerequisite for Peace", 1991: 259-60.
2. See Malanczuk, 1997: 326.
3. Menon, "The Right to Self-Determination: A Historical Appraisal", Revue de droit International, Vol. 53, 1975: 187.
4. Article 1 (2), the Chapter of the United Nations, 1945, in Bennett, A. LeRoy, International Organisations: Principles and Issues, 5th edition, 1991, p. 436.
5. Ibid., p. 452-53.

6. Declaration on the Granting of Independence to Colonial Countries and Peoples, of 14 December 1960, General Assembly Official Records, 15th Session, Supplement No. 16 (A/4884), p. 66; United Nations Yearbook 1960, p. 49. Musgrave explains "[c]laims to self-determination are also put forward by ethnic groups. Such claims often involve secession from an existing state, and consequently have not generally been accepted by members of the international community. Most states in the post-war period, whatever their political motivation, maintained a policy of not recognizing entities which had seceded from independent states. This situation, however, appears to have changed with the dissolution of the Soviet Union and of Yugoslavia into a number of ethnically based nation-states. These successor states have been recognized by the international community and accepted as member states of the United Nations. This response by the international community has been particularly important with regard to Yugoslavia, where the dissolution of the state and the emergence of internationally recognized successor states occurred unilaterally. The response of the international community to the dissolution of the Soviet Union and of Yugoslavia therefore calls into question the extent to which self-determination based on ethnic criteria may now constitute an element of international law, and the circumstances in which it may happen." (Musgrave, Self-Determination and National Minorities, 1997: 125).
7. Johnson, Harold S. Self-Determination within the Community of Nations, 1967: 200.
8. Walker quoted in Przetacznik, 1991: 262-63.
9. Krys, Roman, 1985: 292-93.
10. Donnelly argues as follows: What does respecting the right to self-determination involve? Roughly, it involves respecting all other human rights, and in particular rights to political participation and freedom of speech, press, assembly, and association. If these rights are fully respected, it is difficult to see how the right to self-determination could be denied. Conversely, denial of the right to self-determination takes place principally through the denial of these individual human rights (and is likely to have further deleterious consequences for most other individual rights). There is little or nothing that can be done with the right of self-determination that cannot be accomplished by the exercise of other human rights (Donnelly, Universal Human Rights in Theory and Practice, 1989: 148).
11. Przetacznik, 1991: 263.
12. When it comes to secession, it is noted "while international law does not acknowledge a general right to secession, it also generally agreed that it does not prohibit secession" (Malanczuk, 'Minorities and Self-Determination: Reflections on International Law in General, Including Some Recent Developments in Ethiopia', in Neri Sybesma-Knol en Jef Van Bellingen (eds.), Naareennieuweinterpretatie van het Recht op Zelfbeschikking?, Vubpress, 1995: 180; see also Hannum, Hurst, "Self-Determination in the Post-Colonial Era", in Clark and Williamson (eds.), 1996:25-27. Rudnitsky also argues "the establishment of a new sovereign state as a mode of self-determination for smaller social groups should be a 'last

resort' when: (1) all other means and social remedies within the state in question have been tried and proved ineffective for the purpose of protecting the existence and development of the identity of stable social groups and the human rights of their members on an equal basis; (2) it has been proved on the basis of international standards that such guarantees or mechanisms cannot be established in the given society and state in a reasonable time and without endangering either the identity of such groups or the fundamental rights of their members; and (3) the applicability of all the other modes of the realization of self-determination has been examined and tested without success." (Rudnitsky, "Self-Determination in a Modern World: Conceptual Development and Practical Application", in Sellers (ed.), 1996: 78-79).

13. According to UNESCO Experts "people" is defined as a group of individual human beings who enjoy some or all of the following common features: a) a common historical tradition; b) racial or ethnic identity; c) cultural homogeneity; d) linguistic unity; e) religious or ideological affinity; f) territorial connection; g) common economic life. (UNESCO Experts quoted in Thornberry, in Tomuschat (ed.), 1993: 124).
14. In relation to the above discussion, Stavenhagen remarks "The link between self-determination and democracy must be strengthened, in theory as well as in practice, in policy as well as in process. The violence we see around us is not generated by the drive of self-determination, but by its negation. The denial of self-determination, not its pursuit, is what leads to upheavals and conflicts. And the denial of self-determination is essentially incompatible with true democracy. Only if the peoples' right to self-determination is respected can a democratic society flourish, and only within a truly democratic framework, in which all other human rights are given due recognition, will the right to self-determination be freed from the 'demons' – real or putative- which now envelop it." (Stavenhagen, Rodolfo, "Self-Determination: Right or Demon", in Clark and Williamson (eds.), Self-Determination: International Perspectives, 1996: 8).
15. See Marcus, A History of Ethiopia, 1994: 99; Marcus, The Life and Times of Menelik II, 1995: 176-77; and Zewde, A History of Modern Ethiopia 1855-1974, 1991: 83-84.
16. See the Treaty between Italy and Ethiopia for the Delimitation of the Frontier between Eritrea and Ethiopia, signed at Addis Ababa, 10th July 1900, in Ethiopia and Eritrea: A Documentary Study, Compiled with an introduction by HabtuGhebre-Ab, 1993: 10-11.
17. Ibid., p. 39-40; Section IV, Article 23 of the Treaty of Peace with Italy reads as follows: 1) Italy renounces all rights and title to the Italian territorial possessions in Africa, i.e. Libya, Eritrea and Italian Somaliland. 2) Pending their final disposal, the said possessions shall continue under their present administration. 3) The final disposal of these possessions shall be determined jointly by the Governments of the Soviet Union, of the United Kingdom, of the United States of America, and of France within one year from the coming into force of the present Treaty, in the

manner laid down in the joint declaration of February 10, 1947, issued by the said Governments, which is reproduced in Annex XI.

18. See UN General Assembly, A/2188, Supplement No. 15, 11 December 1952: Final Report of the United Nations Commissioner in Eritrea.
19. See Text of Resolution 390 A (V) adopted on December 2, 1950 by the General Assembly of the United Nations, in Tekeste Negash, *Eritrea and Ethiopia: The Federal Experience*, 1997: 184.
20. Ibid., p. 185.
21. Ibid., p. 188.
22. See Revised Constitution of Ethiopia, Negrit Gazeta, 15th Year, No. 2, Addis Ababa, November 4, 1955.
23. Andargatchew Messay quoted in Tekeste Negash, 1997: 102.
24. See Tekeste Negash, 1997: 146.
25. See Iyob, The Eritrean Struggle for Independence, 1995: 108-22.
26. The EPLF and TPLF relationship has been rocky at times during the armed struggle. Initially, EPLF's close relationship with EPRP and low attention to its collaboration with the TPLF, and its negligible support to the latter's cause was a source of tension between them. It was later compounded by differences in their characterization of the Soviet Union, the issue of self-determination, military strategy and other related issues. The relationship reached its worst stage when the EPLF decided to block the road that was used to transport relief assistance at the height of the North-Ethiopian famine in 1984/85. In 1988, leaders of both organizations met and discuss how to coordinate their struggle against the regime despite their political differences, which paved the way for their collaboration in defeating the Derg in 1991. (for detail Discussions, see Negash and Tronvoll, Brothers at War, 2000: 12-21).
27. The Eritrean demand for independence was very controversial and open to different interpretations. However, the member-organizations of the Transitional Government agreed to allow referendum in Eritrea despite differences of positions on the characterization of the case. (for further discussion on the issue, see Malanczuk, "Minorities and Self-Determination," 1995: 188-193; see also Anna Mamalakis Pappas, Eritrea, in Bernhardt(ed.), Encyclopedia of Public International Law, Volume International Law, Volume Two, 1995: 113-114; Bereket Habte Selassie, Eritrea and the United Nations and other essays, 1989; and Ruth Iyob, The Eritrean Struggle for Independence, 1995.
28. See Joint Statement by the EPRDF, EPLF, and OLF, London, May 28, 1991.
29. The EPLF decision to hold an internationally supervised referendum was a far-sighted arrangement. Henze explains the factors that influenced such decision as follows: a) the likelihood that Eritrean independence would not be recognized by any major Western Country and would not be welcomed in most of Africa; b) the fact that recognition by radical Arab countries would not be beneficial from the viewpoint of basic Eritrean interest; and C) the concern of the EPLF leadership that Ethiopia, freed of the Derg, should evolve peacefully and constructively , an

evolution on which a unilateral declaration of independence would have a negative influence . (Henze, in Charles Gurdon (ed.), 1994:20.

30. See the Principles of Co-operation between the Transitional Government of Ethiopia and the Provisional Government of Eritrea, July 1991.
31. See UN General Assembly, A/C. 3/ 47/ 5, 1992.
32. Provisional Government of Eritrean, Proclamation No. 22/1992, April 7, 1992, Article 5 (1).
33. Ibid., Article 2.
34. For details, see Proclamation No. 21/1992, Eritrean Nationality Proclamation, April 6, 1992, Articles 2-4.
35. Referendum'93: The Eritrean People Determined Their Destiny, Report of the Referendum Commissioner of Eritrea, August 1993: 77.
36. See Minutes of the 5th Special Session of the Council of Representatives of Ethiopia, April 29, 1993.
37. Statement on the Recognition by Ethiopia of the Sovereignty and Independence of Eritrea, Ministry of Foreign Affairs, Addis Ababa, April 1993.
38. Ibid.
39. A National Charter for Eritrea: For a Democratic, Just and Prosperous Future, Approved by the Third Congress of the Eritrean People's Liberation Front, Nakfa, February 1994: 40-41.
40. Ibid., p. 41.
41. Ibid., p. 45, Chapter One.
42. Ibid., p. 58.
43. See Sorensen, 1995: 13-14.
44. See Iyob, 'The Eritrean Experiment: A Cautious Pragmatism?', In the Journal of Modern African Studies, 35 (4), 1997: 655.
45. A Proclamation to Provide for the Establishment of the Constitutional Commission, April 1994. Article 5 of the Proclamation empowered the Commission with the preparation of a draft constitution, and the organization of a public debate on the draft document.
46. See Constitutional Commission of Eritrea. Draft Constitution, July 1996, Asmara, Eritrea.
47. Ibid.
48. Hadas Ertra, 24 May 1997, quoted in Iyob, 1997.
49. See Iyob, 1997: 656-67.
50. Final Report of the Joint Review Committee on the Implementation of the Ethio-Eritrean Economic Agreements, January 1, 1997, p. 1.
51. Trade Agreement between the Transitional Government of Ethiopia and the Government of the State of Eritrea, September 27, 1993.
52. Ibid.
53. The Memorandum of Understanding on Liberalizing Trade, October 7, 1994.

54. See the Agreement on the Establishment of a Free Trade Area, April 3, 1995.
55. See the provisions of the Agreements for a full understanding of the contents.
56. Final Report of the Joint Review Committee, January 1, 1997, p. 11-12; For the provision, see the Memorandum of Understanding on Liberalizing Trade, October 7, 1994.
57. See Minutes of Understanding between the Trade Delegation of the FDRE and the Trade Delegation of the State of Eritrea, August 16, 1996.
58. See Final Report of the Joint Review Committee, January 1, 1997, p. 12-13; the Ethiopian government contended that the prohibition of the franco-valuta imports were intended to tackle the problems of the proliferation of black market and unfair trade practices. It also reminded its counterpart that the measure of franco-valuta imports were employed when the foreign exchange reserve was very scant and that situation improved satisfactorily which required a return to the normal practice of importing goods through bank procedures. However, the Ethiopian explanation was not well received by the Eritrean delegation and was understood as a measure to block the re-export trade, which would mostly hurt Eritrea. The difference of opinion persisted and become one of the causes for the non-cooperative attitude of the Eritrean government in curbing illegal trade. (Ibid., p. 36).
59. Ibid.
60. Ibid., p. 13-14.
61. See the Protocol Agreement on Harmonization of Economic Policies between the Government of the State of Eritrea and the Transitional Government of Ethiopia, September 27, 1993.
62. Ibid., Article 4.
63. See Agreed Minutes of the Fourth Ethio-Eritrean Joint Commission Meeting, August 18-19, 1996.
64. Many Eritreans residing in Ethiopia have had both passports of the two countries. Eritrea allows its citizens to acquire dual citizenship but Ethiopian laws indicate citizens would lose their citizenship the moment they acquire another one. However, due to lack of agreement to sort it out, the task of determining the citizenship of Eritreans residing in Ethiopia remained in suspense until the May 1998 conflict erupted.
65. The Transits and Port Services Agreement of 29th September 1993 implementation process was evaluated as "fairly good" by the Joint Review Committee. However, there were some disagreements such as on the payment system, the rate of the Ethiopian Shipping Lines charges on Eritrean cargo, dwelling time for cargo, responsibility for pilferage and damage at the ports, allowing Ethiopian transistors to work in the ports and other related issues. For example, when the Ethiopian government issued licenses for Eritrean nationals to engage in clearing activities in Ethiopia and requested on reciprocity basis the same right be extended to Ethiopian nationals to render same services in Eritrea, the Eritrean government insisted that the Ethiopian request had to be addressed together

with the issue of allowing Eritreans to operate in road transport in Ethiopia. The Ethiopian side opposed to the tactics of the Eritrean government to extract concessions by mixing two different sectors, but the Eritrean side was unwilling to separately resolve the issues, and persisted in using the transit services sector as leverage. (See the Ethio-Eritrean Joint Meeting on Port and Transit Services, Asmara, March 19, 1996).

66. Final Report of the Joint Review Committee, January 1, 1997, p. 58.
67. The Trade Agreement, September 27, 1993, Article V states "the Contracting Parties agree that all payments for the transaction concluded in the implementation of the present agreement shall be made in Birr as long as the Birr remains common currency".
68. See Directives on the Payment Mechanisms for the Trade and Services Transactions between Ethiopia and Eritrea, Ethiopian Prime Minister's Office, November 18, 1997. (In Amharic).
69. See the Border Trade Directives, Ministry of Trade and Industry, 1997.
70. Interview, Aser (a Tigrigna magazine), Vol. 2, No. 9, December-February 1998, p. 9.
71. Isaias Afwerki, interview with Aser magazine, quoted by Solomon Inquai, in Ethioscope, Vol. 4, No. 2, 1998, p. 13-14.
72. Neway Gebre-Ab, interview, January 6, 1999.
73. Ibid.
74. For example the 1997 remittances were estimated to be about $200 million and the 1998 estimates would be much more for the more contributions made to finance the war effort with Ethiopia. (See The Economist Intelligence Unit. Country Report: Ethiopia, Eritrea, Somalia, and Djibouti, 3rd Quarter, 1998).
75. See Treaty between Italy and Ethiopia for the Delimitation of the Frontier between Eritrea and Ethiopia, signed at Addis Ababa, 10th July 1900, in Ghebre-Ab, 1993: 14-15.
76. Treaties between Great Britain and Ethiopia, and between Great Britain, Italy and Ethiopia, Relative to the Frontiers between the Sudan, Ethiopia, Eritrea, signed at Addis Ababa, 15th May, 1902, in Ghebre-Ab, 1993: 14-15.
77. See Italian colonial maps found in the archives of the Ministry of Foreign Affairs of Italy. (Copies of maps collected by the Ethiopian Ministry of Foreign Affairs).
78. See the Economist, 14 October 1995, p. 54.
79. See the Eritrea-Yemen Arbitration Decision in the International Boundaries Research Unit at http:// www.ibru.dur.ac.uk.
80. Agence France Presse, Djibouti asks Asmara to withdraw map of Eritrea, Djibouti, April 25, 1996.
81. See Aide Memoire sent by Prime Minister to African Heads of State and Government before the OAU Central Organ's Summit Meeting in Ouagadougou on 17-18 December, 1998.

82. Djibouti Foreign Ministry, Statement on Severance of Diplomatic Relations with Eritrea, November 18, 1998.
83. The border issue was initially raised by the ELF in 1976. It claimed that the boundary of Ethiopia and Eritrea was far deeper than what was later claimed by the EPLF. The TPLF had consistently declared that the border issue should be only addressed by legitimate governments. Thus, it should be differed until such situations are created in both sides. Then it was only in 1997 border issues began to resurface after relations started to suffer because of differences in trade and economic relations.
84. See Minutes of the Meeting of the Joint Commission of November 14, 1997.
85. Minutes of the Meeting of the Joint Commission of May 8, 1998.
86. The Statement of the Council of Ministers of the Federal Democratic Republic of Ethiopia, May 13, 1998.
87. Interview with journalists, May 1998. (Quoted from recorded videocassette distributed by the Ethiopian Ministry of Foreign Affairs).
88. President Isaias quoted by Eritrea Profile, May 14, 1998.
89. Statement of the Cabinet of Ministers of the Eritrea Government, May 14, 1998.
90. Ibid.
91. Eritrea Government Statement, May 20, 1998.
92. Recommendations submitted by the Governments of Rwanda and the United States, May 30, 1998.
93. Isaias Afwerki, Interview with the BBC, May 30, 1998.
94. See Resolutions of the 68th Ordinary Session of the OAU Council of Ministers, Ouagadougou, June 5, 1998.
95. See Resolutions of the 34th Ordinary Session of the Assembly of Heads of State and Government, Ouagadougou, June 10, 1998.
96. See Report on the Efforts made by the OAU High Level Delegation on the Dispute between Ethiopia and Eritrea, 4th Ordinary Session of the Central Organ of the OAU Mechanism for Conflict Prevention, Management and Resolution at Summit Level, 17-18 December 1998, Ouagadougou, Burkina Faso.
97. The Statement of the High Level Delegation, Addis Ababa, June 19, 1998.
98. Report on the Efforts made by the OAU High Level Delegation, p. 3; the need to determine by which authority Badme was administered before 12 May 1998 was prompted by the insistence of the Eritrean Government that Badme has always been under Eritrean administration. However, when the Committee was formed, Eritrea showed reservation on its task by stating "we fail to see the rationale of this task. It must be born in mind that Badme is one of the several towns "contested" by Ethiopia... administration by itself does not have any meaning if the process by which this administration was installed is illegal. What of critical importance is where Badme, Adi-Murug and other areas lie within the recognized boundary". (Ibid., p. 4).
99. United Nations Security Council, Resolution 1177 (1998), 26 June 1998.
100. Reuters News Agency, June 9, 1998.

101. Report on the Efforts made by the High Level Delegation, p. 5.
102. Ibid., p. 8-9.
103. Ibid., p. 10; the Eritrean Minister objected to the conclusion that Badme and its environs were administered by Ethiopia prior to May 12. He also objected to the statement that what happened in Badme between 6 and 12 May was a fundamental element of the crises'. (Ibid.).
104. Ibid., p. 15-18.
105. See the Office of the Spokesperson of the Government of the Federal Democratic Republic of Ethiopia, Press Release, November 9, 1998; Clarification was asked on some parts of the Framework Agreement, such as whether the forces to be redeployed to their original positions were the Eritrean troops (as Ethiopia believed that such a recommendation should only concern the Eritrean forces); on the definition of Badme town and its environs, Prime Minister Meles' understanding was all Ethiopian territory occupied after May 6, 1998, which the High Level Delegation took note; and the civilian administration should include its law enforcement organs minus regular troops. (Report on the Efforts made by the High Level Delegation, p. 18).
106. See Press Release issued on 9 November 1998 by the Ministry of Foreign Affairs of Eritrea.
107. See Document Handed over to the Secretary General of the OAU during the Meeting with the President of Eritrea in Asmara, on 12 December 1998; some of the questions asked for clarification seem strange as Eritrea is a member country of the OAU. For example question no. 10 reads as follows: what is the mandate of the Central Organ?; what can we expect from forthcoming meeting of the Central Organ? (Ibid.). The OAU's response to the mentioned questions was: See the 1993 Cairo Declaration of the OAU Summit establishing the Mechanism for Conflict Prevention, Management and Resolution; See the Communiqué adopted by the Central Organ at the end of its deliberations. (Issues Raised by the Eritrean Side Requiring Clarification, Document the OAU gave to the Eritrean government on January 26, 1999).
108. See the above document handed over to the Secretary General by the Eritrean side, 12 December 1998.
109. President Isaias Afwerki's Speech to the OAU Central Organ Meeting, Ouagadougou, 17 December 1998.
110. See A Transcribed Impromptu Statement by H. E. Prime Meles Zenawi, at the Fourth OAU Central Organ Summit, 17 December 1998, Ouagadougou.
111. Ibid.
112. Dispute between Ethiopia and Eritrea, Statement of the OAU Central Organ, Ouagadougou, 17-18 December 1998.
113. United Nations Security Council, Resolution 1226 (1999), January 29, 1999.
114. Ibid.
115. Declaration by the Presidency on behalf of the European Union on the Conflict between Eritrea and Ethiopia, 15 January 1999.

116. Hiruy Amanuel, interview.
117. Verbatim Briefing to the African Diplomatic Community by Prime Minister, January 27, 1999.
118. President Isaias, interview with the Eritrean National Television Network, January 31, 1999.
119. See Office of the Government Spokesperson (Ethiopia), February 06, 1999; and the Press Release of the Foreign Ministry of Eritrea, February 06, 1999.
120. Statement by the Secretary General of the OAU on the Current Situation between Eritrea and Ethiopia, February 8, 1999.
121. Letter to the Secretary General of the UN, Kofi Annan, Asmara, 27 February 1999.
122. Prime Minister, Letter to Ambassador Qin Huasun, President of the Security Council, March 8, 1999.
123. Ibid.
124. Ibid.
125. Press Statement, Ministry of Foreign Affairs of the State of Eritrea, March 10, 1999.
126. Eritrea Profile, Vol. 6, No. 2, March 20, 1999.
127. Ibid.
128. See endnote no. 105 for the clarification sought by the Prime Minister during the November 7and 8, 1998 meeting of the OAU High Level Delegation.
129. See Article 51 of the Charter of the United Nations, in Bennett, International Organizations, 1991: 447; see also Malanczuk, 1997: 311.
130. Letter from President Compaore to President Isaias Afwerki, 08 May 1999 (English translation).
131. Letter from President Compaore to President Isaias Afwerki, 20 May 1999 (English translation).
132. OAU. Modalities for the Implementation of the OAU framework Agreement on the Settlement of the Dispute between Ethiopia and Eritrea, July 12, 1999.
133. Ibid.
134. Ibid.
135. OAU. Transcript of the Proceedings relating to the Ethio-Eritrea Dispute at a Closed Session of Heads of State and Government in Algiers, on Wednesday, July 14,1999.
136. Ibid.
137. Ibid.
138. Letter from Prime Minister to President Abdulaziz Bouteflika of Algeria, 20th of July 1999.
139. Ibid.
140. Letter from Prime Minister to President Abdulaziz Bouteflika of Algeria, 29th of July 1999.

141. Ibid.
142. OAU, Technical Arrangements for the Implementation of the OAU Framework Agreement and its Modalities, August 1999.
143. Ibid., Article 2 and Annex IV.
144. Ibid., Article 2 and 4.
145. Ibid., Article 9 (a) (2.1).
146. Ibid., Article 9 (a) (2.3) and Article 9 (b. 2).
147. See Proposals for A Framework Agreement for a Peaceful Settlement of the Dispute between Eritrea and Ethiopia, November 1998.
148. For the detail questions and comments on the Technical Arrangements, see the Letter from Prime Minister to President Abdulaziz Bouteflika of 13th August of 1999 and its Annex.
149. News Briefing by Isaias Afwerki, President of Eritria, on the Ongoing Conflict between Ethiopia and Eritrea, and the Prospect for Peace, the National Press Club, Washington D.C., Transcript by the Federal News Service, Federal Information Systems Cooperation, August 16, 1999.
150. See Clarifications of the Organization of African Unity in Response to the Questions Raised by Ethiopia relating to the Technical Arrangements, August 1999, (B) Cessation of Hostilities and Redeployment.
151. See Consolidated Technical Arrangement (Non-Paper), May 07, 2000.
152. OAU, Press Release, No. 21/2000, March 6, 2000.
153. Statement of the Cabinet of Ministers on the Peace Process, Ministry of Foreign Affairs of Eritrea, March 21, 2000.
154. Communiqué of the Office of the Current Chairman of the OAU on the Proximity Talks, May 5, 2000.
155. See U.S. Statement, Distributed by the Office of International Information Programs, U.S. Department of State. Web site: usinfo.state.gov, May 5, 2000.
156. See Statement from the Ministry of Foreign Affairs, Ethiopian Memorandum on the Origins and Current Status of the Ethio-Eritrea crisis, May 11, 2000; and see Algiers Peace Talks End without Success due to Ethiopia's Refusal to Sign OAU Peace Plan and Cease-fire, Ministry of Foreign Affairs of Eritrea, May 5, 2000.
157. Minutes of the Meetings of Prime Minister and the Delegation of the United Nations Security Council, May 8 and May 9, 2000.
158. Minutes of the Meeting between Prime Minister and the Diplomatic Community, May 8, 2000.
159. Full Text of Meles Zenawi's Impromptu Speech to Resident Diplomats, May 8, 2000.
160. Letter from Ethiopian Foreign Minister, Seyoum Mesfin to the President of the Security Council, 12th of May 2000.
161. UN Security Council Resolution on Eritrea and Ethiopia (Resolution 1297/2000), May 12, 2000.

162. Communiqué of the 64th Session of the central Organ of the OAU Mechanism for Conflict Prevention, Management and Resolution at Ambassadorial Level on the Conflict between Ethiopia and Eritrea, Addis Ababa, May 14, 2000.
163. The Office of the Ethiopian Government Spokesperson, Press Release, May 13, 2000.
164. See the U.S proposed draft text, Draft Security Council Resolution, 15 May 2000, No. 6.
165. See Russia's proposed draft text, Draft Resolution on Eritrea/Ethiopia, 15 May 2000.
166. See United Nations Security Council Resolution 1298 (2000), 17 May 2000, No. 6.
167. Ibid., No. 16.
168. Ibid., No. 17.
169. Letter from President Isaias Afwerki to Mr. Kofi Annan, Secretary General of the U.N, 17 May 2000.
170. Statement by the Foreign Ministry, Addis Ababa, 18 May 2000.
171. Ibid.
172. Prime Minister, Impromptu Speech Delivered to African Resident Diplomats, May 22, 2000.
173. Prime Minister Meles, Briefing to the Diplomatic Community, Addis Ababa, 23 May 2000.
174. Communiqué of the OAU on the Conflict between Ethiopia and Eritrea, P.R. No. 49/2000, 24 May 2000.
175. The Ethiopian Herald, Vol. LVI, No. 220, 25 May 2000.
176. Statement of the Government of Eritrea Concerning the Appeal Issued by the Current Chairman of the OAU, Ministry of Foreign Affairs, Asmara, 24 May 2000.
177. The Office of the Ethiopian Government Spokesperson, Victorious Ethiopian Forces Liberated Zalanbessa, 25 May 2000.
178. Press Release, Eritrea Completes Redeployment to May 6 Positions, Ministry of Foreign Affairs, Asmara, May 25, 2000.
179. Statement from the Ministry of Foreign Affairs, Ethiopia's Commitment to Peace Unchanged, Addis Ababa, May 25, 2000.
180. Ibid.
181. Ibid., see also Prime Minister Meles Zenawi's Briefing to the Diplomatic Community, Addis Ababa, May 23, 2000.
182. The Office of the Government Spokesperson, After Successfully Completing their Mission, Ethiopian Defense Forces Withdraw from Western Eritrea, May 30, 2000.
183. Statement of the Ministry of Foreign Affairs, Addis Ababa, May 30, 2000.
184. Statement of the Council of Ministers of the Federal Democratic Republic of Ethiopia, Addis Ababa, May 31, 2000.
185. Prime Minister Meles Zenawi's Briefing to the Diplomatic Community, May 31, 2000.

186. OAU, Proposal of the O.A.U. for an Agreement on Cessation of Hostilities between the Government of the Federal Democratic Republic of Ethiopia and the Government of the State of Eritrea, June 10, 2000.
187. Ibid., from Paragraph 1 to Paragraph 5.
188. Ibid., Paragraph 9.
189. Ibid., Paragraph 12.
190. Letter from Haile Weldensae, Eritrean Foreign Minister to Ahmed Ouyahia, Special Envoy of the Current Chairman of the OAU, Algiers, 10 June 2000.
191. FDRE. Office of the Government Spokesperson, Facts and Figures on Victims of the Eritrean Government's War of Aggression, March 18, 1999.
192. Eritrean UN Mission Letter to the UN Security Council, January 29, 1999.
193. On 12 June 1998 Ethiopia announced that it has decided to deport those Eritreans who were considered to be a threat to national security. It also confirmed its position that there was no change of policy on Eritreans living and working peacefully in Ethiopia, and that peaceful Eritreans should not worry about their safety. Those mentioned to be included in the deportation categories were: a) Ex-combatants of the EPLF and conscripts of the Eritrean regime suspected of posing a threat to national security on account of their training has been detained at temporary camps, while they make a choice of the country where they wish to go. They have been visited at the temporary camp by international bodies interested in the issue; b) Functionaries and officials of the EPLF office and other party interests in Addis Ababa; and c) Individual Eritreans who were found engaged in spying activities and mobilizing financial and other resources to support the Eritrean aggression.
194. See Reuters, Geneva, June 9, 2000.
195. FDRE Office of Government Spokesperson, Eritrean Regime Increases its Brutal Abuse against Ethiopian Civilians Residing in Eritrea, June 8, 2000.
196. Tefai Ghermazien, Permanent Secretary of the Eritrean Foreign Ministry, interview to the BBC, June 8, 2000.
197. See Agreement Between the Government of the Federal Democratic Republic of Ethiopia and the Government of the State of Eritrea, 12 December 2000.
198. Ibid.
199. See letter of Ethiopian Government regarding the Request for Interpretation, correction and consultation, May 13, 2002
200. Eritrea-Ethiopia Boundary Commission Decision Regarding the "Request for Interpretation, Correction and Consultation" Submitted by the Federal Democratic Republic of Ethiopia on 13 May 2002, June 24, 2002.
201. For example, see Eritrea-Ethiopia Boundary Commission, order pursuant to Article 27(1) of the Commission's Rules of Procedure, July 17, 2002.
202. See submission by the FDRE, January 24, 2003.
203. Ethiopia submitted detailed objection to the Commission's Observation, which had no effect on the decision for details, see 2 May 2003 Comments to the Eritrea-Ethiopia Boundary Commission Submitted by the FDRE.

204. Eritrea-Ethiopia Boundary Commission, Statement, November 27, 2006.
205. See Letter of the Ethiopian Foreign Minister to the UN Secretary General and Chairperson of the African Union, October 16, 2003.
206. See Letter of the President of the Eritrea-Ethiopia Boundary Commission, October 7, 2003.
207. See Speech by H.E. Prime Minister of F.D.R.E to Members of the House of People's Representatives on the Ethiopia-Eritrea Boarder Issue, 25 November 2004.
208. See Letter of the Minister of Foreign Affairs of Ethiopia to the President of the United Nations Security Council, June 8, 2007.
209. United Nations, Statement by the President of the Security Council, 14 December 2005.
210. Special Report of the Secretary General on the United Nations Mission in Ethiopia and Eritrea, 7 April 2008.
211. Ibid.
212. United Nations, Security Council Resolution 1827(2008), 30 July 2008.
213. United Nations Report of the Secretary General on Ethiopia and Eritrea, 19 September 2006.
214. See letter of Ato Seyoum Mesfin, Minister of Foreign Affairs of Ethiopia sent to Osman Saleh, Minister of Foreign Affairs, the State of Eritrea, 22 September 2007, see also similar letter sent to the Secretary General of the United Nation, 22 September 2007.
215. See Eritrea-Ethiopia Claims Commission, Partial Award Jus Ad Bellum, Ethiopia's Claims 1-8, between the Federal Democratic Republic of Ethiopia and the State of Eritrea, The Hague, December 19, 2005.
216. Eritrea-Ethiopia Boundary Commission, Press Release, 30 November 2006.
217. See Letter of the President of Eritrea to the President of the Eritrea-Ethiopia Boundary Commission, 19 November 2007.
218. See Letter of the Foreign Minister of Ethiopia to the President of the Eritrea-Ethiopia Boundary Commission, 27 November 2007.
219. Letter of the President of Eritrea to the United Nations Secretary General, December 21, 2007.
220. Letter of the Foreign Minister of Ethiopia to the United Nations Secretary General, January 18, 2008.
221. Examples see Resolutions passed in 2002 and Resolutions of 2003 such as Resolution 1466(2003) and Resolution 1507(2003).
222. See Resolution 1531 (2004)
223. For example see Resolutions 1560(2004) and 1586 (2004).
224. See Report of the Secretary General on Ethiopia and Eritrea, January 23, 2008:5.
225. Letter of the President of Eritrea to the President of the Eritrea-Ethiopia Boundary Commission, September 5, 2007.

226. Nigeria and Cameroon entered into dialogue on the Implementation of the International Court of Justice judgment of October 2002 and agreed to form the Cameroon- Nigeria Mixed Commission to follow up the judgment which is currently working to speed up the demarcation process.
227. Africa Union, 140th Meeting of the Peace and Security Council, 29 June 2008, Sharm El-Sheikh (Egypt), Communiqué.
228. Security Council Resolution 1862(2009), 14 January 2009.
229. See Decision on the Report of the Peace and Security Council on its Activities and the State of Peace and Security in Africa, Doc. Assembly/AU/6(XIII), Adopted by the Thirteenth Ordinary Session of the Assembly, in Sirte, Great Socialist People's Libyan Arab Jamahiriya on 3 July 2009.
230. Security Council, Resolution 1907(2009), December 23, 2009.
231. Security Council, Resolution 2023(2011), December 5, 2011.
232. See Communiqué of the 18th Extra-Ordinary Session of the IGAD Assembly of Heads of State and Government on the Activities in Sudan, Somalia and Eritrea, Addis Ababa, 4 July 2011.
233. See Report of the Somalia/Eritrea Monitoring Report, 18 July 2011. (S/2011/433).
234. For details, see Security Council, Resolution 2023(2011), December 5, 2011.
235. IGAD; Communiqué of the 20th Extraordinary Session of the IGAD Assembly of Head of State and Government on the situation in Somalia, The Republic of Sudan and South Sudan, IGAD Minimum Integration Plan and Piracy Off the Coast of Somali, Addis Ababa, Ethiopia, January 27, 2012.
236. See for details, UN Monitoring Group Report on Somalia and Eritrea, July 13, 2012(S/2012/545).
237. Ibid.
238. The Monitoring Group indicated that although it has seen no evidence to suggest that the Eritrean Government bears direct responsibility for the killings, it has confirmed Eritrea continues to host, train and support ARDUF, and that some recent ARDUF trainees many have been involved in the action. Hence, the Group found Eritrea not only acted in violation of Resolution 1907(2009), but also bears indirect responsibility for the killings of 17 January 2012. (See Monitoring Group Report, July 13, 2012; 12-14).
239. In May 2009, the Ethiopian Council of Ministers, at its 85th Regular Session, approved a directive granting the deported Eritreans the right to return, claim and repossess their properties and also develop their businesses. The only restriction the directive made was for those involved with the Eritrean government or the ruling party in their security apparatus and trading companies. (See Council of Ministers, Directive to Enable Eritreans Deported during the Ethio-Eritrean war to Reacquire and Develop their Properties and Businesses, May 20, 2009).
240. See Letter of Eritrean President to the President of the Eritrea-Ethiopia Boundary Commission, 5 September 2007.

Chapter 8

Economic Development under the New Regime

Problems and Reform Policies

The Ethiopian economy languished for seventeen years under the command economy introduced by the military government. What was first the Transitional government of Ethiopia, and then the Federal Government adopted a long-term strategy which included long term sector policies aimed at reversing the prevailing economic deterioration, in an attempt to create favorable conditions for the expeditious recovery of the economy. This Chapter examines the contents of the strategy and the policies formulated since 1991 and show their eventual development. As discussed below, the gradual implementation of the economic policies and the evolving theoretical awareness and recognition of the need to create conducive environment to attract foreign investment and the limited capacity of the State to involve itself in a wide-range of economic activities. Undoubtedly, the substances of these policies and the degree and scope of their implementation have had, and will continue to have a decisive impact on the performance of the economy.

The first part of the Chapter begins with a review of general economic development policies. The 1991 economic policy is briefly discussed to indicate the initial thinking of the transitional government and the resultant reform measures. The Agricultural Development Led Industrialization Strategy (ADLI) will be examined in detail, since the policies of the government have been derived from this strategy. Furthermore, a summary of selected socioeconomic strategies are discussed to show how the ADLI strategy is implemented and how it worked and evolved in the process in terms of sector strategies and policies.

In the second part of this Chapter, selected socioeconomic sectors' performances will be discussed briefly to identify the overall problems, proposed solu- tions and prospects for the country's development, and derive some useful lessons for the future. Furthermore, the discussion is subdivided into two parts to show the differences between the first and the second decade. Evidently, the socioeconomic directions, policies and strategies evolved very well in depth and better articulated in the latter decade. Here also the actual implementation of the strategies and policies is discussed to assess the relationship between theory and practice.

Some Reflections on Economic Development Policies

The Concept of Economic Development

As discussed before,[1] economic development is a broad and multidimensional concept. Todaro notes that the concept involves not only economic growth and poverty eradication but also vital transformations of social structures, popular attitudes and national institutions.[2] Similarly, Adelman and Morris define economic development as "widely shared, sustainable economic growth accomplished by significant structural change in production patterns and in economic and political institutions and by generalized improvements in living standards".[3]

Governments usually formulate strategies and policies to achieve specific objectives of economic, political and social change. Content and direction of major policies will largely determine whether the set objectives are attainable. Defining the course of action and methods to pursue the specified goals, based on the formulated strategy, is tantamount to accomplishing a substantial part of the implementation process. However, the hardest part of such endeavors is not the designing of specific and tangible strategies and policies but their implementation. It requires leadership, vision and deep commitment of both government and society to translate these set of strategies into economic, social and political achievements.

The formulation of development strategies has never been easy and free of controversy. There has always been extensive debate on which strategies developing countries should pursue in order to extricate themselves from the quagmire of poverty and economic decline. In the 1950s and early 1960s the dominant thinking on development economics was the structuralism approach from which the import substitution strategy was derived.[4] This particular strategy views foreign trade as a constraint on developing countries to industrialize. It rejects the theory of comparative advantage since the existing trade regime disadvantages developing countries by allowing the terms of trade to constantly deteriorate, and by favoring those countries that are already developed.

Many analysts suggest that the policies employed to reverse the unfavorable environment of the trade regime and bring about industrialization to the developing nations was not successful.[5] The import substitution strategy was blamed for creating inefficient non-competitive industries secured behind protective tariffs; encouraging the importation of capital-intensive industries that limited the expansion of employment; discouraging exports by maintaining and overvaluing exchange rates; undermining the growth of the manufacturing sector and failing to create connections with other sectors of the economy; aggravating income inequalities within the various sectors of the economy; and other related deficiencies and difficulties.[6] The individual solutions presented differ depending on which school of thought they come from. The neoclassical school recommends the liberalization of the trade regime and opening up of the economy as a stimulant to growth. On the contrary, the structuralists advocate the imperative of taking substantial steps to change the structure of the economy in terms of land redistribution, increasing public ownership and other related measures.[7]

The other contending school of thought has been the neoclassical paradigm that prescribes the adoption of an export-oriented industrialization strategy. Balassa argues in favor of the export-oriented industrialization strategy as follows:

> ...export-oriented policies lead to better growth performance than policies favoring import substitution. This result is said to obtain because export-oriented policies, which provide similar incentives to sales in domestic and in foreign markets, lead to resource allocation according to comparative advantages, allow for greater capacity utilization, permit the exploitation of economies of scale, generate technological improvements in response to competition abroad, and, in labor-surplus countries, contribute to increased employment.[8]

He further contends that "countries applying outward-oriented development strategies performed better in terms of exports, economic growth, and employment than countries that continued inward orientation, which encountered increasing economic difficulties".[9] Similarly, Bhagwati explains that "a number of international research projects have now thoroughly examined these questions, and the evidence is overwhelming that the countries that adhered to IS [import substitution strategy] too long, instead of shifting to EP [export-promotion strategy], lost out on the opportunity for an impressive economic performance that the growing post-war economy liberally provided".[10] The proponents of the neoclassical thought have exhibited the newly industrialized countries (NICs) as good examples of the export-oriented industrialization strategy's success. However, others doubt the assertions that export success was due to the adoption of free trade regime, since the NICs' history shows a strong hand of the State in managing their economic incentives' system to promote exports.[11]

Some scholars argue that the success of the NICs has been the result of the combination of both strategies. The NICs, especially Taiwan and Korea, initially pursued import substitution and then changed to export promoting policies.[12] Kirkpatrick also argues that "the issue is... much more of the optional sequence of ISI and EOI phases in the industrialization process than of the relative merits of EOI and ISI as alternative and competing strategies".[13] Kirkpatrick et al. argue that elements of both strategies may be employed depending on the economy's level of industrialization, its size and resource endowments, and its overall development objectives.[14]

Nevertheless, the neoclassical development theory underpins the economic reform program that has been prescribed to deal with the deteriorating economies of many developing countries. Both the International Monetary Fund (IMF) financial reform program and the World Bank development programs, and the subsequent conditions imposed on reforming countries, are mainly based on the neoclassical strategies and policies. Open and competitive markets, a protected and unrestricted private sector, and minimal State involvement in the economy are the core issues of the economic reform package promoted by these international financial institutions.[15] In short, their policies negate the active involvement of the State in economic sectors. These institutions have failed to appreciate the extent of market failure and the weakness of the private sector which is incapable of bridging those gaps. By discouraging the State to play its part, they have been part of the problem. Experiences have started to show that the State has to play an active role in economic activities in order to narrow the gap created by market failures as well as support the private sector to strengthen its capabilities and contribute better.[16] Evidently, the State owing to its limited capabilities, need to carefully choose areas of investment that will bring about tangible contributions which will play major roles in the growth and transformation of the overall economic situation of the country. What is important here is that the State has to try to overcome its institutional inadequacies by making its initiatives as transparent and accountable as possible in order to frustrate any rent-seeking tendencies. After all, development first and foremost requires political commitment, stability and continuity of policies for reasonable length of period. Therefore, it requires a democratic developmental State in place to alleviate the wide range of challenges for nations like Ethiopia are facing at this stage.

Although the success of the newly industrialized countries (NICs) might seem to provide the international financial institutions with some of their arguments, it failed to support their prescription of forbidding the government from taking any role in economic affairs. In fact, the governments of the NICs have not only managed their economies well, by all measures, but have also been providing enterprises with essential incentives and various forms of assistance to promote exports.[17]

After reviewing the experiences of NICs, Wah and Jomo state that "the government has been involved in establishing priority sectors; mobilizing resources to hasten their development; protecting infant industries; allocating foreign exchange credit; regulating technological flows; controlling direct foreign investment; organizing rationalization and recession cartels; pacifying and co-opting labor; ensuring the effective flow of financial resources to designated priority sectors".[18] Similarly, Amsden argues that "Korea...provides supporting evidence for the proposition that economic expansion depends on state intervention to create price distortions that direct economic activity toward greater investment. State intervention is necessary even in the most plausible cases of comparative advantage, because the chief asset of backwardness and low wages is counterbalanced by heavy liabilities. Where Korea differs from most other late industrializing countries is in the discipline its state exercises over private firms".[19] She explains discipline in terms of penalizing poor performers and rewarding only efficient and well performing enterprises.[20]

The 1991 Economic Policy of the Transitional Government

The Economic Policy for the Transitional Period was formulated in 1991 by the Transitional Government to address the problems that crippled the country during the military government's rule. The government, in its early months, recognized the need to adopt coherent economic policies to correct entrenched macroeconomic imbalances and inefficiencies. The Transitional Economic Policy was based on the consensus of the political parties and groups which formed the Transitional Government. While the Policy confined itself to addressing the most pressing problems, it avoided the controversial issues that might have divided the participants.[21]

The Policy, besides providing a coherent economic direction, became the basis of forming the structural adjustment program negotiated with the IMF. The major policy issues were basically reflected in the policy framework papers (PFP) 1992/93 and 1994/95,[22] which served as a guide for economic reforms implemented by the government. The reform program in time progressed from economic stabilization arrangements to structural reforms, which were made to strengthen with time and change of economic conditions.

The major change which the economic policy introduced has everything to do with the role of the State. As discussed above, the military government was in control of all major economic enterprises in accordance with the Proclamation No. 26 of 1975.[23] Such centralization of economic activities became one of the main sources of economic decline and inefficiency. Hence, in order to reverse the situation, the Transitional Economic Policy underlined that the role of the State in economic activities needed to be radically changed.[24] It was basically a reversal of the policies of the military government, which were not only reflected in many of the proclamations but also underlined in the 1987 Constitution.[25]

The second important issue addressed by the economic policy was the role of the State in encouraging the private sector. During the previous regime, the private sector was totally discouraged by the near total nationalization implemented in the mid-1970s and the consequent government policies, which suppressed its growth and expansion. Hence, the new economic policy underlined the need to promote private investment and detailed the necessary steps to improve the environment. These steps included the abolition of capital limitations in investment ventures, improvement of government procedures, and the introduction of a wide-range of incentives.[26]

In order to implement these policy items, an investment law was enacted in 1992. Proclamation 15/1992 generally reflected the spirit of the economic policy by creating conditions and incentives for private investment. However, it reserved several important economic activities for government investment.[27] In 1996 the Investment Law was revised to allow private investment in areas previously reserved only for government except for power, telecommunications and defense industries.[28] The Law was again revised, in 1998, to open some of the reserved sectors for joint ventures with foreign investors and made other sectors available only for domestic investment.[29] The government preferred a gradual opening of the most sensitive areas, and the reluctance to open up these areas had sometimes become an issue of controversy with the IMF.[30] The government insisted that it had created a reasonably conducive environment for private investment while protecting the interest of the nation as a whole. However, implementing the provisions of the Investment Law had sometimes been difficult because of bureaucratic problems and inefficiencies in implementing agencies.

The Economic Policy envisaged that the formulation of new macroeconomic policies would reverse the damage incurred by the command economy. The monetary and financial plans were reflected in the PFP, 1992/93 and 1994/95, which the IMF agreed, would enable a structural adjustment program.[31] These plans were further deepened and expanded by subsequent PFP documents.[32] Similarly, a new labor law[33] was enacted, while the national population policy[34] and the national science and technology policy[35] were launched. All these initiatives helped in clarifying the government's objectives and directions.

Among the policies adopted during the transitional period was the agricultural policy which advocated the importance of giving priority to small-scale agriculture.[36] Small-farming sector contributes over 95 percent of the country's food production but it was denied a proper share of the governments' budget. This choice of priority signified the total change from the former ideological preoccupation with the State farms.

The matter of land ownership was a very sensitive and controversial issue among the members of the Council of Representatives as the participating organizations had differing policies. On the one hand, there were organizations with the view that rural land should remain under public ownership with guaranteed usage rights. On the other, some groups argued for the adoption of the farmer's rights to sell and exchange their land in order to encourage proper management of their holdings. As a result, the Council of Representatives chose to postpone the land ownership issue, but decided to avoid as much as possible the fragmentation of current land holdings by ensuring farmers could lease land, pass it on to family members, and freely sell their produce.[37]

In general, the economic policy for the transitional period ended the excessively dominant and rent collecting role of the State in the economy, which the Derg regime had maintained until it lost power. Despite the State's intention to retain some strategic sectors, the new economic policy created an environment that encouraged the private sector to participate in numerous activities. Clearly, the government was initially extremely cautious about withdrawing from its perceived strategic sectors. Notwithstanding, even in those areas reserved for the State, state ownership has gradually shrunk and is currently limited to very few areas such as telecommunication, power and very selected vital investments that are considered to be beyond the capabilities of the private sector. In light of these changes in Economic policy the regeneration of the private sector by terminating the repressive command economic system became one of the most important achievements of the economic transformation. The other important advantage of the Economic Policy was that the government was able to use it as a basis to negotiate with the multilateral financial institutions. Undoubtedly, the government had a strong sense of ownership of the reform for it was not merely a prescription by the IMF. This assists the proper implementation of the corrective measures created to revitalize the economy and the evolvement of a receptive environment which helped to properly utilize the country's resources.

The Agricultural Development-Led-Industrialization Strategy (ADLI)

In most discussions of development economics of the 1950s, agriculture was not taken seriously as a sector with a potential for growth that can make a significant contribution to the overall economic development.[38] It was much later on that agriculture in developing countries started to be considered as a viable sector on the bases of which one can commence serious development programs since it constitutes a dominant social and economic base.[39] Since then many scholars have written on the need to invigorate the agriculture sector in order to register tangible improvements in economic growth, as well as to reduce the abject poverty entrenched in many developing countries.[40]

The strategy that revolves around the agriculture sector, which is designed to promote overall economic and social changes is called the "agricultural-development-led-industrialization strategy" (ADLI).[41] As previously noted, various scholars have discussed the strategy's main contents in more or less similar terms, although they have given it different names.[42] The major essence of the strategy lies in shifting a greater share of the nation's investment to the agriculture sector in order to increase agricultural productivity. The strategy takes agriculture as a leading sector whose improved productivity would at the same time induce growth in consumer goods and agricultural import industries.[43]

In comparing the ADLI with an export-led strategy, Adelman argues that "the ADLI strategy generates the same rate of industrialization as does export-led growth but leads to a higher rate of labor absorption, a better distribution of income, better balance-of-payments results, less poverty, and a higher rate of growth per capita gross national product (GNP)..."[44] She attributes the result to a combination of factors such as the greater increase in total factor productivity, the larger reduction in unemployment and the resource reallocation effects.[45] In explaining the mentioned factors, some authors detail the main reasons for the favorable result of the ADLI strategy as follows:

1. Strong domestic linkages of agriculture with manufacturing, through both the demand and the input sides, lead to high domestic multipliers for agricultural output;
2. Investment in agriculture is less import and more labor intensive than investment in industry and so is agricultural production;
3. The rate of return to investment in agriculture is high, equal to, or exceeding that of investment in industry as indicated in the World Bank study devoted to agriculture (World Bank, 1982);
4. As long as the agriculture sector is poorer than the urban sector, policies that raise the incomes of farmers improve the domestic size distribution of income.[46]

Similarly, Mellor argues for the adoption of a rural-led strategy, in which the central directions would be the accelerated expansion of food grains production; building massive rural infrastructure and a shift in the structure of industrial production toward small-scale enterprises producing consumer goods; and agricultural inputs mainly to the agriculture sector. In this regard, he explains that" a rural-led strategy of development is likely to produce high average rates of returns to investment in agriculture; rapid growth of small-scale rural industry receiving direct capital from cultivators; price relationships for industrial consumer goods which facilitate high profits and reinvestment; and an income base in agriculture sufficient to support taxes to self-finance much of the infrastructure requirements. The resulting substantial net outflow of resources from agriculture will spur growth in other sectors of the economy even while agriculture itself is expanding rapidly and profitably."[47]

Under this strategy, the first priority is to accelerate growth in the agricultural sector by providing fertilizers and other agricultural inputs; encouraging major investment in water conservation with an emphasis on small-scale and well-controlled schemes; expanding research and implementing the results of the research; and by expanding supplies of trained manpower to assist the small-scale farmers. The second priority is to facilitate the expansion of small-scale industry mainly through investment in the infrastructure of transport and power. The third priority is to expand and diversify exports in order to cover the expenses of the growing capital-intensive imports.[48] The other major issue is the adoption of appropriate and modern technology to increase productivity in the agricultural sector, which is one of the major components of the ADLI strategy and needs considerable attention from both the farmers and the government. In order for technology to make a difference, it must be sustainable and affordable to the farmers. Apart from imported industrial inputs such as fertilizers, pesticides and machinery, research work on the use of other appropriate technologies may have a major impact on the availability of domestic and affordable inputs to many small-scale farmers. Research results are likely to have tangible effects if they are intertwined with extension services.[49]

Moreover, the technology adopted needs to be acceptable from the farmers' social and cultural viewpoint, as it would be useless to force any application without their active cooperation and dedication. Weitz's assessment reflects the reality of many small-scale farmers when he remarks:

> For the vast number of farm families, whose members constitute the main agricultural work force, agriculture is not merely an occupation or a source of income; it is a way of life. This is particularly evident in traditional societies, where farmers are closely attached to their land and devote long, arduous days to its cultivation. Any change in farming methods per force brings with it changes in the farmer's way of life. The introduction of biological and technical innovations must therefore be adapted not only to the natural and economic conditions, but perhaps even more to the attitudes, values, and abilities of the mass of producers, who must understand

> the suggested changes, must be willing to accept them, and must be capable of carrying them out.[50]

The State plays a crucial role not only in the diffusion of technology but also in the overall implementation of the ADLI strategy, as the activities mainly encompass small-scale farmers whose resources are extremely limited. To materialize the intentions of the ADLI strategy, the government has to invest in the agricultural sector, transportation, power, communication, research, education, and input supply systems.[51] The State must also encourage and promote government agencies to provide export promotion, agricultural extension, and small-business credit and advisory services in order to maximize the strategy's results.[52] In addition, the government needs to provide farmers with secured tenure rights to promote their sense of ownership and protect them from any coercion that would hamper farming initiatives. Furthermore, government's intervention might be needed in situations where price instabilities occur. After adopting new technologies, agricultural production in some specific regions might increase much faster than demand can be created. This can happen mainly due to lack of adequate rural roads and transportation services. In such a situation, the government may act to stabilize prices by buying and transporting the stocks to areas where demand is higher.[53] And for long term stabilization, establishing a modern marketing system, which reduces expensive transactions costs, should receive proper attention to mitigate the difficulties in narrowing the gap between supply and demand of the produces. This would help to bolster annual farmers' productivity and production, and improve their livelihood.

The implementation of the above policies and strategies may bring the desired results; however, it depends on the political commitment of the leadership and the specific country's economic situation. Notwithstanding, the general features of African economies are similar to one another and might respond to the prescriptions of the ADLI strategy. In this regard, Adelman remarks, "unlike other development strategies which cater to international demand, ADLI is uniquely capable of stimulating balanced, equitable growth in the economies of Sub-Saharan Africa".[54] In order to increase productivity, substantial foreign exchange would be needed to import fertilizers and other inputs, and to a certain extent, consumer goods that would not be available in the initial years by the domestic manufacturing sector. Hence, a prudent and selective use of the scarce foreign exchange at hand, and soliciting foreign aid and assistance for the purchase of imports of agriculture inputs, is essential to the initially intensification of production.

As discussed earlier, it is clear that Ethiopia needs to reverse economic malaise by adopting a long-term strategy which will eventually alleviate its food deficiency, and concomitantly, promote the manufacturing sector to provide essential consumer goods. Agriculture, especially smallholder farming, was neglected and, as a result, food production could not match the growth of the population. The use of better technology, even fertilizers, had been far below the Sub-Saharan African average as well as other farming practices, such as water conservation, irrigation, and rural infrastructure, were minimal. Hence, it would be difficult for the country to hope for economic development if it continues to neglect the agricultural sector.

The new strategy has to revolve around agriculture. Some groundwork has been laid by the adoption of the economic policy during the transitional period, recognizing the agriculture sector as the starting point for initiating structural transformation of the economy. As examined above, Ethiopia's economy has a deep-rooted problem that is structural in nature, which requires a long-term strategy to resolve it. Accordingly, the adopted development strategy, the agricultural development-led-industrialization strategy (ADLI), which takes agriculture as its point of departure and growth-engine, paved the way for the adoption of detailed policies and strategies of all sectors of economy including the agriculture sector in 2002.

Major Policies and Strategies of Socio-Economic Sectors

The Agriculture Sector

The initiatives to devise appropriate agricultural policies and strategies started right from the beginning of the Transitional Government, and continued to be refined and diversified in the following years. However, the breakthrough of adopting a comprehensive and all-encompassing policy directions and strategies came after the months of discussions within the EPRDF which ended in the walkout of a splinter group, which had been stonewalling any initiative to the betterment of the organization as well as carrying out development endeavors. A document containing policies and strategies of agriculture development namely, the rural development policies, strategies and tactics of the Federal Government, was published in November 2002.

The rural development policies and strategies attempted to address the above-mentioned deficiencies and create conditions for the total transformation of the rural sector. The major policies and strategies are detailed as promoting labor intensive agricultural development; maximum usage of the land for enhanced benefit; continuous improvement of agricultural practices; devising appropriate directions targeting different agro-ecological zones; and pursuing a development path coordinated and intertwined with other sectors of the economy.

These strategies are further detailed to ensure their appropriate implementation. The significant ones are the imperative need of building the productivity of the labor force by enhancing capacity of production; increased availability of inputs and appropriate technology and enhance the speed and means of distribution; the continuous development of growth packages that could be implemented in various conditions by integrating both diversification and commercialization as their focus; and providing special attention to drought prone areas.

The government clearly delineated its policy as a market-led agricultural development and specifies initiatives to build a new marketing system. Accordingly, it subscribes the importance of building market information system. The essential role of cooperatives, the private sector and rural financial institutions is also widely discussed. Consequently, the policy encouraged the indispensable role of the private sector including foreign investment.

The policy emphasizes that rural transformation will not be achieved without the expansion and development of infrastructure. It details the expansion and improvement of education and health services, rural road and transport services, safe drinking water and other essential services. It also gives due attention to encouraging off-farm activities. Above all, it advocates the imperative need of promoting popular participation in designing local development plans and programs, and improvement of overall good governance in order to enhance belongingness and conviction that would highly contribute to the appropriate implementation of the above discussed policies and strategies.

In general, the policies and strategies summarized above are designed not only to avoid mistakes of past regimes but also to designate the agricultural sector as the engine of overall development endeavors of the country. Apparently, the strategies are capable of transforming the rural sector from subsistence farming to diversified and commercialized one with strong links to the urban sector. However, it is obvious that the results will depend on the success of the implementation process. The success of the implementation process again depends on the ability of the leadership in tirelessly motivating the rural population and continuously building upon achievements and reviewing processes, directions and initiatives.

The Industrial Sector

As discussed before, the industry sector remained minuscule because of multifaceted constraints. The past regimes' policies were unfavorable to industry as the private sector had been discouraged from playing its pivotal role. Other impediments such as deficient roads, shortage of energy, inadequate water and other basic services were unable to offer encouragement and support to the industrialization process.

Agriculture also failed to support the process of industrialization because it could not provide essential raw materials, and its diminishing role in the export market over the years failed to garner enough foreign exchange for necessary imports. Furthermore, as the farmers' income continued to decline, their capacity to absorb the commodities produced by the industry deteriorated, hampering industrial expansion. The linkage of the sector within itself, and with other sectors, also remained low, making it dependent on imports from machinery to spare parts and raw materials. Moreover, the role of the small and medium scale industries was not properly recognized and appreciated until recently, and little incentive and support was provided for. A failure to prioritize and apply incentives led to the establishment of some capital-intensive enterprises, which did little to expand employment, and at the same time, created dependence on imports for their production. Furthermore, little attention was given to the development of appropriate institutions and skilled manpower to assist in the selection, transfer, adoption and diffusion of technology. The industrial sectors, especially private entrepreneurs, were left alone without government direction and support, sometimes to squander their capital on unprofitable and unproductive ventures.

After the adoption of ADLI strategy, there was an attempt to draft a comprehensive industrial strategy. However, it didn't happen until August 2001 when the government published an industry development strategy which addresses almost all the then prevailing challenges. The industry development strategy followed basic principles in addressing the challenges of solving the constraints and paving the way for its development. The role of the private sector as the most important component of the engine of industrial development was recognized as the corner stone of these principles as well as setting ADLI Strategy as its basis; adhering to export-led industrial development; providing priority to labor intensive industries; tackling shortage of capital by coordinating local with foreign investors; and promoting society's participation and contribution in all its forms.

The industrialization strategy envisages that industrial development can be attained by creating conducive environment for its success. Some of the conditions are detailed as combating rent-seeking mindset and activities; maintaining favorable macroeconomic situation; establishing modern and supportive financial system; building and expanding infrastructure such as roads, railways, telecommunications, power and water services; hugely investing on human capacity building; and developing pro-development administrative apparatus and system which is transparent, accountable, efficient and effective. The government is also supposed to create a situation that promotes strong market competitiveness. In addition, it is required to build a fair and transparent taxation system. This needs to be supported by the availability of information system which will have a vital role in building the market-led economy. In relation to the above, the strategy emphasizes on establishing and promoting an efficient judicial system which would encourage the strengthening of effective contract enforcement, arbitration and other problem solving mechanisms.

In addition to detailing the necessity of creating conducive environment, the strategy identifies priority areas where the government provides leadership and close support to the private sector. These priority areas are basically labor intensive sectors which do not relatively require huge capital for their establishment. Textiles and garment sector, meat and leather industry, agro-processing and construction are discussed in detail as priority areas. Furthermore, micro and small enterprises are provided due attention as huge manpower engaging areas, and also as entities, which would greatly contribute to the expansion and advancement of the industrial base of the country. The strategy also entertained the need to build on future industrial growth area such as information and communication technology and biotechnology, which exploits the massive genetic resources of the country.

The implementation of these objectives has not been easy. It requires adequate human and material resources, and a reasonably developed organizational capacity. It also needed the close cooperation of the private sector with the government. Although the government's capacity building endeavors are likely to continue concentrating on improving its institutional and manpower capabilities, it has also to pay close attention to enhancing the entrepreneurial skills of the private sector, which is still feeble from decades of unfavorable treatment under the command economic system. Ultimately, such partnership will have a significant contribution to the expansion of the sector and the structural transformation of the Ethiopian economy.

Social Sectors

Education

The education strategy was adopted in 1994 with the intention of alleviating the constraints and challenges of the sector in order to produce the required skilled manpower for the development and transformation of the country.[55] The education strategy identifies some constraints in the education system. These are: lack of clear educational objectives; inadequate number of schools ; lack of maintenance of educational infrastructure and absence of appropriate and sufficient educational materials; scarcity of vocational and technical schools with adequate staff and facilities to provide the economy with skilled workforce; low professional competence of existing teachers; shortage of resources to alleviate the difficulties of the educational system; and absence of an institutionalized non-formal education system.[56]

As indicated above, the strategy plans to eliminate numerous constraints and improve the education system. It aims to provide good quality primary education with an ultimate goal of achieving universal primary education within a period of 20 years. It also intends to expand vocational and technical training schools, which produce skilled manpower essential to economic progress. In addition, secondary and higher education would receive proper attention, and efforts would be made to enhance the professional competence of teachers and school administrators.[57]

The strategy advocates the restructuring and improvement of the education system and curriculum in order to attain the above objectives. The general school structure would be rearranged and the components would be:

1. A kindergarten system for children aged 4-6 years;
2. A primary education system from grades 1-8 subdivided into two sections of basic (1-4) and general (5-8);
3. A general secondary education from grades 9-10;
4. A preparatory senior secondary education of 2 years and a system of vocational and technical education parallel to it;
5. Higher education of 1-2 years for diploma and 3-5 years for undergraduate degrees;
6. A system of vocational and technical training coordinated and interlinked with General Academic and a special education and distance learning systems in collaboration and coordinated with the rest of the educational system.[58]

The curriculum would be revised to fulfill the needs of the community by taking into consideration the country's economic and social situation. In the curriculum, science, mathematics and language components would be emphasized and social science subjects would be made relevant to the country's needs.[59]

The education sector strategy indicates that the training and professional competence of teachers would be upgraded by means of formal training and on the job upgrading courses. At the same time, a realistic and encouraging career structure would be formulated. The expansion of the education service throughout the country and the provision of adequate school materials are also indicated as major components of the strategy. In addition, the need to encourage research that would steadily improve the education system is also recognized as a major task.[60] At the same time, the community should be encouraged to send their sons and daughters to school without making any excuse. The community's participation in school matters and their contribution is taken as vital to the teaching and learning process.

Furthermore, the capacity building strategy details the need to change the distribution of higher education institutions in the country and their limited objectives. It further explains that the distribution of universities and other higher learning institutions should be expanded to the regions to support the latter's development endeavors.[61] With their increased numbers, their student acceptance rates are also expected to hugely improve. The tasks of these institutions are not only limited to teaching but also conduct research on various fields that would benefit the regional development effort. Hence, they are supposed to expand their postgraduate studies and strive to be center of excellence in their chosen fields. For better results, government and private sector partnership is highly encouraged.

The objectives and targets set by the strategy are vital to change the education system in the country and increase the number of children provided with the opportunity to attend schools. As discussed, the expansion of schooling has been enhanced with the overall implementation of the ADLI strategy. It is intertwined with the development of rural infrastructure and other social services. Clearly, it requires considerable material and human resources to achieve the stated objectives. Whatever the cost and difficulty to avail good education, it is an indispensable burden and imperative task crucial to the future of the country.

The Health Sector

As with the other social infrastructures, the health service in the country has also been a neglected sector, and has always been inadequate in coping with the population's massive needs, which is exposed to many infectious and communicable diseases. It is said that about 75 per cent of the endemic diseases in Ethiopia are communicable and potentially preventable;[62] however, the abject poverty and poor sanitation have made it difficult to tackle the problem. Every health indicator shows to what extent the Ethiopian people are exposed to life-shortening crises. These figures indicate that Ethiopia is almost at the bottom of the human development index ranking of countries produced by the UNDP. The 2011 Human Development Report recently ranks Ethiopia at 174 out of the 187 countries listed.[63]

The health service had been under-funded, and in the last years of the Derg regime, the situation further deteriorated as the per capita share of public health expenditure declined because of the high population growth and the reallocation of resources to the war effort. Even so, the unsatisfactory budget allocated to health institutions was not used in accordance with the priorities of the health sector. The health sector strategy identifies the following deficiencies: very uneven and urban-biased coverage of both facilities and staff; top-down management; shortage of senior and middle level professionals; decline of health sector in the share of the government budget; excessive share of wages and salaries; excessive share of curative care; inefficient cost recovery system; and poor implementation of capital spending. It is indicated that the average implementation of the allocated budget was just over 50 percent during most of the 1980s.[64]

Recognizing the imperative necessity to reverse the dismal situation, the strategy indicates that the objective of the health service system is to provide a comprehensive and integrated primary health care at the community level.[65] In this regard, the strategy emphasized the priority of the preventive and promotional tasks of the service without neglecting the essential curative aspects. It targets the main communicable diseases, common nutritional problems, and environmental health and hygiene, and indicated that human and material resources would be allocated in accordance with the objectives and priorities stated.[66] Obviously, without the full participation of the community in the health program, it would be futile to achieve visible results. Hence, the strategy emphasizes the central role of the people in preventive activities as well as making the health institutions more productive.

Infrastructure

The Transport Sector Strategy

Until recently, Ethiopia has one of the poorest transport networks in the world, even by Sub-Saharan African standards. It has obviously been inadequate to support an efficient production and distribution system. Before the launch of the Road Sector Development Program (RSDP), the road network was comprised of 28,500 km of roads, of which 15 per cent was paved roads. The density of the roads was 25.8 km per 1000 sq. km, far below the average in Sub-Saharan Africa. It also has about 781 km of railway lines, which are old and in poor condition caused by shortage of spare parts and other essential equipment.[67] Inaccessibility to most of the countryside has been a major impediment for millions of farmers, who need to have easy access to markets. They have had enormous difficulty in selling their products on time at a market price, and also in buying agricultural tools and basic manufacturing commodities. Such restricted flow of marketable goods obviously has had a negative impact on the country's development effort.

The strategy explains that road transport costs in Ethiopia are more expensive when compared to other countries. The lack of inadequate road network, almost non-existent support of railways, application of inferior mode of transport operations and absence of alternatives in the sector are major causes for the high cost. Accordingly, the strategy emphasizes the need to improve and expand the transport network, which has been implemented by devising Road Sector Development Programs (RSDP), Universal Rural Road Assess Program (URRAP), the recently launched railways expansion program and the employment of better logistics system.[68]

The role of the transport sector in realizing the overall ADLI strategy is paramount. Without connecting the vast majority of farmers to the market, it would be absurd to think of using the agriculture sector as a means of promoting overall economic development in the country. Progress of the road program is likely to be relatively slow as building road networks will require a considerable amount of the very limited material and human resources. In addition, the country's rough topography makes any surface transport such as roads and railways much more expensive and time consuming.

The success of the ADLI strategy will depend on how much the Ethiopian farmer is connected to the market. This leaves the government with little option but to persevere and proceed with its objective of expanding the network and connecting the agriculture sector to the main and feeder roads.

Energy

Ethiopia has a large potential for hydroelectric power. The country is a source of many rivers and its topography makes it ideal to generate electricity. Until recently a mere one per cent of this potential had been utilized and installed electricity capacity was only 8 kw per 1000 inhabitants,[69] and energy consumption per capita was 22 kilowatt- hours,[70] far below the average for Sub-Saharan Africa. It was also estimated only 4 per cent of the population had access to electricity. Rural residents, 85 percent of the population, used a mere 6 per cent of the energy supply.[71] The rural population basically uses traditional energy sources, which are dwindling because of resource depletion and environmental degradation.

Recognizing the prerequisite of the availability of adequate energy for any substantial development, the government's strategy will not only focus on developing modern energy resources but also modernize traditional energy sources mainly for household consumption. A pressing issue for most people in rural and urban centers. The objective of the energy sector strategy is "increasing the supply of all forms of energy and reducing reliance on traditional forms of energy in favor of the adoption of local renewable sources".[72]

The energy sector strategy outlines several implementation plans. First, by modernizing traditional energy resources is recognized as one of the major tasks in the sector. In rural areas, a number of targets are designed to realize the strategy. These include promoting the expansion of afforestation and agro-forestry; improving efficiency in end-use technology for harnessing energy from wood fuel and other resources; introducing alternative energy sources such as animal residue and dung, and crop residue for producing biogas and making briquettes; and also encouraging farmers to use some of the energy for income generation purposes - for example, setting up small-scale mills and bakeries.[73]

Moreover, emphasis is given to the construction of micro and small hydro-electric powers to promote rural electrification and facilitate integrated development of water resources. In the urban centers, connecting households to the national electricity grid is the easiest way to provide energy for household utilization. In isolated urban centers, some renewable energy alternatives such as small-scale hydropower and geothermal energy will be explored. In the absence of the above, diesel generators would be made available to provide the necessary power supply gap.[74]

Second, developing modern energy resources is another major task of the strategy. The provision of electricity for development activities and other essential services and functions has been the prime preoccupation of the Ethiopian Electric Power Corporation (EEPCo). The strategy in the electricity sub-sector includes the enhancement of efficiency in order to reduce the supply-demand deficit as much as possible, while undertaking construction to increase the existing capacity. Apart from hydroelectric power, the development of geothermal and wind energy, and natural gas for the national grid needs to be given proper attention.[75]

The energy sector's sole goal is to provide other sectors with energy to enable their efficient function. As stated, the country has a large potential for hydroelectric power generation. The major constraint here is the shortage of skilled manpower and huge capital is required to build dams. Here, the riparian issue will continue to be a major impediment, unless agreement is reached with down-stream countries such as the Sudan and Egypt.[76] Borrowing money for such projects from multilateral institutions may require the agreement of these countries, which might not be sympathetic to Ethiopia's pressing energy needs.[77] Although some progress in the negotiations for equitable and mutual benefit is reported, the issue will remain problematic due to Egypt's reluctance to share what it once regarded as an exclusive natural right.[78] On the other hand, relying on Ethiopia's own capital would make the journey too demanding if not impossible. The energy need of the country is growing fast and shortage of supply is already hindering development efforts. Ethiopia might need to make greater attempt at negotiating an arrangement that benefits all, but at the same time, it should proceed with investing in the sector with whatever capital it can afford or borrow from various quarters. It would be short-sighted for Ethiopia to wait for assistance from others, as the strategy needs to be implemented if the sector is to play its indispensable role in the development of the country.[79]

Concluding Remarks

In summary, the ADLI strategy is comprised of, and integrates all the sector strategies, agriculture being at the forefront. The transformation of agriculture is expected to trigger a structural change in the economy. Clearly, substantial growth and expansion in the agriculture sector would considerably reduce, and ultimately, eradicate poverty from the country, as most of the poor live in rural areas. Furthermore, it would have the same effect in urban centers, as agricultural growth would encourage the expansion and growth in the manufacturing and service sectors. As discussed above, the whole strategy advocates for the building of a market-based and export-oriented economy. The sector strategies and policies indicate that the government will not repeat the previous governments' disastrous path of development.

The present government has an ambitious objective of achieving middle-income country status in fifteen years. Considering the commitment of the leadership and the people to development, the country may very well achieve the objective.[80] However, one must not forget that Ethiopia has been exposed to unpredictable climatic changes and that it is situated in a volatile region; unforeseen challenges have arisen from the war with Eritrea, Somalia's failed State, instability in other neighboring countries, and from their socioeconomic consequences during the implementation of the above-discussed endeavors.[81] These factors have had a negative effect on its development efforts. Lastly, the ADLI strategy and its sector strategies have to be evaluated phase-by-phase and updated and revitalized with the emergence of new conditions. Above all, they must be fully put into practice, not merely documented.

Socio-Economic Performance in Selected Sectors

Reversal of Economic Malaise and Deterioration (1991-2000/01)

As discussed before, the economic performance deteriorated badly during the reign of the military government. The growth of Gross Domestic Product (GDP) by industrial origin was an average of about 1.5 per cent per annum between 1974 and 1991. This was a clear downturn when compared with the performance of the previous regime, which averaged 4 per cent per annum during the period between 1965 and 1973. On the other hand, the average rate of population growth increased from 2.5 per cent, in the years between 1965 and 1973, to an average of 2.9 per cent during 1974 and 1991, which resulted in the decline of the real per capita GDP at an annual average rate of about 1.4 per cent.[82] Similarly, the other economic indicators also declined miserably during the years between 1974 and 1991, when compared with the period between 1965 and 1973. Such a dismal performance resulted in unbearable deterioration of the living standard of the people.

After the demise of the military government, the then Transitional Government and later the Federal government attempted to reverse further deterioration and create a favorable situation for building a healthy economy and improving the lives of the people. As indicated previously, it adopted ADLI strategy based on improving agricultural production and productivity, improving the income and living standards of the rural population, and enhancing investment in the other sectors of the economy by encouraging better export earnings. According to the strategy, the transfer of wealth from the rural sector to industry and other related sectors would happen not by impoverishing the small-scale farmer but by improving his/her living conditions. As a World Bank document clearly explains, a unique and defining characteristic of ADLI is to aim for rapid growth and industrialization without subjecting the rural population to bear the burden that has typically characterized actual industrialization experiences.[83] The strategy advocates a path to industrialization without subjecting the rural population to bear a disproportionately high cost for the process of transformation.

Attempts have been made to implement the strategy through various economic reform programs, medium-term adjustment programs of 1992/93 to 1994/95, 1996/97 to 1998/99 and 1998/99 to 2000/01. Although the results of the implementation of these programs vary, they were instrumental in transforming the economy to a market-led one, facilitating the withdrawal of the State from most of the economic sectors and encouraging the previously deprived private sector to play an indispensable role. These programs have been implemented since 1992, except for the period during the Ethio-Eritrean crisis, which brought it to a halt and eroded some of the achievements to a certain extent.

Under the economic reform programs, Ethiopia was able to attain stable macroeconomic conditions and rated by the World Bank among the better performers. The World Bank acknowledged "the commitment of the Government to an economic agenda is reflected in an exceptionally strong sense of "ownership" of economic policies and to probity in their implementation. Policymakers are given to very serious consideration of policy options, do not make policy commitments lightly and have a solid track-record of delivering on those they do."[84]

Performance in Major Economic Sectors

These reforms produced a reasonable growth rate of the economy. During the period between 1992/93 and 2000/01, the economy grew at annual average rate of about 5 per cent in real terms.[85] The growth rate of the economy was highly affected by the performance of the agriculture sector, which has become more erratic in recent years. Drought is now a permanent threat that may occur every few years. At times, as in the last decade or so, an occurrence is observed once every five to ten years. Between 1992/93 and 2000/2001, the agriculture sector annually grew by about 3.59 per cent on average.[86] It was a relatively encouraging performance when compared with the past but inadequate considering the importance given to the sector in the new economic strategy.

On the other hand, the industrial sector's contribution to the GDP was reversed after declining by 7.11 per cent in 1991/92 from that of the previous year. It grew by 28.4 per cent in 1992/93 because of the availability of badly needed foreign exchange for the sector's inputs through the Economic Recovery and Reconstruction Program (ERRP).[87] It showed a reasonable change by growing on average 6.15 per cent per annum between 1993/94 and 1999/2000. Similar changes were observed in the manufacturing sub-sector. After dismal performance of negative 9.02 (-9.02) per cent in 1991/92, it displayed a strong showing by registering a 49 per cent growth from that of the previous year. It also continued to grow at an annual average of about 8.06 per cent between 1993/94 and 2000/01.[88]

The performance of the manufacturing sector had also improved in terms of the share of value added[89] to its products. The value added in the large and medium manufacturing scale had been declining in the 1980s at an annual average rate of 2.4 per cent.[90] This was mainly because of the dismal record of efficiency of the dominant public enterprises during the past regime. The turnaround occurred because of the abolition of the command economy and the managerial autonomy provided to public enterprises, and competition and the profit motif created the motivation for better efficiency and utilization of inputs. The rate of value added at factor cost showed significant increase and reached an annual average of 27.3 per cent between 1991/92 and 1999/2000.[91] The achievements became remarkable considering the devaluation of Birr and its subsequent depreciation. Among the best performers were industrial groups such as metal, non-metal, and food and beverages that registered average growth rates of 53.3, 36.5 and 31.6 per cent respectively.

Since the introduction of the economic reforms and the enactment of the investment law in 1992, the private sector started to participate in almost every sector of the economy. The number of establishments formed by the private sector rapidly overtook that of public enterprises. By 1995/96, the share of private establishments, in terms of numbers, reached almost 74 per cent of total enterprises and this percentage increased to about 82 per cent in 1999/2000.[92] The number of public enterprises had continued to drop because of privatization and the scarcity of newly formed establishments. In terms of gross value of production, the public sector continues to dominate even if the share declined from almost 94 per cent in 1992/93 to slightly over 59 per cent in 1999/2000. Moreover, it has continued to employ most of the work force, and by 1999/2000 its share was still 59.4 per cent of the manufacturing sector employees.[93] The private sector has come a long way since the abolition of the command economy. However, it is still a nascent player. Not only does it need to acquire entrepreneurial skills but also to garner the support of the government, especially in creating an environment conducive for its development.

Most of the manufacturing establishments such as food processing, beverages, textiles and leather products have a significant potential backward linkage with the agriculture sector, which they have not fully exploited to enhance their comparative advantage.[94] On the contrary, the large and medium scale industries are excessively dependent on imported raw materials. The share of imported materials reached 55 per cent in 1993/94, when the desired foreign exchange was made available through ERRP, by way of the biweekly and then weekly auctions. Although the shares in the following years showed some reduction, it continued to be around half of the raw materials made available to the industrial groups. Industrial groups such as basic iron and steel, rubber and plastic products, assembly of motor vehicles, fabricated metal products, chemicals and chemical products and tobacco products continued to consume the highest proportion of imported raw materials to that of total cost of raw materials ranging from 70 to 98 per cent in 1999/2000.[95] The dependency of the large and medium scale industries is better revealed when the costs of the imported raw materials are compared with the foreign exchange they were able to earn. For example, in 1995/96 these group industries used imported raw materials at the cost of Birr 1.3 billion while they were only able to earn Birr 401.1 million, which was only 31 per cent of the expenses in foreign currency.[96]

Another problem in the manufacturing industry is the absence of interlinkages among the various groups. Every group stands by itself and is connected to world market mainly for the purpose of import of raw materials and spare parts. There had been no serious policy or effort made until recently to create backward and forward linkages around the most important groups of the manufacturing sector.

The most important industries, especially textiles, metal, and chemicals and chemical products did not performed well, and their very survival was at stake. Their multiplier effect has yet to be observed in the future. Undoubtedly, the manufacturing industry has shown some revival and progress, but its overall contribution to the economy is still inadequate and it has a long way to go to transform the structure of the economy, and ultimately, play its expected role.

For decades now, Ethiopia's external trade has been characterised by a huge deficit. Export earnings usually cover a small share of imports and the gap has been covered through external assistance and loans. The trade deficit decreased in 1993/94 and 1994/95 from US$829 million in 1992/93 to US$635 million and US$609 million respectively. Since 1995/96, it has started increasing and showed a large rise, in 1998/99 to over US$1.07 billion and in 1999/2000 to over US$1.12 billion, mainly due to defence materials for the war effort with Eritrea.[97] The later years were further worsened because of the severe deterioration of Ethiopia's terms of trade. The trade deficit is likely to continue to widen until Ethiopia's exports expand and diversify, and export earnings increase, changing the country's vulnerability to world trade shocks and reverse the ever-deteriorating terms of trade.

The country's reserve position plummeted in 1991/92 with reserves for only 1.3 weeks of imports. The situation improved in subsequent years reaching as high as 6.6 months of imports in 1995/96. Since 1995/96 the reserve position continued to decline reaching an equivalent of 2.7 months of imports in 1999/2000.[98] Such a situation might persist until the terms of trade improve, although this in itself is a short-term solution to reserves. Long-term solutions have to be sought in the overall development of the economy and in the expansion and diversification of exports in particular.

The government also pursued a prudent monetary policy and made tangible fiscal policy reforms. Inflation dropped from 21 per cent in the early 1990s to 1.2 per cent in 1993/94 and figures in subsequent years remained reasonably low.[99] Even in the aftermath of the Ethio-Eritrean war inflation was expected to remain at about 5 per cent in 2000/01 and 2001/02.[100] On the other hand, Ethiopia has remained a highly indebted country. Although it benefited from its arrangement with the Paris Club, Russia and other countries, the debt burden remains an obstacle to rapid development.

In 1999/2000 the debt burden was 243 per cent of exported goods and non-factor services (net present value terms) and rose to 266 per cent in 2002/03 because of the reconstruction and rehabilitation needs that require external borrowings.[101] Hence, Ethiopia critically needed to obtain a debt relief under the HIPC Initiative, to which it qualified in order to save resources that were diverted to development and poverty reduction programs.[102]

Ethiopia's economy had been exposed to major shocks during the discussed period. Subsequent drought conditions thwarted the agriculture sector from growing adequately, and the lack of adequate growth in this sector affected possible subsequent industrialisation. This was compounded with sharp decline in terms of trade, which affected its export earnings. Moreover, the situation was worsened by the conflict with Eritrea, which siphoned off its reserve and aggravated its budget deficit, and also inhibited donor support. For example, defence expenditure rose sharply from below 3 per cent of GDP before 1998 to an average of 10.7 per cent during 1998/99 and 1999/2000. As a consequence, the gap between fiscal and balance of payments fronts widened markedly with deficits of 8.8 and 8.7 per cent respectively, and money supply increased at an average rate of 10.4 per cent.[103] With the prevalence of peace, the situation changed and external resources started to flow; however, Ethiopia had to strive to reach to its pre-war levels. The economy started to recover and grew by 7.9 per cent in 2000/01 and 7 per cent in the fiscal year of 2001/02.[104]

Ethiopia's infrastructure development had been one of the lowest in the world. Successive governments had given little attention to the development of the sector. Difficult geographical conditions, bad policies, inadequate investment and widespread poverty had played their role in retarding the expansion and improvement of infrastructural services. Beyond these causes, Ethiopia's past instability and civil war had not only discounted government investment initiatives for improvement and expansion but also destroyed road networks, communication systems, power generation and transmission networks, and other related services. These dismal conditions also had their effect on the economic development of the country.

The introduction of telecommunication services in Ethiopia started at the end of the 19th century but remained underdeveloped. These services had slowly grown from merely 52,100 telephone main lines in 1975 to 64,080 in 1980 and then to 125,398 in 1990.[105] 127, 041 main lines were in operation in 1992, which represented only 0.25 main lines per 100 inhabitants. The 1992 figures were still extremely low as the average for Sub-Saharan African countries was about 1 for 100 people.[106] Moreover, the services were mainly concentrated in larger cities. Addis Ababa's share was about 69 per cent of the country's main telephone lines.

The installed capacity of the telephone lines increased from 172,742 in 1993/94 to 458,247 in 1999/2000 and the number of subscribers also increased from 141,650 in 1993/94 to 238,495 in 1999/2000, which was an annual average growth of 20.0 and 9.2 per cent respectively. The telephone main lines per 100 inhabitants increased from 0.25 in 1992 to 0.37 in 1999/2000, which is a modest improvement but yet far below the Sub-Saharan Africa's average.[107] Other services such as internet and mobile phones were in their infancy. In fact, the mobile phone service was limited to Addis Ababa and its environs.

Apparently, the expansion and improvement of the road network is directly linked to the level of development of a country. Expansion of roads, market integration, low cost transportation and increased production flow has again major impact on further development of the network. Ethiopia had 8450 km of total road network in 1970 and increased to 12,208 and 18,946 km in 1980 and 1990. The figure came down to 18,081 km in 1992 as Eritrea's share of the road network was deducted. Of more concern than the size of the road network was its deteriorating condition, which made it almost unserviceable as a result of years of neglect. Apparently, the regime of the day was busy with making wars and infrastructure building was not a priority.

After 1991, the government indicated that without a relatively expanded road network the country's market could not be integrated and developed, and special attention should be accorded to the sector. As discussed before, major rehabilitation of the main roads was undertaken under the ERRP, and other road works that fell within the budget capability of the government were also carried out. The most important initiative has been the formulation of the Road Sector Development Program (RSDP), which has been implemented since 1997. The main purpose of this program is to upgrade the main roads of the country, linking Addis Ababa to major towns and seaports of neighbouring countries, and also significantly expand the rural road network.

The total size of the national road network has showed a remarkable increase since 1995. The total road network increased from 23,442 km in 1995 to 29,571 km in 2000. The figures for the year 2000 include 3,824 km of paved roads, 12,267 km of gravel roads and 13,480 km of rural roads. This increase had also an impact on the road density in the country. The road density increased from 0.43 km per one-thousand people in 1997 to 0.45 in 2000 and from 21 km of road per one-thousand square km to 27 km during the mentioned period.[108]

The other feature of the road sector in Ethiopia has been the absence of a system of maintaining expensive high quality roads.With the objective of maintaining good roads, the government promulgated Proclamation No. 66/1997 to establish a Road Fund to finance maintenance activities. The Road Fund has been formed through funds raised by indirect taxes including a fuel levy, vehicle axle load levy, and overloading fines. The road fund had allocated a budget of over Birr 1.163 billion to the Ethiopian Roads Authority, urban administrations and regional authorities for road maintenance programs between 1997/98 and 2001/02.[109]

In the energy sector, various studies indicate that Ethiopia has a potential of 45,000 megawatt of hydroelectric power. So far, it has been able to develop insignificant percentage of its generating potential that is still way below the country's future needs. The country's generating capacity grew from 95 megawatt in 1960 to 167 megawatt and 316 megawatt in 1970 and 1980 respectively.[110] In 1999/2000, its electric generation capacity was only about 421 megawatt, which increased later on with the completion of some projects that were under construction.[111]

Ethiopia's per capita electric power production and consumption has been low when compared to other African countries. In 1999/2000, Ethiopia's per capita energy production was 27.4 kilowatt hours compared with Uganda's 40, Kenya's 150 and Sudan's 50 kilowatt hours. In terms of electric power consumption per capita in 1998, Ethiopia's 22 kilowatt hours was below Kenya's 129 and Sudan's 47 kilowatt hours, and was far below the average for low income countries and Sub-Saharan Africa, which stood at 362 and 454 kilowatt hours respectively.[112]

Although the electric energy supply registered some increments, it has not been able to satisfy the growing demand in the country. Electricity demand has substantially grown since the liberalisation of the economy, which released the private sector to participate in production and service provision sectors. Clearly, it wasn't hard to imagine that the country needed to take tangible initiatives to satisfy the growing demand of electric power for economic growth and social services needs.[113] The completion of the Gilgel Gibe I hydroelectric power station eased the problem at the time; however, it did not solve the gap between supply and demand. The government had to expedite the constructions of the Tekeze and Gojeb hydroelectric powers, with estimated generation capacities of 300 and 150 megawatts respectively, to meet the growing demand in the country. Undoubtedly, government investment and public participation have to be encouraged and accelerated not only to satisfy the demand within the country but also to export to neighbouring countries as a foreign exchange earner.

On the other hand, the government has shown visible interest in improving the social services sector by not only formulating long term strategies and programs but also by increasing funds for it. It has repeatedly indicated that without major improvement in the education and health conditions of the country, it is difficult to attain meaningful economic development. Undoubtedly, only an educated and healthy society can achieve sustainable economic development.

As discussed before, the education levels in the country were far below satisfactory in 1991/92. The coverage of education was narrow and the quality was under the desired standard that can produce trained manpower essential for the development of the country. Understanding the deficiencies in the education system, the government introduced the Education Sector Strategy, and the Education and Training Policy in 1994. These documents were aimed at changing the curriculum and the organisational orientation of the education system, as well as increasing the availability of qualified teachers and essential school materials and equipment.[114]

The government designed a twenty-year program in 1994 which extends to 2015. The objective of the program is to achieve universal primary education by the year 2015. As part of the long-term program, the Education Sector Development Program (ESDP) was introduced as the first five-year program for the years between 1997/98 and 2001/02. The ESDP gave priority to the expansion of primary education with special emphasis to encouraging girls' participation and providing better services in rural and underserved regions. The program planned to raise primary enrolment from 3.1 to 7 million and achieving an average gross enrolment ratio of 50 percent for primary education, and improving the quality of education by achieving a better ratio of teachers to pupils and improved access to education materials. In general, it detailed indicators intended to be achieved by the year 2001/02.[115]

Since 1992/93 the gross enrolment ratio has been growing for primary as well as secondary education. From below 20 per cent in 1992/93 and 26.2 per cent in 1994/95 the gross enrolment ratio for primary education reached 57.4 per cent in 2000/01. The ratio for secondary education increased from 6.6 per cent in 1994/95 to 12.9 per cent in 2000/01. Between 1996/97 and 2000/01, enrolment in primary education increased at an average of 13.4 per cent per annum and enrolment for secondary education grew at an annual average of 14.6 per cent. These figures point to a significant increase in access to primary education in a short period of time.[116]

Similarly, the higher education enrolment increased from 35,027 in 1995/96 to 87,431 in 2000/01. That was an increased by an average of 20.1 per cent per annum.[117] The number of graduates grew from 5394 in 1995/96 to 17,969 in 2000/01, which was an annual average increase of 27.2 per cent, and the number of teachers grew by an average of 14.3 per cent per annum within the above period. The number of students and graduates significantly increased because of the newly established universities and the emergence of private colleges. Technical and vocational training institutions have also been given increased attention under the current education strategy. These technical and vocational training institutes have been expected to receive students who exited from 8th and 10th grades, since 11th and 12th grades are now considered as preparatory level for higher education.

The gender disparity in enrolment ratios has been narrowing but remains an area where more effort should be made. The female enrolment ratio increased from 26 per cent in 1996/97 to 47 per cent in 2000/01. Out of the primary school enrolment, the percentage of female students grew from 36.4 per cent in 1996/97 to 40.3 per cent but for secondary education the 41.5 per cent for female students remain unchanged. In higher education, there were 18,707 female students in 2000/01 out of the total of 87,431, which accounted for 21.4 per cent. During the 2000/01 school year, the national gender parity index, in primary education that is the ratio of female to male enrolment ratios, stood at 0.7, which signifies that female participation was lower than male and further efforts had to be made to narrow the gap.[118]

Health status of the country is related to nutritional, sanitary, and other similar prevailing conditions. Access to clean water and sanitary services as well as the nutritional in take of the population, and the coverage of the health services was extremely low compared to other developing countries.[119] The previous governments' priority, curative services, did not help in expanding the lower level services and reducing many of the preventable water born and communicable diseases. With the adoption of the new health sector strategy, the priority of the health system has become preventive services and there has been a reorganisation of institutions to provide relatively better services in terms of cost-effectiveness and efficiency.

Parallel to developments in the education sector, the government has prepared a twenty-year plan to improve the health services together with a five-year program, called the Health Sector Development Program (HSDP), covering the period of 1997/98-2001/02. The main objectives of the HSDP were increasing coverage of the healthcare system from 48.5 per cent in 1996/97 to 60 per cent; improving the quality of the services through training and enhancing the supply of necessary inputs; strengthening management capacity at federal and regional levels; and encouraging participation of the private sector and NGOs in providing health services by creating a favourable environment. The program had been implemented with financial contributions from donor countries and international financial institutions as well as government budget and users' fees.

Health care infrastructure has improved after decades of crippling neglect. The primary health care coverage increased from 38 per cent in 1992/93 to 50.7 per cent in 1999/00 and then to 51.2 per cent in 2000/01. The number of hospitals, health centres and health stations had increased by 50.8, 143.3, and 9.87 per cent respectively between 1992/93 and 2000/01. The immunisation coverage for Diphtheria, Pertussis and Tetanus (DPT) increased from 14 per cent in 1992/93 to 84.9 per cent in 1996/97 but there has been difficulty in keeping up with the population increase. The coverage for BacilleCalmette Guerin (BCG) and Measles reached 56.0 and 36.48 per cent of the target population in 2000/01.[120] However, the proportion of the population which was fully immunised was only 21.12 per cent and the achievements in one or the other antigen had to be attained by providing all the necessary antigens as a package.[121] Similarly, although the maternal and child health coverage showed visible progress during the reform period, it did not increase concomitantly with the rapidly growing population numbers. The antenatal health coverage reached 34.7 per cent in 2000/01, and family planning services only cover 18.67 per cent.[122] In 1998/99, population per hospital and health centre was 616,720 and 202,864 respectively. Although there were major improvements since 1992/93, the figures were extremely high, signifying that enormous efforts need to be made to enhance the availability of health services to the people.

In general, health services coverage reached 51.24 per cent. However, this national average does not show the disparity of coverage among the regions. The health service coverage percentage in some major regions such as Amhara and Oromia was below the national average. The most underserved region in terms of health services coverage was the Somali region whose coverage percentage stood at 30.55.[123]

Government's health expenditure showed significant improvement since 1991/92. From 3.99 per cent of the total national expenditure in 1991/92, the health sector's share rose to almost 6 per cent in 1996/97 and 5.88 per cent in 1997/98. The expenditure share showed some decrease in 1998/99 and 1999/2000 as a consequence of the war with Eritrea, however, with the prevalence of peace and a decrease in defence expenditures,[124] it continued to significantly increase in the following years. On the other hand, expenditure continued to rise significantly in absolute terms.

Rapid Economic Growth and Social Transformation (2001- 2012)

By in large, Ethiopia was able to achieve a respectable rate of growth in the first decade of the EPRDF rule. The 5 percent average growth was substantial compared to other African countries' performance. However, it was inadequate to solve the multifaceted problems of the country. Poverty, wide-spread unemployment and other social ills have been prevalent for decades and the situation prescribes rapid economic growth and social transformation.

Towards the start of the Ethio-Eritrean war in 1998, differences on building democratic system, economic policies, on directions to combat corruption and bad governance within the leadership of the EPRDF visibly started to emerge. The war was unfortunate and hindered the leadership to sort out its differences. After the end of the war, the leadership attempted to clarify its political positions and directions through marathon like discussions but end up with a splinter group leaving the organization. The split, on one hand, seriously shaken the foundation of the organization, but on the other hand, it created an opportunity to formulate and disseminate clear and well thought policies, strategies including tactics that immediately brought surge of economic growth. Subsequently, it developed well articulated and deeply analyzed policies and strategies on building a democratic system and practice good governance. It also adapted detailed policies and strategies to improve and bring about structural changes in agriculture, industrial and other socio-economic sectors. These newly articulated directions have been spearheading the concerted effort to escape from poverty and decades of humiliation. These initiatives were also supported by capacity building strategies and programs, and foreign affairs and national security policy and strategy which have been designed to support and create favorable environment for the development effort. In general, these policies and strategies have overhauled not only development directions but also brought a qualitative change to the thought of development and its implementation among stakeholders.

Consequently, the mentioned policies and strategies were translated into development plans. Initially, the government devised the three year plan, the Sustainable Development and Poverty Reduction Program (SDPRP), which was implemented between 2002/03-2004/05. It was then followed by five-year plan, the Plan for Accelerated and Sustained Development to End Poverty (PASDEP), which was carried out between 2005/06 and 2009/10. Recently, Ethiopia has devised an ambitious five-year plan named as the Growth and Transformation Plan (GTP) for the period between 2010/11-2014/15. The plan champions the country's vision of becoming a middle- income economy between 2020 and 2023. The main objectives of GTP are detailed as achieving at least average real GDP growth rate of 11 per cent and fulfilling Millennium Development Goals (MDGs), expanding and attaining the prescribed qualities of education and health services with the intention of achieving MDGs in the social sector; developing a stable democratic and developmental State[125]; and maintaining a stable and predictable macroeconomic framework.[126]

The GTP advocates for a high growth economic performance with a stable macroeconomic environment. The growth scenarios are specified as base case and high case economic performances. In the base case scenario real GDP is expected to grow by an average of 11.2 percent, while in the high case one the expectation is indicated at 14.9 percent, which would be, if achieved, a spectacular performance for a non-oil exporting country.

The successful implementation of the GTP will expedite and facilitate the structural transformation of the economy to a larger extent. Growing diversification and commercialization of the agriculture sector will definitely enhance the productivity and production of crops, which will result in food self-sufficiency. The attainment of food self-sufficiency by itself will contribute to the structural transformation of the economy. Apparently, such achievement can be realized by transforming self-sufficient farmers to commercial farmers, which is in and by itself a structural transformation. In addition, as outlined in the GTP, industry is expected to grow by about 20 percent per year, which is envisioned to expedite the transformation, and consequently take over the leading role of the economy in a relatively shorter period. Evidently, the fast industrial development can only be realized by enhancing the technological capability of the country. A modest development in technological capability will definitely herald the beginning of the structural transformation of the economy. These targets require support by extensive investment in infrastructure. Information and communications technology, railways, road network, and energy are some of the growth sectors, which play an indispensable role in expediting the growth of the economy. Here the education and training system will highly contribute by producing the necessary educated and trained manpower to carry out the transformation endeavor.

Measuring growth performance, the economy has been almost growing every year since 2003/04 by an average of some double digit. After the severe drought of 2002/03, the economy rebounded and grew by 11.7 percent in 2003/04 and continued to grow in 2004/05 by 12.6 percent.[127] This high growth was followed by an average of 11 percent for the period of the PASDEP implemented between 2005/06 and 2009/10.

The growth of the economy as well continued during the GTP period in 2010/2011.The economy registered an average growth of 11.4 per cent.[128] This confirms that Ethiopia achieved a double digit growth of the economy for nine successive years. Ethiopia's achievement not only has been one of the fastest growing economies in Sub-Saharan Africa but also in the world.[129] As a result, absolute poverty head count index was reduced from 38.7 percent in 2004/05 to 29.6 percent in 2010/11, and in fact, it is planned to reduce it to 22.2 percent by the end of the GTP period.[130]

This achievement has not been without challenges. Inflation has been a threatening challenge with a potential of derailing the high performance of the economy in recent years. In 2008/2009 annual average inflation rate reached 40.6 percent, and for food components it was 54.1 percent. It started showing improvements in the following two years and started climbing in 2011/2012 to an annual average of 31.4 percent. After some fluctuations, it has recently started to come down and reached single digit figure that the government aspires.[131]

The reasons for such surge of inflation rate can be numerous. Apparently, the fast growth rate can be one source of inflation, but there are other factors, which have significant impact on the prices of consumer goods. The existence of inefficient market structure; changes in demand created by fast growth; imported inflation which has been displayed by prices of fuel, fertilizer, construction materials and food items; and of course, inflationary expectation are some of the causes that exasperated the inflation situation.

Although the ultimate solution would be to strengthen the growth drive, the government in the meantime, has attempted to take several measures to dampen the inflationary surge. Availing wheat, edible oil and sugar for distribu- tion in subsidized prices, and measures to curb the supply of money and intro- ducing relevant instruments have produced results but to keep it for long within the government's target is a formidable challenge. The inflation problem continues to hurt the low income urbanites as well as salaried portion of the population. In any case, the basic solution lies on the performance of the agriculture sector, which has the capacity to pull forward the rest of the economy.

The exchange rate of Birr to Dollar had almost been stable until 2010/11 when it was made to depreciate by 25 percent from the preceding year. The government stated that the major reasons for depreciating currency is to encourage the growth of exports, and to a certain extent, discourage imports that would result in taming the balance of payments deficit. The initiative could have an impact on narrowing the deficit, however due to massive imports of capital and consumer goods, the deficit further worsened, which has required additional intervention.[132]

Savings and flow of foreign investment had showed little change until the end of the PASDEP. There have recently been some signs of growth. In 2011/12, savings grew to about 10 percent of GDP, and foreign investment has shown modest improvement during the last decade.[133] The recent expansion and reach of banks and microfinance institutions to small towns and rural areas has a major impact on promoting savings. In addition, the government has instituted pension schemes for employees of private enterprises and also promoted the purchase of bonds to finance power projects. The recently invigorated housing saving scheme will also have a positive influence on changing the saving culture of the people.[134] On the other hand, revenue collection of the government has improved even though it has not yet reached the level of the averages Sub-Saharan African countries. External debt also stood at 7.8 billion USD during 2010/11.[135] World Bank report indicates that public debt has a declining trend and stood at 35 percent of GDP in 2011/12 and the country has a low risk of external debt distress.[136] Apparently, the country requires to prudently managing its debt to sustain a stable macroeconomic environment.

Overall, Ethiopia's economic performance is impressive for a non oil producing country. It is rated as one of the fastest growing economies from not only Sub-Saharan Africa but the world.[137] The double digit rate of growth is basically driven by the agriculture sector and massive investment in infrastructure projects. The agriculture sector still has a huge capacity to grow, which will infuse further strength to the economy. The other significantly relevant side of the economy's growth is its emphasis to distribute the created wealth among the entire population as much as possible. That is why Ethiopia's development projects and its expenditure are geared towards benefiting the lower income population. This in part will play to check the gap between income groups as it is essential to encourage fast growth but also maintain peace and stability, which is prerequisite for sustainable development.

Agriculture

Agriculture accounts for about 41 percent of the gross domestic product (GDP).[138] Its share of the economy declined recently, though it continues to be the largest employer and producer of raw materials to domestic industries as well as exports.[139] As discussed above, the major initiative in the sector is the effective diffusion of best practices which are found within the farmers themselves. Furthermore, the proper implementations of diversification intertwined with commercialization, and supported by the drive to modernize the agricultural marketing system have started to produce tangible results.

Consequently, despite the drought of 2002/03, the economy has significantly grown and the main drive for the growth has been the agriculture sector. Agriculture grew at an annual average of 10.2 percent between 2003/04 and 2010/11.[140] Total crop production increased from 106.16 million of quintals in 2000/2001 to 221.8 million in 2011/2012.[141] The increase has been substantial but short of the government's expectation. It has not yet met the ever-increasing demand for food, industrial raw materials and export earnings that are essential for fast development. The bottleneck here is the sluggish diffusion of important technologies and inputs that have tangible impact on the productivity of the sector. One of the challenges is the difficulty in diffusing technologies and farming techniques used by successful farmers to the rest of the farming community. The other challenge is the weak link between research and the beneficiary population. The government has been working to solve the above challenges with results that differ from region to region. The most successful campaign has been the water and soil conservation works performed every year in villages throughout the country. The other drive to have one source of water for a household that can be used either to compensate rainfall shortages or to produce extra earnings is being implemented by the small-holding farming households. This initiative has been successful, especially in Tigray, which even helped the people to mitigate last year's drought without much assistance from the centre.

In addition, the regional governments are striving to irrigate their farm lands as much as possible. This endeavor will not only help mitigating the effects of drought, as mentioned above, but also enable the farmers to produce twice even thrice which will have an immediate impact on reducing poverty and improving the overall living conditions in the rural areas. The expansion and proper utilization of the farming and water harvesting technology packages will evidently improve productivity and total production.

The other major sub-sector whose potential contribution to the GDP has not been exploited is the country's large resources of livestock. Animals are poorly reared by mixed farming population and the remaining stocks raised by pastoralists are no better. The most outstanding problems are lack of animal feed, poor veterinary services, deficient infrastructure and marketing system. The livestock product development extension program devised to address the major impediments to the improvement of the sub-sector has not yet produced tangible results. The government's effort to achieve better results need to be strengthened, and the country has to benefit better from the sector, which is merely statistical mirage at the moment.

The most outstanding problem for agriculture is the dismal function of the market. Modest results have so far been achieved in improving agriculture products and inputs marketing and also in creating a link among producers, agro-processors and exporters. Most of the market players do not yet have access to market information that may help shape their decisions on production, storing, transporting, marketing and other related activities. The institutions created so far to alleviate this problem are still in infancy. Poor conditions of transport and communication infrastructure, scarcity of market information, inadequate access to credit system, shortage of storage facilities and other related deficiencies will continue to adversely affect the success of the sector and harm the interests of market players, especially farmers and small traders.

Realizing the adversities and their consequences, the government has been trying to reduce their impact by introducing a number of initiatives. In addition to facilitating access to inputs and technologies, the starting of a new marketing system, easing access to credit system, massive investment in roads and other infrastructure, and diverse initiatives to reduce the impediments in production are showing tangible results. The task of strengthening and capacitating farmers' cooperatives to help solve difficulties in availing inputs and enhancing their access to the new marketing system has yet to get center stage in the effort to reduce and eradicate poverty from rural areas. Evidently, the challenges are not easy and they are not going to disappear in short time, notwithstanding, the way to betterment seems clear. With better commitment and enhanced implementation capacity success is very possible.

Industry

The contribution of the industrial sector to gross domestic product (GDP) in the year 2010/11 was about 13.4 percent. The industrial sector has evidently shown tangible progress since 2001. It has grown at annual average of 13.35 percent between 2001/02 and 2010/11.[142] Looking at the sub-sectors, the figures indicate that the construction sub-sector is performing better than manufacturing. Between 2005/06 - 2009/10, the industry sector grew at an annual average rate of 10.06 percent. Within the industry sector, during the same period, construction grew at an annual average rate of 11.1 percent while manufacturing registered 9.6 percent.[143] Similarly, during the first year implementation of the GTP, the industry sector grew by 13.4 percent and construction and manufacturing sub-sectors grew at 12.8 percent and 12.1 percent respectively.[144] In the coming years, manufacturing is expected to lead the sector and sustain the growth to bring about the structural change of the economy.

As stated above, the GTP indicates that contribution of the industrial sector to GDP is expected to grow from 13 percent in 2009/10 to 18 percent in 2014/15, meaning it has to grow at an average annual growth rate of 20 percent.[145] This implies it has to grow faster than the agriculture sector if it is to have a tangible impact on the transformation of the structure of the economy. In this regard, the government has been persistently working to build the technological capability of the sector. It has been investing in sectors such as metallurgy and engineering, sugar and fertilizer industries, which will have a significant contribution to enhance the industrial capabilities of the country.

In the manufacturing sector, the government has been providing substantial support to textiles and garment, leather and leather products and agro-processing industries. These sectors not only have a strong linkage to the agriculture sector but also employ substantial number of the labor force.[146] They have been given a substantial target to meet in terms of export earnings. The textile and garment industry had been given the target of reaching export earnings of USD 500 million at the end of PASDEP and similar targets was assigned to leather and leather products sector. However, performance had been unsatisfactory and well below the ambitious targets. In the GTP, by the end of the year 2014/15, textiles and garment, leather and leather products and agro-processing sector are given similar ambitious foreign exchange targets of USD one billion, 496.5 million and 300 million respectively.[147] Learning from the past experience, the government has been supporting these industries in many ways. These initiatives are supports of capacity building made in terms of introducing twinning program with Indian textiles and leather industry research institutions, production benchmarking, implementing the KAIZEN system,[148] creating access to financial and other necessary resources, and extensive human resource development. The performance of the first year of the GTP was below the target. Only 58.8 percent of the targets for textile and garment, leather and leather products, agro-processing and pharmaceuticals and chemical products were achieved.[149] This indicates that performance needs to vigorously accelerate if the GTP targets are to be met. In this regard, the above mentioned support initiatives have to be invigorated to bring about the intended results.

In addition to the export targets, the government has been working on import substituting industries. These industries are promoted to replace imports that are siphoning the scarce foreign exchange earnings of the country. This needs to receive similar support as the exporting counterparts to enhance the contribution to the transformation process. Apparently, these import substituting efforts are mainly done by micro and small enterprises. The government played a pivotal role in organizing, capacity building: availing working places mainly shades and providing access to loans to these enterprises. Attempts have also been made to provide better technology, equipment and tools to increase capacity. Within the PASDEP period, these initiatives created about 1.5 million jobs.[150] Extension agents were also trained to train and support these enterprises and strides have been made to provide one-stop services. Though in its infancy, effort has been made to link higher learning institutions and vocational and technical schools to provide skilled manpower based on the demand of the market. Evidently, these enterprises face difficulties from low entrepreneurial capacity as well as financial and technical difficulties. However, they have been playing a significant role in providing jobs and a means of earning income for thousands of other jobless youth.

The country has been trying to attract foreign direct investment (FDI)[151] since the downfall of the Derg with mixed results. The flow of FDI started to increase substantially since 2003/04. In 2003/04 347 projects with investment capital of 7.2 billion Birr were licensed. In 2007/08 and 2008/09 1651 and 1613 projects with capital of 92.2 billion and 73.1 billion were licensed respectively. Even in 2009/10 and 2010/11 the figures were not bad considering the global financial and economic crises.[152]

The other initiative that has been recently gaining momentum is the building of industrial zones to attract FDI. The China Eastern Industrial Zone at Dukem, near Addis Ababa, has been under construction for some time now. The Addis Industrial Village, though limited in capacity, has been operational. Others such as the Ethio-Turkish, the Kombolcha textile cluster, Dire Dawa and Hawassa are designated as industrial zones and attempt is currently underway to expedite their development.

There have been a number of multi-faceted constraints that are responsible for the low performance of the sector. Notwithstanding the current attempts to resolve outstanding issues, it is important to discuss their extent and forward some recommendations. The most significant deficiency in the Ethiopian industrial development endeavor had been the absence of a clear and defined policy and strategy until 2001. Although the ADLI strategy indicated agriculture-led development has to give way to industrial-led one, it lacked details and clear cut directions. Such gap had its own impact on the promotion and support the sector deserves, and obviously, it is not difficult to recognize that some opportunities were wasted. With the adoption of the industry strategy in 2001 and the subsequent issuance of related directives and regulations, and the implementation of some support packages, the development drive has been made to take the desired strides.

The private sector is a fledgling business community with insufficient entrepreneurial skills. It is receiving inadequate support in its business undertakings. Recently established institutions have yet to strengthen and equip themselves in order to assist the business community. Adequate package of support should be prepared with the participation of all stake-holders to solve the outstanding constraints in the sector. This implies benchmarks should be identified by studying international experiences and our own, clearly indicating what is specifically expected from the priority sub-sectors and the pertinent government ministries and institutions. On the other hand, creating and strengthening leading companies in important sub-sectors should be strongly adhered. They have to play the role of attracting centers to other establishments in creating clusters which can promote inter-industry collaboration to enhance efficiency, productivity, and sharing of technological and managerial expertise. On a similar note, the drive to assist and expand micro and small enterprise should continue with improving support packages to enable them play their role in enhancing the industrial development.

A shortage of skilled manpower is another impediment to the expansion of the sector. There are shortages of trained people in business and industrial management, engineering, information technology and other desired technical skills. It has become one of the sources of low productivity. Recently, there has been a major government drive to establish and expand higher learning institutions and technical and vocational training schools. This will have a major contribution in providing the sector with middle and lower level technicians. These institutes need to produce capable technicians, and training should be guided by market demands. Despite the attempt, producing graduates in accordance with market demand is yet to be mastered.

The country's low level of savings and the private sector's lack of adequate capital are also fundamental difficulties in expanding the industrial sector. These problems have been exacerbated by the deficiencies in the banking system. The banks prefer to provide loans to merchandise businesses rather than finance industrial projects. Hence, the government is expected to introduce measures that lessen the difficulty of obtaining loans to those who have credible projects, and even provide some interest rate subsidy as one form of incentive. It would be prudent to maximize efforts to increase domestic savings as a major contributor of resources to national economic development. Concomitant with its economic development strategy, the government has been implementing policies and regulations to encourage development-oriented entrepreneurs. So far the effort has produced limited success.

The government has already embarked on massive programs to improve the existing infrastructure; however, concerted efforts are needed to reach an acceptable level. Efforts must also be made to involve the private sector in building infrastructure projects, as that will reduce the heavy financial burden on the government. It will also be wise to expedite the development of the designated industrial zones as areas with better infrastructure that are capable of attracting investors with substantial capital, relevant technolog y and managerial capability.

Problems in the taxation system also cause some difficulties to the private sector. In a country where the taxation system is inefficient, only those who visibly own property or production plant pay taxes. Those with rent collecting businesses avoid government duty, as their transactions are untraceable in an unsophisticated system. Thus the burden falls mainly on state-owned enterprises and private industrial establishments. Hence, the government needs, on the one hand, to further expand its revenue base by developing systems and capabilities to prevent tax avoidance by those with a genuine tax liability. On the other hand, it should provide encouragement to enterprises which take an active part in developing the country's economy by continuing to introduce further reforms to the taxation system whenever necessary.

Efforts also have to be made to address market difficulties facing producers. Market information services are at their infant stage in the country and there is a need to further strengthen them. Information is needed not only to sell products but also to import raw materials and spare parts at competitive prices. The government should encourage public private enterprise partnerships in order to penetrate world markets, and also, employ sub-contracting arrangements with well-placed foreign enterprises in world market. Undoubtedly, an enterprise's achievement in export market should be used as a yardstick to measure the state of performance of individual establishments as well as the industrial sector as a whole.

The government must continue to intervene in sectors that are critical to the country's economic development, especially those with extensive forward and backward linkages. Apart from those businesses needing cross-subsidies, and better suited to government administration, the private sector should be encouraged to take opportunities whenever it can and the government should shift its focus to technologically advanced enterprises where the private sector does not have the required resources. In conjunction, it has to expedite privatization and withdraw from sectors in which it should not be involved.

Improving the judicial system will help encourage domestic as well as foreign investment. The existing judicial system is inefficient, undermanned and has few resources. This situation impacts unfavorably on the private sector, in particular on foreign investors. Major steps must be taken to increase the number of judges and upgrade their skills. It is also essential to strengthen an arbitration mechanism whereby business disputes can be expeditiously settled.

Ultimately, the government as well as the private sector has to bring about structural change in the industrial sector. The industry must eventually shift production from consumption commodities to include capital and intermediate goods, which will facilitate the transfer of technology and the development of heavy industry with multiplier effects. Moreover, the industry must develop linkages between its sub-sectors and with other sectors of the economy, especially agriculture, which would reduce the sector's dependence on imports.

Without such a change, it will be difficult to achieve tangible development based on a strong foundation. The recent initiatives by the government are encouraging and it deserves support from every corner for a successful implementation.

In conclusion, it is clear that the industrial sector as well as the private sector have many deficiencies and have not performed to the level of expectations. The government has to further refine its policies and support packages with the active participation of the private sector. This will pave the way for a far-sighted and focused long-term industrial development system. Without active and enthusiastic participation of the private sector, it will be difficult to promote industrial growth and bring about structural change in the sector and in the economy as a whole. It has also to improve its global competitiveness and image to attract the direly needed FDI to support its efforts.[153] Hence, the government, in one hand, investing in major projects that are beyond the private sector and in those that bridge crucial gaps in the industrial sector, and on the other hand, by encouraging and supporting the private sector with appropriate policies and packages to enable it to play its indispensable role, will likely bring about the intended results and expedite the attainment of the country's aspiration of joining the middle income countries' club.

Infrastructure

Ethiopia's infrastructural development has shown significant increase in the last decade. Substantial investments have been carried out in telecommunications, roads, energy and recently railways. These investments are expected to accelerate the economic growth, which the country is endeavoring to achieve. Evidently, the visible infrastructure building and expansion has a major impact on the pace of development, which has recently been registered, and the Growth and Transformation Plan will continue to benefit from the achievements in the sector by enhancing the competitiveness of the country in the world market.

Notwithstanding, the current available infrastructure is yet far from adequate to support the desired acceleration of socioeconomic change. Enhanced infrastructure network and services have direct impact on the increase of per capita growth. In this regard, a World Bank estimate indicates that raising infrastructure services of all Sub-Saharan countries to the level of the regional leader Mauritius could add 2.2 percentage points to per capita growth.[154] If the level is improved to the Republic of Korea, it would add up to 2.6 percentage points per annum to per capita economic growth. Similarly, in the same report, it is indicated that rural Ethiopia's improved access to quality roads increased consumption growth by an estimated 16 percent and reduced poverty by 7 percent.[155] That is why investment in infrastructure has direct effect on increasing economic growth and reducing poverty, which hugely contributes to the socioeconomic transformation of a country.

Telecommunications

As mentioned above, telecommunication has received a huge attention from the federal government in the last decade. The implementation of the Next Generation Network (NGN) with an investment of USD 1.5 billion by a Chinese company has built a big capacity with a variety of services of information technology. Within the above project, over 10 thousand kilometers of fiber optic cables have been deployed in all directions, which have also been connected to neighboring countries' networks to facilitate international connectivity.[156]

With the growth of the capacity, the number of installed line subscribers increased from 283,683 in 2000/01 to 804,635 in 2011/12, and the number of mobile phone subscribers increased from 27,532 in 2000/01 to about 17.26 million in 2011/12. Similarly, the number of internet users increased from 4,073 in 2000/01 to 221,542 users of a variety of data and internet receiving technologies in 2011/12.[157] Substantial strides are being made in installing methods of e-government. The government has started providing several services through the internet and non-internet applications. Services such as woreda-net, video conferencing and school-net are some of the services that help disseminate information and data to many corners of the country. The country has shown substantial progress in its electronic services and has also significantly improved its rankings on the online service component of e-government index.[158]

Ethiopia has invested a substantial amount of resource to build the telecom infrastructure. It will enable the sector to provide a variety of services by using the existing infrastructure and also by continuously adopting new technologies. Accordingly, the country has planned to widen and diversify the services within the GTP period. The plan indicates by 2014/15, the number of installed line users will be increased to 3.05 million; the mobile phone subscribers to 40 million; and the internet users to 3.69 million. Apparently the figures are ambitious, however, considering the country's fast economic growth and the government's appetite to support and expedite the country's transformation with the best available information and communication technologies, their attainment might not be too remote.

Despite its remarkable achievement, the sector faces a number of challenges requiring proper attention from the government. The qualities of the services are not yet up to standard. Periodic interruptions of services have a substantial impact on the country's economic activities. This also have a negative role in undermining the image of the country as a fast growing and transforming country. Some of the problems of quality come from the overall low human resource capacity but they are exacerbated by the frequent damage made on the optic fibers and also by the overcrowding of the available capacity. The other obvious challenge is the constraint of resources to finance the adoption and expansion of the ever-changing technologies.

The government has taken several steps to ease the difficulties in the sector. The sector has been recently reorganized to make it more efficient and effective in providing its services. A contact management agreement was signed with France Telecom not only to run the corporation better but also to learn from its vast experience and managerial skills in the process. The Financial constraint is also expected to ease by using the vendor financing method to improve and expand the technologies and services. In addition, Ethio-telecom has also started working with Ethiopian Electric Power Corporation to deploy optical ground wire, which is expected to reduce the damage made on the cables.

In general, the telecom services have made a visible progress in terms of expansion and it has availed a variety of services. As seen above, the government is determined to expand and improve the services as they have significant impact on the economic development of the country. However, the expansion and improvement of the services will depend on how fast and to what extent the aforementioned major constraints are tamed.

Road Development

As discussed before the road sector received huge investment because of the realization that it has a great deal of impact on the socio-economic development of the country. The Road Sector Development Program (RSDP) that started in 1997 continued to be carried out by phases. The current one is the RSDP IV which runs from July 2010 to June 2015. By way of the four RSDP phases significant achievements have been registered in connecting the county with better road networks.

During the last fourteen years, the total road network has expanded from about 26,550 km in 1997 to 63,083 km in 2012. The road density per 1000 sq. km increased from 24.14 in 1997 to 57.3 and the road density per 1000 population improved from 0.46 in 1997 to about 0.75 in 2012.[159] The accessibility to all weather roads has also improved significantly in the last decade. The proportion of area further than 5 km from any all weather roads has been reduced from 79 percent in 1997 to 56.4 percent in 2012.[160]

The financing of RSDP has been a major part of the federal government's annual budget. The total fund spent for the implementation of the RSDP in the last 13 years was about USD 4.7 billion. Out of the total, 71 percent of the expenditure was financed from internal resources while the rest came from international donors.[161]

In terms of building the capacity of local contractors, there has been a visible improvement not only in their participation in carrying out projects but also in their capacity to participate in major projects. The government played a major role in the development of internal capacity and continuously encouraged these entities to learn from each experience. Out of 765 contracts awarded, both construction and consultancy, since 1997 around 469 contracts were taken up by local companies. The trend shows that over time local companies are acquiring the capacity to take major road construction projects, which in fact will have a major impact on the country's infrastructural development.[162]

The GTP indicates that the road sector continues to receive substantial resources from the government. The plan indicates that the federal and regional total road length will expand to 64,522 kms and woredas' all-weather roads will amount to 71,522 kms by 2014/15. All kebeles will be connected to all weather roads by the end of the plan. Areas further than 5km from all-weather roads will be reduced to 29 percent, and road density per 1000 sq.kms and road density per 1000 population will increase to 123.7 and 1.54 respectively. The implementation of these targets required a substantial amount of resources, which will be a major challenge considering the total amount of resource needs to carry out the GTP as a whole.[163]

Despite the remarkable achievements, there are major challenges that will affect further implementation of the projects. The major constraint has been and will continue to be shortage of resources. Allocating significant amount of resources locally has been always challenging. The solicitation of funds from external resources as well as allocating these funds on time has considerable challenges. Furthermore, the capacity of local operators in carrying out projects has been below expectations, both in terms of quality and delivery per schedule. Such instances of capacity limits have been exacerbated by the low capability of the regulatory body in the control and implementation of the projects at hand. The timely completion of projects has also been affected by the low cooperation of regional and local stakeholders.

Initiatives to address the most outstanding challenges have been recently carried out. The capacity building of local contractors has been underway in terms of training as well as providing sufficient advance payment. The regulatory body is also being reorganized into two organizations, which will separately handle regulatory and operational tasks. In addition, the capacity building of regional and local authorities will also continue. Evidently, the implementation of the road sector projects has significantly contributed to the economic growth of the county by enabling the movement of people, economic transaction that encourages production as it enables the creation of jobs for a substantial number of people. With the planned extensive expansion of the road network, the resultant social and economic contribution will immensely increase in bringing the county together.

Energy

Ethiopia's hydropower potential generating capacity is estimated to be about 45,000 MW. The actual generation capacity reached 2147.65 MW in 2012, which constitutes 1969.35 MW from hydropower, 89.8 MW from diesel engines, 7.5 MW from geothermal power and 81 MW from wind power. The hydropower generating capability is only 4.3 percent of the estimated potential resources.[164] Currently, there are major projects that are under construction. The Gebe III hydroelectric power project with a capacity of 1870 MW and the Great Renaissance Dam with a capacity of 6000 MW are under construction with an estimated completion date of 2014 and 2015 respectively. These two projects alone are expected to substantially enhance the country's capacity of providing energy for production and other services.

The Growth and Transformation Plan has given due attention to increase the energy generating capacity of the country. It is projected to achieve hydroelectric generation capacity of 10,000 MW in 2014/2015.[165] This is designed to increase the per capita consumption of electricity not only in urban centers but also in rural areas through the ongoing rural electricity access program. Accordingly, the coverage of electricity services will be increased from 41 percent in 2009/10 to 75 percent in 2014/15.[166] In addition to the effort to narrow the gap between demand and supply for internal consumption, it will be possible to export to neighboring countries.

The challenges of building large dams are enormous as there is no easy alternative to harness energy, which is urgently need to power the fast economic growth in the country. Obviously, the major bottleneck in expanding hydroelectric power is the shortage of finance, which is always difficult to secure. Looking for and finding financiers have not been easy. The opposition from environmental groups and some riparian countries has made the issue more complicated. Therefore, securing the necessary finance in the required amount and on time will continue to be a challenge, which demands active and forceful political and diplomatic efforts. On the other hand, other alternatives such as thermal and wind power should also have to continue receiving proper attention as the potential is substantial.

Shortcomings in providing quality services have also been challenging not only to the provider but also to the user, especially to industrial and service establishments. Power interruptions and occasional surge have been costly by disrupting production, and damaging machinery and equipment. The main source of the problem is the obsolete transmission lines, which require replacement and regular repairs.

The other major predicament is the shortage of skilled manpower and its high attrition. It is indicated that training and retaining manpower is very crucial to the delivery of services. In fact, this task has to be invigorated to bring about changes of attitude within the core management and the general work force. Everyone needs to understand that every person's contribution is important to avail the required energy, which is a prerequisite to transform the country.

As discussed above, generating and availing power that is necessary for growth and transformation is paramount to the country. Restructuring and reforming the corporation into generating and distributing entities may enhance the efficiency and effectiveness of the service. In addition, capacity building through attitudinal change and skill development will play a pivotal role in the quality and quantity of the provision of the service. Apparently, providing solutions to the obstacles noted and other challenges should be shouldered not only by the pertinent institutions but also by the county's leadership at the top.

Railway Transport

Considering the fast economic growth, it is noted in the GTP that railway transport is more efficient and effective in moving bulky produces and raw materials from place to place. In this regard, connecting major production and other economic activity centers by railways is vital for promoting economic growth and enhancing competitiveness in global markets. The construction of railways requires substantial financial resources and every avenue has to be explored to reduce the cost, especially the hard currency demand. Consequently, domestic manufacturing and engineering establishments will be encouraged and supported to produce substantial amount of parts to sustain the railway network.

The target during the GTP period is calculated to be 2,395 km of network of which 1807.9 km will be completed by the end of the plan's conclusion. The 1807.9 km includes the 656 km from Addis Ababa to Dewele, 556.2 km from Awash to Mekelle via Woldiya, 256.4 km from Woldia to Galafi, and 339.3 km from Addis Ababa to Bedele via Jimma. The remaining 587.1 km will be a line to Southern Ethiopia, specifically from Mojo to Weyto.[167] These railway lines are planned to connect the major industrial and agricultural production areas. In addition, a light railway network of 34 km is intended to be constructed in Addis Ababa to ease the existing transport problems, which is having a significant impact on the movement of people and goods.[168] Apparently, the introduction of light railway network in Addis Ababa may pave the way to expanding it to other cities by getting appropriate experience and capabilities.

In the last two years, the preparation phase has been underway with satisfactory results. Surveying and designing has been completed and some tenders were floated, where some of the projects have been awarded to winners. The search for financiers has also been done with encouraging results.[169] The actual construction of the lines may start soon and the completion on time will have a major impact on the transport industry. In addition, the projects will encourage the expansion and consolidation of construction companies, and metal and electro-mechanical industries to sustain and expand the networks. The benefit of technological transfer will also be substantial.

Social Services

The standard of living is still extremely low in Ethiopia. According to the Human Development Report 2011, Ethiopia ranks 174th in the human development index out of the ranked 187 countries. The index considers the health, education and income levels in a county. This indicates that despite Ethiopia's double digit growth in the last nine years, it has a long way to go before it brings tangible changes in the living standard of the people.

As discussed above, Ethiopia has been making real progress not only in economic growth but also in education and health sectors. The government has been trying to bring real change in these areas by motivating the people. Ethiopia is expected to achieve most of the Millennium Development Goals by 2015. If successful in its millennium development goals, the achievement will bring fundamental changes in society which will accelerate the reduction of poverty and the improvement of overall living conditions of the people.

Education

Education is a sector by which educated, trained and skilled human resources is developed. This is considered by all as a key to economic development and social progress. It is also one of the major ways of creating opportunities to bring about change to an individual's life as well as narrowing the gap in standard of living within the population. That is why the government has detailed its importance not only in its development strategies but also has executed successive programs as its priorities in allocating human and material resources. The implementation process has been carried out in phases, which are called Education Sector Development Programs. Since 1997/98 three programs have been completed and a fourth one, ESDP IV has been devised to be implemented within the GTP period, from 2010/11 to 2014/15.

The gross enrolment ratio for primary education had grown from 57.4 per cent in 2000/01 to 96.4 percent in 2010/11. Similarly, the gross enrolment for secondary education had increased from 12.9 percent in 2000/01 to 23.7 percent in 2010/11.[170] Kindergarten was never heard of or experienced in most parts of the county. Recently, the pre-school enrolment has shown substantial increases. It had grown from 2.2 percent in 2003/04 to 5.2 percent in 2010/11.[171] Apparently, kindergarten expansion has to receive appropriate attention, as its role in teaching and shaping children is imperative.

Technical and Vocational Education and Training (TVET) enrolment has shown substantial increase in the last few years but is still well short of the required numbers for the fast economic growth in the country. The enrolment to TVET increased from 87,158 in 2007/08 to 371,347 in 2010/11. The higher education enrolment has also significantly increased with the expansion of tertiary educational institutions. First year undergraduates input increased from 98,404 in 2003/04 to 447,693 in 2010/11. The number of graduates also surged from 7,600 to 75,348 by almost ten folds during the same period. Graduate school enrolment also showed some increment by growing from 2560 in 2003/04 to 20, 150.[172]

The effort to narrow the gender disparity in enrolment ratios has been bearing fruits and the result has been encouraging. The female enrolment ratio in primary education showed tangible progress by growing from 40.3 percent in 2000/01 to 47.5 percent in 2010/11. In secondary education enrolment, it showed significant improvement by increasing from 35.3 percent in 2003/04 to 44.8 percent. When it comes to females joining undergraduate studies, the gap with their peer male students is significant. The enrolment grew from 20.8 percent in 2003/04 to 27 percent in 2010/11. The percentage of female graduates in 2003/04 was 15.2 and grew to 27.3 in 2010/11.[173] As shown, the female student numbers in tertiary institutions are not registering substantial increases. Hence, special attention has to be paid to assist female students in secondary schools to prepare them to join higher education institutions and also create an enabling environment for them to graduate.

The disparity of regional performance in the sector remains to be an area of concern. The primary education total enrolment ratios for some of the regions with substantial nomadic populations are far lower than other regional states with less or no nomadic populations. In 2000/01, the primary education gross enrolment ratio for Afar and Somali was 11.5 and 10.6 percent respectively.[174] In 2010/11, the figures significantly improved but short of satisfactory. The ratio's for Afar and Somali stood at 40.1 and 61.3 percent respectively but far lower than the average gross primary education ratio of 96.4 percent for the country as a whole.[175] The secondary school enrolment shows similar trends with much lesser figures, which indicate the matter calls for further effort to improve the situation.

Although there have been significant improvements in access to education, the quality of the services has not reached the desired standards. The primary pupil-teacher ratio has significantly decreased from 60 in 2000/01 to 51 in 2010/11, which is almost similar to the set national standard. The secondary pupil-teacher ratio has also substantially improved.[176] The major problem here is the quality of teachers, the availability of adequate educational materials and facilities, the low level of community participation in supporting the management and the teaching and learning process. The primary repetition and drop outs rate, which are 8.5 percent and 13.1 percent in 2009/10 respectively, are also areas of concern, which are closely connected to the quality of education and management.[177] The quality of education in higher learning institutions is also in need of major improvement. The fast expansion of the institutions has had its own negative impact on the quality of teachers, facilities, and management. There is acute shortage of qualified teachers and staff, especially in science, mathematics, engineering and technology education, which is expected to rapidly increase with the enrolment ratio of 70 to 30 percent.[178] The information and communication technology usage has also been low and yet to increase to facilitate the teaching and learning process.

The Education Sector Development Program IV (ESDP IV) is expected to be implemented within the GTP period. The Program envisages producing relevant trained and skilled manpower to the development of the country. It plans to mitigate the problems that spillover from the previous programs at all levels of education. In general education, the focus will be availing education services to all and achieving the Millennium Development Goals. In TVET and higher education, the targets are designed to ensure their contribution to providing education and training relevant to industrial and manufacturing as well as other socio-economic sectors' growth and transformation.[179]

There are a number of constraints affecting the performance of the education sector. One of the major deficiencies is the existing low management and planning capacity both at Federal and regional levels. The scarcity of trained and experienced manpower has been affecting the performance of all sectors of the economy and a similar situation is observed in the dispension of educational services. The government has already identified capacity building program as the top priority.

The expansion of primary education should continue to bring schools nearer to the community, it is meant to benefit, and rural areas must be provided with improvements in service and quality available to the urban areas. However, primary education usually suffers from losing experienced teachers because of upgrading, and the rural areas are more affected due to teachers' desire to be transferred to urban centers. Low income levels also force many teachers to seek other income-earning part-time jobs, affecting their quality of teaching. In addition, the attrition rate of teachers in the sector as a whole is considered to be too high. Hence, efforts have to be made to retain teachers in their working areas by improving their working conditions and providing better remuneration. In addition, access to education in rural areas has to be improved by building schools closer to villages. The presence of a school in the neighborhood encourages improved participation of village children, especially girls as parents feel more comfortable sending them to attend schools not only because of the short distance, but also because it minimizes lunch and other additional costs.

The low quality of education is also another issue creating concern among many parents as well as educators. The shortage of qualified teachers, scarcity of essential school facilities, overcrowded classes and inadequate supply of text books have played a major role in undermining the quality of teaching and learning process. The efficiency of the school system has also been affected by high number of dropouts and repeaters. The scarcity of pre-school education denies children an early education which can help them to perform better in primary schools. Moreover, poverty and parents' low expectation of girls and social problems aggravate incidents of repetition and dropout. The government has been carrying out extensive initiative to improve the quality of education; however, there is a need to increase the effort to bring a tangible qualitative change in the near future.

Another section in the educational services that has not received proper attention until recently is technical and vocational training. As mentioned above, there is a strong drive from the government to expand these institutions not only to accommodate students exiting early from the school system but also to produce technically capable low and middle level workforce for production and service sectors. These institutions and their curricula need to be evaluated periodically, and improved and adjusted to meet the demand in the market. It has to be emphasized that these institutions have to produce technicians and other skilled people in accordance with the market demand. In addition, proper attention should also be given to upgrading the capacity of universities and colleges to enable them to produce the required higher level trained manpower that can bolster management, planning and research capabilities of the country.

Apparently, there have always been financial constraints in the implementation of the Education Sector Development Programs. In addition to the government's generous budget allocation, soliciting donor and community contributions remains to be critical to narrow the gap of financing. The time consuming negotiations and the slow pace of disbursements has negative impact on the implementation process. Notwithstanding, the problems at hand, concerted effort needs to be made to effectively and efficiently carry out the current program. Besides, the notion of maximizing value for money should be at the centre of the availed resources.

Private sector participation in the sector has been limited, and needs to be better promoted. With proper encouragement and incentive, the private sector can play a visible role in improving the access and quality of educational institutions. This will help in easing the burden on the government, and at the same time, the people can be better served with the availability of increased alternatives. Non-governmental organizations (NGOs) can also play a complementary role in this endeavor.

The expansion and improvement of the education sector is at the heart of the capacity building effort of the government. As discussed above, enhancing the capacity of management and implementation capability in the education sector itself will also contribute to the improvement of the implementation capacity in the other sectors. Hence, it requires the involvement of all sections of society and total collective effort to ensure the betterment of the school system in the country. By bringing together the resources of the government, the private sector, non-governmental organizations and the community at large better achievements can be registered in the coming years.

Health

Since 1997/98 three Health Service Development Programs (HSDPs) were implemented to improve the health sector situation of the population. HSDP IV has also been devised and started to be implemented beginning 2010/11 and will extend until 2014/15. The main objectives of the HSDP have been increasing the coverage of the health care system, improving the quality of services, and strengthening the management capacity of federal and regional service providers, and encouraging the participation of other stakeholders in providing health services. The results achieved through the past programs have been encouraging and they were used as basis to prepare HSDP IV.

The principal priority areas of the program will continue to be maternal and new born care, child health and preventing and controlling the spread of the most common communicable disease such as HIV/AIDs, Tuberculosis and Malaria. The HSPD IV is intended to address ten objectives to improve the health care system at its conclusion. The objectives include improving access to health services; enhancing community ownership; maximizing resource mobilization and utilization; advancing quality of health services; improving public health services; improving public health, emergency preparedness and response; increasing pharmaceutical supply and services; developing regulatory system;

promoting evidence based decision making; enhancing health infrastructure; and strengthening human capital and leadership.[180]

The most innovative scheme, the Health Extension Program (HEP) was introduced in 2002/03. It has been designed to diffuse the relevant health knowledge and skill to households to safeguard their own and community health conditions. Since its initiation significant efforts and resources have been spent to bring it into fruition. The HEP has been implemented by developing 16 health intervention packages to bring health situation changes at community level. These packages include prevention and control of major diseases, personal hygiene and neighborhood cleanness, maternal neonatal and child health, nutrition and provision of first aid care.

By 2012, 34,382 women health extension workers were trained and deployed in more than 15,000 Kebeles (villages) to implement these packages. By supplying two extension workers to a village, full coverage of the villages in the country has been attained. Similarly, 5080 health extension workers have also been trained and assigned to urban centers to carry out health extension program. As indicated above, the HEP will have a major role in preventing the most prevalent diseases affecting the community. Apparently, these initiatives are supported by local health institutions which provide the workers with technical support.

Health care infrastructure has significantly improved in recent years. With the assumption of attaining universal primary health care coverage, one health centre to 25,000 people, it was planned to avail a cumulative total of 3,329 health centers in 2011/12. The number of health centers increased from 644 in 2005/06 to 2,999 in 2011/12, and with another 449 under construction it will bring the figure up to a total of 3, 448 health centers in few months. In addition, the number of health posts reached 15, 668 and 125 hospitals are availed in 2011/12 and 129 hospitals are under construction.[181] Accordingly, primary health service coverage reached 96 percent in 2010/11. This is a significant achievement when compared to 51.2 percent in 2000/01.

The immunization coverage for Diphtheria, Pertussis, and Tetanus (DPT) increased from 14 percent in 1992/93 to 84.9 percent in 2011/12. It also shows the coverage has been stable since the end of the nineties. The coverage for Measles reached 79.5 percent of the target population in 2011/12. The percentage of fully immunized children also reached 71.4 percent, which is a significant improvement from 2000/01. The major concern here is the achievements vary from region to region. For example, the highest coverage was attained in Southern Region with 86 percent while the lowest was registered in Gambella Region with 14.8 percent.[182] The figures indicate that special attention should be given to Afar, Somali, Gambella, and Benishangul, which have significant numbers of nomadic populations.

Similarly, the maternal and child health coverage has shown visible progress during the last decade. Maternal Mortality Ratio (MMR) has improved from 871 deaths per 100,000 live births in 2000 to 676 deaths per 100,000 live births in 2011.[183] Apparently, the figures are still high requiring significant improvements. Visible achievement has been observed in child health services. The Under 5 Mortality Rate (U5MR) has decreased from 217 in 1990 to 88 per 1000 live births in 2011. The performance attained in this area is much more outstanding when compared to other Sub-Sahara African Countries. Similarly, the Infant Mortality Rate (IMR) has also decreased from 97 deaths per 1000 live births in 2000 to 59 in 2011.[184] There has also been substantial improvement in fertility and family planning. According to Ethiopia Demographic and Health Survey, the Contraceptive Prevalence Rate (CPR) increased from 8.1 percent in 2000 to 28.6 percent in 2011. The CPR has shown significant increase in rural areas, which is a very important sign of change in women's exposure and empowerment to lead their lives. The Total Fertility Rate (TFR) also declined from 5.9 in 2000 to 4.8 in 2011.[185] The improvement of CPR and TFR has and will continue to substantially impact on MMR by reducing unwanted and unplanned pregnancies. Moreover, the antenatal care health coverage and postnatal care coverage reached 85.1 and 60.1 percent respectively in 2011/12.[186]

Tangible progress has also been made in the prevention and control of communicable diseases. According to 2011 Ethiopia Demographic and Health Survey, the adult HIV prevalence (age 15-49) has declined to 1.5 percent, which is 1.9 percent for women and 1.0 percent for men. The HIV prevalence differs from urban to rural ones. It is 4.2 percent for urban centers while 0.6 percent for rural areas.[187] Malaria prevalence has also decreased because of the extensive usage of insecticide treated nets, indoor residual spraying, community's activities in drying stagnant water near villages and other preventive actions. The prevalence of tuberculosis is also showing some improvements, however, still it warrants concerted effort by all stakeholders.[188]

Ethiopia's availability of medical doctors is below the World Health Organization's standard set for developing countries, one physician for 10,000 people. It currently stands one physician per 36,158 people. The training intake of medical school students have significantly improved recently. In 2011/12, a total of 8,060 medical students are under training in universities and medical institutions in the country.[189] With both increase in intake and the number of graduates, the ratio of physician for number of people is likely to improve in the near future. Similarly, the training of other health professionals has also shown visible progress, which has enabled the functioning of health centers, health posts and other health institutions. The deployment of professions supported by the reform underway to improve services in hospitals and the rest of health institutions will have a visible impact on the contribution of the sector to the welfare of the community. Evidently, the effort to avail pharmaceuticals and medical equipment has to be enhanced to achieve better results in the provisions of acceptable services.

There has been some visible progress in terms of service coverage, immunization and the availability of drugs and medical supplies. There are a number of major constraints thwarting the sector from reaching its objectives. Many of the diseases are communicable and infectious ones, which are related to malnutrition and poor living conditions. These diseases undoubtedly will decrease with the improvement in living conditions. While endeavoring to develop the economy, steps should be taken to minimize the effect of disease on the working force by prioritizing preventive measures. A system to sustainably involve the community in preventive actions has been developed. While providing preventive education to bring about cultural change in sanitation and other health related activities, the government in collaboration with the community has to be able to provide clean drinking water, toilets, waste bins and other hygienic services as much as the resources allow. Preventive education and community participation has been encouraged and should continue to lower the rate of the HIV/AIDs pandemic. Similarly, cultural changes as well as the continuation of the provision of preventive supplies will be required to further reduce the spread.

Financial constraints play a major role in thwarting expansion and upgrading the quality of health care services. Despite the increase in the coverage of health services, the quality of services and the availability of basic drugs and supplies are relatively low. In implementing the HSDP, the delay in the flow of foreign funds has been an impediment in carrying out projects. Furthermore, alternatives to providing a sustainable supply of drugs have to be devised. Establishing revolving drug funds, encouraging the production of generic products and other solutions can be considered to ease the scarcity of supplies. Moreover, the Federal as well as regional governments has to be able to strike a balance between their recurrent and capital budgets.

The shortage of trained manpower is also affecting the provision of quality services. Management and planning capacity of all levels of government is inadequate to the enormous task at hand. It is being adversely affected by the high attrition rate from the public service. Hence, capacity building initiatives in terms of training professionals of all levels, enhancing the managerial and planning capability, and detailing and refining policies, rules and regulations have to occupy the center stage of the health care program. Of course, it has also to include the adjustments of remuneration to retain the professionals on the job. Moreover, the expansion of health care services to rural areas has to go hand in hand with the provision of housing and other services to retain professionals from flocking to urban centers. It is also important to acquire the capacity to control the quality and standard of imported medical supplies, food and beverages, as there is no adequate institution and laboratory to safeguard the country from being affected by transported diseases.

The equitable provision of health care services among regions has to seriously be considered. The low trained manpower capacity in some of the regions is affecting their utilization of resources made available to them, and as a result, they are lagging behind. If such a situation continues, they will undoubtedly have not only socio-economic consequences but a political price will have to be paid. Hence special attention should be given to raise the capacity of implementation in these regions. The coordination between federal and regional governments in all aspects has to be enhanced through regular consultation, forums and other means of communication.

Undoubtedly, there should be a coordinated and persistent effort to improve health in the country in proportion to the gravity of prevailing problems. Although the dedication of the government to improve health care is commendable, the burden cannot be alleviated by the state's contribution alone. It has to devise a system by which the private sector, the NGOs, and the community at large can be active participants in such a difficult endeavor. The public mobilization system which the government is trying to employ will have profound results if properly applied. The collaboration among the ruling party, the government and the community to implement the health program in conjunction with the current endeavor to improve the socioeconomic conditions of people will have visible results in improving the living situation of the people. As discussed above, improving and sustainably developing the capacity of management as well as producing professionals of all levels have to be pursued vigorously and persistently.

Conclusion

The situation during the previous regime was not favorable to Ethiopia and it suffered more than its share. Poor growth rates under the command economy, inadequate social and infrastructure coverage, recurrent droughts and famines, wide-spread poverty, extensive vulnerability to external shocks, and above all, the prevalence of a bloody civil war were the distinguishing features of the country. Therefore, after the demise of the military regime, the major challenge the new government faced was the restoration of peace, and the reduction and eventual eradication of poverty.

The Agricultural Development-Led Industrialization (ADLI) strategy and the economic reform programs formulated by the government were targeted at reducing poverty. The reforms, as discussed above, include not only economic and financial stabilization and recovery but also sector development programs in the areas of infrastructure and social services that have direct impact on the performance of the former. These reforms paved the way for the withdrawal of the State from monopolizing economic activities, and the recognition of the private sector as the major force in the economic development of the country.

As a result of the economic reforms undertaken, Ethiopia had been able to enjoy a relatively stable macro economy and a constant rate of economic growth during the first decade. The economic and financial reforms agreed with the IMF had been carried out. As the government was able to negotiate based on its prepared program, the sense of ownership of the reforms was significantly high. This led to the speedy implementation of the reforms without hesitation. This does not mean that the relationship with the international financial institutions had been smooth. With all its variables, prudent implementation had produced tangible results in terms of stabilizing the economy and initiating recovery and growth. Concerning the achievements registered during the first decade, the World Bank declares "the economic reforms and performance of the last six years in Ethiopia have provided a promising platform for sustained and rapid economic growth and poverty reduction".[190] Certainly, Ethiopia needs further extensively and deeply articulated directions and strategies to bring about faster economic growth and poverty reduction.

After the end of the Ethio-Eritrean war and the crisis within the ruling party, the EPRDF was able to design and articulate its long-term socioeconomic development directions and strategies, which brought faster economic growth and signs of transformation in the country. The country has registered commendable economic growth of an annual average of 11 percent for the last nine years. It has also achieved visible results in education, health and infrastructure development, which have had a significant role in the distribution of economic gains. These well-thought and designed endeavors were supported by the extensive effort to create jobs to millions of youth. As indicated above, visible strides have been made in poverty reduction. The achievements have been recognized by international financial institutions and many foreign partners.

The government's Growth and Transformation Plan (GTP) designed to be implemented between 2010/11–2014/15 is a very ambitious plan. It is a vehicle to realize the Millennium Development Goals (MDGs) by 2015, and of course, the grand vision to transform the country into a middle income country by 2020-23.

Obviously, the successful implementation of successive five year plans requires the close collaboration of the ruling party, the government apparatus and the people at large. National consensus on poverty eradication and development need to be built as the task requires the participation of all stakeholders. The community's active participation has to be promoted and encouraged.

One of the challenges that thwart an expedited economic development is the shortage of financial resources. The government has to strive to weaken rent-seeking activities which drains resources from the rightful owners, the people and slows development efforts. It has to endeavor to promote transparency and accountability, and act on those loopholes that allow rent-seekers to flourish. Promoting good governance evidently facilitates economic development and vice versa. Encouraging savings, revenue collection and resource mobilization will continue to be one of the major tasks of the government. Concomitantly, it has also to endeavor to solicit external resources to fill the gap in financing the extensive socioeconomic and infrastructural projects and programs and locally available finance.

The second challenge which requires due attention is the improvement of production and increased productivity in all sectors. In agriculture, scaling up best practices and expansion of irrigation is likely to bring visible improvement in production and productivity, which will have a major contribution to overall transformation of the country. Similarly, the industrial sector needs to bring about structural change by enhancing productivity and intensifying its competitiveness in the global market. The industrial sector, by bring about real change in its production size and productivity, has to take over lead from the agriculture sector if the county is going to join the middle-income countries' club.

The third challenge would be to maintain macroeconomic stability while continuing to grow in double digit figures. Here, inflation and unhelpful balance of payments will continue to be formidable foes. Evidently, the long term solution would be accelerating the pace of economic growth and intensifying socioeconomic structural transformation. Notwithstanding, the current problem should also be tamed by implementing prudent policies, which should be updated concomitant with the changes in the economy. In general, the monetary and fiscal policies of the country have to be updated and upgraded with the growth and structural changes in the economy.

The fourth challenge is the state of the infrastructure and the transport logistics system, which still continues to affect the pace of development as well as the country's competitiveness in the global market. Evidently, the government is trying to expand and elevate the infrastructure network and services within its capabilities. However, it has to be recognized that the infrastructure required for faster development remains to be desired. Similarly, the underdeveloped trade logistics system in the country has negative effect in promoting modern marketing system in the country, which is one of the prerequisites to higher development stage. In addition, it has been tremendously affecting the country's competitiveness in global market. The government's drive to improve the logistics system should be expedited and properly implemented to contribute to the development endeavor.

The fifth and the most challenging undertaking will continue to be the human factor. The capacity building program of the government has to continue to be a priority area. The civil service reform has to vigorously be implemented without hesitation. As discussed above, the higher learning institutions and TVET have to produce skilled manpower that the economy requires. Every inch of success in this endeavor will have a major impact on the acceleration of the transformation of the country in every aspect. In conclusion, the country's struggle against poverty and ensuring the betterment of the living conditions of the society will much depend on the level of success in human and institutional capacity building efforts.

Notes

1. See Chapter Two.
2. See Todaro, Economic Development, 1996: 16.
3. Adelman, Irma and Cynthia Taft Morris. "Editorial: Development History and Its Implications for Development Theory", 1997: 831.
4. Felix defines the import substitution approach as "a development strategy by which a technologically backward economy tries to accelerate industrial investment primarily for the home market through heavy reliance on government manipulation of market prices, barriers to entry and access to imports and finance". Flex, "Import substitution and Late Industrialization: Latin America and Asia Compared". In Adelman and Thorbecke (eds.), World Development, 17(9), 1989: 1455.
5. For detailed analysis, see Little, Ian, TiborScitovsky, and Maurice Scott, Industry and Trade in Some Developing Countries, 1970; Kirkpatrick, "Trade Policy and Industrialization", in Gemmell (ed.), 1987: 71- 75; See also Hunt, Economic Theories of Development: An Analysis of Competing Paradigms, 1989.
6. Kirkpatrick, "Trade Policy and Industrialization", in Gemmell (ed.), 1987: 73; Todaro, op. cit. p. 494-496.
7. Kirkpatrick, 1987: 75.
8. Balassa, B. "Exports and Economic Growth", 1978: 181.
9. Balassa, B. "The Process of Industrial Development", in Adelman and Taylor (eds.), 1986: 233.
10. Bhagwati, Jadish N. "Rethinking Trade Strategy", in Lewis and Kallab (eds.), 1986: 95.
11. See Kirkpatrick, in Gemmell (ed.), 1987: 79; See also Chang, Bad Samaritans, 2008:120-21; and 215-17; Lin, The Quest for Prosperity, 2012:39-42 and 97-101; see also Sainsbury, Progressive Capitalism, 2013:247-58.
12. See Yu-Kang Mao and Chi Schive, "Agricultural and Industrial Development in Taiwan", in Mellor (ed.), 1995: 38-48.
13. See Kirkpatrick, in Gemmell, 1987: 80.

14. Kirkpatrick et. al., 1984: 200. See Wah and Jomo, "Economy Theory and Industrial Policy in East Asia", in Fitzgerald (ed.), 1995:48-49; Amsden, Asia's Next Giant, 1989: 14-15.
15. See Lensink, Structural Adjustment in Sub-Saharan Africa, 1996: 92-93.Lensink argues that "the extremely positive note concerning the effectiveness of adjustment programs, expressed by the World Bank..., seems to have been based on its faith in the positive effect of the policy adjustments it considers desirable rather than on concrete empirical outcomes". He suggests that further in-depth research on the effectiveness of the adjustment programs needs to be conducted to have an exact picture of the process. Lensink, 1996: 108; Callaghy also remarks, it has been "learning by doing and often experimenting without buffering much of the negative consequences of their efforts". See Callaghy, in Apter and Rosberg (eds.), 1994: 187.
16. For discussions on the role of the State and State owned enterprises, see Chang, Ha-Joon, Bad Samaritans, 2007: 106-116, 120-21, and 215-17; Lin, The Quest for Prosperity, 2012:39-42 and 97-101; see also Sainsbury, Progressive Capitalism, 2013:247-58.
17. Bello and Rosenfeld, in Seligson and Passé-Smith (eds.), 1993: 425-26. See also the World Bank. The East Asian Miracle: Economic Growth and Public Policy, 1993: 23-26.
18. Wah and Jomo, "Economic Theory and Industrial Policy in East Asia", in Fitzgerald (ed.), 1995: 48-49.
19. Amsden, Asia's Next Giant, 1989: 14.
20. Ibid., p. 15.
21. Ethiopia's Economic Policy During the Transitional Period, November 1991: 15-16.
22. See Policy Framework Paper, 1992/93- 1994/95, October 6, 1992.
23. See Proclamation No. 26/ 1975. A Proclamation to Provide for the Ownership and Control by the Government of the Means of Production, March 11, 1975.
24. Ethiopia's Economic Policy During the Transitional Period, November 1991: 17-18.
25. Article 13 states that "the state, through the ownership of key production, distribution and service enterprises, plays the leading role in the economy", the Constitution of the People's Democratic Republic of Ethiopia, September 12, 1987.
26. Ethiopia's Economic Policy During the Transitional Period, November 1991: 18.
27. See Proclamation No. 15/ 1992. A Proclamation to Provide for the Encouragement, Expansion and Coordination of Investment, May 25, 1992, Articles 4 and 5.
28. Proclamation No. 37/ 1996. Investment Proclamation, Federal Negarit Gazeta, June 18, 1996.
29. Proclamation No. 116/ 1998. Investment (Amendment) Proclamation, Federal Negarit Gazeta, June 11, 1998.

30. See IMF. Ethiopia: Briefing Paper – 1997 Article IV Consultation Discussion and Mid-term Review of the 1996/97 Program under the Enhanced Structural Adjustment Facility, March 12, 1997.
31. See Policy Framework Paper, 1992/93-1994/95, October 6, 1992.
32. See the PFP, 1994/95-1996/97, October 1994; and the PFP, 1998/99-2000/01, September 28, 1998.
33. See Proclamation No. 42/ 1993, January 20, 1993.
34. TGE, Office of the Prime Minister: National Population Policy of Ethiopia, April 1993.
35. TGE, Ethiopian Science and Technology Commission: National Science and Technology Policy, December 1993.
36. Ethiopia's Economic Policy, 1991, p. 21.
37. Ibid.
38. See Little, I.M.D. Economic Development: Theory, Policy and International Relations, 1982: 106; Todaro, Economic Development, 1994: 282; Binswanger, Hans P. "Agricultural and Rural Development: Painful Lessons; in Eicher and Staatz (eds.) 1998: 287; Staatz and Eicher, "Agricultural Development Ideas in Historical Perspective", in Eicher and Staatz (eds.), 1998: 9; Timmer, Peter C. " The Agricultural Transformation", in Eicher and Staatz (eds.) 1998: 122; Ruttan, Vernon W. and Yujiro Hayami, "Induced Innovation Model of Agricultural Development", in Eicher and Staatz (eds.) 1998: 163; and Mellor, "Foreign Aid and Agriculture-Led Development", in Eicher and Staatz (eds.) 1998: 61.
39. See Rosenzweig, Mark R. "Agricultural Development, Education and Innovation", in Gersovitz et al. (eds.), The Theory and Experience of Economic Development, 1982: 107; Mellor and Johnston, "The World Food Equation: Interrelations among Development, Employment, and Food Consumption", Journal of Economic Literature, 22, 1984: 567-668; Adelman," A Poverty-Focused Approach to Development Policy, in Lewis and Kallab (eds.), Development Strategies Reconsidered, 1986: 57-60; Todaro, Economic Development, 1994: 282; Mellor, "Introduction", in Mellor (ed.), Agriculture on the Road to Industrialization, 1995: 5-7. Timmer, Peter C. "The Agricultural Transformation" in Eicher and Staatz (eds.), 1998: 123 and 129; and Binswanger, Hans P., "Agricultural and Rural Development: Painful Lessons", in Eicher and Staatz (eds.), 1998: 228-90.
40. Adelman explains ADLI as follows: The argument in favour of this strategy [ADLI] rests both on its linkage effects, in creating a domestic mass market for industrial products through intermediate and final demand linkages, and on its distributional impact, through increasing the supply of wage goods and the incomes of the poorer members of society. The proposed strategy is simultaneously a growth programme and employment programme since agriculture is considerably more labour intensive than even labour-intensive manufacturing, basic needs, food security and income distribution programme and an industrialization programme. It also constitutes a foreign-exchange-saving programme by reducing the need for food imports... Finally, the proposed strategy is also a risk-reducing

programme since some of the investments required for its implementation (e.g. investments in water control and pesticides) reduce weather dependence and environmentally induced fluctuations in agricultural yields and since the strategy substitutes a development dynamic based on the more controllable increases in domestic demand for the less controllable increase in world demand. See Adelman, "Beyond Export-Led Growth", 1984; Mellor, The New Economics of Growth, 1976; Mellor (ed.), Agriculture on the Road to Industrialization, 1995; Eicher and Staatz (eds.), International Agricultural Development, 3rd edition, 1998; and Todaro, Economic Development, fifth edition, 1994.

41. See Adelman, "A Poverty-Focused Approach to Development Policy", in Lewis and Kallab (eds.), 1986: 58; and Adelman, Irma, Jean-Marc Bourniaux and Jean Waelbroeck, Agricultural Development-led Industrialization in a Global Perspective, in Adelman, Institutions and Development Strategies, 1995: 304.
42. For example, Mellor calls the strategy agriculture - and employment - based strategy and Adelman sometimes calls it agriculture - demand - led - industralization. It is also called rural - led strategy of development. (See Mellor, The New Economics of Growth, 1976: 177; Mellor," Agriculture on the Road of Industrialization, in Eicher and Staatz (eds.), 1998: 143; Todaro, Economic Development, 1994: 282; and Adelman, "Beyond Export-Led Growth" 1984: 937.
43. Adelman, "Beyond Export-Led Growth", 1984: 938.
44. Ibid., p. 939.
45. Ibid; see also Adelman, in Lewis and Kallab (eds.), 1986: 60.
46. Adelman et. al., "Agricultural Development- Led- Industrialization in a Global Perspective", in Adelman, 1995: 304.
47. Mellor, the New Economics of Growth, 1976: 177.
48. Ibid., p. 284-85; see also Mellor, "Agriculture on the Road to Industrialization", in Lewis and Kallab (eds.), 1986: 67-89.
49. Kaimowitz identifies five mechanisms to enhance linkages between research and extension: 1) integrate the organization; 2) establish liaison units; 3) organize committees for coordination purposes; 4) have members of the respective institutions carry out joint activities; and 5) communicate better. Kaimowitz quoted in Antholt, "Agriculture Extension in the Twenty-first Century", in Eicher and Staatz (eds.), 1998: 362.
50. Weitz, Raanan, From Peasant to Farmer: A Revolutionary Strategy for Development, 1971: 9.
51. Mellor, in Lewis and Kallab (eds.), 1986: 84.
52. Melllor, the New Economics of Growth, 1976: 293.
53. Mellor, in Lewis and Kallab (eds.), 1986: 85.
54. Adelman and Vogel, "The Relevance of ADLI for Sub-Saharan Africa", in Adelman, 1995: 337.
55. The strategy was further elaborated in 2002 when the government published its strategy and programs on capacity building.

56. TGE, The Education Sector Strategy, September 1994: 11-12.
57. For details of the objectives, see ibid., p. 13.
58. Ibid., p. 14.
59. Ibid., p. 14-16.
60. Ibid., p. 16-18.
61. See FDRE. Capacity Building Strategy and Programs, February 2002.
62. TGE, The Health Sector Strategy, April 1995: 1.
63. See UNDP: Human Development Report, 2011: 126.
64. TGE, The Health Sector Strategy, April 1995: 6-11.
65. Ibid., p. 12.
66. Ibid.
67. UNCTAD. The Least Developed Countries 1998 Report, 1998: 185; The railway lines are under construction at the moment.
68. See FDRE, Industrial Development Strategy, August 2002.
69. UNCTAD. The Least Developed Countries 1998 Report, 1998: 186.
70. Human Development Report, 1999: 204.
71. Energy Sector Strategy, February 23, 1994: 9-10.
72. Ibid., p. 11.
73. Ibid., p. 11-15.
74. Ibid., p. 15-16.
75. Ibid.
76. Okidi notes the relations among the riparian countries until recently as follows: The Ethiopian Ministry of Foreign Affairs issued a series of terse and non-conciliatory responses directed largely to Egypt and in part, to the Sudan. Their position was that 'Ethiopia has all the rights to exploit her natural resources'. Purportedly the statements also remind Egypt that, even though it receives 85 per cent of its Nile waters from Ethiopia, it has never shown friendship nor sought cooperation from Ethiopia. The Ethiopian statement points out that Egypt went ahead and built the Aswan Dam which has to depend on the Blue Nile waters, 'without even consulting Ethiopia'. In the ultimate analysis, the situation illustrates a trend which will develop if basin states do not consult one another and develop a framework for cooperative utilization of the waters of an international river. (Okidi, "History of the Nile and Lake Victoria Basins through Treaties", in Howell and Allan (eds.), The Nile: Sharing a Scarce Resource, 1994: 341.
77. Waterbury remarks "[t]he World Bank has steadfastly maintained its commitment to protect acquired rights, enshrined in its Operational Directive 7.50... The general guideline is that the World Bank will fund a project on an international water-course only if it has been fully explained to the other riparian and their acquiescence sought... After the current Ethiopian Republic was established... the new authorities sought World Bank financing of agricultural resettlement projects to absorb some of the demobilised soldiers from the previous regime.

The schemes required modest amounts of irrigation water from streams feeding into the Blue Nile... It took four years for the World Bank to go through all the processes of notification and assessment of downstream effects. Egypt tried to stall the project by repeatedly seeking additional information, but ultimately Egypt could not demonstrate appreciable harm. Despite the outcome, some professionals in the World Bank see the endorsement of the protection of acquired rights as tantamount to an award of veto power that can be used frivolously by those with senior rights." (Waterbury, 2002: 32).

78. See Tvedt, Terje, " The Management of Water and Irrigation: The Blue Nile", in Doornbos, M. et. al. (eds.) Beyond Conflict in the Horn, 1992: 79-93; Markakis, Resource Conflict in the Horn of Africa, 1998: 181-82; see also Abraham, Kinfe, "Nile Hurdles", The Ethiopian International Institute for Peace and Development (EIIPD), Occasional Papers, Vol. 5, No. 14, June-July 2000, and Abraham, Kinfe, "Nile Imperatives", The EIIPD, Occasional Papers, Vol 5, No. 15, June-July 2000; Waterbury remarks on the Egypt's perceived potential damage that could be done by the upper-riparian countries as follows: It could be argued that water is like no other resource. It is vital to life itself, and there are no substitutes for it. But if this were the underlying rationale for the principle of appreciable harm, then we should invoke it in transboundary water disputes only when the actions of a riparian are seen as life-threatening, such as cutting off all water to a given population or contaminating a water supply. (Waterbury, The Nile Basin, 2002: 29).

79. In this regard, Abate remarks "[i]n the final analysis, a meaningful cooperative alliance needs to be established, which will only be durable when Governments and peoples of the Nile Basin see that the rewards of cooperative association would improve the chances of providing adequate and secure food supplies, harmonious relations based on peace, stability and a sustainable environment. Any binding treaties should be equipped with processes and procedures for the settlement of disputes, and be self-adjusting to the evolving natural realities of the region and the social needs of its peoples in the future." (Abate, "The Integrated Development of Nile Basin Waters", in Howell and Allan (eds.), 1994: 241.

80. Recently, The World Bank acknowledges that Ethiopia can achieve a middle income country status by 2023 as long as it repeats the fast growth seen in the last decade. For details, see The World Bank, Ethiopia Economic Update II, June 2013: 19-31.

81. Some of the economic consequences of the war are discussed in the next section 8.2

82. MEDaC, Survey of the Ethiopian Economy September 1999:1

83. World Bank, Ethiopia: Transitions in a Poor Economy, June 30, 2000: iv

84. See the World Bank, Memorandum of the President of the International Development Association to the Executive Directors on a Country Assistance Strategy of the World Bank Group for the Federal Democratic Republic of Ethiopia, August 19, 1997: 2.

85. See IMF and IDA, Ethiopia: Decision Point Document for the Enhanced Heavily Indebted Poor Countries (HIPC) Initiative, October 15, 2001: 11; the United Nations Economic Commission for Africa (UNECA) report puts the average real GDP growth between 1992 and 2001 at 6 per cent a year (see UNECA, Economic Report on Africa 2002: Tracking Performance and Progress, 2002: 6).
86. See Central Statistics Agency (CSA), Statistical Abstracts for 1997/98 and 1998/99; Statistical Bulletin No. 277, May 2000 and No. 257, December 2001.
87. The Economic Recovery and Reconstruction Program was prepared to reverse the social and economic situation resulting from almost two decades of devastating civil war and economic mismanagement that the Transitional Government of Ethiopia inherited when it came to power in May 1991. It was a multi-donor financed program which covers infrastructure, in puts for industries, construction materials and other essential projects.
88. See Ministry of Finance and Economic Development, and IMF mission, November 2001.
89. Value added refers to the net contribution to the economy of a given economic activity expressed in terms of the difference between gross value of production and cost of intermediate input consumption.
90. See Survey of the Ethiopian Economy, September 1999: 210.
91. See CSA, Statistical Abstract, 1996, 1998, 2000; and see Statistical Bulletin, No. 248, October 2001: 185.
92. CSA, Statistical Abstract, 1998 and 2000; Statistical Bulletin, No. 248, October, 2001: 89.
93. Ibid.
94. See Solomon Wole, "Some Issues on Industrialization Strategy", in Mulat Demeke and Tassew Woldehanna (eds.), Explaining Economic Growth and Development in Ethiopia, November 2001: 79-81.
95. See CSA, Statistical Bulletin, No. 191, June 1998: 24 and No. 248, February 2001: 22.
96. The Evaluation of the Ethiopian Economy, Industry, June 1999: 48.
97. Information provided by the National Bank of Ethiopia, November 2001.
98. Information provided by the National Bank of Ethiopia, November 2001.
99. Inflation figures for year 1996/97, 1997/98, 1998/99, 1999/00 and 2000/01 were 0.3, 3.9, 3.9 4.2 and -7.2 per cent respectively. See National Bank of Ethiopia, Quarterly Bulletin, Vol. 17, No.1, First Quarter, 2001/02, p. ii.
100. IMF Statement by Mr.Rustomjee on Ethiopia: Executive Board Meeting 01/19, February 28, 2001: 3.
101. IMF. IMF Approves in Principle US$112 Million PRGF Arrangement for Ethiopia, March 20, 2001: p. 4.
102. The Heavily Indebted Poor Countries (HIPC) Debt Initiative provided a framework for implementing a strategy of burden sharing among all creditors to reduce the debt of the HIPCs to a sustainable level. The countries eligible to the ini-

tiative were helped to achieve overall debt sustainability and gradually exit from the rescheduling process. The beneficiaries need to show a track record of good policy performance as monitored by the IMF and the World Bank. The HIPC initiative built on the existing mechanisms for providing debt relief, particularly the Paris Club (using the Naples terms as the starting point for debt relief measures). Other bilateral and commercial creditors were required to provide treatment comparable to that provided by the Paris Club. Where existing mechanisms would not permit the achievement of sustainability upon completion of a first stage of adjustment and reform, enhanced action under a second stage is envisaged, including a deepening of relief in the Paris Club and action by multilateral creditors. Paris Club creditors have indicated a willingness to provide debt reduction of up to 80 per cent in net present value terms on a case-by-case basis during the second stage. Multilateral creditors have also provided additional support and relief. (For further details see International Monetary Fund and the World Bank, the HIPC Debt Initiative -Elaboration of Key Features and Proposed Procedures, August 26, 1996; and also the UNCTAD, Trade and Development Report, 1997: 48-49).

103. Ethiopia: Interim Poverty Reduction Strategy Paper 2000/01- 2002/03, November 2000:7
104. IMF. IMF and World Bank Support U.S$1.9 Billion in Debt Service Relief for Ethiopia Under Enhanced HIPC Initiative, Press Release No. 01/45, November 12, 2001: 2; Ethiopia, Memorandum on Economic and Financial Policies for 2000/01-2002/03, January 29, 2001: 5.
105. World Development Report 1994, 1994: 143.
106. See Yearbook of Statistics, Telecommunication Services 1989-1998, February 2000: 59; The World Bank. African Development Indicators 2001, 2001: 249.
107. Information provided by the Ethiopian Telecommunications Corporation, November 15, 2001.
108. Information Provided by the Ethiopian Roads Authority, November 15, 2001.
109. Ibid.
110. See World Development Report 1994, 1994: 140.
111. Information provided by the Ethiopian Electric Power Corporation, November 20, 2001.
112. World Development Indicators 2001, 2001: 302-304.
113. See also Getahun Moges, "The Electric Sector in Ethiopia: Policy, Performance and Problems", in Alemu Mokennon and Dejene Aredo (eds.), Institutions, Resources and Development in Ethiopia, September 2000: 216-217.
114. See the Education Sector Strategy and the Education Sector Development Program, 1994.
115. Ibid.
116. See Education Statistics, Annual Abstract 1996/97, May 1998: 16; and Table 5.9.
117. See Education Statistics Annual Abstract, 2000:20 and 2001: 20.

118. See Education Statistics, Annual Abstract 2000/01, August 2001: 7-8, and Table 5.10.

119. See the UNDP. The Human Development Report 2001, p. 161; and Human Development Report 2000, 2000: 240.

120. See Ministry of Health, Health and Health Related Indicators, 1998/99 and 2000/01.

121. See also the Health and Health Related Indicators, 2000/01: 13.

122. See Ministry of Health, Health and Health Related Indicators, 1998/99 and 2000/01.

123. Ministry of Health: The Health and Health Related Indicators, 2000/01: 21.

124. Defence expenditure rose from below 3 per cent GDP before 1998 to an average of 10.7 per cent during 1998/99 and 1999/2000. After the signing of the peace agreement in December 2000, defence expenditure has significantly decreased. Defence expenditures amounted to 6.2 per cent of GDP (lower than the programmed 7.3 per cent of GDP in 2000/01 (Ethiopia: Interim Poverty Reduction Strategy Paper 2000/01- 2002/03, November 2000:7; and see IMF. Ethiopia: Second Review Under the Three-Year Arrangement Under the Poverty Reduction and Growth Facility, Requests for Augmentation of Access and for Waiver of Performance Criterion, and Second Annual Program, March 1, 2002: 9-10.

125. The Economic Commission for Africa and the Africa Union discuss in detail that it is imperative to build a developmental state in Africa. They recommend that " (t)he role of the African state in achieving rapid and sustained economic growth and development combined with deep structural transformation must be channeled through a disciplined planning approach based on a comprehensive development framework." For details, see United Nations Economic Commission for Africa, Economic Report on Africa 2011, 2011.

126. The GTP indicates that the objectives and strategies for sustaining rapid and broad-based economic growth path are dependent on the following strategic pillars: 1. Sustaining rapid and equitable economic growth; 2. Maintaining agriculture as major source of economic growth; 3. Creating conditions for the industry to play key role in the economy; 4. Enhancing expansion and quality of infrastructure development; 5. Enhancing expansion and quality of social development; 6. Building capacity and deepen good governance; and 7. Promote gender and youth empowerment and equity. See for details, FDRE. Growth and Transformation Plan 2010/11- 2014/15, Volume I, Main Text, Ministry of Finance and Economic Development, November 2010, Addis Ababa, p. 22-27.

127. FDRE. Growth and Transformation Plan 2010/11- 2014/15, Volume I, Main Text, Ministry of Finance and Economic Development, November 2010, Addis Ababa, p. 4-5; and See also Ministry of Finance and Economic Development, Annual Report on Macroeconomic Development in Ethiopia, 2010/2011: 4-6.

128. FDRE. Growth and Transformation Plan (2010/11-2014/15), Annual Progress Report for F.Y. 2010/11, MOFED, June 2012, Addis Ababa, p. 13. The contribu-

tion of the sectors in 2010/11 was agriculture 41 percent, industry 13.4 percent and service 45.6 percent. The growth of industry is yet to be desired. Ibid: 14.

129. The World Bank states "growth over the last nine years was far beyond the growth rates recorded in aggregate terms for Sub-Saharan Africa(SSA), which on average only reached 5.2 percent, less than half of Ethiopia's average real GDP growth rate during that period." The World Bank, Ethiopia Economic Update, November 2012: 1.
130. Ministry of Finance and Economic Development, Annual Report on Macroeconomic Development in Ethiopia, 2010/2011: 17.
131. FDRE. Central Statistics Agency, Country and Regional Level Consumer Price Indices, November 2012. (The inflation rate was down to 6.3 percent in May 2013).
132. Ministry of Finance and Economic Development, Annual Report on Macroeconomic Development in Ethiopia, 2010/2011.
133. For detail figures, see Ethiopian Investment Agency: Summary of Licensed FDI Projects, which are Operational and Under Implementation, between 1992 and September 28, 2012, 2012.
134. Among some important factors, the Growth Report explains that high rates of saving and investment had enabled the East Asian countries to achieve higher growth rates and details some aspect of promoting saving in those counties. See *The Growth Report*, 2008: 24-25.
135. Ministry of Finance and Economic Development, Annual Report on Macroeconomic Development in Ethiopia, 2010/2011: 33-34.
136. World Bank, Ethiopia Economic Update, November 2012: 7.
137. 135 Ibid, P.1.
138. See National Bank of Ethiopia, Annual Report 2010/11, 2012:6
139. National Bank of Ethiopia: 2010/11Annual Report, 2011:9.
140. MOFED. Annual Report on Macroeconomic Development in Ethiopia, 2010/11: 4.
141. Ministry of Finance and Economic Development, Annual Report on Macroeconomic Development in Ethiopia, 2010/2011: 30.
142. Ministry of Finance and Economic Development, Annual Report on Macroeconomic Development in Ethiopia, 2010/2011: 4.
143. Performance Report of the Five-Year Plan (PASDEP) between 2005/06-2009/10, MOFED, December 2011.
144. Ibid.
145. FDRE. Growth and Transformation Plan (2010/11-2014/15), MOFED, November 2010, Addis Ababa, p. 28.
146. Lin emphasizes that although the interventions differ from country to country, the recent successful economies followed similar patterns of industrial development. He said they all started from resource intensive industries or labour-intensive industries such as mining, agriculture, garments, textiles, toys, and electronics

in the early stage of development and moved up the industrial ladder step by step to more capital-intensive industries. (Lin, *The Quest for Prosperity*, 2012:94).

147. FDRE. Growth and Transformation Plan 2010/11- 2014/15, Volume I, Main Text, Ministry of Finance and Economic Development, November 2010, Addis Ababa, p. 59.
148. FDRE. Growth and Transformation Plan (2010/11-2014/15), Annual Progress Report for F.Y. 2010/11, MOFED, June 2012, Addis Ababa, p. 37-38.
149. Ibid, p. 36.
150. Performance Report of the Five-Year Plan (PASDEP) between 2005/06-2009/10, MOFED, December 2011.
151. The IMF defines FDI as "the objective of obtaining a lasting interest by a resident entity in one economy in an enterprise resident in another economy. The lasting interest implies the existence of a long-term relationship between the direct investor and the enterprise and a significant degree of influence by the investor on the management of the enterprise." Furthermore, the OECD defines it as "an incorporated or unincorporated enterprise in which a foreign investor owns 10 per cent or more of the ordinary shares or voting power of an incorporated enterprise or the equivalent of an unincorporated enterprise." It has also been defined as "an investment involving a long-term relationship and reflecting a lasting interest and control of a resident entity in one economy (foreign direct investor or parent enterprise) in an enterprise resident in another economy (FDI enterprise or affiliate enterprise or foreign affiliate)." See Economic and Social Commission for Western Asia (ESCWA), The Role of Foreign Direct Investment in Economic Development in ESCWA Member Countries, 2000: 5.
152. 1413 projects with a capital of 55billion Birr were licensed in 2009/10, and the 2010/11 number of projects were 33 percent lower than the preceding year which was 952. See National Bank of Ethiopia, Annual Report 2010/11, 2011: 96-97.
153. Ethiopia ranks 110th of 146 countries world-wide in World Economic Forum's Global Competitiveness Index of 2011/12; Ethiopia's Ease of Doing Business ranking stood at 127 out of 185 considered countries. It indicates a lot of effort is expected in terms of improving business environment as well as image building. See World Bank, Doing Business Rankings, 2012.
154. Dercon, Stephan et.al. quoted in Ibid.
155. The World Bank. The Growth Report, 2008:19-28.
156. Ministry of Information Technology and Communications: Report on Telecommunication and Postal Services, October 2012. See also Ethio Telecom 2004 EFY (2011/12) Annual Performance Report, August 2012.
157. Ibid.
158. See www.unpan.org.
159. The figures include roads constructed under the Universal Rural Road Access Program (URRAP).

160. FDRE. Ethiopian Roads Authority, Assessment of 14 Years Performance of Road Sector Development Program, November 2011; See also Ethiopian Roads Authority, 2010/11 and 2011/12 performance Report, August 2012.
161. Ibid.
162. Ibid.
163. FDRE. Growth and Transformation Plan, 2010/11-2014/15, November 2010: 69-69.
164. See Ethiopian Electric Power Now and In the Following Years, December 13, 2011; See also National Bank of Ethiopia, Annual Report 2010/11, 2012: 24-25.
165. FDRE. Growth and Transformation Plan 2010/11- 2014/15, November 2010: 71-72.
166. Ibid: 72.
167. FDRE. Growth and Transformation Plan 2010/11- 2014/15, November 2010: 70.
168. Ibid.
169. FDRE. Growth and Transformation Plan (2010/11-2014/15), Annual Progress Report for F.Y. 2010/11, MOFED, June 2012, Addis Ababa, p. 51.
170. See Education Statistics: Annual Abstract, 2001: 20 and Education Statistics: Annual Abstract, September 2011: 5.
171. See Education Statistics: Annual Abstract, January 2005: 2 and Education Statistics: Annual Abstract, September 2011: 5.
172. Ibid.
173. Ibid.
174. Education Statistics: Annual Abstract, 2001: 24.
175. Education Statistics: Annual Abstract, September 2011: 25-28.
176. Ibid: 29-30.
177. Ibid: 32-35.
178. Higher Learning institutions enroll students in the proportion of 70 percent into Mathematics, Science, Engineering and Technology faculties while 30 percent to Social Sciences.
179. FDRE. Growth and Transformation Plan 2010/11- 2014/15, November 2010: 86-91; Education Sector Development Program IV, 2010/11-2014/15, Ministry of Education, August 2010.
180. FDRE. Health Sector Development Program IV, 2010/11-2014, November 2010: 45-50.
181. FDRE. HSDP IV Annual Performance Report, 2011/12, Ministry of Health, 2012: 69-74.
182. Ibid: 18-21.
183. Ibid: 9-10.
184. Ibid: 18.

185. Ibid: 9-10.
186. Ibid: 11.
187. Ibid: 26-28.
188. See Ibid:38-40.
189. Ibid: 75-79.
190. The World Bank, Promise and Challenge in Ethiopia, Press Release, Addis Ababa, January 27, 1998.

Chapter 9

Democracy and Economic Development in Ethiopia: A Synthesis?

In this Chapter, the interaction of democracy and economic development in Ethiopia under the successive regimes of the monarchy, the military government and the current government is discussed in details. An attempt is also made to discuss and analyse whether democracy is compatible with economic development, under what conditions they are compatible, and whether these conditions can eventually be created.

In the first section, democracy under the three regimes is discussed, and an attempt is made to use the major political freedoms and rights as a yardstick to evaluate the performance of each regime. The issues are whether political freedoms and rights have been respected and protected, and what contribution they have made in creating a conducive or detrimental environment for peace and economic development.

The socioeconomic performance of each regime is discussed in the second section. Comparison is made between each regime by using major indicators. The interaction of democracy and economic development is discussed in the third section. In this regard, the experiences of the three regimes are detailed and an attempt is made to analyse the relationship between democracy and economy development under each regime. Some analysis is made to see whether democracy is compatible with economic development, and how these conditions can be created and strengthened in the future. Finally, some useful points are summarized as conclusions in the last section.

Observations on the Democratization Process

As discussed before, democracy is a method of organizing governance through elections and in which the people extensively participate in the activities of government and also enjoy a reasonable level of civil and political freedoms. The most important concepts in this process are contestation and inclusiveness, meaning there has to be meaningful and extensive competition among individuals and political groups; an inclusive participation of the people in electing leaders and choosing their policies; and a certain level of civil and political freedoms has to be ensured to enable the people to freely express their preferences.[1]

Ethiopia had no experience of democracy until the fall of the military government in 1991. Until 1974, Ethiopia had languished under an absolute monarchy, which had little interest in introducing civil and political freedoms. The monarch claimed to have a vision to modernize the country, but without bringing himself under the law and providing the people with the mechanism to exercise their rights. As discussed before[2], the constitutions of 1931 and 1955 provided some civil and political rights but remained on paper with little effect on the lives of the people. The people were only allowed to choose representatives to the lower house of parliament, which had little influence on the Emperor's government and its policies. It was the deprivation of political rights compounded with the economic difficulties that triggered a popular revolution, resulting in the demise of the monarchy in 1974. However, the aspiration for democracy and better life did not materialize as the military usurped power.

Under the military government, Ethiopia experienced one of the most horrendous human and political rights violations that occurred in the African continent. From the start, the government suspended the constitution and promulgated prohibition of any strikes, demonstrations and public meetings.[3] Using the proclamations as a pretext, the government moved to eliminate the student movement and other opponents. The military government never hesitated in using excessive force against any perceived threat to its power.

The "Red Terror" was one of the ruthless campaigns waged by the government to liquidate its opponents between 1976 and 1978. The campaign was not only designed to destroy the opposition but also to terrify and humiliate the people into submission.[4] The exact number of those killed is not yet known but there is no doubt that they were in their tens of thousands.[5]

The suppression of civil and political rights and the absence of any mechanism to air grievances created the ground for the emergence of liberation fronts in many parts of the country. The right of self-determination became a rallying objective for many people in the country. The government responded with brute force to quell the armed opposition and showed no interest in looking for a political solution.

Excessive force was systematically used on the civilian population during the civil war. Aerial bombardments of towns, village and markets were frequently conducted. Large-scale military offensives were carried out, targeting not only rebel forces, but also civilian population. Killings of civilians and burning of houses and crops were part of the military campaigns. The government also attempted to use famine as a political weapon. The government's military counter-insurgency and social control policies turned the drought of the early 1980s into a devastating famine.[6] It did not hesitate to deny the distribution of famine relief supplies when thousands perished from hunger in 1984/85. It also used famine as an excuse for implementing a government campaign for forced resettlement designed to minimise popular support to rebel forces. Out of the estimated six hundred thousand people that were forcibly dislocated from their native villages, about fifty thousand died during the harsh relocation process or because of starvation and disease in the resettlement camps.[7]

The government, after ruling by decree for a decade, decided to create a constitution in 1987. The constitution was designed in line with the former Soviet bloc countries to inaugurate a "Marxist regime". The government also attempted to introduce new administrative restructuring that created "autonomous regions" as a response to the wide-spread armed insurgency for political freedom and self-determination. Nevertheless, the regime's efforts to consolidate its power failed to produce results as they fell short of people's expectations, and because the government's legitimacy was already tarnished beyond repair. In 1991 the government was thrown out and the country was offered another opportunity to rectify the past mistakes and build a democratic system where all its people can live together based on their free will.

Since 1991, both during the transitional period and under the federal government, a wide-range of political reforms has taken place. The reforms started with the adoption of the Transitional Charter and continued with the new constitution entering into force. Several steps have been taken to ensure and strengthen civil and political liberties, such as freedom of expression, freedom of the press, freedom of association and human rights in order to promote political competition and participation, and protect human dignity. Above all, the right of nationalities to self-determination has been recognized and its implementation has been instrumental in introducing federalism and other basic changes to the Ethiopian political landscape, and a new relationship among the various nationalities.

As discussed before, the abuse of human rights was rampant during the military government and the current government chose to bring the offenders to trial in order to draw out lessons for the future. The process of laying charges took a long time. The task had been enormous and arduous considering the Special Prosecutor Office's limited material and human capabilities. There was some truth in the criticisms of human rights groups concerning the speed of the process since the Office could have done more to expedite it. On May 26, 2008, the Derg higher officials, 73 of them, were convicted for crime against humanity and genocide, and sentenced from life imprisonment to death penalty. 34 of the accused had attended the court process, 14 had died in prison and 25 were tried in absentia. In December 2010, the President of Ethiopia commuted the death sentence of 23 Derg officials to life imprisonment. The convicts then requested for pardon by accepting responsibility for the crimes they were accused of. The government accepted their request for pardon and 16 of them were released on October 4, 2011 on parole after 20 years in jail. It was a highly emotional situation for thousands of their victims. Notwithstanding, many are supportive of closing this appalling and deplorable chapter of the county's history.

Although there have been major improvements in the efforts of human rights protection, these are still some reports of human rights violations perpetuated by enforcement agencies. Weaknesses in the judiciary and the police force might have contributed to some of the violations. The judiciary need to perform better by implementing the judicial reform to the fullest extent. The law enforcement institutions, especially the training of the police force on protection of citizens' rights should be strengthened. Furthermore, institutions such as the Human Rights Commission and Ombudsman should contribute to the human rights protection of the people as well as promote transparency and accountability in the affairs of government.

The freedom of expression is one of the fundamental rights meriting constitutional protection and is indispensable for democracy to flourish. Right of assembly and demonstration are recognized provided they are conducted peacefully. The freedom of the press is recognized in the constitution and the Press Law has been enacted to lay down the regime in which the press is expected to function. However, the criminal and civil liability section of the law remains to be controversial, especially those sections regarding defamation and false reporting.

As a result of the new press freedoms, apart from government television and radio services, five commercial radio and eight community radios currently function, and 33 periodicals and 19 magazines are regularly published.[8] There is no censorship; however, the government prosecutors have taken some journalists to court for violations of the Press Law. On one hand, many of the journalists lack the necessary professionalism in the field and have no self-restraint from spreading false rumours and offending or inciting materials. On the other hand, the government has not done enough to build the bridge between itself and the private press and assist them to raise their professional capacity. Whilst some of journalists might have their own political agenda, there are others who violate the Law due to lack of professionalism. The government has to be able to distinguish between the two and has to provide some help for those in need. Moreover, the Law also needs to be revised with time and changes on the ground in order to narrow the list of violations as long as it does not affect Ethiopia's progress to democracy.

Government offices and officials have to understand that they have the duty to provide information and be more accessible to the press. Even now, many institutions and officials tend to avoid any press scrutiny or systematically refuse to provide any requested information. The government has recently declared that it will cooperate with the private media as long as it restrains itself from illegal activities. Whatever the case, the private press will make a great contribution in consolidating democracy and the government has to develop a cordial relationship and work to enhance its positive input and the private sector has to be further encouraged to enhance its participation in radio broadcasting, as the print media's reach will continue to be limited to urban centres.

The existence of political parties is fundamental in mobilizing the people to bring about socio-economic progress. Political pluralism is considered to be a major ingredient in the consolidation of a democratic system. Accordingly, the Constitution as well as Proclamation No. 46/1993 as amended by Proclamation No. 573/2008 provides the right to organize political parties. The only restriction here is that it is forbidden to organize parties along religious lines and those determined to overthrow the constitutional order by force are banned from participating.[9] Over 79 political organizations have been registered but only a few have political coherence and organizational cohesiveness.[10]

Smaller parties may need to put aside non-basic differences and amalgamate if they are to have any chance of success. Diamond rightly remarks that "the issue of time represents one of the great dilemmas of the transition from authoritarianism. Democratic parties need time to develop their identities, leaderships, principles, and organizations, free from pressures of an imminent election in which everything will be at stake".[11] The opposition parties should not show up in the eve of elections, and break up into several groups and subsequently disappear from the political radar. They need to strive to spread their influence and create mass support. Otherwise, as Douglas put it, party leaders may have ideologies and programs, but without mass organization their political influence will remain limited to the cafes of the capital city.[12]

There have been a number of elections conducted in the country which the opposition boycotted until the 2000 national elections. The opposition was able to win 12 seats and made itself present in the parliament. It was a significant improvement to the process as the opposition took up their seats and used the opportunity to entertain their political stances in parliamentary debates and forums. It was in the 2005 elections that the opposition parties were able to draw substantial support from the population. The support came mainly not from the clarity of their alternative policies and strategies but from "protest vote" against the ruling party. Rather than using its political acumen for further gain in the next elections, the opposition damaged itself by boycotting parliament. Such unfortunate decision led to the opposition parties' rout in 2010 elections as the ruling party took lessons from the 2005 elections and performed better in its socioeconomic agenda as well as in improving its records in good governance. [13]

The government still needs to work with the opposition in levelling the field of competition. The opposition parties also need to formulate their own strategies and policies in order to cooperate with the ruling party on their similar positions and compete based on their differences. Apparently, these opposition groups lack the necessary human and material resources to perform the mentioned task. However, it should be understood that is the way to develop cooperation and accommodation while competing to win. Otherwise, opposing for the sake of opposition will be detrimental to democratic system consolidation and stability.

Contending parties and groups have to gradually learn to tolerate one another, not only for the benefit of the country but also for them as long as they remain committed to win through competitive elections. As Diamond remarked, they have "to trust that defeat will not mean elimination, that victory will be limited by accountability, and that power will be wielded responsibly."[14] With time and experience, Ethiopian politics should improve and start to shed its venomous and disruptive features. The political environment should gradually develop into moderation, tolerance and compromise among the power contenders for the democratic system to take root in the country.

Other salient features of Ethiopia's political reform are the institution of parliamentary democracy and a federal system. The House of People's Representatives has the exclusive powers of legislation in all matters assigned to federal jurisdiction while the House of Federation has the ultimate power in interpreting the constitution. The other major task of the House of the Federation is to decide on the allocation of subsidies that the federal government may provide to the states in accordance with agreed formula for grant determination.[15] Although the House of Peoples' Representatives has been active in enacting the necessary laws, it has not done enough to oversee the performance of the executive. The legislative body has to practically assume its responsibility by attentively and vigorously scrutinizing the activities of the executive branch.

At the regional level, not only has oversight and scrutiny been weak but also the executive and legislative branch had been fused under one leadership for considerable time. The President of the state government was at the same time the chairman of the regional council, the legislative branch. This defect has been rectified by amending the regional constitutions at the end of 2001.[16] However, the flaw made the regional legislative organs merely appendant of the executive branches for a relatively long time.

The federal system has evolved from the recognition of the right of nationalities to self-determination. The constitution delegates powers to the federal government and reserves the remaining powers for the states. The states are also delimited by ethno-linguistic criteria.[17] Although many opponents of the federal system regard it as a recipe to destruction, the experience shows that it has helped bring internal peace and stability. The self-rule by itself has been instrumental in localizing conflicts, which could have otherwise converged around the central government.

Although substantial powers have been devolved to the regions, the same pattern did not follow when it comes to the lower levels of government. The regional governments wasted substantial time in devolving appropriate powers to the lower administrations. It was only in 2001 that many of the regional constitutions were amended to provide substantial powers to district (woreda) and other lower levels of administrations.[18]

In terms of fiscal decentralization, the regional governments have full expenditure powers, as the subsidies from the federal government are provided as block grants. The weakness is on the revenue side as the regional governments only cover small part of their expenditures. The limited economic space has restricted the tax base of the regions. Even the federal government is mostly dependent on trade taxes. The regional governments' capacity to exhaustively exploit what is available has also been unsatisfactory. Although income growth will eventually increase regional revenues, other means or new tax instruments need to be devised to reduce the absolute dependence of the regional governments on the federal government.

The federal system is a relatively new phenomenon and it may have a number of deficiencies. There are many aspects of the system that need refinement and improvement by learning from own and other older federal systems' experiences. Notwithstanding, it has played a major role in improving the relations among various nationalities who had been suspicious of each other's motives and attitudes. It has mitigated conflicts, especially over the question of the right of self-rule, which could have been the cause for disintegration. Above all, in conjunction with other reforms, it has helped to bring peace and stability that is conducive for socio-economic progress.

The other issue worth discussing concerns consociational democracy. As discussed before, consociational democracy advocates that a democratic system can be built in fragmented societies by emphasizing the principles of accommodation and cooperation between segmental leaders, since the role of leadership is taken as a crucial element in such endeavours. The four principles that distinguish a consociational one from other forms of democracy are: a substantial segmental autonomy; a formal or informal grand coalition of government at the centre; a formal or informal veto power for the minority segments; and proportional representation or overrepresentation of the minority in all affairs.[19]

Ethiopia is a country of not only tens of nationalities but it also witnessed a protracted war for self-determination which left the country on the verge of collapse in 1991. The convening of the National Conference was designed to bring together various armed movements and other political groups who had diverse political agendas for the country. One of the uniting factors was the recognition of the right of self-determination in the National Charter adopted in the Conference. The Charter and later the federal constitution delimited the regional state boundaries based on settlement patterns, languages, identity and consent of the people and also provide substantial powers to the regional states.[20] Hence, it is clear that the regional states enjoy a substantial autonomy in administering their internal affairs.

Secondly, in terms of organizing a grand coalition at the centre, the Ethiopian system shows the existence of the main elements of this principle. The ruling party is a coalition of four organizations from the four biggest regional states. Moreover, one of the four organizations, the Southern Ethiopia Peoples' Democratic Movement (SEPDM) is itself an amalgamation of around 20 organizations from different nationalities. In addition, the EPRDF works with other organizations from other regions such as Somali, Benishangul-Gumuz, Gambella, Afar and Harari. Periodic consultations are held around federal issues as well as specific regional concerns. Furthermore, the Cabinet is deliberately formed with people of appropriate qualifications but their nationality background is also taken into consideration. It clearly exhibits a representation aspect in its formation.

Thirdly, the minority veto aspect is reflected in the constitution regarding amendments to its articles. The Ethiopian constitution applies a combination of qualified majority at federal level and sub-national governments' approval. The part of the constitution which contains all rights and freedoms requires the approval of all state councils for any proposed amendment. It also requires two-thirds majority vote from both houses of parliament.[21] Hence, the important point is theoretically a small state as Harari whose population is a little over 180,000 can block any amendment of the mentioned category in a country of about 85 million people. Such stringent process was preferred to safeguard the freedoms and rights of the people, especially the right of the people to self-determination from being easily amended as it may cause harm to the unity of the country.

Fourthly, aspects of overrepresentation of minorities can also be found in various forms. The representation of minorities in the House of Federation is ensured by the Constitution. Article 61(2) states that "each nation, nationality and people shall be represented in the House of Federation by at least one member".[22] This indicates, whatever the size of the ethnic group, it is ensured to have a voice in the upper house of parliament. In addition, although the latest amended electoral law, Proclamation No. 532/2007 decides that the number of constituencies shall not exceed 550 and accordingly those constituencies would contain proportional number of people, it exempts the minority nationalities' constituencies from such restriction.[23] In this regard, Article 20(d) explains that "minority nationalities believed to require special representation shall be determined in advance by the House of Federation based on clear criteria."[24] Therefore, the minority nationalities are entitled to representation in the House of People's Representatives as long as they fulfil the criteria approved by the House of Federation, where all nationalities have representation irrespective of their number of population. Until now, minority nationalities with over ten thousand population have been eligible to a special representation in the House of People's Representatives.

The above-mentioned features of the Ethiopian constitution and political system are similar to those principles of a consociational democracy. The political system is in the process of evolving and the features will be more institutionalized and better refined. These aspects of the political system are introduced to ensure that every nationality has a voice in formulating strategies and policies as well as their implementation, and also to safeguard its interests. In a very fragmented society like Ethiopia extensive participation of all stake-holders in major decisions is important to ensure peace and stability, and continuity of the process. This may eventually lead to stronger trust and bond among the diverse peoples, and also to consolidation of democracy in the country.

Comparison of Socio-Economic Performances

As discussed in Chapter II, development is economic growth as well as changes of social and institutional processes designed to achieve a better standard of living.[25] In order to achieve this goal, a number of development theories, have been entertained as detailed before.[26] Successive regimes in Ethiopia have also pursued diverse development paths with the aim of achieving social and economic progress. In the following, an attempt is made to compare the paths of development chosen by the different regimes and their consequences and effects on the people's lives.

The monarchy attempted to modernize the country by introducing a capitalist mode of production to a very traditional and subsistence-oriented society. Social services, telecommunications, transport and road networks began to appear, but at a very slow pace. Until the end of 1950s, Ethiopia's economy largely remained self-sufficient with very limited contact with the global economy. At the end of the 1950s, in pursuit of modernization, the government started formulating comprehensive development plans every five years.

The regime pursued an import substitution strategy with heavy dependence on foreign aid and foreign private funds. Successive legislations were enacted to attract foreign investment but remained extremely low and contributed little to the efforts of expanding the industrial sector. Agriculture was not a priority in the government's economic policy. Little was done to integrate the small-scale farmers to the emerging market economy and the government showed little interest to reform the land tenure, which had become the source of serious political and social tensions.[27]

As a result, the agriculture sector suffered significantly and after the late 1950s the country became a net importer of cereals. Even those sectors such as industry and commercial plantation, which received more attention from the government, failed to perform as expected. In a country where a large part of the population is landless peasants, it is impossible to imagine the emergence of a reasonable consumption rate to encourage other sectors of the economy.

Nevertheless, the economy grew, between 1960-1974, at an annual average of 3.69 per cent. The rate of growth had significantly declined in the early seventies as the 1960s' rates were much higher. As the population grew at annual rate of 2.3 per cent during the same period, it was possible for the per capita GDP to increase by 1.39 per cent per annum.[28]

Of course, the above figures do not show the whole picture of the country at that time. As mentioned above, the landless peasants were always on the verge of starvation even in years of good harvest. When drought hit, it is clear that many of those peasants were left without adequate food. During the 1973 drought, the monarchy attempted to hide the existence of a famine in the country which claimed the lives of about 300,000 people, and caused the displacement and ruins of the livelihood of over two million people. Such irresponsible handling of the crisis spelled the beginning of the demise of the monarchy altogether.

Although the monarchy embarked on the path of modernization to change the Ethiopian economy from a traditional subsistence one into a modern economy, integrated to the rest of the world, it failed to take the necessary reforms to bring about these changes. The monarchy attempted to introduce modern institutions and aspects of the capitalist economy while remaining an absolute monarchy and keeping the feudal economic system in the rural areas. It tried to fuse urban capitalist economic relations with the rural feudal land lordism, which, in fact, caused economic stagnation and political unrest in the country. The attempt failed and spurred the desire for a change, which brought the end of the regime.

In 1974, the military took power using the unrest in the urban centres led by student and teachers' demonstrations. It usurped power promising to bring change and socioeconomic progress to the devastated country. It declared socialism as the guiding ideology in its struggle against backwardness and poverty. It nationalized rural land and abolished tenancy, and farmers were permitted to farm their share of land. It also nationalized urban land and dwellings except one for the owner. Private ownership was depicted as a source of exploitation and misery. Accordingly, the economic policy declared that the government had to control key industrial, commercial and financial establishments "in the interest of the mass of Ethiopian workers and peasants".[29] Consequently, it nationalized commercial and industrial enterprises including retail shops, restaurants and coffee shops.[30]

The military government's economic policies were detrimental to the economy. The nationalization of companies and the restrictions against private investment had a negative effect on the performance of the industrial sector. Hansson rightly remarks that "as a result of the extensive nationalization, initially without compensation to the former owners and with the threat to further nationalizations whenever the government should find it preferable, Ethiopia experienced a severe loss of entrepreneurs, and thereby of private capital and know how".[31] Such atmosphere of uncertainty was compounded by the enactment of successive proclamations which were intended to curb the activities of the private sector from participating in meaningful production sectors.[32]

The agriculture sector suffered because of various misguided policies pursued by the government. Policies discriminating against small-holding farmers while favouring state farms and producer cooperatives; state fixed low prices that depressed farmers' income and curbed their purchasing ability of necessary farming inputs and other essential items; agricultural surplus extraction policy enforced through compulsory deliveries of grain quotas; the imposition of the collectivization, villagization and resettlement programs; and the civil war that had taken away the productive force of the society were some of the causes of the deterioration of the agricultural economy.[33] As a result, food production per head declined by an annual average rate of -1.4 per cent between 1979 and 1991.[34] Furthermore, as indicated in Chapter 3(1), Table 4, the available food supply per head (in grain equivalent) decreased from 201.4 kilograms in 1980 to about 125 kilograms in 1991.[35]

Similarly, the balance of payments deteriorated in the 1980s because of export stagnation and massive imports, especially arms and military hardware. The overvalued exchange rate further harmed the export trade by undermining Ethiopia's competitiveness. It encouraged the expansion of parallel markets of foreign exchange, denying the government a valuable resource.

As a result of the above-mentioned misguided policies and practices, the average real GDP growth between 1974 and1991 was only about 1.5 per cent per annum, which was far below the annual average population growth rate of 2.9 per cent during the same period.[36] Consequently, the country remained desperately poor. It lost over a million people in the famine of 1984-85, and was rocked by a destructive civil war that shook its foundation. The neo-Marxist policies of the government left the country poorer and more miserable than it was under the monarchy. The downfall of the military government in 1991 provided the country another chance to adopt a well-thought development paradigm that might help to rescue itself from the devastation and destitution incurred.

After 1991, a development strategy which regarded agriculture as a sector capable of surplus creation and generated demand linkages with the rest of the economy was adopted. This was a shift from the past regimes' policy of surplus extraction, which not only devastated agriculture but also harmed other sectors that could have benefited from its development.

The major point about the strategy, the ADLI, is that it shifted a greater share of the nation's investment to increase agricultural productivity. Agriculture is the leading sector whose improved productivity will stimulate consumer goods production and agricultural import industries. It also encourages free-market as well as export-oriented policies.[37] In line with the central role of agriculture, other sectoral strategies have been formulated and an attempt has been made to implement them.

Ethiopia has carried out a wide range of economic reforms since 1992 with the cooperation of multinational financial institutions. The performance of the government in implementing the agreed reforms has been praised by the World Bank and the IMF for having a strong sense of ownership, consistency and probity.[38] Notwithstanding, the negotiations carried out between the government and the international financial institutions have always been difficult as differences usually exist on the pace, sequence and scale of the reforms. In addition, the reform packages were suspended twice, once because of differences in the content of the reforms and the other time during the conflict with Eritrea. After the signing of peace treaty with Eritrea, the co-operation with the international financial institutions started again under the Poverty Reduction and Growth Facility (PRGF) and Ethiopia had become once again eligible for financial assistance and loans under the Facility.[39] In general, Ethiopia is considered among the best performers in Africa in carrying out structural adjustment reforms.[40]

The adoption of favourable economic policies complemented by peace and stability created conducive environment for the economy to respond positively. During the period 1992/93-2000/01, the economy grew at annual average rate of 5 per cent.[41] Similarly, the United Nations Economic Commission for Africa (UNECA) explains "[i]n 1992-2001 real GDP growth averaged 6 per cent a year. Exports grew by about 5 per cent a year, though there was considerable volatility. Inflation averaged about 4 per cent a year. And by 2000/01 investment had risen to 16 per cent of GDP. These outcomes reflect big improvements over 1975-1991, suggesting that the policy stance has helped to strengthen economic performance. And the positive trends are expected to continue, with GDP growth of 8.7 per cent in 2000/01 and 7.0 per cent in 2001/02."[42] The economic growth had been severely thwarted by the recurrent droughts repeatedly affecting the agriculture sector. Although droughts are not new to the country, the recent ones occurred in very short intervals or subsequent years in a row. Nevertheless, when compared with the performance of the economy during the military government, which was an average of 1.5 per cent per annum between 1974 and 1991, the rates were significantly high.

During the first decade of the reform, the economy performed reasonably well when compared with other countries' achievements. According to the African Development Indicators 2001, Ethiopia's annual average growth between 1990 and 1999 was 4.1 per cent, and the average for sub-Saharan Africa and all Africa was 2.1 and 2.4 per cent respectively during the same period.[43] This span of time includes the two worst years of turmoil and economic deterioration in Ethiopia's recent history. Considering the reform period alone, between 1992/93 and 2000/01, the annual average growth rate was about 5 per cent.[44] This is a creditable achievement considering the recurrent droughts with abnormal frequency and the unfortunate war with Eritrea.

During the second decade, between 2003/04 and 2010/11, the economy grew by an annual average of about 11.1 per cent. This indicates that Ethiopia grew by a double digit percentage for successive nine years. The World Bank explains that "growth over the last nine years was beyond the growth rates recorded in aggregate terms for sub-Saharan Africa (SSA), which on average only reached 5.2 per cent, less than half of Ethiopia's average real GDP growth rate during that period." [45] It is also envisaged that the economy will continue growing in the coming years.

In terms of the structure of the economy, the agriculture sector continues to be dominant and some improvements have also been achieved in the share of the industrial sector. In 2010/11, the agriculture sector contributed 41 per cent of the gross domestic product while industry's and services' shares were 13.4 and 45.6 per cent respectively.[46] Although the manufacturing sector was promising during the imperial regime, it was made to languish and deteriorate under the neo-Marxist regime. Manufacturing lost its competitiveness under public ownership and the private sector was stifled by restrictive regulations. Currently the sector stands to benefit not only from the recently stimulated private sector activities but also from the efforts made to increase agriculture productivity.

Agriculture is still the problematic sector in the development effort. Its high dependence on rains has exposed it to the effects of frequent droughts.

Agriculture grew at an annual average of about 3.6 per cent between 1992/93-2000/01. When compared with performance of the previous regime, which was an average of 1.22 per cent per annum, the achievement is very significant. It has reversed the declining trend of food production of 1980s.[47] With extensive efforts made in introducing better farming technologies and techniques, water management, inputs and improved marketing system, the agriculture sector showed some improvement in production and productivity between 2003/04 and 2010/11. During the mentioned period, it grew by an annual average of 10.2 per cent.[48] Still by alleviating the major challenges, the sector has a high potential to grow in the next few years in terms of total production as well as productivity. However, it is clear that it has not yet been enough to ensure food sufficiency, let alone food security, in a country that has suffered enormously from food deficiency.

As discussed before, external trade had been affected by stagnation and decline during the previous regime. The command economy, the overvalued currency, heavy taxation and the shortage of exportable commodities because of the civil war were the causes of such dismal performance. After 1991, these deficiencies were tackled to encourage the sector. As a result, between 1992/93-1999/2000, total export volume grew at annual average of 8.1 per cent and export earnings increased by an average of 15.06 per cent per annum. Imports also reached about 19.6 per cent of GDP in 1994/95 and continued in the same range until 1999/2000. The major weakness in the sector that continued to persist was the structure of the export sector. Agricultural exports accounted for about 90 per cent of the total export earnings and coffee averaged over 60 per cent of the total exports between 1992/93 and 1999/2000. Subsequently, with the achievement of substantial growth, the export sector grew at annual average of 24 per cent between 2001/02 and 2011/12. Although the agricultural sector exports still remain dominant, the number of products has substantially increased during the same period. The share of coffee declined from 60 per cent on average to 33 per cent, and in fact, in 2011/12 it further declined to 26.4 per cent. Manufacturing exports share has shown some increase but still remains modest and expected to significantly increase in the coming years. Nevertheless, the amount of export earnings increased from USD 452 million in 2001/02 to USD 3.2 billion in 2011/12.[49]

The industrial sector has shown little change in its contribution to gross domestic product, which stood at 13.4 per cent in 2010/11. With the abolition of the command economy, the private sector has been active in investing in the manufacturing as well as other sectors although the savings in the country are low.[50] After a dismal situation in 1991, the industry revived and grew by about 28.4 per cent in 1992/93, and grew on annual average of about 6.15 per cent between 1993/94 and 2000/01.[51] For example, in 2000 Ethiopia was one of the best performers in Africa with 7.5 per cent annual growth rate in its industrial sector. In the mining sector, it was the best performer in 2000 with an annual growth rate of 13 per cent.[52] Similarly, the sector grew at an annual average of 13.35 per cent between 2001/02 and 2010/11.[53] However, as indicated above, at the end of the Growth and Transformation Plan, the share of the sector is expected to grow to 18 per cent by growing at an annual average of 20 per cent.

It has been discussed that one of the impediments to Ethiopia's development is the low level of its infrastructure sector. Energy production has shown a significant increase in the last decade. The country's generating capacity grew from 316 megawatt in 1980 to 2147.65 megawatt in 2012.[54] There are some mega projects such as the Gilgel Gibe III and the Great Renaissance Dam with expected capacity of 1800 Megawatts and 6000 Megawatts respectively. Ethiopia has already signed agreements with almost all neighbouring countries for exporting energy. In most cases, the constructions of transmission lines are underway and providing Djibouti with some power has already started. With the addition of the projects under construction and those under study, Ethiopia will have a sustainable renewable energy supply and extra substantial amount for export.

The other major drive made during the reform period is the efforts being implemented to expand and improve the country's road network. The government has started implementing the Road Sector Development Program (RSDP) in 1997 with extensive international assistance. The road network has expanded from about 26,550 km in 1997 to 63,083 km in 2012. This expansion has brought significant changes on the availability of road transport in many parts of the country. In this regard, the road density per 1000 sq.km increased from 24.14 in 1997 to 57.3 and the road density per 1000 population improved from 0.46 in 1997 to about 0.75 in 2012.[55] In the last decade, the accessibility to all weather roads visibly increased, and as a result, the proportion of area further than 5 km from an all-weather road has been reduced from 79 per cent in 1997 to 56.4 per cent in 2012.[56] Such an improvement will have a significant impact in the country's economic development endeavours and in building better functioning domestic markets.

Telecommunication services have shown significant improvement in the last decade. Extensive infrastructure expansion has been carried out in the last few years. Over ten thousand kilometres of optic fibre cables have been deployed in all directions of the country and also connecting with neighbouring counties to facilitate international connectivity. By enhancing its capacity, the number of installed line subscribers increased from 283,683 in 2000/01 to 804,635 in 2011/12, and the number of mobile phone subscribers increased from 27,532 in 2000/01 to about 17.26 million in 2011/12. The number of internet users also increased from 4,073 in 2000/01 to 221, 542 in 2011/12.[57] As indicated in the Growth and Transformation Plan, the availability of information and communication technologies will be expanded to expedite the socioeconomic transformation of the country.

The education sector has been one of the sectors where major improvements occurred. The gross enrolment ratio for primary education increased from below 20 per cent in 1992/93 to 57.4 per cent in 2000/01. Similarly, the ratio for secondary education increased from 6.6 per cent in 1994/95 to 12.9 per cent in 2000/01. Enrolment in primary education increased at an annual average of 13.4 per cent and for secondary education at an average of 14.6 per cent per annum between 1996/97 and 2000/01. Such achievement has been sustained and substantially improved in the last decade. The gross enrolment for primary education has grown to 96.4 per cent in 2010/11. Similarly, secondary education gross enrolment improved to 23.7 per cent in 2010/11. Pre-school enrolment has started to pick up. The Technical and Vocational Education and Training (TVET) have shown substantial progress in the last few years. The enrolment increased from 87,158 in 2007/08 to 371,347 in 2010/11. Higher education enrolment also registered significant increase. The first year enrolment increased from 98,404 in 2003/04 to 447,693 in 2010/11.[58] As indicated the education sector has received huge attention, and as a result, the achievements are substantial in enhancing the human resource capacity of the country. Evidently, enhancing the quality of the education and delivery system will require proper attention in the coming years.

Gender disparity in primary and secondary education enrolment has significantly narrowed in the last few years. The female enrolment ratio for primary and secondary education reached 47.5 per cent and 44.8 per cent respectively in 2010/11. The gap grows visibly when it comes to higher education. The female enrolment ratio reached 27 per cent in 2010/11. This signifies that there needs a lot of effort to be done to encourage female enrolment in higher education institutions in the coming years. Similarly, the disparity in regional performance still remains area of concern. The primary education enrolment ratio in Afar and Somali regions reached 40.1 and 61.3 per cent respectively.[59] Although they have come a long way and the achievements are undeniable, special effort is required to bring them to the national average figures considering the regions are mostly inhabited by nomadic populations.

In the health sector, after year of neglect during the imperial and military governments, the primary health care coverage increased from 38 per cent in 1992/93 to 96 per cent in 2010/11. The Health Extension Program introduced in 2002/03 has brought significant changes in the health situation of the country, especially in the rural areas. 34,382 women health extension workers were deployed in more than 15,000 kebeles (villages) by 2012. Similarly, 5080 health extension workers have also been assigned to urban centres. The health care infrastructures have also shown significant increases. The number of health centres, health posts and hospitals reached 2,999, 15,688 and 125 respectively in 2011/12.

The immunization coverage has also registered significant improvement. Coverage for Diphtheria, Pertussis, and Tetanus (DPT) increased from 14 per cent in 1992/93 to 84.9 per cent in 2011/12. The coverage for Measles also reached 79.5 per cent of the target population in 2011/12. Overall, the percentage of fully immunized children reached 71.4 per cent, which is a major achievement but still short of the desire target set to reduce child mortality.

In many respects, the quality of life in Ethiopia has not changed significant enough. Quality of life was bad during the imperial regime and became worse under the military dictatorship. Although efforts have been made in the last decade, the changes are still inadequate in bringing about qualitative difference. Life expectancy at birth increased from 41.8 years in early 1970s to 56.56 years in 2012. Infant mortality rate decreased from 160 per 1000 live births in 1970 to 59 in 2011. Similarly, under-five mortality rate decreased from 239 per 1000 live births in 1970 to 88 in 2011.[60] Maternity Mortal Ratio (MMR) has also improved from 871 deaths per 100,000 live births in 2000 to 676 deaths per 1000 live births in 2011.[61] As mentioned above, one of the major reasons for the improvement is the expansion of the health care system in recent years. Still the figures are high and concerted effort has to be made to achieve the millennium goals.

In the nineties, the spread of HIV/AIDS was a major menace and was threatening the very foundation of the country. The prevalence rate in the age group of 15-49 was estimated to be 10.63 per cent at the end of 1999.[62] With concerted efforts of all stakeholders, the adult HIV prevalence rate (age 15-49) has declined to 1.5 per cent, which is 1.9 per cent for women and 1.0 per cent for men. Other communicable diseases are also showing a decrease of their prevalence rate in recent years.[63] In health, the government has given more attention than any regime before. It prepared the Health Sector Development Program (HSPD) in which various international donors have also extensively participated.

The drive to improve the health situation of the people is not without challenges. There are many challenges that affect the quantitative and qualitative progress in the sector. The major problems are financial constraints, shortage of trained manpower, the disparity of services in the regions and the overall quality of the delivery system. Evidently, the government has accomplished a commendable job and the results are admirable. However, considering the remaining tasks and the challenges ahead, the mission requires appropriate leadership and substantial resources to attain qualitative changes in the country's health system delivery. Apparently, it has to contribute massively to the transformation of the socioeconomic situation of the country.

With all the above activities, the level of poverty is still distressing. It is obvious Ethiopia's relatively strong economic growth has achieved some improvement in the living condition of the people. It is reported "the growth reversed the secular decline in per capita income, and the national poverty rate dropped significantly. Per capita consumption spending rose in both urban and rural areas. Moreover, net school enrolment ratios moved up, and both child mortality and malnutrition rate declined. Still Ethiopia remains one of the World's poorest countries."[64]

The above statement explains the achievement of the first decade after the fall of the military government. Subsequently, in the second decade, Ethiopia has shown significant progress in terms of reducing poverty. Food poverty line per adult person per year was estimated to be Birr 1,985 and the total poverty line per adult person per year was Birr 3,781 in 2010/11. According to the 2010/11, Household Income Consumption & Expenditure Survey (HICES), the proportion of poor people (poverty head count index) in the country is estimated to be 29.6 per cent. Apparently, although much more is desired, the reduction of poverty from the 1996 level is commendable. The percentage of the population below the poverty line decreased from 45.5 per cent in 1996 to 29.6 per cent in 2010/11. [65]

The government's commitment to eradicate poverty was demonstrated by devising three consecutive development plans in the last decade. The government first devised the Sustainable Development and Poverty Reduction Program (SADRP) implemented between 2002/03 -2004/05. The next one was the Plan for Accelerated and Sustained Development to End Poverty (PASDEP), which was implemented from 2005/06 to 2009/10. The Growth and Transformation Plan (GTP) is also currently in the process of implementation which covers from 2010/11–2014/15. As discussed above, substantial results are expected from the implementation of GTP, which will reduce percentage of people under poverty line to 22.2 per cent and the attainment of the Millennium Development Goals (MDGs) by 2015.[66] Apparently, poverty reduction initiatives will continue to be the core of the country's development agenda. The struggle against poverty and its results will determine how fast and to what extent Ethiopia will achieve a significant socioeconomic progress.

Ethiopia's socioeconomic performance since 1991 is not comparable to the situation during the military government. The misguided policies of the previous government and their consequences had gravely devastated the country. When such situation was compounded with civil war that spread to all corners of the country, the result was not only poverty and destitution but also a real danger of disintegration and destruction. The grave situation was lessened through political reforms and the economic efforts to alleviate poverty and desolation. However, what has achieved so far is not yet adequate to ease the poverty burden of the people. Further effort is required to expedite socioeconomic progress with poverty reduction endeavours at its core. Otherwise, the existing internal peace and stability cannot be indefinitely taken for granted.

The Interaction of Democracy and Economic Development

As discussed in Chapter Two, there have been differing views on the compatibility of democracy and economic development. Some theorists argue that there is a trade-off between democracy and economic development. They argue that democracy creates obstacles to economic development by exposing the government to a wide-range of pressures to squander the country's resources on immediate consumption. Hence, they advocate for restricting political participation in order to create the environment for the government to concentrate on its development agenda.[67]

Alternatively, others argue that democracy creates conducive conditions encouraging economic development. Some also contend that there has not been a one-to-one relationship between the type of regime and development, and other factors contribute to development achievements. Apparently, it seems there has not been a clear consensus on the compatibility of democracy and economic development among theorists.[68]

Ethiopia has experienced different regimes with diverse political orientation and economic development agendas. Until recently, the ever-deteriorating situation saw people sinking into an abyss of poverty. Poverty eradication has continued to elude Ethiopia for a long time now.

The imperial government had advocated that economic development would be achieved through the modernization process. It had attempted to encourage private investment and market-based economy in the urban centres while trying to keep the rural areas out of the modernization initiative. The government kept resisting any pressure to abolish the feudal production relations in the rural areas in order to protect its power base. It was not even ready to introduce a limited reform to quell the brewing unrest in the countryside. The oppressive land tenure system was one of the sources of fierce opposition to the regime.

The government was also in favour of expanding commercial plantations. These plantations were not established in open land, but by evicting peasants from their homes. Although over 85 per cent of Ethiopia's people live on small plots of land, the government had not paid any attention to assist peasant farming.

On the other hand, the monarchy had attempted to embrace modernization without reforming the political environment. The Emperor continued to be above the law and preferred to remain an absolute monarch. There was little space for popular participation and the only "popular participation" the Emperor gave "as a gift to his subjects" were the periodic elections conducted to elect members of parliament to the lower house. The upper house membership was filled by the nobility and landlords through appointment. In fact, there was no significant difference between both houses in their composition. All were controlled by the upper strata of the society. Moreover, the parliament had little power in influencing the country's political and economic policies. It was just an appendage of the monarchy, which was created in the first place for the monarch's image building in the eyes of foreign powers. In addition, although the 1955 Revised Constitution detailed various freedoms and rights, they were not intended to be used or invoked by anybody.[69] In this respect, it was only a constitution that was supposed to remain on paper.

The monarchy had ruled the country with half-hearted modernization program and with little freedoms and participation of the people. It was clear that the economy could not achieve the intended results by neglecting the rural people and agriculture. The enactment of unfriendly policies compounded with recurrent drought, and the attempt made to hide the famine crisis in the country shook the government to its foundation. On the other hand, the absence of freedoms and participation created the ground for a wide and strong opposition from the urban population. Dissatisfaction and hostility against the regime rapidly grew as most of the people were excluded from economic benefits and the fruits of modernization, which sounded the death knell of the monarchy. Hence, the limited modernization process with scant democratic freedoms and participation failed to bring about economic development in the country.

The military government, during the early days of its rule, declared that the guiding ideology of the regime was Marxism and intended to build Socialism by nationalizing private enterprises and dwellings. It abolished the feudal land ownership in rural Ethiopia but built a mechanism for maximum extraction of resources from agriculture. It confiscated all major production, trading and financial enterprises, and controlled the external sector of the economy. It also pursued an import-substitution strategy, which left the small manufacturing sector sluggish and incompetent in the face of fierce international competition.

On the other hand, from the start, it attempted to rule the country by decrees, which excluded people from exercising their rights. It managed to crush the urban opposition through brute force and intimidation. The "Red Terror" campaign was instituted claiming the lives of thousands of students, intellectuals and workers. The military government also carried out massive military campaigns to crush national liberation movements. At the end of its rule, it had the largest army in sub-Saharan Africa.[70]

After the consolidation of its regime, the Derg organized a "Marxist-Leninist" party, which was designated to lead the country to Socialism. Consequently, a constitution designed to resemble the former Soviet Union and Romanian constitutions was promulgated. The basic freedoms and rights were indicated to be decreed by law. The regime, throughout its stay in power, ruled the country through intimidation and brute force. Popular participation did not go far from being rhetoric and remained only on paper.[71]

Neo-Marxist economic policies combined with lack of any elements of democracy and democratic participation brought the country to its knees. In 1984/85, about a million people lost their lives because of the famine that gripped the nation, which was mainly a man-made phenomenon. It was the saddest period of the Ethiopian people, when human life lost its value and dignity. At the end of the regime, Ethiopians found themselves poorer and more desperate than they were under the monarchy. Authoritarianism not only postponed the country's development thirst by almost two decades, but also severely damaged what it had during the downfall of the imperial regime.

As discussed before, the current regime inherited an economically devastated country, a country on the verge of disintegration. The first task of the provisional government was to bring all liberation movements and political groups together to form an interim government. The right of nationalities to self-determination, including the right to secede, and other freedoms and rights were recognized in the National Charter which paved the way for the establishment of the Transitional Government.[72]

The implementation of the right of self-rule began with the creation of regional states based on language and cultural affinity and devolving power from the centre. These rights and freedoms were later consolidated by the formulation and ratification of the federal constitution. As discussed before, the constitution and the system as a whole contain significant elements of consociational democracy. Whatever shortcomings it has, democracy is not just an alternative to Ethiopia; it is the most important ingredient, essential for its survival as a united country. A country that was expected to repeat the carnage of Somalia and Liberia has been largely successful in establishing a largely peaceful and stable environment internally.[73]

From the outset the country adopted an economic reform program with the cooperation of the IMF and the World Bank. Steps have been taken to change the command economy into a market-oriented one. Agriculture, for the first time, has been taken not as a sector for resource extraction, but as an area where large investment has to be made to increase productivity and to enable it to take along other sectors of the economy to better performance. Instead of an import substitution strategy, the new policies have been designed to promote exports and to enhance global integration. The policies adopted and are being implemented have more or less the support of the IMF and other international donors. Basically, these policies can be regarded as market oriented with the state playing a significant role in selected and limited sectors.

In spite of much cooperation with the IMF, Ethiopia's relations with the IMF have not been smooth. Its program with IMF lapsed twice, in 1997 and 1998. The first on differences of policies and the second one during the war with Eritrea. It was difficult for Ethiopia to understand the position taken by the IMF in 1997. The IMF demand for financial market liberalization was not based on the specific situations in the country. Stiglitz (winner of the 2001 Nobel Prize in economics) rightly remarks "to the Fund, a liberalized financial system was an end in itself... The IMF was so certain about the correctness of its dogmatic position that it had little interest in looking at actual experiences... Ethiopia resisted the IMF's demand that it "open" its banking system, for good reason. It had seen what happened when one of its East African neighbours gave in to IMF demands".[74] Stiglitz criticizes the IMF for its "one-size-fits-all" approach.[75] Of course, its position on the role of the state also arises from such approach. The cooperation between the Ethiopian government and the IMF has once again resumed after the end of the war with Eritrea but differences have still persisted.

As mentioned above, the Ethiopian government has been participating in selected economic activities. The feebleness of the private sector warrants the participation of the state in selective and important sectors that are indispensable for the development of the private sector as well as Ethiopia's economy as a whole. The intervention should not impede any step towards strengthening the market economy and also facilitate the process through assisting the private sector to develop, and reducing the effect of the market failure that is common in undeveloped economies. Some relevant lessons can be learned from the experiences of the East Asian countries where the state played a prominent role in achieving respectable level of economic development. The governments pursued market friendly approaches while maintaining selective intervention in allocating resources and participating in useful ventures.[76] For example, Oyejide states Taiwan's development strategy clearly signifies "the weaving together of three key strands: the maintenance of macroeconomic stability, the participation of a vibrant and active private sector, and the use of strategic and selective state intervention".[77] It also sounds reasonable when he argues that "the SSA [sub-Saharan Africa region] cannot achieve rapid and sustainable growth unless developmental states are established that are capable of articulating a long-term vision of development and of exercising sufficient policy autonomy not only in implementing strategies constructed around such a vision but also in disciplining the private sector. Seeking refuge in a "minimalist" state could, in this context, amount to abandoning the quest for sustainable and equitable growth."[78]

In this regard, the Ethiopian government's hesitance to hasten financial market liberalization and its difference with the IMF regarding the role of the state makes sense provided they are better utilized to strengthen the market economy and bring about economic development. As discussed above, Ethiopia has been able to maintain macroeconomic stability but its private sector has not yet reached the stage of playing visible and dominant role in the economy. On the other hand, some measures of intervention stated in the strategy and sector programs to assist the private sector and promote economic development should be carried out more vigorously and persistently than before. Ethiopia has so far learned a lot and has to continue learning from other countries' experience, especially from the East Asian countries in promoting economic development and eradicating poverty.

The democratic reforms, including devolution of power, the recognition of freedoms and rights, and the wide-spread participation of the people ranging from periodic elections to taking part in their local affairs have produced a relatively stable and peaceful environment in a country that had been rocked with decades of civil war and unrest. Such an environment has encouraged not only the private sector to participate in the economic development endeavours but also the international community to extend its support. As discussed above, Ethiopia benefited from substantial aid and financial flows as well as debt cancellation and rescheduling.

The situation has become conducive for economic development efforts to bear fruits. As a result, the economy has significantly responded but short of bringing a qualitative change to people's lives. Obviously, there is an acute shortage of human and material capabilities in the country, which need to be prudently addressed. The compatibility between the democratic reforms and economic development endeavours is not difficult to notice. However, the results are determined not only by adopting proper policies and creating conducive environment but also by the availability of human and material resources. As Sorensen rightly remarked democracy offers the opportunities, but it does not offer guarantees of success.[79]

The government has to further improve its performance. Poverty reduction and gradually eradication will continue be the core of its development endeavours. Certainly, freedom raises expectations and if the government cannot expedite its effort to mitigate the despicable poverty and desolation, there can possibly be a backlash. As Przeworki et.al.remarked it seems certain that poverty breeds poverty and dictatorship.[80]

Hence, the government needs to work hard to improve its democratic credentials by addressing its shortcomings, and building and strengthening democratic institutions. It also has to periodically evaluate and rectify its deficiencies in its economic efforts. By combining these initiatives, it can possibly create an environment that better encourages the two factors, democracy and economic development, work hand in hand to alleviate the country's predicaments, and eventually create a level of progress that can bring out its people from the present quagmire.

Conclusions

The interaction of democracy and economic development has had diverse features under the successive regimes that ruled Ethiopia during the past century. The monarchy that ruled Ethiopia for most of the past century attempted to introduce modernization but with little effect on society. Although it allowed the private sector to have a role in the urban centres, it was unable to introduce reform to the countryside, especially to accommodate the millions of landless peasants. Hence, the government attempted to advance partial modernization in socioeconomic sectors with almost no popular participation in the affairs of the country. As a result, Ethiopia's development efforts declined to a point where millions died of hunger while the government failed to act, and even worse, attempted to hide the existence of the disaster.

The military came to power with the promise of improving the living conditions of the people and cleaning society of the aristocratic blunders and corruption of the previous regime. It declared that Socialism was the guiding ideology to bring about social change and development. It tried unsuccessfully to crush the aspirations of many peoples through sheer military might. The combination of command economy and undemocratic and nonparticipatory system of government destroyed the people's hope for improved and better livelihood. Near the conclusion of the regime's era, the country found itself in a deep economic mess and political disintegration. It clearly signified how authoritarianism brought destruction, destitution, and extensive damage to the social fabric of the country.

After 1991, political and economic reforms have been simultaneously implemented. The recognition of self-determination of nationalities and devolution of power, and the effort made to promote basic freedoms and rights have created a relatively peaceful and stable environment for the first time in decades. The economic reform program designed with the cooperation of the IMF was instrumental in changing the command economy into a market-oriented one. The periodic programs implemented between 2002/03 and 2009/10 had produced substantial results. Currently, the GTP, a five year plan, is expected to bring commendable achievements that will serve as spring board for the structural socioeconomic transformation, which will enable Ethiopia to join the middle-income countries' club in about a decade time. With all its shortcomings, one can see the compatibility of democracy with economic development even at this stage. The conducive business climate created by the political reform has produced a reasonable uplift to the whole economy, although it has a long way to go to bring about a substantially qualitative difference in the lives of the people.

The democratic system needs further institutionalization. In Ethiopia, poverty is the most challenging factor that heavily affects the transition towards democracy. People who live under difficult circumstances lack the capability and time to exercise their rights. Hence, the process of strengthening democracy has to go hand in hand with poverty eradication endeavours. The economic development exercise carried out so far has to continue and further deepen to a point where it will eliminate major obstacles to faster and sustainable economic growth and the development of a dynamic and viable economic environment. Obviously, the economy needs to continuously grow around the rate that is planned in the GTP if a structural socioeconomic change is to be observed. Only through significant growth can democracy and economic development be further enhanced and consolidated, and their interrelation and interdependence can be sustained and strengthened. As repeatedly discussed before, democracy is not an option but the only means of survival for Ethiopia.

Notes

1. For further discussion, see Chapter Two, The Theoretical Framework.
2. For further discussions, see Chapter Four.
3. See Proclamation on the Establishment of a Provisional Military Government in Ethiopia, Published by the Co-ordinating Committee of the Armed Forces, Police and Territorial Army, Addis Ababa, 12 September 1974.
4. de Waal, Evil Days: 30 Years of War and Famine in Ethiopia, 1991: 101.
5. Brietzke estimates the number of victims of the Red Terror as 32,000. However, some observers' estimates are by far higher (Brietzke, quoted in Tiruneh, 1993: 223).
6. See de Waal, 1991: 175-176.
7. Ibid., p. 224-227.
8. Broadcasting Authority, List of Broadcasters, Periodicals, and Magazines, December 2012.
9. For further discussions, see Chapter Five.
10. See NEB, List of Political Parties and Organizations, December 2012.
11. Diamond, "Beyond Authoritarianism and Totalitarianism", 1989:145.

12. Douglas, in Raymond D. Gastil (ed.), 1984:102.
13. For detail discussion, see Chapter 5.
14. Diamond, "Beyond Authoritarianism and Tolitarianism", 1989: 144.
15. See Proclamation No. 1/1995. Proclamation of the Constitution of the Federal Democratic Republic of Ethiopia, August 21, 1995.
16. See the Amended Constitution of the Tigray National Regional State, Proclamation 45/2001, November 15, 2001; The Amended Constitution of the Amhara National Regional State, Proclamation 59/2001, November 5, 2001; and The Amended Constitution of the Oromo National Regional State, Proclamation 49/2001, October 27, 2001.
17. See Proclamation No. 1/1995.
18. See the above amended regional constitutions.
19. See Lijphart, 1979: 505; for further discussion, see Chapter Two.
20. See Proclamation No. 1/1995, Article 39.
21. Constitutions employ various means to amend or make changes in some of their provisions. Lane details some of the methods in which amendments could take place: no change; referendum; delay; confirmation by a second decision; qualified majorities; and confirmation by sub-national governments (Lane, 1996: 114). In most cases, there exists a mechanism that combines some of the mentioned institutions. One of the most rigid constitutions to amend is the German Constitution. Article 79 (2) declares that amendments "require the consent of two-thirds of the members of the Bundestag and two-thirds of the votes of the Bundestrat". On the other hand, Article 79 (3) states that "amendments of this Basic Law affecting the division of the Federation into Länder, the participation on principle of the Länder in legislation, or the basic principles laid down in Articles 1 and 20 shall be inadmissible" (Finer et al., 1995: 163-64; Articles 1 & 20 contain the fundamental rights and freedoms of the people and federal form of government which are categorized by the Constitution beyond any amendment. Ibid., p. 128 and 137). Others employ the combination of qualified majorities and confirmation by sub-national governments. In the United States, amendments can be valid only when "ratified by the Legislatures of three fourths of the several states, or by Conventions in three fourths thereof, as the one or the other Mode of Ratification may be proposed by the Congress" (Ibid., p. 113, the American Constitution, Article V). The only item beyond amendment is the right of state to have equal suffrage in the Senate unless it chooses otherwise. The Ethiopian Constitution applies the combination of qualified majority and sub-national governments' approval. Besides, the constitutional contents are categorized into two parts requiring different grades of majorities. The formal initiation of constitutional amendment takes place by a two-thirds majority vote in the House of Peoples' Representatives or in the House of the Federation. Similarly, one-third of the State Councils of the member states of the federation, by a majority vote in each Council can propose and initiate amendments (Proclamation No.1/1995, Article 104). As mentioned above, the first category that contains all rights and

freedoms specified in Chapter Three of the Constitution and Articles 104 and 105 needs to pass through a stringent process of amendment. The proposed amendment can be valid: a) When all State Councils, by a majority vote, approve the proposed amendment; b) When the House of Peoples' Representatives, by a two-thirds majority vote, approves the proposed amendment; and c) When the House of the Federation, by a two-thirds majority vote, approves the proposed amendment (Ibid., Article 105). The amendment process was made stringent in order to prevent any encroachment to the fundamental rights and freedoms. As the right of nations, nationalities and peoples, to self-determination is the corner stone of the Constitution, special care is taken to protect it from any easy alteration, which many believe would spell disaster to the unity of the country.

22. Ibid., Article 61(2).
23. Proclamation No. 532/2007, The Amended Electoral Law of Ethiopia, June 25, 2007 Article 20(b).
24. Ibid, Article 20(d).
25. See Todaro, Economic Development, 2000:16; see also Adelman and Cynthia Taft Morris, "Editorial: Development History and Its Implications for Development Theory", 1997: 831.
26. See Chapter Two.
27. See Chapter Three.
28. Ibid.
29. The Declaration on the Economic Policy of Socialist Ethiopia, Addis Ababa, February 7, 1975: 3 (in Amharic).
30. For detail discussion, see Chapter Three.
31. Hansson, the Ethiopian Economy, 1995: 25.
32. See Proclamation No. 76 of 1975 and other related directives.
33. See Hansson, 1995: 29-34; Kebede, 1992: 16-26.
34. See Chapter Three, Table 3.3.
35. Ibid., Table 3.4.
36. Ethiopia: Policy Framework Paper, 1992/93-1994/95, October 1992:2.
37. For further discussion on the ADLI, see Chapter Five.
38. See the World Bank, Memorandum of the President of the International Development Association to the Executive Directors on a Country Assistance Strategy of the World Bank Group for the Federal Democratic Republic of Ethiopia, August 19, 1997: 2.
39. The Enhanced Structural Adjustment Facility (ESAF) was renamed as the Poverty Reduction and Growth Facility (PRGF) on November 22, 1999. Under this Facility, programs based on country-owned poverty reduction strategies and adopted in participatory process involving civil society and development partners, are entitled to the support of international financial institutions and other development partners.

40. IMF, World Economic Outlook, April 1998: 50; see also UNECA, Economic Report on Africa 2002, 2002: 6.
41. See Chapter Eight.
42. UNECA, Economic Report on Africa 2002, 2002: 6.
43. The World Bank. African Development Indicators 2001, 2001: 15.
44. See Appendix, Table 1; according to UNECA's report the growth in the same period averaged 6 per cent (see UNECA, Economic Report on Africa 2002, 2002: 6).
45. The World Bank, Ethiopia Economic update, November 2012:1.
46. See National Bank of Ethiopia, Annual Report 2010/11, 2012.
47. World Development Indicators 2001, 2001: 134.
48. MoFED. Annual Report on Macroeconomic Development in Ethiopia, 2010/11:4.
49. MoFED, Economic Performance (2001/02 – 2011/12), 2013; see also National Bank of Ethiopia, Annual Report 2010/11, 2012.
50. It is only in 2011/12 that savings grew to about 10 per cent of GDP.
51. See Chapter Five, Industrial Production.
52. UNECA, Economic Report on Africa 2002, 2002: 35.
53. MoFED, Annual Report on Macroeconomic Development in Ethiopia, 2010/11:4.
54. See The Ethiopian Electric Power Corporation (EEPCO) Report, 2013.
55. The density figures include roads constructed under the universal Rural Road Access Program (URRAP).
56. FDRE. Ethiopian Roads Authority, Assessment of 14 years Performance of Road Sector Development Program, November 2011; See also Ethiopian Roads Authority, 2010/11 and 2011/12 Performance Report, August 2012.
57. Ethio-Telecom 2004 EFY (2011/12), Annual Performance Report, August 2012.
58. See Education Statistics: Annual Abstract, January 2005:2 and Education Statistics: Annual Abstract, September 2011:5.
59. See Education Statistics: Annual Abstract, September 2011: 5 and 25-28.
60. UNDP. Human Development Report 2001, 2001: 169; See also FDRE: HSDP IV Annual Performance Report, 2011/12, Ministry of Health, 2012:18.
61. FDRE, HSDP IV Annual Performance Report, 2011/12, Ministry of Health, 2012: 9-10.
62. UNDP. Human Development Report 2001, 2001:165.
63. HSDP IV, Annual performance Report, 2011/12, 2012: 26-28.
64. UNECA, Economic Report on Africa 2002, 2002: 6-7.
65. FDRE Ethiopia's progress Towards Eradicating Poverty: An Interim Report on Poverty Analysis Study(2010/11), MoFED, March 2012:7-10.

66. FDRE Growth and Transformation Plan 2010/11 – 2014/15, volume I, MoFED, November 2010: 22-27.
67. See Chapter Two.
68. Ibid.
69. See Chapter Three and Four.
70. See Chapter Three.
71. See Chapter Four.
72. For further discussion, see Ibid.
73. Ibid.
74. Stiglitz, Joseph E. Globalization and its Discontents, 2001: 31 – 32; Stiglitz argues that "the IMF had insisted on financial market liberalization, believing that competition among banks would lead to lower interest rates. The results were disastrous: the move was followed by the rapid growth of local and indigenous commercial banks, at a time when the banking legislation and bank supervision were inadequate, with predictable results- fourteen bank failures in Kenya in 1993 and 1994 alone. In the end, interest rates increased, not decreased" (Ibid.).
75. Ibid., p. 34; see Stiglitz's whole discussion on the differences and conflicts between Ethiopia and the IMF. It provides a good picture on the relationship between the powerful international institutions and poor sub-Saharan Africa nations (Ibid., p. 25-36).
76. The World Bank report states that the governments of the East Asian countries intervened "systematically and through multiple channels - to foster development, and in some cases the development of specific industries. Policy interventions took many forms: targeting and subsidizing credit to selected industries, keeping deposit rates low and maintaining ceilings on borrowing rates to increase profits and retained earnings, protecting domestic import substitutes, subsidizing declining industries, establishing and financially supporting government banks, making public investments in applied research, establishing firm- and industry-specific export targets, developing export marketing institutions, and sharing information widely between public and private sectors. Some industries were promoted, while others were not." (World Bank, the East Asian Miracle, 1993: 5-6; see also Ibid., p. 87-90).
77. Oyejide, "What can Sub-Saharan Africa Learn from the Taiwanese Development Experience?", in Thorbecke and Wan, Taiwan's Development Experience, 1999: 367.
78. Ibid., p. 377; see also Adelman's discussion on the qualities and policies of the Korean and Taiwanese governments that enabled them to achieve high and sustainable economic development (Adelman, "State and Market in Economic Development of Korea and Taiwan", in Thorbecke and Wan, 1999: 313-316).
79. Sorensen, Democracy and Democratization, 1993: 89.
80. Przeworski et. al., "What Makes Democracies Endure?", in Diamond and Plattner (eds.), 2001: 177.

Chapter 10

Concluding Remarks

The introduction to this book stated that the purpose of the study is to contribute to the general and continuing debate on the relationship between economic development and democracy by analysing the experience of Ethiopia under its last three regimes. The conclusions at the end of each chapter provide specific answers to the questions posed. This chapter has the purpose to summarize these conclusions and to draw some more general conclusions on the basis of the preceding chapters.

As in the case of many African countries, modern Ethiopia was created by expansion and conquest. Ethiopia's rulers expanded the empire of Abyssinia to the southeast and south by conquering many nationalities. They were also able to forge treaties with European colonialists which gave recognition to their conquest. Ethiopia itself was also a target for European conquest but managed to survive by defeating the Italians at Adwa and also by skilful diplomatic manoeuvring.

In the first half of the 20th Century the monarchy embarked on modernizing the country, initially to weaken the competing regional power centres and create a centralized country. However, the centralization went too far in denying the identity of the various nationalities, and the imposition of the Amhara culture brewed dissatisfaction and rebellion in some parts of the country. This was further compounded with the limited modernization steps, which neglected the countryside and avoided any reform to the monarchy itself. The government was not ready to introduce reforms to change the archaic land tenure system that created millions of poor landless peasants. Moreover, the Emperor chose to remain an absolute monarch with no check and balance on his powers. Even the parliament which was largely established in the first place for international image building purposes had little influence on the policies and decisions of the government. Such a half-hearted modernization drive failed to produce the intended development results. The failure to reform the political system and to change the oppressive land tenure system compounded with the war in Eritrea tarnished the image of the monarchy and expedited its demise.

The military government came to power in 1974 by exploiting the people's desire for a change and hope that it might bring them better political system and economic development. However, the government suspended the constitution and all freedoms and rights, and declared that its objective was to build Socialism. Starting from its early days in power, the government attempted to defeat the various nationalities' demands for self-rule, including the Eritrean demand for independence by force. Moreover, it waged a campaign called the "Red Terror" to quell urban opposition, which resulted in the deaths of thousands of people. The government attempted to bring the people to the point of submission and helplessness through brute force and intimidation.

It openly declared that private ownership was the source of misery and destitution, and embarked on the process of nationalization. It nationalized major production and financial establishments, and in some cases, small retails shops, restaurants and other small businesses. It abolished the land tenure system and provided the landless peasants with the rights to farm a plot of land, but built institutions to forcefully extract resources from the sector, denying small farmers any benefit from their new usufructuary rights. The command economy and slogan of "all to the war effort" exacerbated poverty and desolation in the country. At the end of the regime, the country was on the verge of disintegration and its coffers were literally bankrupt.

The 1991 London Conference agreement between the major liberation movements and the subsequent steps turned the development and economic situations around from their state of decline. The fear that the scenarios of Liberia and Somalia would be repeated evaporated when the EPRDF took power and positive changes, started to materialize. The July 1991 National Conference and the adoption of the National Charter signified the start of the democratization process. The acceptance of the right of nationalities to self-determination, up to and including secession, was a radical change in a country, where suppression of nationalist aspirations had been the norm. Moreover, the recognition of individual rights based on the 1948 Universal Declaration of Human Rights of the United Nations was a stark departure from the past.

Over 25 political organizations and groups participated in the Conference and then in the Council of Representatives that assumed the functions of a legislative organ. Despite their differences in various political issues, they managed to lead the transitional period in a relatively peaceful manner. The exception was when the OLF decided to withdraw from the government, and ordered its armed units to leave their camps. However, the government managed to contain the problem, and within a short time, the rebellion was suppressed.

Apart from internal forces, external forces also played a significant role in shaping the transitional period. For example, the EPLF had played a major role not only by agreeing to an orderly resolution of the Eritrean question through an internationally supervised referendum, but also contributed to the effort made to bring the OLF into the process even after the latter's withdrawal from the government in June 1992. The U.S administration was also instrumental in convening the London Conference which paved the way for the establishment of the Transitional Government. The major donor countries have promoted democratic transition not only by providing badly needed resources but also by encouraging the government to pursue a wide-range of reform programs. Similarly, the IMF and the World Bank have assisted in the implementation of the economic reform programs and stabilizing the economy. There has been an agreement on the general content of the reform programs, however, differences especially on timing, sequencing and pacing have had their impact on the process. Other external forces such as international NGOs have made their contribution to the process. Notwithstanding, the study does not contain detailed discussion and analysis of the role of the external forces as it is beyond the scope of this presentation. However, the subject matter is worthy of closer examination and another careful study.

One of the major objectives of the National Charter was the establishment of the Constitutional Commission, which was entrusted with leading the process of drafting and ratification of the federal constitution. The federal constitution has further enriched and deepened the reforms initiated by the Transitional Charter. It articulated fundamental freedoms and rights, the right of self-determination and the establishment of a federal structure based on the criteria of language, identity, and settlement patterns.

There have been efforts to carry out the democratic reforms envisaged in the National Charter and later in the federal constitution. Despite some shortcomings, the Ethiopian people have been able to exercise their rights more than any time in their history. Even so, further efforts have to be made to improve the political environment. Lack of democratic experience and the existence of extreme poverty are some of the impediments affecting the consolidation of democracy. This situation is, of course, aggravated by the infancy and feebleness of the existing democratic institutions. Democratic institutions should not only be strengthened and made effective but also efforts have to be made to expedite the establishment of new ones to enhance the democratization process.

The federal constitution confirmed and consolidated the devolution of power to the regional states started during the transitional period. It delegates various powers to the federal government and the residual powers rest in the hands of the member states. As discussed above, there have been major transfers of powers to the regional administration; however, the further devolution of powers to the lower levels of government has been relatively slow. It is only after a decade that the regional state constitutions were amended to empower the lower levels of government.

In terms of fiscal decentralization, the regional states are empowered to collect some of the revenues provided to them by the constitution, prepare their budgets, and carry out their development programs. However, the regional states are excessively dependent on the grants from the federal government. The major reason is the existence of narrow economic capacity but there are also obvious shortcomings in the effort of expanding and diversifying the tax base in the country. Currently even the federal government is primarily dependent on trade taxes.

With all their weaknesses, the democratic reforms have brought peace and stability to the country that has been damaged by decades of civil war. The proliferation of political groups and parties has contributed to the articulation of various interest. Similarly, the development of significant numbers of private newspapers, in spite of their unsatisfactory professionalism and quality, has made some contribution to the same purpose. Although critics of the constitution have argued that the recognition of self-determination is a recipe for, and first step to disintegration, the country has achieved reasonable internal stability and made visible strides in uniting the people. However, it would be too early to say that it is securely safe from the dangers of centrifugal forces.

Economic reforms have been carried out concomitant with the democratic process. The main purpose of the early economic reform program was the transformation of the command economy into a market-oriented one. The first step was the formulation of appropriate strategies and policies to guide the economic reform program. The transitional government adopted an economic policy in 1991, and this policy indicated the withdrawal of the State from monopolizing economic activities and the recognition of the private sector as the major driving force in the economic development endeavours of the country. It also served as a base for negotiations with the IMF to formulate an economic reform program reflected in the policy framework paper of 1992.

The other major step in this direction was the adoption of a long-term development strategy, the Agricultural Development-Led Industrialization (ADLI), in 1993. The strategy regards agriculture as a leading sector of the economy, which is expected to encourage growth in other sectors through interlinks. Ultimately, the strategy envisages bringing about economic structural transformation, in which the industrial sector will take over the leading role. The implementation of the strategy has been carried out through the formulation of sectoral strategies and successive five-year development programs.

The government's drive to bring about socioeconomic transformation has gained accelerated pace in the last nine years. The three year plan, the Sustainable

Development and Poverty Reduction Program (SDPRP), implemented between 2002/03 and 2004/05 and the subsequent five-year plan, the Plan for Accelerated and Sustained Development to End Poverty (PASDEP) achieved a double digit growth, which made Ethiopia one of the fastest growing countries in the world. Based on the experience of those plans and their implementation process as well as the disposition to move towards the structural transformation of the socioeconomic situation of the country, the government has introduced a very ambitious five year plan, the Growth and Transformation Plan (GTP), since 2010/11.

In the last two years, Ethiopia was able to again achieve double digit growth. However, enormous effort and dedication is required in the next three years to attain the planned rate of growth as the challenges are formidable. Apparently, the successful implementation of the GTP will serve the country as a spring board towards the start of the structural change of the economy. It will also enhance the ability of the country to achieve its long-term vision of joining the middle income countries' club in the next 10 to 12 years.

As discussed above, poverty reduction and food security will continue to be at the centre of the governments' economic development endeavours. As the overwhelming majority of the population lives in rural areas, brining structural change to the rural economy is the primary challenge. Introducing improved technologies and enhancing the capacity of the farmers to utilize them need to receive more and better attention. The weakness of the market and the scarcity of credit facilities available to the farming population have continued to affect the sector. The markets in the country are not yet integrated and farmers have not yet fully acquired the idea of producing in accordance with market demands.

The marketing system has to help farmers in their production decisions in order to earn better prices for their produces. Although the introduction of modern marketing system, the Ethiopia Commodity Exchange, is one step forward, it has to be supported at the grassroots level by strengthening the primary markets, and also organizing and consolidating cooperatives with the intention of making them the main actors in the modern marketing system besides their task of funnelling inputs, encouraging savings and also providing credit to the farmers. Eventually, the cooperatives' role has to be elevated to even investing in agro-processing projects to add value to the farmers' produces.

The industrial sector has shown reasonable improvement in the last decade. The investment environment has significantly improved and the privatization process continues, although its pace has been slower than expected. Despite its visible growth, the external sector has been affected by recurrent droughts and the extreme deterioration of the terms of trade. Ethiopia has not yet exploited its comparative advantage and is still dependent on a small number of agricultural commodities. The recent slump in world coffee prices strongly signals on-going balance of payments difficulties. The government and private sector's consultation and cooperation has to be enhanced and the institutionalization process has to continue to improve the country's capability to exploit the opportunities, and at the same time, to develop new sectors of the economy. The government's recent effort to develop industrial zones need to get better momentum. These zones will play a major role in attracting foreign investment to the country. Evidently, sustainable economic growth cannot be achieved without technological and industrial advancement and structural transformation of the economic sector. In addition, the government's major investments such as metallurgy and metal works, sugar industry, and fertilizer and chemical industry should be expedited as they are going to create major clusters of small and medium industries around them.

One of the major deficiencies affecting the performance of the economy has been the weakness of the infrastructure. The recent construction of extensive road network, which is almost bringing every corner of the country nearer to the feeder roads will significantly contribute to market integration and expedite other economic activities. The expansion of information and communication technology has started playing a visible role in supporting the socioeconomic transformation endeavour. By envisaging major increase of production in the next few years, the plan to expedite the railway system will help the country to reduce its transport costs, and as a result, products will have a better chance of competing in the global market. Evidently, a major task that still remains is the formulation of a competitive transport logistics ecosystem, which seems to lag behind. The recent activities to formulate one have to be expedited to go along with the fast growth the country is registering. On the other hand, significant strides have been made in the expansion of social services. Primary school enrolment has expanded from a dismal low to almost fulfilling the target in a short span of time. The secondary and higher education sectors are also gradually improving. The major task which is still expected to show significant change is the quality of education. The effort that is underway to improve the quality of education should continue to receive high attention. Evidently, the economy demands trained people with quality education. Similarly, the health sector coverage has shown impressive increase and the availability of services has registered commendable improvement. However, improvement of the availed services remains to be a major task. In addition, efforts have to be made to sustain the achievements gained through the health extension system by continuously nurturing the participation of the people.

The economy has substantially responded to economic reform and the implementation of development programs and plans. Apart from the deficiencies mentioned above, the country's low level human and material resources has also played a major role in slowing down the acceleration of change. The government has to focus on capacity building initiatives to improve human and institutional capabilities, which are vital instruments for expedited development results. Improvements in human and institutional capacity compounded with initiatives to improve physical infrastructure and allure material resources will create a better environment for further results in socioeconomic progress.

As discussed in Chapters Two and Eight, theorists have divergent views on the compatibility of democracy and economic development. While some argue the existence of a trade-off between democracy and economic development, others try to establish their compatibility in the socio-economic advancement endeavour. There appears to be no distinct consensus on the compatibility of democracy and economic development.

Ethiopia's experience regarding the two objectives has varied tremendously from regime to regime in the last century. The monarchy embarked on the modernization process but attempted to shield the rural society from its impact. It chose to remain an absolute monarchy with almost no tangible participation of the people in the business of government. There were nominal freedoms and rights provided by the constitution but were not intended to be invoked by any citizen. In the economic sphere, the government encouraged private investment but maintained the archaic land tenure system, which made millions of peasants landless and miserable. Hence, modernization with very little participation of the people, and market-oriented policies in urban centres mixed with unfavourable land tenure system was unable to bring the envisaged results, and gradually, eroded the base of the monarchy, resulting in its demise.

The military government that overthrew the monarchy espoused a neo-Marxist path of development to bring about radical changes to the Ethiopian economy and society. From the start, it banned all freedoms and rights of the people and was resolute in crushing any opposition by force. It killed thousands of people suspected of harbouring anti-government sentiment, and waged unrelenting military campaigns to destroy nationalist liberation movements. Its campaigns were designed to carry out scorched earth policies, and aerial bombardments intended to force the people into submission. Hence, the government not only disallowed any participation, rights and freedoms but was also determined to stay in power through intimidation and terror.

It also nationalized almost all major production and financial enterprises, and created a command economy. It discouraged private investment as its economic policy put private capital as the source of exploitation and misery. It abolished the oppressive land tenure system and allowed peasants to have usufructuary rights, but immediately built mechanisms and institutions to extract their produces. Moreover, whatever resource it managed to collect was wasted on waging war against its opponents. Eventually Ethiopians found themselves poorer than they were under the monarchy. The government's rule of terror combined with not only command economy but also with a war economy brought despicable poverty and desolation, and left the country on the verge of disintegration.

After 1991, the new government was destined to reverse the deteriorating political and economic situations in the country. It recognized the people's freedoms and rights, including self-determination up to and including secession. It opened the door for the people to participate at all levels of government and devolved power to lower levels of administrations to pave the way for the materialization of the right to self-rule. The federal constitution also contains significant elements of consociational democracy, creating the opportunity for minorities to be overrepresented in the legislative and executive organs.

Paul Henze who had followed closely developments in Ethiopia remarked that "Ethiopia's experience in establishing democracy in the 1990s is enlightening for both would be democrats and democratizers. In some ways, its present leaders' efforts to establish democracy have succeeded to a remarkable degree. The administrative structure of the country has been transformed, and a new form of government- ethnic federalism - has been adopted. The peasants who make up approximately 85 per cent of the population have been freed to make their own decisions about which crops to plant and when and where to sell their produce. In fact, Ethiopia's new leaders have been conducting one of today's more dramatic experiences in governance".[1] As discussed before, the changes that have taken place in the last two decades have instituted new relationship between the government and the people. As also discussed, it is a relatively new experiment in governance, which will require further refinement and elaboration.[2]

In the economic sphere, Ethiopia has embarked on economic reforms that were designed to transform the command economy into a market-oriented one. It has adopted the ADLI strategy, which transformed agriculture from a victim of extraction to a sector where a great part of the country's resources are invested to increase productivity and enable it encourage other sectors of the economy to respond positively. The policy also makes it clear that the country has to adopt export-oriented strategy to promote the country's competitiveness and integration to the global economy. In general, the economic reform program formulated with the cooperation of the IMF and the World Bank, which had been implemented prudently, had the major elements to develop a market-based economy.

In addition, since 2002 the development strategies and policies were further deepened, detailed and elaborated in order to accelerate the achievements gained in the first decade of the regime. Based on these strategies and policies, successive development plans targeted at reducing poverty were successfully implemented. The recently adopted which is in the middle of implementation, the Growth and Transformation Plan, is intended not only to result in impressive growth rates but also to serve as a spring board to induce the start of the socioeconomic structural changes. Besides, in the next 10 to 12 years, the country's vision is to ensure its ascendancy to the middle-income countries' club.

As a result of the prudent implementation of the economic reform program and the sectoral development programs, the economy has positively responded.[3] Ethiopia achieved an annual average growth rate of 5 per cent between 1992/93 and 2000/01. This achievement has been further enhanced and it has been able to grow in double digit rates for nine years, and it is well positioned to even grow in greater rates in the coming years.

With all its shortcomings, there is a visible compatibility between the democratization process and the economic development endeavours. The democratization process not only allowed and enhanced people's participation but also created relatively peaceful and stable internal conditions that have been conducive to economic progress. The economic policies, on the other hand, encouraged private investment and the emergent market-based economy, creating the ground for the consolidation of democracy. This situation has also been reinforced by the proliferation of political parties and groups, and the private press, which are usually expected to originate alternative ideas and positions.

The Ethiopian experience indicates that a country that was on the verge of collapse and disintegration in the early 1990s has been able to transform itself into a relatively peaceful country internally. As discussed above, the country has also performed economically way above the average for African countries. During the discussed period, as Stiglitz remarks "not only did Ethiopia have a sound macroeconomic framework but the World Bank had direct evidence of the competence of the government and its commitment to the poor".[4]

The democratization process has been helpful in establishing stability in the country. The implementation of democratic reforms with substantial elements of consociational democracy has contributed to building confidence and trust among the tens of nationalities in Ethiopia. As one of the fragmented populations in Africa, these consociational principles detailed by Lijphart have contributed to narrowing the rift between former competing and warring nationalities. The devolution of power and self-rule, overrepresentation of minorities in federal institutions, the power of minorities to exercise a veto on constitutional matters and grand coalition of government have paved the way for the environment of accommodation and cooperation to evolve. Although the system has to pass the test of time and various challenges, it provides some lessons to many African countries which have similar fragmented communities.

Poverty reduction initiatives have been given priority in Ethiopia's economic development endeavour. The rural-centred strategy was formulated to assist the fight against poverty for the mass of the population which happens to reside in the rural areas. This poverty has not only been an affront to human dignity but also a source of instability in Ethiopia. It is also a major obstacle thwarting the people from properly exercising their constitutionally provided freedoms and rights. The government's commitment to poverty reduction programs has been commendable and appreciated by the international financial institutions and donor countries. The experience of the implementation of these programs is providing valuable lessons on how to better tackle and reduce poverty.

For the democratization process and poverty reduction strategy to succeed, Ethiopia needs to strengthen its human and institutional capacities. The reform of the civil service has to be pursued to create a relatively efficient and transparent system. Moreover, the reform of law enforcement institutions has to be carried out more vigorously than before. Without achieving visible improvements in these institutions, especially in the judiciary and police force, it will be difficult to ensure and safeguard the human and political rights of the people. In addition, special attention has to be given to consolidate the Human Rights Commission and the Ombudsman to discharge their responsibilities and contribute to the development of democracy. Enhancing human and institutional capabilities of these institutions will continue to be critical in the effort to consolidate democracy in the country. Furthermore, the attention given to civic education in educational institutions has to be strengthened. Its contribution cannot be taken easily in a country where democracy is a new acquaintance.

From the Ethiopian experience, one can easily see that carrying out democratic transition concomitant with economic reforms has not been a matter of choice among alternatives. Without promoting democratic participation and carrying out devolution of power, it is difficult to see a peaceful and united country. On the other hand, poverty is not conducive to building democracy. As discussed above, poverty breeds discontent and frustration, and in the end, dictatorship. Hence, the country is obliged by the existing situations to carry out democratization process hand in hand with economic development. By doing so, it creates the general conditions for the consolidation of both endeavours and the so far experience indicates that there is a strong possibility of developing favourable environment in the country to achieve the intended objectives. The process is very difficult and uneven, and demands persistent and vigorous struggle. In this regard, Shihata rightly remarks that "as we come to accept that development is a costly and time-consuming process, fraught with ups and downs, we should be able to accept that the transition to democracy is also a complex process and we should not expect a country with no democratic history to convert overnight to a successful Western-style democracy. If such a miracle were to happen, it is likely to be short-lived. We should aim at a democracy which lasts, a sustainable democracy".[5]

However, experiences of the last few years indicate that internal peace and stability is not enough to promote development. Stable external relations, especially with neighbouring countries has a major impact on the country's socioeconomic performance. The border war with Eritrea wasted enormous human and material resources that could have been used to fight poverty. The signed agreements and the verdict of the Border Arbitration Commission,[6] how unjust and outrageous it may be, have to be used as instrument to normalize relations and build a peaceful environment in the border areas. Ethiopia has to close this chapter of its history and concentrate on its development agenda to defeat its worst enemy, poverty. Moreover, it is in its own interest to continue providing its indispensable contribution to peace and stability in Africa, especially in the Horn of Africa.

The Growth Report explains that five striking points emerge when the sustained and high growth of thirteen counties is analyzed. These points are: they fully exploited the world economy; maintained macroeconomic stability; mustered high rates of saving and investment; let markets allocate resources; and had committed, credible, and capable governments.[7] The fifth point, the role of the state, had a pivotal place in the much faster rate of growth and transformation achieved by the East Asian countries. The state, on one hand, had to invest in sectors highly essential to the development of the country as well as beyond the capabilities of the private sector, and on the other hand, continuously improved the business environment and provided the critical and multifaceted support to enable the private sector to play its role.

Evidently, the Ethiopian government has to pay attention to the experiences of those success stories and adopt them to Ethiopia's realities. On the one hand, it has the responsibly of filling the gap created by the existence of wide market failure and weaknesses of the fledgling private sector, and on the other hand, building conducive environment and providing the necessary support to enable the private sector to play its indispensable role. Accordingly, the government has, more than ever, to give proper attention to the creation and development of institutions, which contribute to expediting the crucial socio-economic structural changes. As discussed above, the building of an increasingly capable, credible and committed developmental state with democratic credentials is indispensable to the transformation of Ethiopia into a country that provides respectable livelihood to its citizens. Apparently, the Ethiopian experience of the last decade indicates that the future looks bright as long as it vigorously pursued its agenda of building democracy concomitant with economic development.

This study is far from being exhaustive in discussing all the factors affecting the political and economic transformation in Ethiopia. Moreover, the Ethiopian experience with democracy is only a few years old and it is a process in the making. It will be too early to conclude the outcome altogether as it will take decades to prove itself beyond doubt. Further and periodic research is needed to look into the interaction of democracy and economic development as the situation unfolds in the future.

Notes

1. Henze, "Is Ethiopia Democratic? A Political Success Story", *Journal of Democracy*, vol. 9, no. 4, October 1998: 41.
2. For further details, see Chapter six.
3. Ethiopia has been designated as one of the strong performers by the IMF (see IMF, World Economic Outlook, April 1998, Vol. 1, p. 50).
4. Stiglitz, *Globalization and Its Discontents*, 2002: 28.
5. Shihata, "Democracy and Economic Development", International and Comparative *Law Quarterly*, vol. 46, July 1997: 638.
6. See Agreement between the Government of the Federal Democratic Republic of Ethiopia and the Government of the State of Eritrea, December 12, 2000; and Eritrea-Ethiopia Boundary Commission Decision: Regarding Delimitation of the Border between the State of Eritrea and the Federal Democratic Republic of Ethiopia, April 13, 2002.
7. The World Bank. The Growth Report, 2008:19-28.

Bibliography

Addona, A.F. *The Organisation of African Unity*. Cleveland and New York: The World Publishing Company, 1969.

Adelman, Irma. "Beyond Export-Led Growth", World Development, 1984, 12, 9, p. 937-949.

Adelman, Irma. *Institutions and Development Strategies: The Selected Essays of Irma Adelman*, Vol.I. Aldershot: Edward Elgar, 1995.

Adelman, Irma and Cynthia Taft Morris. "Editorial: Development History and Its Implications for Development Theory", World Development, 25 (6), 1997, p. 831-40.

Ake, Claude. *Democracy and Development in Africa*. Washington D.C: The Brookings Institution, 1996.

Almond, G. and G. B. Powell, *Comparative Politics: System, Process and Policy*. Boston: Little Brown, 1978.

Ambrose, Brendalyn P. *Democratization and the Protection of Human Rights in Africa: Problems and Prospects*. Westport and London: Praeger Publishers, 1995.

Amin, Samir. *Accumulation on a World Scale: A Critical of the Theory of Underdevelopment*. New York and London: Monthly Review Press, 1974.

Amsden, Alice H. *Asia's Next Giant: South Korea and Late Industrialisation*. New York and Oxford: Oxford University Press, 1989.

Annan, Kofi A. *We the Peoples: The Role of the United Nations in the 21st Century*, United Nations,2000.

Bagchi, Amiya Kumar. *Democracy and Development: Proceedings of the IEA Conference held in Barcelona, Spain*. New York: St. Martin's Press, 1995.

Balassa, B." 'Exports and Economic Growth", Journal of Development Economics, 5, 1978, p. 181-9.

Barro, Robert J., "Democracy and Economic Growth", Journal of Economic Growth, 1, March 1996, p. 1-27.

Barro, Robert J. *Determinants of Economic Growth: A Cross-Country Empirical Study*. Cambridge, Massachusetts and London: The MIT Press, 1997.

Bauer, P.T. and B.S. Yamey.*The Economics of Underdeveloped Countries*.Cambridge University Press, 1959.

Bauzon, Kenneth E. *Development and Democratization in the Third World: Myths, Hopes and Realities*. Washington, D.C.: Crane Russak, 1992.

Bennett, A. LeRoy. *International Organizations: Principles and Issues*, 5th edition. Eaglewood Cliffs: Prentice Hall, 1991.

Bennett, Jon (ed.). *Meeting Needs: NGO Co-ordination in Practice*. London: Earthscan Publications, 1995.

Berg-Schlosser, Dirk. "Africa Political Systems: Typology and Performance", Comparative Politics Studies, 1984, 17, 1, p. 121-151.

Birch, Anthony H. *The Concepts and Theories of Modern Democracy*. London and New York: Routledge, 1993.

Blomstrom, Magnus and Bjorn Hettne.*Development Theory in Transition: The Dependency Debateand Beyond*. London: Zed Books, 1984.

Boadway, Robin, Sandra Roberts and Anwar Shah.*The Reform of Fiscal Systems in Developing and Emerging Market Economics: A Federalism Perspective*. World Bank Policy Research Working Paper 1259, February 1994.

Bogdanor, Vernon (ed.). *Constitutions in Democratic Politics*. Aldershot: Gower, 1988.

Bogdanor, Vernon and David Butler (ed.). *Democracy and Elections: Electoral Systems and Their Political Consequences*. New York: Cambridge University Press, 1983.

Bollen, Kenneth A. "Issues in the Comparative Measurement of Political Democracy", America Sociological Review, 1980, 45, June, 370-390.

Bulcha, Mekuria. *Flight and Integration: Causes of Mass Exodus from Ethiopia and Problems of Integration in the Sudan*. Uppsala: Scandinavian Institute of African Studies, 1988.

Burkhart. Ross E. and Michael S. Lewis-Beck, "Comparative Democracy: The Economic Development Thesis", American Political Science Review, Vol. 88, No. 4, December 1994, p. 903-910.

Callaghy, Thomas M. and John Ravenhill (eds.). *Hemmed In: Responses to Africa's Economic Decline*. New York: Columbia University Press, 1993.

Calvert, H. *British Constitutional Law*. London: Blackstone Press, 1985.

Cappelli, Vanni. "The Oromo of Ethiopia- Africa's Nation Manqué". Horn of Africa, Vol. XV, Numbers 1,2,3,4, December 1997, p. 81-91.

Cassese, Antonio. *Self-determination of Peoples: A Legal Reappraisal*. Cambridge: Cambridge University Press, 1995.

Chang, Ha-Joon. *Bad Samaritans: The Myth of Free Trade and the Secret History of Capitalism*. New York: Bloomsbury Press, 2008.

Chole, Eshetu. *The Ethiopian Economy: An Overview*. Geneva: International Institute for Relief and Development, 1988.

Clapham, Christopher. *Haile Selassie's Government*. London: Longman, 1970.

Clapham, Christopher. *Transformation and Continuity in Revolutionary Ethiopia*. Cambridge: Cambridge University Press, 1988.

Clapham, C. "Constitutions and Governance in Ethiopian Political History", in Constitutionalism: Reflections and Recommendations, Symposium on the Making of the New Ethiopian Constitution, May 17-21, 1993, p.29-39.

Clark, Donald and Robert Williamson (eds.). *Self-Determination: International Perspectives*. Houndmills, Hampshire and London: Macmillan Press Ltd., 1996.

Cohen, Herman J. The Political Crisis in Ethiopia and the Role of the United States, Statement to the Sub Committee on Africa of the Committee on Foreign Affairs, House of Representatives, June 18, 1991.

Cohen, Herman J. *Intervening in Africa: Superpower Peacemaking in a Troubled Continent*. Houndmills, Hampshire and London: Macmillan Press Ltd., 2000.

Cooding, Jr., G. A. *The Federal Government of Switzerland*. Boston: Houghton Mifflin Company, 1961.

Crawford, James, "Democracy and International Law", British Yearbook of International Law, 1994, p. 113-133.

Daalder, Hans. "The Consociational Democracy Theme", World Politics, 1974, 26, July, p. 604-621.

Dahl, Robert A. *Polyarchy: Participation and Opposition*. New Haven and London: Yale University Press, 1971.

Dahl, Robert A. *Democracy and Its Critics*. New Haven and London: Yale University Press, 1989.

Dahl, Robert A. *Modern Political Analysis,* 5th edition. New Jersey: Yale University, 1991.

Demeke, Mulat and Tassew Woldehanna (eds.). *Explaining Economic Growth and Development in Ethiopia*, Proceedings of the 10th Annual Conference on the Ethiopian Economy November 3-5,2000, Addis Ababa, November 2001.

Dessalegn, Gebremeskel et. al. Market Structure, Conduct, and Performance: Constraints on Performance of Ethiopian Grain Markets, Grain Market Research Project, MEDaC, Addis Ababa, January 1998 (manuscript).

De Villiers, Bertus (ed.). *Evaluating Federal Systems*. Dordrecht: Martinus Nijhoff Publishers, 1994.

De Waal, Alex. *Evil Days: 30 Years of War and Famine in Ethiopia*. New York: Human Rights Watch, 1991.

De Waal, Alex. *Famine Crimes: Politics and the Disaster Relief Industry in Africa*. Oxford: James Currey, 1997.

Diamond, Larry. Class, *Ethnicity, and Democracy in Nigeria*. London: Macmillan Press, 1988.

Diamond, Larry, Juan J. Linz and Seymour M. Lipset. (eds.) *Democracy in Developing Countries: Africa,* Vol II. Boulder and London: Rienner Publishers and Adamantine Press Ltd., 1988.

Diamond, Larry. "Beyond Authoritarianism and Totalitarianism: Strategies for Democratisation". The Washington Quarterly, 1989, 12, 1, p. 121-163.

Diamond, Larry. *The Democratic Revolution: Struggles for Freedom and Pluralism in the Developing World*. New York: Freedom House, 1992.

Diamond, Larry (eds.). *Political Culture and Democracy in Developing Countries*. Boulder and London: Lynne Rienner Publishers, 1993.

Diamond, Larry and Marc F. Plattner (eds.). *Economic Reform and Democracy*. Baltimore and London: The Johns Hopkins University Press, 1995.

Diamond, Larry, Juan J. Linz and Seymour M. Lipset (eds.). *Politics in Developing Countries: Comparing Experiences with Democracy*, 2nd edition. Boulder and London: Lynne Rienner Publishers, 1995.

Diamond, Larry and M. F. Plattner (eds.). *The Global Resurgence of Democracy*, 2nd edition. Baltimore and London: The Johns Hopkins University Press, 1996.

Diamond, Larry. *Developing Democracy: Toward Consolidation*. Baltimore and London: The Johns Hopkins University Press, 1999.

Diamond, Larry and Marc F. Plattner (eds.). *The Global Divergence of Democracies*. Baltimore and London: The Johns Hopkins University Press, 2001.

Dicey, A. V.*An Introduction to the Study of the Law of Constitution*, 10th edition. Basingstoke and London: Macmillan, 1959.

Dick, G.William, "Authoritarian Versus Nonauthoritarian Approaches to Economic Development", Journal of Political Economy, 1974, 82, 4, p. 817- 827.

Donnelly, Jack. *Universal Human Rights in Theory and Practice*. Ithaca and London: Cornell University Press, 1989.

Doornbos, M. et. al. (eds.). *Beyond Conflict in the Horn: The Prospects of Peace, Recovery, and Development in Ethiopia, Somalia, Eritrea and Sudan*. London: James Currey Ltd., 1992.

Dritz, N. J. (ed.). *Transitional Justice: How Emerging Democracies Reckon with Former Regimes*, Vol. I, II & III. Washington D.C: United Institute of Peace, 1995.

Economic and Social Commission for West Asia.*The Role of Foreign Direct Investment in Economic Development in ESCWA Member Countries*. New York: United Nations, 2000.

Eicher, Carl K. and John M. Staatz (eds.). *International Agricultural Development*, 3rd edition. Baltimore and London: The Johns Hopkins University Press, 1998.

Eide, Asbjorn and Bernt Hagtvet (eds.). *Human Rights in Perspective: A Global Assessment*. Oxford: Blackwell Publishers, 1992.

Elazar, Daniel J. "Federalism", in Sills, David L. (ed.), *International Encyclopaedia of Social Sciences,* Vol. 5. New York: The Macmillan Company &The Free Press, 1972, p. 353-367.

Elazar, Daniel J. *Exploring Federalism*. Tuscaloosa: University of Alabama Press, 1987.

Elazar, Daniel J. "International and Comparative Federalism". PS Political Science and Politics, 26,2, June 1993, p. 190-195.

Epstein, Leon D. *Political Parties in Western Democracies*. New Brunswick and London: Transaction Books, 1982.

Erlich, Haggai. *Ethiopia and the Challenge of Independence.* Boulder: Lynne Rienner Publishers, 1986.

FDRE.Growth and Transformation Plan 2010/11- 2014/15, Volume I, Main Text, Ministry of Finance and Economic Development, November 2010, Addis Ababa.

Finer, S. E. *Comparative Government.* Harmondsworth, Middlesex: Penguin Books, 1978.

Finer, S. E. Five *Constitutions: Contrasts and Comparisons.* Harmondsworth, Middlesex: Penguin Books, 1979.

Finer, S. E., Vernon Bogdanor and Bernard Rudden.*Comparing Constitutions.* Oxford: Clarendon Press, 1995.

Fitzgerald, Robert (ed.). *The State and Economic Development: Lessons from the Far East.* London: Frank Cass, 1995.

Flex, David. "Import Substitution and Late Industrialisation: Latin America and Asia Compared", in Adelman and Thorbecke (eds.), World Development, 17 (9), 1989, p. 1455- 69.

Franck, Thomas M., "The Emerging Right to Democratic Governance", The American Journal of International Law, Vol. 86, 1992, p. 46-91.

Frank, Andre Gunder, *Capitalism and Underdevelopment in Latin America: Historical Studies of Chile and Brazil.* New York and London: Monthly Review Press, 1969.

Fukui, Katsuyoshi and John Markakis (ed.). *Ethnicity and Conflict in the Horn of Africa.* London: James Currey, 1994.

Fukuyama, Francis. *The End of History and the Last Man.* London: Penguin Books, 1992.

Furley, Oliver (ed.). *Conflict in Africa.* London and New York: I.B. Tauris Publishers, 1995.

Furtado, C. *Development and Underdevelopment.* Berkeley and Los Angeles: University of California Press, 1964.

Galenson, Water (ed.). *Labour and Economic Development.* New York: John Wiley & Sons, Inc., 1959.

Gersovitz, M. et. al. (eds.). *The Theory and Experience of Economic Development.* London: Allen and Unwin, 1982.

Ghai, Yashi, "Human Rights and Governance: The Asia Debate", Australian Year Book of International Law, 15, 1994, p. 1-34.

Gorman, Robert F. *Political Conflict on the Horn of Africa.* New York: Praeger, 1981.

Greenberg, Douglas et al., (ed.). *Constitutionalism and Democracy: Transitions in the Contemporary World.* New York and Oxford: Oxford University Press, 1993.

Griffin, Keith. *The Economy of Ethiopia.* New York: St. Martin's Press, 1992.

Gupta, Sanjeev et. al., *Ethiopia: Issues in Intergovernmental Fiscal Relations.* International Monetary Fund, January 1996.

Gurdon, Charles. *The Horn of Africa.* London: UCL Press Limited, 1994.

Habte Selassie, Bereket. *Conflict and Intervention in the Horn of Africa*. New York and London: Monthly Review Press, 1980.

Habte Selassie, Bereket. *Eritrea and the United Nations and Other Essays*. Trenton, NJ: The Red Sea Press, Inc., 1989.

Hadenius, Axel (ed.). *Democracy's Victory and Crisis*, Nobel Symposium No. 93. Cambridge: Cambridge University Press, 1997.

Hadjimichael, Michael T. et. al. *Sub-Saharan Africa: Growth, Savings, and Investment, 1986-93*. Washington D. C., IMF, January 1995.

Halliday, Fred and Maxine Molyneux.*The Ethiopian Revolution*. London: Verso Editions, 1981.

Hannum, Hurst (ed.). *Guide to International Human Rights Practice*, 2nd edition. Philadelphia: University of Pennsylvania Press, 1992.

Hannum, Hurst. *Autonomy, Sovereignty and Self-determination: The Accommodation of Conflicting Rights*, Revised Edition. Philadelphia: University of Pennsylvania Press, 1996.

Hansson, Gote. *The Ethiopian Economy 1974-94: Ethiopia Tikdem and After*. London and New York: Routledge, 1995.

Harbeson, John W. *The Ethiopian Transformation: The Quest for the Post-Imperial State*. Boulder and London: Westview Press, 1988.

Havnevik, Kjell J. (ed.) *The IMF and The World Bank in Africa: Conditionality, Impact and Alternatives*. Uppsala: Scandinavian Institute of African Studies, 1987.

Hayek, F. A. *Law, Legislation and Liberty, Vol. 3: The Political Order of a Free People*. London: Routledge and Kegan Paul, 1979.

Healey, J. and Mark Robinson.*Democracy, Governance and Economic Policy: Sub-Saharan Africa in Comparative Perspective*. London: The Overseas Development Institute, 1992.

Helleiner, G. K. "The IMF, The World Bank and Africa's Adjustment and External Debt Problems: An Unofficial View", World Development, Vol. 20, No. 6, 1992, p. 779-792.

Henze, Paul B. *The Horn of Africa: From War to Peace*. London: Macmillan, 1991.

Henze, Paul B., "Is Ethiopia Democratic? A Political Success Story", Journal of Democracy, Vol. 9, No. 4, 1998, p. 40-54.

Henze, Paul B. *Layers of Time: A History of Ethiopia*. London: Hurst and Company, 2000.

Himmelstrand, Ulf, Karibu Kinyanjui and Edward Mburugu.*African Perspectives on Development: Controversies, Dilemmas and Openings*. New York: St. Martin's Press, 1994.

Howell, P. P. and J. A. Allan (eds.). *The Nile: Sharing a Scarce Resource-An historical and Technical Review of Water Management and of Economical and Legal Issues*. Cambridge: Cambridge University Press, 1994.

Hueglin, T. "Legitimacy, Democracy, and Federalism", in H. Bavkis and W. Chandler (eds.), *Federalism and the Role of State*. Toronto: University of Toronto Press, 1987.

Hunt, Diana. *Economic Theories of Development: An Analysis of Competing Paradigms*. London: Harvester Wheatsheaf, 1989.

Huntington, Samuel P. *Political Order in Changing Societies*. New Haven and London: Yale University Press, 1968.

Huntington, Samuel P. and Jorge I. Dominguez, "Political Development", in Greenstein, Fred I. and Nelson W. Polsby (eds.), *Handbook of Political Science: Macropolitical Theory*, Vol.3. Reading, Massachusetts: Addison-Wesley Publishing Company, 1975, p. 1-114.

Huntington, Samuel P. and Joan M. Nelson.*No Easy Choice: Political Participation in Developing Countries*. Cambridge, Massachusetts and London: Harvard University Press, 1976.

Huntington, Samuel P. "Will More Countries Become Democratic?", Political Science Quarterly, 1984, 99, 2, p. 193-218.

Huntington, S. P. *The Third Wave: Democratization in the Late Twentieth Century*. Norman and London: The University Oklahoma Press, 1991.

Huntington, Samuel P. Challenges Facing Democracy: What Cost Freedom? Current, 1993, p. 22-27.

Huntington, Samuel P. *The Clash of Civilizations and the Remaking of World Order*. New York: Simon and Schuster, 1996.

IMF. *Ethiopia: Recent Economic Developments*, Washington D.C, 1988.

IMF. *World Economic Outlook*, Washington D.C, May 1999.

Iyob, Ruth. *The Eritrean Struggle for Independence: Domination, Resistance, Nationalism, 1941-1993*. Cambridge: Cambridge University Press, 1995.

Jackson, R. H. and C. G. Rosberg.*Personal Rule in Black Africa: Prince, Autocrat, Prophet, Tyrant*. Berkeley CA: University of California Press, 1982.

Jacquin-Berdal and Martin Plaut (ed.). Unfinished Business: Ethiopia and Eritrea at War. The Red Sea Press, Inc., 2004.

Jalata, Asafa. *Oromia and Ethiopia: State Formation and Ethno-national Conflict, 1868-1992*. Boulder and London: Lynne Rienner Publishers, 1993.

Jalata, Asafa (ed.). *Oromo Nationalism and the Ethiopian Discourse: The Search for Freedom and Democracy*. Lawrenceville: The Red Sea Press, Inc., 1998.

Kamrava, Meharan. *Politics and Society in the Third World*. London and New York, Routledge, 1993.

Kapuscinski, Ryszard. *The Emperor: The Downfall of an Autocracy*. London and New York: Quartet Books Limited, 1983.

Karl, Tery Lynn. "Dilemmas of Democratization in Latin America", Comparative Politics, 23, October 1990, p. 1-21.

Kassa, Belay. "Instability of Ethiopia's Export Earnings: The Contribution of Major Agricultural Export Commodities", Ethiopian Journal of Agricultural Economics, Vol. 2, No. 1, January 1998,p. 27-54.

Kebbede, Girma. *The State and Development in Ethiopia.* New Jersey and London: Humanities Press, 1992.

Keller, Edmond J. "Ethiopia: Revolution, Class and the National Question", African Affairs, 80, 1981, p. 519-49.

Keller, Edmond J. *Revolutionary Ethiopia: From Empire to People's Republic.* Bloomington: Indiana University Press, 1988.

Keller, Edmond J. "Revolution and the Collapse of Tradition Monarchies: Ethiopia" in Schutz and Slater, *Revolution and Political Change in the Third World*, Boulder: Lynne Rienner Publishers, 1990, p. 81-98.

Kello, Abdulhamid Bedri (ed.). *Privatisation and Public Enterprise Reform in Ethiopia.* Addis Ababa: Ethiopian Economic Association, 1994.

King, Preston. *Federalism and Federation.* London and Canberra: Croom Helm, 1982.

Kirkpatrick, C. H., N. Lee and F. I. Nixson (eds.). *Industrial Structure and Policy in Less Developed Countries.* London: George Allen and Unwin, 1984.

Kitching, Gavin. *Rethinking Socialism.* London and New York: Methuen, 1983.

Korn, David A. *Ethiopia, the United States and the Soviet Union.* London and Sidney: Croom Helm, 1986.

Krys, Roman. "The Right of Peoples to Self-Determination", Revue de droit International, Vol. 63, 1985, p. 289-307.

Landau, Daniel, "Government and Economic Growth in the Less Developed Countries: An Empirical Study for 1960-1980", Economic Development and Cultural Change, Vol. 35, No. 1, October 1986, p. 35-75.

Lane, Jan-Erik.*Constitutions and Political Theory.* Manchester and New York: Manchester University Press, 1996.

Larkins, Christopher M. "Judicial Independence and Democratisation: A Theoretical and Conceptual Analysis", The American Journal of Comparative Law, Vol. 44, 1996, p. 605-626.

Lefort, Rene. *Ethiopia: An Heretical Revolution?* London: Zed Press, 1983.

Legum, Colin. *Ethiopia: The Fall of Haile Selassie's Empire.* New York: Africana Publishing Company, 1975.

Lehmbruch, Gerhard. "Consociational Democracy in the International System", European Journal of Political Research, 1975, 3, p. 377-391.

Lehner, Franz. "Consociational Democracy in Switzerland: A Political-Economic Explanation and Some Empirical Evidence", European Journal of Political Research, 1984, 12, p. 25-42.

Lensink, Robert. *Structural Adjustment in Sub-Saharan Africa.* London and New York: Longman, 1996.

Lerner, D. *The Passing of Traditional Society: Modernizing the Middle East*. Glencoe, The Free Press, 1958.

Levine, Donald. *Greater Ethiopia: The Evolutions of a Multi-ethnic Society*, 2nd edition. Chicago: Chicago University Press, 2000.

Lewis, John P. and Valeriana Kallab (eds.). *Development Strategies Reconsidered*. Brunswick and Oxford: Transition Books, 1986.

Lijphart, Arend. "Consociational Democracy", World Politics, 1969, 21, 2, January, p. 207-225.

Lijphart, Arend. *The Politics of Accommodation: Pluralism and Democracy in the Netherlands*, 2ndedition. Berkeley, Los Angeles, London: University of California Press, 1975.

Lijphart, Arend. "Consociation and Federation: Conceptual and Emprical Links", *Canadian Journal of Political Science*, 1979, 12, 3, p. 499-515.

Lijphart, Arend. *Democracy in Plural Societies: A Comparative Exploration*. New Haven and London: Yale University Press, 1980.

Lijphart, Arend. "Consociational Theory: Problems and Prospects", Comparative Politics, 1981, April, p. 355-360.

Lijphart, Arend. "Advances in the Comparative Study of Electoral Systems", World Politics, April 1984, 36, 3, p. 424-436.

Lijphart, Arend. *Democracies: Patterns of Majoritarian and Consensus Government in Twenty-One Countries*. New Haven and London: Yale University Press, 1984.

Lijphart, Arend. "The Puzzle of Indian Democracy: A Consociational Interpretation", American Political Science Review, 1996, 90, 2, p. 258-268.

Lin, Justin Yifu. *The Quest for Prosperity: How Developing Economies Can Take Off*. New Jersey and London: Princeton University Press, 2012.

Linz, Juan J. and Alfred Stepan. *The Breakdown of Democratic Regimes*. Baltimore and London: The Johns Hopkins University Press, 1978.

Linz, Juan. "Transition to Democracy", Washington Quarterly, Vol. 13, No. 3, 1990, p. 143-164.

Lipset, Seymour Martin. "Some Social Requisites of Democracy: Economic Development and Political Legitimacy", The American Political Science Review, 1959, 53, 1, p. 69-105.

Lipset, Seymour Martin. *Political Man: the Social Bases of Politics*. Baltimore: The John Hopkins University Press, 1981.

Lipset, Seymour Martin. "The Social Requisites of Democracy Revisited", American Sociological Review, Vol. 59, No. 1, February 1994, p. 1-22.

Little, I.M.D. *Economic Development: Theory, Policy and International Relations*. New York: BasicBooks, 1982.

Mahbubani, Kishore. *Can Asians Think?* Singapore: Times Books International, 1998.

Makinda, Samuel M. *Superpower Diplomacy in the Horn of Africa*. London and Sidney: Croom Helm, 1987.

Malanczuk, Peter, "Minorities and Self-Determination: Reflections on International Law in General, Including Some Recent Developments in Ethiopia", in Neri Sybesma-Knol en Jef Van Bellingen (eds.), *Naar een nieuwe interpretatie van het Recht op Zelfbeschikking?*, Vubpress, 1995, p. 169-193.

Malanczuk, Peter. *Akehurst's Modern Introduction to International Law*, 7th revised edition. London: Routledge, 1997.

Malanczuk, Peter. The Universality of Human Rights and Differences in Asian and European Values from the Perspective of International Law, Paper for the Informal ASEM Human Rights Seminar, Beijing, 28-29 June, 1999 (manuscript).

Marcus, Harold G. *Ethiopia, Great Britain, and the USA 1941-74*. Los Angeles: University of California Press, 1983.

Marcus, Harold G. *A History of Ethiopia*. London: University of California Press, 1994.

Marcus, Harold G. *The Life and Times of Menelik II: Ethiopia 1844-1913*. Lawrenceville, NJ: The Red Sea Press, 1995.

Marcus, Harold G. *Haile Selassie I: The Formative Years 1892-1936*. Lawrenceville, NJ: The Red Sea Press, 1996.

Markakis, John and Nega Ayele.*Class and Revolution in Ethiopia*. Trenton, NJ: The Red Sea Press, 1986.

Markakis, John. *National and Class Conflict in the Horn of Africa*. Cambridge: Cambridge University Press, 1987.

Markakis, John. *Resource Conflict in the Horn of Africa*. London: SAGE Publications, 1998.

Marsh, R. M. "Does Democracy Hinder Economic Development in the Latecomer Developing Nations", Comparative Social Research, 1979, 2, p. 215-48.

Marte, Fred. *Political Cycles in International Relations: The Cold War and Africa, 1945-1990*. Amsterdam: VU University Press, 1994.

McClintock, Cynthia. "The Prospects for Democratic Consolidation in a "Least Likely" Case: Peru", Comparative Politics, 1989, 21, January, p. 127-148.

McDonald, Ronald H. and J. Mark Ruhl.*Party Politics and Elections in Latin America*. Boulder and London: Westview Press, 1989.

MEDaC.*Survey of the Ethiopian Economy, Review of Post-Reform Developments (1992/93-1997/98)*, September 1999.

Mellor, John W. *The New Economics of Growth: A Strategy for India and the Developing World*. Ithaca and London: Cornell University Press, 1976.

Mellor and Johnston, "The World Food Equation: Interrelations among Development, Employment,and Food Consumption", Journal of Economic Literature, 22, 1984, p. 567-668.

Mellor, John W. (ed.). *Agriculture on the Road to Industrialisation*. Baltimore and London: The Johns Hopkins University Press, 1995.

Menon, P. K. "The Right to Self-Determination: A Historical Appraisal", Revue de droit International, Vol. 53, 1975, p. 183-200.

Monshipouri, Mahmood. *Democratization, Liberalisation and Human Rights in the Third World*. Boulder and London: Lynne Rienner Publishers, 1995.

Montesquieu, C. de S. *The Sprit of the Laws*. New York: Cambridge University Press, 1989.

Moore, Jr. Barrington. *Social Origins of Dictatorship and Democracy*. Harmondsworth: Penguin Books, 1977.

Musgrave, Richard A. and Peggy B. Musgrave.*Public Finance in Theory and Practice*, 5th edition, New York: McGraw-Hill, Inc., 1989.

Musgrave, Thomas D. *Self-Determination and National Minorities*. Oxford: Clarendon Press, 1997.

Negash, Tekeste. *Eritrea and Ethiopia: The Federal Experience*. Uppsala: Nordiska Afrikainstitutet, 1997.

Negash, Tekeste and Kjetil Tronvoll. Brothers at War: Making Sense of the Eritrea-Ethiopia War. James Curry Ltd, 2000.

Neubauer, Deane E. "Some Conditions of Democracy", American Political Science Review, 1967, 61, 4, p. 1002-9.

Oates, Wallace E. *Fiscal Federalism*. Aldershot: Gregg Revivals, 1993.

Oates, Wallace E.(ed.). *The Economics of Fiscal Federalism and Local Finance*. Cheltenham, UK: Edward Elgar Publishing Limited, 1998.

Ottaway, Marina.*Soviet and American Influence in the Horn of Africa*. New York: Praeger, 1982.

Ottaway, Marina (ed.). *The Political Economy of Ethiopia*. New York: Praeger, 1990.

Ottaway, Marina (ed.). *Democracy in Africa: The Hard Road Ahead*. Boulder and London: Lynne Rienner Publishers, 1997.

Oyugi, W. O. , E. S. A. Odhiambo, M. Chege and A. K. Gitonga. *Democratic Theory and Practice in Africa*. Portsmouth and London: Heinemann and James Currey, 1988.

Pateman, Carole. *Participation and Democratic Theory*. London: Cambridge University Press, 1970.

Pausewang, Siegfried et al. (ed.). *Ethiopia: Rural Development Options*. London and New Jersey: Zed Books Ltd., 1990.

Perham, Margery. *The Government of Ethiopia*. London: Faber and Faber Ltd., 1969.

Pickett, James. *Economic Development in Ethiopia: Agriculture, the Market and the State*. Paris: OECD, 1991.

Preston, P. W. *Theories of Development*. London, Boston, Melbourne and Henley: Routledge and Kegan Paul, 1982.

Prouty, Chris. *Empress Taytu and Menilek II: Ethiopia 1883-1910*. Trenton, NJ: The Red Sea Press, 1986.

Przetacznik, Frank. "The Basic Collective Human Right to Self-Determination of Peoples and Nations as a Prerequisite for Peace: Its Philosophical Background and Practical Application", Revue de Droit International, Vol. 69, 1991, p. 259-317.

Przeworski, Adam. *Democracy and the Market: Political and Economic Reforms in Eastern Europe and Latin America*. Cambridge: Cambridge University Press, 1991.

Przeworski, Adam, Michael E. Alvarez, Jose Antonio Cheibub and Fernando Limongi. *Democracy and Development: Political Institutions and Well-Being in the World, 1950-1990*. Cambridge: Cambridge University Press, 2000.

Putnam, Robert D. *Making Democracy Work: Civic Traditions in Modern Italy*. Princeton: Princeton University Press, 1993.

Riker, William H. *Federalism: Origin, Operation, Significance*. Boston and Toronto: Little, Brown and Co., 1964, p. 93-172.

Riker, William H., "Federalism", in Fred I. Greenstein and Nelson W. Polsby (eds.). *Handbook of Political Science, Vol. 5: Governmental Institutions and Processes*. Reading, Mass: Addison-Wesley, 1975, p. 93-172.

Rao, Vaman, "Democracy and Economic Development", Studies in Comparative International Development, 1984, 19, 4, p. 67-81.

Rosas, Allan and Jan Helgesen.*The Strength of Diversity: Human Rights and Pluralist Democracy*. Dordrecht: Martinus Nijhoff Publishers, 1992.

Rostow, W. W. *The Stages of Economic Growth: A Non-Communist Manifesto*. New York: Cambridge University Press, 1960.

Rousseau, J. J. *The Social Contract*. Harmondsworth: Penguin, 1968.

Rubenson, Sven. *Wichale XVII: The Attempt to Establish a Protectorate over Ethiopia*. Addis Ababa, 1964.

Rubenson, Sven. *The Survival of Ethiopian Independence*. Addis Ababa: Kuraz Publishing Agency, 1991.

Rueschemeyer, Dietrich, Evelyne H. Stephens and John D. Stephens.*Capitalist Development and Democracy*. Cambridge: Polity Press, 1992.

Sainsbury, David. *Progressive Capitalism: How to Achieve Economic Growth, Liberty and Social Justice*. London: Biteback Publishing Ltd, 2013.

Sarkar, R. C. S. *The Constitution of India*. New Delhi: National Publishing House, 1991.

Sartori, Giovanni. *Comparative Constitutional Engineering: An Inquiry into Structures, Incentives and Outcomes*. London: Macmillan Press Ltd., 1997.

Sbacchi, Alberto. *Legacy of Bitterness: Ethiopia and Fascist Italy, 1935-1941*. Lawrenceville, NJ: The Red Sea Press, Inc., 1997.

Scholler, Heinrich. "Strengthening and Capacity Building of the Regional Judiciary in Ethiopia", Recht in Afrika, 1999, p. 51-90.

Schraeder, Peter J. "The Horn of Africa: US Foreign Policy in an Altered Cold War Environment", The Middle East Journal, Vol. 46, No. 4, Autumn 1992, p. 571-593.

Schumpeter, J. A. *Capitalism, Socialism and Democracy*. London: Unwin Paperbacks, 1987.

Schwab, Peter. *Ethiopia: Politics, Economics and Society*. London: Frances Printer, 1985.

Scully, Gerald W. *Constitutional Environments and Economic Growth*. Princeton, New Jersey: Princeton University Press, 1992.

Seligson, Mitchell A. and John T. Passé-Smith (eds.). *Development and Underdevelopment: The Political Economy of Inequality*. Boulder and London: Lynne Rienner Publishers, 1993.

Sellers, Mortimer (ed.). *The New World Order: Sovereignty, Human Rights, and the Self-Determination of Peoples*. Oxford and Washington D.C: Berg, 1996.

Shah, Anwar.*Fiscal Federalism and Macroeconomic Governance: For Better or For Worse?*, World Bank Policy Research Working Paper 2005, 1998.

Shah, Anwar. *The New Fiscal Federalism in Brazil*, World Bank Working Paper, December 1990.

Shetreet, Shimon and Jules Deschenes.*Judicial Independence: The Contemporary Debate*. Dordrecht: Martinus Nijhoff Publishers, 1985.

Shihata, Ibrahim F., "Democracy and Development", International and Comparative Law Quarterly, Vol. 46, July 1997, p. 635-643.

Sorensen, Georg. *Democracy, Dictatorship and Development: Economic Development in Selected Regimes of the Third World*. London: Macmillan Press Ltd., 1991.

Sorensen, Georg. *Democracy and Democratization: Processes and Prospects in a Changing World*. Boulder, San Francisco and Oxford: Westview Press, 1993.

Sorenson, John (ed.). *Disaster and Development in the Horn of Africa*. New York: St. Martin's Press, 1995.

Stiglitz, Joseph E. *Globalization and Its Discontents*. New York and London: W. W. Norton and Company, 2002.

Taddesse, Mokonen (ed.). *The Ethiopian Economy: Structure, Problems and Policy Issues*. Proceedings of the First Annual Conference on the Economy, Addis Ababa, 1992.

Tareke, Gebru. *Ethiopia: Power and Protest*. Cambridge: Cambridge University Press, 1991.

Tarlton, Charles D. "Symmetry and Asymmetry as Elements of Federalism: A Theoretical Speculation", *Journal of Politics* 27, No. 4, November 1965, p. 861-874.

Tavares, José and Romain Wacziarg, "How Democracy Affects Growth", European Economic Review, Vol. 45, No. 8, August 2001, p. 1341-1378.

Ter-Minassian, Teresa (ed.). *Fiscal Federalism in Theory and Practice*. International Monetary Fund, Washington, D. C., 1997.

Thorbecke, Erik and Henry Wan (eds.). *Taiwan's Development Experience: Lessons on Roles of Government and Market*. Boston, Dordrecht and London: Kluwer Academic Publishers, 1999.

Tibebu, Teshale. *The Making of Modern Ethiopia, 1896-1974*. Lawrenceville, NJ: The Red Sea Press INC., 1995.

Tiruneh, Andargachew. *The Ethiopian Revolution, 1974-1987*. Cambridge: Cambridge University Press, 1993.

Todaro, Michael P. *Economic Development,* 7th edition. New York: Addison-Wesley, 2000.

Tomuschat, Christian (ed.). *Modern Law of Self-Determination*. Dordrecht: Martinus Nijhoff Publishers, 1993.

Toye, *Dilemmas of Development*. Oxford: Basil Blackwell, 1987.

Trimingham, J. S. *Islam in Ethiopia*. London: Oxford University Press, 1952.

Tripathy, `R. N. *Federal Finance and Economic Development in India*. New Delhi: Sterling Publishers Private Ltd., 1982.

Tronovoll, K., "Voting, Violence, and Violations: Peasant Voices on the Flawed Elections in Haddiya, Southern Ethiopia", *Journal of Modern African Studies*, Vol. 39, No. 4, 2001, p. 667-716.

UNCTAD. *Trade and Development Report, 1997*. New York and Geneva: United Nations, 1997.

UNDP. *Human Development Report 2000*. New York and Oxford: Oxford University Press, 2000.

UNDP. *Human Development Report 2001*. New York and Oxford: Oxford University Press, 2001.

UNDP. *Human Development Report 2002*. New York and Oxford: Oxford University Press, 2002.

UNDP. *Human Development Report 2011*. New York and Oxford: Oxford University Press, 2002.

United Nations. *Human Rights: A Compilation of International Instruments*, Vol. I, 1994.

United Nations. *United Nations and the Independence of Eritrea*, Blue Books Series, Vol. XII, 1996.

United Nations. *Report of the Secretary-General on the Work of the Organization*, General Assembly, Official Records, Fifty-sixth Session, Supplement No. 1 (A/56/1), New York, 2001.

United Nations Economic Commission for Africa. *Economic Report on Africa 2002: Tracking Performance and Progress*, Addis Ababa, Ethiopia, June 2002.

Vaughan, Sarah. *The Addis Ababa Transitional Conference of July 1991: Its Origins, History and Significance*, Occasional Papers No. 51, Edinburgh University, 1994.

Wallerstein, Immanuel. *The Modern World-System*. San Diego: Academic Press, Inc., 1974.

Warren, W., *Imperialism: Pioneer of Capitalism*. London: New Left Books, 1980.

Waterbury, John. *The Nile Basin: National Determinants of Collective Action*. New Haven and London: Yale University Press, 2002.

Weiner, Myron and Ergun Ozbudun. *Competitive Elections in Developing Countries*, Duke University Press, 1987.

Weitz, Raanan. *From Peasant to Farmer: A Revolutionary Strategy for Development*. New York: Colombia University Press, 1971.

Wheare, K. *Federal Government*. London: Oxford University Press, 1963.

Wheare, K. *Modern Constitutions*. New York: Oxford University Press, 1966.

Wheatley, Steven, "Democracy in International Law: A European Perspective", International and Comparative Law Quarterly, Vol. 51, April 2002, p. 225-247.

Woll, Peter. *Constitutional Democracy*. Boston and Toronto: Little Brown and Company, 1986.

World Bank.*Accelerated Development in Sub-Saharan Africa*, Washington, D.C., 1981.

World Bank.*Ethiopia: Agriculture Sector, An Interim Report*, Washington D.C, January 1983.

World Bank.*From Crisis to Sustainable Growth: A Long-term Perspective Study*. Washington D.C.,1989.

World Bank.*Ethiopia's Economy in the 1980s and Framework for Accelerated Growth*, 1990.

World Bank.*Adjustment lending.Policies for Sustainable Growth*, Washington, D. C., 1990.

World Bank.*The East Asian Miracle: Economic Growth and Policy*. Oxford: Oxford University Press, 1993.

World Bank.*Adjustment in Africa: Reforms, Results, and the Road Ahead*. Oxford: Oxford University Press, 1994.

World Bank.*Ethiopia: Emergency Recovery and Reconstruction Project, A Retrospective Review OfBest Practices and Lessons Learned*, September 1995.

World Bank. *Case Studies in War- to- Peace Transition: The Demobilisation and Reintegration of Ex-combatants in Ethiopia, Namibia and Uganda*, 1996.

World Bank.*Ethiopia: Regionalisation Study*, Report No. 18898-ET, June 15, 2000.

World Bank.*Ethiopia: Transitions in a Poor Economy*, June 30, 2000.

World Bank. The Growth Report: Strategies for Sustained Growth and Inclusive Development. Commission on Growth and Development, 2008.

Wubneh, Mulatu and Yohannes Abate. *Ethiopia: Transition and Development in the Horn of Africa*. Boulder: Westview Press, 1988.

Young, John. *Peasant Revolution in Ethiopia: The Tigray People's Liberation Front, 1975–1991*. Cambridge: Cambridge University Press, 1997.

Zartman, I. William.*Collapsed States: The Disintegration and Restoration of Legitimate Authority*. Boulder and London: Lynne Rienner Publishers, 1995.

Zewde, Bahru. *A History of Modern Ethiopia, 1855-1974*. London: James Currey, 1991.

Index